Perspectives from *Historical Archaeology:*

African Diaspora Archaeology

Compiled by:

Christopher Fennell

SOCIETY *for* HISTORICAL ARCHAEOLOGY

Compiled with an Introduction by Christopher C. Fennell

Contact information:

Christopher C. Fennell
Department of Anthropology
University of Illinois at Urbana-Champaign
109 Davenport Hall, MC-148, 607 S. Mathews Ave., Urbana, IL 61801.
Office telephone: (217) 244-7309
Email address: cfennell@uiuc.edu
Fax number: (217) 244-3490

Cover photograph: Library of Congress, *Carte générale de l'Océan Atlantique ou Occidental, dressée au Dépôt général des cartes, plans, et journaux de la marine, et publiée par ordre du Ministre pour le service des vaisseaux français en 1786*. Paris, 1792

Perspectives from Historical Archaeology is a reader series providing collected articles from the journal of the Society for Historical Archaeology (SHA). Published since 1967, *Historical Archaeology* is the oldest North American scholarly publication on the archaeology of sites and materials from the historic past, and one of the world's premier publications on this subject. Each volume in the *Perspectives* series is developed on either a subject or regional basis by a compiler who selects the articles for inclusion and their order. The compilers also provide an introduction that presents an overview of the substantive work on that topic. *Perspectives* volumes offer non-archaeologists a convenient source for important publications on a subject or a region; an excellent resource for students interested in developing a specialization in a specific topic or area; as well as a convenient reference for archaeologists with an interest in the material.

The *Perspectives* series is managed by the SHA's Journal Editor and Co-Publications Editor and is published through the SHA's Print-On-Demand Press. Individuals interested in compiling a volume for publication through this series are encouraged to contact the Series Editors:

J. W. Joseph, PhD, RPA
Journal Editor, SHA
New South Associates, Inc.
6150 East Ponce de Leon Avenue
Stone Mountain, GA 30083
jwjoseph@newsouthassoc.com

Annalies Corbin, PhD
Co-Publications Editor, SHA
The PAST Foundation
1929 Kenny Road, Suite 300
Columbus, OH 43210
annalies@pastfoundation.org

Formed in 1967, the SHA is the largest scholarly group concerned with the archaeology of the modern world (A.D. 1400-present). The main focus of the society is the era since the beginning of European exploration. SHA promotes scholarly research and the dissemination of knowledge concerning historical archaeology. The society is specifically concerned with the identification, excavation, interpretation, and conservation of sites and materials on land and underwater. Geographically, the society emphasizes the New World, but also includes European exploration and settlement in Africa, Asia, and Oceania. To learn more about the SHA and historical archaeology, visit www.sha.org.

Perspectives from Historical Archaeology: African Diaspora Archaeology

Part I. Introduction

Part II. Perspectives from Historical Archaeology in Africa

Part III. African Heritage in the Caribbean, Central and South America

Part IV. African Descendant Communities in North America

CHRISTOPHER C. FENNELL

African Diaspora Archaeology in Multiscalar and Multivariate Perspectives

ABSTRACT:

This introduction addresses historical trends in African diaspora archaeology over the past several decades, assesses ongoing debates in theories, research questions, and interpretative frameworks, and provides an overview of the selected readings included in this volume.

Archaeological research of African diasporas has expanded dramatically in scope and the diversity of research questions over the past few decades. In this regard I use the term "diaspora" generally to encompass the dispersion of people to new locations as a result of adverse and hostile circumstances in the areas from which they were abducted or departed. A 2007 forum convened at the annual meeting of the Society for Historical Archaeology (SHA) in Williamsburg, Virginia, focused on the theme of "Research Designs for Atlantic Africa and African Diaspora Archaeologies." On that occasion, Merrick Posnansky spoke with great enthusiasm about how much progress has been made in the past 30 years through the work of historical archaeologists focusing on regions of Africa and the African diaspora. He believes we can all look forward with great excitement as to what the next 30 years will likely yield (Posnansky pers. comm. 2007). The SHA has helped promote this tremendous growth through the publication of numerous articles in its *Historical Archaeology* journal over those decades. This book presents a sampling of the many studies disseminated to thousands of readers through that peer-reviewed journal.

In addition to exchanging information, theories, and data through published articles and books, archaeologists working on African diaspora subjects have also collaborated through research networks. The "African-American Archaeology Network" was organized by Theresa Singleton and others by 1990 and published a newsletter of research projects, conferences, and commentary on ongoing interpretative debates. A regular forum meeting of this group has convened each year since then at SHA's annual conferences. The *African-American Archaeology Newsletter* was later edited and published by Thomas Wheaton and then John McCarthy up through 2000. Starting in 2005, this group was renamed as the "African Diaspora Archaeology Network" (ADAN), to emphasize a global geographic scope of interest, and a new *African Diaspora Archaeology Newsletter* was launched as an online publication. The increasing levels of activity in African diaspora archaeology subjects are evident in the fact that in the period of 2005 through 2007 the ADAN Newsletter published 66 articles or essays, 99 news items and announcements, 67 conference announcements and calls for papers, and 34 book or film reviews (ADAN 2005-2007). The ADAN also maintains extensive online bibliographies and resource information for readers interested in African heritage worldwide (e.g., ADAN 2008).

Other highly valuable online resources for researchers include the *Digital Archaeological Archive of Comparative Slavery* (or DAACS), funded and maintained by the Thomas Jefferson Foundation (2008). In addition, a monumental, multi-year research program has resulted in publication of the digital resource entitled *The Trans-Atlantic Slave Trade: a Database on CD-ROM* (Eltis et al. 2000). This database provides detailed information on over 27,000 trans-Atlantic slave ship voyages in the period of 1595 through 1866, encompassing over two-thirds of all trans-Atlantic slave ship voyages undertaken after 1600 (Eltis et al. 2000). Turning to visual depictions of the operations of the trans-Atlantic slave trade and its impact on past events and lives, Jerome Handler, Michael Tuite, Jr. (2008) and their colleagues have compiled a substantial online database of such historical images, entitled the *Atlantic Slave Trade and Slave Life in the Americas: a Visual Record*.

Researchers and commentators have pursued a multiplicity of perspectives in this period of growth for African-American archaeology and African diaspora archaeology. Their work has also traversed spatial scales across the local, regional, inter-regional, and global. Some scholars call for a focus on the contours of racial ideologies and capitalist economies on a global scale (e.g., Mullins 2008; Orser 1994). Other studies recommend rich, contextual analysis at the local and regional scales (e.g., Armstrong 2008; Brandon 2008; Mullins 2006). A breathtaking diversity of research questions has been pursued by researchers over the past decades, often employing investigative strategies informed by the interests of local and descendant communities (e.g., McDavid 1997), in addition to an engagement with ongoing theoretical debates concerning such themes as racism, power, agency, ethnicity, social group identity, class structures, and self-determination.

This diversity of studies includes a focus on racism and racial ideologies underlying economic structures (e.g., Babson 1990; Joseph 1993; Orser 2003, 2007) and African Americans in industrial settings (e.g., Gradwohl and Osborn 1984; Shackel and Larsen 2000). Extensive analyses of consumer choices and dietary and culinary practices (e.g., Mullins 1999; Reitz 1994; Wilkie 2000a) provide data on multiple spatial scales and time periods. Continuing developments of cultural beliefs and practices related to particular African cultures (e.g., Brown and Cooper 1990; Deetz 1996; Ferguson 1992; Samford 2007) and material expressions of African-American spirituality (e.g., Fennell 2003; Leone and Fry 1999; Ruppel et al. 2003; Russell 1997) have been explored in-depth. The contours of social networks and ethnic group identities (e.g., Ogundiran and Falola 2007; Wilkie 2000b) and processes of creolization, syncretism, and ethnogenesis (e.g., Armstrong 2003; Fennell 2007) have been the subject of extensive analysis. Other researchers have studied instances of self-determination, "maroon" communities, and resistance against oppression (e.g., Agorsah 2006; Weik 1997), as well as the operations of escape networks combating slavery in North America (e.g., Delle 2008; Delle and Shellenhamer 2008; LaRoche 2004).

Studies of mortuary traditions (e.g., Armstrong and Fleischman 2003; Davidson 2004; McCarthy 2006) and health care practices (e.g., Cabak et al. 1995), and bioarchaeological investigations of past lifeways, health, and the impacts of enslavement (e.g., Blakey 2001; Handler 1994; Mack and Blakey 2004) have also greatly enriched our knowledge of African diaspora histories. Gender dynamics within African diaspora communities (e.g., Galle and Young 2004; Wilkie 2003) and analyses of spatial and landscape contours from household to community and region (e.g., Battle-Baptiste 2007; Chan 2007; Delle 1998; Heath and Bennett 2000; Upton 1985) provide rich contexts on which future studies can continue to build. In addition to this expanding body of work in the Americas, a rapidly increasing program of historical archaeology analyses in locations in Africa impacted by the trans-Atlantic slave trade (e.g., DeCorse 2001; Kelly 2004; Ogundiran and Falola 2007; Reid and Lane 2004; Stahl 2004a, 2004b) presents tremendous promise for comparative analyses in future diaspora studies.

Consider how far this field of research has evolved since early steps just decades ago. Among the earliest studies in African-American archaeology was Adelaide and Ripley Bullen's (1945) analysis of the late 19th-century Foster site in Andover, Massachusetts. Lucy Foster was a formerly enslaved laborer, and the remains of her household were studied by the Bullens, who described their excavations, the recovered material remains, and related historical data. The Bullens did not approach this study with a particular theoretical framework. As Anna Agbe-Davies (2007:413) recently observed, at the time of the Bullens' work "there was little precedent for excavating post-contact North American sites, let alone those associated with ordinary people and everyday life." In a comprehensive overview of studies in the United States and Caribbean, Agbe-Davies (2007:414) provides a concise chronology of the subsequent increase of projects in the 1960s and 1970s:

In the United States, African-American archaeology emerged in earnest in the late 1960s and early 1970s. Excavations of free black communities like Weeksville (1968), Sandy Ground (1971), the African Meeting House in Boston (1975), and Parting Ways (1975), as well as the plantation quarters at Kingsley (1968), Cumberland Island (1969), Kingsmill (1972), and Cannon's Point (1973), were spurred by a heady mix of civil rights activism, new historic preservation laws, and the twin influences of the new social history and Black Power on the academy. Soon, even at sites previously concerned with the glorification of the elite and powerful, attention turned toward the previously ignored black presence, for example, at Monticello (1981), Colonial Williamsburg (1986), and Annapolis (1989). Important early research elsewhere in the Americas included the plantations at Newton (1971),

New Montpelier (1973), Drax Hall (1980), and Gallways (1980).

Within this increasing field of studies, a creative project undertaken by Robert Ascher and Charles Fairbanks (1971) focused on a plantation quarters for enslaved laborers in the sea islands region of Georgia. Their report on the archaeological record of this residential site on Cumberland Island was among the first such articles on African-American heritage published in SHA's *Historical Archaeology* journal. Like the Bullens' earlier study, Ascher and Fairbanks did not pursue a particular theoretical framework, nor directly address issues such as the contours of racism within the institution of slavery. Yet, they utilized an innovative approach to reporting their perspectives on this research by including "soundtracks" of excerpts from literary, political, and public record documents that provided a poignant backdrop of commentary on the impacts of slavery and racism in American history (Ascher and Fairbanks 1971; Orser 2007:16).

Projects conducted by archaeologists working in cultural resource management (CRM) settings have also contributed greatly to the development of African diaspora archaeology in the United States. For example, Thomas Wheaton, Amy Friedlander, and Patrick Garrow (1983) conducted excavations at Yaughan and Curiboo plantations in South Carolina, which uncovered the remains of dwellings constructed with building styles related to vernacular traditions in West Africa and evidence of African-American production of "colonoware" earthenwares. In part, the extensive contributions of CRM researchers to African-American archaeology reflects the frequency with which sites of African diaspora heritage are often subjected to disturbance by new construction projects and resultant analysis through CRM procedures (Joseph 2004:18-20).

The following chapters of this book are divided into three collections, focusing in succession on articles from the *Historical Archaeology* journal that present studies in Africa (Part II), the Caribbean, Central and South America (Part III), and finally on research concerning sites in North America (Part IV). Contextual commentary on the significance and implications of these studies is also provided.

PERSPECTIVES FROM HISTORICAL ARCHAEOLOGY IN AFRICA

Part II assembles three chapters on historical archaeology in the regions of Africa impacted by trans-Atlantic diasporas. Chapter 2 presents an article published by Merrick Posnansky and Christopher DeCorse in 1986 on historical archaeology projects in sub-Saharan Africa. One approach to African diaspora archaeology could be to first undertake an exhaustive program of historical archaeology within the regions of Africa from which people were drawn into diasporas. Researchers could then use that collection of studies as a baseline for comparative analysis and predictive modeling of later developments throughout the diaspora (Ogundiran and Falola

2007:7-9). Posnansky and DeCorse describe progress in historical archaeology within Africa up through 1986, and four of the five primary regions of research they discuss related directly to trans-Atlantic African diasporas.

For example, research in the region of West Africa, including fortified towns such as Elmina on the Gold Coast, provided evidence of the significant cultural diversity of Africans captured and transported through these regional ports of the Atlantic slave trade (Posnansky and DeCorse 1986:5). The authors recommended that historical archaeology within Africa focus more on settlement sites and understanding particular African societies in full detail and historical context, rather than continue to focus on descriptions of the remains of fortified colonial facilities that had previously been undertaken (Posnansky and DeCorse 1986:10). Such a broad research focus on the characteristics of particular African societies later impacted by the trans-Atlantic slave trade would provide a highly valuable body of data and analysis for comparative studies and predictive modeling of later developments in African diasporas. Posnansky and DeCorse (1986:10-11) recommended that archaeologists working within Africa should undertake an ongoing and evolving dialogue with archaeologists working on diaspora sites in North America and the Caribbean to continually formulate and revise their mutual research questions to facilitate such comparative analysis over time.

Approximately two decades after Posnansky and DeCorse made those recommendations, a rich body of studies of historical archaeology within Africa was being published. For example, Andrew Reid and Paul Lane edited a volume of articles in 2004 entitled *African Historical Archaeologies* that included 14 studies ranging in locations from the Middle Nile, Kenya, Tanzania, Nigeria, Zimbabwe, and South Africa. Reiterating Posnansky and DeCorse's recommendations, Ken Kelly (2004) authored an article included in that volume entitled "The African Diaspora Starts Here: Historical Archaeology of Coastal West Africa." Other publications included DeCorse's (2001) study of historical archaeological sites in West Africa in locations spanning a region from Senegambia to the area of Cameroon. Peter Schmidt's (2006) long-term studies in East Africa provided another regional counter-point. An edited volume focusing on historical studies (Philips 2000) provided 20 chapters with detailed consideration of research methodologies and findings concerning both written and oral histories in a variety of African societies impacted by the Atlantic slave trade and other diasporas. Among the 20 chapters of Akin Ogundiran and Toyin Falola's (2007) edited volume entitled *Archaeology of Atlantic Africa and the African Diaspora,* 7 historical archaeology studies focus on locations in Africa, including the Gold Coast, the Yoruba-Edo hinterland, the Bight of Benin, Senegal, northern Yorubaland, East Africa, and Ghana.

Chapter 3 presents a 1995 study by Anne Markell, Martin Hall, and Camile Schrire focusing on Vergelegen, an 18th-century farmstead on the Cape of Good Hope in South Africa. The research questions in this study included a comparison of the structure of enslavement in this Dutch colony and the patterns of plantation organization seen in some examples in North America (Markell et al. 1995:12). The authors also applied research questions as to whether enslaved laborers at Vergelegen exercised daily acts of self-determination in a manner similar to examples in North America, such as hunting and fishing to supplement their diets (Markell et al. 1995:12). Many of the enslaved laborers at Vergelegen were captives from the region of Madagascar and East India (Markell et al. 1995:29).

Markell, Hall, and Schrire provide a rich presentation of data concerning the layout of the farmstead, dependencies, a mill, a wine cellar, and changing patterns of spatial use in the housing for enslaved laborers spanning the 18th and early 19th centuries. Analyses of material culture, landscapes, dietary remains, and health indications from skeletal remains are discussed in detail. Artifacts from the space of slave housing included a predominance of hollow wares, a variety of porcelain, stoneware, and earthenwares, Dutch manufactured tobacco pipes, iron tools, fishing equipment, and sewing implements (Markell et al. 1995:24-26). The researchers found no overt differences in the types of material culture remains uncovered in the houses of enslaved laborers and European house sites in the Cape (Markell et al. 1995:29).

A unique form of architectural style for laborers' housing was utilized at Vergelegen, influenced by building traditions from northern Europe (Markell et al. 1995:28). Yet, in some structures, a form of pit hearth consistent with vernacular practices in Madagascar was added to an otherwise Dutch-influenced architectural style in what the authors interpret to indicate "some retentions and adaptations of traditional practices in the syncretic Vergelegen slave culture" (Markell et al. 1995:29). Little evidence was uncovered to indicate that the laborers at Vergelegen engaged in hunting and gathering to supplement their diets in a manner similar to that found in some North American plantations (Markell et al. 1995:30). Applying a comparative analysis of plantation management in examples in North America and South Africa, the authors hypothesize that the basic dietary provisions in Vergelegen made supplementation less necessary than in locations such as South Carolina plantations (Markell et al. 1995:30).

Chapter 4 continues this consideration of comparative data from locations and cultures within Africa and later cultural developments within African diasporas. Ross Jamieson's 1995 study focuses on mortuary practices on both sides of the Atlantic. He advocates that historical archaeologists working in the Americas need to undertake an interdisciplinary, ethnohistorical approach that examines comparative data from historical, archaeological, and ethnographic data concerning particular African cultures impacted by the trans-Atlantic slave trade. Jamieson (1995:41-46) provides rich analysis of evidence of mortuary practices in several cultures in West and West Central Africa during the period of the slave trade, as well as bioarchaeological evidence concerning those societies. He then provides a comprehensive survey of studies in North America and the Caribbean, including a variety of research questions and findings emerging from

Jerome Handler and Frederick Lange's (1978) detailed studies in Barbados and data results from the African Burial Ground in New York City (Jamieson 1995:46-54).

AFRICAN HERITAGE IN THE CARIBBEAN, CENTRAL AND SOUTH AMERICA

Part III of this book focuses on African diaspora sites in the Caribbean, Central America, and South America. Jane Landers' overview in Chapter 5 provides valuable historical contexts for studies and research questions concerning communities in the Spanish colonial sphere within this region. While her article does not discuss archaeological findings, it provides historical contexts of Africans in Spain and in the areas of Spanish colonial influence in the Americas. She provides an overview of historical dynamics in which Africans and African descendants were "agents of change who have gone little noticed, although their tenure in the Americas matches that of the Spaniards" (Landers 1997:84). In turn, Terrance Weik's (2004) study in Chapter 6 provides a number of case studies of archaeological findings within African diaspora sites in "Latin America," including Hispaniola (later Haiti and the Dominican Republic), Cuba, Brazil, Jamaica, and Florida. Weik (2004) also raises a number of interpretative and theory debates, including the value of conceptualizations of social processes such as creolization, ethnogenesis, mestizaje, and maroonage, and the dearth of studies that focus on the rich interactions of Native American populations with Africans and African descendant groups.

Paul Farnsworth turns our attention in Chapter 7 to the history of African diaspora communities in the plantations of the Bahamas in the 18th and 19th centuries. He provides a detailed consideration of market production and distribution networks that impacted the availability of goods in both Nassau and more remote locations of the North Caicos (Farnsworth 1996). His study demonstrates that large-scale economic models of commodity distribution must be refined with an analysis of local conditions and the final stages of product availability. For example, the remote location of Wade's Green plantation on the North Caicos section of the Bahamas resulted in enslaved African laborers possessing types and frequencies of material culture, such as ceramics, tobacco pipes, and personal adornments, which differed notably from plantation locations in Nassau or the southern United States (Farnsworth 1996).

Moving to Jamaica, James Delle's study in Chapter 8 addresses facets of creolization. He examines ethnohistorical evidence for the development of "Afro-creole" identities in Jamaica in the 19th century, which were distinct from "Euro-creole" social groups and from the social affiliations of recently arrived Africans. Delle (2000) analyzes both cognitive and material culture manifestations of multi-faceted creolization processes as modalities in which new social group identities were formed. Among the material culture expressions of Afro-creole social groups were distinctive modes of housing, yard, and garden landscapes. In contrast to the remote locations Farnsworth analyzed in the Bahamas, plantations in Jamaica were occupied by African descendants who made their own forms of "Yabba" redware ceramic vessels for preparing and serving food (Delle 2000: 65-66). These were mostly hollowwares and were used in culinary traditions that focused on preparation and serving of stews containing a wide variety of ingredients. Yard spaces were important activity and production areas surrounding houses made typically of earthfast construction, wattle-and-daub, and thatched roofs (Delle 2000:62-63). Gardens or "provision grounds" for production of food for the laborers were also of great importance within these landscapes shaped by the Afro-Creole population.

Examining ethnohistorical evidence concerning the health of Afro-creoles, Delle (2000: 67-68) finds that the disease of yaws, which is a form of spirochete infection, likely traveled with captive Africans from West Africa to Jamaica. He observes that very little archaeological research on the health of African diaspora populations has yet been undertaken in regard to locations in the British West Indies. Delle (2000:69) recommends future work on, among other sources, plantation hospital sites, including flotation of soil samples from privies and wells to examine "floral evidence of the types of herbs used by Afro-creole healers in specific remedies."

The bioarchaeological evidence of physical impacts of slavery upon captive Africans provides a focus of David Watters' study in Chapter 9, which examines the remains of 17 individuals buried in an 18th-century cemetery in Montserrat in the northern Lesser Antilles.

Having conducted a salvage archaeology project under very constraining conditions when construction crews in Montserrat disturbed the remains of an early cemetery, Watters (1994) presents evidence and comparative analyses that yield valuable insights from a dire circumstance. He presents new data from that analysis and a survey of comparative studies from sites in Barbados, Jamaica, and Dutch Guiana (now Suriname in South America). A review of evidence of disease, injuries, malnutrition, pathologies, and trauma reflected in the remains of individuals at these 18th and 19th century sites provides a testament to the brutal character of slavery across the region (Watters 1994:58-60, 66). Comparative analysis of burial practices and potential grave goods included with the deceased provides indications of intriguing variations over time and space in directional orientation of interments and the ritual compositions included in mortuary rites (Watters 1994:60-70).

Barbados was the target of Britain's earliest colonial ventures in the Caribbean, with enterprises investing in sugar plantations operated with enslaved African laborers starting in the early 1600s (Handler 1996:76). Jerome Handler, Frederick Lange, Robert Corruccini, and their colleagues under took an intensive archaeological and historical research program focusing on the plantation cemetery at Newton, on the southern portion of the island, in the period of 1972-1973. The remains of 104 individuals, interred from approximately 1660 through 1820, were excavated and analyzed along with the material culture that accompanied the deceased and the mortuary practices evident in the contexts of the burials. In addition to the archaeological investigations, a program of extensive historical, ethnohistorical, and comparative studies was undertaken (Handler 1996:76). Among many publications of their findings, Handler and Lange's (1978) study entitled *Plantation Slavery in Barbados: An Archaeological and Historical Investigation* remains a foundational work in the field of African diaspora archaeology.

Chapter 10 presents Handler's 1996 article focusing on one of those 104 burials at Newton plantation. He presents an array of evidence from skeletal analysis to ethnographic analogies and ethnohistorical data from particular West African cultures that he brings to bear on interpreting the likely meaning and significance of the mortuary practices utilized in that interment. An individual who suffered significant lead poisoning during life likely experienced dramatic behavioral symptoms that were interpreted by community members through particular cultural beliefs resulting in distinctive treatment of the deceased (Handler 1996).

Shifting our focus to the African diaspora communities of South America, Chapter 11 presents Charles Orser's study of Palmares, in the Pernambuco state of Brazil, which was "without doubt one of the most important maroon settlements in the history of the New World" (Orser 1994:7). Orser analyzes the archaeological and historical evidence of Palmares from a perspective of the modern world system of economic and social interactions operating across the Atlantic hemisphere, including Portuguese and Dutch colonial regimes, Native American populations, and captive

Africans from the area of Angola. Portuguese colonial interests developed sugar plantations in Brazil by 1570, and Dutch colonial interests established sugar processing facilities and shipping operations nearby. Captive Africans and Native Americans escaped from Portuguese plantations and created the Palmares settlements, located some 50-75 miles inland, by the early 1600s (Funari 2003:83-84; Orser 1994). By the mid-1640s there were 9 separate Palmares villages, and by the late 1600s, Palmares settlements likely contained 20,000 people – up to a third of the enslaved population had escaped to Palmares.

In the 1670s, the defense of Palmares was supervised by one of their own members, called King Zumbi (Orser 1994:8-9). Portuguese and Dutch colonial forces began expeditions against the Palmares settlements as early as 1612. The settlements withstood and repelled those attacks until 1694, when the Portuguese destroyed them with the use of hired mercenary forces, and King Zumbi and the other leaders of Palmares were executed (Orser 1994:9-10). Archaeological investigations at the sites of Palmares villages revealed evidence of self-sufficient production of material culture and trade with coastal settlements in the late 1600s. Pottery forms in the villages showed a blending of African and indigenous Tupinamba pottery traditions and decorative techniques. Clay smoking pipes with forms and decorative motifs consistent with West African production methods were also recovered (Funari 2003:86-87; Orser 1994:11-13). In his related study of Palmares, Pedro Paulo Funari (2003:83) emphasized the ways in which these historical and archaeological analyses demonstrated a remarkable complexity, heterogeneity, and fluidity of the populations and cultural networks within those settlements.

AFRICAN DESCENDANT COMMUNITIES IN NORTH AMERICA

Part IV focuses on African descendant communities in North America, and the 13 chapters in this collection provide just a sampling of the many studies published in *Historical Archaeology* that concentrated on research projects conducted in the United States. This part of the book starts with three chapters addressing issues concerning the politics of African-American archaeology and trends in overall interpretative biases and challenges for improvement. The following seven chapters then discuss studies presented along a geographic trajectory from locations in the northern United States to southern locations and plantation archaeology. Finally, the last three chapters in this collection focus on interpretations of the economic, social, and religious meanings and significance of particular categories of material culture uncovered at an array of African-American sites across the United States.

Maria Franklin's 1997 critique of African-American archaeology begins this overview of work in North America in Chapter 12. She lauds historical archaeology's goal of providing a voice to people of our past who are largely omitted from past documentary records and traditional historical accounts of America's heritage and accomplishments (Franklin 1997:36). However, Franklin demands that historical archaeologists critically consider why and how they work to provide such understandings of African-American histories. The stakes for such self-reflection by archaeologists are high, because many historical accounts in the United States have served to legitimize a present "social order permeated by racism, classism, and gender bias" (Franklin 1997:38).

Franklin (1997:38) insists that to be "critical, responsible, and accountable," historical archaeologists must actively engage with members of the African-American communities they purport to serve in their research. Archaeological research undertaken without community engagement and expressed in jargon-laden reports and biased exhibits fails to meet such goals. Moreover, if historical archaeologists "continue to ignore the needs and interests of descendant groups, we will foster antagonism, and our research will mean little to nothing to the segments of society whose ancestors we choose to study" (Franklin 1997:39). While the Society for American Archaeology had adopted a principle of accountability to groups impacted by archaeologists' research, the Society for Historical Archaeology (SHA) did not express a direct counter-part of that commitment at the time of Franklin's analysis (1997:46-47). The SHA "Statements of Ethics," adopted in 2003, now include provisions requiring archaeologists to "respect the dignity and human rights of others" and to "strive to engage citizens in the research process" (SHA 2003: principles 5, 7), but continuing improvements in our organization's commitments in this regard remain vital. Full community engagement in archaeological practice should involve members of such groups in the full array of project elements, including "conception of research questions, excavation, data analysis, and interpretation" (Franklin 1997:40).

Franklin's commentary does not issue naïve calls for improvement. She provides a nuanced consideration of the challenges facing both archaeological researchers and members of community groups in grappling with often painful histories of past subjugation and the institution of slavery in America. Archaeologists face challenges in that community and descendant groups are by no means monolithic in their views (Franklin 1997:41-44). Impassioned conflicts and debates will often arise within and across community groups as to the significance and contours of particular archaeological projects. Other challenges arise through the highly interdisciplinary character of studies concerning African-American history. A fully interdisciplinary approach to African-American archaeology requires researchers to be as conversant with the accomplishments of scholars in Black studies, such as Frederick Douglass, St. Claire Drake, W. E. B. Du Bois, Zora Neale Hurston, Arturo Schomburg, Booker T. Washington, George Williams, and Carter Woodson, as they are with the methods for conducting excavations and analyzing material culture (Franklin 1997:44-45; Mullins 2008:105-07).

J. W. Joseph addresses the tremendous contributions of archaeologists working in cultural resource management (CRM) projects to our understanding of African-American history and archaeology. CRM archaeology projects have produced valuable research concerning African-American communities in plantation contexts, freedmen's settlements, late 19th century tenant households, urban archaeology settings, and analysis of cemetery contexts (Joseph 2004:19). Joseph's survey of these accomplishments, presented in Chapter 13, also outlines a series of interpretative biases that have emerged in many CRM studies. For example, important studies such as those at Yaughan and Curiboo Plantations in South Carolina (Wheaton et al. 1983) recovered evidence of continuing developments of particular African cultural practices, such as architectural and pottery styles, during the 18th century (Joseph 2004:19). However, many CRM archaeologists have also developed working assumptions that African Americans experienced assimilation and acculturation within European-American cultural traditions by the start of the 19th century, and that one can expect to see no continuing developments of African cultural influences on material culture found at residential sites after that time (Joseph 2004:18-19). Joseph outlines the reasons and evidence of why these latter assumptions are invalid and he advocates that CRM research designs and questions concerning 19th century sites must become more flexible in future projects.

The extensive studies undertaken on African-American work and residential sites by CRM researchers also presents evidence of the continuing impacts of racism in today's society. Such CRM projects are typically undertaken when a large-scale development project will likely destroy the archaeological record underlying existing real estate. As Charles Orser (2007:36) recently observed, the locations of home and work spaces of past and present African-American families are far more frequently targeted "for urban renewal, gentrification, or some other project involving land modification and federal funding" than are the spaces of past and present European-American residences. The apparent racial biases of large-scale development projects present CRM researchers with a constant challenge of working to mitigate the impacts of developers' purposeful or unintended effects of erasing material facets of African-American heritage from the current landscape.

Kerri Barile (2004) published an insightful study that illuminated an additional trend of biases that work to the detriment of preserving African-American heritage. She outlines a number of points for improvements in the methods of CRM projects and the guidelines utilized by State Historic Preservation Officers (SHPOs) who are responsible for administering the regulations of cultural resource management efforts. Barile (2004) details a growing tendency of SHPOs in a number of states to view late-19th and early-20th century residential sites as insignificant due to the standardization of mass-produced consumer goods often uncovered at sites from those periods. She recommends that CRM researchers combat this tendency by focusing more intensively on aspects of intangible cultural heritage of each locality and region. Greater exploration of oral histories, regional and local contours of racialization, and more contextual data of aspects of heritage beyond archaeological remains will aid in

demonstrating the historical significance of such sites (Barile 2004).

Excavations at the African Burial Ground in lower Manhattan, New York, in 1991 and 1992 started as a CRM project related to construction of a new federal office building. Chapter 14 presents Cheryl LaRoche and Michael Blakey's (1997:100) compelling account of how the African-American community in New York City succeeded in seizing "power and control" and not just an "afterthought of inclusion" in the guidance of this large-scale archaeology project. Excavations on a 6-acre portion of an early burial ground uncovered over 400 burials of Africans and African descendants interred in the period of approximately 1712 through 1794 (LaRoche and Blakely 1997:84-85). A powerful collaboration of "influential and determined African Americans" that included officials in the federal and municipal governments, journalists, local clergy and church congregation members, and an array of civic groups, developed during the excavations and shaped the procedures and research questions applied in the project (LaRoche and Blakey 1997:85-86).

Among the intellectual influences applied in the investigations of the New York African Burial Ground were the concerns of "vindicationist" efforts in which scholars of African-American studies from the 19th century to the present have emphasized the need to "correct the demeaning distortions of the culture, biology, and history of the Africana world" (LaRoche and Blakey 1997:90; Mullins 2008:108). As also emphasized by Franklin in Chapter 12, LaRoche and Blakey (1997:99) caution that while "there is general unity surrounding the major issues, the African descendant community speaks with many voices" and researchers should not assume that such community concerns will be simplistic or monolithic in character. Similarly, one should not confuse vindicationist efforts with a simplistically celebratory perspective. For the African-American community in New York City, "the excavation of our ancestors" was both "a cathartic and wrenching experience" (LaRoche and Blakey 1997:100).

Four primary research questions were pursued in the New York African Burial Ground project: determining the likely cultural, population, and geographic origins of the individuals; examining evidence of the physical quality of their lives; analyzing the biological and cultural impacts of life in America for captive Africans; and examining any evidence of modes of resistance against structures of enslavement (LaRoche and Blakey 1997:86-87). Chapter 15 provides a summary of some of the results from this research, with findings detailed in a 2004 article by Mark Mack and Michael Blakey. The project employed an array of interdisciplinary methods, including insights from the fields of "[o]steological and dental radiology and chemistry, molecular genetics, history, archaeology, botany, and African art history," among others (Mack and Blakey 2004:10). The collaborating researchers on the African Burial Ground project have continued to publish comprehensive and updated reports of the results of these interdisciplinary studies (e.g., General Services Administration 2007).

Continuing a focus on studies of African-American heritage in the northern United States, Chapter 16 presents Robert Fitts' 1996 study of the "landscapes of bondage" in that region. Using a detailed case study of enslavement in Rhode Island as a focal point, Fitts (1996) provides evidence refuting stereotypical views that slavery in northern states was somehow "mild and paternalistic" in contrast to greater brutalities of the plantation South. Fitts applies concepts of landscape analysis in this study, examining the ways in which northern plantation owners attempted to control and manipulate domestic and work spaces to "instill their ideology of alienation" of African Americans to deprive them of capacities of self-determination (Fitts 1996:67). In response, captive African Americans pursued acts of resistance in a variety of settings within those northern landscapes of oppression. During decades of bondage, such moments of resistance played out in private dwellings, during the laboring hours in work spaces and running errands between plantations, and through subversive interactions at church, funeral, and festival gatherings (Fitts 1996:66-67).

Lu Ann De Cunzo's archaeological study and narrative storytelling shift our consideration to the post-bellum decades of freedom in Delaware in Chapter 17. She provides a conjectural reconstruction of the events and lifeways in two, neighboring African-American households from the 1870s through the 1920s that produced the artifacts and features uncovered in archaeological excavations (De Cunzo 1998:42). The defeat of slavery won by the Civil War was succeeded in many regions by renewed forms of virulent racism. De

Cunzo provides interpretations of the material culture of these residences within the contexts of racism that presented these African-American families with the challenges of confronting enduring social and economic adversities. This chapter presents a persuasive view of archaeological evidence by envisioning the social events and lifeways in which the objects of their daily activities were embedded. Paul Mullins' (1999) study of African-American households in Annapolis during the same period offers similar insights. His research findings, presented in Chapter 18, provide a compelling interpretation of household remains that demonstrate the ways in which African Americans subverted racism through strategic choices within the realm of product consumption, local merchant interactions, and patronage of national brands (Mullins 1999:24-26). The relationship of labor opportunities, racial distortions of economic and social structures, and changing culinary preferences are similarly analyzed (Mullins 1999:26-34).

The remaining seven chapters in Part IV largely concern archaeological and historical research of African-American communities and plantations in the southern United States. Theresa Singleton's 1990 article in Chapter 19 provides an overview of the development of "plantation archaeology" in the United States and the strengths and weaknesses of the research designs developed within that field of specialization. Approaches to plantation archaeology projects varied from Charles Fairbank's (1974) studies of the "extent to which an African heritage was transplanted, modified, and replaced in slave material culture" (Singleton 1990:71) to John Otto's (1984) research concerning differences in socioeconomic status and class evident in the material culture of plantation owners, overseers, and enslaved laborers. Other approaches include Charles Orser's (1988) critical analysis of southern plantations as a form of capitalist economic enterprise dependent upon the expropriation of enslaved labor and enforcement of social domination through manipulations of the built environment. Similarly, Terrance Epperson (1990) and David Babson (1990) analyzed the cultural landscapes of plantations as involving a class structure built upon evolving racist ideologies (Singleton 1990:73).

Fairbanks did not succeed in his own projects in identifying the influences of particular African cultural traditions in the material culture of enslaved laborers at plantations such as Kingsley in Florida (Singleton 1990:74). However, recent work at Kingsley by James Davidson and his colleagues (2006) uncovered the remains of a ritual composition dating to the early 1800s that was very likely part of spiritual observances that represented continuing developments of particular beliefs and practices related to cultures in the Bight of Biafra region of West Africa. Many of the Kingsley plantation laborers were abducted from that region (Davidson et al. 2006).

Archaeological studies of the production and use of "colonoware" pottery on plantations in Virginia and the Carolinas have similarly involved heated debates concerning the degree to which these materials provide evidence of continuing influences of African pottery traditions in the Americas (Singleton 1990:74-75; Singleton and Bograd 2000:5-

8). Investigations by Wheaton and his colleagues (1983) at Yaughan and Curiboo plantation, by Leland Ferguson (1992) at Middleburg plantation, and by James Deetz (1993) at Flowerdew Hundred, to name just a few, provide ample evidence that colonoware pottery was produced by African Americans in those regions in the period of the late 17th through the early 19th centuries (Singleton 1990: 74-75). Other analysts nonetheless maintain that colonoware was principally manufactured by Native American potters in North America who traded with such plantations (Mouer et al. 1999). While current interpretative models for colonoware in locations such as the Carolinas are growing more refined and multi-faceted (Espenshade 2007; Ferguson 2007; Joseph 2007), an expanding body of studies in the Caribbean and South America also provides comparative data of particular African-influenced pottery traditions evolving in those locations (e.g., DeCorse and Hauser 2003; Hauser 2007; Symanski 2006).

Singleton concludes Chapter 19 with proposals of areas for future expansion of research designs focused on plantation structures. Among other avenues of investigation, she proposed a greater focus on region by region variations in the economic and social organization of plantations and how these regional differences impacted the lives of African Americans living and working in those spaces (Singleton 1990: 76). Singleton's advocacy of far-reaching research designs no doubt laid the foundations for a current global-scale perspective that the "historical legacy and implications of the plantation system in terms of the modern realities of racial ideologies, the world economy and globalization to name a few, are of great social significance" (Kraus-Friedberg and Fellows 2008).

Jean Howson's 1990 review and critique of trends within plantation archaeology, presented in Chapter 20, addresses ways for applying practice theory and the interdependence of structure and agency in analyzing developments and changes in particular cultures. Detailed, interdisciplinary, and contextual studies of particular locations, populations, and cultural elements should replace earlier tendencies to search for simplistic "Africanisms" in the 17th and 18th centuries and "acculturation" of African-American lifeways to Anglo-American material culture in the 19th century (Howson 1990:79-80). Similarly, earlier trends of searching for an "African American pattern" of material culture in a particular century and region should be superseded by contextual analysis of specific communities within more refined time periods (Howson 1990:79-80). Where Singleton's (1990) critique principally lauded a move away from studying variations in "status and class" within plantations to an analysis of the impacts of "economy and power" at broader geographic scales, Howson (1990) advocated a greater focus on the meanings of material culture within the context of particular cultural traditions and the ways those cultural elements changed over time.

Ten years later, Barbara Heath and Amber Bennett (2000) presented a study that provided one example of the type of detailed, interdisciplinary, and contextual analysis that Howson and Singleton had advocated. Ranging from broader-scale questions of power relations within plantations to closer-scale spatial analysis, Heath and Bennett focused on analyzing the uses, meanings, and significance of the yard areas surrounding African-American dwellings in plantations. This finely delimited spatial analysis, presented in Chapter 21, is employed in exploring an array of topics, from community interactions, to a range of work and leisure activities, to landscape aesthetics and culture change over time. At a broader scale, the analysis is also comparative and interdisciplinary, presenting historical, ethnographic, and archaeological data from landscape studies in West Africa, locations of African diaspora communities in the Caribbean, and the plantations of the American south (Heath and Bennett 2000: 39-44).

If any archaeologists harbored a belief that African-influenced cultural beliefs and practices had disappeared in North America by the 19th century, Kenneth Brown and Doreen Cooper (1990) laid such misgivings to rest with their study of the Levi Jordan plantation in Brazoria, Texas, presented here in Chapter 22. Started in 1848, the Jordan plantation included 8 barracks-like buildings with quarters for some of the 140 enslaved African Americans who worked the sugar and cotton cash crops before the Civil War (Brown and Cooper 1990:9-10). After emancipation, over 100 African Americans and their families remained on the plantation land and farmed parcels as tenant sharecroppers, staying in the same dwellings (Brown 2004:85). Descendants of the plantation owner instigated summary evictions of those families in the early 1880s, causing tenants to leave much of the material culture of their households behind when they departed (Brown and Cooper 1990:9-10). Applying rigorous excavation techniques at the Jordan plantation, archaeologists uncovered a remarkable collection of material culture compositions in these house sites, dating to the middle of the 19th century. Their findings provided highly persuasive interpretations of the ways those materials related to the evolving cultures of African Americans, Afro-Cubans, and descendants of the BaKongo and Yoruba cultures (Brown and Cooper 1990). These features, artifact assemblages, and related interpretations were approached through rigorous, interdisciplinary methods that included close attention to spatial and cultural contexts and employed careful uses of ethnographic and ethnohistorical analogies (Brown and Cooper 1990:18-19). The artifacts, when analyzed within these spatial and cultural contexts, included items that very likely functioned to express social group affiliations, the occupation and social status of individuals within the community, and compositions related to cosmological beliefs and religious practices derived from particular African cultures.

In a study published in 2004, Kenneth Brown revisited the contextual and interdisciplinary methods he and colleagues utilized in analyzing the African-American dwellings at the Jordan plantation site. Careful use of ethnographic and ethnohistorical analogies based on studies of Yoruba, BaKongo, and Afro-Cuban cultures richly informed his interpretations of the material culture uncovered in Texas. Turning to new African-American sites in the location of the modern-day Gullah and Geechee culture of the Carolina Lowcountry, Brown's 2004 study recommends that historical archaeologists also utilize analogic reasoning based on the modern-day Gullah and Geechee cultural elements when seeking to interpret 19th century remains of African-American communities in those coastal locations (Brown 2004:87-88).

The challenges of interpreting the meaning and significance of personal items with African diaspora archaeology are taken up further in Chapter 23. Linda Stine, Melanie Cabak, and Mark Groover (1996) focus on a particular category of material culture – blue beads – uncovered in the archaeology of African-American work and dwelling spaces and for which there exists extensive and varied data. These items provide a test case with which to address issues concerning the multiple functions such material culture could have served, and the range of meanings that potentially entangled such an object. Combining data from oral histories, folklore studies, ethnographic investigations in particular African cultures, and historical documentary evidence, the authors demonstrate the range of social status, personal adornment, and religious functions and meaning such material culture could have served in different settings. How then does an archaeologist correctly interpret the past use and significance of a particular artifact? Stine, Cabak, and Groover (1996) join Brown and Cooper (1990) in a profound and vital refrain – context is everything.

Laurie Wilkie's 1997 review and critique of studies concerning the material culture of spiritual beliefs and practices among African Americans, presented in Chapter 24, concludes this book's collection of articles. Wilkie provides a comprehensive overview of the ways in which such spiritual beliefs and practices were integrated with community relations, family roles, gender dynamics, medicine, childcare, and household efforts to combat adversities. Changes over time in the beliefs and practices related to particular African cultures included the interactions of multiple African religions within diasporic communities in the Americas, and the impacts of socially dominant religions including Christian and Muslim denominations. Wilkie (1997:96-103) outlines a diachronic model for analyzing these cultural changes over time in African America.

PROMISING PROSPECTS

This collection of articles from past issues of *Historical Archaeology* hopefully provides a representative sample of the remarkable array of insightful studies in the expanding field of African diaspora archaeology. It is impracticable to fully review all of the developments and published studies over the past several decades in the limited space available here. As Merrick Posnansky recently observed, the future for the field is extremely promising for even greater developments to come. We can look forward to undertaking synthetic and comparative studies based on an expanding field of analysis in the areas of the Caribbean, Central and South America, and the regions of Africa impacted by the trans-

Atlantic slave trade. As African diaspora questions reach global scales, the archaeology of communities in locations of Europe, Asia, and the Pacific rim also awaits future expansion. Rapid developments in bioarchaeology include isotope analysis and DNA studies that provide data on potential links between populations across time and space.

Expanding landscape and spatial analyses are aided by ever-improving capabilities of computer-generated databases, mapping programs, and spatial modeling techniques. New survey methods include remote sensing, such as low altitude aerial surveys with high resolution thermal imaging, which may detect more sites in a highly cost-effective manner. Such increasingly sophisticated survey methods will aid an expansion of studies in an increasing diversity of sites, from dense urban areas to remote "maroon" community locations and the short-term sites of African descendant soldiers in military services throughout history in the Americas. Throughout these trends, we can expect to see researchers continuing in their intensive engagement with local and descendant communities in the formulation of key questions and investigative strategies for each project. The current focus on undertaking rich, contextual investigations of each site and then relating those findings in comparative analysis with other studies will yield a period of maturity in the field of African diaspora archaeology.

REFERENCES

AFRICAN DIASPORA ARCHAEOLOGY NETWORK (ADAN)
2005-2007 *African Diaspora Archaeology Newsletter*. Department of African American Studies and Department of Anthropology, University of Illinois Urbana-Champaign.
http://www.diaspora.uiuc.edu/.
2008 *African-American Archaeology, History, and Cultures*. Department of African American Studies and Department of Anthropology, University of Illinois Urbana-Champaign.
http://www.diaspora.edu/bookmark3.html.

AGBE-DAVIES, ANNA S.
2007 Practicing African American Archaeology in the Atlantic World. In *Archaeology of Atlantic Africa and the African Diaspora*, edited by Akinwumi Ogundiran and Toyin Falola, pp. 413-425. Indiana University Press, Bloomington, IN.

AGORSAH, E. KOFI
2006 The Other Side of Freedom: The Maroon Trail in Suriname. In *African Re-Genesis: Confronting Social Issues in the Diaspora*, edited by Jay B. Haviser and Kevin C. MacDonald, pp. 191-203. University College London Press, New York, NY.

ARMSTRONG, DOUGLAS V.
2003 *Creole Transformations from Slavery to Freedom: Historical Archaeology of the East End Community, St. John, Virgin Islands*. University Press of Florida, Gainesville, FL.
2008 Excavating African American Heritage: Towards a More Nuanced Understanding of the African Diaspora. *Historical Archaeology* 42(2):123-137.

ARMSTRONG, DOUGLAS V., AND MARK FLEISCHMAN
2003 House-Yard Burials of Enslaved Laborers in Eighteenth-Century Jamaica. *International Journal of Historical Archaeology* 7(1):33-65.

ASCHER, ROBERT, AND CHARLES H. FAIRBANKS
1971 Excavation of a Slave Cabin: Georgia, U.S.A. *Historical Archaeology* 5:3-17.

BABSON, DAVID W.
1990 The Archaeology of Racism and Ethnicity on Southern Plantations. *Historical Archaeology* 24(4):20-28.

BARILE, KERRI S.
2004 Race, the National Register, and Cultural Resource Management: Creating an Historic Context for Postbellum Sites. In Transcending Boundaries, Transforming the Discipline: African Diaspora Archaeologies in the New Millennium, edited by Maria Franklin and Larry McKee, thematic issue, *Historical Archaeology* 38(1):90-100.

BATTLE-BAPTISTE, WHITNEY L.
2007 "In This Here Place:" Interpreting Enslaved Homeplaces. In *Archaeology of Atlantic Africa and the African Diaspora*, edited by Akinwumi Ogundiran and Toyin Falola, pp. 233-248. Indiana University Press, Bloomington, IN.

BLAKEY, MICHAEL L.
2001 Bioarchaeology of the African Diaspora in the Americas: Its Origins and Scope. *Annual Review of Anthropology* 30: 387-422.

BRANDON, JAMIE C.
2008 Disparate Diasporas and Vindicationist Archaeologies: Some Comments on Excavating America's Metaphor. *Historical Archaeology* 42(2):147-151.

BROWN, KENNETH L.
2004 Ethnographic Analogy, Archaeology, and the African Diaspora: Perspectives from a Tenant Community. In Transcending Boundaries, Transforming the Discipline: African Diaspora Archaeologies in the New Millennium, edited by Maria Franklin and Larry McKee, thematic issue, *Historical Archaeology* 38(1):79-89.

BROWN, KENNETH L., AND DOREEN C. COOPER
 1990 Structural Continuity in an African-American Slave and Tenant Community. *Historical Archaeology* 24(4):7-19.

BULLEN, ADELAIDE K., AND RIPLEY P. BULLEN
 1945 Black Lucy's Garden. *Bulletin of the Massachusetts Archaeological Society* 6(2):17-28.

CABAK, MELANIE A., MARK D. GROOVER, AND SCOTT J. WAGERS
 1995 Health Care and the Wayman A.M.E. Church. *Historical Archaeology* 29(2):55-76.

CHAN, ALEXANDRA A.
 2007 Bringing the Out Kitchen In? The Experiential Landscapes of Black and White New England. In *Archaeology of Atlantic Africa and the African Diaspora*, edited by Akinwumi Ogundiran and Toyin Falola, pp. 249-276. Indiana University Press, Bloomington, IN.

DAVIDSON, JAMES M.
 2004 Rituals Captured in Context and Time: Charm Use in North Dallas Freedman's Town (1869-1907), Dallas, Texas. *Historical Archaeology* 38(2):22-54.

DAVIDSON, JAMES M., ERIKA ROBERTS, AND CLETE ROONEY
 2006 Excavations at Kingsley Plantation, Florida. *African Diaspora Archaeology Newsletter*, September, 2006. Department of African American Studies and Department of Anthropology, University of Illinois Urbana-Champaign. http://www.diaspora.uiuc.edu/news0906/news0906.html.

DECORSE, CHRISTOPHER R.
 2001 *West Africa During the Atlantic Slave Trade: Archaeological Perspectives.* Leicester University Press, New York, NY.

DECORSE, CHRISTOPHER R., AND MARK W. HAUSER
 2003 Low-Fired Earthenwares in the African Diaspora: Problems and Prospects. *International Journal of Historical Archaeology* 7(1):67-98.

DE CUNZO, LU ANN
 1998 A Future after Freedom. In *Archaeologists as Storytellers*, edited by Adrian Praetzellis and Mary Praetzellis, thematic issue, *Historical Archaeology* 32(1):42-54.

DEETZ, JAMES
 1993 *Flowerdew Hundred: The Archaeology of a Virginia Plantation, 1619-1864.* University Press of Virginia, Charlottesville, VA.
 1996 *In Small Things Forgotten: An Archaeology of Early American Life*, expanded and revised from 1977 edition. Anchor Books, New York, NY.

DELLE, JAMES A.
 1998 *An Archaeology of Social Space: Analyzing Coffee Plantations in Jamaica's Blue Mountains.* Plenum Press, New York, NY.
 2000 The Material and Cognitive Dimensions of Creolization in Nineteenth-Century Jamaica. In Creolization, edited by Shannon Lee Dawdy, thematic issue, *Historical Archaeology* 34(3):56-72.
 2008 A Tale of Two Tunnels: Memory, Archaeology, and the Underground Railroad. *Journal of Social Archaeology* 8(1):63-93.

DELLE, JAMES A., AND JASON SHELLENHAMER
 2008 Archaeology at the Parvin Homestead: Searching for the Material Legacy of the Underground Railroad. *Historical Archaeology* 42(2):38-62.

ELTIS, DAVID, STEPHEN D. BEHRENDT, DAVID RICHARDSON, AND HERBERT S. KLEIN
 2000 *The Trans-Atlantic Slave Trade: A Database on CD-ROM.* Cambridge University Press, Cambridge, UK.

EPPERSON, TERRANCE W.
 1990 Race and the Disciplines of the Plantation. *Historical Archaeology* 24(4):29-36.

ESPENSHADE, CHRISTOPHER
 2007 Building on Joseph's Model of Market-Bound Colonoware Pottery. *African Diaspora Archaeology Newsletter*, September

2007, Department of African American Studies and Department of Anthropology, University of Illinois Urbana-Champaign. http://www.diaspora.uiuc.edu/news0907/news0907.html

FAIRBANKS, CHARLES
1974 The Kingsley Slave Cabins in Duval County, Florida, 1968. *Conference on Historic Sites Archaeology Papers* 7:62-93.

FARNSWORTH, PAUL
1996 The Influence of Trade on Bahamian Slave Culture. *Historical Archaeology* 30(4):1-23.

FENNELL, CHRISTOPHER C.
2003 Group Identity, Individual Creativity and Symbolic Generation in a BaKongo Diaspora. *International Journal of Historical Archaeology* 7(1):1-31.
2007 *Crossroads and Cosmologies: Diasporas and Ethnogenesis in the New World.* University Press of Florida, Gainesville, FL.

FERGUSON, LELAND G.
1992 *Uncommon Ground: Archaeology and Early African America.* Smithsonian Institution Press, Washington, DC.
2007 Early African-American Pottery in South Carolina: A Complicated Plainware. *African Diaspora Archaeology Newsletter,* June 2007, Department of African American Studies and Department of Anthropology, University of Illinois Urbana-Champaign. http://www.diaspora.uiuc.edu/news0607/news0607.html.

FITTS, ROBERT F.
1996 The Landscapes of Northern Bondage. *Historical Archaeology* 30(2):54-73.

FRANKLIN, MARIA
1997 "Power to the People": Sociopolitics and the Archaeology of Black Americans. In In the Realm of Politics: Prospects for Public Participation in African-American and Plantation Archaeology, edited by Carol McDavid and David W. Babson,

thematic issue, *Historical Archaeology* 31(3):36-50.

FUNARI, PEDRO PAULO A.
2003 Conflict and the Interpretation of Palmares, a Brazilian Runaway Polity. *Historical Archaeology* 37(3):81-92.

GALLE, JILLIAN E., AND AMY L. YOUNG (EDITORS)
2004 *Engendering African American Archaeology: A Southern Perspective.* University of Tennessee Press, Knoxville, TN.

GENERAL SERVICE ADMINISTRATION
2007 *African Burial Ground: Return to the Past to Build the Future.* http://www.africanburialground.gov/.

GRADWOHL, DAVID M., AND NANCY M. OSBORN
1984 *Exploring Buried Buxton: Archaeology of an Abandoned Iowa Coal Mining Town with a Large Black Population.* Iowa State University Press, Ames, IA.

HANDLER, JEROME S.
1994 Determining African Birth from Skeletal Remains: A Note on Tooth Mutilation. *Historical Archaeology* 28(3):113-119.
1996 A Prone Burial from a Plantation Slave Cemetery in Barbados, West Indies: Possible Evidence for an African-type Witch or Other Negatively Viewed Person. *Historical Archaeology* 30(3):76-86.

HANDLER, JEROME S., AND FREDERICK W. LANGE
1978 *Plantation Slavery in Barbados: An Archaeological and Historical Investigation.* Harvard University Press, Cambridge, MA.

HANDLER, JEROME S., AND MICHAEL L. TUITE, JR.
2008 *The Atlantic Slave Trade and Slave Life in the Americas: A Visual Record.* Virginia Foundation for the Humanities and the Digital Media Lab at the University of Virginia, Charlottesville, VA. http://www.slaveryimages.org.

HAUSER, MARK W.
2007 Between Urban and Rural: Organization and Distribution of Local Pottery in Eight-

eenth-Century Jamaica. In *Archaeology of Atlantic Africa and the African Diaspora*, edited by Akinwumi Ogundiran and Toyin Falola, pp. 292-310. Indiana University Press, Bloomington, IN.

HEATH, BARBARA J., AND AMBER BENNETT
2000 "The Little Spots Allow'd Them": The Archaeological Study of African-American Yards. *Historical Archaeology* 34(2):38-55.

HOWSON, JEAN E.
1990 Social Relations and Material Culture: A Critique of the Archaeology of Plantation Slavery. *Historical Archaeology* 24(4):78-91.

JAMIESON, ROSS W.
1995 Material Culture and Social Death: African-American Burial Practices. *Historical Archaeology* 29(4):39-58.

JOSEPH, J. W.
1993 White Columns and Black Hands: Class and Classification in the Plantation Ideology of the Georgia and South Carolina Lowcountry. *Historical Archaeology* 27(3):57-73.

2004 Resistance and Compliance: CRM and the Archaeology of the African Diaspora. In Transcending Boundaries, Transforming the Discipline: African Diaspora Archaeologies in the New Millennium, edited by Maria Franklin and Larry McKee, thematic issue, *Historical Archaeology* 38(1):18-31.

2007 One More Look into the Water -- Colonoware in South Carolina Rivers and Charleston's Market Economy. *African Diaspora Archaeology Newsletter*, June 2007, Department of African American Studies and Department of Anthropology, University of Illinois Urbana-Champaign. http://www.diaspora.uiuc.edu/news0607/news0607.html

KELLY, KENNETH
2004 The African Diaspora Starts Here: Historical Archaeology of Coastal West Africa. In *African Historical Archaeologies*, ed-

ited by Andrew Reid and Paul Lane, pp. 219-241. Kluwer Academic/Plenum Press, New York, NY.

KRAUS-FRIEDBERG, CHANA, AND KRISTEN R. FELLOWS
2008 A Report from the SHA Meetings in Albuquerque: Exploring a More Global Perspective on Plantation Archaeology. *African Diaspora Archaeology Newsletter*, March, 2008, Department of African American Studies and Department of Anthropology, University of Illinois Urbana-Champaign. http://www.diaspora.uiuc.edu/news0308/news0308.html.

LANDERS, JANE
1997 Africans in the Spanish Colonies. In Diversity and Social Identity in Colonial Spanish America: Native American, African, and Hispanic Communities During the Middle Period, edited by Donna L. Ruhl and Kathleen Hoffman, thematic issue, *Historical Archaeology* 31(1): 84-91.

LAROCHE, CHERYL J.
2004 On the Edge of Freedom: Free Black Communities, Archaeology, and the Underground Railroad. PhD Dissertation, University of Maryland, College Park, MD.

LAROCHE, CHERYL J., AND MICHAEL L. BLAKEY
1997 Seizing Intellectual Power: The Dialogue at the New York African Burial Ground. In In the Realm of Politics: Prospects for Public Participation in African-American and Plantation Archaeology, edited by Carol McDavid and David W. Babson, thematic issue, *Historical Archaeology* 31(3):84-106.

LEONE, MARK P., AND GLADYS-MARIE FRY
1999 Conjuring in the Big House Kitchen: An Interpretation of African American Belief Systems Based on the Uses of Archaeology and Folklore Sources. *Journal of American Folklore* 112(445):372-403.

MACK, MARK E., AND MICHAEL L. BLAKEY
2004 The New York African Burial Ground Project: Past Biases, Current Dilemmas, and Future Research Opportunities. In Transcending Boundaries, Transforming the Discipline: African Diaspora Archaeologies in the New Millennium, edited by Maria Franklin and Larry McKee, thematic issue, *Historical Archaeology* 38(1):10-17.

MARKELL, ANN, MARTIN HALL, AND CARMEL SCHRIRE
1995 The Historical Archaeology of Vergelegen, an Early Farmstead at the Cape of Good Hope. *Historical Archaeology* 29(1):10-34.

MCCARTHY, JOHN P.
2006 African Community Identity at the Cemetery. In *African Re-Genesis: Confronting Social Issues in the Diaspora*, edited by Jay B. Haviser and Kevin C. MacDonald, pp. 176-183. University College London Press, New York, NY.

MCDAVID, CAROL
1997 Descendants, Decisions, and Power: The Public Interpretation of the Archaeology of the Levi Jordan Plantation. In In the Realm of Politics: Prospects for Public Participation in African-American and Plantation Archaeology, edited by Carol McDavid and David W. Babson, thematic issue, *Historical Archaeology* 31(3):114-131.

MOUER, L. DANIEL, MARY E. HODGES, STEPHEN R. POTTER, SUSAN L. RENAUD, IVOR NOËL HUME, DENNIS J. POGUE, MARTHA W. MCCARTNEY, AND THOMAS E. DAVIDSON
1999 Colonoware Pottery, Chesapeake Pipes, and "Uncritical Assumptions." In *I, Too, Am America: Archaeological Studies of African-American Life*, edited by Theresa A. Singleton, pp. 83-115. University Press of Virginia, Charlottesville, VA.

MULLINS, PAUL R.
1999 Race and the Genteel Consumer: Class and African-American Consumption, 1850-1930. *Historical Archaeology* 33(1):22-38.

2006 Racializing the Commonplace Landscape: An Archaeology of Urban Renewal along the Color Line. *World Archaeology* 38(1):60-71.
2008 Excavating America's Metaphor: Race, Diaspora, and Vindicationist Archaeologies. *Historical Archaeology* 42(2):104-122.

OGUNDIRAN, AKINWUMI, AND TOYIN FALOLA
2007 Pathways in the Archaeology of Transatlantic Africa. In *Archaeology of Atlantic Africa and the African Diaspora*, edited by Akinwumi Ogundiran and Toyin Falola, pp. 3-45. Indiana University Press, Bloomington, IN.

OGUNDIRAN, AKINWUMI, AND TOYIN FALOLA (EDITORS)
2007 *Archaeology of Atlantic Africa and the African Diaspora*. Indiana University Press, Bloomington, IN.

ORSER, CHARLES E. JR.
1988 The Archaeological Analysis of Plantation Society: Replacing Status and Caste with Economics and Power. *American Antiquity* 53:735-751.
1994 Toward a Global Historical Archaeology: An Example from Brazil. *Historical Archaeology* 28(1):5-22.
2003 *Race and Practice in Archaeological Interpretation*. University of Pennsylvania Press, Philadelphia, PA.
2007 *The Archaeology of Race and Racialization in Historic America*. University Press of Florida, Gainesville, FL.

OTTO, JOHN SOLOMON
1984 *Cannon's Point Plantation, 1794-1850: Living Conditions and Status Patterns in The Old South*. Academic Press, New York, NY.

PHILIPS, JOHN E. (EDITOR)
2000 *Writing African History*. University of Rochester Press, Rochester, NY.

POSNANSKY, MERRICK, AND CHRISTOPHER R. DECORSE
1986 Historical Archaeology in Sub-Saharan Africa – A Review. *Historical Archaeology* 20(1):1-14.

REID, ANDREW M., AND PAUL J. LANE (EDITORS)
2004 *African Historical Archaeologies*. Kluwer Academic/Plenum Press, New York, NY.

REITZ, ELIZABETH J.
1994 Zooarchaeological Analysis of a Free African Community: Gracia Real de Santa Teresa de Mose. *Historical Archaeology* 28(1):23-40.

RUPPEL, TIMOTHY, JESSICA NEUWIRTH, MARK P. LEONE, AND GLADYS-MARIE FRY
2003 Hidden in View: African Spiritual Spaces in North American Landscape. *Antiquity* 77(296):321-335.

RUSSELL, AARON E.
1997 Material Culture and African-American Spirituality at the Hermitage. *Historical Archaeology* 31(2):63-80.

SAMFORD, PATRICIA E.
2007 *Subfloor Pits and the Archaeology of Slavery in Colonial Virginia*. University of Alabama Press, Tuscaloosa, AL.

SCHMIDT, PETER R.
2006 *Historical Archaeology in Africa: Representation, Social Memory, and Oral Traditions*. AltaMira Press, Walnut Creek, CA.

SHACKEL, PAUL A., AND DAVID L. LARSEN
2000 Labor, Racism, and the Built Environment in Early Industrial Harpers Ferry. In *Lines that Divide: Historical Archaeologies of Race, Class, and Gender*, edited by James A. Delle, Stephen A Mrozowski, and Robert Paynter, pp. 22-39. University of Tennessee Press, Knoxville, TN.

SINGLETON, THERESA A.
1990 The Archaeology of the Plantation South: A Review of Approaches and Goals. *Historical Archaeology* 24(4):70-77.

SINGLETON, THERESA A., AND MARK BOGRAD
2000 Breaking Typological Barriers: Looking for the Colono in Colonoware. In *Lines that Divide: Historical Archaeologies of Race, Class, and Gender*, edited by James A. Delle, Stephen A Mrozowski, and Robert Paynter, pp. 3-21. University of Tennessee Press, Knoxville, TN.

SOCIETY FOR HISTORICAL ARCHAEOLOGY
2003 *SHA Ethics Statement*. Adopted June 21, 2003.

STAHL, ANN B.
2004a Making History in Banda: Reflections on the Construction of Africa's Past. In <u>Transcending Boundaries, Transforming the Discipline: African Diaspora Archaeologies in the New Millennium</u>, edited by Maria Franklin and Larry McKee, thematic issue, *Historical Archaeology* 38(1):50-65.
2004b Political Economic Mosaics: Archaeology of the Last Two Millennia in Tropical Sub-Saharan Africa. *Annual Review of Anthropology* 33:145-172.

STINE, LINDA F., MELANIE A. CABAK, AND MARK D. GROOVER
1996 Blue Beads as African-American Cultural Symbols. *Historical Archaeology* 30(3):49-74.

SYMANSKI, LUIS C. P.
2006 *Slaves and Planters in Western Brazil: Material Culture, Identity and Power*. PhD Dissertation, Department of Anthropology, University of Florida, Gainesville, FL., and UMI/Proquest Ann Arbor, MI.

THOMAS JEFFERSON FOUNDATION
2008 *Digital Archaeological Archive of Comparative Slavery*. Thomas Jefferson Foundation, Charlottesville, VA. http://www.daacs.org/.

UPTON, DELL
1985 White and Black Landscapes in Eighteenth-Century Virginia. *Places* 2(2):59-72.

WATTERS, DAVID R.
1994   Mortuary Patterns at the Harney Site Slave Cemetery, Montserrat, in Caribbean Perspective. *Historical Archaeology* 28(3):56-73.

WEIK, TERRANCE
1997   The Archaeology of Maroon Societies in the Americas: Resistance, Cultural Continuity, and Transformation in the African Diaspora. *Historical Archaeology* 31(2):81-92.
2004   Archaeology of the African Diaspora in Latin America. In Transcending Boundaries, Transforming the Discipline: African Diaspora Archaeologies in the New Millennium, edited by Maria Franklin and Larry McKee, thematic issue, *Historical Archaeology* 38(1):32-49.

WHEATON, THOMAS R., AMY FRIEDLANDER, AND PATRICK GARROW
1983   Yaughan and Curiboo Plantations: Studies in African American Archaeology. Soil Systems, Inc., Marietta, GA.

WILKIE, LAURIE
1997   Secret and Sacred: Contextualizing the Artifacts of African-American Magic and Religion. *Historical Archaeology* 31(4):81-106.
2000a Culture Bought: Evidence of Creolization in the Consumer Goods of an Enslaved Bahamian Family. *Historical Archaeology* 34(3):10-26.
2000b *Creating Freedom: Material Culture and African American Identity at Oakley Plantation, Louisiana, 1840-1950.* Louisiana State University Press, Baton Rouge, LA.
2003   *The Archaeology of Mothering: An African American Midwife's Tale.* Routledge, New York, NY.

MERRICK POSNANSKY
CHRISTOPHER R. DECORSE

Historical Archaeology in Sub-Saharan Africa— A Review

ABSTRACT

Relatively few historical archaeology projects have been carried out in Sub-Saharan Africa, yet the area presents a wide variety of research potentialities from both historical and theoretical viewpoints. Various definitions of historical archaeology and their application to Africa are examined, and the research undertaken thus far is reviewed. Previous work has largely focused on the larger fortified sites of 15th to 19th century European construction. On the East African Coast archaeolological fieldwork has also been carried out on Islamic sites where limited documentation is provided by Arabic writings. Directions for future research are discussed, including the possibility of examining the socio—cultural background of the African diaspora. Particular stress is placed on the necessity for intensified regional studies, cognizant of the contacts between well documented historical sites and the villages and resource areas with which they interacted.

Introduction

Though historical archaeology as currently understood in Europe and North America has been undertaken in Africa since World War II, it has neither been defined as such nor has it received recognition as a separate sub-discipline. Archaeology itself has a respectable antiquity in Africa (Posnansky 1982), but its early practitioners placed their emphasis on the Stone Age, which in several parts of Africa lasted into the second millennium A.D., to the detriment of the Iron Age and Historic period. Even as late as the 1950s many prominent European scholars disparaged the idea of African history as a worthwhile endeavour. Both African history and the detailed study of Africa's more recent archaeological past awaited the independence era when most countries moved rapidly to expand their nascent universities and to vigorously search for their historical antecedents in order to establish their cultural integrity and promote national pride.

With independence came national museums and antiquities services, at first manned by expatriate Europeans and later by nationals trained in local universities. New priorities for research were established which shifted the emphasis from the Stone Age to the cultural history of the component populations of the new states. There was also a reaction against the study of the history of the colonizers about whom it was felt enough was already known. Those historical archaeology projects that have been initiated have largely been incidental to other activities such as the preservation of national monuments or as isolated projects carried out in cooperation with historians to locate, describe, and date sites known from documentary sources. Less than 25 archaeologists have undertaken historical projects in an area three and a half times the size of the United States. Most excavations have been brief, lasting two weeks or less.

Definitions of Historical Archaeology

Definitions of "Historical Archaeology" posited thus far are not appropriate descriptions of the field as it applies to sub-Saharan Africa. Schuyler's definition of "Historic Sites Archaeology" as "the study of the materal manifestation of the expansion of European culture into the non-European world starting in the 15th century and ending with industrialization or the present depending on local conditions" (Schuyler 1978:28), though superficially accepted is nevertheless unsuitable. The problem with this definition is not the contact implication that it represents but the emphasis in some of the literature on the one sided impact of that contact. The colonial adaptations under study were adaptations to new physical and human environments. They were not straightforward cultural transplantations. The acculturation and reactions of the indigenous groups they met should form an equally important part of any such definition.

Various American definitions which limit historical archaeology to "archaeology carried out on sites of the historic period" (South 1977:25; Also Schuyler 1978:27) or to the "cultural remains of literate societies" (Deetz 1977:5) are inappropriate in that many of the societies studied, though existing in the relatively recent past, were neither literate nor in close contact with literate societies. In much of sub-Saharan Africa documentary history has a short time span. The first Arabic accounts date back to approximately A.D. 800 for the Sudanic belt and to the 15th century for much of the west and central African littoral. The east African Coast has scattered isolated documents, with the emphasis on the isolated nature of the accounts, rather than a continuous history from Classical times until the advent of the Portuguese in A.D. 1497–1498. Much of the interior of Africa is lacking in literary sources until the later part of the 19th century.

In the sense that we are dealing with some areas which have excellent documentary records and that the arteries of international trade penetrated to quite remote areas, some scholars have considered it appropriate to use the term protohistoric for a greater part of the second millennium A.D. (e.g., Mauny 1967). The east African coast and Sudanic belt had Islamic societies which were culturally reinforced by trade with the Middle East and North Africa. Towns with mosques and centers of learning such as Timbuktu were established, while contacts were maintained through pilgrimages and commerce with the heartland of the Islamic world (Levtzion and Hopkins 1981). In this sense, parts of Africa have an active Islamic archaeological tradition which on the Kenyan Coast dates back to 1948 when James Kirkman began his work at Gedi. It is notable that Kirkman (1957), referring to his research, was the first to use the term historical archaeology in Africa.

In many cases the documentary source material which does exist is incomplete and ethnocentric and so provides only limited insight into the history and development of indigenous societies (Figure 1). Archaeologists in Africa have therefore commonly utilized approaches other than archaeology or documentary sources. Oral history and linguistic data have perhaps been used more inten-

sively by historians in Africa than in most other parts of the world (eg., Miller 1980; Ehret and Posnansky 1982). The term historical archaeology has in fact been quite legitimately used by Schmidt (1977; 1983) to include those periods for which ample information from oral history exists. These sources often provide more details in terms of family, clan, or state history than later periods supposedly covered by written sources. Though this usage is attractive for later Iron Age African situations, some aspects of such research might be better included within the rubric of ethnohistory or occasionally ethnoarchaeology both in terms of source material and objectives (Atherton 1983). Historically and methodologically the later periods of African archaeology reflect a closer involvement with history as a discipline than with anthropology, which is completely unrepresented in many African universities.

In this paper the definition employed approximates the current sense of the term widely used in North America. A straightforward definition of historical archaeology for Africa is "archaeology undertaken in periods or for areas in which the principal source of contextual information is provided by documentary evidence." The context as here understood is the general historical framework rather than the socio-cultural background. In this sense it applies particularly, but not exclusively, to the activities of European societies and the communities which are known better from European documents than from oral history and other sources. The definition can be expanded to those coastal societies covered by Islamic archaeology, though by and large before A.D. 1500 there are only discontinuous literary sources and chronicles based on oral traditions.

Historical archaeological research in Africa has largely been focused on five regions: the West African coast, the Zambesi River valley, South Africa, the east African coast, and the upper Nile in Uganda. In recent years five significant shipwreck projects have also been undertaken, one in East Africa, two in South Africa, one in the Madeiras, and another at St. Helena. These research areas will be discussed in turn. Sites referred to in the text are shown in Figure 2.

Perspectives from Historical Archaeology: African Diaspora Archaeology

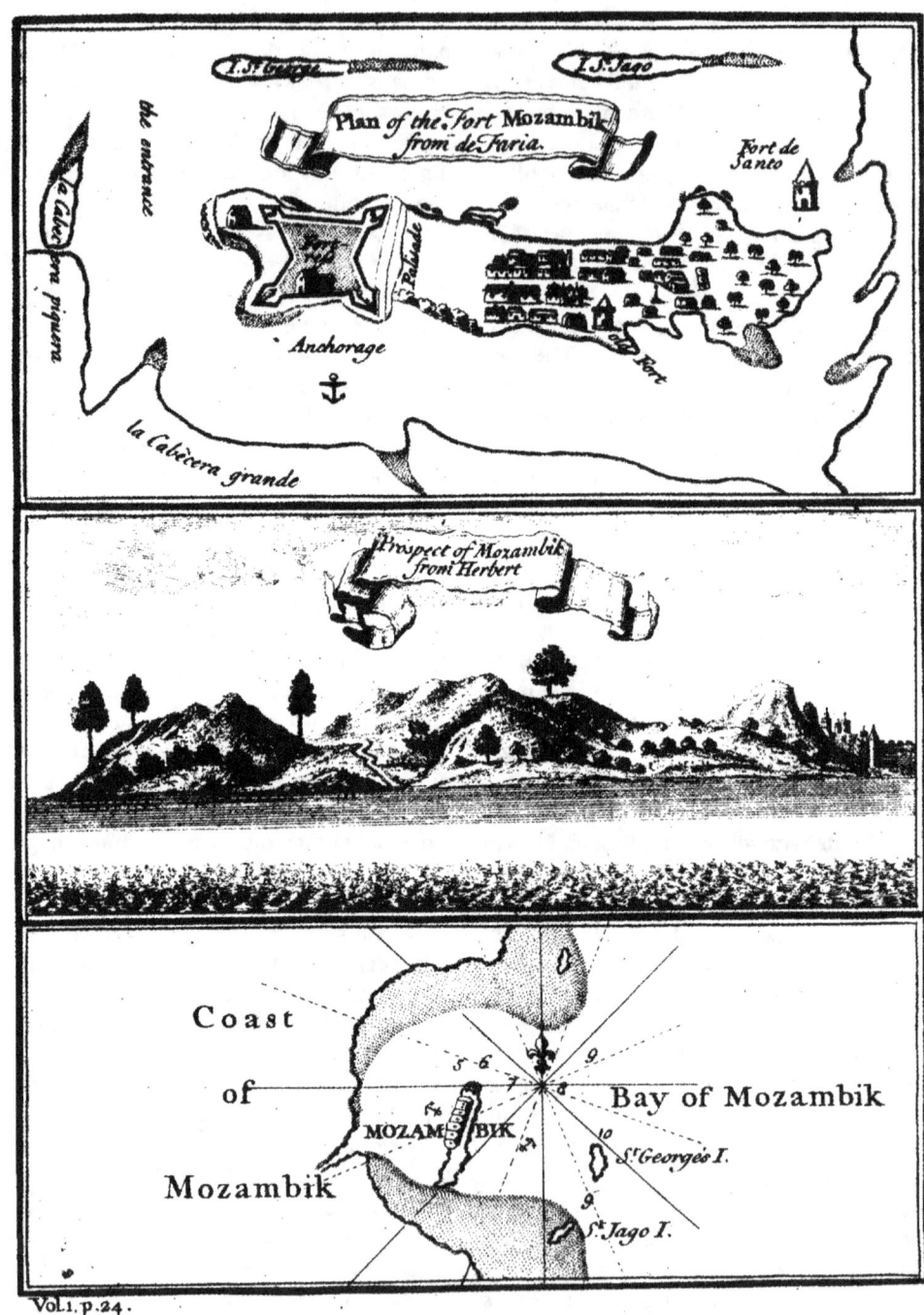

FIGURE 1. Numerous documentary sources exist for Africa, yet most focus on the European presence and are often biased and incomplete, as evidenced by this eighteenth century illustration which includes a fanciful rendering of the "Prospect of Mozambik" (From an unknown 18th century source).

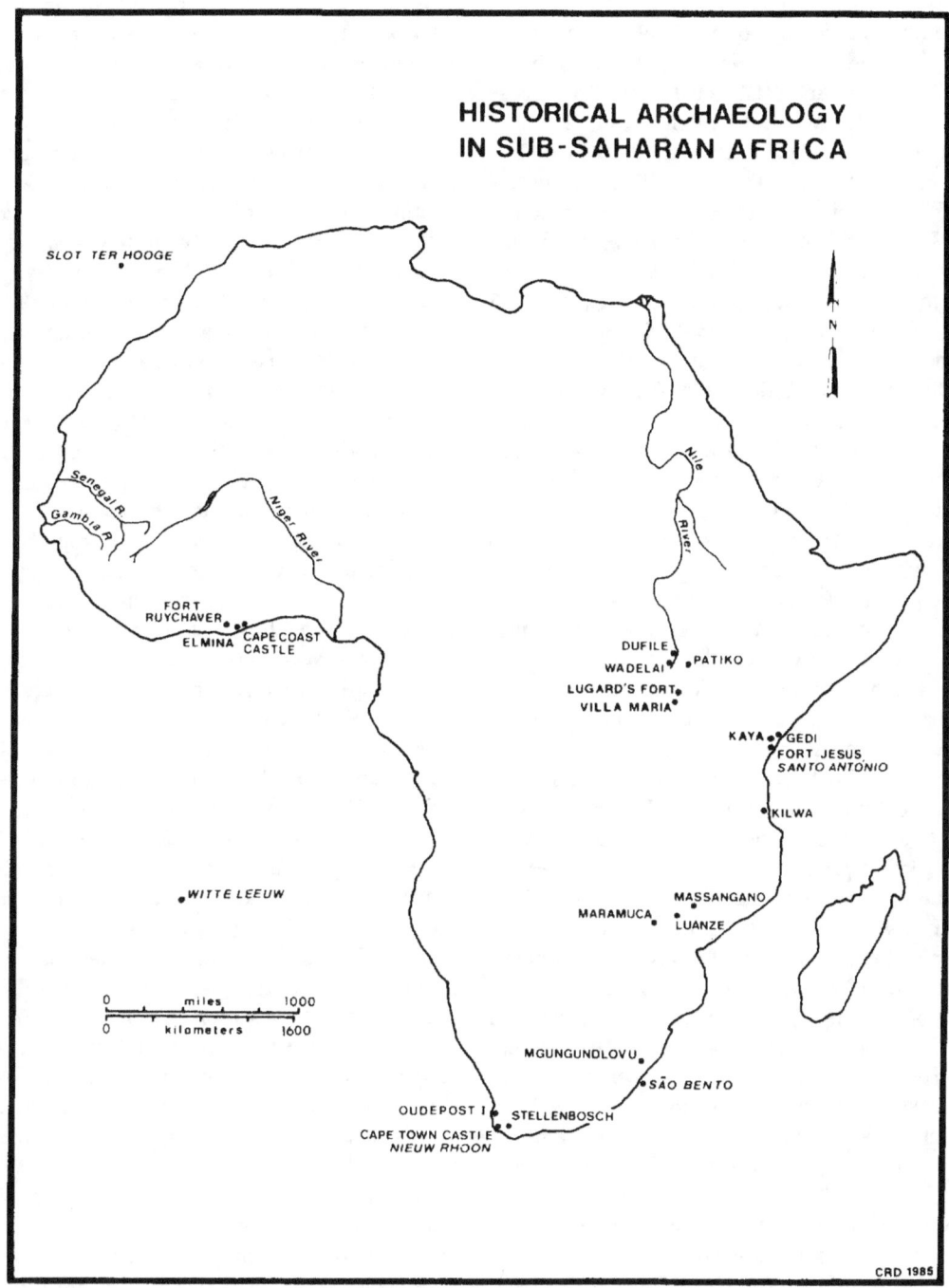

FIGURE 2. Map showing the locations of sites referred to in the text.

West Africa

The fortified trading posts of West Africa, some well deserving of their popular appellation "castles," were first established by the Portuguese who constructed a fort at Arguin in Mauretania in the mid-15th century. Later came the Dutch, English, French, Swedes, Danes, and Brandenburgers who founded forts or trading posts along much of the West African coast, particularly in the Senegambia and the Gold Coast. On the Gold Coast alone more than 50 posts were built between 1482 and 1787 (Van Dantzig 1980). Except for Fort Ruychaver in Ghana and a number of smaller outposts along the Senegal and Gambia rivers (Wood 1967), the activities of European factors were largely confined to the coastal zones. Trading opportunities offered by the Europeans presented what the late K.O. Dike (1956) termed a "frontier of opportunity." Towns like Elmina on the Gold Coast, which expanded rapidly after the founding fort *Sao Jorge da Mina*, were initially ethnically heterogeneous but eventually established cultural identities of their own. It is the appreciation of the historical and cultural development of societies such as these that provide the challenge for the historical archaeologist.

The material culture of the West African forts is dominated by cannon, cannon balls, brass fuses, drink bottles, nails, and tobacco pipes (Walker 1975) with surprisingly small quantities of ceramics. The male oriented European fort communities presumably relied heavily on local services of the domestic kind. Historical archaeology projects undertaken in West Africa thus far have concentrated on cataloging European monuments and discussions of their structural history (Bessac and Dfkeyser 1951; Bessac 1952; Lawrence 1963; Wood 1967). The few excavations that have been conducted have either focused on problems of chronology and cultural ascription (e.g., Calvocoressi 1977) or been undertaken to facilitate restorations (e.g., Van Dantzig 1972).

Two exceptions are projects undertaken at Cape Coast Castle and Fort Ruychaver in Ghana. Excavations at Cape Coast in 1973 were aimed at examining a slave dungeon in order to illuminate one of the points of departure for the African diaspora (Figure 3). Total excavation provided data on the meager possessions of the slaves just prior to their departure and on their treatment in crowded, hot, damp, and dark basement confines (Simmonds 1973). Fort Ruychaver, 40 miles up the Ankobra River, was the only trading post ever established in the hinterland of the Gold Coast. Completely forgotten, it was rediscovered archaeologically in the Dutch archives and in the oral traditions of the local inhabitants (Posnansky and van Dantzig 1976). Excavations in 1975 confirmed the temporary nature of the outpost, which only lasted from 1655 until 1659. This attempt to tap directly into the gold trade in the interior ended in disaster when the Dutch factor, unable to meet his obligations, blew himself up along with many of the neighboring chiefs in an explosion which completely consumed the building. The finds, while including few items of European origin, were indicative of the commercial policy of the Dutch who rather than manufacture local roof tiles exported the identical type to West Africa, South Africa, and New York.

In addition to forts and castles several of the 18th and 19th century Danish plantations on the Gold Coast have been located and planned (Jeppesen 1966). These agricultural projects were quite different in character from the slave plantations of the West Indies as they developed, at least in part, as a response to the abolitionist movement. Plantations were established during the late 18th century with the hope that crops supplied by the West Indian plantations could be produced in Africa and thus make slavery unnecessary. An additional impetus was provided after 1800 when the effects of legislation for the suppression of the slave trade and anti-slaving squadrons started to interfere with the supply of slaves to the Americas. Support also came from the Danish government that no doubt saw the plantations as a means of supplying Danish tradeposts. Coffee, cotton, tobacco, fruits, hides and various other products were produced, but only with very limited success and no substantial European settlement was ever made. The sites of Daccubie and Fredriksgave, two of the larger

FIGURE 3. Cape Coast Castle, once headquarters of the Royal Africa Company, it now houses the National Museum of Ghana.

plantations, were recently visited to assess their potential as training sites for archaeology students from the University of Ghana. Both sites, though heavily overgrown, are relatively well preserved. Excavation might provide interesting comparative data with other European sites.

The Zambezi Valley

There were numerous Portuguese trading stations in the Zambesi valley which in course of time developed into *prazos* or estates engaged in both agriculture and trade which by the 19th century included a lucrative market in slaves. Built of mudbrick, wattle, and daub with low surrounding banks, surmounted in their prime by palisades,

they are far from obvious on the Zambian and Zimbabwean landscape. Painstaking research by Newitt and Garlake (Garlake 1967; Newitt and Garlake 1967) on historical sources has led to the correct identification of several of the more important posts. Excavations and surface collections have been carried out at sites ranging in age from the 17th century trade posts of Luanze and Maramuca, to the 19th century *aringa* at Massangano (Clark 1967; Garlake 1967, 1970; Phillipson 1972). Data from documentary records provides a tapestry of Portuguese-African interaction against which archaeological data can be used to complement a story rich in enthnohistorical documentation. Unfortunately other than providing descriptions, chronological parameters, and sections of embankments, the scale of the excavations has not generated much new data on the social and economic life of their inhabitants. It is obvious from the few finds recovered that gold mining and trade were important activities in the 17th century, while the later *prazos* present a picture of a creole population whose ceramics were more closely allied to their African neighbors than to their European homeland or even to the larger towns on the coast.

South Africa

Work in South Africa has focused on Dutch colonial sites of the 17th and 18th centuries, though a variety of materials have received attention ranging from early postal stones or pillars, to a collection from a dump site of World War I German and English bayonets (Abrahams 1984). Much of the excavation that has been undertaken has been aimed at the salvage of sites threatened with destruction or has been part of restoration projects. The earliest of these efforts dates to 1926 when some material was gathered in connection with the restoration of Groot Constantia (Vos 1981:354). Intermittent work has been carried out at a variety of sites since then.

Systematic salvage work at Stellenbosch was initiated by Vos in 1975 and continued over the next five years as part of a research program to examine colonial life between 1680 and 1850 (Vos 1981). The analysis of material from 25 excavated sites has not yet been completed, but results promise to provide a greater understanding of the unique character of Cape society. Preliminary work indicates that imported Chinese porcelain was common in everyday use during the Colonial Period (Deacon 1984). This is in contrast to Western Europe and the Americas where such wares remained at a premium. Faunal analysis has revealed that the Stellenbosch colonists relied on domesticated animals such as sheep and cattle, as well as fish, hares, ostriches, and tortoises.

Much work has also been initiated in the Cape Town area. Abrahams has excavated on the Grand Parade of Cape Town Castle to locate the 17th

.century remains of Van Riebeck's Fort. Portions of the southwestern bastion and the adjacent moat were identified and a great deal of cultural material was collected (Abrahams 1984). This provides an interesting comparitive collection for material recovered by the Fagans within Cape Town Castle (Deacon 1984; Potgieter and Abrahams 1984). Abrahams (1984) has also done extensive documentary research to produce several overlay maps of central Cape Town development over the past 330 years. This will be invaluable in urban planning and cultural resource management.

A fascinating excavation to the northeast was conducted by Parkington and Cronin (1979) to examine spatial arrangements within the Zulu King Dingane's capital kraal at Mgungundlovu. Between 1829 and 1838 various European visitors, mainly missionaries and traders, left a series of conflicting reports and sketches of the capital. The excavators, through careful planning and excavation, were able to establish that the site had approximatly 1100 dwellings arranged in a circular pattern. Some indications of the status and occupational divisions referred to in historical accounts were discovered.

East Africa

On the east African coast there has been a continuity of activity ranging from research on Islamic towns such as Kilwa to work on the Portuguese and Omani Arab forts (Chittick 1975, 1984). The largest project to date is Kirkman's excavation at Fort Jesus, which was constructed by the Portuguese in 1593 and held until 1698 when it was captured by forces of Saif bin Sultan I (Kirkman 1974). The fortress remained in use as a prison under the British Protectorate until 1958 when it was declared a historical monument and archaeological and reconstructive work was initiated. Kirkman supplemented documentary sources with archaeological data to provide a detailed structural history of the fort. His research also gives a description of the associated material culture spanning the late 16th through 19th centuries.

The work at Fort Jesus, along with the excavation of a Portuguese frigate which sank near the fort in 1697 (see discussion below), has shed invaluable light on the nature of Portuguese societies in the Indian Ocean, including the strong links which existed between Mombasa and Mocambique and their reliance on African potters for domestic ware. Unfortunately, little work has been carried out on the Portuguese forts further south or on the associated African and creole communities.

The Upper Nile

In the upper Nile and Uganda there are also numerous forts, including some of the largest and most massive European earthworks in Africa. One of the latest is Lugard's fort in Kampala built in 1890. This fortification prompted the late Sir Mortimer Wheeler, who visited the site in 1961, to wax lyrically about it being "the last true hill-fort of the British Empire." The earliest of the forts, Patiko, was established in northern Uganda in 1872 as a base for the control of the slave trade by Sir Samuel Baker, then in the Egyptian Service (Thomas 1963). Later, Emin Pasha, cut off by the Mahdi's rebellion in the Sudan, built other forts like Wadelai and Dufile on the Nile to control his isolated province of Equatoria (Langlands 1967; Figure 4). Other forts were established early in the colonial era to subdue the Banyoro and Nandi in the Uganda Protectorate (Matson and Sutton 1965). Excavations at these sites has largely focused on their structural history. At Wadelai the presence of tin cans is an indication of an early adoption of canned goods by a colonial army. Most of the later forts have been surveyed but not excavated (Imperial College 1966).

As in other parts of Africa some of the early Christian mud brick buildings, such as the early Catholic mission at Villa Maria, have been given minimal protection (Figure 5). Uganda also witnessed some early experimental railways including a pre World-War I monorail. A study of the Kampala to Bombo locotractor railway (Peal 1963) clearly indicates the potential that exists for industrial Archaeology.

Nautical Archaeology

Five underwater projects have been undertaken in various parts of Africa. Work on the Pondoland Coast in South Africa by Auret and Maggs focused on material collected from the wreck site of the mid-16th century Portuguese ship *São Bento* which sank in 1554 (Auret 1977; Auret and Maggs 1982). Much of the material was recovered by private individuals and is now divided among several public and private collections. Lightley (1976) salvaged a portion of a wreck near Cape Town, South Africa, which was exposed as a result of construction activities. Excavation suggested that the vessel might be the Dutch East Indiaman *Nieuw Rhoon* which was purposefully beached and stripped after floundering in 1776. Two other Dutch East India vessels have been investigated by Sténuit: the *Witte Leeuw* which sank at St. Helena in 1613 and the *Slot ter Hooge* which went down at Porto Santo in the Madeiras in 1724 (Sténuit 1975; 1978). These projects recovered large amounts of trade goods, including both commodities outward bound to the Orient as in the case of the *Slot ter Hooge* and those being carried back to Holland as in the case of the *Witte Leeuw*. Published accounts of the finds provide some tantalizing photographs of a portion of the material salvaged (van de Pijl-Ketel 1982).

It is not by coincidence that the most thoroughly examined wreck site is that of the Portuguese warship *Santa Antonio da Tanna* which sank while attempting to relieve the garrison at Fort Jesus, Mombasa, in 1697. Systematic archaeological work on the 42 gun frigate was initiated by Kirkman (1972a; 1972b), and later continued by Piercy (1977; 1978; 1979; 1981). Excavation provided a quantity of information on the construction of the vessel as well as the material on board. A detailed description of the vessel's ceramics is provided by Sassoon (1981).

Summary and Conclusion

Although the preceding provides only a brief survey of historical archaeology in sub-Saharan

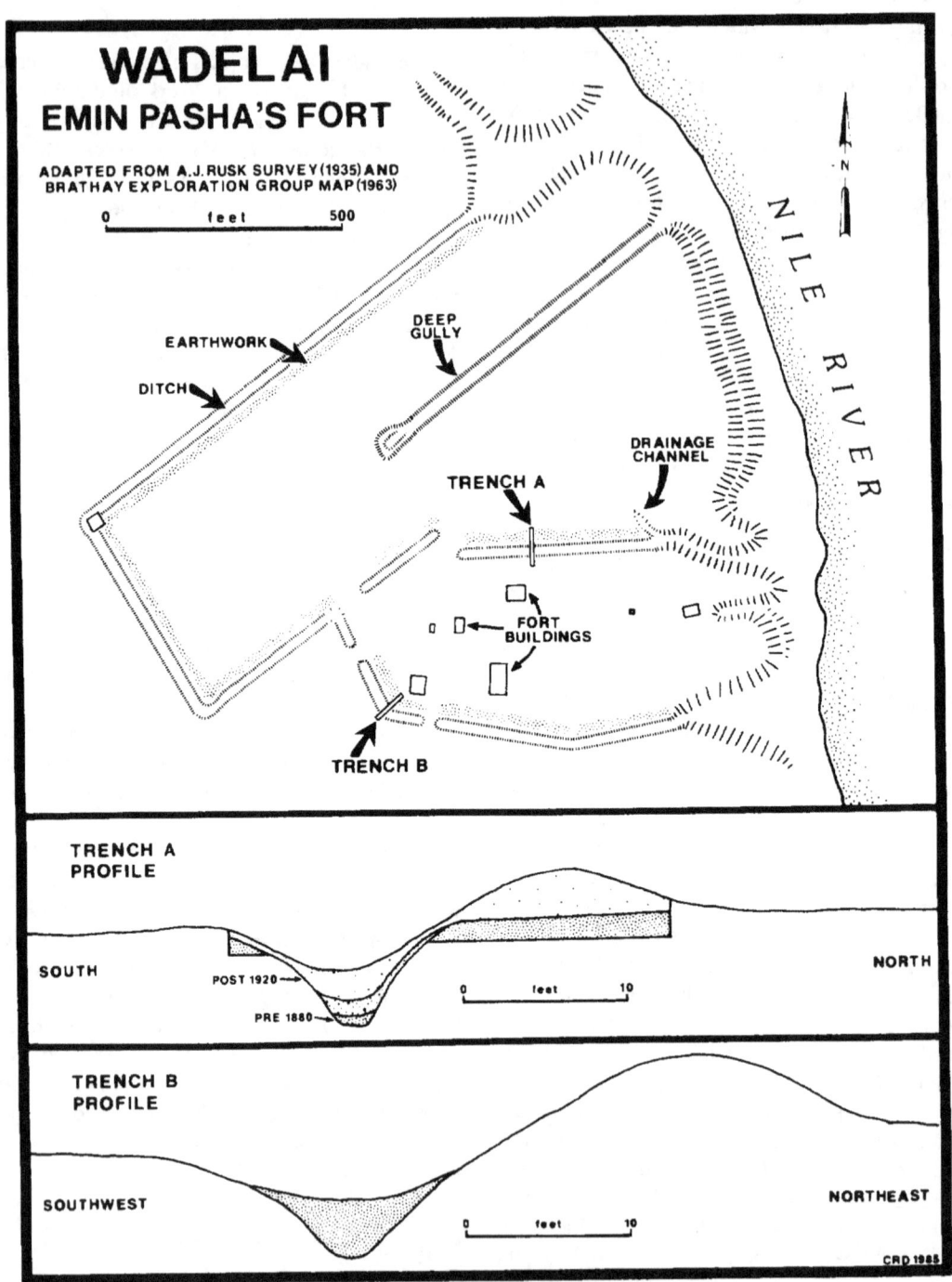

FIGURE 4. Emin Pasha's fort at Wadelai, Uganda.

FIGURE 5. A 19th century mud brick drum tower at the early Catholic Mission Villa Maria in Uganda.

Africa, at least four common features are apparent. First, there has been an undue though perhaps understandable emphasis on the larger, obvious military or fortified sites. Secondly, though the sites that have received attention include some of the major historic period sites of sub-Saharan Africa, their locations mirror the areas where there has been significant fieldwork in other periods, and they largely reflect their proximity to such centers as Dakar, Accra, Mombasa, Kampala, Livingstone, Harare, Cape Town, and Durban. Thirdly, what little work has been done is at the pioneering descriptive stage, reflecting relatively little concern with the development of societies within their larger social context. Lastly, a chief identifying feature in all areas has been the close cooperation between historians and archaeologists and the effective use in several areas of oral traditions.

The future for historical archaeology in Africa is encouraging, particularly where the aim is not solely to describe the European presence but to integrate the sites into the broader historical picture. There has been no quantitative analyses of artifact patterning, most studies having remained largely descriptive. Except to a limited extent on the east African Coast and in the Zambesi valley, no attempt has been made to examine how the forts, prazos, and other expatriate settlements interacted in the wider natural and cultural environments. Future work should include an examination of the associated African settlements. One clearly cannot understand the later archaeology of much of coastal Africa without an appreciation of the familial and other interactions that existed with the hinterland. Germaine to all studies should be an attempt to examine the dynamics of the changes which occurred in both the African societies and expatriate communities.

Several projects that have been recently initiated

will provide a clearer picture of the acculturation of African societies which came in contact with Europeans. A study to examine African-European interaction at Elmina, the African settlement which grew up adjacent to the first of the European forts established on the Gold Coast, is being planned by Christopher DeCorse. Carmel Schrire is conducting excavations at Oudepost I, a small Dutch trading station in South Africa, to examine Khoi-Dutch interaction between 1666 and 1800. Work by others on the late prehistoric period will help in evaluating the changes that occurred in later time periods. Studies in Kenya on the *kaya* settlements of the Midjikenda, being undertaken by Henry Mutoro of the University of Nairobi and the University of California, Los Angeles, will provide a model which will aid in understanding the development of later coastal towns. The town houses of stone are linked to the wattle and daub village houses by intricate ties of clan and societal obligations.

Another challenging theme that calls for research includes an examination of the slave trade in its' West African setting. The archaeological study of the Black diaspora (Posnansky 1983) depends on the excavation of the castle dungeons and barracoons as well as studies of the wider social and economic environment. Slaves were employed on the west African coast as servants, artisans, and soldiers. Whether their presence will be manifest in an area where much of the material culture is ephemeral and whether they can be distinguished from the general population is problematical. There is also a need for a comparative study of the diet of west African populations of known dates and of their skeletal remains in order to examine the effects of poor or changed nutrition on peoples of similar ethnic origin in the New World. A further important study should concern the investigation of the sites of those ex-slaves who were returned to Liberia and Sierra Leone in the early 19th century. These would represent a distinct ex-slave group who could be compared with groups of comparable date in the immediate hinterland and also with Free Blacks in America.

Perhaps most importantly, Africanist archaeologists interested in the areas from which the slaves originated should be brought into a continuous and mutually reinforcing dialogue with their North American and Caribbean colleagues who are interested in the archaeology of slavery. Few objects made the crossing to the New World but people *did* who continued behavioral practices which might be familiar to Africanist archaeologists and leave activity patterns which would otherwise go unnoticed by archaeologists without African experience.

The study of those sites associated with the development of legitimate trade would also be beneficial. Closely dated European trade goods provide a means of dating African sites of the past four or five hundred years which are often difficult to date by other means. Potential research in this area includes underwater projects at the wreck sites of European ships and at the remains of the trading hulks once moored in the mud of the Niger Delta that have not as yet been located or studied.

Great potential in Africa also exists for industrial archaeology. Detailed work is now being undertaken on the latest phases of pre-European iron technology which in many parts of Africa approached industrial proportions and drastically polluted the landscape (Warnier and Fowler 1979; Goucher 1981; Pole 1982). However, little is known about early European industrial activity. Many late 19th century entrepreneurs left few documents, yet they had profound environmental and social impacts. Aside from occasional notes on early railways, mining is the only activity that has received even scant attention. In a different vein, explorers, traders, and colonial armies of conquest used cans, bottles, and other items easily recognized in the exploration and colonization of Africa. What information can these items provide about the nature of expeditions which often numbered thousands of heterogeneous individuals?

Success of future work depends on the protection of historic sites which still exist. Problems of preservation in Africa are immense where mud brick disintegrates within 15 years without constant care, and vegetation can quickly destroy stone walls. Despite these difficulties there are surprisingly large numbers of historic buildings which have until recently been little threatened by

destruction. A start has been made in some countries, as for instance Ghana and Nigeria, to prepare
an architectural register of some of the more
significant sites (Murray 1966; Nunoo 1972).
South Africa has also seen a growing interest in
both the preservation and excavation of historic
sites (Abrahams 1984; Deacon 1984). It is notable
that many of the larger forts have continued in use
to the present day as prisons, resthouses, museums, and in the case of Accra, the Presidential
House, and are often excellently maintained. Yet
numerous sites are threatened with destruction and
many countries do not have adequate funding
available for the preservation and maintainance of
sites. It is in these cases that international organizations have played, and must continue to play a
role (Unesco 1983; 1984). Protection must be
extended not only to large European forts, but to
African and creole settlements which have heretofore received little attention.

To summarize, historical archaeology in Africa
is still in its pioneer descriptive state. The future
must bring the same explanatory and analytical
approaches that have been applied successfully to
other aspects of African archaeology. It is hoped
that an integrated study of Africa's recent past will
emerge without a separation between research on
the European and African components.

REFERENCES

ABRAHAMS, GABBEBAH
    1984 The Development of Historical Archaeology at the
        Cape, South Africa. *Bulletin of the South African
        Cultural History Museum* 5:20–32.

ATHERTON, JOHN HARVEY
    1983 Ethnoarchaeology in Africa. *The African Archaeolog-
        ical Review* 1:75–104.

AURET, C. H. N.
    1977 Preliminary Notes on the Msikaba Wreck Site.
        Africana Notes and News 22(6):231–35.

AURET, CHRIS and TIM MAGGS
    1982 The Great Ship São Bento: Remains From a mid-
        Sixteenth Century Portuguese Wreck on the
        Pondoland Coast. *Annals of the Natal Museum*
        25(1):1–39.

BESSAC, H.
    1952 L'emplacement des Forts de Portendick. *Notes
        Africaines* 54:50–52.

BESSAC, H. AND P.-L. DFKEYSER
    1951 Les Ruines du Fort de Merinaghen en Marge de la
        Mise en Valeur du Senegal de 1817 a 1854. *Notes
        Africaines* 49:18–21.

CALVOCORESSI, DAVID
    1977 Excavations at Bantama, Near Elmina, Ghana. *West
        African Journal of Archaeology* 7:117–41.

CHITTICK, NEVILLE
    1975 *Kilwa: an Islamic Trading City on the East African
        Coast.* Thames and Hudson, London.
    1984 *Mande: Excavations at an island Port on the Kenya
        Coast.* Thames and Hudson, London.

CLARK, J. DESMOND
    1967 The Portuguese Settlement at Feira. *The Northern
        Rhodesian Journal* 6:275–92.

DEACON, JANETTE
    1984 Editorial. *South African Archaeological Bulletin,*
        39(139):3–4.

DEETZ, JAMES
    1977 *In Small Things Forgotten: The Archaeology of Early
        American Life.* Anchor Books Doubleday, New York.

DIKE, K. ONWUKA
    1956 *Trade and Politics in the Niger Delta.* Clarendon
        Press, Oxford.

EHRET, CHRISTOPHER and MERRICK POSNANSKY (editors)
    1982 *The Archaeological and Linguistic Reconstruction of
        African History.* University of California Press, Los
        Angeles.

GARLAKE, P. S.
    1967 Seventeenth Century Portuguese Earthworks in Rho-
        desia. *South African Archaeological Bulletin*
        21(4):157–70.
    1970 Excavations at the Seventeenth Century Portuguese
        Site of Dambarare, Rhodesia. *Transactions of the
        Rhodesia Scientific Association* 54(1):23–61.

GOUCHER, CANDICE L.
    1981 Iron is Iron 'Til it is Rusts: Trade and Ecology in the
        Decline of West African Iron-Smelting. *Journal of
        African History* 22(1):179–89.

IMPERIAL COLLEGE
    1966 Final Report of the Imperial College Uganda Expedi-
        tion. Mimeographed. Imperial College Exploration
        Board, Imperial College, London.

JEPPESEN AF HENRIK
    1966 Danske plantageanlaeg pa Guildkysten 1788–1850.
        *Kobenhavns Universitets Geografiske Institute,
        Publikation nr. 91.*

KIRKMAN, JAMES S.
    1957 Historical Archaeology in Kenya 1948–1956. *The
        Antiquaries Journal* 37:16–29.
    1972a The Mombasa Frigate. *Kenya Past and Present* 1
        (2):25–26.

Perspectives from Historical Archaeology: African Diaspora Archaeology   37

1972b The Portuguese Wreck off Mombasa, Kenya. *International Journal of Nautical Archaeology* 1:153–57.

1974 *Fort Jesus: A Portuguese Fortress on the East African Coast.* Clarendon Press, Oxford.

LANGLANDS, B. W.
1967 *The Chronicle of Dufile,* Uganda Museum Occassional Papers 11, Kampala.

LAWRENCE, A. W.
1963 *Trade Castles and Forts of West Africa.* Jonathan Cape, London.

LEVTZION, NEHEMIA AND J. F. P. HOPKINS (eds.)
1981 *Corpus of Early Arabic Sources for West African History.* Cambridge University Press, New York.

LIGHTLEY, ROBERT ALLEN
1976 An 18th Century Dutch East Indiaman, Found at Cape Town, 1971. *International Journal of Nautical Archaeology* 5(4):305–16.

MATSON, A. T., AND J. E. G. SUTTON
1965 The role of forts in safeguarding the Uganda Road. *Uganda Journal* 29(2):163–84.

MAUNY, RAYMOND
1967 Bibliographie de la Prehistoire et de la Protohistoire de l'Ouest Africain. *Bulletin de l'IFAN, series B* 29.

MILLER, JOSEPH C. (ed.)
1980 *The African Past Speaks.* Dawsons and Sons, Hamdem Connecticut.

MURRAY, K. C.
1966 A List of Sites, Buildings etc. in Nigeria Declared as Monuments Under the Antiquities Act. *West African Archaeological Newsletter* 4:31–33.

NEWITT, M. D. D. AND P. S. GARLAKE
1967 The 'Aringa' at Massangano. *Journal of African History* 8:133–56.

NUNOO, R. B.
1972 A Note on the Scheduling of Monuments in Ghana. *West African Journal of Archaeology* 2:119–20.

PARKINGTON, JOHN AND MIKE CRONIN
1979 The size and Layout of Mgungundlovu 1829–1838. *South African Archaeological Society: Goodwin Series* 3:133–45.

PEAL, W. J.
1963 The Kampala to Bombo Railway. *Uganda Journal* 27:61–70.

PHILLIPSON, D. W.
1972 Kasoko, a Portuguese Entrepot in the Middle Zambezi Valley. *Zambia Museums Journal* 3:35–48.

PIERCY, R. C. M.
1977 Mombasa Wreck Excavation: Preliminary Report, 1977. *International Journal of Nautical Archaeology* 6(4):331–47.

1978 Mombasa Wreck Excavation: Second Preliminary Report. 1978. *International Journal of Nautical Archaeology* 7(4):301–19.

1979 Mombasa Wreck Excavation: Third Preliminary Report, 1979. *International Journal of Nautical Archaeology* 8(4):303–09.

1981 Mombasa Wreck Excavation: Fourth Preliminary Report, 1980. *International Journal of Nautical Archaeology* 10(2):109–18.

POLE, L. M.
1982 Decline or Survival? Iron Production in West Africa From the Seventeenth to the Twentieth Centuries. *Journal of African History* 23:503–13.

POSNANSKY, MERRICK
1982 African Archaeology Comes of Age. *World Archaeology* 13:345–58.

1983 Towards an Archaeology of the Black Diaspora. *Proceedings of the Ninth International Congress for the Study of the Pre-Columbian Cultures of the Lesser Antilles, Santa Domingo 1981.* Centre de Researches Caraibes, University of Montreal.

POSNANSKY, MERRICK and ALBERT VAN DANTZIG
1976 Fort Ruychaver rediscovered. *Sankofa* 2:7–18.

POTGIETER, SUZANNE AND GABEBAH ABRAHAMS
1984 Gouda Clay Pipes From Excavated Historical Sites in Cape Town. *Bulletin of the South African Cultural History Museum* 5:42–53.

SASSOON, HAMO
1981 Ceramics From the Wreck of a Portuguese Ship at Mombasa. *Azania* 16:97–130.

SCHMIDT, PETER
1977 *Historical Archaeology: A Structural Approach in an African Culture.* Greenwood Press, Westport, Connecticut.

1983 An Alternative to a Strictly Materialist Perspective: A Review of Historical Archaeology, Ethnoarchaeology, and Symbolic Approaches in African Archaeology. *American Antiquity* 48(1):62–79.

SCHUYLER, ROBERT (editor)
1978 *Historical Archaeology: A Guide to Substantive and Theoretical Contributions.* Baywood Publishing Co., Farmingdale, New York.

SIMMONDS, DOIG
1973 A Note on the Excavations in Cape Coast Castle. *Transactions of the Historical Society of Ghana* 14(2):267–69.

SOUTH, STANLEY
1977 *Method and Theory in Historical Archaeology.* Academic Press, New York.

STÉNUIT, ROBERT
1975 The Treasure of Porto Santo. *National Geographic* 1 48(2):260–73.

1978 The Sunken Treasure of St. Helena. *National Geographic* 154(4):562–76.

THOMAS, I. F.
1963 Baker's Fort at Patiko. *Uganda Journal* 28(2):195–204.

UNESCO
1983 Ruins of Kilwa Kisiwani and Songo Mnara. *World Cultural Heritage Information Bulletin* 21–22: 15–16.
1984 Gorée, Historic Island. *World Cultural Heritage Information Bulletin* 23–24:28–33.

VAN DER PIJL-KETEL, C. L. (ed.)
1982 *The Ceramic Load of the 'Witte Leeuw.'* Rijksmuseum, Amsterdam.

VAN DANTZIG, ALBERT
1972 A Note on Fort "Batenstein" and Butri. *Ghana Notes and Queries* 12:16–19.
1980 *Forts and Castles of Ghana*. Sedco, Accra.

VOS, H. N.
1981 Excavating Our Colonial Past: Some Recent Discoveries. *Southern African Museums Association Bulletin* 14(8):354–57.

WALKER, IAIN C.
1975 The Potential Age of European Clay Tobacco Pipes in West African Archaeological Research. *West African Journal of Archaeology* 5:165–93.

WARNIER JEAN PIERRE AND IAN
1979 A Nineteenth-Century Ruhr in Central Africa. *Africa* 49(4):329–51.

WOOD, W. RAYMOND
1967 An Archaeological Appraisal of Early European Settlement in the Senegambia. *Journal of African History* 8:39–64.

MERRICK POSNANSKY, DIRECTOR
INSTITUTE OF ARCHAEOLOGY
UNIVERSITY OF CALIFORNIA, LOS ANGELES
LOS ANGELES, CALIFORNIA 90024

CHRISTOPHER R. DECORSE, LECTURER
DEPARTMENT OF ARCHAEOLOGY
UNIVERSITY OF GHANA
P.O. BOX 3
LEGON, GHANA

ANN MARKELL
MARTIN HALL
CARMEL SCHRIRE

The Historical Archaeology of Vergelegen, an Early Farmstead at the Cape of Good Hope

ABSTRACT

Excavations at Vergelegen, a large estate in the Western Cape of South Africa that dates to the earliest years of the 18th century, have allowed archaeologists to address a number of questions about the nature of colonial settlement in this former Dutch colony. Primary among these were questions about slavery and about the interrelationships between slaves, colonists, and the indigenous inhabitants of the Cape of Good Hope. This article offers some of the results of this investigation, and an interpretation of those results in light of the original questions about slave community, slave–indigenous interaction, and early colonial architecture in the Cape.

Introduction

At the turn of the 18th century the new governor of the Cape of Good Hope, Willem Adriaan van der Stel (1699–1708), son of former Governor Simon van der Stel, built himself a substantial estate with a house, garden, and outbuildings laid out on a symmetrical plan. He called it Vergelegen—"Far Away"—to mark its position, a good day's ride from Cape Town, across a sandy isthmus still frequented by lions, hippos, and elephants (Figure 1). At least 60 Dutch East India Company servants, including subalterns, soldiers, and sailors, were commandeered to work here (Leibbrandt 1897:53; Fouche 1970:239) and the governor also acquired some 200 slaves. Most were put to work in the orangery, the mill, the outbuildings, and especially in the vineyards and fields. This ambitious display provided the perfect vehicle for an official complaint about gubernatorial privilege. Accustomed though they were to the venality of the Dutch East India Company, a group of wealthy and influential

Historical Archaeology, 1995, 29(1):10–34.
Permission to reprint required.

burghers used this exhibition of status and wealth as a springboard for a long list of grievances about conditions at the Cape of Good Hope. A prolonged dispute and investigation followed and Van der Stel was recalled to the Netherlands in 1708, leaving the estate to be subdivided and sold.

Although the house was scheduled for destruction after the dispute, the estate continued to sport a fine mansion, with its octagonal garden and outbuildings, 80 years later. The legend of its splendor clung so tenaciously that, although it fell into disrepair, it was reborn in the 1920s under the ministrations of Randlord Sir Lionel Phillips and his imaginative, if insistent, wife. Famous people gathered there, including General Smuts, photographically captured while smiling benevolently under the trellis with "Lady Li-Phi" (Gutsche 1966:facing page 356). Today Vergelegen remains one of the most beautiful Cape Dutch estates, under the ultimate ownership of the Anglo American Corporation. The core of the estate survives in the ruined water mill and the octagonal garden facing the blue Hottentots Holland mountains. Gnarled camphor trees, their burled trunks like the feet of great mastodons, stand stolid on the manicured lawns between the new English rose garden and the homestead (Figure 2).

Vergelegen stirs the imagination. Rian Malan set the roots of his familial apostasy there in a speculative account of the elopement of his ancestor with a young slave woman (Malan 1990). General Smuts visited, to contemplate the future in the cool shade of the past. The setting was leased for parties, hunts, and fashion shows. The present owners have restructured the farm and its new winery and, in doing so, funded research to set the entire enterprise in its historical perspective through a major program of archaeological research.

Vergelegen offers rich possibilities for historical archaeology. In contrast with some other parts of the world, the Cape documentary record lacks the evidence of daily life kept by overseers, owners, and slaves. Court and census records mitigate this lack (Ross 1983; Worden 1985; Shell 1986, 1993), but archaeological data can provide the elements of everyday existence that allow a fuller interpretation of what it was like to live, survive, endure, and

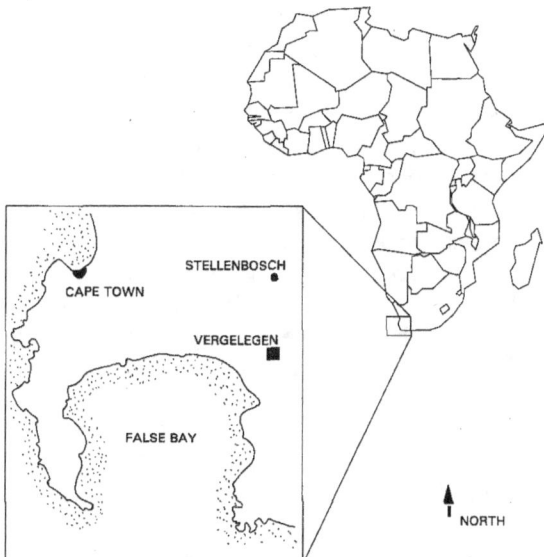

FIGURE 1. Location map showing the position of the site within the Cape peninsula.

FIGURE 2. Late 19th-century photograph of Vergelegen and the camphor trees. (Courtesy of the South African State Library, Cape Town).

enjoy life in those days. Because of the virulence of the dispute between Willem Adriaan van der Stel and his accusers—a group of prominent Cape citizens—Vergelegen was documented and counter-documented, providing details about those living and working on the estate, about building

materials and provisions, and providing views, plans, and diagrams. Inspired by the archaeological possibilities of Van der Stel's estate, the research team began, in 1989, a three-year program of excavation and research.

Archival sources identified and located three buildings specifically associated with daily work: a slave lodge, a water mill, and a wine cellar. Documentary plans proved excellent predictors of the buried outbuildings, and the archaeological investigations have been able to expose in plan the complete foundations of both the wine cellar and the slave lodge. The water mill was still partially standing, although much modified in later years. Again, extensive excavation has revealed the full plan and details of the building's subsequent architectural history.

Here, then, was the opportunity to pull back the curtain of silence about daily life in the early Cape by excavating identified living and working areas. Specifically, the archaeologists were interested in evaluating three propositions about the 17th- and 18th-century Cape.

The first proposition, deeply embedded in South African architectural history, is that there is a direct line of continuity between "Cape Dutch" architecture and that of the initial Dutch colonial settlement in the mid-17th century. This argument has two forms. The first, perhaps best represented in the work of Hans Fransen (1987), is that Cape colonial architecture can best be understood through reference to the grand stylistic traditions of Europe: the baroque, rococo, and neoclassical. The second approach, influenced by vernacular architectural studies and represented in the work of James Walton (1965, 1989), infers an evolutionary sequence, starting with simple, rectangular thatch cottages from which complex house plans developed. Van der Stel's governorship came at a critical juncture in the history of the Cape—a time when the colony was firmly established, when farming expansion into the interior was beginning, and when a distinct class of colonial gentry was emerging. The architecture of his estate—and in particular the buildings allocated for everyday purposes—might thus reveal the interplay of architectural forms in the early colonial Cape.

Secondly, the research team was interested in Nigel Worden's (1985) suggestion that there was no "slave culture" at the Cape. Worden argued that the bonds of language, family, and belief that underlay a sense of common purpose among American slaves were lacking in Cape society. Instead, according to Worden, owners deliberately chose rural slaves from widely separated sources, from areas including Madagascar and Malabar. Female slaves were in the minority and often infertile, and even when children were present the overseers undercut parental authority on numerous occasions. Slaves were rarely incorporated into their masters' religion, in contrast with the United States. For these reasons, Worden claimed, a common cause—a unified revolt—never emerged. Slaves betrayed each other, and never appeared united against their oppressors.

But unified revolt is only one—quite overt—indicator of the existence of community. Cultural identity is one of the most cogent inferences that can be drawn from archaeology. Whether it is expressed openly or not, it is invariably encoded in the subconscious patterns of material residues. It emerges in diet, where food is prepared using methods learned in childhood and according to culturally acquired tastes. It may be seen in carvings on a pipe, as in the designs similar to Western African symbols that were scored into clay pipes in Virginia (Emerson 1988). It may be found in the use of snares and hunting weapons, in embellished buttons, in the ways in which rubbish is disposed, and in the pattern of hearths around which people eat and sleep. These are the humble residues that can be scrutinized to test the question of slave memories, identity, and culture.

Thirdly, Robert Ross (1983) has argued that runaway slaves, known at the Cape as *drosters,* could not live well off the land because they did not understand its potential, and that their relations with indigenous Khoikhoi pastoralists, who might have protected them, varied considerably.

Of course, colonists as well as slaves needed to learn the nature of the land before they could exploit its resources. The archaeological evidence for the Dutch intrusion into the indigenous niche is well illustrated by the archaeology of the Com-

pany's outpost at Saldanha Bay on the Cape west coast (Schrire 1988, 1990; Cruz-Uribe and Schrire 1991). The excavation and analysis of dietary residues from Vergelegen might show whether slaves, as well, supplemented their diet by hunting and gathering food beyond the borders of the farm. This situation has proved to be the case for many American plantation slaves, who seem either to have had enough time and freedom to exploit alternative food sources (Otto 1984; Fairbanks 1984), or to have been encouraged in this by owners seeking to cut expenses (Mintz and Price 1992: 30).

"A country seat, large beyond measure"

In the early years of the 18th century, the image of Vergelegen depended on whose opinion was canvassed. For Governor Willem Adriaan van der Stel it was "merely a house with one story . . . [including] a labourer's cottage, with six or seven enclosures in all, a horse stable, a wine press, and slave quarters" (Leibbrandt 1897:7). But according to the governor's antagonists, Vergelegen was ". . . a country seat, large beyond measure and of such broad dimensions, as if it were a whole town" (Leibbrandt 1897:53).

Similar ambiguity characterizes the record of the original land grant made to the governor. In 1686 Adriaan's father, Governor Simon van der Stel, ordered that a Dutch East India Company outpost be set up in the Hottentots' Holland area of the Stellenbosch district (South African State Archives [SASA] 1686:842–844). This outpost was to straddle the road between Cape Town and the mountains, thus blocking the route allegedly used by the colonists to trade cattle illegally with Khoikhoi pastoralists. The exact location of the outpost is unknown, but a 1695 map of the colony shows a Company settlement where Vergelegen was later to be built, and it is likely that the later grant to Willem Adriaan van der Stel incorporated the Company's land (Sleigh 1982).

The core of the Vergelegen estate was 413 morgen in extent—one morgen being the amount of land that could be plowed in a morning, or an area

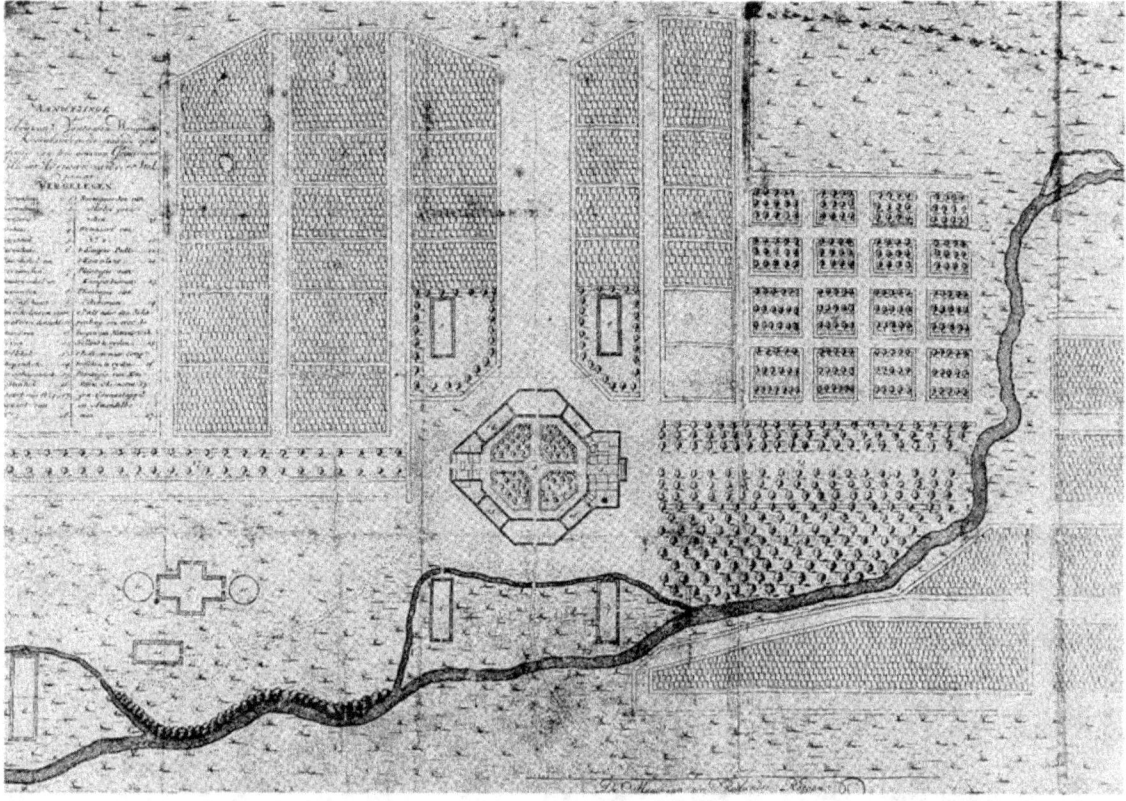

FIGURE 3. Plan of Vergelegen estate from the *Contra Deductie* (Tas and Van der Heyden 1712).

equivalent to about 2 acres. Van der Stel later expanded the estate to comprise 613 morgen, enlarging the original grant to an area of about 1,226 acres, most of it arable land (Heap 1977:33). Oak and camphor trees and fruit orchards were planted and wheat was sown. In particular, Van der Stel wanted a major share in the lucrative Company-controlled trade in wine and fresh meat. It was claimed that, by 1706, more than 400,000 vines had been planted, accounting for about one-fourth of the colony's wine production in that year. Cattle and sheep were kept in vast numbers, both at the estate and at cattle stations on the other side of the mountains (Theal 1913:211).

The focal point for these farm and grazing lands was Van der Stel's house, built in the tradition of the fashionable country dwellings of the contem-

porary European gentry. The building was fronted by an octagonal, double-walled garden that incorporated a range of outbuildings. Flanking these structures, and providing the symmetry of the plan, were the wine cellar, slave house and water mill, as well as a dovecote. A tannery and smithy, a corn store, threshing floors, and a brick kiln were built a short distance upriver (Figure 3).

Resplendent though it might have been, Vergelegen was consistent with the perquisites that accompanied gubernatorial office at the Cape. Willem Adriaan's 613 morgen was comparable with 900-odd morgen held by his father at Constantia (Fouche 1970:332–335; Schutte 1989:193), though it far exceeded the holdings of even the most prosperous burghers (Schutte 1989:193). The more central problem was that, after Willem Adri-

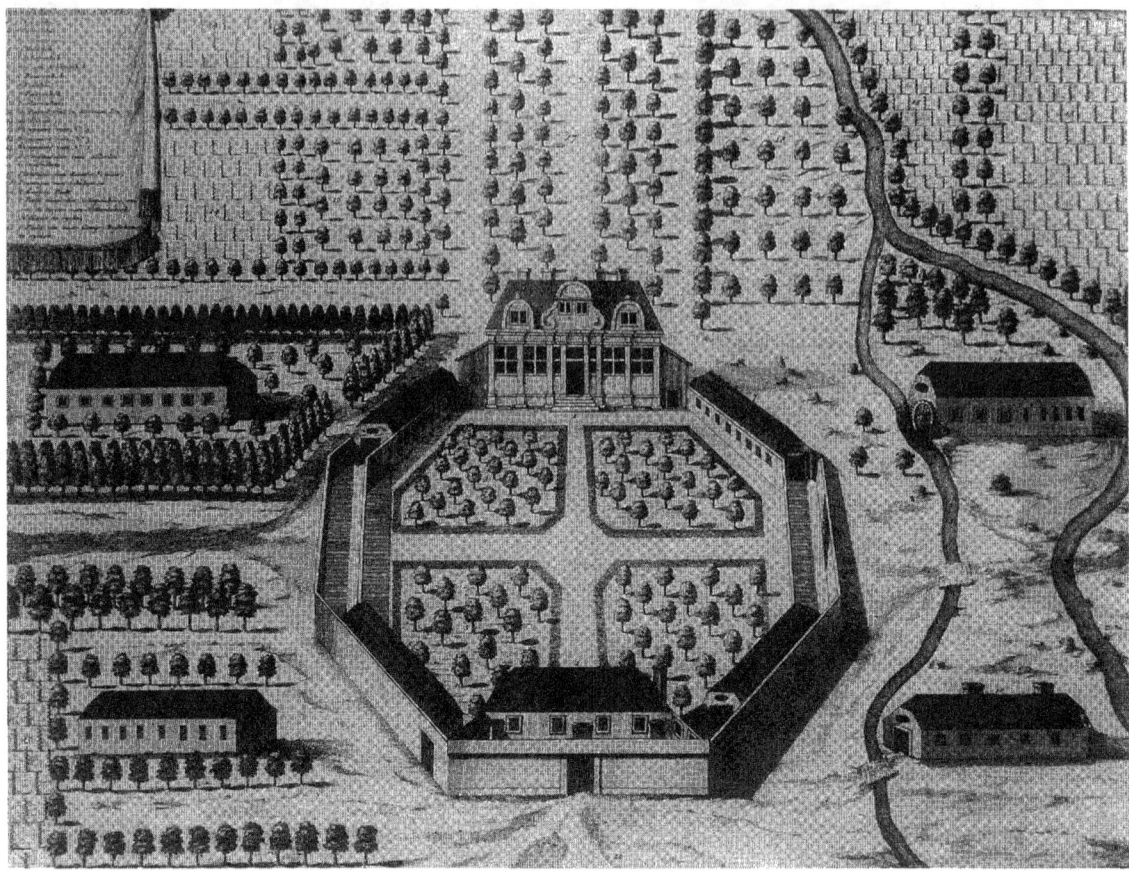

FIGURE 4. View of Vergelegen from the *Contra Deductie* (Tas and Van der Heyden 1712).

aan set about stimulating agriculture, productivity outweighed demand, forcing the Governor into the traditional VOC, or Dutch East India Company, stance of protecting his self interest. This position threw him into direct conflict with a group of prosperous burghers who in 1706, posing to some extent as pitiful victims, drafted a clever appeal known as the Contra Deductie (Tas and Van der Heyden 1712) to free them of their tyrannical overlord (Fouche 1970).

The Contra Deductie (Tas and Van der Heyden 1712) included detailed charges of malpractice, lists of those whose services were misappropriated in the construction of Vergelegen, lists and sources of building materials, and a view and plan of the estate (Figures 3, 4). The Council of Seventeen weighed both sides and, for a variety of reasons, recalled Van der Stel, less for his despotism than for the inconvenience of having fomented strife (Schutte 1979:192–196). Van der Stel departed for the Netherlands in 1708 and later that year countered with the Korte Deductie, or "Brief Statement" (Bogaert 1711), where he posited his adversaries as anarchic democrats and defended his palatial holdings as a modest achievement, standing against wild nature (Figure 5).

Vergelegen was divided into four sections in preparation for its sale, and an official evaluation was prepared, including measurements and architectural descriptions of the standing buildings

FIGURE 5. View of Vergelegen from the *Korte Deductie* (Bogaert 1711).

(SASA 1710:68–70). The Company ordered the manor house itself destroyed:

> for the Company, nothing more shall be taken over than the stables, slave quarters and similar useful and serviceable buildings, but by no means his dwelling house, which we desire shall be broken down by him, as such buildings which are for ostentation and more for pomp than use have been built by the Company's servants at the Cape and elsewhere in India greatly to our annoyance, and in a very prominent fashion. This is to be taken as a general remark for the information of those who might in future wish to undertake anything of the kind (SASA 1706, in Leibbrandt 1896:433–434).

The instruction to raze Van der Stel's house seems not to have been carried out completely at this stage; although probably not as resplendent as in its builder's day, a house and precinct still formed a unified whole late in the century. In July 1774, Vergelegen was visited by a Dutch admiral, Jan Splinter Stavorinus:

The front of the house faced the east. Before it lay a large garden, of a regular octagon form, enclosed by a wall. The walk which led up to the house, was bordered on each side by orange and lemon trees; but the outer avenue was planted with large oak-trees; they were, however, less in size than those of Europe; between these, stood almond trees, which were then in blossom, and did not contribute a little to embellish those pleasant walks. . . . The dwelling-house, not to say any thing of the other buildings, as slave-houses, warehouses, stables, &c. is a handsome edifice, though of only one story (as, in fact, all the countryhouses here are, as well as most of the houses at Capetown), with a long and broad gallery, which is the sitting and eating-room of the family, and many large apartments on each side. The garden, the buildings, and the plantations, all bore very evident signs of the magnificence and wealth of the founder, who spent large sums of money upon this spot; but every thing is now much decayed, as the succeeding proprietors did not possess the same means as Mr. Van der Stel, to keep it in proper repair (Stavorinus 1969:87–89).

Vergelegen passed through many changes of ownership before the estate was acquired in 1987

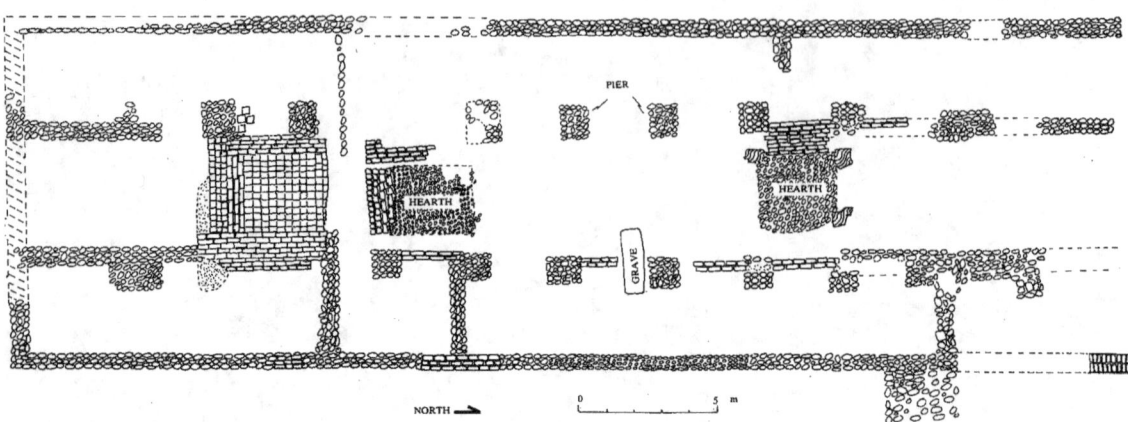

FIGURE 6. Archaeological plan view of the Vergelegen slave lodge.

by the Anglo American Corporation. There were frequent modifications to the stock of buildings, and at some point—exactly when is not clear—the original outbuildings were razed. But the estate's distinctive layout, centered on the octagonal walled garden, remained intact, and there was every reason to expect that the richness of the archival record would be matched by substantial archaeological deposits preserved beneath verdant lawns and pastures.

The Outbuildings: Adapting the Hallehuis to Colonial Needs

Although the documentary record of the Van der Stel affair was often contradictory, both parties agreed about the existence of the slave house and its position relative to the octagonal garden and the other outbuildings. And, although nothing was to be seen above the present-day ground surface, test excavation revealed wall foundations of cobblestones and traces of early brickwork.

The foundations and floors were the remains of a structure that measured some 40 × 12 m. The Company's estate evaluation of 1709 described the slave house as 122 Cape ft. in length and 38 Cape ft. broad (SASA 1710:68–70); dimensions that closely match the excavated structure (Figure 6). A Cape foot, probably the same as a Rhineland foot, was equal to 1.03 English ft., or 0.315 m. Excavation also exposed 11 pairs of small, square cobblestone platforms equally spaced in two rows running the length of the building, originally built as piers to support uprights of wood or masonry. As the 1709 document recorded that the roof of the slave house was supported by 11 cross beams, a very good fit exists between the archival and archaeological sources.

There is little place for a house plan such as is shown in Figure 6 in the conventional architectural history of the colonial Cape (Fransen and Cook 1980). While contemporary descriptions of the exterior dimensions of some 17th-century buildings suggest that they may correspond to this plan (see Conclusions), the only excavated, free-standing 17th-century structure—the lodge at Oudepost I, the Dutch East India Company's outpost at Saldanha Bay (Schrire 1987, 1988, 1990)—does not seem to conform to these specifications. While this two-room building had outer dimensions of 63 by 18 Rhineland ft.—much smaller than the Vergelegen slave house, but of similar overall proportions—it is probable that the walls of the Oudepost lodge supported the full weight of the roof structure, as there was no evidence for uprights supporting cross beams. This building, in common with later vernacular houses in the Cape, was built

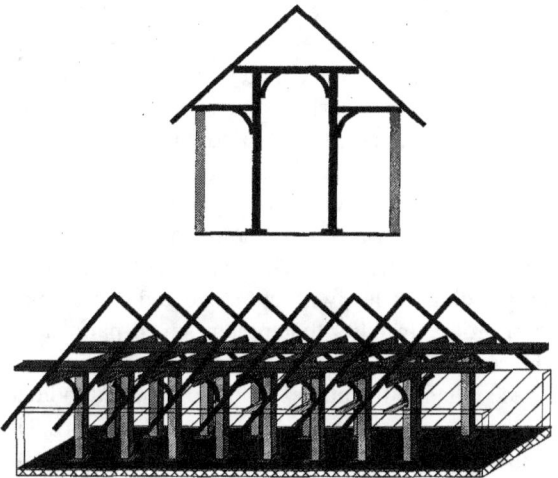

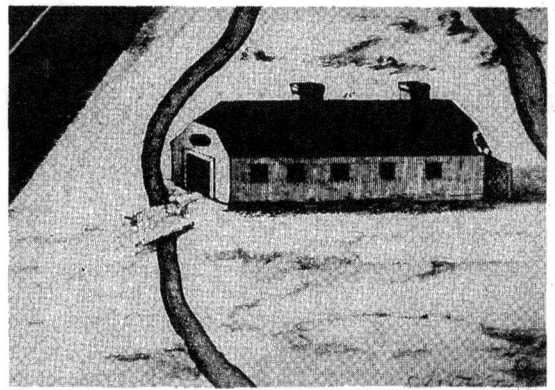

FIGURE 8. The slave lodge at Vergelegen (enlargement from Figure 4).

FIGURE 7. Schematic reconstruction of the Vergelegen slave lodge.

with load-bearing walls, while the Vergelegen slave house was based on the principles of timber-frame construction (Markell 1993).

Although no certain precedents for the form of the Vergelegen slave house have yet been found in the Cape, there are clear models in the vernacular building traditions of northern Europe, with roots as far back as 350 B.C. (Van Wijk 1987:162) and direct continuity from late medieval times (Prudon 1986:212). Known as a *hallehuis,* hall house, or *loshuis,* open house, such a building (Figure 7) was broken into three longitudinal aisles, formed by a frame of uprights and cross beams with anchor braces at the joints to give rigidity to the structure (Zantkuyl 1985). The uprights were typically seated on masonry platforms. Rooms were often defined simply by changes in floor surface rather than by interior partitions.

Hallehuisen were most often used as combination farm buildings, but the basic structural form was also adapted to more specific uses such as housing for laborers, as dwellings alone, and as outbuildings or barns. The basic form, incorporating the transverse anchorbent, was versatile and could be shortened or narrowed. Exterior aisles could be placed on only one side, or removed altogether.

Documentary sources clearly show that the Vergelegen slave house was equipped with two chimneys (Figure 8). No evidence was found for chimney structures or for the raised hearths characteristic of the established Cape vernacular building tradition (Woodward 1982:76; Cook [1970]), but cobble surfaces, with discoloration suggesting burning, were found in positions which would have been beneath the chimneys shown in the archival drawing. Electron spin resonance spectroscopy, carried out on cobble samples, confirmed localized burning at temperatures commensurate with domestic cooking (Miller et al. 1993). Beneath the cobbles was clay paving with charcoal inclusions and blackening, suggesting that the hearths had been resurfaced with the cobbles. Again, this is consistent with the typical *hallehuis* form where the hearth was often in the center of the general living space, consisting of no more than a hearth plate or a pit in the cobbled floor surface (Wilcoxen 1981:93). In the absence of a brick chimney structure a wooden smoke hood was often present (Wilcoxen 1981). At the corners of one of the burned cobble areas in the Vergelegen slave house were flat, cut blocks of granite that could well have been used as bases for posts supporting a smoke hood (Figure 6).

Excavation revealed that the slave house had a partition with a cobble foundation that divided the

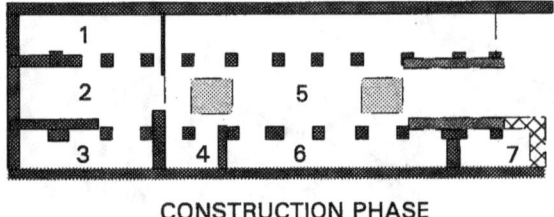

CONSTRUCTION PHASE

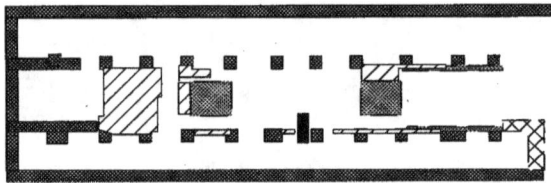

POST REMODELING PHASE

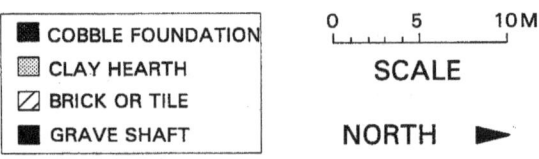

■ COBBLE FOUNDATION

▦ CLAY HEARTH

▨ BRICK OR TILE

■ GRAVE SHAFT

0   5   10M

SCALE

NORTH ▶

FIGURE 9. Plan view of the Vergelegen slave lodge, showing room divisions and changes during remodeling.

building horizontally into two sections, the northern portion comprising two-thirds of the entire building. This northern end contained three divisions in its eastern aisle, again with the partitioning indicated by cobble foundations; two small rooms, and one long room (Figure 9). At the south end of the building the side aisles were both separated from the central aisle by cobble foundations, effectively breaking this area into three rooms as well.

The position of the wine cellar was also shown clearly on contemporary plans (Figures 3, 4), and again, the documentary record was crucial in locating a building which had no visible remains above the modern land surface. As with the slave house, the excavated plan of the wine cellar (Figure 10) corresponded with archival descriptions: 150 Cape ft. by 38 Cape ft. in the Company's specifications (SASA 1710:68–70) and 47 m by 12

m measured from the outer faces of the foundations. Like the slave house, the wine cellar foundations were of river cobbles mortared with clay, the walls were of brick, and enough of the floor surfaces remained to determine that they had been of crushed brick and clay.

This was also clearly a *hallehuis* type of building, although varying in some details from the slave house. The wine cellar was divided into three longitudinal aisles, with cut stone and cobble piers supporting uprights that ran in seven pairs down the center of the structure. These were more widely spaced than in the other two buildings, and indicate fewer cross beams used for structural support. The wine cellar had, in addition to the interior supports, brick buttresses on the building's exterior and although some were destroyed by later road building along the western side of the cellar, evidence of seven pairs remains along the eastern wall (Figure 10).

Unlike the slave house, there was no indication of partitioning within the outside aisles, but there was, as in the slave house, a solidly built wall that divided the building horizontally. There are remains of a threshold of crushed brick and clay leading through this wall, indicating that it had a doorway passing through it (Figure 10). There were no clear indications of an exterior doorway, but the building configuration suggests that there may have been an end entrance on the south side.

Part of the water mill was still standing although most of it had undergone extensive modifications through the years. Its last function had been as a "wild garden," utilizing the crumbling walls to fulfill an early 20th-century Gothic dream (Walgate 1926). As a result of this history, the architecture was more complicated to unravel.

The mill was described in the 1709 evaluation as a combination water mill and horse stable, with five sheds. Sixty Cape ft. of its length was besoldert, indicating that there was a ceiling either of planks for overhead storage, or of clay to minimize the danger of fire to the thatched roof (SASA 1710: 68–70). Excavation showed that, again, these needs had been met by a *hallehuis* with overall dimensions the same as those of the slave house (Figure 11). The part of the building used as a mill

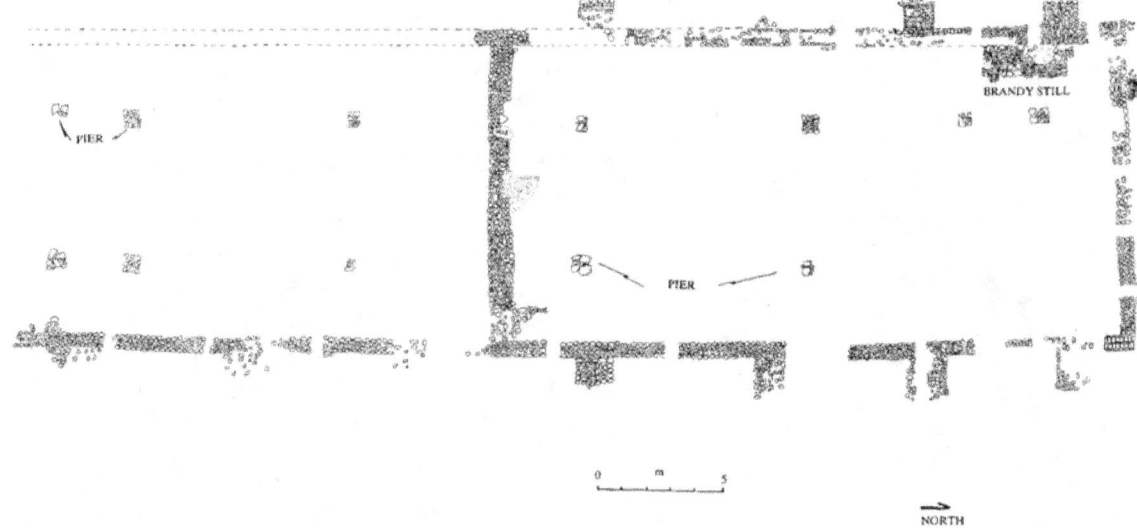

FIGURE 10. Archaeological plan view of the wine cellar.

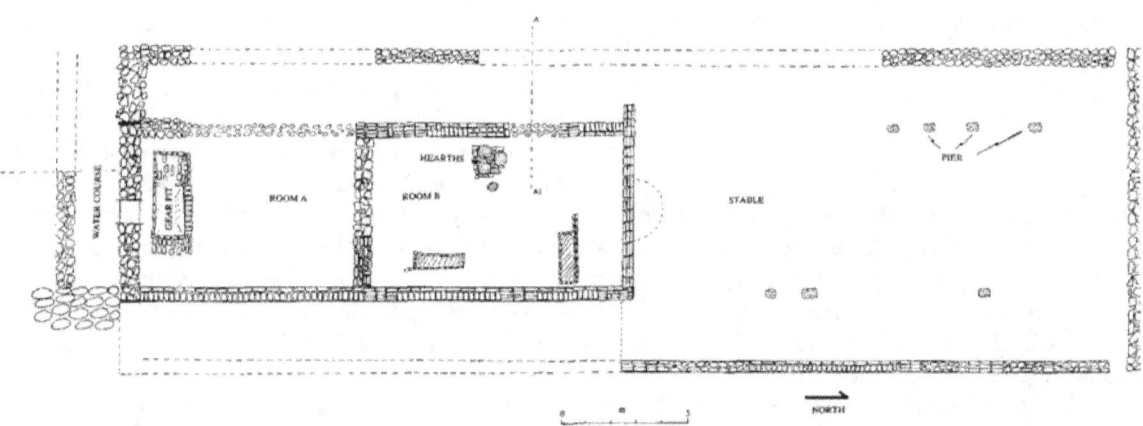

FIGURE 11. Archaeological plan view of the Vergelegen water mill.

was delineated by cobble foundations and brick walls in the central aisle of the southern end of the building. This was in turn divided into two rooms with crushed brick and clay floors; one contained the mill machinery while the other was probably used for storage and as living quarters. The five sheds listed in the Company's evaluation were in the exterior aisles alongside these two rooms. The northern end of the building apparently served as the stable, occupying both central and exterior aisles, and had a cobbled floor (Figure 11).

The Vergelegen water mill was extensively re-modelled in later years. The stables at the northern end and the outer aisles alongside the rooms were removed. The south wall was partially rebuilt to carry a new overshot mill wheel, and the mill race was raised for this purpose. These renovations transformed the mill into a far smaller structure

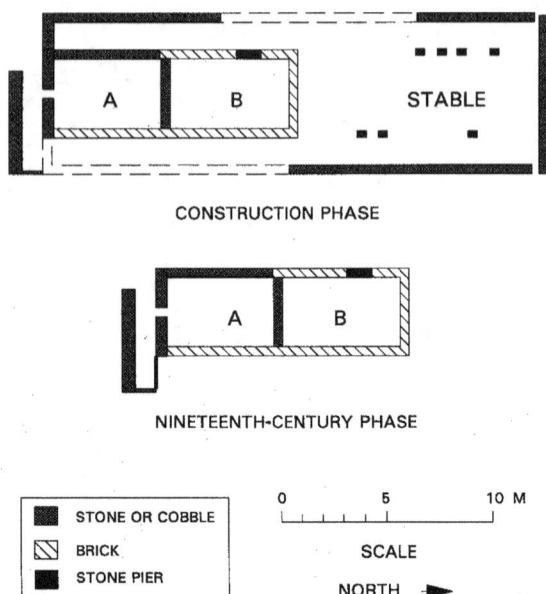

CONSTRUCTION PHASE

NINETEENTH-CENTURY PHASE

■ STONE OR COBBLE
▨ BRICK
■ STONE PIER

0   5   10 M

SCALE

NORTH ➤

FIGURE 12. Plan view of the mill showing room designations and changes during the last, 19th-century, remodeling.

with load-bearing walls supporting the full weight of the roof, effectively disguising its *hallehuis* origins (Figure 12). But in Willem Adriaan van der Stel's day, water mill, wine cellar, and slave house—along with the unexcavated dovecote—formed a suite of large timber, masonry, and thatch farm buildings, carefully balancing the planned symmetry of the manor house and walled garden.

Patterns of Living

A surprising aspect of the excavations at Vergelegen is the paucity of archaeological finds from all parts of the site. Test pits were excavated at various positions away from the outbuildings, but there was no evidence for any dump areas. Nowhere was there a density of material comparable to that in contemporary urban sites (e.g., Hall 1991), rural outposts (Schrire 1988; Cruz-Uribe and Schrire 1991; Hall et al. 1993; Schrire et al. 1993) or, for that matter, in plantations of similar

scale in North America (Kelso 1984). This paucity was constantly echoed in the extensive excavations of the three buildings.

A number of explanations can be explored here. The slightly acidic soils may have been inhospitable to bone preservation, although the presence of a largely intact 18th-century burial militates against this as a general explanation. Then there are the cultural norms that dictated garbage disposal throughout the 18th century. It is commonly held that general European disposal practice until the mid-18th century included wide broadcasting of refuse. Towards mid-century, a gradually increasing sense of order prompted more frequent use of pits for rubbish (Deetz 1977:125–126). A pattern of broadcast rubbish is also found on indigenous sites and in the urban backyard sites occupied by non-Europeans (Hall 1992; Hall et al. 1993). Researchers would therefore have expected both pits and a wide spread of residues here; neither is evident. Then again, there is the likely possibility that garbage was dumped in a watercourse, two of which—the Lourens River and the mill stream—run right alongside the slave quarters and the mill. Close scrutiny of the river bank failed to reveal any concentrations of debris, a fact all the more surprising since the equally fluctuating Eerste River at Stellenbosch has yielded large amounts of 18th-century porcelain from its banks (Vos 1993), but throughout the 20th century the river bank in this area has been subjected to extensive flood control construction, certainly affecting the visibility of any earlier deposits. Except for a concentrated deposit of early 20th-century material close to the mill structure, test excavations in the area of the mill stream at Vergelegen have been as unproductive as the rest of the site.

The key to understanding the lack of residues at Vergelegen lies in the virtual absence of collapsed building debris in the slave quarters and the wine cellar. It would seem that the superstructures of the buildings, the walls, and parts of the foundations were carried away in a comprehensive clearing operation that probably also obliterated larger garbage dumps and broadcast debris, leaving behind only floor surfaces, lower foundations, and artifacts tucked into corners or level with the ground.

This taphonomic history limits interpretation of diet, behavior, fashion, gender, and other aspects of life at Vergelegen to inferences based on the small collection that escaped the shovels and wheelbarrows of demolition, and on changes that were made to the living arrangements within the buildings with the passage of time.

The documentary evidence clearly indicated that the recall of Adriaan van der Stel did not break the continuity of occupation and use of the farm buildings for some considerable time. The estate continued under new ownership, and slaves continued to live in the outbuildings and provide essential labor on the estate, as Stavorinus (1969[1798]) noted in 1774. However, archaeological stratigraphies reveal extensive alterations to the slave house and water mill, not detailed in the documentary sources, which must have had considerable implications for those living and working in these buildings. In contrast, the wine cellar *hallehuis* remained much the same in appearance between its construction and eventual demolition.

Excavations have shown that, in its earliest form, the slave *hallehuis* included at least seven distinct living areas: the large, open space with two fireplaces occupying two-thirds of the northern end of the building, the three aisle rooms leading off this, and the three additional rooms at the south end of the building (Figure 9). Sometime later, internal modifications were made. Floors were leveled with a layer of soil and resurfaced with clay and, in one section, a red tile floor. The two cobble surfaces were added to the hearths in the central aisle of the lodge, and at the same time, some of the interior partitions were removed (Figure 9).

The water mill fulfilled an important function on the governor's estate. When Vergelegen was first built there were few mills for grinding the colonial farmers' wheat into flour; Adam Tas and his contemporaries all brought their crops to the mill in the small hamlet of Stellenbosch, where they complained to one another about the governor's rapacity (Fouche 1970). But despite the critical importance of the mill machinery to the success of Van der Stel's farming enterprise, the building was also used for other purposes and, like the slave house, was modified with the passing of time.

As it was first built, the water mill combined two rooms and five sheds—in the *hallehuis* aisle—associated with the mill in the southern end of the building, and a stable in the northern part of the structure, backing onto the Lourens River (Figure 11). In contrast with the slave house, there was no evidence of formal hearths in the mill. But in one of the rooms in the south end of the mill building, Room B (Figures 11, 12), several shallow circular pits with brick surrounds, filled with charcoal-rich soil and containing burned bone and shell fragments, were cut into the lowermost floor surface (Figure 11). These might have been used for cooking. Also in the floor of Room B were two rectangular pits lined with brick and lime plaster which may have been used for storing food (Figure 11). An identical feature was found in an early 18th-century context in the floor of a kitchen in nearby Stellenbosch (Vos 1993).

After it had been used for some years, the floor of Room B was resurfaced with brick paving and a mixture of crushed brick and clay. One of the two brick storage pits was filled and covered, while the other, as well as the circular "cooking pits," remained in use. The aisle sheds continued in use, but their floor levels were steadily raised through the accumulation of debris. Later again, the threshold of the door leading between Room B and the aisle room was strengthened with a surface of hard, packed clay and rubble (Figure 13).

Although the documentary sources make it clear that the northern part of the mill building served as stabling for horses, the archaeological evidence suggests that it also served as a living area. A heat-reddened patch of cobbling indicated the location of a hearth against the brick wall separating the stable and Room B. When the water mill was remodelled in its final form, this northern part of the structure was demolished. A thick lime floor was laid over the earlier stratigraphic layers in Room B in the southern part of the mill (Figures 13, 14); this surface was subsequently disturbed, probably by Lady Phillips's vigorous gardening forays in the 1920s (Walgate 1926).

Because this building work is not detailed in the documentary sources it is difficult to narrow the chronological occurrence of these changes to less

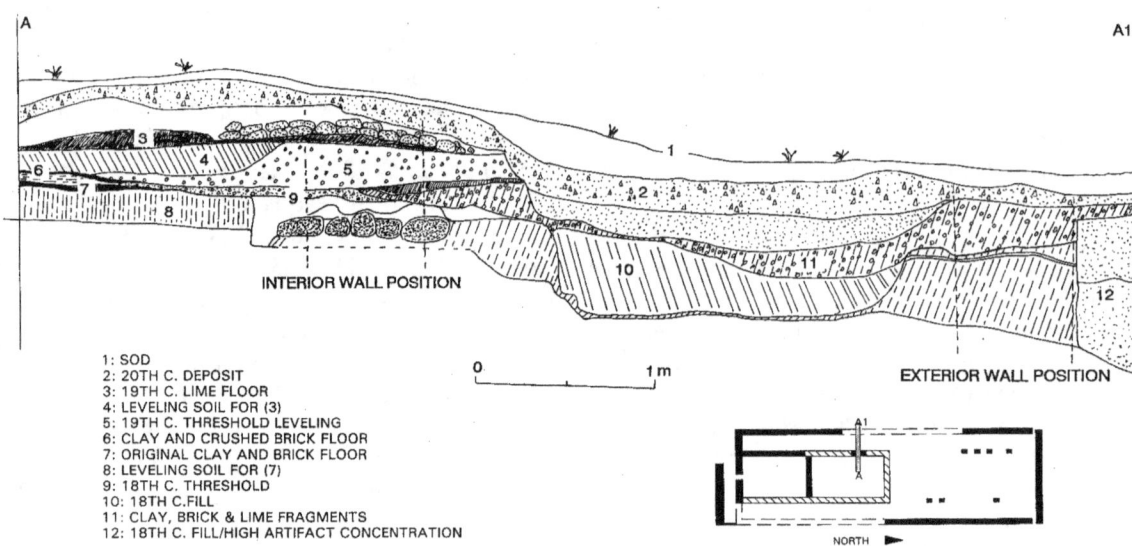

1: SOD
2: 20TH C. DEPOSIT
3: 19TH C. LIME FLOOR
4: LEVELING SOIL FOR (3)
5: 19TH C. THRESHOLD LEVELING
6: CLAY AND CRUSHED BRICK FLOOR
7: ORIGINAL CLAY AND BRICK FLOOR
8: LEVELING SOIL FOR (7)
9: 18TH C. THRESHOLD
10: 18TH C.FILL
11: CLAY, BRICK & LIME FRAGMENTS
12: 18TH C. FILL/HIGH ARTIFACT CONCENTRATION

FIGURE 13. Stratigraphic section showing the threshold between Room B and the aisle room of the water mill.

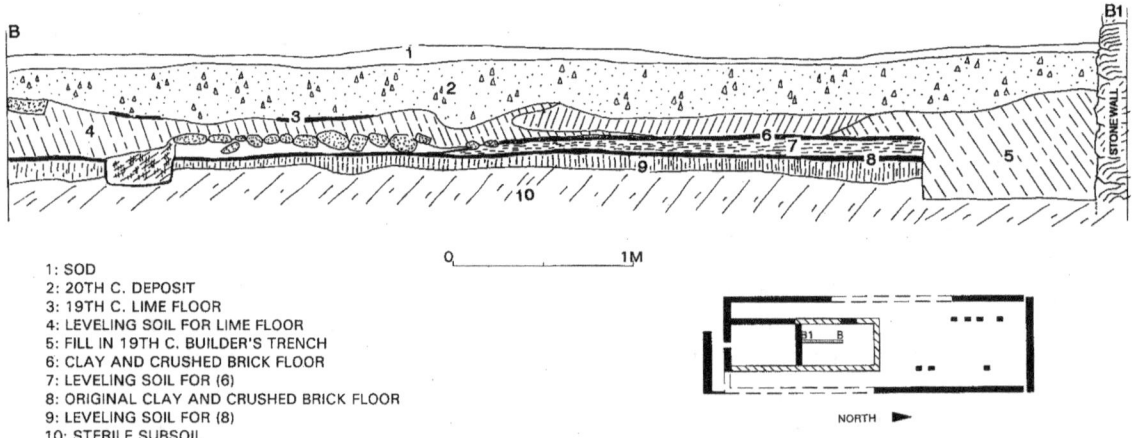

1: SOD
2: 20TH C. DEPOSIT
3: 19TH C. LIME FLOOR
4: LEVELING SOIL FOR LIME FLOOR
5: FILL IN 19TH C. BUILDER'S TRENCH
6: CLAY AND CRUSHED BRICK FLOOR
7: LEVELING SOIL FOR (6)
8: ORIGINAL CLAY AND CRUSHED BRICK FLOOR
9: LEVELING SOIL FOR (8)
10: STERILE SUBSOIL

FIGURE 14. Stratigraphic section showing the builder's trench of the stone wall separating rooms A and B in the water mill.

than 20- or 30-year periods, and more difficult to determine whether slave house and water mill were remodelled at the same time. However, there is some circumstantial evidence that alterations might have been carried out in the latter part of the 18th century. When Vergelegen was sold on the instructions of the Company it was divided into four sections; the slave house and water mill were in different sections and were sold to different people. The Company stipulated that the four sections could not be recombined. This condition was met until 1757, when the two sections which include the excavated buildings were brought together under the ownership of Abraham Maasdorp. It is possible that Maasdorp carried out some changes on his newly acquired estate, and it seems unlikely that anyone before Maasdorp would have undertaken these widespread renovations on a still-divided farm. But Stavorinus (1969[1798]:89), writing in 1774, described the estate as "much decayed," suggesting that extensive renewal had not yet taken place. One year after Stavorinus wrote this description, the property was purchased by Johannes de Waal for 6,000 rixdollars (Cape Town Deeds Office [CTDO] 1775). Five years later it was sold for 27,000 rixdollars to David Malan (CTDO 1780). And again, in 1792, it sold for 45,000 rixdollars (CTDO 1792). These huge price increases over relatively short time periods were unequalled by any previous or subsequent purchases of the estate. The low price of 6,000 rixdollars may reflect fluctuation in the prices of agricultural commodities (Guelke 1989:81), but a 450 percent increase over the following five years seems likely to have been precipitated, at least partially, by improvements to the estate. The property transfers are dealt with in detail in Markell (1993).

In 1802 Vergelegen was acquired by the Theunissen family that was to own it throughout most of the 19th century. Stratigraphic and artifactual evidence suggest that, within the first few decades of the 19th century, the slave lodge and wine cellar were demolished and the water mill was extensively remodelled. In 1816, a new wine cellar was built a short distance from the original building. By 1850 the former slaves had been lodged in "good cottages with sufficient ground for a fruit and vegetable patch" (Heap 1977:48), and the water mill was a far smaller building with a new overshot wheel.

As has already been noted, assemblages from the buildings excavated at Vergelegen have been small. In the slave house, most artifacts and food debris were found against the foundations of the walls, rather than scattered over the floor surfaces—bits and pieces that had escaped the broom. In particular, there were concentrations of rubbish against the side wall of the largest of the three aisle rooms, Room 6 (Figure 9), and around a patch of smaller, more even cobbling in the eastern wall that may represent a door threshold. In contrast, the large open space formed by the center of the *halle-huis* and the western aisle contained far fewer artifacts, although some ceramic sherds and two flints, probably from strike-a-lights, were found near the southernmost hearth. The southern end of the slave house had noticeably fewer artifacts than the north end of the building. However, just outside the south foundation there was a small concentration of debris, close to the position of the exterior doorway suggested by the documentary evidence.

At the southern end of the water mill, most of the artifactual material was concentrated in Room B and in the aisle rooms. The clay and rubble threshold between these two areas (Figure 13) contained numerous fragments of ceramics, glass, bone, as well as more individualized objects such as a coin, a buckle, and a padlock. Some material was also found in the fill of a builders' trench dug during the last phase of building alterations (Figure 14). There was also a concentration of bone, ceramics, and glass in a sealed context just outside the eastern exterior wall of the *hallehuis,* which suggests the possibility of an exterior doorway in this position.

Deposits in the northern, horse stable section of the mill *hallehuis* did not provide a clear stratigraphic pattern as in the rest of the structure. They were mixed into a single soil layer probably laid down at the time of destruction of the stable at the beginning of the 19th century. The random distribution of some of the materials across the cobble-paved stable floors also suggests that they were deposited with the destruction fill. There were clear areas of disturbance caused by later road-building, the construction of a flood bank in the 1920s, and by vigorous tree growth. In these easily identified areas, the artifacts included recent 20th-century debris in addition to the expected 18th-century and early 19th-century material. Frequent ceramic crossmends with the 18th-century materials from the stratigraphically intact areas of Room B and the aisle rooms indicate that these artifacts derived from the same source, however, and they serve as a reminder that during the 18th century this was a single building used in a variety of farm tasks.

Excavation of the wine cellar resulted in the smallest assemblage of artifacts, mostly associated with wine making, brandy distilling, and barrel coopering. The poverty of this collection contrasts with documentary evidence of the early 18th century. Van der Stel's detractors claimed, perhaps with exaggeration, that the building housed four pressing vats, each operated by four slaves (Tas and Van der Heyden 1712:205). In addition one slave, Adam by name, had been trained as a cooper (Tas and Van der Heyden 1712:205). Each Sunday, Vergelegen's slaves were allotted a half bottle of wine each; their share of the huge quantity of wine and brandy that was made in the cellar (Tas and Van der Heyden 1712:147). After Van der Stel's departure, the wine cellar continued in its original use. A daybook kept by Hendrik van Heezel, a cooper at the estate in 1721 and 1722, records that slaves were issued wine in wooden buckets, and were at times given brandy in bottles (SASA [1721]). Although 50 years later, Stavorinus did not specifically mention the wine cellar, it seems a fair assumption that the activities carried out in the building had changed little since Van der Stel's day. Any timber or other materials that could be reused were probably employed in the construction of the new cellar in about 1816, the date on the gable of the new building.

Living and Dying

The distribution of residues across floors and around hearths and doorways—potsherds, food waste, and the occasional personal item, as well as implements associated with the everyday life of a slave on the Vergelegen estate—begin to amplify the imprint of people on the archaeological record. And then, of course, there are the details of these assemblages—grist to the mill of archaeological interpretation.

One of the consequences of the unusual taphonomic history of the Vergelegen buildings is a difficulty in tracking changes with time. Just as the architecture of the slave house and water mill was volatile, with the layout of living and working spaces changing through the 18th and into the 19th

centuries, so the everyday implements and foodstuffs available to the estate's residents changed through the years. However, the radical demolition of the slave house, the severity of the restructuring of the water mill, and the degree of later disturbance over parts of the site render any strict chronological implications extremely tenuous.

In the slave house, most of the artifacts, bones, and shells are sealed by the floor surfaces laid down during the 18th-century remodelling episode, which is in turn sealed by the early 19th-century destruction debris. Those artifacts that can be dated are consistent with this interpretation. In the water mill, the stratigraphic sequence rests mainly on the sequence of deposits that make up the threshold between Room B and the aisle rooms (Figure 13). In this case, earlier floor surfaces in Room B could be tied to deposits of fill that were sealed by the later thresholds. Artifacts in these sealed deposits were used to infer broad chronological sequences for the floor surfaces and their occupation periods. Elsewhere in the mill building the sequence has been disturbed by later activities—in particular, by Lady Phillips's gardening. In addition, it must be remembered that only tenuous circumstantial evidence exists that building alterations in the slave house and the water mill happened at corresponding time periods (Markell 1993). For these reasons, researchers have avoided arranging the Vergelegen assemblages in a chronological sequence, rather trying to outline patterns in general terms.

The most durable, and consequently the most common, artifacts were those made of ceramic and glass. Table 1 shows profiles of the ceramic assemblages in the slave house, water mill, and wine cellar. Porcelains in these assemblages were imported from China or Japan, and were commonplace in households throughout the domain of the Dutch East India Company (Woodward 1974; Klose and Malan 1992). The majority of these pieces are hollow forms—bowls, shallow dishes, saucers, and tea bowls. Less than 10 percent of the porcelain vessels were plates.

Some of the stonewares were also imported from the East, but others came to the Cape from Europe, originating in the specialized German potteries (Hurst et al. 1986; Von Bock 1986). All were

TABLE 1
CERAMIC ASSEMBLAGES FROM THE SLAVE LODGE, WATER MILL, AND WINE CELLAR

Type	Lodge		Mill		Cellar	
	MNV	%	MNV	%	MNV	%
Porcelain						
Chinese/Japanese	42	48	88	40	22	20
Provincial	8	9	67	30	21	20
Stoneware						
German	10	12	12	5	10	9
Oriental	2	2	10	4	0	0
Coarse Earthenware	22	25	18	8	8	7
Refined Earthenware	2	2	22	10	44	41
Other Wares	2	2	6	3	3	3
Total	88	100	223	100	108	100

either jugs or large storage jars. The coarse earthenwares, probably used in a wide variety of everyday tasks, may have been made at the Cape—where a pottery was established soon after the initial Dutch settlement some 50 years before Vergelegen was built—or may have been imported from the Netherlands. Most are lead-glazed redwares, either tripod-footed cooking pots or dishes.

Two of the earthenware vessels—one from the slave house and the other from the stable area of the water mill—are large, globular, flat-based pots or jars of unknown provenance. They are burnished with black slip on both interior and exterior and show evidence of burning on the lower areas, indicating that they may have been used for cooking. The bodies of these ceramics bear little similarity to ceramics thought to have been made with local clays, or to the fabric of locally made bricks, but petrographic analysis has shown that they are quite similar to sherds excavated at the Castle in Cape Town (Miller 1990). While the provenance of these vessels is as yet unidentified, they do bear some formal similarities with ceramics from the Indonesian archipelago, India, and perhaps Madagascar (Verin et al. 1965:281; Fernandez 1970:33; R. Wright 1993, pers. comm.). Another earthenware vessel found at the lodge is a crudely handbuilt, unglazed redware pot that appears to have been fired at an extremely low heat and may have been manufactured locally. It also shows signs of burning, indicating its probable use as a cooking vessel.

Variations in the proportions of the ceramic types from the individual Vergelegen buildings are probably as much a function of the small samples as of meaningful differences between the material culture sets of the people who lived there. However, it should be noted that the higher proportion of refined earthenwares found at the water mill (Table 1) is probably the result both of the longer lifespan of the building and of dumping on the site after the northern portion of the building had been razed; later disturbances have considerably compromised the stratigraphy of certain levels. It should also be noted that there is evidence of variation between the buildings in the nature of the porcelain collections. The proportion of high-quality export pieces relative to the coarser provincial wares is much higher at the slave lodge site than at the water mill (Table 1). At the mill, 43 percent of the porcelain assemblage consisted of almost identical, coarser porcelains produced in the Chinese provinces and very likely purchased in a single lot (Jane Klose 1993, pers. comm.). Again, the small sizes of the assemblages have accentuated such variability.

Clay tobacco pipes, all of Dutch manufacture, corroborate the documentary evidence that slaves were issued rations of tobacco during Van der Stel's tenure (Tas and Van der Heyden 1712:147). The mean pipe stem bore diameters for the slave house (2.25 ± 0.17 mm [n = 289]) and for the water mill (1.97 ± 0.19 mm [n = 538]) reflect the differing life spans of the two structures. The taphonomy of the lodge site probably affected it also; the later occupation residues of the slave house were stripped away when the building was razed. The collection from the wine cellar was negligible. There is, as yet, insufficient evidence from colonial sites in the Cape to construct a general relative chronology based on pipe stem bore diameters.

Compared with ceramics, glasswares from both slave house and water mill were few in number, 14 and 24 vessels respectively. With the exception of one 19th-century bottle from the upper part of the dump at the south end of the slave house, all glass from this building was manufactured in the 18th century. The assemblage included mallet or onion wine bottles and case-type bottles, small medicine bottles, and parts of the bases of stemmed and *roemer*-type drinking glasses. Glassware from the water mill was more diverse, and included an 18th-century glass beaker, mallet-type wine bottles (but no case bottles), and 19th-century bottle forms from the stable area.

Glasswares excavated in the wine cellar reflected the lack of stratigraphic clarity in this building. The majority of the glass vessels were found in the central and northern areas of the *hallehuis,* and most of them are 19th- and 20th-century forms, post-dating the demolition of the building. Only one 18th-century case bottle was found, at the spot where it was broken, the shattered pieces lying against the exterior of the western wall.

Ceramic and glassware assemblages give a generalized profile of some aspects of the equipment of those who lived and worked in Vergelegen's slave house, water mill, and wine cellar. Other artifacts, although less numerous, widen further this impression of everyday life.

Iron tools were found in all three buildings. Some relate to woodworking, such as a well-used iron chisel from the slave house, a similar one from the wine cellar, and the blade from a plane or adze found in the deposit in the stable of the mill complex. Several iron barrel straps were found just outside the northeast corner of the wine cellar. Other iron objects were used in agricultural activities—the collar of a hoe and two spades from the stable, one of a design depicted in Dutch genre paintings, and two more spades of the same type from the wine cellar, one found near the brandy still.

All three buildings also had bits and pieces of fishing equipment. Sinkers of rolled lead, identical to those pictured in an 18th-century engraving of French fishing equipment (Diderot 1959[1763]), were found at both the slave house and at the water mill, in the stable. One smaller weight was found in the wine cellar. A fragment of a barbed brass trident, or fish spear, came from the mill.

Impressions of the people using such hoes, spades, and fishing lines are, not surprisingly, fleeting. Personal items found in the slave house included flints, probably from strike-a-lights, a silver two-stuiver piece dated 1678—from the dump at the south end of the building, a copper *liard* from Liege, datable to the first half of the 18th century, a brass sewing thimble, and a William and Mary *jetton* or casting counter made in Nuremburg, probably ca. 1689 (Forrer 1907:333; Baart et al. 1977:409; Noël Hume 1985:158), and similar to one found at Oudepost, Cape (Schrire and Meltzer 1992:105). These last were all found in the eastern aisle room of the lodge. Fabrics have not survived and, anyway, would rarely make their way into archaeological deposits. The collection from the slave house does, however, include a brass buckle from the long aisle room and 10 domed brass buttons, molded in two pieces and soldered, from different parts of the building. Otto Mentzel (1921 [1785]:169), describing the Cape in the first half of the 18th century, wrote of male Company slaves as equipped with a "doublet . . . adorned with 12 brass buttons."

Personal items found in the rooms of the water mill included one domed brass button, similar to those from the slave house but larger, an iron buckle, and a fragment of a bone hair comb, undecorated, and of typical 17th- to 18th-century design. A brass casting counter with the words "Louis . . . Roi" on the face was found embedded in the clay of the threshold between interior room and aisle, and a silver coin—unfortunately too worn for identification—was found in the stable area.

However, one feature of Vergelegen's archaeology does provide more direct contact with the people who left these traces of their lives behind them. In the slave house a grave about 1 m deep, and oriented on an east-west axis, was cut through the clay floor surface that marked the remodeling of the building's internal architecture. In turn, this burial was sealed by the stratigraphic layer of clay and brick rubble that marks the demolition of the building. If the tentative chronology for the slave house is correct, then burial took place sometime between the last quarter of the 18th century and the early decades of the 19th century.

The grave received a coffin made from planks of wood tentatively identified as local yellowwood, hammered together with a rough assortment of iron nails. Identification of wood samples from the coffin was by E. February (1992, pers. comm.) of the South African Museum. Thirty-six iron nails were excavated, ranging in size between 18 mm and 105 mm. This variation suggests that the nails were reused—gathered together from around the estate.

The coffin was barely large enough to contain the body which was that of a woman aged about 50, buried on her back with her hands crossed over her abdomen. The skeletal material provides some evidence of diet. Firstly, the teeth are complete and have no caries; although crippled with osteoarthritis, this woman suffered no tooth decay, indicating a diet very low in refined carbohydrates. Secondly, comparative isotopic and trace element analyses of tooth dentine, formed largely in childhood, and bone tissue, replaced throughout life, suggests that she had a childhood diet that included tropical grain foods such as sorghum, millet, and maize and little, if any, seafood. But as an adult, temperate climate grains (e.g., rice, wheat, rye) were added and seafood became a larger component of her diet for many years (Sealy et al. 1993). While many of the slaves were brought to the Cape from the islands of the eastern archipelago and Madagascar, this does not presuppose a diet based on seafood. Many of the groups indigenous to these islands lived in interior areas with little access to the sea. Even in those areas with easy access to water, this proximity often had little to do with the consumption of fish (Linton 1933; Evans 1968; Rakotoarisoa 1986).

This woman's last years could not have been easy, as she suffered from extensive osteoarthritis, particularly in her back and hands (Sealy et al.

TABLE 2
WATER MILL FAUNAL ASSEMBLAGE

Species	MNI		NSIP	
	N	%	N	%
Sheep (*Ovis aries*)	9	41	210	54
Cattle (*Bos taurus*)	6	27	111	28
Pig (*Sus scrofa*)	2	9	6	2
Chicken (*Gallus* sp.)	2	9	22	6
Dog (*Canis canis*)	2	9	32	8
Tortoise (*Chersina angulata*)	1	5	5	2
Total	22	100	386	100

1993). Her physical disability implies that, towards the end of her life, she was cared for by others. The fact that, of all those who must have died in servitude at Vergelegen, this woman was the only person to have been buried beneath the floor of the slave house suggests that she may have held some status in the community.

Food residues also provide a generalized impression of diet, although of the three buildings excavated, the faunal assemblage from the water mill was the only one large enough for analysis. Much of this assemblage was recovered from the units in the shed area of the mill and is assignable to the second half of the 18th century. The Minimum Number of Individuals (MNI) identified for different animal species from this building are given in Table 2. Although sheep were the most numerous species in the assemblage, cattle must have been of at least equal importance in terms of meat yield. Other domesticated animals—pig and fowl—were represented in far smaller proportion, as were wild animals hunted, snared, or collected around the Vergelegen estate. This fact that the first half of the century is not well represented in this assemblage should be borne in mind when assessing these results.

Fish remains from the water mill assemblage are listed in Table 3. The three identified species would have been obtained from False Bay or from the estuary of the Lourens River, both within a few miles of the estate. Table 4 lists shellfish. Although some whelks and limpets were collected, and a few perlemoen and alikreukel were taken from the

TABLE 3
WATER MILL FISH ASSEMBLAGE

Species	MNI		NSIP	
	N	%	N	%
White Steenbras (*Lithognathus* sp.)	1	33.3	6	9.5
White Stumpnose (*Rhabdasorgus globiceps*)	1	33.3	1	1.6
Musselcracker	1	33.3	1	1.6
Unidentified species	0	0	55	87.3
Total	3	100	63	100

TABLE 4
WATER MILL SHELLFISH ASSEMBLAGE

Species	Weight	
	g	%
GASTROPODA		
Limpets		
Patella argenvillei	0.7	0.05
Patella barbara	115.4	8.67
Patella granatina	0.3	0.02
Patella longicosta	1.7	0.13
Patella sp.	1.2	0.09
Whelks		
Oxystelle sinesis	51.4	3.86
Oxystelle sp.	2.9	0.22
Creppidula porcelana	2.0	0.15
Argobuccinum pustulosum	87.3	6.56
Bullia digitalis	0.5	0.04
Whelks unidentified	56.4	4.24
Alikreukel		
Turbo sarmaticus	194.8	14.63
Turbo sp.	11.2	0.84
BIVALVES		
Choromytilus meridionalis	12.2	0.92
Crassotrea margaritacae	474.3	35.62
Pecten maximus sulciostatus	20.4	1.52
Scissodesma spengleric	7.0	0.52
Gastrana matadoa	3.0	0.22
Donax serra	249.1	18.71
Venus verrucosa	9.8	0.74
NON-MOLLUSCAN SHELL		
Cirripedia (barnacle)	5.2	0.39
UNIDENTIFIED SHELL	24.7	1.86
Total	1,331.5	100.00

rocks at low tide, the shellfish most commonly eaten in the mill were white mussels and oysters, taken from the shoreline. As with the fish, all the

shellfish could have been obtained from the near-by False Bay coast. Small amounts of ostrich egg-shell found among the bone and shell in the 18th-century deposits of Room B and the aisle room of the mill suggest the occasional exploitation of this food source, also.

Documentary sources are unequivocal on the subject of the diet of Company slaves at the Cape—mutton and fish, usually dried and salted, and sometimes the entrails and the tougher and discarded cuts of beef (Mentzel 1925[1785]:168–169, 1944[1787]:203; Armstrong and Worden 1989:146). In addition, the faunal assemblage from Cape Town's Castle shows that slaves were able to scavenge additional food, such as birds and small animals, during their everyday activities (Hall 1992). One of the specific complaints against Van der Stel was that the governor monopolized the False Bay fishery in order to cater to the needs of his and his friends' slaves (Tas and Van der Hey-den 1712:146; Kolb 1968[1731]:29). The isotopic, and trace element, analysis of the slave house burial is consistent with the documentary evidence, as is the archaeological evidence from the water mill, which indicates a diet dominated by beef and mutton, and with occasional delicacies such as mussels and oysters and, perhaps, tortoise and os-trich eggs.

Discussion

What, then, of the three propositions that were addressed in excavating at Vergelegen? Firstly, Van der Stel's estate included a type of architec-ture previously unencountered archaeologically in South Africa. The use of the *hallehuis* type struc-ture for farm outbuildings is consistent with the way this building type was used in northern Eu-rope, where *hallehuisen* housed farm laborers and fulfilled a variety of farm functions (Netherlands Open-Air Museum 1990).

Vergelegen's outbuilding architecture thus brings into question the assumption of a unilinear line of vernacular tradition in the Cape (De Bosdari 1953; Walton 1965; Fransen 1987). In the light of this new evidence, it seems likely that timber frame buildings were constructed elsewhere in the early colony—perhaps at the first outpost of *Paradys,* on the slopes of Table Mountain, prior to the stone and brick construction that was put up sometime after 1720 (Hall et al. 1993)—perhaps on the site of the new Castle in 1666, where a *boerehuys* measuring 96 by 33 Rhineland ft. was built as temporary housing and stores for slaves and Company soldiers (Ras 1959). The Vergelegen evidence suggests the need to reassess the nature of early colonial architecture at the Cape; a point recently made by Brink (1992), who has argued that the "Cape Dutch" tradition only originated in the third decade of the 18th century, more than 80 years after the initial colonial settlement on the shores of Table Bay.

Secondly, the assorted debris of everyday living from the excavated deposits of the Vergelegen outbuildings does begin to suggest the outline of a slave material culture, countering Nigel Worden's suggestion of social disablement. With few exceptions, the slaves in the Cape colony were brought from Madagascar, the East Indian archipelago, and the Dutch-held colonies in India and Ceylon. The majority (65%) officially brought by the Dutch East India Company itself were from Madagascar, with smaller numbers coming from Indonesia and India (Shell 1986). This percentage was based, however, on male slaves resident in the Company lodge, and a 25 percent figure for Malagasy slaves might be more realistic (Robert Shell 1993, pers. comm.). A small number came from Delagoa Bay, now Maputo, on the southeastern African coast, and after 1776 significant numbers were brought from Mozambique (Armstrong and Worden 1989: 121). Of the slaves owned by the freeburghers, or farmers, a higher proportion was brought from the East Indies—originally from islands like Timor or Macassar, or from Bengal, Malabar, or Cormandel on the coast of India (Shell 1986). From the list of Governor Adriaan van der Stel's slaves, it appears that 11 came from Cape Verde, and one from Guinea, which could be the Guinea Coast of West Africa (Robert Shell 1992, pers. comm.). Although the diversity of origins of the slaves has been used as argument against the development of strong community ties amongst the slaves, it should be remembered that there was also a good deal of

cultural and linguistic diversity among the West and Central African peoples brought to the Americas as slaves (Mintz and Price 1992:14). Just as the slaves brought to the New World shared a generalized African heritage, so the slaves imported into the Cape Colony shared a background of contact with or exploitation by Malay, Arab, Indian, and Chinese traders, as well as by Portuguese, Dutch, and other Europeans (Cooper-Cole 1945).

As has been found on plantation sites in the United States, there is little overt difference between the specific material goods found on slave sites and on European sites in the Cape. Even the argument for colonoware as a conscious Africanism and a regular component of regional North American slave material culture (Ferguson 1992) is unlikely to find a correlate in the ceramics of the Cape. Because of the geographic and cultural origins of some of the slaves, or their parents, living and working at Vergelegen, they would likely have been familiar with porcelain bowls and dishes similar to those imported to the Cape by the Dutch East India Company for the use of its employees. Even if the porcelain material were unfamiliar, the form of these ceramics bore a close correspondence to the traditional foodways of the slaves. As Ferguson (1992) and others (Joyner 1984; Otto 1984; Mintz and Price 1992) have concluded for North American sites, it is likely that the differences between slave and European assemblages will be found in the more subtle patterns of use, reuse, and adaptation, rather than in the identification of specific "ethnic markers."

While ceramics still prove elusive, there are some small aspects of the outbuildings' archaeology that do hint at wider cultural connections. The pit-hearths found in the floor of the water mill do not form part of Dutch domestic practice, but are similar to hearths known from other parts of Africa, including Madagascar (Linton 1933:66–67), from where many slaves were brought to the Cape. They suggest that there were some retentions and adaptations of traditional practices in the syncretic Vergelegen slave culture.

Some elements in the small assemblages of personal items found in the slave house and water mill may also have contributed to a sense of identity. Coins and counters may have been part of an undercurrent of circulation within the protective walls of the *hallehuisen.* Buttons may simply have been lost at a careless moment. But they may also have been part of a system of slave currency, as Robert Shell (1986) has suggested. Ostrich eggs were also said to have been gathered by slave herders, who found them in the veld, and were often sold to ships' crews (Thunberg 1986: 168). Thus the small quantity of ostrich eggshell from the water mill may indicate another facet of internal trade.

Of course, other personal items will not have survived the passage of time. Contemporary 18th-century descriptions of urban Cape Town offer vivid images of slave hairstyles and clothing with close connections to the East (Mentzel 1921[1785]: 131; Thunberg 1986:26). Mentzel (1921[1785]: 131) describes the practice of chewing betel nut, a traditional habit apparently tenaciously followed by many slaves, but one which would have left few tangible remains. When the Company-owned slave Rangton van Balij died in 1720, his goods were sold at a *vendue* or public auction. They consisted of two empty chests—probably of wood, tobacco boxes, baskets, a blanket, miscellaneous items termed "lumber"—used in the inventories to denote various items of little value, and not worth enumerating, a small amount in wages, and two packets of playing cards (SASA 1720; Shell 1991). Few of these items would have lasted in an archaeological context.

The third question posed was about the extent of the Vergelegen slaves' knowledge of local wild resources. An answer to this might also have led, as Ross (1983) has suggested, to some illumination of the nature of the interaction between slaves at early 18th-century Vergelegen and the Khoikhoi pastoralists who at the beginning of the century were still moving seasonally in and out of the higher ground closely bordering Van der Stel's estate. Unfortunately, the material culture assemblages from both water mill and slave house provided no unequivocal evidence of contact between slaves and Khoikhoi; neither did they suggest that contact did not take place. The faunal material recovered from the site is inadequate for a proper assessment of this ques-

tion, since little of it can be clearly dated to the earliest years of the 18th century.

Other interesting questions are raised, though, by the virtual absence—save for the occasional tortoise, the fish, and the ostrich eggs—of the remains of wild animals snared and trapped in the woodlands and heaths that pressed around Vergelegen. This stands in marked contrast to faunal assemblages from North American plantation sites, where hunting and gathering provided meat for the table and, it has been argued, offered a form of resistance to slave owner control (Otto 1984; Reitz et al. 1985). Ferguson (1992:95–96) ties this supplementary hunting to the nutritional deficiencies of the maize staple diet of American slaves, and points out that a diet based on rice rather than maize as a staple offered a more complete range of amino acids and other nutrients, and thus made meat consumption less crucial. Documentary evidence indicates that rice, wheat, and vegetables were major components of the slave diet during the 18th century in the Cape (Leibbrandt 1896:270; Mentzel 1925[1785]:130, 168–169; see also Armstrong and Worden 1989:146). While the specific rations given to the slaves at Vergelegen are unknown, their diet probably included whole wheat—possibly supplemented with rice as was the case on some estates, vegetables, additional rations of fish and shellfish, and occasionally mutton or beef. A diet like this would have been nutritionally adequate. This argument, coupled with the fact that the traditional diets of most of the slaves brought to the Cape were not heavily weighted towards meat (Linton 1933:68; Evans 1968), may help to explain the absence of larger numbers of wild fauna in the archaeological record at Vergelegen.

Van der Stel's self-imposed psychological isolation from his compatriots in the Cape, so well expressed by his commissioned engraving of the estate as an enclave of buildings faced by wild animals on one side and uncivilized Khoikhoi on the other, may not have extended in the same manner to his slaves. Despite being forced by physical circumstance to look inward for social resources to those who shared the slave house, mill, or stable floor, the archaeological evidence hints at their ability to adapt the scant material possessions available to them to a developing culture that drew on both their former experiences and on their new situation in the Cape.

ACKNOWLEDGMENTS

The authors would like to thank the Anglo American/De Beers Chairman's Educational Trust for their generous support of this project. We would also like to thank the many people of Vergelegen who offered encouragement and assistance throughout our work there. We would like to extend thanks to Sarah Winter, the site assistant; to the crew—headed by Robert Tonis; to Jane Klose for her preliminary analysis of the ceramics; and to all of the many people who have provided assistance and support.

REFERENCES

ARMSTRONG, JAMES C., AND NIGEL WORDEN
1989   The Slaves, 1652–1834. In *The Shaping of South African Society, 1652–1840*, edited by Richard Elphick and Hermann Giliomee, pp. 109–183. Maskew, Miller, and Longman, Cape Town, South Africa.

BAART, JAN, WIARD KROOK, AB LAGERWEIJ, NINA OCKERS, HANS VAN REGTEREN ALTENA, TUUK STAM, HENK STOEPKER, GERARD STOUTHART, AND MONIKA VAN DER ZWAN
1977   *Opgravingen in Amsterdam, 20 jaar stadskernondersoek.* Fibula-van Dishoek, Amsterdam.

BOGAERT, ABRAHAM
1711   *Historiche reizen door d'oosersche deelen van Asia.* Nicolas ten Hoorn, Amsterdam.

BRINK, YVONNE
1992   Places of Discourse and Dialogue: A Study in the Material Culture of the Cape during the Rule of the Dutch East India Company, 1652–1795. Unpublished M.A. thesis, Department of Archaeology, University of Cape Town, Cape Town, South Africa.

CAPE TOWN DEEDS OFFICE (CTDO)
1775   Transfer of property from N. Vlok to J. de Waal, No. 1775/4731. Deeds Office, Cape Town, South Africa.
1780   Transfer of property from J. de Waal to D. Malan, No. 1780/5277. Deeds Office, Cape Town, South Africa.
1792   Transfer of property from D. Malan to R. Loubser, No. 1792/6678. Deeds Office, Cape Town, South Africa.

COOK, MICHAEL
[1970]   *The Cape Kitchen.* Stellenbosch Museum, Stellenbosch, South Africa.

COOPER-COLE, FAY
1945   *The Peoples of Malaysia.* Van Nostrand, New York.

CRUZ-URIBE, KATHRYN, AND CARMEL SCHRIRE
1991   Analysis of Faunal Remains from Oudepost I, an Early Outpost of the Dutch East India Company, Cape Province. *South African Archaeological Bulletin* 46:92–106.

DE BOSDARI, C.
1953   *Cape Dutch Houses and Farms.* A. A. Balkema, Cape Town, South Africa.

DEETZ, JAMES F.
1977   *In Small Things Forgotten: The Archaeology of Early American Life.* Anchor Press/Doubleday, New York.

DIDEROT, DENIS
1959   *Recueil de planches, sur les sciences, les arts liberaux, et les arts mechaniques, avec leur explication,* Vols. 1–2. Facsimile reprint of 1763 edition. Dover, New York.

EMERSON, MATTHEW C.
1988   *Decorated Clay Tobacco Pipes from the Chesapeake.* Ph.D. dissertation, Department of Anthropology, University of California, Berkeley. University Microfilms, Ann Arbor, Michigan.

EVANS, I. H. N.
1968   *The Negritos of Malaya.* Frank Cass, London.

FAIRBANKS, CHARLES
1984   The Plantation Archaeology of the Southeastern Coast. *Historical Archaeology* 18:1–14.

FERGUSON, LELAND
1992   *Uncommon Ground: Archaeology and Early African America, 1650–1800.* Smithsonian Institution Press, Washington, D.C.

FERNANDEZ, M. F.
1970   Contribution a l'étude du peuplement ancien du Lac Alaotra. *Taloha* 3:3–48. Revue du Musée d'Art et d'Archaeologie, Annales de l'Université de Madagascar.

FORRER, LOUIS
1907   *Biographical Dictionary of Medallists,* Vol. 3. A. H. Baldwin and Sons, London.

FOUCHE, LEO
1970   *The Diary of Adam Tas, 1705–1706.* Van Riebeeck Society, Cape Town, South Africa.

FRANSEN, HANS
1987   Classicism, Baroque, Rococo and Neo-Classicism at the Cape: An Investigation into Stylistic Modes in the Architecture and Applied Arts at the Cape of

Good Hope, 1652–1820. Unpublished Ph.D. dissertation, Department of History, University of Natal, South Africa.

FRANSEN, HANS, AND MICHAEL A. COOK
1980   *The Old Buildings of the Cape.* A. A. Balkema, Cape Town, South Africa.

GUELKE, L.
1989   Freehold Farmers and Frontier Settlers, 1657–1780. In *The Shaping of South African Society, 1652–1840,* edited by Richard Elphick and Hermann Giliomee, pp. 66–101. Maskew, Miller, and Longman, Cape Town, South Africa.

GUTSCHE, THELMA
1966   *No Ordinary Woman.* Howard Timmins, Cape Town, South Africa.

HALL, MARTIN
1991   Archaeological Work at Sea Street, Cape Town. Report on file, Archaeological Contracts Office, University of Cape Town, South Africa.
1992   Small Things and the Mobile, Conflictual Fusion of Power, Fear, and Desire. In *The Art and Mystery of Historical Archaeology; Essays in Honor of James Deetz,* edited by Anne Yentsch and Mary Beaudry, pp. 373–399. CRC Press, Boca Raton, Florida.

HALL, MARTIN, ANTONIA MALAN, SHARON AMANN, LYNN HONEYMAN, TAFT KISER, AND GABRIELLE RITCHIE
1993   The Archaeology of Paradise. *South African Archaeological Association, Goodwin Series* 7:40–58.

HEAP, PEGGY
1977   *The Story of Hottentot's Holland.* Peggy Heap, Sir Lowry's Pass, South Africa.

HURST, JOHN G., DAVID S. NEAL, AND H. J. E. VAN BEUNINGEN
1986   Pottery Produced and Traded in North-West Europe, 1350–1650. *Rotterdam Papers VI: A Contribution to Medieval Archaeology.* Museum Boymans-van Beuningen, Rotterdam, The Netherlands.

JOYNER, CHARLES
1984   *Down by the Riverside: A South Carolina Slave Community.* University of Illinois Press, Urbana.

KELSO, WILLIAM
1984   *Kingsmill Plantation, 1619–1800.* Academic Press, New York.

KLOSE, JANE, AND ANTONIA MALAN
1992   Ceramics of the Southwestern Cape, 1650–1850. *HARG Handbook* 1. Historical Archaeology Research Group, University of Cape Town, South Africa.

KOLB, PETER
1968   *The Present State of the Cape of Good Hope.* Reprint of 1731 edition. Johnson Reprint Corporation, London.

LEIBBRANDT, H. C. V.
1896   Letters received, 1695–1708. *Précis of the Archives of the Cape of Good Hope.* W. A. Richards and Sons, Cape Town, South Africa.
1897   The Defense of Willem Adriaan van der Stel. *Précis of the Archives of the Cape of Good Hope.* W. A. Richards and Sons, Cape Town, South Africa.

LINTON, RALPH
1933   *The Tanala, a Hill Tribe of Madagascar.* Field Museum of Natural History, Chicago, Illinois.

MALAN, RIAN
1990   *My Traitor's Heart.* Bodley Head, London.

MARKELL, ANN B.
1993   Building on the Past: The Architecture and Archaeology of Vergelegen. *South African Archaeological Society, Goodwin Series* 7:71–83.

MENTZEL, OTTO F.
1921   *A Geographical and Topographical Description of the Cape of Good Hope,* Vol. 1. Reprint of 1785 edition. Van Riebeeck Society, Cape Town, South Africa.
1925   *A Geographical and Topographical Description of the Cape of Good Hope,* Vol. 2. Reprint of 1785 edition. Van Riebeeck Society, Cape Town, South Africa.
1944   *A Geographical and Topographical Description of the Cape of Good Hope,* Vol. 3. Reprint of 1787 edition. Van Riebeeck Society, Cape Town, South Africa.

MILLER, DUNCAN E.
1990   Petrographic Description of Two Specimens of Pottery of Suspected Local Manufacture from the Western Cape. Report submitted to the Vergelegen Project, University of Cape Town, South Africa.

MILLER, D. E., J. H. N. LOUBSER, SR., AND A. B. MARKELL
1993   Electron Spin Resonance Thermometry Applied to Quartzite Cobbles from Vergelegen Slave Lodge, Somerset West, South Africa. *Archaeometry* 35(1): 1–9.

MINTZ, SIDNEY W., AND RICHARD PRICE
1992   *The Birth of African-American Culture, an Anthropological Perspective.* Beacon Press, Boston, Massachusetts.

NETHERLANDS OPEN-AIR MUSEUM [Arnhem]
1990   *Guide.* Special Images b.v., Enschede.

NOËL HUME, IVOR
1985   *A Guide to Artifacts of Colonial America.* Reprint of 1978 edition. Alfred A. Knopf, New York.

OTTO, JOHN SOLOMON
1984   *Cannon's Point Plantation, 1794–1860: Living Conditions and Status Patterns in the Old South.* Academic Press, New York.

PRUDON, THEODORE
1986   The Dutch Barn in America: Survival of a Medieval Structural Frame. In *Common Places: Readings in American Vernacular Architecture,* edited by Dell Upton and John Vlach, pp. 204–216. University of Georgia Press, Athens, Georgia.

RAKOTOARISOA, J. A.
1986   Principaux aspects des formes d'adaptation de la société traditionelle Malgache. In *Madagascar, Society and History,* edited by C. Kottak, J. A. Rakotoarisoa, A. Southall, and P. Verin, pp. 89–106. Carolina Academic Press, Durham, North Carolina.

RAS, A. C.
1959   *Die Kasteel en ander vroeë Kaapse vestingwerke, 1652–1713.* Tafelberg, Cape Town, South Africa.

REITZ, ELIZABETH, TYSON GIBBS, AND TED A. RATHBURN
1985   Archaeological Evidence for Subsistence on Coastal Plantations. In *The Archaeology of Slavery and Plantation Life,* edited by Theresa Singleton, pp. 163–191. Academic Press, New York.

ROSS, ROBERT
1983   *Cape of Torments: Slavery and Resistance in South Africa.* Routledge and Kegan Paul, Cape Town, South Africa.

SCHRIRE, CARMEL
1987   The Historical Archaeology of Colonial–Indigenous Interactions in South Africa: Proposed Research at Oudepost I, Cape. In Papers in the Prehistory of the Western Cape, edited by John Parkington and Martin Hall. *British Archaeological Reports, International Series* 332:424–461. Oxford.
1988   The Historical Archaeology of the Impact of Colonialism in 17th-Century South Africa. *Antiquity* 62: 214–225.
1990   Excavating Archives at Oudepost I, Cape. *Social Dynamics* 16:11–21.

SCHRIRE, CARMEL, KATHRYN CRUZ-URIBE, AND J. KLOSE
1993   The Site History of the Historical Site at Oudepost I, Cape. *South African Archaeological Society, Goodwin Series* 7:21–32.

SCHRIRE, CARMEL, AND LALOU MELTZER
1992   Coins, Gaming Counters and a Bale Seal from Oudepost, Cape. *South African Archaeological Bulletin* 47:104–107.

SCHUTTE, GERRIT
1989   Company and Colonists at the Cape, 1652–1795. In *The Shaping of South African Society, 1652–1840,* edited by Richard Elphick and Hermann Giliomee, pp. 283–323. Maskew Miller Longman, Cape Town, South Africa.

SEALY, J. C., A. MORRIS, R. ARMSTRONG, A. MARKELL, AND C. SCHRIRE
1993   Archaeological, Biological and Isotopic Observations on a Historic Skeleton from the Slave Lodge at Vergelegen. *South African Archaeological Society, Goodwin Series* 7:84–91.

SHELL, ROBERT
1986   *Slavery at the Cape of Good Hope, 1680–1731.* Ph.D. dissertation, Department of History, Yale University, New Haven, Connecticut. University Microfilms, Ann Arbor, Michigan.
1991   The Short Life and Personal Belongings of One Slave: Rangton of Bali (1673–1720). *Kronos* 18:1–7.
1993   The Slave Trade to the Cape of Good Hope, 1652–1808. Manuscript on file with the author.

SLEIGH, DANIEL
1982   The Outposts of the D.E.I.C. on the Border of the Cape Settlement. Unpublished M.A. thesis, Department of History, University of Stellenbosch, Stellenbosch, South Africa.

SOUTH AFRICAN STATE ARCHIVES (SASA)
1686   Daghregister, VOC 10. Cape Depot of the South African State Archives, Cape Town, South Africa.
1706   Letters Received. Letter from the Committee of the Directors of the Dutch East India Company, 30 October 1706. Cape Depot of the South African State Archives, Cape Town, South Africa.
1710   Daghregister, VOC 1454, 30 March 1710. Cape Depot of the South African State Archives, Cape Town, South Africa.
1720   List of Goods of Rangton van Balij Sold at Vendue. Mooc 10/2, No. 14. Cape Depot of the South African State Archives, Cape Town, South Africa.
[1721] Daghboek van Hendrik van Heezel. Misc. 8/5, 49a. Cape Depot of the South African State Archives, Cape Town, South Africa.

STAVORINUS, JAN SPLINTER
1969   *Voyages to the East Indies,* translated by Samuel Hull Wilcocke. Reprint of 1798 edition. Dawsons, London.

TAS, ADAM, AND NICOLAAS VAN DER HEYDEN
1712   *Contra Deductie.* Nicolas ten Hoorn, Amsterdam.

THEAL, GEORGE MCCALL
1913   *Willem Adriaan van der Stel and Other Historical Sketches.* Thomas Maskew Miller, Cape Town, South Africa.

THUNBERG, CARL PETER
1986   *Travels at the Cape of Good Hope, 1772–1775,* edited by Prof. V. S. Forbes. Van Riebeeck Society, Cape Town, South Africa.

VAN WIJK, PIET
1987   Form and Function in the Netherlands Agricultural Architecture. In *New World Dutch Studies: Dutch*

Arts and Culture in Colonial America, 1609–1776, edited by R.H. Blackburn and N.A. Kelley, pp. 161–169. Albany Institute of History and Art, Albany, New York.

VERIN, P., R. BATTISTINI, AND D. CHABOUIS
  1965 L'Ancienne civilisation de l'Isandra. *Taloha* 1:249–285. Revue du Musée d'Art et d'Archaeologie, Annales de l'Université de Madagascar.

VON BOCK, G. R.
  1986 *Steinzeug.* Kunstgewerbemuseum der Stadt Köln, Köln.

VOS, H. E.
  1993 An Historical and Archaeological Perspective of Colonial Stellenbosch, 1680–1860. Unpublished M.A. thesis, Department of Archaeology, Stellenbosch University, Stellenbosch, South Africa.

WALGATE, C. P.
  1926 Vergelegen. *South African Archaeological Record,* December: 100–101.

WALTON, JAMES
  1965 *Homesteads and Villages of South Africa.* Van Schaik, Pretoria, South Africa.
  1989 *Old Cape Farmsteads.* Human and Rousseau, Cape Town, South Africa.

WILCOXEN, CHARLOTTE
  1981 *Seventeenth Century Albany: A Dutch Profile.* Albany Institute of History and Art, Albany, New York.

WOODWARD, CAROLYN S.
  1974 *Oriental Ceramics at the Cape of Good Hope, 1652–1795.* A. A. Balkema, Cape Town, South Africa.

  1982 The Interior of the Cape House, 1670–1714. Unpublished M.A. thesis, Department of Art History, University of Pretoria, Pretoria, South Africa.

WORDEN, NIGEL
  1985 *Slavery in Dutch South Africa.* Cambridge University Press, Cambridge.

ZANTKUYL, HENK
  1985 Reconstuctie van enkele Nederlandse huizen in Nieuw-Nederland uit de zeventiende eeuw. *New Netherlands Studies Bulletin* 84(2/3):166–181.

ANN MARKELL
DEPARTMENT OF ARCHAEOLOGY
UNIVERSITY OF CAPE TOWN
RONDEBOSCH 7700
SOUTH AFRICA

MARTIN HALL
DEPARTMENT OF ARCHAEOLOGY
UNIVERSITY OF CAPE TOWN
RONDEBOSCH 7700
SOUTH AFRICA

CARMEL SCHRIRE
DEPARTMENT OF ANTHROPOLOGY
DOUGLASS COLLEGE
RUTGERS UNIVERSITY
NEW BRUNSWICK, NEW JERSEY 08903

ROSS W. JAMIESON

Material Culture and Social Death: African-American Burial Practices

ABSTRACT

Orlando Patterson has proposed that the institution of slavery caused the "social death" of slaves, in that the inherited meanings of their ancestors were denied to them through control of their cultural practices by slave owners and overseers. A survey of archaeological evidence for mortuary practices in African-American society, however, shows that this was not the case, as such inherited meanings were present throughout the early historical period, and in some communities are still present. The careful identification of such occurrences can only be made through comparison to African archaeological and ethnographic evidence. Such occurrences do not negate the horrors of the dominance of slaveholders over slaves in the New World, but do give an opportunity to celebrate the unique nature of African-Atlantic culture.

Introduction

In a recent review, Parker Potter (1991:95) has warned plantation archaeologists about the "inseparability of knowledge and human interests." For Potter, and I am in basic agreement with him, plantation archaeologists must struggle to celebrate the unique African-American heritage forged while under the dominance of Euroamerican society (Potter 1991:99). Archaeologists of the African-American past have a social responsibility constantly to remind themselves of "*who controlled* the quality of life," and also a responsibility to ask African Americans what interests they have in their cultural heritage, and how these can be related to archaeological research (Potter 1991:98–100).

The recent excavation of a portion of the colonial African Burial Ground in New York City (Harrington 1993) has brought the study of African-American mortuary remains into the public and archaeological spotlight. The wholesale excavation

Historical Archaeology, 1995, 29(4):39–58.
Permission to reprint required.

of cemeteries merely to answer the research questions of archaeologists can validly be classified as desecration, and thus a certain reticence on the part of archaeologists to include discussion of African-American burials when outlining archaeological research potential (cf. Singleton 1990) is understandable. The developments in New York City (Harrington 1993), however, have demonstrated that contract archaeologists are required to deal with such remains, and that a solid understanding of the historical and anthropological aspects of African-American mortuary practices is necessary before interpreting them.

Funerals in plantation slavery contexts in particular appear to have afforded African Americans an opportunity to develop African-American cultural practices in the New World based at least partially on African practices (Genovese 1972:194–202; Thornton 1992:228). Several archaeological excavations of African-American burials have now been carried out (Thomas et al. 1977; Parrington and Wideman 1986; Owsley et al. 1987), although large New World cemeteries from before emancipation are restricted to Handler and Lange's (1978) Barbados sample and the recent New York City excavations (Harrington 1993).

In order to understand fully the cultural implications of such burials, there is a need for historical archaeologists to consider the work of historians of slavery, art historians, Africanist ethnographers, and Africanist archaeologists. Only with such a wide-ranging, "ethnohistorical" approach can historical archaeologists begin fully to put the burial practices of African Americans in context. The interpretation of mortuary rituals and material culture is contingent on the wide-ranging chronological, geographical, and social contexts which characterize the long history of African descendants in the New World.

Burials, Social Death, and Africanisms in the New World

The excavation of burials has always been central to archaeology, and up until the mid-20th century, the emphasis was usually on the "flow of traits" visible in mortuary remains that defined culture areas and cultural diffusion (Chapman and Rands-borg 1981:2–3). Since the 1960s archaeological interest in mortuary patterns has grown to include individual status, modes of death, rites of passage, group affiliations, and many other types of specific cultural information. By the early 1970s it became clear that the relationship of mortuary practices to status, group membership, and other societal factors was not a simple one. A debate began as to whether mortuary variability could really prove much about societal structures (Chapman and Randsborg 1981: 4–8). Mortuary data have now been used extensively by archaeologists, ethnographers, and ethnohistorians to study many anthropological and historical issues (Ucko 1969; Brown 1971; Tainter 1978; Chapman et al. 1981; Humphreys and King 1981; Parker Pearson 1982; Johnson et al. 1994).

The study of African-American heritage has broadly paralleled that of the discipline of anthropological archaeology. An emphasis on the "flow of traits" is clear in the anthropological work of Melville Herskovits, whose 1920s scholarship concentrated on African "culture areas." Herskovits (1958[1941]) created the first full formulation of the concept of "African retentions" in the New World with his 1941 book *The Myth of the Negro Past.* Herskovits' affirmation of the existence of an African heritage in the New World was the basis for much of the "black studies" scholarship in the United States, Cuba, Haiti, and other countries from the 1960s onward (Cole 1985:120–124).

During the 1970s anthropologists and historians studying African-American culture began to shift their emphasis from Herskovitsian "survivals," and instead began to concentrate on certain "basic values" and "phenomenology" as defining African-American relationships to Africa (Cole 1985: 120–124). Sidney Mintz and Richard Price in 1976 called for the definition of a "generalized West African heritage" for African Americans, defined by emphasizing cognitive orientations rather than the more formal elements concentrated on by Herskovits. Mechal Sobel (1979:xvii) proposed that in the New World "African worldviews coalesced over time into one neo-African consciousness." For Sobel, West African peoples did not have one Sacred Cosmos, but they did share enough of a world-view to create one worldview in America (Sobel 1979:21).

It is clear that the institution of slavery severely restricted the ability of African Americans to maintain cohesive cultural identities from Africa. Orlando Patterson has attempted to show that the cultural practices of slaves were greatly influenced by the definition of slavery "as a substitute for death, usually violent death":

> Slaves differed from other human beings in that they were not allowed freely to integrate the experience of their ancestors into their lives, to inform their understanding of social reality with the inherited meanings of their natural forebears, or to anchor the living present in any conscious community of memory. That they reached back for the past, as they reached out for the related living, there can be no doubt. Unlike other persons, doing so meant struggling with and penetrating the iron curtain of the master, his community, his laws, his policemen, or patrollers, and his heritage (Patterson 1982:5).

Slaves had to resist this desocialization in countless ways (Patterson 1982:337). The lack of ability to import material culture from their homeland, and prohibitions on many cultural practices, created great difficulties in undertaking such resistance (Genovese 1972). Despite these difficulties, historians of the African-American diaspora have now clearly shown that African culture, and particularly religion, have made important contributions to the African-American experience (Raboteau 1978; Sobel 1987; Creel 1988).

Neither a search for "survivals," nor an anthropological emphasis on "phenomenology" seems suited to the study of African-American mortuary practices. Jean Howson (1990:79–80) has pointed out that the search for formal elements, or "survivals," of African practices in the Americas was and is naive. Attention to specific material traits and their disappearance over time as a way to construct a universal sequence of acculturation is a dangerous oversimplification. James Garman (1994:90) calls for a holistic picture "that does not reduce African Americans to a collection of material traits with links to Africa."

The key that is missing from sterile studies of "Africanisms" and "survivals" is cultural context. The historian John Thornton (1992:211) emphasizes that the dynamics of cultural change in African-American society worked very differently on different elements of culture, such as political systems, language, aesthetics, and religion. Howson (1990:84) advocates the careful interpretation of material culture in all its contexts, a position that is important for research on African-American burials.

The mortuary context was a place within slave culture where in some cases some "freedoms" were allowed by the slave owners. For Parker Potter, the ability of slaves to hunt game or to purchase their own ceramics—or, to bury their own dead—were not really "freedoms"; they were traded off against "the more powerful unfreedoms" of the institution of slavery (Potter 1991:98). Potter goes so far as to suggest that "placing too much emphasis on . . . the ability of slaves to create certain aspects of their own world could do a disservice to contemporary African Americans in the attempt to identify and challenge the racial discrimination that still exists in contemporary American society" (Potter 1991:101). His point is valid; the existence of a burial that shows African religious practices in the New World should not and cannot be used to argue that slavery was a benign institution—and yet African influences cannot be ignored, and should be celebrated. As the art historian Robert Farris Thompson (in Cosentino 1992:59) put it, "Yes, I *am* political if it is a political statement to say that African-Atlantic culture is fully self-possessed, an alternative classical tradition; that one studies Mbanza Kongo, Ile-Ife, and Kángaba as one might study Carthage, Jerusalem, Rome, and Athens."

Historic Burial Studies in Africa
and the Americas

The lack of a well-researched ethnohistorical approach has been a serious limitation of many studies of African-American material culture. Douglas Armstrong (1990:7) has rightly pointed out the seriousness of the "problem encountered in the study of cultural transformations among Africans in the New World . . . the tendency to over generalize West African cultures." In his studies of 18th-century slave houses he felt "forced to rely on vague comparisons and incidental observation to establish elements of African continuity" (Armstrong 1990:8), a problem which seriously compromises the validity of the undertaking. He points out the need for more interaction between historians and archaeologists of West Africa and the Americas, and also the paucity of archaeological work on West African sites contemporary with the period of slaving for the Americas (Armstrong 1990:8).

This is in part due to the lack of focus on the colonial period by governments of independent African countries and Africanist archaeologists. Most Africanist archaeologists are concerned with concentrating on the prehistoric cultural heritage of Africa. The archaeology of the colonial period in Africa is a very new, and still very limited, field of study (DeCorse 1987, 1991, 1993). A major new contribution to the study of African historical mortuary archaeology is the work of Christopher DeCorse at ElMina, Ghana (Figure 1c). His excavations of urban domestic contexts adjacent to the Dutch fort at ElMina, dating to the 17th through late 19th centuries, has recently revealed 200 burials in sub-floor domestic contexts (DeCorse 1992:184). Analysis of this material was still in progress in 1992, but when published it will be an important comparative sample for New World archaeologists. This is just one excavation location, however, and if African-American practices are to be traced to Africa, the historical period must be fully studied on both sides of the Atlantic.

Archaeological excavation of African-American mortuary remains has been undertaken in North America and the Caribbean since the early 1970s, but the pressures of salvage situations have meant that in many cases little attention has been paid to the historical context of burials. Salvage excavation of a slave cemetery by a prehistorian on Montserrat, West Indies, and the discovery of two slave burials on St. Catherine's Island, Georgia, were not accompanied by any historical research other than to find that early maps showed the cemeteries to have been part of a plantation (Thomas et al. 1977:401; Watters 1987:312, 1994:56). David Watters (1994: 56) validly points out that, in the case of the Eastern Caribbean, severe funding problems, the lack of

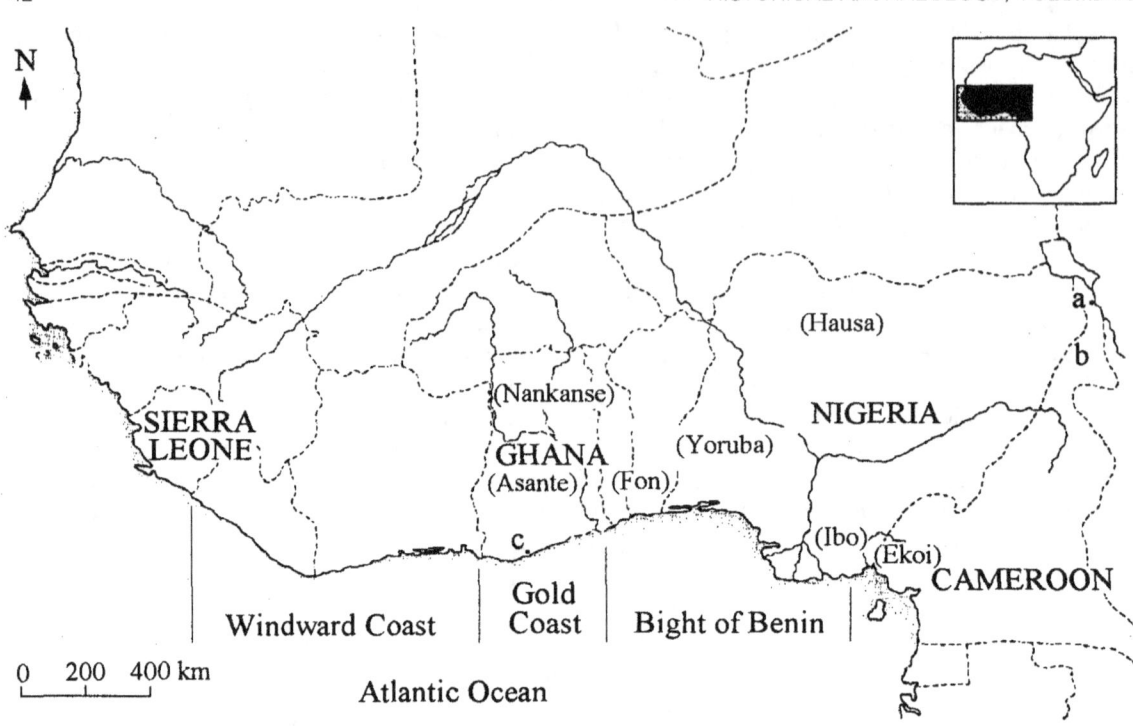

FIGURE 1. Map of West Africa: *a*, Holouf Cemetery site, Cameroon; *b*, Mandara Highlands of Cameroon; *c*, ElMina site, Ghana.

professional archaeologists, and the rapid development of tourist sites have made short salvage projects by avocational archaeologists an unfortunate reality.

Handler and Lange's (1978) work on Barbados is the only major published archaeological case explicitly using an ethnohistorical approach to the study of New World slave mortuary practices. Their research, based on excavation and historical documents, is by far the best archaeological study of mortuary practices of Africans and their descendants in the Americas. They found the excavation of a slave cemetery on Barbados to be of limited use in reconstructing mortuary ideology, with documents as a more useful source. The documents had their own limitations, however, in being very anecdotal and heavily affected by a European bias. The time span and extent of particular mortuary practices were often difficult to define, but the doc-

uments were in the end an extremely useful addition to the archaeological data (Handler and Lange 1978:171). Handler's later attempt deliberately to locate other slave cemeteries in Barbados was unsuccessful; the invisibility of many slave cemeteries may thus be a factor in their preservation, or a factor in their untimely destruction at the hands of developers who are not even aware of their existence (Handler 1989).

The excavation of African-American burials has so far been limited, which has created great limitations on interpretation. Up until the excavation of the African Burial Ground in New York City (Harrington 1993), Handler and Lange's (1978:21, 171) Barbados excavation was the largest group of slave burials (N = 104) excavated in the New World, and also—dating between 1660–1820—the earliest group. Handler and Lange (1978:28) state that with such a small database generalization is premature, but the ongoing research on the African Burial Ground in New York City (Harrington 1993) will soon give archaeologists a large 18th-century sample for comparison to Handler and Lange's excavation. Other published excavation reports (Combes 1972; Thomas et al. 1977; Parrington and Wideman 1986; Bell 1990; Cheek and Friedlander 1990) have been rescue excavations of 19th-century burials, and thus largely post-emancipation, although one salvage exavation of a pre-1800 cemetery on Montserrat has been carried out (Watters 1987, 1994). This gives a good chronological range of data, but more data for the period of slavery in the United States would be desirable.

The limited use of comparative data from Africa on burial practices is perhaps the most serious shortcoming of New World studies to date. Inadequate ethnographic research is notorious for resulting in underestimation of variability in mortuary practices (Chapman and Randsborg 1981:14). Handler and Lange (1978:317) saw great difficulty in using African ethnographic sources because they are often "directly contradictory of each other," but this may be due more to Handler and Lange's attempt to simplify the huge range of African cultural practices than to any real contradictions. Slaves came from wide geographical regions of Africa which changed over time. Thus the wide variation in ethnographic practices, rather than being contradictory, are, in fact, of great relevance to the study of American practices.

Handler and Lange (1978:210) validly point out that the comparison of modern African ethnographic studies to New World burials from the 18th century is in itself not ideal and, in addition, points to a great need for data on West African burial practices from the European colonial period. An even greater problem is outlined by Merrick Posnansky (1989:4), in that in West Africa "it was not major states like Benin, Asante, or the Hausa city-states which contributed the major numbers of slaves but rather the weaker societies, societies which lost out in the process of state formation." This creates a problem in comparative archaeological data, as such societies are very rarely studied by Africanist archaeologists, and by the time ethnographers began to record details about such societies

in the early 20th century they had been displaced, marginalized, and ravaged by the slave trade (Posnansky 1989:4).

For the Kongo region, where huge numbers of slaves originated, the problem is even worse, as the pre- and protohistory of the modern nations of Zaire and Angola remains largely unexplored (Posnansky 1989:6). The first scientific archaeology in the entire Lualaba River basin, for example, began only in 1957 (Hiernaux et al. 1972:148).

The lack of such data has created many false generalizations. David Roediger (1982:170) has claimed that the common burial practice on both continents of orienting the body in an east–west direction is a West African practice "against burying a corpse crossways to the world," something which may well be true but which ignores both the great variation in West African burial orientations and the Christian tradition of east–west body orientation. Handler and Lange (1978:214) concur with this attempt to define broad West African and even Sub-Saharan African beliefs which would override specific differences in mortuary patterns in African-American practices, a type of syncretism built from the varying backgrounds of slaves. Merrick Posnansky (1989:1), however, calls it a naive assumption "that there is a commonality of African traditional culture spread over a wide geographical area and over a long time period."

It is clear that ethnoarchaeological, ethnographic, and historical literature on African burial practices must be used to create valid comparisons. It is also evident that research must focus on the range of areas that slaves came from, and not just be limited to the Yoruba, a single West African culture, and the Kongo, a huge geographic region made up of many groups, two areas which are usually emphasized in the comparative American literature. Nicholas David's (1992:181) caution that ethnoarchaeologists in West Africa have given little attention to mortuary practices is well taken, and brings forward once again the problem of adequate African published data. The influences of Muslim, and perhaps even Christian, religion on African mortuary practices further complicate the African templates from which American practices were drawn.

Cultures of Origin

The mixing of ethnic groups brought about by the slave trade must have caused great changes in African-American burial practices in the New World. The African origin of first-generation slaves in a particular location is a very important factor to consider in research.

The origins of slaves in the British colonies changed over the period of the slave trade, and are of central concern in any future use of African burial data to compare to American practice. Philip Curtin's (1969) data on the ports from which slaves were taken on the African coast (Figure 1) shows that for the 1680s approximately 27 percent of slaves came from the "Windward Coast," or modern Liberia and the Ivory Coast, with another 21 percent from the Gold Coast, modern Ghana, and 15 percent from the Bight of Benin region, Togo, Dahomey, and Nigeria. By the 1750s this had shifted to only 32 percent of slaves coming from Sierra Leone, the Windward and Gold Coasts, combined, and a full 40 percent from the "Bight of Biafra," Cameroon and Nigeria. In 1800 the trade had shifted southward (Figure 2), with 45 percent of slaves coming from the Bight of Biafra, and 34 percent from the Central Africa/Angola region (Curtin 1969:129). A point of origin on the coast does not reveal the ethnicity of the slaves, however, and this "mystery of the ultimate origin of slaves in the African interior" (Handler and Lange 1978: 28) is a very complex topic (cf. Lovejoy 1983; Thornton 1992).

Curtin's (1969) publication of an 1850 census of Freetown, Sierra Leone, taken by ethnic group, is a good indication of the diversity of peoples enslaved at that time. The sample was 54 percent Yoruba, 9 percent Ibo, 8 percent Fon, and apart from that was made up of 160 additional, different ethnic groups—defined by their languages—from mainly West and Central Africa, but also from East Africa and other regions. What ethnic groups are we to use for comparison of burial traits? In the end this question seems to address a moot point. Kongo and Yoruba groups, with high populations enslaved in the American trade, have commonly been compared to African-American examples (Vlach 1978;

Thompson and Cornet 1981; Thompson 1983), but vast numbers of other peoples from many parts of Africa were enslaved as well (Curtin 1969; Lovejoy 1983).

Thornton (1992:192–195) emphasizes that in most cases a single slave ship would pick up its entire cargo from one port, thus increasing the chances of cultural homogeneity. In the common case that slaves were war captives they all could have been from one cultural group. It is in the New World that the separation of African slaves from others of their own ethnic group would more commonly have occurred. The purchasing policies of plantation owners varied greatly. Some felt that deliberate mixing of Africans of different ethnicities prevented rebellions, whereas others preferred having slaves from a particular ethnic group in order to form a stable plantation community (Thornton 1992:195–196). More focused research at the local or plantation level, emphasizing the trade and purchase records for a particular place and time, is one of the few ways to get closer to the ethnic origins in Africa of particular first-generation slave populations.

The Bioarchaeology of African Ancestry

Before African-American burials can be studied, they must be identified as African-American. This identification can be done using cultural material associated with the deceased, using historical evidence for an African-American cemetery in the location, or, finally, by identifying the physical remains themselves as of African descent, using osteological techniques.

Physical identification would seem to be the most objective initial step, and yet it is problematic in itself. The identification of "race" in physical anthropology has a long and infamous history in America, exemplified by the racist work of Samuel George Morton in the 1820s to 1850s (Gould 1981: 51–62), and the 18th- and 19th-century practice of using African-American dead as scientific specimens (Humphrey 1973). In 1962 Frank Livingstone published his now classic 1-page argument in *Current Anthropology*. It urged anthropologists to re-

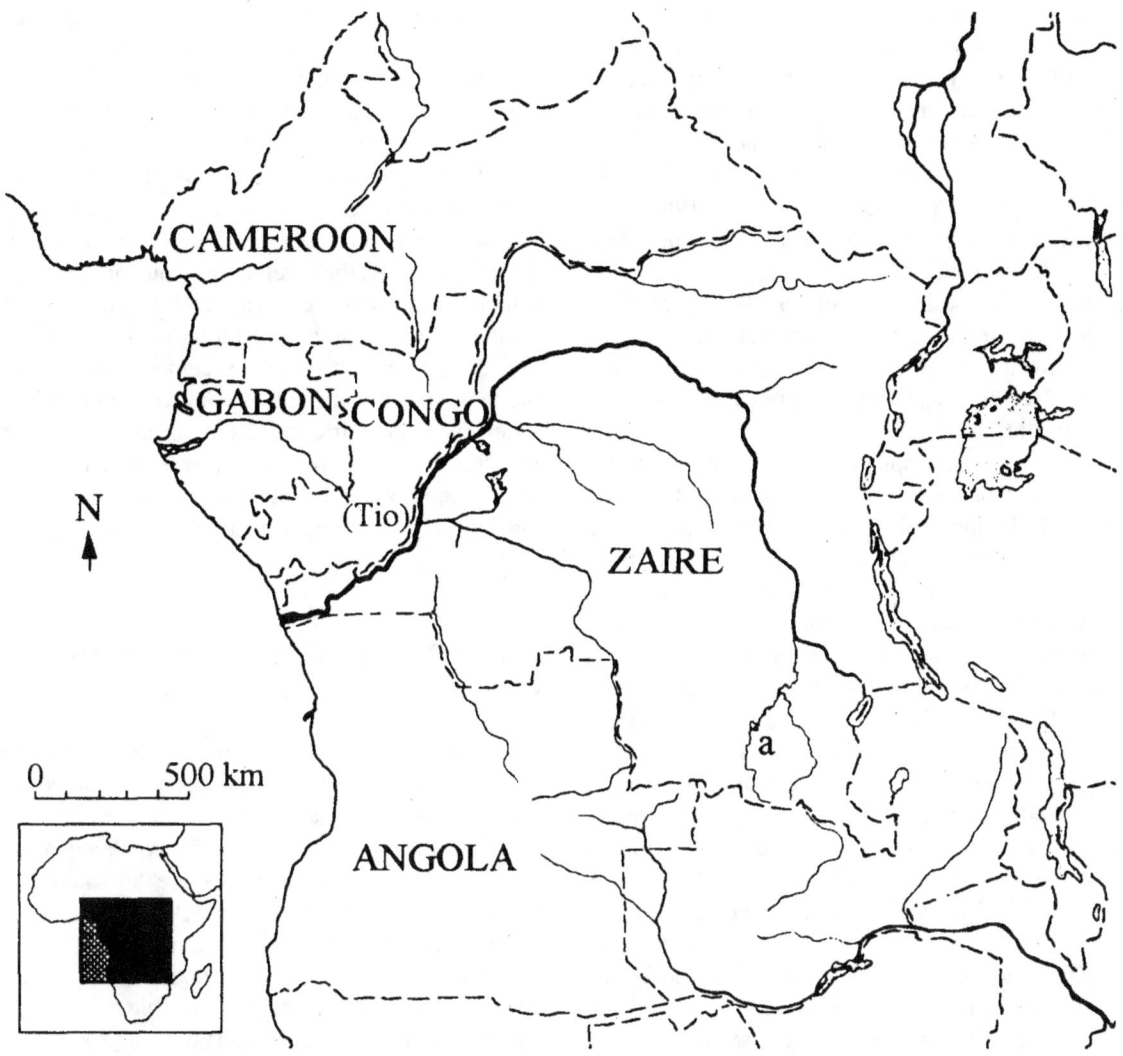

FIGURE 2. Map of Central Africa: *a*, Katoto Cemetery site, Zaire.

ject the concept of "race," because within *Homo sapiens* "variability does not conform to the discrete packages labelled races" (Livingstone 1962: 279).

Within modern forensic anthropology, however, the race concept is still in use (Krogman and Işcan 1986:270; Işcan 1988:209), in order to "categorize the skeletal remains of unknowns in terms that reflect racial reality as locally understood" (Stewart 1979:227). The tacit acceptance of such fuzzy categorizations has led to a schizophrenic response by physical anthropologists, denying the validity of racial categorization while simultaneously trying to describe its morphology.

Some researchers working with African-American burials have made no attempt to identify the ancestry of their sample through the physical remains, since the historical documentation of the cemetery is taken as sufficient proof (Handler and Lange 1978:105). In other research the ancestry of the individuals is reported, but the methodology used to infer ancestry is not published (Owsley et al. 1987:188–190). When the methodology is reported, it varies widely among researchers (Blakely and Beck 1982:193–195; Angel et al. 1987:216–226; Rathbun 1987:241; Harris and Rathbun 1989:411). Many of these techniques appear to depend greatly on the skill of the analyst; the problem of subjectivity in this type of study can lead dangerously toward assigning skeletal remains to an ancestry that the researcher was predisposed toward for other reasons.

Craniometrics, despite a common reaction to reject the methodology because of its racist past, may ironically be the tool needed to break free of the flawed concept of race, and create the most effective criteria for the assignation of ancestry. T. L. Woo in the 1930s began to realize that cranial measurements commonly in use were often an invalid attempt ''to give quantitative value to the differences that were obvious to them at first sight'' (Hershkovitz et al. 1990:307). This methodology emphasized measures heavily influenced by environmental selection. The emphasis should rather have been put on those regions of the skull, such as the calvarium and base, which show ''little obvious adaptive significance'' (Hershkovitz et al. 1990: 307, 318; Yongyi et al. 1991:274). Since the pioneering work of E. Giles and O. Elliot (1962), the methodology of bio-distance measurement and statistics on cranial remains has been steadily improving (Gill 1984; Krogman and Işcan 1986:275–280; Brace and Hunt 1990; Hershkovitz et al. 1990; Pietrusewsky 1990). Such modern bio-distance studies look at the polygenic traits of bone or tooth shape, data which include both a genetic and environmental component, and attempt to define patterns in the data thought to reflect degrees of genetic relatedness (Buikstra et al. 1990:1–6).

The almost complete lack of data on the range of variation within most skeletal populations is the first major stumbling block to such cranial studies (St. Hoyme and Işcan 1989:54). This limitation has begun to be remedied in recent research, although a need still exists for data from Africa before a true

comparison can be made to African-American remains. A need also exists for further research on worldwide craniometrics before the complex issue of bio-distance measures in the ethnically diverse American case becomes more clear.

At the individual level it is possible that assessment of ancestry is in fact impossible, since idiosyncratic variation may effectively counteract any inherited traits. At the level of the group or cemetery population, however, geographical origins may be possible to ascertain, and different populations, for instance within archaeological cemeteries, may be able to be sorted out. In cases where clear historical evidence for an African-American cemetery does not exist, the osteological remains may be the only way to identify the cemetery as an African-American burial ground without a reliance on cultural practices.

Material Culture: African Practices in the New World

African influence on mortuary practices in the Americas is evident in both living communities and in archaeological contexts in the United States and the West Indies. Practices may have been more widespread in earlier periods, and are rare today, but they were not extinguished by the Atlantic crossing. Evidence comes from diverse sources.

It is clear that in many contexts of the earlier colonial period slaves were mostly able to maintain control over burial practices. Thornton (1992:206) specifically rejects Mintz and Price's (1976) idea that barriers to cultural transmission from Africa were overwhelming. This cultural transmission appears to have been strongest in the practice of funerary rituals. In Barbados from the 1600s up until the 1780s slaves were usually responsible for burying their own dead, in their own cemetery. Slaves were often not baptized Christians, and whites considered slaves ''idolatrous''; thus, slave control over funeral rites seems to have been fairly complete (Handler and Lange 1978:173, 209). In Jamaica in 1688 Hans Sloane noted that slaves from the same ethnic group in Africa would gather at a plantation for the funeral of one of their members

(Sloane 1707:xlviii; cf. Thornton 1992:200). In 1712 in New York the Reverend John Sharpe (in Raboteau 1978:66) complained that slaves "are buried in the common by those of their country and complexion without the office; on the contrary the Heathenish rites are performed at the grave by their countrymen."

Sharpe may have been referring specifically to the African Burial Ground now being investigated (cf. Harrington 1993). This cemetery was founded around 1712 just outside the New York city limits, as church burial had been denied slaves in New York since 1697. Church authorities did not dedicate the burial ground, and control of the funerals, mortuary, and burial practices at the cemetery seems to have rested mostly within the African-American community (Harrington 1993:30). Funerals were in fact the only time slaves in 18th-century New York were permitted to gather in groups larger than three people (Harrington 1993:30), and thus little doubt remains that such events were of key importance in maintaining many cultural ties.

Up until the late 18th century in English-speaking North America and the Caribbean a general feeling prevailed among slave owners that teaching Christian doctrine to slaves would undermine the authority of the masters (Patterson 1982:73); thus, Christian practice was not at first forced upon slaves in the Protestant New World. In North America from the 16th to the 19th centuries slaveholders were always concerned about the "conspiratorial" or "heathenish" aspects of slaves holding funerals for fellow slaves, but did not forbid the practice. In some cases they felt it callous to do so; in other cases they felt that such a prohibition could cause embitterment leading to slave rebellions (Genovese 1972:194–195).

On some plantations, special groups of slaves appear to have prepared the corpse, with taboos against others touching it, a practice similar to many African cases (Roediger 1981:169). This practice is reflected in David's (1992:187) Mandara Highlands data from Cameroon (Figure 1b), which show that in some societies male "transformers" are responsible for carrying out the funeral, but in others the funeral is carried out by the family of the deceased.

Among the Yoruba the blacksmiths are called upon to put the body in the coffin and seal it (Ojo 1976: 105). A cemetery dating to A.D. 1500–1600 excavated by Augustin Holl at Houlouf in Cameroon (Figure 1a) was within a separate area of the walled house compound of a blacksmith, which Holl (1994:164–165) relates to the modern "recurrent feature in the ethnography of Chadic-speakers of the Mandara Mountains" of having blacksmiths as undertakers and gravediggers.

The age and gender of slaves brought from Africa thus may have been of critical importance in the transmission of burial practices between the cultures of the two continents. As an example, the 18th-century British trade into Jamaica was predominantly in adult males "in the prime of life," with around 58 percent males, 35 percent females, and 7 percent children as fairly standard (Klein 1986:254). The age and gender of the slaves would have influenced their cultural knowledge. Age-grade systems and secret societies in some African groups may have limited the knowledge of burial practices to within certain groups of older, often male, individuals. Thus, transmission of cultural practices to the Americas would have been highly dependent on whether such specialists were present. It can be fairly safely assumed, however, that in most situations at least some of the males would have been old enough to have been versed in the burial practices of their culture.

The physical location of the burials may be another clue to African practices. Separate burial practices for different social groups is a common occurrence in many African societies, with the location of burials often tied to the symbolism of a group's cosmology (Chapman and Randsborg 1981:15, 17). In DeCorse's (1992:183) excavations at ElMina in Ghana, 200 burials were found under the house floors, at least one in each house excavated.

In some African societies those who died a "natural death" were distinguished from those who died in childbirth, from infectious disease, from being struck by lightning, from committing suicide, and as victims of murder or drowning. Among the Yoruba, burial of the dead generally occurred within the town boundary, under a room in their house, whereas those who died "unnaturally" were relegated to outside the town for burial (Ojo 1976:99). Drowning victims specifically were interred at the riverbank where they had died (Ojo 1976:100).

"Natural deaths" in the Mandara Mountains of Cameroon are buried in the clan cemetery, whereas a list of "others" similar to the Yoruba case are often buried at the cemetery margins. Infants are generally interred behind the mother's hut, and clan chiefs may be buried within their house or compound. An emphasis on "belonging" is clear in some groups in the Mandara Highlands, where chiefly and other land-holding clans have separate cemeteries, and "strangers" are buried on the side of the road leading back to their village, explicitly denying their descendants land rights (David 1992: 188). In the Houlouf cemetery in Cameroon the 25 burials were all interred in an upright or seated position, and from ethnographic analogy Holl (1994:139, 168) proposes that these were members of the elite, while other members of the society were buried in other locations. Four empty marked graves may be symbolic burials of those who died away from the town and could not be brought back for burial (Holl 1994:136). Among several Ghanaian tribes burial of children occurred separately, at a crossroads. Among the Asante, children under eight days old were buried in pots in the town (Ucko 1969:271).

Placing multiple individuals in one grave is also an important trait. A cemetery consisting of 47 tombs and dated to ca. A.D. 1100 was excavated at Katoto in Zaire in the 1960s (Figure 2a; Hiernaux et al. 1972). The cemetery contained 32 single burials, and also 14 multiple burials, usually with a woman and infant, or a man, woman, and children together (Hiernaux et al. 1972:148). Two burials in the Barbados cemetery appear to have been of two individuals each, although the reason for this may have been expediency in time of disease rather than any cultural preference (Handler and Lange 1978: 193).

Subfloor burials within the house, as in the El-Mina sample from Ghana, was clearly carried to the Caribbean by slaves. Slaves in Jamaica in the late 18th century were said "sometimes" to bury family members under the bed in their house (Moreton

1790:162; cf. McDonald 1993:110). Handler and Lange have historical evidence of subfloor graves in Barbados slave houses, although the burial plot was a more common place. In the Newton Plantation cemetery child/infant burials are underrepresented. This may mean that they were buried elsewhere, or may simply be a reflection of differential bone preservation (Handler and Lange 1978:124, 174). One male adult at the Drummond Plantation near Jamestown, Virginia, dated to the 1680–1720 period, was buried away from the others and "very near a servants' quarter." This occurrence is interesting, although the ancestry of the individual is not clearly stated as African (Aufderheide et al. 1985: 357–358). In South Carolina in the 1970s the most important aspect of burial for African Americans was to be buried with other family members. Late 19th- and early 20th-century burials were not in church cemeteries in coastal South Carolina, and when church burial became commonplace the power of the clergy in being able to refuse burial in the family plot was much resented (Combes 1972: 56).

Burial in mounds seems to have been desired by many African-American groups. The slave cemetery at Newton Plantation has three mounds, each ½–1 m high, and 4½–7½ m wide, presumably built by the slaves, with burials in and around the mounds (Handler and Lange 1978:107). David Hurst Thomas and other excavators were surprised to come upon two 19th-century plantation slave burials in a native mound group on Saint Catherine's Island, Georgia. Only one mound was partially excavated, but an 1890 map had a cemetery marked in the vicinity, so presumably the mound group was used extensively by the slaves as a burial ground. Slave burials were also found in the Mississippian period temple mounds in Moundville, Alabama, but apparently have not been published (Thomas et al. 1977:412, 417). The reuse of prehistoric mounds was not an exclusively African-American practice, however, as evidenced by the Euroamerican family cemetery located in the Irene Mound near Savannah, Georgia (Aufderheide et al. 1985:358).

Grave goods placed with the body afford the most obvious evidence in an archaeological context of African influences on the burial. The type and placement of grave goods with the corpse varies widely in African practice. In the Mandara Highlands grave goods placed with the body are limited in nature: "The overall concern . . . is to provide the departed with items either of sentimental value to them or that will serve them in good stead in the land of the dead, where they will live a life that is, it would seem, perceived as being on the whole pretty similar to the one they are leaving" (David 1992: 197). At the Houlouf cemetery Holl (1994:140) reports the inclusion of a smoking pipe, lots of stone tools, copper artifacts, and a large number of imported carnelian beads, with a maximum of 174 beads in one tomb. At ElMina the grave goods included ceramic vessels, beads, and tobacco pipes. A 1602 document from ElMina claimed that the Africans would bury all of the deceased's belongings in the grave (DeCorse 1992:183).

High-status chiefs among the Tio were reported in the late 19th century as being buried with plates, guns, and lots of other European items, but low-status burials did not emphasize grave goods (Vansina 1973:211–212). The 13th-century Katoto cemetery in Zaire had multiple ceramic vessels, iron tools, and iron jewelry in the graves (Hiernaux et al. 1972:150–153).

Peter Ucko (1969:265) provides the cautionary note that among the Nankanse of Ghana the grave goods are actually objects owned by a living person which are placed with the dead to get their soul out if it is trapped by the grave, and thus have little to do with the role of the deceased in life. Yoruba grave goods may include items of personal equipment, but do not include valuables, as these are displayed at the funeral but not placed in the grave (Ucko 1969:267). It should also be noted that funerary items, and in particular ceramics associated with the deceased in African practice, may be permanently positioned in an area of spiritual significance other than the burial site, such as the sites for clan spirit pots in Akan funerary customs (Vivian 1992). No reports have been made of such separate areas for "spirit pots" in African-American practice, but perhaps that is because they have gone unrecognized by researchers.

Documentary evidence from the New World gives an interesting example of the belief that death would mean a return to Africa, and of the need for grave goods for the journey. A slave in the southern United States in the 1830s reported on a funeral of the son of African-born slaves, into the grave of whom they placed

> a small bow and arrows; a little bag of parched meal; a miniature canoe and a little paddle (with which he said it would cross the ocean to his own country) . . . and a piece of white muslin with several curious figures painted on it . . . , by which . . . his countrymen would know the infant to be his son (Charles Ball, quoted in Roediger 1981:178).

The clearest New World archaeological example of African influence on grave goods is the "old" adult male from the Newton Plantation buried wearing three copper bracelets; one copper and two white metal finger rings, with a metal knife in the left hand; and a necklace of cowrie shells, dog canines, glass beads, fish vertebrae, and an agate bead; plus an earthenware pipe at the pelvis that was identified as a 17th-century pipe from Ghana (Handler and Lange 1978:129–131; Handler 1981).

The cowries are Indo-Pacific in origin, and served as a West African form of currency (Hogendorn and Johnson 1986). They are also present as grave goods at the Katoto cemetery in Zaire (Hiernaux et al. 1972:154).

The burial thus seems to be an example of slave access to goods from Africa, perhaps brought over by the deceased. The social role of the deceased is unknown, but some sort of special position in the slave community is certainly implied (Handler and Lange 1978:129–131). The other burials at Newton Plantation showed European clay pipes as the most common grave item, in 17 of the 92 burials (Handler and Lange 1978:123). One burial had a large fragment of a shallow red earthenware bowl located under the pelvis (Handler and Lange 1978:136). European-made glass beads, dating mostly to the first half of the 18th century, were found in eight of the burials, with two particular burials containing over 200 beads each (Handler and Lange 1978: 145). Placing a relatively large number of grave goods with the deceased was thus a practice which was present in the New World, but one which is so far only recorded for pre-1820 contexts.

The earth put into the grave, and human relationships to it, may also have had significance to

African Americans. A presumably 19th-century practice of each funeral attendant tossing a handful of earth into the grave is purported to be "in conformity with [unspecified] West African traditions" (Roediger 1981:173), although this also conforms to European Christian traditions. In courts of law in Barbados the practice of drinking grave dirt mixed with water was a form of oath taken by slave witnesses. This practice is not known from Africa, but was certainly not European in origin (Handler and Lange 1978:207). The sacredness of earth from a grave is also evident in Kongo practice, in which it is a part of "nkisi" medicine bags, and is said to embody the spirit of the deceased which can come back to serve the owner of the charm (Thompson 1983:117).

The surface material placed above the grave appears to be the most enduring material marker of African influences in the New World. In the Mandara Highlands pots are usually placed on the graves of adults, with a "variety of pots that are used by different groups to signal a limited range of statuses." The most common and obvious distinction is by gender, as certain pots are only associated with males or females (David 1992:197).

In North America the surface decoration of graves with ceramics and other objects is the most commonly recognized African-American material culture indicator of cemetery sites. William Faulkner, in *Go Down, Moses,* described a black cemetery with "shards of pottery and broken bottles and old brick and other objects insignificant to sight but actually of a profound meaning and fatal to touch, which no white man could have read" (Faulkner 1942:135; cf. Vlach 1978:139).

The 20th-century manifestations of this practice have appeared to some researchers to be miscellaneous piles of "junk" (Combes 1972:54), and include arrangements of a vast array of articles including ceramics, glassware, clocks, lamps, seashells, spoons, doll heads, lightbulbs, flashlights, false teeth, eyeglasses, cigar boxes, piggy banks, gun locks, razors, knives, tin cans, marbles, pebbles, and at least one example of a ceramic toilet tank (Vlach 1978:139). The material is still not always clearly reported and published, as with the Charleston County, South Carolina, cemetery, 38

CH 778, which had unspecified "surface materials" present (Rathbun 1987:240–241).

The earliest published example of material evidence of the practice in the New World appears to be a blue shell-edged plate, dated 1800–1818, found in the surface humus directly above the head of an excavated burial in South Carolina (Thomas et al. 1977:406). This of course does not preclude the use of artifacts as grave markers from the first arrival of Africans in the New World, as such surface remains would be particularly susceptible to disturbance by many processes including reuse of the land for purposes other than as a cemetery. Handler and Lange (1978:205–206) report documentary evidence that post-interment ceremonies in which food and drink were placed on the grave for the dead were common among Barbadian plantation slaves until the 1820s, when a major Christianization period ended them. The practice of placing the last article used by the deceased on the grave was recorded in Georgia in 1850 (Thompson 1983:134).

Early recognition of the relationship of this practice to African customs is related in correspondence in the *Journal of American Folklore* of 1891 and 1892, in which South Carolina graves with oyster shells, white pebbles, ceramics, glass bottles, and other "nondescript bric-a-brac" were described, all "broken and useless," and were compared to such items illustrated in *Century Magazine* from the Congo (Bolton 1891; Ingersoll 1892; Vlach 1978: 142). It is interesting that in this African instance locally made grave goods had by this time been replaced by European trade items, perhaps reflecting high-status associations with such goods in Africa.

What materials were placed on graves, and ethnographic testimony on the meaning of such materials, varies widely. Vansina (1973:217) describes Tio late 19th-century practice, in which a little house was often built over the grave to protect the crockery or jugs left on the mound. John Vlach records several African and American instances of surface grave decoration. A variation on the practice was noted among the Ekoi of Nigeria in 1912, with a low mud mound built over the grave and plates pressed into it all along the edges. Testimony from Alabama in the 1920s and Georgia in the

1930s stated the surface grave goods were what the person owned or used, and were to satisfy the spirit and keep it from wandering. Other 1930s Georgia testimony stated that it was important ritually to break the containers, in order to break the chain of death in the community. Graves in Gabon in the 1970s were noted to be similarly covered with diverse objects. In the United States such surface grave markers are much more common in the South, but Vlach (1978:140–147) points out that they have been recorded as far north as Staten Island, New York.

Particular categories of material have been favored in surface assemblages. The color white, evident in ceramics, shells, and pebbles, is of importance. Association with water is also evident, which took the form of water jugs, marine shells, or mirrors which served as a metaphor for water. Clocks are a 20th-century addition, and may be set either at 12 o'clock to wake the dead on Judgment Day, or at the time of the deceased's death (Vlach 1978: 140–147). White marine shells are reported on graves as wide-ranging as the Kongo, the southern United States, Haiti, and Guadeloupe. A 1912 burial in South Carolina had a large number of pressed glass hens arranged on the surface, a South Carolina grave of a child from 1967 includes a single white rooster statue, and white chicken images are known to have been placed on tombs in the Kongo. These images are perhaps related to the sacrifice of a live white chicken over the grave, a practice reported in the Caribbean in 1816 on each Christmas morning, in the Kongo in the 1880s, and at a wake in Georgia in 1939 where it was claimed to "keep the spirits away" (Thompson 1983:134–135).

Pots that had been deliberately pierced and turned upside down to symbolize the realm of the ancestors or death were reported in the Kongo in the 1970s. The practice was explained by an informant as the last strength of the dead person contained in the last objects that they used. It was repeated that the items kept the spirit in the grave, and kept it from harming the living. When the informant touched the items on his mother's tomb he later dreamed the things she wanted to tell him (Thompson 1983:134, 142).

An informant in Mississippi in the 1920s stated that the last cup and saucer used by the deceased should be put on the grave, as well as the last medicine bottles used. If medicine is still in the bottles they should be turned upside down so that the medicine goes into the grave. Cups, cut glass, bottles, and lamps were common, and it was explained that something that was "the best in the house" was more important than something used by the deceased. Cut flowers and conch shells were said to be just for "dressing up" the grave. A particularly vivid account from South Carolina in the early 1970s stated that a woman whose daughter had died had had repeated dreams of the daughter asking for her hand lotion, dreams which only stopped bothering her when she took the lotion and placed it on the grave (Combes 1972:56, 58).

If there is a general pattern to such practices, it can perhaps be related to the "liminal state" of the deceased in the belief systems of many African groups, formulated in anthropology by Robert Hertz, a student of Émile Durkheim, and further elaborated by Arnold Van Gennep. In Hertz's model the deceased is removed from the social realm through a primary funeral, but then enters a rite of passage in which the living mourn, and the deceased lingers in an ambiguous state and may intervene in human affairs, particularly if the funeral preparations are not correctly carried out (McCaskie 1989:426). Yoruba informants state that for three years after the funeral the deceased is "on his knees," i.e., only after the three years does the spirit go to heaven (Ojo 1976:108). A belief that the spirit component of the individual had to be "managed back" into the spirit world through burial ritual is stated in Asante mortuary customs as well (McCaskie 1989:428). The Tio in the late 19th century also clearly stated that the dead would often come in dreams to tell their needs or to accuse those who had bewitched them (Vansina 1973:218). African beliefs are thus clearly continued in many aspects of American mortuary practices throughout the historical period. Such practices are, however, very rare today.

The End of African Mortuary Practices

No single period exists in the history of African-American burial practices that marks the end of

African influence in the New World. Differences in community cohesion and/or isolation, the change from plantation to urban life, the influence of Christianity, and attempts to gain power in mainstream economic and political structures in the Americas all no doubt contributed to a growing marginalization and syncretization of African burial practices in the Americas. Only in rural African-American communities have practices related to an African past continued into the modern era.

The case of New Orleans provides an interesting early example of a forced end to African-American practices. As early as 1724 Catholic law required Christian slaves to have Christian burial and all New Orleans slaves to be baptized. Parish priests demanded disinterment and reburial in church cemeteries when non-Christian burials were discovered to have occurred. Thirteen African-American skeletons were excavated from a New Orleans cemetery, dating 1720–1810, with no evidence of any African practices in these church-controlled burials (Owsley et al. 1987:185–188).

The orientation of the burial appears to have been one of the first practices to become standardized. African burial orientation varied widely within and between groups. For instance, in the Mandara Highlands burial orientation ranges through seated corpses in boot-shaped tombs, "sleeping position" flexed burials in bell-shaped tombs, urn burials for some potters, and supine burials in sub-rectangular graves. The most common Mandara burial orientation was the flexed burial with the body on its side. Which side the body is laid on is often dependent on gender, and orientation of the body is related to a general concern with the east–west axis. David (1992:195) concludes that with such a variety of burial styles in the Mandara Mountains, inference of the symbolism of the body orientations solely from archaeological remains would probably be impossible. The A.D. 1500–1600 cemetery at Houlouf consisted entirely of individuals in an upright or seated position, facing to the southwest. This orientation is taken from ethnographic analogy to be a sign of high status (Holl 1994:138). For the Asante of Ghana the orientation is usually lying on the side, with the key being that the deceased must face away from the village (Ucko 1969:273).

Among the Tio of the Kongo the corpse was tied into an "N-shaped," flexed position before burial on its side in a round shaft, with a small mound on top (Vansina 1973:209). The cemetery at Katoto had both supine burials and flexed burials on their sides. Orientation was widely varying, with no single direction prevalent (Hiernaux et al. 1972: 148).

In the Americas the variation in burial orientation seems to be minimal. Fifty-five of the 58 burials at Newton Plantation for which orientation was clear were supine and on an east–west axis, 38 with the head to the west and 17 with the head to the east (Handler and Lange 1978:185). This pattern shows only minor variation from the almost universal Christian orientation of supine burial with the head to the west. In the African Burial Ground in New York City all burials seem to have been supine, with Michael Blakey stating that the majority were head to the west, and some with the head to the east. He suggests the head to the east burials may indicate Muslim practice (Harrington 1993:36). John Vlach (1978:147) sees orientation with head to the west as an African practice, "a shared African concept of the cosmos, that the world is oriented following the sun," but Handler and Lange (1978:317) correctly contradict this interpretation in pointing out the great variety of burial orientations in West Africa, some with orientation to the sea, others differentiated on the basis of gender, et cetera.

A brief description of burials at the Drummond Plantation, near Jamestown, Virginia, dating to the 1650–1720 period, suggests that "servants" of both African and European origin may have been buried together. Three adults buried in the same vicinity all had their heads to the north (Aufderheide et al. 1985:357). All burials in the Montserrat mid-18th-century cemetery that were identifiable were supine, head to the west burials (Watters 1987:301, 1994:60), and the supine, head to the west orientation of burials is universal in excavated African-American burials from the beginning of the 19th century onward in both the United States and the Caribbean (Combes 1972:54; Thomas et al. 1977: 410; Blakely and Beck 1982; Parrington 1986). In general it would seem that supine, head to the west burial was common as slaves became Christianized, but may have been more easily accepted than other Christian concepts as it is syncretic with common African associations of life and death with the path of the sun.

The position of one Newton Plantation cemetery burial is of interest, a solitary interment of a woman in a separate mound, in a prone position, face down. Handler and Lange (1978:198–199) point out that burial face down is a practice used for "Nyongo" witchcraft practitioners in coastal Cameroon, in an effort to confuse the spirit so that if it attempted to leave the grave it would go the wrong way. Ethnographic testimony from African Americans in Georgia in the 1940s stated that if repeated deaths of children in a family occurred, burial face down of the last child to die would ensure that the next child would live to adulthood (Combes 1972:58). It is important to note, however, that prone burial was also practiced historically in Europe, particularly in the burial of suspected witches.

Grave goods in 19th-century African-American burials appear to be, in almost all cases, in line with European and Christian practice. Of 140 burials in the First African Baptist Church cemetery in Philadelphia, all dating between 1824 and 1842, eight had a single coin near the head, six had a single shoe placed on the coffin lid, and in two cases a ceramic plate had been placed on the stomach. The plate, although interestingly similar to the surface material common to many African-American burials, is taken as possibly related to the European practice of placing a plate of salt on the corpse to prevent it from bloating and to keep the devil away (Parrington and Wideman 1986:60–61).

The validity of these interpretations is unfortunately not substantiated with any historical documentation of such practices by local Philadelphians. A burial from South Carolina had a penny placed over each eye, conveniently dating the burial as after the 1882—latest—date on the pennies. Placing pennies over the eyes was a common 19th-century practice in many Christian burials to keep the eyes closed (Combes 1972:54). All 17 late 19th-century burials in Atlanta, Georgia, had no grave goods apart from clothing and some jewelry (Blakely and Beck 1982).

James Garman has recently completed an interesting study of the Newport, Rhode Island, "Common Burying Ground," focusing on the headstones in the spatially segregated African-American section of the cemetery that date from the 1720–1830 period. These head and footstones were purchased by Euroamerican masters in the pre-emancipation period, up until the year 1800, and Garman (1994: 80–82) concludes that the headstones are more a representation of the desired virtue of the master to the community than they are a representation of the lives or culture of the slaves. After emancipation there are a series of stones commissioned by African Americans themselves. These are mostly identical to Euroamerican headstones of the same period. This may be either a representation of the desire of African Americans to be admitted into the culture of the new republic or due to fear of calling attention to any cultural differences within an overwhelmingly white society (Garman 1994:87–88).

The use of coffins also became increasingly common, and eventually universal, over time, and apparently was not common practice in African traditions. Until the 17th century in Europe, coffins were considered a high-status item, and the poor were not buried in them (Parker Pearson 1982:110). At ElMina, burial was in a specially prepared shroud up until the introduction of coffins in the late 19th century (DeCorse 1992:183). Historical evidence from Barbados shows that, in the 17th through early 19th centuries, coffins were supplied by plantation owners as a final reward for devoted slaves, and were thus an incentive toward acceptance of the dominant European ideology. They were certainly not always used (Handler and Lange 1978:191–192).

A cemetery identified as mid-18th century from a Montserrat plantation had probable coffin nails in five of nine burials, and copper stains from the pins of burial shrouds in the others (Watters 1987:303, 1994:62–63). Two early 19th-century people from a plantation in Georgia were both buried in coffins, without coffin hardware. Coffin hardware was, however, rare for any ethnic group before 1830 in North America (Thomas et al. 1977:410, 412).

By the late 19th century, African-American burials in the United States included coffins with the elaborate mass-produced hardware common to all ethnic groups. These were essentially "high-status" coffins, but the skeletal remains of these free blacks show high trauma rates and low nutritional status. This may demonstrate an attempt by free blacks to negate the socioeconomic differences between them and other ethnic and higher-status groups. Mortuary ritual thus continued to be an opportunity in the late 19th century for expressing the symbolic ideals of African Americans. The ideals, however, had shifted from more directly African-based ones, to an attempt at the time of death to mask the socioeconomic differences between African Americans and other parts of American society (Combes 1972:54; Genovese 1972:201–202; Blakely and Beck 1982; Bell 1990:67–70).

The rise of "fundamentalist Protestantism" in the 1790–1830 period in the English-speaking Americas created an emphasis on Christian piety and obedience. This change resulted in a desire, or pressure, on slave masters to have all slaves made Christian (Patterson 1982:73). Handler and Lange (1978:213) conclude that by the late 18th century, African influences in Barbados mortuary practices were "fading out." Another important influence began in the 1820s, as both European and North American society began moving toward an emphasis on "sanitation," with new municipal cemeteries set up to replace church burial by the 1850s in most urban areas (Parker Pearson 1982:106; Blakely and Beck 1982:178). This, too, may have resulted in less control over their own burial rites by African Americans. Thus, in many cases African-American burials by the mid-19th century, and in some cases well before that date, had become indistinguishable from the burials of any other ethnic group in America.

The Future

There is a clear need in formulations of African burial practices in the New World to have a much larger database of published excavated material. Handler and Lange's Barbados excavation is the only thoroughly researched and published pre-1800 cemetery of African Americans, and in itself has shown the great difference between such early practices and the 19th-century practices which have

been shown by other excavations. The recent New York City finds (Harrington 1993) have demonstrated the importance of descendant community—in this case African-American—involvement in the excavation and research of African-American burials. Despite any controversy involved, or perhaps in this case because of it, an opportunity is provided for greater community involvement in their own heritage. Both the descendant group itself, and all members of society, are shown the key contributions and role that that group has played in American history.

Most, if not all, future African-American burial excavations will probably be undertaken through salvage archaeology efforts. The negative consequences of this are clear, in the minimization of time and investment involved in properly researching and excavating burials which are threatened by development. It is essential that a coordinated historical, biological, and archaeological research effort be made to recognize African-American burials, to protect them from destruction, to maximize the information gained from them when excavation is inevitable, and to publish the results in an accessible format. It is difficult to place such a heavy burden on contract archaeologists alone, and thus the solution for the future may be a coordinated effort between contract archaeologists and university- or museum-based archaeologists when important finds such as the recent New York City burials are initially discovered.

Conclusions

Mortuary remains are a form of ritual communication in which fundamental social values are expressed (Parker Pearson 1982:100). The control of symbolic instruments such as mortuary practices by slave owners and overseers was an attempt to alienate the slaves from claims of belonging to a legitimate social order, and instead to make the master–slave relationship the dominant cultural force (Patterson 1982:5). Yet, did African Americans really cease to have any control over such symbolism and practice?

A 19th-century master in Georgia objected to, but

did not end, the use of African drums to announce slave funerals (Roediger 1981:168). Handler and Lange have shown significant African-American practices in excavated burials. If any conclusions are valid for the limited data available, they would seem to indicate that African Americans before 1800 had control over their own burial practices in many cases, and with that control they chose to practice much of what their ancestors had emphasized for proper burial. The burial practices of the late 19th-century urban, predominantly Christian, African-American communities in centers such as Philadelphia and Atlanta had very different concerns. These focused more on Christian piety and on the denial of the economic hardships that their communities faced in life, through use of dominant-culture symbols such as elaborate industrially produced coffins.

Funerals may have been one of the few times that antebellum slave communities could assume control of the symbolism around them, and thus create the dignity at death that negated the "social death" of their slave status. In the burial practices of many cultures we see an area in which social groups are afforded the possibility of reviewing the past, and thus both reaffirming cultural consent for particular relationships, and also disputing other traditional power relationships. The end of the liminal state for the deceased can also be seen as the reconciliation of cultural ideals with the new power structure (McCaskie 1989:430). For antebellum African Americans the power structure was, however, further complicated by the slave relationship. We see rapid shifts toward more European practices in various African-American communities at widely varying periods in their history. In other communities, however, African Americans continue practices which are not of Euroamerican origin, despite the immense difficulties of adapting to Euroamerican cultural, religious, and economic domination.

ACKNOWLEDGMENTS

My thanks to Laurie Beckwith, Nicholas David, Brenda Kennedy, Scott MacEachern, and anonymous *Historical Archaeology* reviewers, all of whom read and commented on earlier versions of this paper.

REFERENCES

ANGEL, J. LAWRENCE, JENNIFER O. KELLEY,
MICHAEL PARRINGTON, AND STEPHANIE PINTER
1987 Life Stresses of the Free Black Community as Represented by the First African Baptist Church, Philadelphia, 1823–1841. *American Journal of Physical Anthropology* 74:213–229.

ARMSTRONG, DOUGLAS V.
1990 *The Old Village and the Great House: An Archaeological and Historical Examination of Drax Hall Plantation, St. Ann's Bay, Jamaica.* University of Illinois Press, Urbana.

AUFDERHEIDE, A. C., J. LAWRENCE ANGEL,
JENNIFER O. KELLEY, A. C. OUTLAW,
M. A. OUTLAW, G. RAPP, AND L. E. WITTMERS
1985 Lead in Bone III: Prediction of Social Correlates from Skeletal Lead Content in Four Colonial American Populations (Catoctin Furnace, College Landing, Governor's Land, and Irene Mound). *American Journal of Physical Anthropology* 66:353–361.

BELL, EDWARD L.
1990 The Historical Archaeology of Mortuary Behavior: Coffin Hardware from Uxbridge, Massachusetts. *Historical Archaeology* 24(3):54–78.

BLAKELY, ROBERT L., AND LANE A. BECK
1982 Bioarchaeology in the Urban Context. In *The Archaeology of Urban America: The Search for Pattern and Process*, edited by Roy S. Dickens, Jr., pp. 175–207. Academic Press, Toronto.

BOLTON, H. CARRINGTON
1891 Decoration of Graves of Negroes in South Carolina. *Journal of American Folklore* 4:214.

BRACE, C. LORING, AND KEVIN D. HUNT
1990 A Nonracial Craniofacial Perspective on Human Variation: A(ustralia) to Z(uni). *American Journal of Physical Anthropology* 82:341–360.

BROWN, JAMES A.
1971 Approaches to the Social Dimensions of Mortuary Practices. *Memoir of the Society for American Archaeology* 25. Published as *American Antiquity* 36(3), pt. 2.

BUIKSTRA, JANE E., SUSAN R. FRANKENBERG, AND
LYLE W. KONIGSBERG
1990 Skeletal Biological Distance Studies in American Physical Anthropology: Recent Trends. *American Journal of Physical Anthropology* 82:1–7.

CHAPMAN, ROBERT, I. KINNES, AND KLAUS RANDSBORG
(EDITORS)
1981   *The Archaeology of Death.* Cambridge University Press, Cambridge, U.K.

CHAPMAN, ROBERT, AND KLAUS RANDSBORG
1981   Approaches to the Archaeology of Death. In *The Archaeology of Death,* edited by Robert Chapman, I. Kinnes, and Klaus Randsborg, pp. 1–24. Cambridge University Press, Cambridge, U.K.

CHEEK, CHARLES D., AND AMY FRIEDLANDER
1990   Pottery and Pigs' Feet: Space, Ethnicity and Neighborhood in Washington, D.C., 1880–1940. *Historical Archaeology* 24(1):34–60.

COLE, JOHNNETTA B.
1985   Africanisms in the Americas: A Brief History of the Concept. *Anthropology and Humanism Quarterly* 10: 120–126.

COMBES, JOHN D.
1972   Ethnography, Archaeology, and Burial Practices among Coastal South Carolina Blacks. *Conference on Historic Sites Archaeology Papers* 7:52–61.

COSENTINO, DONALD J.
1992   Interview with Robert Farris Thompson. *African Arts* 25(4):53–63.

CREEL, MARGARET WASHINGTON
1988   *''A Peculiar People'': Community Life and Religion among the Gullah.* New York University Press, New York.

CURTIN, PHILIP D.
1969   *The Atlantic Slave Trade: A Census.* University of Wisconsin Press, Madison.

DAVID, NICHOLAS
1992   The Archaeology of Ideology: Mortuary Practices in the Central Mandara Highlands, Northern Cameroon. In *An African Commitment: Papers in Honour of Peter Lewis Shinnie,* edited by Judy Sterner and Nicholas David, pp. 181–210. University of Calgary Press, Calgary, Alberta.

DeCORSE, CHRISTOPHER
1987   Historical Archaeological Research in Ghana, 1986–1987. *Nyame Akuma* 29:27–31.
1991   West African Archaeology and the Atlantic Slave Trade. *Slavery and Abolition* 12:92–96.
1992   Culture Contact, Continuity and Change on the Gold Coast, A.D. 1400–1900. *African Archaeological Review* 10:163–196.
1993   The Danes on the Gold Coast: Culture Change and the European Presence. *African Archaeological Review* 11:149–173.

FAULKNER, WILLIAM
1942   *Go Down, Moses.* Random House, New York.

GARMAN, JAMES C.
1994   Viewing the Color Line Through the Material Culture of Death. *Historical Archaeology* 28(3):74–93.

GENOVESE, EUGENE D.
1972   *Roll, Jordan, Roll: The World the Slaves Made.* Vintage Books, New York.

GILES, E., AND O. ELLIOT
1962   Race Identification from Cranial Measurements. *Journal of Forensic Sciences* 7:147–157.

GILL, G. W.
1984   A Forensic Test Case for a New Method of Geographical Race Determination. In *Human Identification: Case Studies in Forensic Anthropology,* edited by Ted E. Rathbun and Jane E. Buikstra, pp. 329–339. C. C. Thomas, Springfield, Illinois.

GOULD, STEPHEN JAY
1981   *The Mismeasure of Man.* W. W. Norton, New York.

HANDLER, JEROME S.
1981   A Ghanaian Pipe from a Slave Cemetery in Barbados, West Indies. *West African Journal of Archaeology* 11:93–99.
1989   *Searching for a Slave Cemetery in Barbados, West Indies: A Bioarchaeological and Ethnohistorical Investigation.* Center for Archaeological Investigations, Southern Illinois University, Carbondale.

HANDLER, JEROME S., AND FREDERICK W. LANGE
1978   *Plantation Slavery in Barbados: An Archaeological and Historical Investigation.* Harvard University Press, Cambridge, Massachusetts.

HARRINGTON, SPENCER P. M.
1993   Bones and Bureaucrats: New York's Great Cemetery Imbroglio. *Archaeology* 46(2):28–38.

HARRIS, EDWARD F., AND TED A. RATHBUN
1989   Small Tooth Sizes in a Nineteenth-Century South Carolina Plantation Slave Series. *American Journal of Physical Anthropology* 78:411–420.

HERSHKOVITZ, I., B. RING, AND E. KOBYLIANSKY
1990   Efficiency of Cranial Measurements in Separating Human Populations. *American Journal of Physical Anthropology* 83:307–319.

HERSKOVITZ, MELVILLE J.
1958   *The Myth of the Negro Past.* Reprint of 1941 edition. Beacon Press, Boston, Massachusetts.

HIERNAUX, J., E. MAQUET, AND J. DE BUYST
1972   Le Cimetière Protohistorique de Katoto (Vallée du Lualaba, Congo-Kinshasa). In *Sixième Congrès Panafricain de Préhistoire, Dakar 1967,* edited by Henri J. Hugot, pp. 148–158. Les Imprimeries Réunies de Chambéry, Chambéry, France.

HOGENDORN, JAN S., AND MARION JOHNSON
1986 *The Shell Money of the Slave Trade.* Cambridge University Press, Cambridge, U.K.

HOLL, AUGUSTIN
1994 The Cemetery of Holouf in Northern Cameroon (A.D. 1500–1600): Fragments of a Past Social System. *African Archaeological Review* 12:133–170.

HOWSON, JEAN E.
1990 Social Relations and Material Culture: A Critique of the Archaeology of Plantation Slavery. *Historical Archaeology* 24(4):78–91.

HUMPHREY, DAVID C.
1973 Dissection and Discrimination: The Social Origins of Cadavers in America, 1760–1915. *Bulletin of the New York Academy of Medicine* 49:819–827.

HUMPHREYS, S. C., AND H. KING (EDITORS)
1981 *Mortality and Immortality: The Anthropology and Archaeology of Death.* Academic Press, New York.

INGERSOLL, ERNEST
1892 Decoration of Negro Graves. *Journal of American Folklore* 5 (Jan.–Mar.):68–69.

IŞCAN, MEHMET Y.
1988 Rise of Forensic Anthropology. *Yearbook of Physical Anthropology* 31:203–230.

JOHNSON, JAY K., JENNY D. YEAROUS, AND NANCY ROSS-STALLINGS
1994 Ethnohistory, Archaeology and Chickasaw Burial Mode during the Eighteenth Century. *Ethnohistory* 41:431–446.

KLEIN, HERBERT S.
1986 *African Slavery in Latin America and the Caribbean.* Oxford University Press, Oxford, U.K.

KROGMAN, WILTON M., AND MEHMET Y, IŞCAN
1986 *The Human Skeleton in Forensic Medicine.* Charles C. Thomas, Springfield, Illinois.

LIVINGSTONE, FRANK B.
1962 On the Non-existence of Human Races. *Current Anthropology* 3(3):279–281.

LOVEJOY, PAUL E.
1983 *Transformations in Slavery: A History of Slavery in Africa.* Cambridge University Press, Cambridge, U.K.

MCCASKIE, THOMAS C.
1989 Death and the Asantehene: A Historical Meditation. *Journal of African History* 30:417–444.

MCDONALD, RODERICK A.
1993 *The Economy and Material Culture of Slaves: Goods and Chattels on the Sugar Plantations of Jamaica and Louisiana.* Louisiana State University Press, Baton Rouge.

MINTZ, SIDNEY W., AND RICHARD PRICE
1976 *An Anthropological Approach to the Afro-American Past: A Caribbean Perspective.* Institute for the Study of Human Issues, Philadelphia, Pennsylvania.

MORETON, J. B.
1790 *Manners and Customs in the West India Islands.* N.p., London.

OJO, JEROME O.
1976 Yoruba Customs from Ondo. *Acta Ethnologica et Linguistica* 37. Elisabeth Stiglmayr, Wien.

OWSLEY, DOUGLAS W., CHARLES E. ORSER, ROBERT W. MANN, PEER H. MOORE-JANSEN, AND ROBERT L. MONTGOMERY
1987 Demography and Pathology of an Urban Slave Population from New Orleans. *American Journal of Physical Anthropology* 74:185–197.

PARKER PEARSON, MICHAEL
1982 Mortuary Practices, Society and Ideology: An Ethnoarchaeological Study. In *Symbolic and Structural Archaeology,* edited by Ian Hodder, pp. 99–113. Cambridge University Press, Cambridge, U.K.

PARRINGTON, MICHAEL, AND JANET WIDEMAN
1986 Acculturation in an Urban Setting: The Archaeology of a Black Philadelphia Cemetery. *Expedition* 28:55–62. Philadelphia, Pennsylvania.

PATTERSON, ORLANDO
1982 *Slavery and Social Death: A Comparative Study.* Harvard University Press, Cambridge, Massachusetts.

PIETRUSEWSKY, MICHAEL
1990 Craniofacial Variation in Australian and Pacific Populations. *American Journal of Physical Anthropology* 82:319–340.

POSNANSKY, MERRICK
1989 West African Reflections on African-American Archaeology. Paper presented at the Conference "Digging the Afro-American Past: Archaeology and the Black Experience," University of Mississippi, University.

POTTER, PARKER B., JR.
1991 What Is the Use of Plantation Archaeology? *Historical Archaeology* 25(3):94–107.

RABOTEAU, ALBERT J.
1978 *Slave Religion: The Invisible Institution in the American South.* Oxford University Press, Oxford, U.K.

RATHBUN, TED A.
1987 Health and Disease at a South Carolina Plantation: 1840–1870. *American Journal of Physical Anthropology* 74:239–253.

ROEDIGER, DAVID R.
  1981   And Die in Dixie: Funerals, Death, and Heaven in the
         Slave Community, 1700–1865. *Massachusetts Review* 22(1):163–183.

ST. HOYME, LUCILE E., AND MEHMET Y. IŞCAN
  1989   Determination of Sex and Race: Accuracy and Assumptions. In *Reconstruction of Life from the Skeleton*, edited by Mehmet Y. Işcan and Kenneth A. R. Kennedy, pp. 53–93. Alan R. Liss, New York.

SINGLETON, THERESA A.
  1990   The Archaeology of the Plantation South: A Review of Approaches and Goals. *Historical Archaeology* 24(4):70–77.

SLOANE, HANS
  1707   *A Voyage to the Islands of Madeira, Barbados, Neives, S. Christopher and Jamaica*, Vol. 1. N.p., London.

SOBEL, MECHAL
  1979   *Trabelin' On: The Slave Journey to an Afro-Baptist Faith*. Greenwood Press, Westport, Connecticut.
  1987   *The World They Made Together: Black and White Values in Eighteenth-Century Virginia*. Princeton, New Jersey.

STEWART, T. D.
  1979   *Essentials of Forensic Anthropology: Especially as Developed in the United States*. Charles C. Thomas, Springfield, Illinois.

TAINTER, J. A.
  1978   Mortuary Practices and the Study of Prehistoric Social Systems. *Advances in Archaeological Method and Theory* 1:104–141. Michael B. Schiffer, editor. Serial Publication Series. Academic Press, New York.

THOMAS, DAVID HURST, STANLEY SOUTH, AND CLARK SPENCER LARSEN
  1977   Rich Man, Poor Men: Observations on Three Antebellum Burials from the Georgia Coast. *Anthropological Papers of the American Museum of Natural History* 54(3):393–420.

THOMPSON, ROBERT FARRIS
  1983   *Flash of the Spirit: African and Afro-American Art and Philosophy*. Random House, New York.

THOMPSON, ROBERT FARRIS, AND JOSEPH CORNET
  1983   *The Four Moments of the Sun: Kongo Art in Two Worlds*. National Gallery of Art, Washington, D.C.

THORNTON, JOHN
  1992   *Africa and Africans in the Making of the Atlantic World, 1400–1680*. Cambridge University Press, Cambridge, U.K.

UCKO, PETER J.
  1969   Ethnography and Archaeological Interpretation of Funerary Remains. *World Archaeology* 1:262–280.

VANSINA, JAN
  1973   *The Tio Kingdom of the Middle Congo, 1880–1892*. Oxford University Press, Oxford, U.K.

VIVIAN, BRIAN C.
  1992   Sacred to Secular: Transitions in Akan Funerary Customs. In *An African Commitment: Papers in Honour of Peter Lewis Shinnie*, edited by Judy Sterner and Nicholas David, pp. 157–167. University of Calgary Press, Calgary, Alberta.

VLACH, JOHN M.
  1978   *The Afro-American Tradition in Decorative Arts*. Cleveland Museum of Art, Cleveland, Ohio.

WATTERS, DAVID R.
  1987   Excavations at the Harney Site Slave Cemetery, Montserrat, West Indies. *Annals of the Carnegie Museum* 56:289–318. Pittsburgh, Pennsylvania.
  1994   Mortuary Patterns at the Harney Site Slave Cemetery, Montserrat, in Caribbean Perspective. *Historical Archaeology* 28(3):56–73.

YONGYI, LI, C. LORING BRACE, GAO QIANG, AND DAVID P. TRACER
  1991   Dimensions of Face in Asia in the Perspective of Geography and Prehistory. *American Journal of Physical Anthropology* 85:269–279.

ROSS W. JAMIESON
DEPARTMENT OF ARCHAEOLOGY
UNIVERSITY OF CALGARY
CALGARY, ALBERTA, T2N 1N4
CANADA

JANE LANDERS

Africans in the Spanish Colonies

Introduction

If the 15th-century history of the Americas was characterized by the drama of first contact and the 16th century by continued exploration, conquest, and expansion of Spanish hegemony, the 17th century has often been described as a time of protracted depression and decline. Pointing to the drain of European wars, metropolitan bankruptcies, depopulation in both the metropolis and the colony, declining mineral revenues and Spain's failures to adequately provision and protect its American colonies, some historians have emphasized the depreciation of the overextended Spanish empire. Indeed Spain was hardpressed to maintain its grip in the face of French, Dutch, and English challenges, most of which focused on the circum-Caribbean arena and the transatlantic trade which was Spain's lifeline (McAlister 1984).

But as all of these problems beset the empire, Spain's colonies were forced to develop their own resources and find ways to provide for and defend themselves. It was a time of improvisation, adaptation, accommodation, and change. Pragmatism ruled. Unenforceable or impractical mercantile and governmental restrictions were more easily ignored than in the past, as were even some social distinctions, which in times of crisis were a luxury colonists could ill afford. It was a moment when demographic determinants, frontier conditions, and external threats to Spanish sovereignty combined to create leverage and opportunities for certain groups. Africans, heavily concentrated in the coastal circum-Caribbean, were embroiled in the imperial contests played out there and, like Europeans and natives, they carefully evaluated their positions and acted in what they perceived to be their own best interests. In short, they made choices and concessions and were agents of change who have gone little noticed, although their tenure in the Americas matches that of the Spaniards.

Historical Archaeology, 1997, 31(1):84-91.
Permission to reprint required.

Africans in Spain

African incorporation into Spanish society predated the American experience. By 1525, 5,271 slaves appeared in the notarial records of Seville, almost 400 of whom were listed as blacks or *mulatos* (Phillips 1985:161). African slaves were an important source of hard and skilled labor in Spanish mines and agriculture and in Spanish port cities. Although excluded from Spanish guilds, Africans were also artisans and petty merchants and domestic servants in Spanish households. In all these capacities they worked alongside slaves of diverse religious and ethnic backgrounds, including Jews and Muslims, Egyptians, Syrians, Greeks, Russians, Sardinians, and even Spaniards, who had been captured in "just wars," been condemned, or had sold themselves into slavery (Phillips 1985:138–139, 155, 160–163).

Just as all slaves in Spain were not Africans, nor were all Africans slaves. Enslaved persons of any race in Spain had many avenues out of bondage. Spanish law and custom granted slaves a moral and juridical personality and legal mechanisms by which to escape abusive owners. Social and religion values promoted paternalism toward "miserable classes" which sometimes led owners to manumit favored slaves. Furthermore, slaves were permitted to hold and transfer property, and with their *peculium* they could purchase their freedom or that of relatives or friends. The emphasis on a slave's humanity and the lenient attitude toward manumission created a free black class that filled accepted economic and social roles, and even at the lowest level, political roles.

In Spain's largest city, Seville, free and enslaved Africans congregated in ethnic enclaves such as San Bernardo, San Roque, and San Idelfonso. As their numbers grew, Isabel and Ferdinand named one Juan de Valladolid, "of noble lineage among Negroes," to regulate the city's African community and be its "Chief and Judge" (Rout in Ortiz de Zuñiga 1975, 3:78). This precedent opened the way for other free blacks and foreshadowed Spanish practice in the Americas of enacting dominion through "natural" leaders of alien communities. The Catholic church also worked in these communities to promote orderly living and conversions among Africans who thereafter enjoyed both its sacraments and its advocacy. By the late 14th century, an African confraternity or *cofradía* had been established to administer the Hospital of Our Lady of the Angels in the African *barrio* of San Bernardo. African brotherhoods played enthusiastic roles in civic and religious rituals such as the processions of Semana Santa and Corpus Christi in Seville, Barcelona, Valencia, and Cádiz and provided social services and fraternal identity for their members (Pike 1972:173–174; Rout 1976:18; Phillips 1985:161).

Africans in the Conquest of Spanish America

Given their roles and numbers in Spanish port cities, it is not surprising that free and enslaved Africans crossed the Atlantic on the earliest voyages of exploration and conquest. With the Spaniards they formed a specialized pool of human resources circulating through the circum-Caribbean. One member of this tightly-knit group, a free African named Juan Garrido, took part in Juan Ponce de León's "pacification" campaigns against the Taino Indians of Hispaniola and then accompanied him in the conquest of Puerto Rico, on slave raids against the Caribs of Santa Cruz, Guadalupe, and Dominica, and on to Florida. Changing patrons, Garrido was at the side of Hernando Cortés when Cortés conquered Tenochtitlán, and when he went in search of black Amazons on the Pacific coast (Alegría 1990:17, 20).

Overlooked for centuries, Africans such as Garrido, the interpreter Juan González, the guide Estévan Dorantes, or the conquistador Juan Valiente (who performed specific valuable functions for the Spaniards) can be found in the records of explorations by Pánfilo de Narváez, Hernando de Soto, Francisco de Coronado, Francisco Pizarro, Pedro de Valdivia, and others. Class and racial biases of the day assure that many more were present than were recorded. For instance, although one can safely assume that a colonization effort such as Lucas Vásquez

de Ayllón's at San Miguel de Gualdape, involving some 600 persons in a new frontier and drawing on the lessons of Hispaniola, must have included a good number of slaves, to date we know little about them. However, these unnamed African slaves played a critical role in the destruction of the colony, setting fire to the houses of only one faction in the mutiny, and escaping to join the rebellious Guale Indians (Hoffman 1990:73–79).

Native uprisings against Spanish exploitation and resettlement began in Hispaniola in 1494 and plagued the Spaniards in almost every new locale they attempted to settle. Although some free Africans fought with the Spaniards in the Indian wars, enslaved Africans often used the occasions to escape. The fear of Indian/African alliance was already reality when Governor Nicolás de Obando arrived in Hispaniola in 1503. He complained of existing *cimarrón* communities and warned of the dangerous consequences of introducing more Africans into the Americas. Like slaveholders everywhere, the Spaniards would be haunted by fears of servile insurrection which proved well-founded. The first recorded slave uprising took place on Diego Colon's sugar plantation in 1522, and thereafter, slave revolts are a leitmotif running through the histories of the Spanish slave-holding nations (Larrazábal Blanco 1967:143–154; Palmer 1976:133; La Roza Corzo 1991:44).

African Slavery in Spanish America

Despite their fears of slave revolts, Spaniards came to consider African slavery the only solution to labor deficits, as warfare, disease, and overwork decimated Indian populations and extensive slave raids failed to satisfy the demands of Spaniards in settlements stretching from the Caribbean to Mexico, Central America, Peru, and northern South America. In 1513, Ferdinand established the *asiento* or licensing system which, it is estimated, sent between 75 and 90,000 enslaved Africans to Spanish America by 1600, and approximately 350,000 by the end of the 17th century. Because contraband trade in slaves was endemic, those may be conservative figures. Philip Curtin (1990) and others have argued that the shift to full-scale plantation economies fundamentally altered Spanish slavery, stripping the slave of many medieval protections, and for plantation settings that was certainly true. Blacks outnumbered whites in Hispaniola and Mexico by an estimated 10 to 1 as early as the mid-16th century, and Spanish officials worried. On various occasions they halted the trade, but the demands of Spanish settlers for more slaves eventually prevailed. The joining of the Spanish and Portuguese Crowns in 1580 facilitated the slave trade and increased the pace of importations into the Americas. Through the 16th century, Portuguese traders drew primarily from West African slave factories such as Arguim, São Jorge da Mina, and São Tomé Island, pushing southward into Angola by the 17th century. The shifting trade is evident in Patrick Carroll's study of slaves introduced into Vera Cruz. During the 16th century, 90 percent of the Vera Cruz slaves came from West African groups such as the Wolof from modern Senegal, Mandinga from modern Gambia, and the Biafara and Bran from modern Guinea-Bissau. By the 17th century, notarial records show that 80 percent of Vera Cruz slaves came from Central Africa—primarily from the Angolan and Congo groups (Carroll 1991:29, 158, 160). Meanwhile, contraband slaves, whose origins are impossible to know, continued to be introduced by Portuguese, Spanish, French, Dutch, and English traders who easily evaded or conspired with Spanish customs officials.

Gold, silver, and copper mining, cattle and sheep ranching, and plantation agriculture of sugarcane and cacao, indigo, wheat, grapes, and olives absorbed many of the newly introduced Africans, or *bozales*, who were already familiar with metallurgy, pastoral activities, and large-scale agriculture. Seventeenth-century Spanish officials realized their heavy dependence on Africans and claimed that ranching, mining, and the burgeoning sugar industry could not be sustained without them (Marcías Domínguez 1978; Ferry 1981:609–635; Carroll 1991).

Cimarronaje

Paradoxically, as plantation regimes were established, Spanish dependence upon African labor intensified and conditions for the *bozales* deteriorated. The grueling work and severe punishments meted out by planters drove many slaves to flight, and *cimarronaje* increased proportionally with the extension of plantations. Studies of maroon communities, or *palenques*, in Hispaniola, Cuba, Mexico, and New Granada (present-day Colombia, Venezuela, and Ecuador) find similar patterns of organization and development. Many originated as remote camps of male runaways who raided Spanish settlements or trade routes for supplies and women of all races. Over time, the successful bands evolved into more settled and sexually balanced communities practicing a mixed economy based on agriculture, animal husbandry, hunting and gathering, and contraband trade. Some runaways sustained themselves by mining copper (in Cuba) and gold (in Hispaniola and New Granada). Although they attempted to be self-sufficient, the maroons made use of their plantation contacts, trading with slaves, and even some poor whites, for materials they could not obtain in the wild. Maroons living near the coasts established similar exchanges with corsairs and pirates. Some groups also received assistance and even members from Indian communities, although in other locations Indians fought with Spaniards to eliminate them (Price 1973).

Over time some of the *palenques* grew to great size and organized multiple village sites. By mid-17th century, the runaways of Hispaniola had established four towns with a combined population of more than 1,000 persons. The *palenques* ringing Cartagena in the same time period had an estimated population of 3,000 persons. These sites were often organized under the leadership of an African and, in some camps, political and military leadership were divided. Outside Veracruz, the African Yanga led a long and determined resistance to Spanish attackers, aided by his war captain Francisco

Angola (Palmer 1976). Organization of the *palenques* outside Cartagena, was even further specialized, divided by ethnicity with four different war captains being responsible for their own compatriots. Little is known of the social life within the *palenque*, except that maroons sometimes practiced a blend of Catholic and African religions, creating churches which they staffed, but also assigning respected roles to African religious leaders or *obeahmen*.

Runaways did not have to form major communities such as San Basilio in order to be a threat. Slave flight cost owners dearly. Not only did they lose their original investment, but sorely-needed labor as well. Slaves were costly, averaging around 400 *pesos* for a healthy hand in the 17th century, yet demand commonly outstripped supply in many areas. Some owners tried to keep slaves through good treatment. Others resorted instead to hiring *rancheadores* to track and capture runaways who were then brutally punished.

Large and notorious communities such as those outside Cartagena and Vera Cruz were the bane of Spanish officials who charged that they controlled river and land trade routes, incited plantation slaves to rebel or flee, disrupted local economies, and were a threat to public order and Spanish dominion. Spaniards were divided on how to respond. Local *hacendados* and political figures usually advocated a hard line against the maroons and were ready to mount and pay for military expeditions against them. The Crown, peninsular officials, and churchmen, on the other hand, usually preferred a more conciliatory approach—offering mediation and pardons to restore order. It was a conservative and less expensive response but one that the locals found unsatisfactory.

The maroons were also divided and had to weigh their options. Most distrusted peaceful overtures since punitive campaigns continued, even when in the case of the Cartagena *palenques*, royal *cedulas* forbade them (Borrego Pla 1973). Usually, it was only after long years of resistance, and when conditions seemed to

demand it, that the communities acceded to mediation by Catholic priests, and then only if they were able to win guarantees of liberty and self-rule. By holding out long enough they won formal recognition of their communities as Spanish towns, replete with corporate status, municipal *fueros* (charters), land ownership, a Catholic parish, and at least a minimal measure of respectability. In return they promised to return future runaways (a promise most often unkept), and to be loyal vassals of the Spanish Crown. Thus were born free Afro-Spanish towns such as San Basilio in Cartagena, San Lorenzo de los Negros de Mina in Hispaniola, and San Lorenzo de Cerralvo in Mexico, to name only a few (Borrego Pla 1973; Palmer 1976; Arróm and García Arévalo 1986).

Ladinos in Spanish America

Meanwhile, acculturated African slaves, or *ladinos*, came to fill a wide range of domestic, artisanal, and lower-status economic roles in Spanish cities, creating in effect a two-tier system of African slavery in the Americas. They were found working in occupations as varied as construction to tailoring. The *ladino* group generally received better treatment, based on older metropolitan slave relations and on their access to legal and religious protections and a cash economy (Landers 1988). As they had in Spain, they organized themselves through *cofradías*, which, at least in the Americas, were organized by nations, often with elected kings and courts. It is interesting to note that contemporary authorities investigating many of the slave revolts also described the election of kings and courts by participants, and such elections were also a feature of later slave revolts in the British Caribbean (Thornton 1991; Mullin 1992). The *cofradías* were active and noted participants in the civic and religious life of Spanish cities. A 17th-century account from Havana describes Africans celebrating and enjoying Carnaval with "picturesque pomp" (Berthe 1971). In Seville, the celebrations had included African song and dance and elaborate costuming—all of which were still part of feast day celebrations in Havana well into the 19th century and were also noted in British Caribbean slaveholding areas (Ortíz 1920:5–16; Pike 1972:188–189; Thornton 1991; Mullin 1992).

The rich social life ascribed to Africans in Havana and other circum-Caribbean cities was possible, in part, because slaveowners sometimes followed metropolitan practice and employed urban slaves in a *jornal* system which allowed them to work at their own devices and live in their own homes in return for a daily payment. In this way owners earned income but escaped many of the responsibilities of feeding, sheltering, clothing, and medicating their slaves. Slaves, on the other hand, gained personal autonomy. One Havana official remarked that the slaves "go about as if they were free, working at whatever they choose, and at the end of the week or the month they give their owners the *jornal*. . .some have houses in which they shelter and feed travellers, and have in those houses, slaves of their own" (Marcías Domínguez 1978). This practice enabled some industrious slaves to purchase their freedom or that of their family members, and some Havana officials worried about the growing numbers of free blacks in their midst, suggesting that they be siphoned off to nearby St. Augustine. Population growth and urban expansion made their small urban properties more valuable, but also more desirable to Spaniards who found many ways to dispossess them (Wright 1916:313). Few slaves actually became property owners, however, and many slaves were unable to pay their required *jornal*, especially in *tiempo muerte*, when no fleets were in town. To avoid punishments, they sometimes fled to become maroons (García del Pino and Melis Cappa 1988:188–199).

Other slaves worked through the *jornal* system to buy their freedom or that of their family and friends. If owners and slaves agreed on a price, self-purchase or *coartación* was a relatively simple process. Once the slave acquired the funds, the owner simply notarized a manumis-

sion document that always stipulated the full rights the ex-slave would acquire. It might take slaves decades to acquire the full sum, but some borrowed funds or received assistance from their *cofradías*, while a lucky few gained freedom when owners manumitted them as a charitable act or in last testaments. If owners and slaves could not agree on a figure, the slaves could, and did, go to court to ask that a "just price" be established. Owner and slave each appointed a person to assess the slave's value, and in cases of wide disagreement the court would appoint yet a third evaluator. With a "just price" established, the slave made a downpayment and became a *coartado*, free of the former owner's control, but not legally emancipated until the set price was paid in full.

Once free, Africans became small property holders and operated a wide variety of small businesses in Spanish America. The men were often skilled artisans—coopers, ironsmiths, masons, carpenters, shoemakers, or butchers—whose very ability had helped them gain the funds for self-purchase. Free women often baked and sold sweets, ran laundry businesses, or raised and sold pigs and chickens to help support their families, and sometimes husbands and wives jointly operated taverns (Landers 1988).

Once free, Africans struggled to make sure their rights were not abridged. They took their complaints to local courts, and if they failed to get satisfaction at that level, they sought it in Spain, from their King. In the early 17th century, the free Africans of Havana registered a series of complaints against local authorities which included charges that authorities entered their homes without permission when searching for runaways and often seized the property of free blacks, and that officials sometimes required free blacks to serve as mail couriers which took them away from their fields at critical periods. The free blacks also complained both about being denied the right to wear capes (a status symbol) and about officials' requiring their wives and daughters to dance in public festivals (when properly married and virtuous unmarried women did not). In their petitions they reminded the King that they were his "good vassals" and "members of his republic." As required by law, these charges were processed by Havana's governor, reviewed by the Council of the Indies, and then sent to the King with a recommendation. The King responded by requiring Cuba's Governor and Captain General to "do justice to the blacks," and to "see to their good treatment." Further, the Crown ordered that no one "disturb their rights to purchase or work lands," or compel them to carry mail or oblige free black women to participate in public ceremonies against their will (Wright 1927:55–95). Such victories did not mean that Africans were thereafter always treated fairly or equally in Cuba, or in any other of the Spanish colonies where free blacks also litigated in the courts to secure their rights. They do demonstrate, however, that free blacks saw themselves as deserving of the rights of Spanish citizens and were willing to pursue them, and that the Spanish legal system and the Crown also recognized them as vassals deserving of the King's protection and intercession.

Africans in the Era of Piracy

Spanish officials were increasingly threatened by even small-scale *cimarronaje*, especially in the circum-Caribbean, where after the 16th century it combined with the threat of foreign attack. The waters near Puerto Rico were said to be "as full of French as Rochelle," and maroons developed a lucrative trade with the foreigners, providing them with cattle and turtle meat, hides, and agricultural products. Spanish officials feared that the maroons would form a fifth column as they had when they helped Sir Francis Drake take Nombre de Dios in Panama (Wright 1916:346).

Seeing an opportunity for both independence and profit, some Africans became pirates themselves. In 1638, after a corsairing career which included many prizes and prisoners taken from Campeche to Veracruz, Capitán Diego Martín, alias Diego el Mulato, offered his service to Spain. Although nothing is known of Martín's crew, later examples of black captains and crews can be found in Spanish records. Captain Martín assured Spanish officials in Havana of his great desire to serve as a *Valeroso Soldado del Rey nuestro Señor*, making appropriate references to the King's championship of the Catholic faith. He promised that if the King agreed to his offer of service, no Dutch ship or any other enemy would any longer stop along Cuba's coasts, "especially knowing that I am here very few would dare pass on to the Indies, for they certainly fear me" (García del Pino and Melis Cappa 1988:139–140). Captain Martín's boast bespeaks a pride which in other times the Spaniards might have thought presumptuous, but his deeds must have merited it. Havana officials forwarded Martín's offer to Spain with a recommendation of royal pardon and a salary equivalent to that of an admiral, an obvious admission of their need. Moreover, the Spaniards made no derogatory mention of Martín's color or class. Four years later, one Diego de los Reyes, "el Mulato," sacked Campeche and kidnapped Indians all the way to Honduras, before taking 16,000 *pesos* in booty from the Spanish mission town of Bacalar. If this was the same *mulato* Diego, it may be that the Crown did not offer him the commission he sought, or perhaps not one that would match his corsairing profits (Jones 1983:226, 229–230).

Military Roles for Africans

Although they worried about maroons and slave revolts, the Spaniards also employed free and enslaved Africans in local self-defense, as plantation and town militias, as coastal sentinels, and even as sailors on locally organized patrol boats (Wright 1916:315; García del Pino and Melis Cappa 1988:8–40). French and English pirates still attacked with impunity and became rich on *rescate*, the practice of holding persons or towns hostage for a ransom. The disastrous raid of Sir Francis Drake in 1585–1586 in which he sacked Santo Domingo, Cartagena, and St.

Augustine marked a turning point for the area. Thereafter the Crown launched a major effort to fortify their Caribbean ports. African masonry and metalworking skills eventually helped erect great stone forts at Havana, Cartagena, St. Augustine, Vera Cruz, San Juan, and Portobelo as well as many minor constructions in lesser ports along the threatened coasts (Chatelain 1941; Arana and Manucy 1992).

As the English and French escalated from piracy to territorial seizures, the Spaniards accepted Africans as welcome additions to chronically understaffed garrisons. Even those Spanish officials holding strong antipathies for blacks recognized that the Crown would never supply enough men to fill their *plazas*, and so they worked with what was at hand, including Africans and Indians. Although William Penn and Robert Venables succeeded in taking Jamaica in 1655, Africans fought bravely alongside Spaniards and after the Spanish evacuation stayed on to man an interior stockade at Los Bermejales and harry the English as maroons (Kopytoff 1978:290). The Spaniards at St. Augustine also employed black guerrillas in raids against the new English settlement at Charles Towne and encouraged them to return with English slaves. Some of these men later saw Spanish service against their former masters (Landers 1990b:9–30). By mid-17th century, free blacks and *mulatos* were serving throughout the circum-Caribbean in more formally organized militias. A Central American roster from 1673 listed almost 3,000 *pardos* (usually meaning *mulatos*, but sometimes referring to non-Europeans of mixed ancestry) serving in infantry units throughout the isthmus (Weber 1987:511–528). Free blacks in St. Augustine also formed themselves into a unit in 1683, commanded, as their Central American counterparts were, by officers of their own election (AGI 1683). Similar units served in Hispaniola, Cuba, Mexico, Puerto Rico, and Cartagena (Klein 1966:17–27; Kuethe 1971:105–115). Blacks and *mulatos* also staffed and sometimes captained Spanish ships in the circum-Caribbean (Hann 1991:370, 391–394, 426).

Most of the black militias were formed by free black artisans and acculturated skilled workers. They were Catholics who lived as Spaniards and were integrated into their communities through powerful social institutions such as *compadrazgo* and patron/client networks. Leading useful and orderly lives, they mirrored the early African communities of Spain and enjoyed the protections promised by Spanish law and custom. Military service was yet another way for free blacks to prove themselves to their community and also advance themselves through occasional opportunities for plunder. Moreover, through the militias free blacks acquired titles and status, and eventually full corporate privileges. It is possible that the units also functioned to reinforce relationships within the African community, as "natural" leaders rose to command and assumed responsibility for their men. In this way they were not unlike the military captains of the *palenques* or the leaders of slave revolts. Parish registers from St. Augustine show that militia families commonly intermarried and served as godparents and marriage sponsors for one another. Church records also suggest that the double connection of family and military corporatism may have worked to move some men out of slavery (Landers 1988). Although their slave past was certainly not forgotten, it was in a sense, excused, by appropriate behavior, valuable services, and the sponsorship of Africans whom the community already approved.

Conclusion

This very superficial review of the choices and concessions and changes made by Africans in the 17th-century circum-Caribbean has attempted to illustrate both the agency and adaptability of Africans who made the most of uncertain times and negotiated lives for themselves throughout the Spanish colonies, despite the oppressions of slavery and racial prejudice. As historians and archaeologists design their future research projects, especially in the circum-Caribbean, they cannot afford to overlook Africans, who were such an integral and often sizeable component of Spanish colonial society. As documented, blacks greatly outnumbered both whites and natives in some areas by the 16th century, and even in the 17th century they still formed 45 percent of Cuba's population (Marcías Domínguez 1978:35).

The historical records are available, and are certainly richer than once was believed, especially on Africans in urban settings. But by their nature historical records are insufficient, and their biases and omissions can best be corrected through historical archaeology. As the exciting collaborations on a variety of Anglo-American slave sites, maroon sites in Brazil and Jamaica, and a free black town in Spanish Florida demonstrate, much is yet to be discovered.

Terrance Weik

Archaeology of the African Diaspora in Latin America

ABSTRACT

Archaeology conducted at Latin American sites in Brazil, Cuba, Florida, Hispaniola, Jamaica, and Peru has made significant contributions to our understanding of African Diaspora history. Historical archaeology of the African Diaspora in Latin America has explored technological innovations in pottery making, resistance to slavery, and everyday life. The unifying theme in these studies, like that of the Anglo colonies, has been ethnic or cultural markers of identity. Maroon studies have predominated, while plantation archaeology in Latin America is developing slowly. By placing Latin American sites within the context of theories such as ethnogenesis, focusing on intercultural interactions in Maroon and slave societies, and rediscovering the forgotten connections between Amerindians and Africans, it is possible to advance our understanding of African Diaspora social formation and culture creation.

Introduction

An African Diaspora approach provides a useful framework for analyzing the myriad interactions that have spread millions of Africans across the globe into places such as Latin America (Figure 1) (Shepperson 1976:4; Harris 1982:5–8; Gilroy 1993; for a broader discussion of diasporas see Tölölyan 1996). A diaspora perspective is one way of reconciling the positions of those who have either overemphasized Africans' historic separation from their homelands or traits of their African cultural background. Another dialectic that is examined in an African Diaspora perspective involves the extent to which people drew on their shared experiences and cultural traditions to affect their condition versus using unique responses to their environments to shape their lives. In the Western hemisphere, the African Diaspora cannot be understood apart from the European race for land, profit, and power that created colonialism and slavery.

Similarly, Latin America resulted largely from the destruction and transformation of Native American and African cultures by Spanish and Portuguese conquests and labor systems (G. Foster 1960; Lockhart and Schwartz 1983; Ewen 2001). Latin American archaeological sites have illuminated the lives of free Blacks, Maroons, and enslaved Africans who rarely had a voice in the documents of their time (Vega 1979; Arrom and García Arévalo 1986; Smith 1986, 1995; Marron 1989; Orser 1992, 1994a, 1996; Herron 1994; Deagan and MacMahon 1995). These studies suggest that Africans and Amerindians were intimately associated within and beyond colonial settlements. I would contend that future archaeological research at African Diaspora sites in Latin America would benefit from a new focus on African and Indian interactions as well as a theoretical framework that accounts for ethnogenetic mechanisms that overlapped with and transcended colonial creolization.

Archaeologists who ignore or underestimate the contacts between Africans and Amerindians risk misunderstanding nuances of cultural identities, and culture change, as they are reflected in the archaeological and historical record. Colonial documents indicate that Europeans actively sought to segregate African and Amerindian peoples, using the strategy of "divide and rule" to overpower these groups (Davidson 1966; Love 1970). Ethnohistorians and anthropologists have been criticized for carrying this Eurocentric bias into their writings and neglecting the productive exchanges between Africans and Amerindians

FIGURE 1. Archaeological sites of the African Diaspora in Latin America.

Historical Archaeology, 2004, 38(1):32–49.
Permission to reprint required.

(Landers 1990; Forbes 1993; Peguero Guzman 1994). "Colonoware" studies have illustrated the complexity of interpreting African and Indian pottery production in North America (Ferguson 1992). Colonowares were originally credited to Native American potters, but an African Diaspora perspective has overturned this assumption in favor of a more likely view that also acknowledges the role of Africans and Blacks in colonoware production (Ferguson 1992).

North American and British West Indian sites have received the most attention from archaeologists studying the African Diaspora; however, this is not because of a lack of suitable or numerous sites in Latin America. Few European nations can match the Spanish and Portuguese in terms of the duration and span of their colonial legacies in the Western hemisphere. Spain and Portugal erected the first European forts and plantations in the Americas, and they were the last nations to abolish slavery (Sauer 1966). The presence of large numbers of Amerindians in Iberian colonial societies created a demographic situation that differed markedly from many British and Dutch colonial societies. The present form of these divergent colonial legacies is evident in linguistic and religious differences as well as in different systems of racism that created bipolar race relations in North America an d the racial continuum in Latin America (Hoetink 1985; Safa 1987). The United Kingdom, France, and the Netherlands continue to maintain Caribbean colonies in the present day. The United States controls Puerto Rico and the Virgin Islands and has not hesitated to send military aid and troops to Latin America when its political and economic interests are challenged. Thus, an important challenge for archaeologists who engage in research on the African Diaspora in Latin America is to address the complex sociopolitical and racial relations there, while avoiding the elitism and the single-minded extraction of resources that have characterized European and U.S. imperialism in the Western hemisphere (Schmidt and Patterson 1995).

Puerto Real

Puerto Real, located on the north coast of Haiti, holds a special significance to African Diaspora studies, as it is one of the first sites in

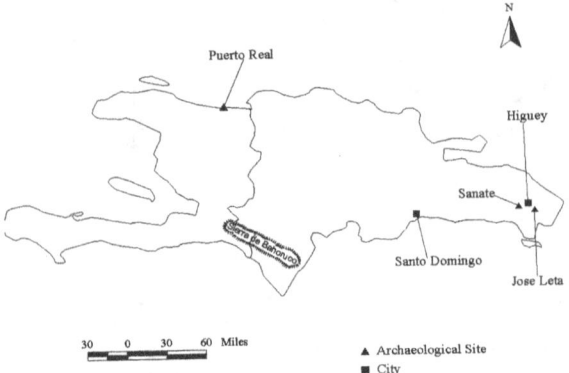

FIGURE 2. Hispaniola.

the Americas to be affected by enslaved Africans. The study of Afro-colonoware production at Puerto Real has important theoretical and methodological implications for other African Diaspora sites in Latin America. Greg Smith's analysis of more than 92,000 ceramics from Puerto Real was designed to account for all non-European pottery production in this Spanish colonial town during the period 1503–1578 (Figure 2). Smith (1995:341–342) examined samples from an early (1503–1550) cattle-processing area, an early domestic household, and a late (1550–1578) high-status domestic occupation. He noted that the destruction of native populations in Puerto Real coincided with the importation of enslaved Africans for work such as copper mining. Using mineralogical and morphological ceramic analysis, stratigraphic data, and historical literature, Smith argued that a new type of African-based pottery called Christophe Plain, a low-fired, thick, utilitarian vessel, resulted from this demographic transformation (Smith 1986, 1995).

Smith (1995) convincingly argued that paste constitution, firing temperature, surface treatment, sherd thickness, and vessel form differences distinguished Christophe Plain as a separate ceramic type. His artifact analyses illustrated how Christophe Plain slowly rose in proportion to other ceramics to dominate the potsherd counts in three areas at Puerto Real. He gave equal consideration to African, European, and Taino pottery-making traditions, avoiding the biases of approaches that seek unilinear causes, compartmentalize past ethnic groups, and overemphasize culture continuity. In addition,

Smith argued that Amerindian, European, and African production techniques contributed to the creation of "transitional" or "unidentified" forms of pottery (Smith 1986:11, 54, 106; 1995). "Unidentified" potsherds differed from Christophe Plain in that they were less thick, had more surface incisions and punctations, and were confined to later contexts (1550–1578) (Smith 1995:365). However, these forms did share the low-fired and blackened characteristics of Christophe Plain.

A more intensive examination of ethnographic and ethnohistoric cases of Afro-Caribbean or African pottery making would strengthen the argument for an African origin of Christophe Plain by defining the range of variation of African Diaspora forms and production techniques (Afro-Jamaican examples can be found in Ebanks 1984 and Reeves 1997; possible Maroon examples include locally made pottery from Jamaica and Palmares [Agorsah 1994; and Allen 1994: 22–24, 42; 1998:148–15]; see ethnohistoric accounts of Matawai Maroon pots summarized by King 1979:299). Interior African archaeological sites of the 16th century are slowly being documented, but more research is necessary to make clear-cut comparisons of ceramic morphology, composition, manufacturing technique, and surface treatment (Agorsah 1985; Posnansky 1989; Stahl 1999). Similarly, contact period sites are not well documented in Hispaniola, making comparisons between unidentified pottery at Puerto Real and other settlements in the Caribbean difficult (Smith 1986; Rouse 1992:139; Deagan 1996; Ewan 2001). Many colonial and aboriginal sites, especially in the east and southwestern part of the Dominican Republic, await study by committed and bilingual archaeologists.

Theorizing Culture Contact in Puerto Real

A question that remains to be answered at Puerto Real concerns the identity of the potters and their role in society. Women were pottery producers in many precolonial and colonial settlements in the Americas (King 1979:299; Nash 1980:144; Ebanks 1984; Knight 1985:121, 165; Ferguson 1991:31). June Nash (1980: 145) observed that "the creative role of Indian women and their *mestizo* offspring in producing a mestizo culture ... has been largely ignored."

Kathleen Deagan addressed this issue by showing how Amerindian women, who were sometimes household heads or servants, created aboriginal cooking technology that complemented the colonizers' influences (i.e., architectural styles) within *mestizo* households at colonial St. Augustine (Deagan 1983; 1985:305). African females may have eventually replaced Amerindian females in Puerto Real, serving an analogous role to that of female Amerindians in early St. Augustine, as pottery producers and reproducers of culturally and racially mixed households.

Although the word *mestizo* has been viewed in a positive light by some, as either a valid social category or a meaningful intercultural identity, its conceptual shortcomings make *mestizo* a problematic option for theorizing about African Diaspora peoples. *Mestizo* was a hybrid class and race category used by chroniclers and historians to refer to the offspring of Iberians (Spanish and Portuguese) and Asians or American Indians (Gibson 1966:116–117; Forbes 1993:128). Portuguese and Spanish chroniclers attributed a cultural meaning to *mestizo* during its earliest usage (1495), and by the colonial period it took on both a racial and cultural connotation. *Mestizo* was used in a variety of ways in colonial times, as in Mexico where the offspring of various combinations of Africans, Spaniards, and Amerindians were sometimes designated as *mestizo* (Forbes 1993:129). They were seen by Spaniards and Indians as low status, and "illegitimate" intermediary populations in many parts of Latin America, until the rise of modern nations (for colonial period views, see Nash 1980:140; Lockhart 1994:185–192; for modern South American views of *mestizos* and blacks, see Whitten 1976; Wade 1993; a view of the Hispanic Caribbean can be found in Safa 1987).

Mestizaje (intermixture or integration) is the process that creates *mestizo* cultures (Rosenblatt 1954; Mörner 1967; Deagan 1983:100). Unfortunately, the way traditional *Mestizaje* theory has been applied, African and Amerindian peoples have been interpreted as both physically and culturally ephemeral, more likely to assimilate or be acculturated into colonial and modern Latin American societies (for a traditional view, see Foster 1960; for a critique, see Whitten and Torres 1998:7). People of Amerindian and African descent continue to struggle against the assimilative *Mestizaje* or *blanqueomiento* (whitening) policies of neocolonial regimes in various parts of Latin America, where many *mestizos* have joined the elite in applying oppressive political and military power in modern nations (Whitten 1976; Safa 1987; Wade 1993; Harrison 1995:55). In light of the shortcomings and the political implications of perpetuating a theory of *Mestizaje*, a more balanced perspective is necessary, one that examines continuity and changes among interconnected cultural groups at different scales of analysis. Smith's (1995) study of Puerto Real is evidence that there are methodological alternatives to *Mestizaje* theory for interpreting Latin American sites in the African Diaspora.

Colonowares and Puerto Real

The non-European pottery at Puerto Real fits into a wider theme of historical archaeology called colonoware studies (Ferguson 1980,1992; Armstrong 1990; Crane 1993; Smith 1995:340; Schavelzon 1999; also see articles in Haviser 1998). Colonoware is a low-fired, plain, bulky, gray-brown pottery that often combined African or Native American production techniques with European vessel forms. One obstacle faced by Smith and others studying colonowares is that there are no documented examples of Africans producing pottery at Puerto Real (Ferguson 1980; Smith 1986, 1995). In a sense, the arguments for African or African American colonoware production are indirect, resting on comparisons made with analogous pot forms in Africa and associations with Africans who were reported to have inhabited locations where colonowares are found (Ferguson 1992). However, such indirect arguments that use independent documentary and material lines of evidence may be the only way of establishing the presence of African Diaspora populations in many places.

The promise of indirect arguments becomes clearer when one considers the problem of the "archaeological invisibility" of Africans who are known to exist from documents for locations such as St. Augustine but are not associated with identifiable African-influenced or African-made objects (Hoffman 1997:29). Smith (1997) has faced the same difficulty in examining a rural *bodega* (winery) called Moquegua in colonial Peru (Rice and Smith 1989). He was aware of a documented, 17th-century, African jug maker but could only discern variability in the ceramics influenced by Spanish or native Andean pottery traditions. As with Puerto Real, Smith's intercultural approach (accounting for African, Amerindian, and European components) balanced his interpretations of Moquegua by accounting for the full range of actors and cultures that affected the archaeological record. Much remains to be learned about those who built and operated the kilns in Moquegua (Rice and Van Beck 1993: 79). Defrance (1996:45) pointed out that a faunal study of areas associated with indigenous or African laborers at Moquegua may inform other questions related to foodways.

Maroon Studies

The majority of published works on historical archaeology of African Diaspora populations in Latin America focuses on Maroons (Funari 1995; Orser 1996; Weik 1997a). *Maroon* is an English derivation of the Spanish *Cimarron*. English colonial documents often refer to Maroons as "runaway slaves" or "fugitives" (Price 1979). Maroon archaeology has examined sites in Brazil, Cuba, the Dominican Republic, Florida, and Jamaica (Montejo 1968; Vega 1979; Arrom and García-Arévalo 1986; Marron 1989; Soto David 1989; Guimarães 1990; Herron 1994; Orser 1994a; Reitz 1994; for a broader summary, see Weik 1997a). Archaeologists studying Maroons have explored themes such as subsistence, everyday life, and world systems, with special emphasis on reconstructions of African ethnicity. Geometrically incised pipes found in Cuba, Brazil, and the Dominican Republic seem to be the best evidence of African-influenced material culture (Arrom and García Arévalo 1986:64; Guimarães 1990:172; Orser 1996). The connection between Maroon pipes and those of African production rests on an association found in Matthew Emerson's (1988, 1999) study of geometrically incised pipes from the Chesapeake Bay. Like Smith's (1995) Puerto Real study, Emerson (1988, 1999) examined African, European, and Native American artifact types in order to delineate Africa-influenced pipes. However, theorizing Maroon archaeological sites should not be merely an exercise in accounting for Africanisms or African connections, for new Maroon cultures emerged that were related to plantation socialization and frontier aboriginal groups.

Maroon Ethnogenesis

Ethnogenesis theory provides an explanatory framework within which we can examine culture contact and sociocultural dynamics in Maroon societies. Ethnogenesis is the formation of *new or different* sociocultural groups from the interactions, intermixtures, and antagonisms among people who took part in global processes of colonialism and slavery. This definition draws on the pioneering theory of William Sturtevant (1971) whose model of Seminole Indian history, ethnography, and linguistics suggests a picture of multilinear group fission and formation, rapid culture change, and cultural diversity (Whitten 1976, 1995; Moore 1994; for criticisms of Sturtevant, see Sattler 1996). Sidney Mintz and Richard Price's (1992:50–51) classic synthesis, *The Birth of African-American Culture*, applied a similar conceptualization as Sturtevant, arguing that African American plantation cultures were "newly-created," dynamic, and internally diverse. Price's (1979) *Maroon Societies* reiterated this view for Maroons in more subtle ways.

I utilize theories of ethnogenesis as an alternative to the creolization model of societies in the African Diaspora (Joyner 1984:xxi; Ferguson 1992; Mintz and Price 1992; for a Caribbeanist critique, see Safa 1987). Ideas about creolization were originally developed by linguists. Archaeologists' version of the linguistic model envisioned Africans using European lexicon or material culture and embedding it in newly created social systems or pre-established African cultural grammars (see Ferguson 2000 for a review of recent creolization theory). Archaeologists borrowed some of their views of creolization from Kamau Brathwaite (1976) who conceptualized slave society in Jamaica as composed of African American and European-American subcultures that resulted from the selective adaptation of Old World cultural antecedents within a system dominated by a slave-owning class and European forms of labor and politics.

Archaeologists have recently articulated alternative views, such as creolization as conflict, a political economic perspective (Mullins and Paynter 2000:73), or the emic, Creole identity perspective (Dawdy 2000). The newer views of creolization address formerly neglected areas such as the unequal power relations within societies, the agency of indigenous and enslaved peoples, and the conflicts that accompanied syncretisms (Dawdy 2000:110). Grey Gundaker's (2000) eloquent critique of the archaeology of creolization suggests guidelines that archaeologists are using to recognize how multiple cultural practices and material assemblages were combined in the past. She advises that archaeologists focus on local contexts in their interpretations while they oscillate between concepts of complexity and reduction. She recommends mapping out networks of use and meaning and discerning the "'timing' of creolization" that determined when and where material culture was created and allocated (Gundaker 2000:132).

Although Maroon studies share the above-mentioned interests of creolization approaches, Maroons must be viewed within the wider range of ethnogenetic factors that shaped their cultural trajectories. Creolization theories have not been able to fully explain Maroon sociocultural formations because they have overemphasized *cladistic*, as opposed to *rhizotic*, processes of cultural genesis. Cladistic processes involve the linear, sequential creation of cultures from the contact among antecedent cultures, in a way similar to the branching family tree created by genealogists (Moore 1994; Gundaker 2000:127 also notes the linear arguments of archaeologists). John Moore (1994) criticized cladistic models of social formation for their assumption that linguistic, cultural, and biological characteristics co-evolved and passed down through societies, changing at constant rates. Moore's (1994) ethnogenesis approach argues that rhizotic processes were equally as relevant to past social dynamics. Rhizomes are roots that continuously branch off into new shoots in search of nourishment and space to grow. Similarly, rhizotic processes feature abrupt additions and subtractions of beliefs, artifacts, and behaviors from cultures facing rapid demographic and structural changes. Maroon social dynamics were different from those of slave societies because Maroons mobilized frequently, incorporated new members, and occasionally splintered into smaller groups. Maroon ethnogenesis was the product of cultural creation as well as intermittent periods of transformation and dissolution that present archaeologists with special challenges.

José Leta

In summer 1996 I set out to explore Maroon ethnogenesis at José Leta, a Maroon site located on the southeastern side of Hispaniola (the Dominican Republic and Haiti) (Weik 1997b). Eastern Hispaniola was the last area to be subdued by the Spanish conquistadors in the 16th century. Its distance from colonial settlements and rough terrain made José Leta an ideal place for a *maniele*, the local Native American word that refers to both African and Indian Maroon settlements. Most Maroons escaped from the numerous plantations built around Santo Domingo. Estates such as Sanate (west of Higuey) also employed some of the 12,000 enslaved Africans on the island in the 1540s (Vega and Deive 1980:151; Guitar 1998). Native Americans worked the sugarcane fields alongside Africans at Sanate and were amongst the 3,000 Maroons reported on Hispaniola in the mid-16th century (Deive 1989:43).

My archaeological survey of José Leta was designed to expand on García-Arévalo's previous survey by conducting excavations that identified the site layout and boundaries (Figure 3) (Arrom and García Arévalo 1986; Weik 1997b). A pedestrian survey by García Arévalo and his team located finds, such as incised clay pipes, copper bracelets, lithic tools, griddle fragments, potsherds, and metal weapons. These items were found on the surface down to a depth of 10 cm (Arrom and García Arévalo 1986:48).

My subsurface testing consisted of 15 shovel tests, spread over a 30 × 30 m area (Weik 1997b). No soil changes were evident in these shovel tests. The small number of Taino ceramics, bone, and metal artifacts recovered were of the type found earlier by García Arévalo during his fieldwork (Arrom and García Arévalo 1986: 48–55; Manuel A. García Arévalo, personal communication 1997). Most potsherds were gray, tan, or light reddish brown with small pebble inclusions (Figure 4). The surfaces of the sherds were either plain or incised, and the interior surfaces were plain. The sherds ranged from 3–13 mm thick. Only one flattened rim sherd was recovered. All other potsherds were unidentified forms, except for the one flat, thick griddle fragment. All sherds were located between surface level and 20 cm deep.

FIGURE 3. The José Leta site.

FIGURE 4. Pottery excavated from José Leta.

One radiocarbon date that García Arévalo obtained from pig remains places the copper bracelets, pipes, and metal weapons somewhere between 1641 and 1791 (Arrom and García Arévalo 1986). However, since many of these surface finds were not in a sealed stratigraphic context with the dated materials, the dates of the Maroon occupations are debatable. The Indigenous Meillacoid and Chicoid pottery fragments found in my excavations were produced from the 13th to the 16th century (Rouse 1992). A small group of aboriginal peoples who produced Amerindian pottery probably occupied José Leta during and prior to the arrival of African Maroons (Arrom and García Arévalo 1986:50; Weik 1997b). The lack of 16th- or 17th-century European artifacts or radiocarbon dates for José Leta suggests that the 16th-century African or Native American Maroons may have relied on indigenous pottery. Better stratigraphic evidence and more dateable artifacts are needed to discover the sequence or interrelations of cultural groups. The harshness of the terrain and the small number of people enslaved in the area may have prevented the group at José Leta from developing into a stable community.

The activities of the *cacique* Enriquillo, who ruled a 16th-century *maniele* in the mountains of Bahoruco (the southwestern part of the Dominican Republic), serve as a useful example of how José Leta may have evolved. Enriquillo organized successful plantation raids against the Spanish, liberating enslaved Africans in areas west of Santo Domingo (Arrom and García Arévalo 1986:24; Deive 1989). Later, African and Black Maroons from Saint Domingue and Hispaniola followed Enriquillo's example by establishing *manieles* in the same mountains of Bahoruco during the 18th century. José Leta may have started as a Taino camp and later became a hideout for Native American Maroons fleeing the Spanish. After Africans were enslaved on the island, they probably joined the Amerindians or replaced them, as in the case of the Maroons of Bahoruco.

Jamaica before British Colonial Rule

Around 1655, the British defeated Spanish forces in Jamaica. Coins that were recovered in the Maroon enclave called Nannytown hint at the fact that Jamaica was originally colonized by

the Spanish (Agorsah 1994). Hence, it is not surprising that the earliest Maroon leaders of Jamaica bore Spanish names, such as Juan de Bolas, that still mark the Jamaican countryside (Campbell 1990). Research on *marronage* during the British colonial period has uncovered a wide range of material culture at Maroon sites such as Nannytown and Accompong (Agorsah 1994).

Kofi Agorsah (1993:187) has suggested that intermixed yabba earthenware sherds, European-made items, and aboriginal artifacts are sufficient evidence to raise the possibility that Arawak peoples survived in Nannytown beyond the early period of destruction caused by disease and colonization in Jamaica (Agorsah 1993: 183). Historians traditionally argue that the 16th century was the period of the demise of Amerindians. Throughout the Americas, Amerindians were the first Maroons because they were the first to be enslaved. African peoples probably merged with aboriginal groups to form highly syncretic societies in a manner similar to the Black Garifuna of the Circum-Caribbean region or the Black Seminole of Florida (Bateman 1990; Mulroy 1993; for archaeological discussions of the Garifuna, see Fewkes 1922:20; Bullen and Bullen 1972:35–58; Gonzalez and Cheek 1980; Gonzalez 1988:24–37).

Patterns of settlement layout remain to be discovered in both Spanish- and British-period Maroon sites in Jamaica. Besides a stone structure built during a British military occupation and the Maroon occupation levels underneath it, other structural remains were not identified at Nannytown. Thus far the *quilombo* (Brazilian word for Maroon villages) called Ambrosio, located in south-central Brazil, is the only other location where archaeologists have discerned Maroon architectural features (Guimarães 1990; see also Castano 2000). A wealth of ceramics recovered from Nannytown, including European, Aboriginal, and locally made Afro-Jamaican ceramics await a comparative analysis like the one Smith conducted in Puerto Real (1995). Hopefully, more archaeologists will develop long-term projects devoted to both sides of the Atlantic, as Agorsah (1993) has done in West Africa and Jamaica. Researchers may then be able to make more explicit links to the material culture, ideas, and behaviors that created the archaeological record at Jamaican Maroon settlements (Agorsah 1993, 1994).

Palmares

Around the same time that the Spanish were attempting to hold off the advances of the British in Jamaica (1650), the Portuguese were defending their holdings in Brazil from the Dutch. During this period, Palmares, one of the largest Maroon societies in the Americas, was established (1605–1694) (Carneiro 1966). According to historians, Palmares had a status system with interdependent monarchy and military leadership, slavery, and birthrights (Cardoso 1983:154). K. R. Kent (1965) and Stuart Schwartz (1992: 104, 117) maintained that an African monarchy reigned over a culturally diverse population. There was a council of *quilombo* chiefs from each of the settlements of Palmares that met only to discuss collective issues such as defense (Cardoso 1983:155). Most settlements had African-derived names, while others were Amerindian or European (Kent 1965). European 17th-century ceramics, clay pipes, and Amerindian artifacts have been located on 10 sites in the mountains of northeastern Brazil believed to be Palmares (Orser 1992, 1994a; Allen 1994, 1998; Orser and Funari 2001).

Historians have debated whether Palmares was a monarchy, a state, or a confederation (Kent 1965; Schwartz 1992; Anderson 1996). The criteria used to apply these types of social organization need to be more closely scrutinized before their relevance to Maroons can be determined. At a basic level, it appears that elements of political centralization, social stratification, intervillage alliance, and monarchy existed at Palmares (Kent 1965; Carneiro 1966; Schwartz 1992). Palmares may have been an amalgamation of political forms instead of one or the other. It is critical that we avoid the typological and evolutionary approaches that merely place sociocultural groups into predetermined forms such as bands, tribes, chiefdoms, confederacies, or states (Renfrew 1984). These categories of social organization have limited applicability, for one cannot assume an archaeological site (or group of sites) is a socially unified or homogenous entity (Renfrew 1984:34, 40–41). The nature of inter- and intravillage politics at Palmares needs to be more clearly determined before an overarching political structure is proposed. Changes in sociopolitical structures also need to be theorized for Palmares' chronology, in light of the likely stresses caused by increasing populations, African to Amerindian ratios and male to female ratios.

Roger Bastide's (1979) idea of Palmares as a "culture mosaic," a mix of disparate African, Amerindian, and European culture traits and syncretisms has survived in the archaeological interpretations of Palmares (Orser 1994a:13). According to Richard Price (1979:26), the "culture mosaic" fails to recognize the diversity of Africans involved, confuses the "ideological commitment of things African with the putative possession of some sort of generalized African culture," and leaves out any discussion of the culture of former slaves who escaped from "plantation-forged Afro-American cultures." The mosaic metaphor seems to perpetuate a view that Maroon culture is the product of various scraps of African and Amerindian cultural traits instead of a new and unique Maroon sociocultural group (Allen 1998).

Ethnogenesis is a useful theoretical alternative that may help Maroon archaeology move beyond historical supplementation. The nature of ethnogenesis in the 10 villages of Palmares is based on the demographic composition of each village as well as on the nature of inter-African, African-Black, and African-Amerindian interchanges. Europeans were enemies and allies (Orser 1994b). A regional scale of analysis that maps out the proximity of Palmares to plantations, frontier settlements, and Amerindian sites is an important first step in understanding trade and military relations as well as cultural exchanges among various sites. Site-level studies that create a database of feature and artifact assemblage characteristics will help archaeologists who are examining Palmares' role in world systems (Orser 1994b, 1996) transcend document-based interpretations. The same applies for those studying ecological adaptation (Agorsah 1994), ethnicity (Arrom and García Arévalo 1986; Nichols 1988; Deagan and MacMahon 1995), or ethnogenesis at Maroon societies.

Florida

Florida was home to some of the latest-occurring Maroon groups in an area that was once a Latin American frontier. "La Florida" was a strategically important territory that the Spanish defended against other European powers from the 16th through the 19th centuries (Chatelain

1941). Blacks fled from British plantations in the Carolinas into Florida from as early as 1687 (Foster 1935; Tepaske 1975). In 1693, the Spanish crown angered the Anglo planters to the north by proclaiming religious sanctuary to runaway converts (Landers 1992). Without their freed Black and Maroon allies, the Spanish in Saint Augustine may not have withheld the British and American incursions of the colonial period. The military fortifications and villages of Fort Mosé were home to more than 80 freed Black militiamen and their families, whom the Spanish subsidized. A British raid destroyed the original village and fort in 1740. From 1753 to 1763, a second village and fort were inhabited. The British occupied St. Augustine from 1763–1783, stimulating the growth of plantation slavery in east Florida. The Spanish regained control of eastern Florida during the period 1783–1821. However, British trade, plantations, and military influence continued to affect Florida as much as Spanish colonialism.

Archaeological research and satellite imagery at Fort Mosé located the second fort as well as European and Native American artifacts (Marron 1989; Deagan and Landers 1999). Test excavations have also established data for a faunal study. It is not surprising that wild food sources were a large component of their diet or that supplies originating from ports antagonistic to Spain found their way to Fort Mosé (Reitz 1994; Deagan and Landers 1999). These Maroons had to be self-sufficient, for the ill-equipped Spanish colonial government, as the documents suggest, could only supply a small number of items (Landers 1990). Future archaeological research at Fort Mosé will hopefully discern the level of interhousehold variability, the types of activity areas, and other documentary and material clues to the Maroons' lives. Similar studies need to take place on the Florida panhandle, where previous research has uncovered the powder magazine and moat at the "Negro Fort" (Griffin 1950; Poe 1963). During the War of 1812, the British armed more than 300 blacks and 20 Amerindians at Negro Fort who harassed American planters until the U.S. Navy destroyed the fort in 1816 (Milligan 1974).

Unlike other Maroon societies, the settlement at Fort Mosé may be best conceived as a product of creolization. Documents describing godparent-

age links with Spanish colonists and baptisms are evidence of the important ties binding Africans to their European allies. Not all Maroons who escaped from South Carolina to St. Augustine became free during the Spanish period. Some were put to work under new masters, despite crown proclamations giving amnesty to all runaways who became Christian. Tensions between the Africans and Spaniards over issues such as cultural practices exposed the colonists' attempts to control their African neighbors. Fort Mosé's African cultural heritage is evident in some of the names and ethnicities described by Spanish documents (Landers 1992). But the discovery of medallions and other religious artifacts at Fort Mosé suggests that African and American-born Black people also integrated European practices and beliefs into their daily activities (Deagan and MacMahon 1995:35).

At about the same time that Blacks were establishing themselves at Fort Mosé, Maroons and enslaved blacks were settling alongside Seminole Indians in the Alachua Prairie of north central Florida (Figure 5) (Mulroy 1993). Estimates for Black Seminoles ranged from 500 to 1,400 people (Mulroy 1993). As with the Spaniards and British, Seminole Indians formed alliances with Maroons. Some have claimed that *Seminole* is a distortion of *cimarrón* (the Spanish word for Maroon) (Covington 1993). Historians agree that a major motivation behind the strong Amerindian resistance during the Seminole Wars with the United States (1812–1855) was the Indian-African link

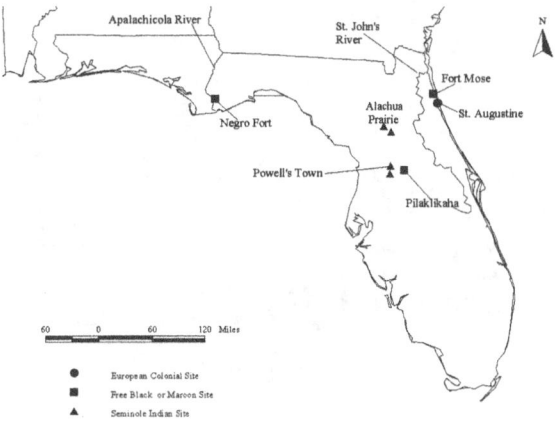

FIGURE 5. Colonial Florida sites.

(Covington 1993; Porter 1996). Blacks assisted the Seminole during military campaigns and during negotiations with the U.S. government. Africans were known on the frontiers for their interpreting skills. The historical literature is less clear on whether "Black Seminoles" were slaves, tribute-paying clients, or social equals to the Seminoles. Historians relying on Anglo travelers and soldiers' accounts have asserted that Blacks lived apart from Seminole Indians, in newly formed Black Seminole villages (Mulroy 1993; Porter 1996). Neglected Spanish documents related to St. Augustine and the Cuban fisherman who visited southwest Florida may help to explain the ethnogenesis of Florida Maroons by introducing new factors of change, by locating new Maroon communities that branched off from known settlements and by identifying emic and etic indicators of sociocultural identity (Saunt 1996). Maroons and freed Blacks probably had a diversity of relationships with the Seminole Indians during the 19th century (Sturtevant 1971; Saunt 1996).

At the Black Seminole site of Pilaklikaha, a surface survey by Jordon Herron (1994) has yielded 18th- and 19th-century ceramics, metal, glass, and stone artifacts. The preliminary findings of recent excavations have produced similar items (Figure 6). Pilaklikaha (1812?–1836) was a Black Seminole town where important Maroon leaders such as Abraham and the Seminole chief Micanopy spent much of their time (Mulroy 1993; Porter 1996). More subsurface testing is necessary for archaeologists to uncover the archaeological remains that will provide clues to the material basis of Black Seminole sociocultural formation. A database of settlement locations and site structures must be analyzed so that the spatial patterns and material assemblages can be compared for Black Seminole and Seminole Indian sites. Artifacts such as "Chattahootchee Brushed pottery" have served as diagnostics for Seminole Indian sites (Weisman 1987). Black Seminole archaeology will discover whether any sort of diagnostic artifacts such as colonowares will allow archaeologists to better distinguish Black Seminole and Seminole Indian sites. The nature of ethnogenesis, as a process of rapid cultural change and intermixture may convince archaeologists to move beyond looking for diagnostic artifacts and, instead, look for processes of interaction and syncretism within and between sites.

A final question that can be addressed by archaeologists studying Pilaklikaha is how did Africans and Amerindians organize their settlement layout? Did they attempt to draw on elements of spatial organization from European, African, or Native American settlements? Rectilinear or grid-like layouts were most closely associated with the settlements and forts of Europeans (Deagan 1996; for a perspective on rectilinear settlement plans found in Amerindian settlements, see Low 1993). One could also pursue this line of research in Brazil, examining whether the soldiers who sketched rectilinear-looking *quilombos* represented their own European ideals of Maroon settlements or the actual layouts of the sites (Kent 1965; Schwartz 1992). Native American patterns of settlement, such as the "square-ground" and "dispersed homestead" of the Creek and Seminole, are found in colonial Florida (Dickinson and Wayne 1985; Weisman 1987). In addition, Maroons may have attempted to re-create the slave housing patterns of plantations (Epperson 1999; Delle 2000; Singleton 2001:104). We must also consider African patterns of settlement, such as clustered compounds (Agorsah 1985). While these patterns only suggest broad cultural associations, they may be the first step in analyzing the social organization of space at Maroon archaeological sites. Future research on spatial aspects of sites may involve a range of ideological, environmental, and social factors beyond the scope of this essay (Hall 1969; Kuper 1972; Kus 1983; Low 1993).

FIGURE 6. Artifacts recovered from Pilaklikaha.

The histories of Jamaica and Hispaniola suggest Maroons situated their houses along hillsides in dispersed or cocentric patterns (Deive 1985:21; Campbell 1990). Defense needs were paramount to Maroons, and documents from South America to Florida speak of special fortifications such as pit traps and natural defenses such as swamps (Price 1979; Orser 1994a). Theresa Singleton's (2001) research at El Padre and Angerona suggests that the walls surrounding slave villages on Cuban plantations may have been erected to prevent escape or attacks by outsiders such as Maroons. Similarly, "defensive" features at Maroon communities could also be viewed as mechanisms to contain untrustworthy new recruits or those re-enslaved in maroon communities.

Seminole wars, labor obligations, kinship ties, and slave catchers all caused Maroons to migrate to central Florida sites such as Pilaklikaha during the 19th century. Maroon mobility may have created such a transitory material record that our methods may have to work at larger regional scales of analysis to pick up the material patterns of seminomadic groups. The archaeological record is made more complex by the possibility that Black Seminoles may have reoccupied Amerindian sites as they probably did at José Leta. Differentiating Maroon from Seminole Indian sites, as well as discerning the material signatures of sites inhabited by Africans and Seminoles, will be a challenging task.

Florida may have become a part of Latin America if the Creek Indians, who were kin and cultural ancestors to the Seminoles of Florida, had not been such numerous and effective allies to the British and American enemies of the Spanish. A segment of aboriginal peoples and Africans intermarried and rebelled against the Spaniards from their earliest interactions in the 16th century (Deagan 1985:297, 306). At other times, Africans and Amerindians fought each other in the service of the colonists (Porter 1996; Saunt 1996). To assume that relations always existed between Maroons and Seminole Indians would be a gross overgeneralization, as there were independent Maroon communities and Seminoles willing to return runaway slaves (Brown 1990; Saunt 1996). Ultimately, their defeat and deportment at the end of the 19th-century Seminole wars signaled the end of a significant historical pattern of Black and Indian alliances in Florida (Mulroy 1993; Porter 1996).

African Diaspora Archaeology: The Past, Present, and Future in Latin America

African Diaspora archaeology in Latin America functions in an atmosphere where African cultures and phenotypes are often not viewed in a positive light, and Blacks are not given much visibility in discussions of national history (Safa 1987; Wade 1993; Funari 1995). Indigenous peoples face a similar dilemma elsewhere in Latin America, as their past is erased or reduced to obscurity because of national policies of racism, ethnocide, and *Mestizaje* (Whitten 1976; Sued-Badillo 1995; Whitten and Torres 1998). African Diaspora populations are not mentioned once in recent edited works on the history of Latin American archaeology (Politis 1992; Oyuela-Caycedo 1994). Palmares is the only site mentioned in articles by Pedro Paulo Funari (1992, 1994) on the historical archaeology of South America (also Castano 2000). The state plays a prominent role in funding archaeology in Latin America (Ewen 2001:4). Thus, support for improved representation in history and archaeology must come from national governments. Unfortunately, state repression and violence have limited social criticism and the diversity of theoretical approaches in Latin America (Oyuela-Caycedo et al. 1997; Patterson 1997:375).

The Dominican Republic has provided me with sobering experiences regarding the obstacles that can impede research as well as some hope for what archaeologists can accomplish in Latin America. In the Dominican Republic and Haiti, local and foreign archaeologists committed to the African Diaspora have been active in the 1970s and early 1980s (Vega 1979; Arrom and García Arévalo 1986; Smith 1986, 1995; Encarnacion Jimenez 1993:35). The few studies of plantations are more architectural than anthropological in nature (Encarnacion Jimenez 1993:29–31). Funari (1995) has made the similar observations for South American historical archaeology. Financial and political factors drive the current government in the Dominican Republic to focus on European sites that symbolize the national heritage, such as La Isabela, one of Christopher Columbus's first settlements.

FIGURE 7. The ruins of Sanate.

Meanwhile, the mammoth remains of Sanate, an early plantation built by African and Indian slaves, is left awaiting decay (Figure 7). Taino sites receive some attention (Rouse 1992); however, my summer survey in the east has shown me that there is a multitude of undocumented Taino sites that end up as fodder for impoverished local peasants whose profit motives for artifact trading outweigh academic concerns.

This small-scale artifact selling is a reminder that we need to actively encourage local stewardship of archaeological resources. Archaeologists have to seriously consider their roles as "wealthy" foreigners whose success and local support may rest on the expedient allocation of resources and employment positions. In addition, developing long-term collaborative projects with local scholars and research centers (Funari 1995) is an important step in building a responsible and critical historical dialogue with our hosts abroad who do not have the government support that is so abundant in the United States.

Conclusion

The long duration of slavery, diversity of cultural groups, and geographical expansiveness of Latin America all make for challenging and unique opportunities for archaeology. Research on free Blacks and Maroons is beginning to mature in Latin America. Singleton's (2001) Cuban plantation studies are helping to fill an important gap in research and bringing to light the efforts of scholars isolated because of modern global politics. New publications concerning places such as Buenos Aires are making

African and Native American contributions to colonial urban life in other regions more visible (Schavelzon 1999:120–131, 139–143). Comparative works on pottery and pipes will benefit from these efforts (Schavelzon 1999:142). While my review of African Diaspora archaeology in Latin America does not fully cover all of the research occurring at the present, it does reflect the general trend for much of Latin America.

In order for archaeology to advance in Latin America, groundwork needs to be laid at individual sites. Theories of social organization and ethnogenesis must be generated so that sociocultural complexity can be examined. Regional approaches that link slaves, colonists, free people of color, Amerindians, and Maroons are necessary for African Diaspora archaeology to proceed on a broader methodological footing than traditional plantation studies in the United States and Caribbean. African Diaspora archaeology in places like the Caribbean will help address the "relative lack of Spanish colonial research" in the region (see the review of Spanish colonial archaeology in Ewen 2001:4).

It remains to be seen whether the new or different sociocultural groups created during Maroon ethnogenesis created new artifact types, production techniques, and spatial relations. Perhaps the changes brought by ethnogenesis will be more subtle and related to different artifact uses and meanings, as opposed to the creation of different items and forms. Another possibility is that Maroon sites will manifest such a mixed, heterogeneous, and random collection of artifacts and feature distributions that the archaeological record will defy our attempts to recognize patterns or intrasite material variability. It is possible that randomness is a part of the patterns we are seeking. Maroon sites were arenas of meaning, and use must be placed within the wider field of ethnogenetic processes that trace origins, migrations, subgroup divergences, and ethnocide.

Issues such as Indian-African interaction will continue to challenge us to be more critical and creative in our analyses of the African Diaspora. Technological and cultural innovations, such as the Christophe Plain pottery at Puerto Real, were facilitated by intercultural exchanges among Africans, Amerindians, and Europeans. Amerindian artifacts have been found in almost all of the Maroon sites that have been excavated in the Americas. Hence, Native American sites may serve as guides in the location of Maroon sites. Some Native American sites could be reinterpreted in light of the known or possible presence of Africans. The archaeology of frontier Maroon settlements such as Pilaklikaha will help us theorize about the gaps in our knowledge of both Afro-Maroon and Amerindian ethnogenesis. As home to the largest number of Maroon sites in North America as well as some of the first archaeological studies of enslaved Africans (Fairbanks 1984), Florida is an ideal setting for African Diaspora archaeology. It must not be forgotten that Florida was originally La Florida, a strategically important border area for the Spanish colonies of Latin America. A greater understanding of the contribution of Latin America to all parts of the Western hemisphere must be generated in the United States and Europe, so that those with access to funding and political influence can help provide information and resources for the critical production of knowledge in Latin America.

ACKNOWLEDGMENTS

An earlier version of this paper was presented to The Society for Historical and Underwater Archaeology meetings in Atlanta, Georgia, during January 1998. I would like to thank Kathryn Burns, Kathleen Deagan, Irma McClaurin, and Peter Schmidt for their critical comments on drafts of this paper. Special thanks to the Center for Latin American studies at the University of Florida and the Tinker Field Research Grant program, both of which were instrumental in helping me fund my research in the Dominican Republic. I also appreciate the editing advice that some of the participants at the SHA meetings generously offered. Finally, I want to thank Larry McKee and Maria Franklin for organizing the conference session that inspired this paper and for their careful editing help.

REFERENCES

AGORSAH, KOFI E.
1985   Excavation in the North Volta Basin. *West Africa Journal of Archaeology,* 15:11–40.
1993   Archaeology and Resistance History in the Caribbean. *The African Archaeological Review,* 11:175–196.
1994   Archaeology of Maroon Settlements in Jamaica. In *Maroon Heritage: Archaeological, Ethnographic, and Historical Perspectives,* Kofi E. Agorsah, editor, pp. 163–187. Canoe Press, Kingston, Jamaica.

ALLEN, SCOTT
1994   Africanisms, Mosaics, and Creativity: The Historical Archaeology of Palmares. Master's thesis, Department of Anthropology, Brown University, Providence, RI.
1998   A "Cultural Mosaic" at Palmares? Grappling with the Historical Archaeology of a Seventeenth-Century Brazilian Quilombo. In *Cultura Material e Archeologia Historica,* Pedro A. Funari, editor, pp. 141–178. Instituto de Filosofia e Ciencias Humanas Universidade Estadual de Campinas.

ANDERSON, ROBERT
1996   The Quilombo of Palmares: A New Overview of a Maroon State in Seventeenth-Century Brazil. *Journal of Latin American Studies,* 28(3):545–566.

ARMSTRONG, DOUGLAS V.
1990   *The Old Village and the Great House.* University of Illinois Press, Chicago.

ARROM, JOSÉ JUAN, AND MANUEL A. GARCÍA ARÉVALO
1986   *Cimarron.* Fundacion García Arévalo, Santo Domingo, Dominican Republic.

BASTIDE, ROGER
1979   The Other Quilombos. In *Maroon Societies: Rebel Slave Communities in the Americas,* Richard Price, editor, pp. 191–201. Anchor Books, New York, NY.

BATEMAN, REBECCA B.
1990   Africans and Indians: A Comparative Study of the Black Carib and Black Seminole. *Ethnohistory,* 37(1): 5–23.

BRATHWAITE, KAMAU
1976   *The Development of Creole Society in Jamaica.* Oxford University Press, Oxford.

BROWN, CANTER, JR.
1990   The "Sarrazota, or Runaway Negro Plantations": Tampa Bay's First Black Community, 1812–1821. *Tampa Bay History,* 12(2):5–19.

BULLEN, RIPLEY, AND ADELAIDE BULLEN
1972   Archaeological Investigations on St. Vincent and the Grenadines, West Indies. *American Studies Report,* 8. William L. Bryant Foundation, University of Central Florida, Orlando.

CAMPBELL, MAVIS C.
1990   *The Maroons of Jamaica, 1655–1796.* Africa World Press, Trenton, NJ.

CARDOSO, GERALD
1983   *Negro Slavery in the Sugar Plantations of Veracruz and Pernambuco, 1550–1680: A Comparative Study.* University Press of America, Washington, DC.

CARNEIRO, EDISON
1966   *O quilombos dos Palmares.* Editôra Civilização Brasileira, Rio de Janeiro, Brazil.

CASTANO, ANA M. MANSILLA
  2000 Patrimonio AfroAmericano en Brasil: Arqueologia
        de los Quilombos. *Artículos,* 2(2). September.
        <www.ucm.es/info/arqueoweb/numero2_2b/
        articulo2_2C.htm>.

CHATELAIN, VERNE E.
  1941 *The Defenses of Spanish Florida: 1565–1763.* Carnegie
        Institution of Washington Publication, Washington,
        DC.

COVINGTON, JAMES W.
  1993 *The Seminoles of Florida.* University Press of Florida,
        Gainesville.

CRANE, BRIAN
  1993 *Colono Ware and Criollo Ware Pottery from Charleston,
        South Carolina, and San Juan, Puerto Rico, in
        Comparative Perspective.* Doctoral dissertation,
        Department of American Civilization, University of
        Pennsylvania. University Microfilms International,
        Ann Arbor, MI.

DAVIDSON, DAVID M.
  1966 Negro Slave Control and Resistance in Colonial Mexico,
        1519–1650. *Hispanic American Historic Review,* 46(3):
        248–50.

DAWDY, SHANNON LEE
  2000 Understanding Cultural Change through the Vernacular:
        Creolization in Louisiana. *Historical Archaeology,*
        34(3):107–123.

DEAGAN, KATHLEEN
  1983 *Spanish St. Augustine: The Archaeology of a Colonial
        Creole Community.* Academic Press, New York,
        NY.
  1985 Spanish-Indian Interaction in Sixteenth-Century
        Florida and Hispaniola. In *Cultures in Contact,*
        William Fitzhugh, editor, pp. 281–317. Smithsonian
        Institution Press, Washington, DC.
  1996 Colonial Transformation: Euro-American Cultural
        Genesis in the Early Spanish American Colonies.
        Journal of Anthropological Research, 52(2):135–
        161.

DEAGAN, KATHLEEN A., AND JANE LANDERS
  1999 Fort Mosé: Earliest Free African-American Town in the
        United States. In *I, Too, Am America: Archaeological
        Studies of African-American Life,* Theresa Singleton,
        editor, pp. 261–282. University of Virginia Press,
        Charlottesville.

DEAGAN, KATHLEEN, AND DARCIE MACMAHON
  1995 *Fort Mosé : Colonial America's Black Fortress of
        Freedom.* University Press of Florida, Gainesville.

DEFRANCE, SUSAN
  1996 Iberian Foodways in the Moquequa and Torata Valleys
        of Southern Peru. *Historical Archaeology,* 30(3):
        20–48.

DEIVE, CARLOS ESTEBAN
  1985 *Los Cimarrones del Maniel de Neiba, historia y
        etnografia.* Publicaciones del Banco Central de la
        Republica Dominicana, Santo Domingo.
  1989 *Los Guerrilleros Engross.* Fundacion Cultural
        Dominicana, Santo Domingo, Republica Domingo.

DELLE, JAMES
  2000 The Material and Cognitive Dimensions of Creolization
        in Nineteenth-Century Jamaica. *Historical
        Archaeology,* 34(3):56–72.

DICKINSON, MARTIN, AND LUCKY B. WANE
  1985 The Seminole Indian Dispersed Settlement Pattern:
        An Example from Marion County, Florida. In *Indians,
        Colonists, and Slaves: Essays in Memory of Charles
        H. Fairbanks,* Kenneth Johnson, Jonathan Leader, and
        Robert Wilson, editors. Florida Anthropology Student
        Association, University of Florida, Gainesville.

EBANKS, RODE RICK
  1984 Jamaica's Ma Lo. *Ceramics Monthly,* 32:63–65.

EMERSON, MATTHEW C.
  1988 *Decorated Clay Tobacco Pipes from Chesapeake.*
        Doctoral dissertation, Department of Anthropology,
        University of California, Berkeley. University
        Microfilms International, Ann Arbor, MI.
  1999 African Inspirations in a New World Art and Artifact:
        Decorated Tobacco Pipes from the Chesapeake. In *I,
        Too, Am America: Archaeological Studies of African-
        American Life,* Theresa Singleton, editor, pp. 47–82.
        University of Virginia Press, Charlottesville.

ENCARNACION JIMENEZ, PEDRO
  1993 Los Negros Esclavos: En la Historia de Bayona,
        Manoguayaba y Otros Poblados. Editora Alfa y
        Omega, Santo Domingo, Republica Dominicana.

EPPERSON, TERRENCE W.
  1999 Constructing Difference: The Social and Spatial Order
        of the Chesapeake Plantation. In *I, Too, Am America:
        Archaeological Studies of African-American Life,*
        Theresa Singleton, editor, pp. 159–172. University
        of Virginia Press, Charlottesville.

EWEN, CHARLES R.
  2001 Historical Archaeology in the Colonial Spanish
        Caribbean. In *Island Lives: Historical Archaeologies
        of the Caribbean,* Paul Farnsworth, editor, pp. 3–20.
        University of Alabama Press, Tuscaloosa.

FAIRBANKS, CHARLES
  1984 The Plantation Archaeology of the Southeastern Coast.
        Historical Archaeology, 18(1):1–14.

FERGUSON, LELAND
  1980 Looking for the "Afro" in Colono-Indian. In
        Archaeological Perspectives on Ethnicity in America,
        Robert L. Schuyler, editor, pp. 14–28. Baywood,
        Farmingdale, NY.

1991   Struggling with Pots in Colonial South Carolina. In *The Archaeology of Inequality*, Robert Paynter and Randall H. McGuire, editors, pp. 28–39. Basil Blackwell, Oxford.

1992   *Uncommon Ground.* Smithsonian Institution Press, Washington, DC.

2000   Introduction. *Historical Archaeology,* 34(3):5–9.

FEWKES, J. WALTER

1922   A Prehistoric Island Culture Area of America. *Annual Report of the BAE,* (1912–13) 34:10–12, 35–281.

FORBES, JACK

1993   *Africans and Native Americans: The Language of Race and the Evolution of Red-Black Peoples.* University of Illinois Press, Chicago.

FOSTER, GEORGE

1960   *Culture and Conquest: America's Spanish Heritage.* Quadrangle Books, Chicago, IL.

FOSTER, LAURENCE

1935   Negro-Indian Relationships in the Southeast. Doctoral dissertation, University of Pennsylvania.

FUNARI, PEDRO PAULO A.

1992   La Arqueología en Brasil. In *Arqueología en América Latina Hoy,* Gustavo Politis, pp. 57–69. Biblioteca Banco Popular.

1994   South American Historical Archaeology. *Historical Archaeology in Latin America,* 2:1–14.

1995   The Archaeology of Palmares and Its Contribution to the Understanding of the History of African-American Culture. *Historical Archaeology in Latin America,* 7: 1–41.

GIBSON, CHARLES

1966   *Spain in America.* Harper and Row, New York, NY.

GILROY, PAUL

1993   *The Black Atlantic: Modernity and Double Consciousness.* Harvard University Press, Cambridge, MA.

GONZALEZ, NANCY

1988   *Sojourners of the Caribbean.* University of Illinois Press, Chicago.

GONZALEZ, NANCY, AND CHARLES D. CHEEK

1980   Black Carib Settlement Patterns in Early Nineteenth-Century Honduras: The Search for a Livelihood. Paper presented at the annual meetings for The American Anthropological Association, Washington, DC.

GRIFFIN, JOHN W.

1950   An Archaeologist at Fort Gadsden. *Florida Historical Quarterly,* 28(4):255–261.

GUIMARÃES, CARLOS MAGNO

1990   O Quilombo do Ambrósio: lenda, documentos e arqueologia. *Estudos Ibero-Americanos,* 16:161–174.

GUITAR, LYNNE A.

1998   Cultural Genesis: Relationships among Africans and Spaniards in Rural Hispaniola, First Half of the Sixteenth Century. Doctoral dissertation, Vanderbilt University, Nashville, TN.

GUNDAKER, GREY

2000   Discussion: Creolization, Complexity, and Time. *Historical Archaeology,* 34(3):124–133.

HALL, EDWARD T.

1969   *Hidden Dimension.* Doubleday & Co, Garden City, New York, NY.

HARRIS, JOSEPH E. (EDITOR)

1982   *Global Dimensions of the African Diaspora.* Howard University Press, Washington, DC.

HARRISON, FAYE V.

1995   The Persistent Power of "Race" in the Cultural and Political Economy of Racism. *Annual Review of Anthropology,* 24:47–74.

HAVISER, JAY B. (EDITOR)

1998   *African Sites Archaeology in the Caribbean.* Markus Wiener Publishers, Princeton, NJ.

HERRON, JORDON

1994   Black Seminole Settlement Pattern. Master's thesis, Department of Anthropology, University of South Carolina, Columbia.

HOETINK, H.

1985   "Race" and Color in the Caribbean. In *Caribbean Contours,* Sidney Mintz and Sally Price, editors, pp. 55–84. Johns Hopkins University Press, Baltimore, MD.

HOFFMAN, KATHLEEN

1997   Cultural Development in La Florida. *Historical Archaeology,* 31(1):24–35.

JOYNER, CHARLES

1984   *Down by the Riverside: A South Carolina Slave Community.* University of Illinois Press, Chicago.

KENT, R. K.

1965   Palmares: An African State in Brazil. *Journal of African History,* 6:161–175.

KING, JOHANNES

1979   Guerrilla Warfare: A Bush Negro View. In *Maroon Societies: Rebel Slave Communities in the Americas,* Richard Price, editor, pp. 298–304. Anchor Books, New York, NY.

KNIGHT, VERNON

1985   Tuckabatchee: Archaeological Investigations at an Historic Creek Town, Elmore County, Alabama. Manuscript, Office of Archaeological Research, Alabama State Museum of Natural History, University of Alabama, Tuscaloosa.

Perspectives from Historical Archaeology: African Diaspora Archaeology   **107**

KUPER, HILDA
1972 The Language of Sites in the Politics of Space. *American Anthropologist,* 74:411–425.

KUS, SUSAN
1983 The Social Representation of Space: Dimensioning the Cosmological and the Quotidian. In *Archaeological Hammers and Theories,* J. Moore and A. Keene, editors, pp. 276–298. Academic Press, New York, NY.

LANDERS, JANE
1990 African and Indian Interaction in Spanish Florida. Paper presented at the annual meeting of the Organization of American Historians, Washington, DC.
1992 Fort Mosé: Gracia Real de Santa Teresa de Mosé, A Free Black Town in Spanish Colonial Florida. *American Historical Review,* 95(1).

LOCKHART, JAMES
1968 *Spanish Peru, 1532–1560: A Social History.* Reprinted in 1994 by the University of Wisconsin Press, Madison.

LOCKHART, JAMES, AND STUART SCHWARTZ
1983 *Early Latin America: A History of Colonial Spanish America and Brazil.* Cambridge University Press, New York, NY.

LOVE, EDGAR
1970 Legal Restrictions on Afro-Indian Relations in Colonial Mexico. *Journal of Negro History,* 55:137.

LOW, SETH M.
1993 Cultural Meaning of the Plaza: The History of the Spanish-American Gridplan-Plaza Urban Design. In *The Cultural Meaning of Urban Space.* Bergin and Garvey, London.

MARRON, JOHN
1989 Preliminary Report on the Excavations at the Site of Fort Mosé, 1988. Florida Museum of Natural History, Gainesville.

MILLIGAN, JOHN D.
1974 Slave Rebelliousness and the Florida Maroons. *Prologue,* 6:4–18.

MINTZ, SIDNEY, AND RICHARD PRICE
1992 *The Birth of African-American Culture,* 2nd edition. Beacon Press, Boston, MA.

MONTEJO, ESTEBAN
1968 *The Autobiography of a Runaway Slave.* Pantheon Books, NY.

MOORE, JOHN
1994 Ethnogenetic Theories of Human Evolution. *Research and Exploration,* 10(1):10–37.

MÖRNER, MAGNUS
1967 *Race Mixture in the History of Latin American.* Little and Brown, Boston, MA.

MULLINS, PAUL R., AND ROBERT PAYNTER
2000 Representing Colonizers: An Archaeology of Creolization, Ethnogenesis, and Indigenous Material Culture among the Haida. *Historical Archaeology,* 34(3):73–84.

MULROY, KEVIN
1993 *Freedom on the Border: The Seminole Maroons in Florida, the Indian Territory, Coahuila, and Texas.* Texas Tech University Press, Lubbock.

NASH, JUNE
1980 Aztec Women: The Transition from Status to Class in Empire and Colony. In *Women and Colonization: Anthropological Perspectives,* Mona Etienne and Eleanor Leacock, editors, pp. 134–148. Praeger, New York, NY.

NICHOLS, ELAINE
1988 No Easy Run to Freedom: Maroons in the Great Dismal Swamp of North Carolina and Virginia, 1677–1850. Master's thesis, Department of Anthropology, University of South Carolina, Columbia.

ORSER, CHARLES
1992 In Search of Zumbi: Preliminary Archaeological Research at the Serra da Barriga, State of Alagoas, Brazil. Manuscript, Sociology and Anthropology, Illinois State University, Normal.
1994a Searching Palmares at the Serra da Barriga, Brazil. *National Geographic Research and Exploration,* 10(4): 480–482.
1994b Toward a Global Historical Archaeology: An Example from Brazil. *Historical Archaeology,* 28(1):5–22.
1996 *A Historical Archaeology of the Modern World.* Plenum Press, New York, NY.

ORSER, CHARLES E., AND PEDRO PAULO A. FUNARI
2001 Archaeology and Slave Resistance and Rebellion. *World Archaeology,* 33(1):61–72.

OYUELA-CAYCEDO, AUGUSTO (EDITOR)
1994 *History of Latin American Archaeology.* Worldwide Archareology Series 15. Avebury, Brookfield, VT.

OYUELA-CAYCEDO, AGUSTO, ARMANDO ANAYA, CARLOS ELERA, AND LIDIO VALDEZ
1997 Social Archaeology in Latin America? Comments to T. C. Patterson. *American Antiquity,* 62(2):365–374.

PATTERSON, THOMAS C.
1997 A Reply to A. Oyuela-Caycedo, A. Anaya, C. G. Elera, and L. M. Valdez. *American Antiquity,* 62(2): 375–376.

PEGUERO GUZMAN, LUIS ALEJANDRO
1994 Contribucion del cimarronaje al desarrollo del campesinado y la cultura popular. *Boletin,* Ano. XX, Num. 26, pp. 112–132. Museo del Hombre Dominicano, Santo Domingo, Republica Dominicana.

POE, STEPHEN
1963 Archaeological Excavations at Fort Gadsden, Florida. *Notes in Anthropology,* 8.

POLITIS, GUSTAVO (EDITOR)
    1992   *Arqueología en América Latina Hoy.* Biblioteca Banco
           Popular, Bogota, Columbia.

PORTER, KENNETH W.
    1996   *The Black Seminoles.* Revised and edited by Alcione
           M. Amos and Thomas P. Senter. University Press of
           Florida, Gainesville.

POSNANSKY, MERRICK
    1989   West African Reflections on African-American
           Archaeology. Manuscript, African Studies Center,
           University of California, Los Angeles.

PRICE, RICHARD
    1979   *Maroon Societies: Rebel Slave Communities in the
           Americas.* Anchor Books, New York, NY.

REEVES, MATTHEW BRUCE
    1997   *By Their Own Labor: Enslaved Africans' Survival
           Strategies on Two Jamaican Plantations.* Doctoral
           dissertation, Department of Anthropology, Syracuse
           University. University Microfilms International, Ann
           Arbor, MI.

REITZ, ELIZABETH J.
    1994   Zooarchaeological Analysis of a Free African
           Community: Gracia Real de Santa Teresa de Mosé.
           Historical Archaeology, 28(1):23–40.

RENFREW, COLIN
    1984   *Approaches to Social Archaeology.* Harvard University
           Press, Cambridge, MA.

RICE, PRUDENCE M., AND GREG C. SMITH
    1989   The Spanish Colonial Wineries of Moquegua, Peru.
           Historical Archaeology, 23(2):41–49.

RICE, PRUDENCE M., AND SARA L. VAN BECK
    1993   The Spanish Colonial Kiln Tradition of Moquegua,
           Peru. *Historical Archaeology,* 27(4):65–81.

ROSENBLATT, ANGEL
    1954   *La Poblacion Indigena y el Mestizaje en America.*
           Editorial Nova, Buenos Aires.

ROUSE, IRVING
    1992   *The Tainos: Rise and Decline of the People Who Greeted
           Columbus.* Yale University Press, New Haven, CT.

SAFA, HELEN
    1987   Popular Culture, National Identity, and Race in
           the Caribbean. *New West Indian Guide,* 61(3/4):
           115–126.

SATTLER, RICHARD A.
    1996   Remnant, Renegades, and Runaways: Seminole
           Ethnogenesis Reconsidered. In *History, Power, and
           Identity: Ethnogenesis in the Americas, 1492–1992,*
           Jonathan D. Hill, editor, pp. 36–69. University of Iowa
           Press, Iowa City.

SAUER, CARL
    1966   *The Early Spanish Main.* University of California
           Press, Berkeley.

SAUNT, CLAUDIO
    1996   *A New Order of Things: Creek and Seminoles in the
           Deep South Interior, 1733–1816.* Doctoral dissertation,
           History, Duke University, Durham, NC. University
           Microfilms International, Ann Arbor, MI.

SCHAVELZON, DANIEL
    1999   *The Historical Archaeology of Buenos Aires.* Translated
           by Alex Lomonaco. Kluwer Academic/Plenum
           Publishers, New York, NY.

SCHMIDT, PETER, AND THOMAS PATTERSON (EDITORS)
    1995   *Making Alternative Histories.* School of American
           Research Press, Santa Fe, NM.

SCHWARTZ, STUART B.
    1992   *Slaves, Peasants, and Rebels: Reconsidering Brazilian
           Slavery.* University of Illinois Press, Urbana.

SHEPPERSON, GEORGE
    1976   Introduction. In *The African Diaspora: Interpretative
           Essays,* Martin L. Kilson and Robert I. Rotberg, editors,
           pp. 1–10. Harvard University Press, Cambridge,
           MA.

SINGLETON, THERESA A.
    1985   Introduction. In *The Archaeology of Slavery and
           Plantation Life,* Theresa A. Singleton, editor, pp.
           1–14. Academic Press, Orlando, FL.
    2001   Slavery and Spatial Dialectics on Cuban Coffee
           Plantations. *World Archaeology,* 33(1):98–114.

SMITH, CHARLES GREG
    1986   Non-European Pottery at the Sixteenth-Century Spanish
           Site of Puerto Real, Haiti. Master's thesis, Department
           of Anthropology, University of Florida, Gainesville.
    1995   Indians and Africans at Puerto Real: The Ceramic
           Evidence. In *Puerto Real: The Archaeology of a
           Sixteenth-Century Spanish Town in Hispaniola,* Kathy
           Deagan, editor, pp. 335–372. University of Florida
           Press, Gainesville.
    1997   Hispanic, Andean, and African Influences in the
           Moquegua Valley of Southern Peru. *Historical
           Archaeology,* 31(1):74–83.

SOTO DAVID, MOISÉS
    1989   Un Hallazgo Arqueologico: Armas y Objetos Del Negro
           Cimarron. *Boletin del Museo del Hombre Dominicana,*
           Ano XVI, No. 22.

STAHL, ANN B.
    1999   The Archaeology of Global Encounters Viewed from
           Banda, Ghana. *African Archaeological Review,* 16(1):
           5–81.

STURTEVANT, WILLIAM C.
    1971   Creek into Seminole. In *North American Indians in
           Historical Perspective,* Eleanor Burke Leacock and
           Nancy Oestreich Lurie, editors, pp. 92–128. Random
           House, New York, NY.

SUED-BADILLO, JALIL
1995 The Theme of the Indigenous in the National Projects of the Hispanic Caribbean. In *Making Alternative Histories*, Peter Schmidt and Thomas Patterson, editors. School of American Research, Santa Fe, NM.

TEPASKE, JOHN J.
1975 The Fugitive Slave: Intercolonial Rivalry and Spanish Slave Policy, 1687–1764. In *Eighteenth-Century Florida and Its Borderlands*, Samuel Proctor, editor, pp. 1–12. University Press of Florida, Gainesville.

TÖLÖLYAN, KHACHIG
1996 Rethinking Diaspora(s): Stateless Power in the Transnational Moment. *Diaspora,* 5(1):3–35.

VEGA, BERNARDO
1979 Arqueologia de Los Cimarrones del Maniel del Bahoruco. *Boletin del Museo del Hombre Dominicana,* 12:11–48.

VEGA, BERNARDO, AND CARLOS ESTEBAN DEIVE
1980 Toponimos Dominicanos Vinculados a Esclavos y a Africa. *Boletin,* 14:147–164. Museo del Hombre Dominicano, Santo Domingo, Republica Dominicana.

WADE, PETER
1993 *Blackness and Race Mixture: The Dynamics of Racial Identity in Colombia.* Johns Hopkins University Press, Baltimore, MD.

WEIK, TERRANCE
1997a The Archaeology of Maroon Societies in the Americas: Resistance, Cultural Continuity, and Transformation in the African Diaspora. *Historical Archaeology,* 31(2): 81–92.

1997b Maroon Archaeology in the Dominican Republic: A Five-Week Research Project in the Dominican Republic. Report to the Tinker Foundation and the Center for Latin American Studies, from the Department of Anthropology, University of Florida, Gainesville.

WEISMAN, BRENT RICHARDS
1987 *Like Beads on a String: A Culture History of the Seminole Indians in North Peninsular Florida.* University of Alabama Press, Tuscaloosa.

WHITTEN, NORMAN
1976 *Sacha Runa: Ethnicity and Adaptation of Ecuadorian Jungle Quichua.* University of Illinois Press, Urbana.
1995 Ethnogenesis. In *Encyclopedia of Cultural Anthropology*, Vol. 2, David Levinson and Melvin Ember, editors, pp. 407–411. Henry Holt and Company, New York, NY.

WHITTEN, NORMAN, AND ARLENE TORRES
1998 General Introduction: To Forge the Future in the Fires of the Past: An Interpretive Essay of Racism, Domination, Resistance, and Liberation. In *Blackness in Latin America and the Caribbean: Social Dynamics and Cultural Transformations*, vol. 1, Norman Whitten and Arlene Torres, editors, pp. 3–33. Indiana University Press, Bloomington.

TERRANCE WEIK
DEPARTMENT OF ANTHROPOLOGY
1350 TURLINGTON HALL
UNIVERSITY OF FLORIDA
GAINESVILLE, FL 32611

PAUL FARNSWORTH

The Influence of Trade on Bahamian Slave Culture

ABSTRACT

The Bahamian plantations of Wade's Green and Promised Land are compared using analyses of ceramics, tobacco pipes, and beads. The differences in the distributions revealed are explained by each plantation's market access. The research is significant because it illustrates conditions where economic models commonly used to interpret archaeological data are mediated by local conditions. Distance and isolation from the point of distribution restricted access to goods and accentuated the planter's control over the goods available to the slaves in the Bahamas.

Introduction

British Loyalists fleeing the 13 American colonies after the Revolution were primarily resettled in England, Canada, Jamaica, and the Bahamas, with smaller populations scattered on other islands in the West Indies. Of the approximately 100,000 people who fled, over 6,000 settled in the Bahamas (Peters 1960; Siebert 1975). The first large group of Loyalists arrived in the Bahamas in 1783 from New York. However, most of the Loyalists who were granted land in the British colony of the Bahama Islands had originally fled from the Southeast, Georgia and the Carolinas in particular, arriving in the Bahamas in 1784 and 1785 by way of East Florida (Craton and Saunders 1992:188).

The Loyalist influx dramatically transformed the Bahamas because the Loyalists brought with them their plantation culture from the Southeast and thousands of slaves to work the previously uncultivated islands (Craton 1986). After a brief period of prosperity growing cotton as the principle cash crop, the combination of poor soils and insect attack led to the decline of the plantations in the early years of the 19th century.

Many planters returned to the southeastern United States, where persecution was no longer a threat. Clearing new land for cotton and raking salt where possible, some of the Bahamian plantations survived and expanded, while most

were abandoned. By the 1820s, cotton production in the Bahamas was minimal, and the surviving plantations practiced mixed agriculture, with salt becoming their primary economic resource. Emancipation of the slaves in 1834 ended the already moribund plantation system (Saunders 1983, 1990).

Archaeological research on the Loyalist period in the Bahamas is beginning to provide new insights on the short-lived plantation period. Research at Wade's Green and Promised Land plantations has provided a new source of information on the ways of life of the Loyalists and the enslaved people they brought with them from America or purchased from slave traders in Nassau. This paper presents one aspect of the results, the significant impact of the isolation of many of the plantations relative to Nassau, the only major source of manufactured goods in the Bahamas.

The research clearly illustrates conditions where economic models commonly used to interpret archaeological data are mediated by local conditions. Neither ethnicity nor socioeconomic factors are the primary variables that explain the ceramic distributions at Wade's Green plantation. The distance and isolation from the point of distribution in Nassau restricted access to goods and accentuated the planter's control over the goods available to the slaves.

After developing this hypothesis from the Wade's Green data in 1989, it was necessary to test it against data from other Bahamian plantations. Unfortunately, although there had been archaeological research published on four Loyalist plantations in the Bahamas (Gerace 1982, 1987; Lawlor 1985; Attrill 1986; cf. Turner 1992), none contained sufficient detailed information to evaluate the hypothesis. Therefore, in 1993, Promised Land plantation was studied, in part, to test the hypothesis.

Promised Land plantation is located on New Providence Island, with easy access to Nassau. If restricted access to goods due to isolation explains the ceramic distributions at Wade's Green, then the distributions at Promised Land should match those found on plantations where access to goods was not restricted. However, if

Historical Archaeology, 1996, 30(4):1–23.
Permission to reprint required.

the same ceramic distributions as at Wade's Green plantation were observed, then the implication would be that factors governing ceramic supply to the colony as a whole were involved.

The Promised Land distributions differed from the Wade's Green distributions and matched those predicted from previous research in the southeastern United States. This supports the hypothesis that it was the remote location and the resultant restrictions on access to goods that were responsible for the Wade's Green ceramic distributions.

The same factors also affected the availability of other goods. Archaeologically, tobacco is the most readily discernible. However, the distribution of tobacco pipes indicates that, while the planter and overseer had access to tobacco, and distributed it to favored slaves working in the kitchen, the planter could effectively prevent the bulk of the slave population from obtaining access to it if he so chose, due to the absence of alternative sources of supply. As a result, the planter's control over some resources was enhanced compared to less isolated locations in the New World.

Glass beads are frequently found on slave sites. However, they were not found in either excavation discussed here. This may indicate that access to some goods was a problem throughout the colony, and not just on the remote islands. Why this should be so, especially for an easily transportable object like beads, remains ambiguous at present. However, their absence serves as a reminder that other, less tangible, perishable materials may also have been in short supply in this remote corner of the British Empire in the late 18th and early 19th centuries.

Transatlantic and Caribbean Trade Patterns

Understanding the distribution of goods found on the plantations in the Bahamas, requires a brief overview of the nature of trade between Britain, its colonies, foreign countries, and their colonies. In particular, four specific trade relations are of importance: 1) between Britain and its colonies in the Caribbean, which includes the Bahamas; 2) between British colonies in the Caribbean; 3) between Britsh Caribbean colonies and the United States of America; and 4) between British colonies and the colonies of other European powers in the Caribbean.

British trade was regulated by the Navigation Acts of 1651 and 1660 and the Staples Act of 1663, which remained in effect until they were repealed in 1848. In essence, these ordered that no produce from a colony could be carried to Britain or any British colony except in British ships and that goods and produce had to be shipped either to Britain or another British colony. All colonial ports were closed to foreign vessels. In addition, foreign goods could only be sent to the colonies after they had first landed in England, so that import and export duties could be collected. The only exceptions were items that Britain did not produce itself, such as wine and slaves (Edwards 1819, 2:445–448; Claypole and Robottom 1980:59, 62, 68; Cash et al. 1991:76–77, 85–87, 124).

The Plantations Duties Act of 1673 further restricted trade between British colonies by placing a heavy tax on goods shipped from one British colony to another, encouraging planters to ship their produce directly to Britain. Initially, planters attempted to evade these restrictive laws whenever possible, usually being acquitted by a jury of fellow colonists if they were caught and brought to trial. As a result, the Consolidating Duties Act of 1676 was passed which summarized all the laws controlling colonial trade and set up an Admiralty Court in each colony to try those breaking the trade laws. The Admiralty Court was a military court without a jury which strictly enforced the trade laws (Edwards 1819, 2:448–451; Claypole and Robottom 1980:68–69).

There were minor changes to these laws over the next century. Most involved including or excluding specific commodities or making exceptions for specific commodities from certain colonies (Edwards 1819, 2:451–454). Significant changes only came about after the American Revolution, when the 13 former colonies became foreign territory and, hence, changed their status under the trade laws. This caused significant economic problems for Britain's Caribbean colonies, as the American colonies had become their major suppliers of lumber, fish, flour, and grain, in return for sugar, rum, molasses, and coffee, which the Caribbean colonies could supply above and beyond European demand (Edwards 1819, 2:484–489). For example, America consumed twice as much rum—the most profitable Caribbean product—as Britain and Ireland combined (Edwards 1819, 2:489).

Responding to complaints of hardship from the British colonies in the Caribbean, the British government gradually relaxed trade restrictions with America. In 1787, the list of British "free ports" was expanded to include St. George (Grenada) and Nassau (Bahamas), in addition to the existing free ports in Dominica and Jamaica, created in 1766. A range of produce, dyewoods, lumber, livestock, coin, and bullion from colonies or plantations belonging to any European state, and in foreign vessels of less than 70 tons belonging to that state, could be imported into these ports. In return, rum, slaves, and virtually all legally imported goods could be exported in the same foreign vessels, back to the European colony in America (Edwards 1819, 2:452–453).

The Free Port Act of 1787 made Nassau a profitable entrepôt for trade with French and Spanish New World colonies until the French Revolutionary Wars (1791–1802) and the Napoleonic Wars (1803–1815) closed French and Spanish ports (Craton and Saunders 1992:192). However, it did not address the fundamental problem of the former British colonies in North America (Ragatz 1975:190–192). In 1788, the British government legalized the importation to the Caribbean colonies from the United States of commodities such as lumber, tobacco, livestock, and various foodstuffs, including all grain, providing they were brought in British ships by British subjects. The same act also prohibited the importation of these same goods from foreign islands except in times of emergency. The export of produce, including sugar, molasses, and coffee, to the United States was legalized, but again only in British ships (Edwards 1819, 2:516–517).

While this change brought some relief to the Caribbean colonists, it was still viewed as too restrictive, especially in the Bahamas, where a significant portion of the salt industry was dependent upon American ships. Consequently, in 1794, the British government finally allowed American ships of less than 70 tons to import any goods or merchandise manufactured or grown in the United States and to export to America any items or produce of the British island colonies (Edwards 1819, 2:524–525).

In addition to the shipping restrictions, the trade laws imposed taxes and customs duties on the goods that could be legally traded. As a result, goods had to pass through specific ports of entry where customs duties were collected. For the Bahamas, throughout the 18th century, the entire island chain was treated as one port, with only one customs house at Nassau on New Providence. As a result, all vessels from outside the Bahamas had to report to Nassau before any goods could be loaded or unloaded (Cash et al. 1991:124).

Pressure from prominent Loyalists gradually forced the British Government to open additional ports of entry in the Bahamas. By 1803, Great Exuma, the Caicos, and Turk's Island had become regular ports of entry (McKinnen 1804:132; Thompson 1812:126; Edwards 1819, 4:226; Craton and Saunders 1992:198). Another was established at Crooked Island by 1812 (Riley 1983:202). These ports of entry were established to promote the salt trade, particularly with the Americans, and none developed as significant mercantile centers (Craton and Saunders 1992:198). Nassau remained the hub for the distribution of supplies and manufactured goods from Britain and supplies from America throughout the Loyalist period in the Bahamas.

While legal trade was strictly controlled, illegal trade with America and other islands flourished throughout Bahamian history (Riley 1983; Craton 1986; Cash et al. 1991:30; Craton and Saunders 1992). The free port acts, the legalization of specific trade goods from America, and the additional ports of entry, were as much a recognition of existing illegal trade relationships as they were a stimulus for the development of new ones. During the Loyalist period, America was the primary foreign power engaged in illicit

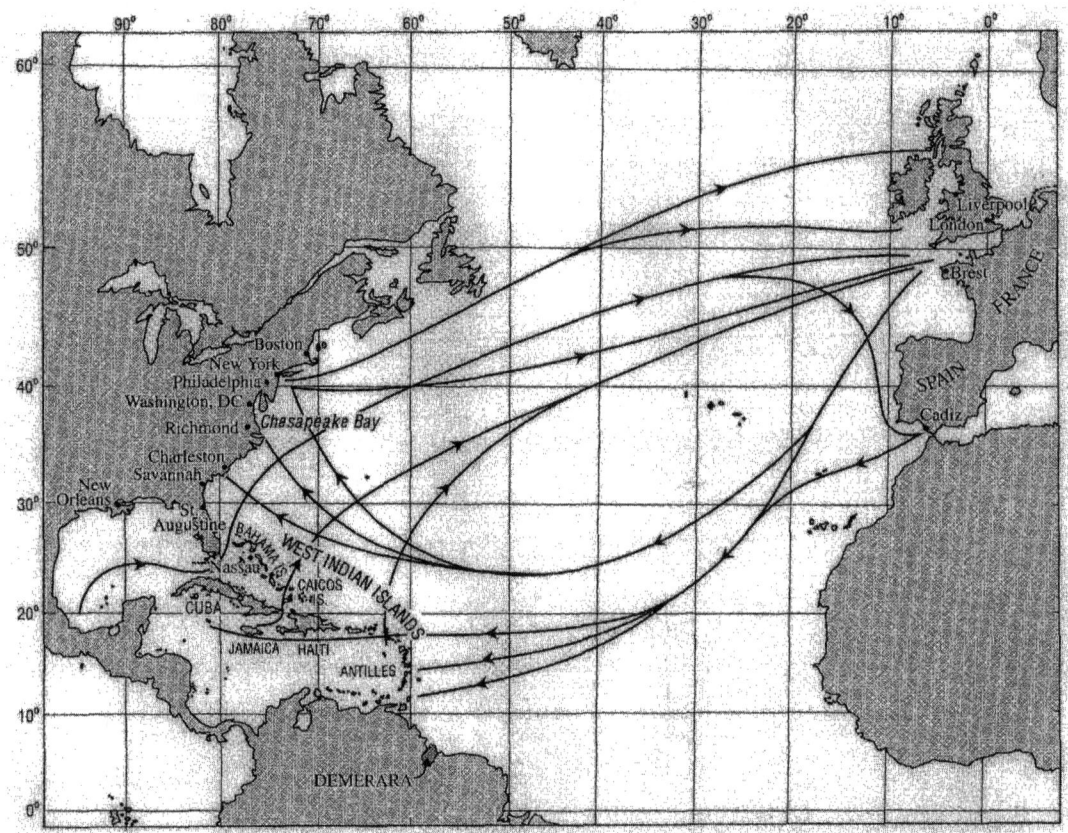

FIGURE 1. The major North Atlantic sailing tracks between Europe and the West Indies or North America in the early 19th century (Treharne and Fullard 1969; Daggett 1988).

trade in the Bahamas (Riley 1983:167–168). The almost constant state of war between Britain, France, and Spain during the Loyalist period severely curtailed legal and illegal trade with French and Spanish vessels. Indeed, the very appearance of French and Spanish vessels in the Out Islands—a term used historically to mean all Bahamian islands other than New Providence—was reported with alarm in the Nassau papers, as most were believed, often quite correctly, to be privateers (e.g., *Bahamas Gazette [BG]*, 31 May 1796a).

Two other significant sources of goods and supplies in the Bahamas warrant brief consideration: wrecking and privateering. With the many cays, reefs, and islands that make up the Bahamas, wrecking was a profitable occupation throughout the colonial period. Goods of all types were recovered from ships throughout the

Bahamas. By law, these salvaged commodities should have been transmitted to Nassau for sale at auction; however, significant quantities were distributed throughout the islands (Deans Peggs 1957:iii; Fries 1968:16–17; Craton 1986:166–167; Cash et al. 1991:30).

The booty from privateering, in essence legalized piracy against the ships of Britain's enemies, was another major source of supply throughout Bahamian history. During the French Revolutionary Wars (1791–1802) and the Napoleonic Wars (1803–1815), French and Spanish vessels were frequently seized, while the War of 1812 resulted in the seizure of large numbers of American vessels. Ships and their cargoes were sold at auction in Nassau (Coker and Watson 1986:203–225; Craton 1986:167; Cash et al. 1991:30–31; Craton and Saunders 1992:213–214).

Cargoes auctioned in Nassau, be they from privateering or wrecking, were advertised in the Nassau papers, sometimes with detailed descriptions. Most cargoes appear to be food supplies and commodities produced in America and the Caribbean. This is almost certainly because of the geography of the region and the prevailing winds. The Bahamas straddle the return leg to Europe and the route to the east coast of North America for vessels coming from European colonies to the south (Figure 1). Vessels from Europe going to North America did not have to put into Nassau unless they chose to do so, even though they made the Atlantic crossing at tropical latitudes. They could head north with the prevailing winds before reaching the dangerous waters of the Bahamas (Figure 1). Only British vessels headed for the Gulf Coast or the Bahamas had to enter Bahamian waters, although many others chose to make port in Nassau before heading for St. Augustine, Savannah, and Charleston (e.g., Colonial Office Records [CO] 1803b, 1803c; Coker and Watson 1986). Foreign vessels headed for the Gulf Coast would stay to the south, going by way of Santo Domingo or Cuba.

Excluding ships sailing directly from Britain, most vessels traversing Bahamian waters were coming from Central America, Caribbean islands to the south, or North America and were carrying supplies and produce from those regions, not manufactured goods from Europe. Thus, manufactured goods from Europe are rarely listed for auction from wrecking or privateering. Only the occasional cargo salvaged from a British ship included manufactured goods from Europe.

In summary, as a result of the British Navigation Acts, European politics, the prevailing winds, and the geography of the region, Britain was the primary source of supplies and manufactured goods in the Bahamas. North America was the second most important source of supplies and the major market for Bahamian salt. The West Indian colonies of the other European powers were another source of supplies, largely through privateering and wrecking, although smuggling also contributed to some degree. However, legal trade remained the major source for manufactured goods from Britain for the Bahamian planters.

Wade's Green Plantation

North Caicos is one of the Caicos Islands, the most remote of the Bahamian Out Islands (Figure 2). The Caicos Islands were part of the British colony of the Bahama Islands until 1848 (Craton 1986:209–210); geographically, environmentally, and geologically, they still are. However, after 1848, the Turks and Caicos Islands were administered from Jamaica, due to their remoteness from Nassau. Today they remain a British Crown Colony, a separate entity from the independent Commonwealth of the Bahamas.

Englishman Wade Stubbs, a Loyalist refugee from British East Florida (Siebert 1972:281), was granted 860 acres on North Caicos in 1789 (Registrar General's Department [RGD] 1789). Stubbs originally called his plantation Bellefield (Department of Archives [DA] 1806:193), but after 1806 he changed the name to Wade's Green, the name still used today (DA 1821).

Little is known of Stubbs's life on the island. Apparently he grew cotton and sugar successfully and added to his holdings while other planters were abandoning theirs. In various legal transactions he usually described himself as a planter, but sometimes as a merchant. Unlike most of the other Loyalist planters, Wade Stubbs still lived on the Caicos Islands until the time of his death on March 4, 1822, in Grand Turk (*Royal Gazette and Bahama Advertiser*

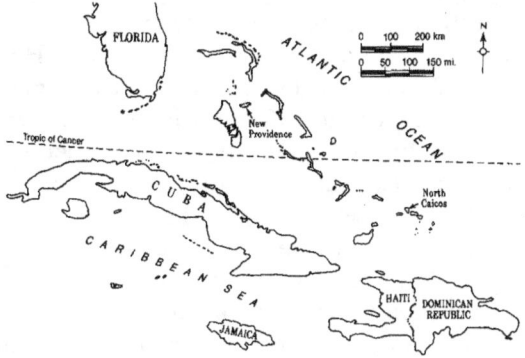

FIGURE 2. The Bahamas showing the locations of North Caicos and New Providence Islands.

[RG&BA], 23 March 1822). He had expanded his Wade's Green estate to approximately 3,000 acres, in addition to his 5,000-acre Cheshire Hall estate on Providenciales, the Caicos Island immediately to the west of North Caicos (DA 1821). According to the triennial slave return for January 1, 1822 (DA 1822), he owned 384 slaves, all but 48 being on the Caicos. This total represents approximately 3.5 percent of all the slaves listed in the Bahamas in the 1822 slave return (Craton and Saunders 1992:Table 14), making Wade Stubbs one of the largest slave owners in the colony. There can be no doubt that Wade Stubbs was one of the wealthiest planters in the Bahamas.

During the summer of 1989 the University of California, Los Angeles, archaeological field school spent four weeks examining Wade's Green plantation. A systematic surface survey revealed 12 structures enclosed by a continuous dry-stone wall (Figure 3). Five structures were cleared of brush, photographed, and drawn: Wade Stubbs's house and kitchen building, the overseer's house, a slave cabin, and a storage shed. One-x-1-m archaeological test units were excavated in and around the structures using trowels and brushes. All dirt was sieved through 1/8-in. mesh. Over 6,000 artifacts were recovered from surface collections and excavations (Farnsworth and Wilkie Farnsworth 1990; Farnsworth 1993).

The vast majority of the artifacts recovered from the excavations were ceramic sherds. All major types of British ceramics from the late 18th and 19th centuries were represented in the collection, ranging from redwares to refined earthenwares, ironstones, and stonewares. However, only three sherds of non-European earthenware were recovered. The origin of these sherds remains ambiguous, as they are not sherds of locally made, prehistoric Lucayan Palmetto ware, nor do they resemble any of the Afro-Caribbean wares from the Greater or Lesser Antilles.

No primary documentation from the Bahamas has yet been found which discusses the distribution of ceramics on the plantations. The only extant plantation journal from the Bahamas was written in 1831–1832 by Charles Farquharson,

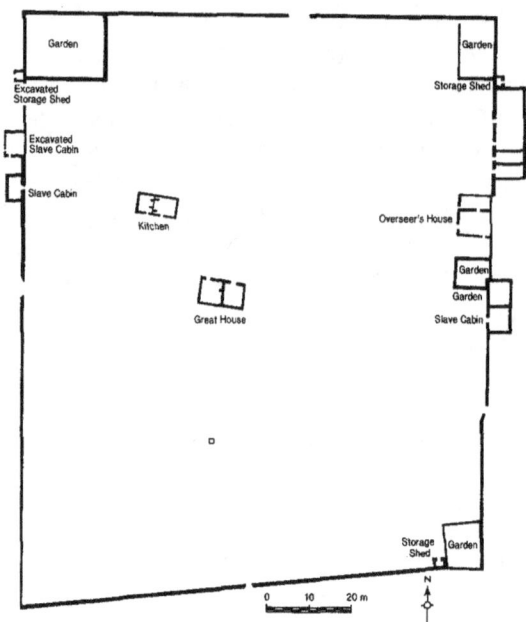

FIGURE 3. The central compound of Wade's Green plantation, North Caicos.

who owned 2,000 acres and 52 slaves on San Salvador Island (Deans Peggs 1957). The journal dates after the heyday of the Bahamian plantations, shortly before emancipation, when Farquharson's estate was failing. Apart from food and drink, the journal only refers to the distribution of cloth and clothing to the slaves over the two-year period it covers. As a plantation established three decades earlier and in its last years of operation, it is not surprising that little other than food was being distributed.

Other documents are frustratingly vague about items other than food supplied to the slaves. For example, Thomas Nattall was a carpenter who was employed on plantations on Crooked Island from 1806 to 1808. In a court case, he testified that the planter who employed him supplied food, medicines, and "living and other necessities" to the slaves (CO 1818). In the same trial, Alexander Mortimer, who worked as an overseer on the same Crooked Island plantations from 1796 to 1801, stated that in addition to food, the planter "supplied medicines and every other necessary for his slaves" (CO 1818). This implies that ceramics and other manufactured

TABLE 1
CERAMIC SHAPE/FUNCTION ANALYSIS

| | Wade's Green | | Promised Land |
| | Planter | Slave | Slave |
	%	%	%
Flat	31.8	47.7	18.8
Hollow	34.1	29.5	34.8
Soup	1.6	1.1	5.4
Serving	3.1	5.7	9.8
Tea/Coffee	7.0	5.7	18.8
Storage	14.0	3.4	10.7
Other	0.0	0.0	1.8
Unidentified	8.5	6.8	0.0
Total	100	100	100

Note. Percentages are based on the following sample sizes: Wade's Green, planter (n = 129), Wade's Green, slave (n = 88), Promised Land, slave (n = 112).

goods found on the plantations were supplied by the planter.

For the slaves, there seem to have been few alternatives for obtaining goods on North Caicos. Hand-me-downs or thefts from the planter seem unlikely to be the main source of goods for Stubbs's 300 slaves. There were no towns on the island, and despite the 33 land grants on North Caicos (Kozy 1983:86), many planters quickly sold or abandoned their grants. McKinnen (1804:132) reports only 12 planter families on all of the Caicos Islands by 1788, the year before Stubbs's grant. Kozy (1983:105) documents land grants to 72 individuals over the next two years on the Caicos but believes that many were too small for agriculture, and they were rapidly sold to larger landholders. Therefore, she estimates 40 families may have actually lived on the Caicos in the early 1790s (Kozy 1983:106), an estimate that corresponds well with a letter of 1796 which lists 35 planters and other principle inhabitants of the islands (CO 1796).

Government documents note only six families on North Caicos in January 1803 (CO 1803a). A letter from Thomas Brown (CO 1803d) states that only four planter families remained on the island in September 1803 and that all the others had fled to America with their slaves, abandoning their estates. On a small island, 400 mi.

from Nassau, the only significant town in the colony, with only four active plantations, there would have been little opportunity to obtain significant quantities of goods other than through the planter. There can be few places where the power the owner exerted over access to goods on the plantation was as complete as it was for the planters on the Bahamian Out Islands.

Ceramic Analyses

The application of ceramic shape and function analysis, following the work of Otto (1984), to the Wade's Green ceramic assemblages (Table 1) shows that the slaves used more flatwares (plates and platters, 47.7%) than hollowwares (bowls, 29.5%), while the planter used approximately equal percentages of flatwares (31.8%) and hollowwares (34.1%). This contradicts the expectation of slaves using more hollowwares based on previous research in the southeastern United States by Wheaton, Friedlander, and Garrow (1983), Otto (1984), Kelso (1984), and Moore (1985). However, Kelso (1986) at Monticello, Virginia, and Adams (1987) at Kings Bay plantation, Georgia, had observed a similar pattern to the one at Wade's Green. To simplify comparison with other sites, the percentage of hollowwares versus flatwares in each assemblage was recalculated, using only the two vessel forms, omitting tea/coffee, serving, storage, and other vessel forms (Table 2). Still the percentages are the reverse of the expected pattern, with the planter using a higher percentage of bowls than the slaves.

The Wade's Green percentages can be compared to those from Southeastern plantations (Table 2). While Georgia data dominate the comparison because they are the most readily accessible, there are also good historical reasons for comparison with Georgia sites. First, a larger proportion of the population of Georgia submitted claims for compensation to the British government than any other colony, and a larger percentage of the population of Savannah submitted claims than any other city (Kozy 1983:79). The Georgia Loyalists had fled to East Florida, and many were compensated with

TABLE 2
PERCENTAGE OF HOLLOWWARE VERSUS
FLATWARE IN ASSEMBLAGES

Assemblage	Percentage of Hollowware
Bahamas:	
Wade's Green Planter	51.8
Wade's Green Slave	38.2
Promised Land Slave	65.0
Southeast Planters:	
Georgia	
Cannon's Point Planter	45.6
Sinclair Planter	44.1
Pike's Bluff Planter	64.8
Kings Bay Planter	45.1
Virginia	
Monticello Planter (approx.)	40.0
Bray's Littletown	66.0
Southeast Slaves:	
Georgia	
Cannon's Point Slave	61.6
Jones Slave	81.0
Sinclair Slave	71.4
Butler Island Slave	80.0
Kings Bay Slave	51.9
Harmony Hall Slave	48.6
James King Plantation Slave	60.7
South Carolina	
Yaughan Slave (1740–1790)	93.1
Yaughan Slave (1780–1820)	82.3
Curriboo Slave (1740–1800)	94.1
Virginia	
Monticello Slave (approx.)	20–40
Littletown Quarter	68.0
Kingsmill Quarter	63.0
North Quarter	65.0

Note. Hollowware + flatware = 100%. Georgia data from Moore (1985:Table 7.4) and Adams (1987:300); South Carolina data from Wheaton, Friedlander, and Garrow (1983:246) and Wheaton and Reed (1990:202–203); Virginia data from Kelso (1984:179, 1986:16).

land grants in the Bahamas. William Wylly states in his book, *A Short Account of the Bahama Islands*, published in 1798, that the Loyalist refugees came principally from Georgia (Kozy 1983:106). According to Kozy (1983:105), 44 percent of the settlers on the Caicos came from Georgia, while 32 percent came from the Carolinas. Another 12 percent

were recorded as coming from East Florida, like Wade Stubbs, but probably had fled there from Georgia like William Moss (*BG*, 6–9 December 1796b). Second, most of the Loyalists who left the Bahamas after the plantations declined in the early 19th century returned to their lands in Georgia and South Carolina (CO 1803a).

For the planter contexts (Table 2), at approximately 50 percent hollowwares, Wade Stubbs's percentage of hollowwares is approximately consistent with Georgia planters on Cannon's Point (45%), Sinclair (44%), and Kings Bay plantations (45%). It is the Wade's Green slave assemblages that diverge from the expected pattern (Table 2). The slaves at Wade's Green used a far smaller percentage of hollowwares (38%) to flatwares than slaves on the Georgia (48–81%) or South Carolina (82–94%) plantations. The same is true for the Virginia slaves at Littletown Quarter, Kingsmill Quarter, and North Quarter (63–68%). Only the slaves at Monticello, Virginia, have an equally low percentage of hollowwares in their assemblages (20–40%).

Kelso (1986:17) explains the low percentage of hollowwares at Monticello as the result of the house slaves bringing garbage and trash from the nearby main house for disposal in their yards. At Jefferson's carefully planned, showplace plantation, this may have been the case, but it seems unlikely that slaves would have dragged garbage and trash 60 m from the main house at Wade's Green to a slave cabin, when similar trash and garbage were being dumped extensively around Wade Stubbs's house and the nearby kitchen.

At Wade's Green, the slave hollowware to flatware percentage (38%) is closer to the percentages of Wade Stubbs (51%) and the planters on the southeastern plantations (40–66%) than to the slave percentages (48–94%, excluding Monticello). That is, it resembles a planter percentage versus a slave percentage. The explanation for the proportion of hollowwares to flatwares in the Bahamian slave assemblage is thought to lie in the nature of the ceramic distribution systems that supplied the Out Island plantations.

Ceramic Distribution Systems

Although there are some exceptions (e.g., Adams and Gaw 1977; Price 1979; Miller and Hurry 1983; Majewski and O'Brien 1987), few archaeologists give much consideration to the means by which the ceramics they recover traveled from the pottery to their site. As the vast majority of the ceramics recovered from the plantations in the Bahamas were manufactured in Britain, a brief overview of the distribution of British ceramics is given here.

Industrialization of the English potters in the second half of the 18th century had outpaced the abilities of the traveling "cratemen," who carried wares on their backs or in small carts, to distribute their wares (Miller 1984a:3). Potters were forced to become merchants marketing their own wares, establishing showrooms in London and other locations, and some established agents abroad. For the most part, general merchants dealt directly with the potters back in Britain. Pottery was only a minor part of the general merchants' business. Some acted as wholesalers as well as retailers, selling to other merchants in remote locations (Miller 1984a:4). In the late 18th century, in urban centers like Philadelphia, New York, and Boston, merchants specializing in ceramics and glass began to develop (Miller 1984a:4). However, none developed in the Bahamas at this time.

Merchants could order complete services, but this was rarely done (Miller 1984b:46; Schwind 1984:23). The only sets found in invoices of this period are tea sets, typically composed of a dozen cups, saucers and (coffee) cans, a teapot, teapot stand, sugar box, cream (pitcher), slop bowl, large plate (8 in.), and small plate (7 in.). The teapot, cream pitcher, and sugar box were often omitted for wealthy clients who would have these items in silver (Whiter 1989:216–217). Most merchants' orders consisted of a mixture of vessels in terms of size, form, decoration, and even ware (e.g., Blaszczyk 1984:11–18; Schwind 1984:23; Whiter 1989:211–217), composed according to the merchants' perception of their local market (Miller 1984a:4). These would usually be packed in crates at the pottery and shipped, with the cost of the crate, straw for packing, and shipping charges added to the cost of the order (e.g., *Antiques* 1934:197; Miller 1984b:43, Figure 1; Whiter 1989:212).

General merchants, especially those in remote locations, paid limited attention to the pottery part of their business, as long as they could obtain a reasonable supply of the basic goods in demand. Most were more concerned with the assortment of vessels than the specific makeup of the crates they obtained. For example, Frederick Rhinelander, a Loyalist merchant in New York wrote in 1776 to his supplier that "a regard must be had to the assortment, otherwise the sales will be much prejudiced" (Schwind 1984:32). Such crates were often destined for Rhinelander's customers in rural locations (Schwind 1984:32).

Many British potters shipped these mixed, prepacked crates of ceramics. These crates contained what the potters in Britain perceived as the vessels desired by their customers. While most were shipped to fill merchants' orders, some were shipped to merchants on consignment (*BG*, 28 December 1798–4 January 1799). During the War of 1812, large quantities of ceramics were warehoused in England for shipment to the United States when hostilities ceased. At that time, the potters were eager to sell these stored ceramics as rapidly as possible and shipped them directly to merchants on commission, without awaiting specific orders. In major ports, such as New York, these ceramics were auctioned, creating a new distribution system that competed with the traditional importing merchants. Ceramics shipped on commission and sold at auction were usually sold at prices below those available for traditional orders. Auction markets grew at most major ports in the United States. Jobbers, who had no contact with the potteries in Britain, became the major suppliers for rural merchants, who did not need special orders or the very latest fashions (Miller 1984b:41). Jobbers depended on what was sent by the potters, dealing more in cheaper wares, surplus production, out-of-style patterns, and standard types such as plain creamware, shell-edged ware, and willowware (Miller 1984b:41).

With no direct order between merchant and potter, the contents of the crates sold at American auctions was determined by the pottery. Therefore, the mixed crates being shipped to the United States should, presumably, be indicative of the contents of crates shipped anywhere else. A one-page broadside advertising 26 crates of ceramics to be auctioned by Boggs, Thompson & Co. in New York in March 1821 (*Antiques* 1934:196) shows the diversity available. Only three crates were composed of just one size of one vessel form with the same decoration. Nine crates contained just one vessel form with the same decoration but in a variety of sizes, ranging from two sizes of "CC hand basins," to three sizes of "edgd muffins" and "dipt bowls" up to nine sizes of "edg'd dishes." Six crates contained multiple vessel forms and sizes, all with the same decoration, while eight contained multiple vessel forms with a variety of different types or patterns of decoration. The maximum number of different vessel forms—excluding differences in size—in a crate was seven, while two was the maximum number of different types of decoration in a crate, although up to five different printed patterns (bird, woodman, milkmaid, pas'l [pastoral?], and vine) were listed in two crates (*Antiques* 1934:196).

Twenty-six crates from one auction provides only a qualitative picture of the contents of mixed crates at one point in time. Analysis of the quantities of vessels shipped by a jobber to a number of rural merchants over a number of years may provide a more generalized, quantitative idea of the nature of ceramic distribution using such crates. Miller (1984b:Table 3) has compiled information on the quantities of ceramics shipped by George M. Coates, a Philadelphia jobber, to five country stores in New Jersey and Pennsylvania over a number—between three and six—of years in the late 1820s (1824–1830).

Dividing Miller's (1984b:Table 3) data into flatware, hollowware, and teaware shows a surprising dominance of the last. Flatwares range from 28 to 53 percent of the ceramics, averaging 36 percent overall, while hollowwares range from 3 to 16 percent, averaging 10 percent over-

all. Tea wares, however, range from 44 to 62 percent and averaged 54 percent overall. Blaszczyk (1984:19) concluded from her study of Maryland merchants that the availability of tea wares increased significantly from the 1770s to the 1790s, and Miller (1984b:47) suggests that this trend continued in the first 30 years of the 19th century, if not beyond. Therefore, the percentage of tea wares (54%) supplied by Coates probably represents a higher percentage than would be expected in earlier years.

Removing tea wares from the analysis renders the data comparable to that given in Table 2. When the percentage of flatwares to hollowwares was recalculated using only the two vessel forms and omitting tea wares, hollowwares comprised between 5 and 36 percent of the various merchants' ceramics, averaging 23 percent. This suggests that, at least in the late 1820s, British potters were shipping crates which would provide at most 36 percent hollowwares in a straightforward hollowware to flatware comparison, with 23 percent more likely to be typical.

TABLE 3
PERCENTAGES OF CERAMIC PRICE LEVELS BY
DECORATION

Assemblage	Percentage by Price Level			
	1	2	3	4
Bahamas:				
Wade's Green Planter	44.7	19.1	11.7	24.5
Wade's Green Slave	49.4	20.3	10.1	20.3
Promised Land Slave	88.2	0.0	11.8	0.0
Georgia Planters[a]:				
Cannon's Point Planter	11.7	3.4	4.2	80.7
Sinclair Planter	58.2	27.3	5.6	8.9
Pike's Bluff Planter	50.4	19.0	4.7	25.9
Georgia Slaves[a]:				
Cannon's Point				
North Slave	20.3	43.9	6.6	29.2
South Slave	36.2	38.1	16.0	9.7
Jones Slave	49.9	28.4	13.4	8.3
Sinclair Slave	61.7	8.8	9.9	19.6
Butler Island Slave	46.0	40.2	10.2	3.6

[a] Georgia data from Moore (1985:Table 7.3).

Ceramic Distribution in the Bahamas

Newspaper advertisements in Nassau mention the availability of prepacked, mixed ceramic crates. For example, on 28 December 1798, Alexander Leckie, Jr., advertised the availability of "Sixty Crates of Queen's Ware" on consignment (*BG*, 28 December 1798–4 January 1799). On 2 May 1800, James Howie advertised the availability of "crates of earthen ware [*sic*]" (*BG*, 2–6 May 1800). Detailed information on the contents of such crates has not been found in the Bahamian advertisements, but the inclusion of sets of ceramics and the mixing of types and styles of decoration in the crates is suggested by certain advertisements. For example, in October 1794, William and James Moss advertised "Liverpool China; Printed and assorted Earthen Ware in small Packs; Small Table Setts of Printed Green, and Blue Edged Ware" (*BG*, 10–17 October 1794). William and James Moss advertised "Earthen Ware and Liverpool China; Table Setts of Ware" on 12 June 1795 (*BG*, 9–12 June 1795), while in December 1799, Alexander Leckie, Jr., was advertising "A few sets of tea and table china" (*BG*, 13–17 December 1799), and James Moss, Jr., advertised "earthen, tin and glass ware, assorted in packages" on 17 August 1804 (*RG&BA*, 17 August 1804). Other similar examples can be found in the newspapers throughout the Loyalist period.

Based on the percentages of vessel forms in the planter and slave assemblages at Wade's Green, it would seem a likely hypothesis that for basic table wares, Wade Stubbs did not seek to supply his slaves with ceramics ordered separately, but purchased what was available to him at the least overall cost in terms of both time and money. This consisted of prepacked, mixed vessel crates with proportions of plates, bowls, and other vessel forms determined by a British pottery rather than a merchant in Nassau and sold at a considerable discount compared to orders specifying the contents. Vessels such as tea wares and serving pieces were often included in the prepacked crates, and the percentages of these vessels are similar in the planter and slave assemblages from Wade's Green (Table 1), fur-

ther supporting the "mixed crate" hypothesis. Finer wares could be purchased separately for the main house to add the appearance of wealth and status required by the plantation owner. Considerable evidence of Chinese porcelain, English bone china, and "black Basaltes" vessels was found at Wade Stubbs' house and kitchen, but minimal quantities were found at the overseer and slave houses. Such crates could be ordered from a merchant in Nassau and shipped to North Caicos without the planter or his manager having to make the long voyage or prepare detailed lists of ceramics, while not knowing their purchase prices.

Hence, for colonies like the Bahamas, where demand was relatively limited and supply to remote locations was difficult, mixed crates of ceramics would have been a logical choice for routine planter household use and for distribution to the slaves. What is not clear, is whether all plantations in the Bahamas purchased their ceramics in this way or whether this pattern is to be found only on the remote Out Islands.

Ceramic Distribution in the American South

In contrast to the Bahamas, North America was the most important export market for the British ceramic industry, which went to considerable lengths to cater to American desires and demands. In comparison to the 400-mi. voyage from North Caicos to Nassau, the Georgia plantations studied by Otto (1984) and Moore (1985) all had easy access to supplies from the port of Savannah, Georgia, some 10 to 12 hours away by rowing boat (Otto 1984:155), while the Kings Bay plantations were only another 25–30 mi. further away (Adams 1987:2). Hence, while the prepacked, mixed crate was also available in Georgia, the supply situation allowed the planter or his manager to travel to a merchant and choose the desired forms and decorations for the slave versus planter households, bringing them directly back to the plantation that day. The total purchase price was probably lower than for a mixed crate due to the predominance of cheap bowls purchased for the slaves and the control over quantities purchased. Hence, there was much greater freedom of ceramic choice for the coastal plantation owner.

Similarly, the South Carolina plantations studied by Wheaton, Friedlander, and Garrow (1983) had access to Charleston via the Santee River to the coast, while the Virginia plantations studied by Kelso (1984) were on the James River with access to the various ports of the Chesapeake. Consequently, it was easier and cheaper for these planters to buy separately the ceramics for distribution to the slaves versus those for the household; therefore, significant differences in the percentages of vessel forms occur between the two contexts.

Only Monticello, located in the Virginia piedmont (Sanford 1994:117–118), approximately 100 mi. from the Chesapeake by river and 60 mi. from Richmond, lacked easy access to a major port. As a result, the piedmont plantations did not practice monocrop agriculture, but mixed commercial and subsistence crops for local and regional markets, seeking self-sufficiency from national and international marketing systems (Sanford 1994:118–119). It may be no coincidence that the slave assemblages at Monticello had only 20–40 percent hollowwares, a percentage similar to that calculated for the crates distributed by George Coates in Philadelphia.

Testing the Mixed Crate Hypothesis at Wade's Green Plantation

To compare the cost of the ceramics in an assemblage, historical archaeologists have used several techniques. The best known is Miller's CC index system (Miller 1980, 1991). Plantation archaeologists have commonly used a simplified variant of Miller's price index in which the percentages of the ceramics in different price groups are compared, as opposed to using the actual CC index values (e.g., Otto 1984; Moore 1985; Orser 1988; Armstrong 1990). Miller defined four price levels for refined earthenwares based on type of decoration: level 1, plain undecorated ceramics, the cheapest available; level 2, minimally decorated vessels such as edged, banded, sponged and mocha; level 3, hand-painted vessels; and, level 4, transfer-printed

vessels (Miller 1980, 1991). Note that porcelains, "black Basaltes," and bone chinas, the most expensive types of ceramics found at Wade's Green, are not included in this analysis.

At Wade's Green, the percentages of the four price levels are similar in slave and planter contexts (Table 3). The slaves were using about 5 percent more of the cheapest vessels than Wade Stubbs, who used 4 percent more vessels in the most expensive category. To this must be added the virtual monopoly on Chinese porcelain, "black Basaltes," and bone china vessels enjoyed by Wade Stubbs. Although the differences are small, Wade Stubbs has a more costly ceramic assemblage.

Comparison with Georgia plantations (Moore 1985:152) suggests a contradiction in wealth as measured by ceramics between the planter and slaves at Wade's Green. The planter comparison (Table 3) places Wade's Green with Pike's Bluff, a small plantation. In contrast, comparison of the slave contexts (Table 3) shows that the Wade's Green slaves had higher percentages of expensive, transfer-printed ceramics than most of the large Georgia plantations studied by Moore (1985). The contradiction supports the hypothesis that Wade Stubbs was purchasing by the mixed crate, providing the same ceramics for use by all segments of the plantation population, and then purchasing porcelains and bone china to embellish his household. The result is that the slaves acquired apparent wealth with their relatively high percentage of transfer-printed ceramics, while Stubbs appears relatively impoverished, despite being one of the wealthiest planters in the Bahamas.

Unfortunately, Miller (1984b) does not provide a complete listing of the ceramics distributed by the Philadelphia jobber, George Coates. He does, however, provide a listing of the percentages of undecorated and transfer-printed vessels by vessel form supplied to six rural merchants (Miller 1984b:Table 1). Fifteen percent of muffins and 17 percent of plates were undecorated, while 31 percent of muffins and 12 percent of plates were transfer printed. Forty-three percent of bowls were undecorated and only 6 percent were transfer printed, while 5 percent of cups

TABLE 4
FUNCTIONAL ANALYSIS OF BAHAMIAN ASSEMBLAGES

Functional Group	Wade's Green				Promised Land	
	Planter %	Kitchen %	Overseer %	Slave %	Slave %	Planter %
Food Consumption	47.2	61.3	53.7	52.4	46.1	18.1
Beverage Consumption	10.4	13.3	4.1	8.5	14.4	12.5
Food Storage	6.9	2.0	3.4	3.7	0.0	1.4
Beverage Storage	15.3	7.3	15.0	18.3	15.6	44.4
Tobacco and Recreational Drugs	6.3	6.7	4.8	1.2	13.8	16.7
Health and Hygiene	3.5	2.0	2.0	7.3	3.0	2.8
Personal Adornment and Clothing	4.2	1.3	7.5	2.4	1.2	0.0
Currency and Tokens	0.7	0.0	0.0	0.0	0.0	0.0
Security and Restraint	0.7	1.3	3.4	0.0	0.0	0.0
Household Decor and Lighting	1.4	1.3	0.7	2.4	4.8	1.4
Domestic Activities	2.8	3.3	4.1	3.7	1.2	2.8
Nondomestic Activities	0.0	0.0	0.0	0.0	0.0	0.0
Communications	0.7	0.0	1.4	0.0	0.0	0.0
Ideology	0.0	0.0	0.0	0.0	0.0	0.0
Total	100	100	100	100	100	100

Note. Total number of artifacts: Wade's Green, planter (n = 144), kitchen (n = 150), overseer (n = 147), slave (n = 82); Promised Land, planter (n = 167), slave (n = 72).

and saucers were plain, with 28 percent transfer-printed. Using the average percentages of the vessel forms discussed earlier, these figures can be used to calculate an overall average percentage of undecorated and transfer-printed vessels supplied by Coates.

The results indicate that approximately 25 percent of the vessels supplied by Coates were transfer printed, while only 13 percent were undecorated. Again, because of the dominance of tea wares, which were most the most likely vessels to be transfer printed, their percentage probably represents a higher proportion than would be found earlier. However, comparison with the Wade's Green percentages (Table 3) shows a correlation with the quantities of transfer-printed ceramics in both the planter (24.5%) and slave (20.3%) assemblages. Again, this supports the mixed-crate hypothesis for ceramic supply at Wade's Green.

Other mechanisms could explain the similar distributions between the planter and slave at Wade's Green; hand-me-downs or theft from the planter could, presumably, produce a similar result, although the scale of such activities would

suggest them to be unlikely as the main source of goods for Stubbs's three hundred slaves. They could, however, account for the distribution at the one cabin excavated for this study. A detailed comparison of ceramic types based on ware, decoration, and color suggests that this is a less probable hypothesis.

There were 49 different types of ceramic recovered from the excavations at the plantation house, planter's kitchen, overseer's house, and the slave cabin at Wade's Green. Twelve of these types were found in all four contexts and account for 52.5 percent of the planter's assemblage, 56.5 percent of the overseer's assemblage, and 66.6 percent of the slaves' assemblage. Eighteen types were shared by both the planter and the slave assemblages, accounting for 83.3 percent of the slave assemblage and 64.6 percent of the planter's assemblage. These included light yellow creamware; blue-edged pearlware; underglaze blue, hand-painted pearlware; broadline, floral hand-painted pearlware; blue transfer-printed pearlware; earth-tone, annular whiteware; dark blue, transfer-printed whiteware; underglaze blue, hand-painted whiteware; bright-palet, broadline, floral, hand-painted whiteware; bright-palet, fineline, floral, hand-painted whiteware; bright colored transfer-printed whiteware; brown-glazed redware; black-glazed redware; and brown stoneware.

Only one type out of 24, represented by one vessel, was unique to the slaves' assemblage, while six types out of 38, were unique to the planter, representing 8.1 percent of his assemblage. Five types were unique to the overseer, representing 8.7 percent of his assemblage.

The 20 types found in the planter's assemblage, but not in the slaves' assemlage, included annular creamware; embossed pearlware; mocha-decorated whiteware; engine-turned whiteware; bright-tone annular whiteware; sponge-decorated whiteware; marbled whiteware; underglaze blue painted, hard-paste porcelain; bone china; semivitreous earthenware; slipware; "black Basaltes"; Jackfield; and gray stoneware.

The existence of a relatively large number of types (n = 20) in the planter's assemblage not found in the slave assemblage, including the most expensive types, argues against hand-me-downs or theft accounting for the basic similarity of the two assemblages. These mechanisms would be expected to leave the same types in both assemblages, just in different proportions. The slaves have only two-thirds as many types in their assemblage, but the types shared with the planter account for over 80 percent of it. This percentage suggests that both assemblages are based on the same 18 types of ceramics, but that the planter has access to additional types not made available to the slaves. The analysis would appear to support the mixed crate hypothesis, which would make the same ceramics available to both planter and slave, but would allow the planter to embellish his household with specially purchased, expensive ceramics. It does not support the hypothesis that the planter purchased ceramics specifically for the slaves and separately for his household. This would be expected to produce a far higher number of types that are unique to the slaves and which would make up a far larger proportion of their assemblage. The detailed ceramic analysis

strongly supports the mixed crate hypothesis of ceramic supply to Wade's Green.

Clearly, the ceramic analyses do not reflect the ethnicity or social or economic status of the slaves at Wade's Green, as would be the usual interpretation. Instead, they reflect the mechanisms of ceramic supply on North Caicos.

The Impact of Limited Access to Goods at Wade's Green

Using a functional analysis (Farnsworth 1992) of the assemblages from Wade's Green (Table 4) reveals some other effects of limited access to goods. For example, tobacco was a common commodity in the American South and was available to planters and slaves alike. Seen in the archaeological record as pipe fragments, tobacco pipes typically comprise approximately 5 percent of the assemblage, included in the tobacco and recreational drugs group in this functional analysis (Table 5). However, the difference in the tobacco consumption of the Wade's Green slaves is striking at only 1 percent. The distribution shows that pipe smoking was restricted to the British population (planter 6.3%, overseer 4.8%) and favored slaves (kitchen 6.7%) at Wade's Green.

This is surprising as tobacco pipes comprise 5–10 percent of the artifacts recovered from slave houses in Jamaica (Armstrong 1990:260). Since slaves elsewhere enjoyed smoking tobacco, why did not the slaves at Wade's Green smoke? So far as can be determined at this time, tobacco was not grown on North Caicos, and,

FIGURE 4. New Providence Island showing the locations of Nassau and Promised Land plantation.

therefore, was available only from other islands. Access was, presumably, controlled by the planter, who apparently chose to distribute it only to his most trusted slaves—those who worked in the kitchen preparing his food. Was this decision based on its scarcity and cost in Nassau, or the cost of getting it to North Caicos, or other, noneconomic factors?

The evidence suggests that a similar situation may have existed on other Out Islands. Excavations on San Salvador have recovered only four pipe bowl fragments—two from the same pipe—from 12 slave houses at Sandy Point Estate, while six pipe stems came from the main house. One pipe stem was recovered from 15 slave houses at Farquharson plantation, while four came from the main house (Gerace 1982, 1987).

Historical research suggests that tobacco was not produced on any of the Bahamian islands for either local sale or export, even though it was considered a potentially significant crop when the Loyalists first came to the Bahamas (*BG*, 3–10 June 1786). No primary or secondary source consulted to date mentions tobacco production or the sale of locally produced Bahamian tobacco during the Loyalist period. Newspapers do, however, occasionally have advertisements listing imported tobacco and pipes for sale (e.g., *BG*, 11 July 1789), although even these are rare.

The Wade's Green slaves also had a lower percentage of personal adornment and clothing artifacts than slaves at sites in Georgia, which typically have over 3 percent (Table 5). Especially surprising at Wade's Green is the complete absence of glass beads in the slave assemblage. Only one glass bead was recovered during the course of excavation at Wade's Green, and this was found at the overseer's house. Glass beads are frequently found in sites associated with slaves in the American South (e.g., Wheaton et al. 1983; Otto 1984; Moore 1985; Wheaton and Garrow 1985; Adams 1987; Sanford 1994) as well as the Caribbean. (For slave villages in Jamaica, see Kelly [1989] and Armstrong [1990]; for a slave cemetery in Barbados, see Handler and Lange [1978]; one exception is the slave cemetery on Montserrat re-

ported by Watters [1994]). It has been suggested by Handler and Lange (1978:148) that glass beads found in the Caribbean were obtained by the planters and then distributed to the slaves as rewards. Apparently, this did not occur at Wade's Green. Again, was this due to high cost and/or limited availability in Nassau or on North Caicos, or was it a decision by Wade Stubbs not to distribute beads to his slaves and a lack of alternative sources of supply for the slaves on North Caicos?

The evidence from other excavations suggests limited bead availability on other Bahamian islands. Excavations on San Salvador recovered one intact glass bead from the 12 slave houses examined at Sandy Point Estate and no beads from either Farquharson or Fortune Hill plantations (Gerace 1982, 1987). However, whether this is due to the availability of goods shipped to the merchants in Nassau or the cost and difficulties in getting goods from Nassau to Out Islands like North Caicos remains open without comparison to assemblages from New Providence.

To understand the artifact distributions on North Caicos, the availability of goods in the Bahamas through the port of Nassau must first be understood. Then it can be determined which of the available goods were not provided to the Out Islands by the planters. If transatlantic trade and distribution problems can be ruled out, then the Bahamian distribution system may be responsible for the absence of certain goods from Wade's Green.

The Bahamas were never a major colony in the British Empire, and ranked far behind the sugar islands, such as Jamaica and Barbados. They represented a relatively remote and small market for British merchants. In addition, the many islands, cays, and reefs presented dangerous waters for shipping and were avoided by vessels headed for the southeastern ports of Charleston and Savannah. Hence, it is plausible that the characteristics of the Wade's Green assemblages indicating limited access to goods could represent a colony-wide phenomenon. After all, Wade Stubbs was a wealthy planter who could probably afford to purchase any goods he chose in Nassau. However, due to a general lack of archaeological research on other Bahamian plantations, and the absence of detailed publications of those few excavations that have been carried out previously, it was not possible to determine whether the characteristics observed in the slave assemblages from Wade's Green are typical of sites throughout the Bahamas or limited to the remote Out Islands or limited to North Caicos. To solve this problem required the excavation of a plantation site on New Providence with direct access to Nassau.

Promised Land Plantation

During the month of July 1993, a Louisiana State University archaeological field school focused on locating, recording, and excavating the buildings and field walls of Promised Land plantation on New Providence Island (Figure 4) (Farnsworth 1994). One goal was to obtain the data necessary to disentangle the influences of the Bahamian distribution system from the transatlantic trade network on plantations in the Bahamas. Promised Land had direct access to Nassau. Hence, the Bahamian distribution system should have had limited effect on the Promised Land assemblage.

Promised Land lies on the southwestern coast of New Providence. It was granted in 1785 to British Loyalist William Moss (Department of Lands and Surveys [DLS] 1785). Upon William's death in 1796 (*BG*, 9 December 1796b), the plantation passed to his brother, James Moss (Aarons et al. 1990:4). William's probate inventory (RGD 1797) lists no improvements or crops at Promised Land, unlike most of his other estates, so it appears that the plantation was developed after 1796 by James. After James's death in 1820 (*RG&BA*, 25 October 1820), the plantation passed to his nephew, James Moss, Jr., who transferred all of the working-age slaves to the colony of Demerara (British Guiana/Guyana, Figure 1), leaving only the old and infirm to eke out a living into the late 1830s, when they appear to have relocated

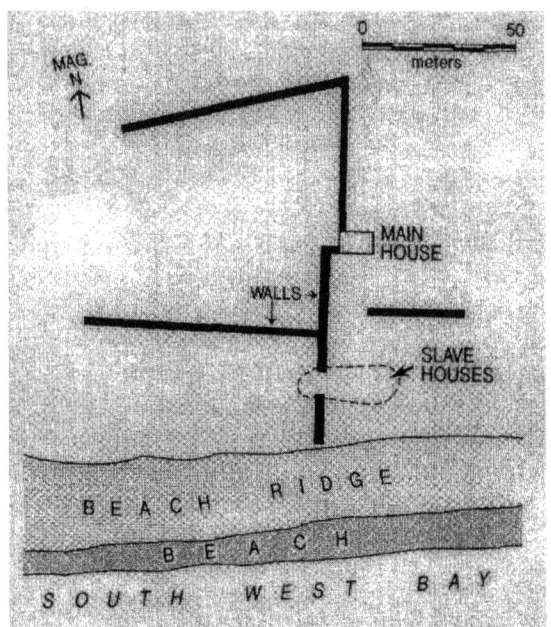

FIGURE 5. Promised Land plantation showing the relationships between the ruins of the main house and field walls, and the slave houses located during shovel testing.

to the nearby, new settlement of Adelaide (DA 1838:964–965).

The ruins of the main house were cleared of brush and 26 1-m^2 test units were excavated in and around the building. As at Wade's Green, all excavations at Promised Land were carried out with trowels and brushes, and all dirt was sieved through 1/8-in. mesh. Although only a small number of artifacts were recovered, these dated to the late 18th and early 19th centuries based upon the quantities of creamware and small amounts of pearlware recovered among the diverse ceramic assemblage. However, no locally made ceramics were recovered. The house was originally at least a two-story structure, with a timber-framed upper story built on a lower story of limestone-block piers. The floor of the house was of lime mortar. Human footprints and animal hoof prints, probably horse, were found impressed in the floor. Preliminary interpretations suggest that the ground floor, or cellar as it is known locally, was used as a barn and storage area, while the upper floor or floors were the living quarters. This plan parallels the arrangement at Wade's Green.

In addition to the excavations at the main house, the students systematically surveyed an area of 28 ha roughly centered on the main house. Systematic shovel testing was carried out at 10-m intervals over the 2-ha area encompassing the house ruins and field walls. Testing located the remains of what appear to be two structures approximately 50 m south of the main house with a yard area between (Figure 5).

Relatively large quantities of domestic artifacts were recovered from the 25 1-m² excavation units in the area around and between these structures. Creamware again dominated the ceramic assemblage, although pearlware, soft-paste porcelain, and two sherds of whiteware were among the other ceramic types recovered. No locally-made ceramics were recovered. The ceramics again suggest a late 18th- to early 19th-century occupation, ending around 1820. The structures are of particular interest for their technique of construction, which was a variant of wattle and daub, presumably with a thatched roof. However, rather than using mud or clay for the daub, these structures used a lime and sand mortar to coat the wattle walls, whose impressions were preserved in the mortar. At least some of the walls were then plastered and painted yellow. The result is an interesting hybrid of African and European construction techniques.

Based on the artifacts and the evidence of William's will, it appears that the occupation dates between 1796 and 1820, the period of James Moss's ownership. James and William were originally partners, being both merchants in Nassau and the principle slave importers to the Bahamas (BG, 1786–1800). William was also one of the richest planters in the colony (RGD 1797). After William's death in 1796, James apparently inherited all of William's plantations and became the wealthiest man in the Bahamas. He was a senior member of the House of Assembly (RG&BA, 25 October 1820), expanding his land and slave holdings over the years until

at the time of his death in 1820, he was the largest slave owner in the Bahamas, with 840 slaves, and numerous plantations (DA 1822). A major portion of the slaves and goods sold in Nassau by James arrived in ships owned by his brother Thomas, a wealthy merchant in Liverpool (Colonial Office Records [CO] 1803e). There can be little doubt that if anyone had access to goods in the Bahamas, it was James Moss.

Promised Land was, however, a very small plantation of little economic importance in the Moss financial empire. There is no reason to suppose that it obtained special goods that were not generally available in Nassau. It was located just over 10 mi. by road from Nassau and was easily accessible by boat. Therefore, obtaining goods from Nassau was not a significant problem. The assemblages from Promised Land should, therefore, accurately reflect the goods available to any planter in Nassau, and they are ideal for comparison with the Wade's Green assemblages.

One problem for the comparison, however, is that, unlike Wade's Green, the main house at Promised Land was not permanently occupied by the planter. James Moss lived in a large, three-story brick house in Nassau (RG&BA, 14 November 1818; Fries 1968:9). Indeed, given the relatively small quantities of artifacts and the types found at the main house compared to the slave houses, it is debatable whether anyone spent many nights in the main house of the plantation. Functional analysis of the assemblage shows it to be dominated by beverage storage items, mostly wine and liquor bottles. Food consumption is next in importance, closely followed by tobacco and recreational drugs and then beverage consumption. The emphasis on alcohol storage and consumption, eating, and smoking resembles more a tavern than a permanent residence, suggesting that the house was used as a weekend retreat. A similar interpretation has been proposed by Watters and Nicholson (1982) for Highland House on Barbuda. Therefore, the main house at Promised

Land does not further the examination of trade networks. The assemblage from the slave houses is far more useful in this regard.

Ceramic Analyses

Ceramic shape and function analysis (Table 1) reveals percentages similar to those from slave sites in Georgia (Otto 1984), although with greater emphasis on storage vessels. Flatware/hollowware analysis (Table 2) shows 65 percent bowls, not atypical for slave assemblages in the Southeast. These percentages are different from those at most planter sites in the Americas and are unlikely to result from any type of prepackaged crate. Analysis of ceramic decoration (Table 3) shows 88 percent to be undecorated (level 1) with the balance hand-painted ceramics (level 3). This is consistent with most slave assemblages. In short, there is no evidence of prepacked, mixed-vessel crates or sharing of ceramics with the planter class in this ceramic assemblage. The ceramics are dominated by the cheapest available—undecorated bowls.

There can be no doubt that when buying ceramics in Nassau it was possible to selectively provide plantation slaves with the cheapest types of ceramics. Therefore, with regard to ceramics, at least, the proportions of vessel forms and decorations at the Wade's Green slave house were apparently not the result of the transatlantic trade network, but the result of the costs and difficulty of distributing goods over the 400-mi. distance from Nassau to North Caicos. This, presumably, represents a decision by Wade Stubbs that it was not worth the time and cost to him to travel 400 mi. to Nassau to provide the slaves with ceramics specifically chosen for their use.

Access to Other Goods

The results of a functional analysis of the entire Promised Land slave assemblage (Table 4) are surprisingly similar to the results of the analysis of the Wade's Green slave assemblage.

The major difference lies in the tobacco group, which makes up almost 14 percent of the slave assemblage. Slaves at Promised Land had access to pipes and, presumably, tobacco. This suggests that at Wade's Green, for the slaves, it was the difficulty of obtaining tobacco that resulted in its absence from the slave assemblage there, not its scarcity or cost in Nassau. Indeed, the planter, overseer, and kitchen assemblages at Wade's Green have relatively typical percentages of pipes. Presumably, therefore, Stubbs could have given, traded, or sold tobacco to his slaves if he so chose, as he apparently did for the kitchen slaves. However, if Wade Stubbs chose not to supply his slaves with tobacco, there appears to have been no other way for them to obtain it on North Caicos. This suggests that tobacco was not available even through the slaves' own exchange system, which presumably existed on North Caicos, as they did on other islands.

Another significant aspect of the Promised Land assemblage is its similarity to the Wade's Green slave assemblage in terms of personal adornment and clothing. The Promised Land slaves had an even smaller percentage of items in this category than the Wade's Green assemblage, and no glass beads were recovered at all. In this regard, one may indeed be seeing a difference in the transatlantic trade network. It appears that glass beads were not readily available even in Nassau. A study of newspaper advertisements in the Nassau papers also sup-

TABLE 5
PERCENTAGE OF SELECTED FUNCTIONAL
GROUPS IN
GEORGIA SLAVE ASSEMBLAGES

Assemblage	Tobacco %	Personal Adornment and Clothing %
Cannon's Point	5.7	3.6
Jones	3.7	
Sinclair	4.8	2.6
Butler Island	30.2	5.2

Note. Calculated from Moore (1985:Table 7.1).

ports the conclusion that glass beads were not readily available, as none has been found listing glass beads for sale.

The Promised Land excavations have helped to define the effects of the transatlantic trade network on the material culture available to planters in the Bahamas. Of the items studied, only glass beads apparently were not supplied in any quantities to the Bahamas through the transatlantic trade network and, therefore, were not available in Nassau, nor on North Caicos. The Bahamas distribution system, however, appears to have had considerable influence on a planter's purchasing decisions on the goods that were available. The cost of transporting goods 400 mi. from Nassau clearly determined the availability of ceramics and tobacco at Wade's Green. When buying ceramics in Nassau it was possible and cheaper to selectively provide plantation slaves with the cheapest types of ceramics. However, it was not worth the time and cost to travel to Nassau from North Caicos to provide the slaves with ceramics specifically chosen for their use. A prepacked, mixed crate available at a discount price was adequate. The Promised Land excavations have also revealed the control that the planter had over the slaves' access to tobacco on plantations in the Out Islands. The planter had the purchasing power to obtain tobacco for himself, the overseer, and favored kitchen slaves at Wade's Green; but the planter could, as Wade Stubbs did, exercise his power to prevent his slaves from obtaining it. This emphasizes the extra level of control that planters could exert over their slaves' access to goods in remote locations such as the Out Islands of the Bahamas.

Conclusions

Archaeological research at Wade's Green and Promised Land plantations has demonstrated that restricted access to manufactured goods due to distance and isolation from the center of distribution in Nassau, explains the ceramic distributions at Wade's Green plantation. At the same time, the ceramic distributions at Promised Land matched those found on plantations where access

to goods was not restricted in the same way.

The same restrictions also affected the availability of other goods. Tobacco is another commodity with an unusual distribution at Wade's Green plantation. However, the distribution of tobacco pipes indicates that, while the planter and overseer had access to tobacco, and distributed it to favored slaves working in the kitchen, the planter could effectively prevent the bulk of the slave population from obtaining tobacco if he so chose, due to the absence of alternative sources of supply. As a result, the planter's control over some resources was enhanced compared to less isolated locations. In contrast, at Promised Land plantation, planter and slave both had ready access to tobacco.

Glass beads are another noticeably absent artifact at Wade's Green plantation. However, they were not found at Promised Land plantation either. This indicates that access to some goods was a problem throughout the Bahamas colony, not just on the remote islands.

This research is significant because it clearly illustrates conditions where economic models commonly used to interpret archaeological data are mediated by local conditions. The distance and isolation from the point of distribution in Nassau restricted access to goods and also served to accentuate the control that the planter could exert over the goods available to the slaves.

Not everything that happened on the Bahamian plantations can be explained and understood in terms of trade networks or planter control over access to goods. Within the framework of the plantation, with all of its restraints and restrictions, Bahamian slaves built a community and a culture that enabled them to survive enslavement.

It is interesting to consider for a moment the meaning of the overall similarity of the functional analyses of the two Bahamian slave assemblages, separated as they are by over 400 mi. of water and different access to goods from Nassau. In the slaves' day-to-day lives and their priorities, at least as represented by their surviving material culture, they are remarkably similar. Thus, while ceramic analysis of the Wade's Green slave assemblage may be misleading with regard to ethnicity and socioeconomic status, the functional analysis provides an incomplete and cursory glimpse of the slaves' lives and culture. Archaeology, combined with the limited documentary sources can provide a general view of Bahamian slave culture on the plantations and the roots of modern Bahamian culture. Building on this framework, using archaeological, documentary, and oral historical evidence, a more complete understanding of the slaves' lives is being developed.

ACKNOWLEDGMENTS

I thank the people and governments of the Commonwealth of the Bahamas and the Turks and Caicos Islands for their cooperation and hospitality. The excavations at Wade's Green were carried out by the students of the 1989 UCLA summer field school and a select group of high school students from the Turks and Caicos Islands. They were codirected by Laurie A. Wilkie. The excavations at Promised Land were carried out by the students of the 1993 LSU summer field school, the staff of the Pompey Museum in Nassau, the staff of the Archaeology Section of the Department of Archives, and volunteers from the Historic Preservation Committee of the Bahamas National Trust, all under the field direction of George W. Shorter, Jr., assisted by Bradley E. Ensor. I thank them all for their dedication and hard work. The Wade's Green project was organized with the assistance of the late Mr. H. E. Sadler and Dr. Nancy A. Whitney-Desautels and carried out by permission of the Government of the Turks and Caicos Islands. The Promised Land project was organized with the assistance of Dr. Gail Saunders and Mr. George A. Aarons, both of the Department of Archives, and Mr. Pericles Maillis of the Bahamas National Trust. Permission for the Promised Land excavation was graciously given by Mr. John Ironson of the New Providence Development Company. The author and his students have spent many hours in the Department of Archives, Nassau, the Department of Lands and Surveys, Nassau, the Registrar General's Department, Nassau, and the Public Records Office, Kew, England, and I thank the staff of each for their patient assistance throughout. I also thank Douglas V. Armstrong, Donna J. Seifert, and two anonymous reviewers for their comments on an earlier version of this manuscript. Finally, I thank Laurie A. Wilkie for her many and varied contributions to my Bahamian research.

REFERENCES

AARONS, GEORGE A., KIM OUTTEN, AND GRACE S. R. TURNER
1990 Historical-Archaeological Research at an 18th-Century Plantation: South Ocean Beach, Divi Bahamas Ltd. Manuscript on file, Department of Archives, Nassau, Bahamas.

ADAMS, WILLIAM HAMPTON (EDITOR)
1987 Historical Archaeology of Plantations at Kings Bay, Camden County, Georgia. Reports of Investigations 5. University of Florida, Gainesville.

ADAMS, WILLIAM HAMPTON, AND LINDA P. GAW
1977 A Model for Determining Time Lag of Ceramic Artifacts. Northwest Anthropological Research Notes 11(2):218–321.

ANTIQUES
1934 Queries and Opinions #900. Antiques 26(5):196–197.

ARMSTRONG, DOUGLAS V.
1990 The Old Village and the Great House. University of Illinois Press, Urbana.

ATTRILL, MOIRA
1986 Bahamas Archaeological Team Report 1985–1986. Journal of the Bahamas Historical Society 8(1):25–26.

BAHAMA GAZETTE (BG)
1786 For the Bahama Gazette. Bahama Gazette 3(97):3–10 June.
1786– Advertisements placed by William and James Moss.
1800 Bahama Gazette, 1786–1800.
1789 Advertisement placed by William and James Moss. Bahama Gazette 6(260):11 July.
1794 Advertisement placed by William and James Moss. Bahama Gazette 11(780):10–17 October.
1795 Advertisement placed by William and James Moss. Bahama Gazette 12(847):9–12 June.
1796a Nassau, May 31, 1796. Bahama Gazette 13(947):28–31 May.
1796b Death. Bahama Gazette 13(1000):6–9 December.
1798 Advertisement placed by Alexander Leckie, Jr. Bahama Gazette 16(1210):28 December 1798–4 January 1799.
1799 Advertisement placed by Alexander Leckie, Jr. Bahama Gazette 16(1307):13–17 December.
1800 Advertisement placed by James Howie. Bahama Gazette 17(1346):2–6 May.

BLASZCZYK, REGINA LEE
1984 Ceramics and the Sot-Weed Factor. Winterthur Portfolio 19(1):7–19.

CASH, PHILIP, SHIRLEY GORDON, AND GAIL SAUNDERS
    1991   *Sources of Bahamian History.* MacMillan Caribbean, London, England.

CLAYPOLE, WILLIAM, AND JOHN ROBOTTOM
    1980   *Caribbean Story.* Book 1, *Foundations.* Longman Caribbean, San Juan, Trinidad.

COKER, WILLLIAM S., AND THOMAS D. WATSON
    1986   *Indian Traders of the Southeastern Spanish Borderlands: Panton, Leslie & Company and John Forbes & Company, 1783–1847.* University Presses of Florida, Gainesville, FL.

COLONIAL OFFICE RECORDS (CO)
    1796   Letter from Planters and Principal Inhabitants of the Caicos Islands to Alexander Murray, 23 November 1796, CO 23/44:101–102. Original Correspondence, Colonial Office Records, Public Records Office, Kew, Richmond, Surrey, England.
    1803a Alexander Murray to the Lords of the Committee of the Privy Council for Trade and Foreign Plantations, 21 January 1803, CO 23/44:106. Original Correspondence, Colonial Office Records, Public Records Office, Kew, Richmond, Surrey, England.
    1803b List of English Ships Cleared Outwards, Nassau, 25th March 1803 –25th June, CO 23/44:56. Original Correspondence, Colonial Office Records, Public Records Office, Kew, Richmond, Surrey, England.
    1803c List of English Ships Cleared Outwards, Nassau, 25th June 1803–25th September, CO 23/44:68. Original Correspondence, Colonial Office Records, Public Records Office, Kew, Richmond, Surrey, England.
    1803d Thomas Brown, Piarra Coffeehouse, Covent Garden, CO 23/44:81–82. Original Correspondence, Colonial Office Records, Public Records Office, Kew, Richmond, Surrey, England.
    1803e Thomas Brown to Lord Hobart, September 1803, CO 23/44:212–215. Original Correspondence, Colonial Office Records, Public Records Office, Kew, Richmond, Surrey, England.
    1818   William V. Mannings to Earl Bathurst, CO 23/67:103–115. Original Correspondence, Colonial Office Records, Public Records Office, Kew, Richmond, Surrey, England.

CRATON, MICHAEL
    1986   *A History of the Bahamas.* San Salvador Press, Waterloo, ON.

CRATON, MICHAEL, AND GAIL SAUNDERS
    1992   *Islanders in the Stream: A History of the Bahamian People.* Vol. 1, *From Aboriginal Times to the End of Slavery.* University of Georgia Press, Athens.

DAGGETT, KENDRICK PRICE
    1988   *Fifty Years of Fortitude: The Maritime Career of Captain Jotham Blaisdell of Kennebunk, Maine, 1810–1860.* Mystic Seaport Museum, Mystic, CT.

DEANS PEGGS, A.
    1957   *A Relic of Slavery: Farquharson's Journal for 1831–1832.* Deans Peggs Research Fund, Nassau, Bahamas.

DEPARTMENT OF ARCHIVES (DA)
    1806   Indenture between James Moss and John McIntosh, and Wade Stubbs, 30 December 1806. Indentures, 6 April 1825–3 October 1826:193–197. Department of Archives, Nassau, Bahamas.
    1821   Last Will and Testament of Wade Stubbs, 17 October 1821. Department of Archives, Nassau, Bahamas.
    1822   Register of Slaves, 1 January 1822. Department of Archives, Nassau, Bahamas.
    1838   John Cockburn to Lord Glenely, Duplicate Despatch #65:964–965, 12 April 1838. Bahamas Duplicate Despatch 1837–1838. Department of Archives, Nassau, Bahamas.

DEPARTMENT OF LANDS AND SURVEYS (DLS)
    1785   Grant Book A, page 21. Department of Lands and Surveys, Nassau, Bahamas.

EDWARDS, BRYAN
    1819   *The History, Civil and Commercial, of the British West Indies.* Five volumes. T. Miller, London.

FARNSWORTH, PAUL
    1992   Comparative Analysis in Plantation Archaeology: The Application of a Functional Classification. Paper presented at the Annual Meeting of The Society for Historical Archaeology Conference on Historical and Underwater Archaeology, Kingston, Jamaica.
    1993   Archaeological Excavations at Wade's Green Plantation, North Caicos. *Journal of the Bahamas Historical Society* 15(1):2–10.
    1994   Archaeological Excavations at Promised Land Plantation, New Providence. *Journal of the Bahamas Historical Society* 16(1):21–29.

FARNSWORTH, PAUL, AND L. A. WILKIE FARNSWORTH
    1990   A Preliminary Report on the 1989 Excavation at Wade's Green Plantation, North Caicos. Manuscript on file, Department of Archives, Nassau, Bahamas.

FRIES, ELEANOR BETHEL (EDITOR)
    1968   *Nassau, Bahamas 1823–1824: The Diary of a Physician from the United States Visiting the Island of New Providence.* Bahamas Historical Society, Nassau, Bahamas.

GERACE, KATHY D.
1982   Three Loyalist Plantations on San Salvador Island,
       Bahamas. *Florida Anthropologist* 35(4):216–222.
1987   Early Nineteenth-Century Plantations on San Salvador,
       Bahamas: The Archaeological Record. *Journal of the
       Bahamas Historical Society* 9(1):14–21.

HANDLER, JEROME S., AND FREDERICK W. LANGE
1978   *Plantation Slavery in Barbados: An Archaeological
       and Historical Investigation.* Harvard University
       Press, Cambridge, MA.

KELLY, KENNETH G.
1989   Historic Archaeology of Jamaican Tenant-Manager
       Relationships: A Case Study from Drax Hall and
       Seville Estates, St. Ann, Jamaica. Unpublished M.A.
       thesis, Department of Anthropology, College of
       William and Mary, Williamsburg, VA.

KELSO, WILLIAM M.
1984   *Kingsmill Plantations, 1619–1800.* Academic Press,
       Orlando, FL.
1986   The Archaeology of Slave Life at Thomas Jefferson's
       Monticello: "A Wolf by the Ears." *Journal of New
       World Archaeology* 6(4):5–20.

KOZY, CHARLENE JOHNSON
1983   A History of the Georgia Loyalists and the Plantation
       Period in the Turks and Caicos Islands. Unpublished
       B.A. dissertation, Department of History, Middle
       Tennessee State University, Murfreesboro, TN.

LAWLOR, JIM
1985   Archaeological Notes: Report of Bahamas
       Archaeology Team on the Archaeological Findings at
       Tusculum, New Providence. *Journal of the Bahamas
       Historical Society* 7(1):27.

MAJEWSKI, TERESITA, AND MICHAEL J. O'BRIEN
1987   The Use and Misuse of Nineteenth-Century English
       and American Ceramics in Archaeological Analysis.
       Advances in Archaeological Method and Theory
       11:97–209.

McKINNEN, DANIEL
1804   *A Tour Through the British West Indies, in the Years
       1802 and 1803, Giving a Particular Account of the
       Bahama Islands.* J. White, London, England.

MILLER, GEORGE L.
1980   Classification and Economic Scaling of 19th-Century
       Ceramics. *Historical Archaeology* 14:1–40.
1984a Marketing Ceramics in North America. *Winterthur
       Portfolio* 19(1):1–5.
1984b George M. Coates, Pottery Merchant of Philadelphia,
       1817–1831. *Winterthur Portfolio* 19(1):37–49.
1991   A Revised Set of CC Index Values for Classification
       and Economic Scaling of English Ceramics from
       1787 to 1880. *Historical Archaeology* 25(1):1–25.

MILLER, GEORGE L., AND SILAS D. HURRY
1983   Ceramic Supply in an Economically Isolated Frontier
       Community: Portage County of the Ohio Western
       Reserve, 1800–1825. *Historical Archaeology*
       17(2):80–92.

MOORE, SUSAN MULLINS
1985   Social and Economic Status on the Coastal Plantation:
       An Archaeological Perspective. In *The Archaeology
       of Slavery and Plantation Life*, edited by Theresa A.
       Singleton, pp.141–160. Academic Press, Orlando,
       FL.

ORSER, CHARLES E., JR.
1988   The Archaeological Analysis of Plantation Society:
       Replacing Status and Caste with Economics and Power.
       American Antiquity 53(4):735–751.

OTTO, JOHN SOLOMON
1984   *Cannon's Point Plantation, 1794–1860.* Academic
       Press, Orlando, FL.

PETERS, THELMA PETERSON
1960   *The American Loyalists and the Plantation Period in
       the Bahama Islands.* Ph.D. dissertation, Department
       of History, University of Florida, Gainesville.
       University Microfilms International, Ann Arbor, MI.

PRICE, CYNTHIA R.
1979   19th-Century Ceramics in the Eastern Ozark Border
       Region. *Southwest Missouri State University, Center
       for Archaeological Research, Monograph Series* 1.

RAGATZ, LOWELL J.
1975   "Upon Every Principle of True Policy": The West
       Indies in the Second Empire. In *The American
       Revolution and the West Indies*, edited by Charles W.
       Toth, pp.183–209. Kennikat Press, Port Washington,
       NY.

REGISTRAR GENERAL'S DEPARTMENT (RGD)
1789   Land Grant to Wade Stubbs, Bahamas Records
       Alphabet Series B-1:12. Registrar General's
       Department, Nassau, Bahamas.
1797   Inventory of Assessment of William Moss, Bahamas
       Records Alphabet Series E-2:34–47. Registrar
       General's Department, Nassau, Bahamas.

RILEY, SANDRA
1983   *Homeward Bound: A History of the Bahama Islands
       to 1850.* Island Research, Miami, FL.

ROYAL GAZETTE AND BAHAMA ADVERTISER (RG&BA)
1804   Advertisement placed by James Moss, Jr. *Royal
       Gazette and Bahama Advertiser* 1(12):17 August.
1818   Most Destructive Fire. *Royal Gazette and Bahama
       Advertiser* 5(521):14 November.
1820   On Monday Last. *Royal Gazette and Bahama
       Advertiser* 7(724):25 October.

1822 Died. *Royal Gazette and Bahama Advertiser* 9(854):23 March.

SANFORD, DOUGLAS W.
1994 The Archaeology of Plantation Slavery in Piedmont Virginia: Context and Process. In *Historical Archaeology of the Chesapeake*, edited by Paul A. Shackel and Barbara J. Little, pp.115–130. Smithsonian Institution Press, Washington, DC.

SAUNDERS, D. GAIL
1983 *Bahamian Loyalists and Their Slaves*. Macmillan Caribbean, London, England.
1990 *Slavery in the Bahamas 1648–1838*. D. Gail Saunders, Nassau, Bahamas.

SCHWIND, ARLENE PALMER
1984 The Ceramic Imports of Frederick Rhinelander, New York Loyalist Merchant. *Winterthur Portfolio* 19(1):21–36.

SIEBERT, WILBUR HENRY
1972 *Loyalists in East Florida, 1774 to 1785; The Most Important Documents Pertaining Thereto, edited with an Accompanying Narrative*. Vol. 2, *Records of their Claims for Losses of Property in the Province*. Reprint of 1929 edition. Gregg Press, Boston, MA.
1975 Loyalist Exodus to the West Indies: Legacy of Revolution. In *The American Revolution and the West Indies*, edited by Charles W. Toth, pp. 210–225. Kennikat Press, Port Washington, NY.

THOMPSON, G. A.
1812 *The Geographical and Historical Dictionary of America and the West Indies*. J. Carpenter, London, England.

TREHARNE, R. F., AND HAROLD FULLARD
1969 *Muir's Historical Atlas: Medieval and Modern*. Eleventh edition. George Philip & Son, London, England.

TURNER, GRACE S. R.
1992 An Archaeological Record of Plantation Life in the Bahamas. *Journal of the Bahamas Historical Society* 14(1):30–40.

WATTERS, DAVID R.
1994 Mortuary Patterns at the Harney Site Slave Cemetery, Montserrat, in Caribbean Perspective. *Historical Archaeology* 28(3):56–73.

WATTERS, DAVID R., AND DESMOND V. NICHOLSON
1982 Highland House, Barbuda: An 18th-Century Retreat. *The Florida Anthropologist* 35(4):223–242.

WHEATON, THOMAS R., AMY FRIEDLANDER, AND PATRICK H. GARROW
1983 Yaughan and Curriboo Plantations: Studies in Afro-American Archaeology. Soil Systems, Marietta, GA.

WHEATON, THOMAS R., AND PATRICK H. GARROW
1985 Acculturation and the Archaeological Record in the Carolina Lowcountry. In *The Archaeology of Slavery and Plantation Life*, edited by Theresa A. Singleton, pp. 239–259. Academic Press, Orlando, FL.

WHEATON, THOMAS R., AND MARY BETH REED
1990 James City, North Carolina: Archaeological and Historical Study of an African American Urban Village. New South Associates, Stone Mountain, GA.

WHITER, LEONARD
1989 *Spode: A History of the Family, Factory and Wares from 1733 to 1833*. Barrie & Jenkins, London, England.

PAUL FARNSWORTH
DEPARTMENT OF GEOGRAPHY AND ANTHROPOLOGY
LOUISIANA STATE UNIVERSITY
BATON ROUGE, LA 70803-4105

James A. Delle

The Material and Cognitive Dimensions of Creolization in Nineteenth-Century Jamaica

ABSTRACT

Creolization is defined as a special form of ethnogenesis that in plantation contexts was a process through which social and material worlds were defined. Using colonial Jamaica as an example, ethnohistorical sources to suggest how creole identities were emically defined by and negotiated between populations of both European and African descent, and suggests how the process of creolization was manifested in the use of space, foodways, and general health of creole populations of both European and African descent.

Introduction: The Dual Process of Creolization

As scholars from such disparate disciplines as linguistics and culinary arts have used the term "creole" in a variety of contexts, it may be difficult if not impossible to create a consensus among archaeologists as to just what the term "creolization" means. For the purposes of this paper, creolization is considered to be a theoretical concept used to explain the processes by which European and African populations adjusted or adapted to conditions in the New World, particularly where plantation agriculture dominated the political economy (Brathwaite 1971; Ferguson 1992:xli). Creolization can be considered as a form of ethnogenesis, specific to plantation contexts. Creolization is a dual process, comprised of both social and material elements, through which distinctive identities, social structures, and material cultures were created, negotiated, and re-negotiated in colonial zones of the New World. As an anthropological concept, creolization can be used in archaeological analysis to interpret how people adapted to the political ecology of, for example, late 18th- and early 19th-century Jamaica. Creolization can be defined both as an emic, cognitive process of defining a distinctly Jamaican social identity on the parts of both European and African peoples and a material process of adaptation to the economic, social, and ecological conditions of colonial Jamaica.

Although archaeologists are most interested with the material remains of colonial society, the material evidence of creolization is best understood in the contextual light of ethnohistorical research. Using the ethnohistorical record of Jamaica in the late 18th and early 19th centuries, this article sets out to: characterize the cognitive, emic definitions of "creole" identities as they were understood by people in that place and time; define creolization as a material process of adaptation for people both of European and African descent, which, in following Richard D. E. Burton's (1997) terminology, are referred to as Euro-creoles and Afro-creoles respectively; and to suggest how the concept of creolization, defined as a dual material and cognitive process, can be used to inform the archaeological analysis of 19th-century Jamaican coffee plantations.

The Cognitive Definition of Creole Identity

In his definitive study of creole society in Jamaica, the Caribbean scholar Edward Brathwaite (1971) revealed the complexity of meanings entwined in the term "creole," particularly when applied to the Caribbean. As Brathwaite (1971:xv) suggests, the term has been applied to descendants both of European colonialists and enslaved Africans; to various "pidgen" languages that have developed, primarily in the New World; and to a sense of cultural authenticity. Now used as an analytical term by scholars generations removed from the people they study, the term "creole" was in general use in 19th-century Jamaica, referring to those members of society–both black and white–born in, native to, and committed to living in Jamaica. From at least the second half of the 17th century, there was a self-conscious distinction made between those born in the Caribbean, and those who had emigrated to the islands. As early as 1689 Sir Hans Sloane, in writing about the population of

Historical Archaeology, 2000, 34(3):56—72.
Permission to reprint required.

Jamaica, distinguished between "Europeans" and what he called "creolians" (Burton 1997:14).

In understanding the nature of creolization as a process of negotiating identity in colonial Jamaica, it therefore seems appropriate to begin with a consideration of how people emically defined their "creole" identities. It should be pointed out that there were at least three distinct forms of creole society forming in Jamaica during this time. Two of these three groups developed in relationship to the slave-based plantation system: Euro-creoles (those who were identified primarily by their European ancestry) and Afro-creoles (those who were identified primarily through their African heritage). A third group, the maroons, was composed of escaped slaves and their descendants, a group that developed a distinct and sovereign identity apart from those integrated into the colonial plantation system (Brathwaite 1971). Despite the importance of the maroons to the development of Jamaican society, this study focuses on those directly involved in the Euro-centric plantation economy: the Euro-creoles and the Afro-creoles.

In the early 19th century a sharp distinction was drawn between "creole" and "new comer," a distinction that was experienced differently by those defined as being of European and African descent. The historical record of Jamaica suggests that the descendants of both Europeans and Africans living in Jamaica self-consciously considered themselves distinctively "creole." This interpretation of how these emic identities were constructed and experienced is drawn from a number of sources, the most important of which are: (1) the diary of Maria Nugent, the daughter of a prominent New Jersey loyalist who eventually became the wife of George Nugent, governor of Jamaica from 1801 to 1805 (Wright 1966); (2) the remarks made by Edward Long, a Jamaican planter who wrote a voluminous history of Jamaican in 1774, in which he described Jamaican society in great detail (Long 1970); and (3) archival and material data from a series of plantation records from those coffee plantations on which the author has worked, including Martin's Hill, Marshall's Pen, Balcarres, Radnor, and several located in the Yallahs district, an upland region that has been the focus of recent research. Taken together these sources offer insight into how the inhabitants of late 18th- and early 19th-century Jamaica created and perceived Jamaican creole identities.

Euro-Creoles

In the early 19th century, white Jamaicans were called "creoles" both by themselves and their European contemporaries if they were born in the West Indies to white parents. Creole identity had to do with much more than simple pedigree, however. Much of creole identity was centered around cognitive constructions; for example, white Jamaican creoles adopted a distinct accent or dialect. According to the diary of Maria Nugent, Europeans disparaged the creole dialect as "gibberish" and "an indolent drawling out of the words" (Wright 1966:76, 98). She noted that a creole language was spoken by both whites and blacks, and considered the language somewhat of a degeneration of English, as is evident in the following passages from her diary:

> The Creole language is not confined to the negroes. Many of the ladies, who have not been educated in England, speak a sort of broken English, with an indolent drawling out of the words, that is very tiresome if not disgusting. I stood next to a lady one night, near a window, and, by way of saying something, remarked that the air was much cooler than usual; to which she answered, 'Yes ma'am, him rail-ly too fraish' (Wright 1966:98). Mrs. Sherriff [wife of a coffee planter] is a fat, good-humored Creole woman, saying dis, dat, and toder . . . (Wright 1966:76). Major and Mrs. Cookson, their two daughters, and a little boy, a black maid, and two men, came on a West India visit, to spend the day. Mrs. C. is a perfect Creole, says little, and drawls out that little, and has not an idea beyond her own Penn (Wright 1966:52).

The dialect was described in similar terms by Edward Long in his voluminous *History of Jamaica*, published in 1774. In arguing that white children should be sent to England for education, Long contended that Euro-creole girls who spent long hours with the enslaved domestic servants attached to their households tended to adopt the "drawling, dissonant gibberish" of the domestics (Long 1970:278).

Maria Nugent did not have a very favorable opinion of the Euro-creole population of Jamaica. She characterized what she calls the Euro-Creole "disposition" as being parochial, overbearing, indolent, and lazy with very unrefined manners; she often commented that Euro-creoles consistently overindulged in food, drink, and sex. She summarized her impressions of the white creole population succinctly:

> It is indeed melancholy, to see the general disregard of both religion and morality, throughout the whole island. . . . It is extraordinary to witness the immediate effect that the climate and habit of living in this country have upon the minds and manners of Europeans, particularly of the lower orders. In the upper ranks, they become indolent and inactive, regardless of everything but eating, drinking, and indulging themselves. . . In the lower orders, they are the same, with the addition of conceit and tyranny; considering the negroes as creatures formed merely to administer to their ease, and to be subject to their caprice . . . (Wright 1966:97-98).

Beyond their comparative immorality from an elite colonial point of view, Euro-creoles developed distinct mannerisms and social characteristics. For example, Mrs. Nugent admitted to indulging herself in an interesting and practical habit known as breezing or "creolizing," a posture that allowed the overdressed Euro-creoles to air themselves out (Figure 1). This practice was described by John McLeod in 1817: "Creolizing is an easy and elegant mode of lounging in a warm climate; so called because much in fashion among the ladies of the West Indies; that is reclining back in one arm-chair, with their feet upon another, and sometimes upon the table" (quoted in Wright 1966:117, note 1).

Long (1970:261-262) perceived Euro-creoles as having developed not only a distinctive social identity, but a set of distinct physical characteristics:

> Creoles . . . are in general tall and well-shaped; and some of them rather inclined to corpulence. Their cheeks are remarkably high-boned, and the sockets of their eyes deeper than is commonly observed among the native of England. . . . Their sight is keen and penetrating. . . . The effect of climate is not only remarkable in the structure of their eyes, but likewise in the extraordinary freedom and suppleness of their joints. . . ."

Although he held a generally favorable opinion of Euro-creoles, Long commented quite frankly on what he defines as the men's "foibles." In describing the flaws of the creole disposition, he used terms like indolent, haughty, vain, and supine. Like Mrs. Nugent, he believed that

FIGURE 1. "Creolizing," or reclining with one's feet resting on a wall or table. (Courtesy of the National Library of Jamaica.)

both men and women engaged too frequently in sex, and were addicted to expensive living, particularly costly entertainments (Long 1970:265). Long described Euro-creole women as being lively, frank, polite, and generous, fond of dancing, gossip, and socializing, and not inclined to drink as heavily as creole men. As was the case with creole men, women engaged, apparently quite commonly, in extra-marital affairs. Long blames this phenomenon on the warm climate which he thought roused human passion to the point where, in his words, chastity required "no mean effort of female fortitude" (Long 1970:283).

Both Long and Mrs. Nugent comment on the racist, segregated reality of Jamaican creole society. Long asserted that Euro-creole men often preferred Afro-creole women as sexual partners, creating what was in his mind a vast population both of white spinsters and mulatto children. He commented that the latter did not have a place in polite Jamaican society and should not be educated, while as the wife of the governor, Mrs. Nugent felt compelled to receive wealthy mulatto women whom she called "the coloured ladies" *but only* after dinner, in her bedroom, segregated from white society (Wright 1966:66).

Afro-Creoles

Slavery was the primary organizing principle of Jamaican society until its full abolition in 1838. As was usually the case in instances where slavery was reified by skin color, creole society in colonial Jamaica was graded by skin color. In the late 18th and early 19th centuries, Jamaican social structure was largely based on distinctions made between those of European, African, and mixed descent, legally termed "white," "black," and "mulatto" or "coloured," respectively (Brathwaite 1971; Heuman 1981; Bakan 1990; Holt 1992).

According to Long's account, the rights and privileges of what he calls "freed blacks and mulattos" were restricted, as only those who could prove that they were at least three generations removed from their nearest African ancestor were allowed the same rights as were whites. All others of mixed European and African heritage were legally defined as "mulattos," in effect creating a tripartite racial structure in the island. The existence of free mulattos was perceived as a problem by many of the Euro-creoles, particularly since there were reputedly a number of white planters who bequeathed significant property to their mulatto children. Other whites struggled to ensure that voting rights enjoyed by this class of people were limited, the Jamaica Assembly going so far as to pass a bill in 1762 which put limits on the amount of property Afro-creoles could inherit from their white fathers (Long 1970:323; Heuman 1981).

Just as he characterized the disposition of Euro-creoles, Long described the character of what he calls the "Creole Blacks." He argued that Afro-creoles were more adept at resisting the designs of overseers not only by intentionally misunderstanding orders, but by studying the personality weaknesses of overseers and playing on their particular weaknesses (Long 1970:405). Although this was by no means his intention, Long provides an image of Afro-creoles being extremely perceptive of the human condition under slavery. This perception inclined many Afro-creoles to distance themselves from white society, which they thought corrupt. Many Afro-creoles, for example, did not drink, believing, in Long's words that the whites "exhibit such detestable pictures of drunkenness, that the better sort of Creole Blacks have . . . conceived a disgust at [the] practice . . . "(Long 1970:409).

Another feature said to characterize the Afro-creoles was their enjoyment of music, at which many were adept. According to Long: "This . . . has also been remarked of the Creole Blacks, who, without being able to read a single note, are known to play twenty or thirty tunes,

country-dances, minuets, airs, and even sonatas, on the violin; and catch, with an astonishing readiness, whatever they hear played or sung . . ." (Long 1970:262-263).

Adopting several names simultaneously or in sequence has been part of Jamaican Afro-creole culture from at least the early 19th century, and may be representative of the dual nature of life for those living between the white and black worlds of Jamaican society. For example, in the early 1820s, the population of Martins Hill was baptized into Christianity. According to the documentary evidence, every one of the enslaved women, most of whom had previously been referred to by a single name, adopted both a Christian first and surname. Of the 138 women listed in the baptismal register, only seven had identifiably African names; all were identified as creoles. Each of these creole women had their names changed to Christian ones: e.g., Beneba and Mimba, both creoles born in 1774, had their names changed to Cecelia Manning and Diana Martin. The youngest of the seven, born in 1804 and previously known as Yabba, had her name changed to Eleanor Robertson. This may reflect a precedent for the current Jamaican custom of adopting more than one name, a "Christian" or "Babylon" name (depending on whether one identifies oneself as Christian or Rastafarian), and a common name that a person generally chooses for themselves as a young adult. Interestingly, none of the African women identified in the Martins Hill record was listed with an African name. It is impossible now to reconstruct whether these women, African and creole alike, commonly used their new Christian names, or whether they continued to use African names without the expressed knowledge (expressed in the documentary record anyway) of the planters.

The historical record suggests that Afro-creoles may have distanced themselves from newly arrived Africans. For example, Long (1970:410) asserted that Afro-creoles had a self-conscious shared identity that they used to distinguish themselves from Africans: "The Creole Blacks . . . hold the Africans in the utmost contempt, stiling [sic] them 'salt-water Negroes' and 'Guiney-birds'."

Long's account suggests that Africans of the various ethnic groups recognized by Europeans exhibited both cultural and physical traits that distinguished them from each other, and from Afro-creoles. The African ethnicities identified by Long include Coromantins from the Gold Coast, Minnahs, Mundingos [sic], Congos, Ebos, Papaws, Conchas, Whidahs, Angolas, and Aradas (Long 1970:403-404). That various personality traits were recognized among the several ethnic groups identified by Long is supported by the West Indian historian Bryan Edwards: "Coromantins, and many others of the Gold Coast slaves, are haughty, ferocious, and stubborn . . . " (Long 1970:403). "The circumstances which distinguish the Koromantyn, or Gold coast negroes . . . are firmness both of body and mind; a ferociousness of disposition . . . courage, and . . . stubbornness . . . " (Edwards 1810:267). "The Congos, Papaws, Conchas, Whidahs, and Angolas, in general, are good field labourers . . . " (Long 1970:403). " . . the people of Whidah, or Fida . . . are called generally in the West Indies *Papaws*, and are unquestionably the . . . best-disposed slaves that are imported from any part of Africa" (Edwards 1810:278). "The Ebo men are lazy, and averse to every laborious employment, the women performing almost all the work in their own country; these men are sullen, and often make away with themselves, rather than submit to any drudgery; the Ebo women labour well, but are subject to obstructions of the *menstrua*, often attended with sterility, and incurable" (Long 1970:404).

> We are now come to the Bight of Benin, comprehending an extent coast of near 300 English leagues, of which the interior countries are unknown, even by name, to the people of Europe. All the negroes imported from these vast and unexplored regions . . . are called in the West Indies *Eboes*. . . . The great objection to the Eboes as slaves, is their constitutional timidity, and despondency of mind; which are so great as to occasion them very frequently to seek . . . a voluntary death. . . . The females of this nation are better labourers than the men . . . (Edwards 1810 :280-281).

Long (1970:403-404) further remarked about the personality and physical traits of other various ethnic groups:

> The Minnahs, timid and desponding, apt to destroy themselves upon the least, and often without any, provocation. The Mundingo Negroes are very subject to worm disorders; the Congos to dropsies . . . The Negroes brought from Senegal are of better understanding than the rest, and fitter for learning trades, and for

> menial domestic services. They are good commanders over other Negroes, having a high spirit, and a tolerable share of fidelity; but they are unfit for hard work; their bodies are not robust, nor their constitution vigorous . . . The Aradas are thought to excel all the rest in the knowledge of agriculture, yet their skill is very incomplete. The Congos, and Gold Coast Negroes, in general, are good fishermen, and excel in making canoes.

Bryan Edwards (1810:283) recognized that the conditions of slavery in the West Indies, and in particular Jamaica, were such that the distinct cultural characteristics of what he calls the "various African nations" combined to create a new creole society. In his words, the circumstances of slavery "soon efface the native original impression which distinguishes one nation from another in negroes newly imported, and create a similitude of manners, and a uniformity of character throughout the whole body" (Edwards 1810:284). In effect, although he does not use the term, he observed the process of creolization as it created a new ethnic identity out of the multitude of cultures imported from Africa. He characterizes this newly emergent creole disposition as being distrustful and not always truthful when dealing with whites. Enslaved creoles would thoroughly ponder questions put to them by their masters, Edwards (1810:284) observed, so that they would have time to consider "not what is the true answer, but what is the most politic one . . . to give." He contrasts the tension that existed between white and black with strong attachments that developed between enslaved men, revealing that the term "shipmate" signified a close bond of friendship. Edwards (1810:290) further noted that enslaved creoles were artful orators who prided themselves on their loquaciousness.

In comparison, Long's (1970:407) description of the Afro-creole disposition, while equally racist, suggests a unified sphere of personality traits that the Europeans and Euro-creoles assigned to the Afro-creoles:

> In their tempers [creoles] are in general irascible, conceited, proud, indolent, lascivious, credulous, and very artful. They are excellent dissemblers, and skillful flatterers. They posses good-nature, and sometimes, but rarely, gratitude. Their memory soon loses the traces of favours conferred on them, but faithfully retains a sense of injuries; this sense is so poignant, that they have been known to dissemble their hatred for many

years, until an opportunity has presented of retaliating; and, in taking of their revenge, they shew a treachery, cowardice, and deliberate malice, that almost exceed credibility. . . .

Whether or not these perceptions about creoles distinguishing themselves from Africans was accurate, it does seem to be the case that Euro-creoles made a distinction between African-born and Afro-creole identities, and that this distinction held some meaning for the planters. The planters distinguished between what they called "creoles" and "Africans" in official plantation and parish records, including such records as slave returns and plantation daybooks or journals. At Radnor plantation when two people shared a name it was common to refer to one as, for example, "Creole King" to distinguish him from, presumably, another man born in Africa and known simply as "King." The distinction was clearly important to the managers of Martin's Hill, a coffee plantation owned by the Earl of Balcarres. Although records of this estate exist from as early as 1807, the first time the distinction was made between African and creole was in 1825, 18 years after the end of the slave trade. At that time, the adult enslaved population of Martins Hill, those over the age of 14, numbered 288; of these 158 were identified as African and 130 as creole.

A Shared Creole Cognition?

The ethnohistoric evidence indicates that a distinct creole consciousness had formed in Jamaica by the beginning of the 19th century. It appears from the contemporary accounts of Long, Mrs. Nugent, and Edwards that those born on Jamaica–whether black or white–shared a cognitive base emerging from both European and African precedents; this may be nowhere more evident than in the creole dialect shared by black and white. The latter was disparaged by European elites, yet fully emerged by the 19th century as the lingua franca of Jamaica. Afro-creole nannies would teach the dialect to the children of Europeans, who would in turn become the Euro-creoles, sharing some measure of their identity not only with their Afro-creole instructors, but with the Afro-creole children with whom they themselves played as children. While grave social distance separated black from white, master from slave, the shared cognition of

being creole intimately linked Euro-creole society to Afro-creole society, while it simultaneously reinforced the racist social hierarchy of colonial Jamaica. In effect, the cognitive dimension of creolization was a complex process of social negotiation through which the descendants of Europeans created a new social milieu with precedents in English culture, but dependent on the existence of a social hierarchy bolstered by the inequalities of slavery. What Long and Edwards poetically referred to as the disposition of Afro-creoles may in fact have been the result of the development of a shared consciousness of struggle against this racist hierarchy. The cognitive dimension of creolization for those of African descent may well have been based on the emergence of a shared identity that created a sense of unity and solidarity among people of color, both enslaved and free, whose recent ancestors may have had little in common beyond the fact that they had been enslaved and brought to Jamaica from various regions in Africa. In sum, creole identities–both Euro-creole and Afro-creole–emerged as the actors negotiated their positions in the social order of colonial Jamaica.

The Material Negotiation of Creole Identity

In colonial Jamaica, creolization involved not only the cognitive process of defining a distinctive identity, but adapting to the material conditions of the island's ecology and the social conditions of the island's society. This in turn was a dual process, involving both biological and social adaptation. It follows that elements of this biocultural process should be recoverable from the archaeological record. From the perspective of historical archaeology, the most recoverable traces of the process of creolization may exist in the material culture of space, health, and foodways.

The Afro-creole Use of Space

While enslaved on plantations, Afro-creoles and Africans alike lived in what were called villages or settlements on the estates to which they were attached. Three spatial areas were of particular importance to the process of creole adaptation: the house, the yard, and the provision ground or farm.

FIGURE 2. Scene showing Afro-creole wattle-and-daub houses with thatched roofs and overhanging porches. (Courtesy of the National Library of Jamaica.)

Most of the surviving descriptions of Afro-creole houses suggest that houses generally had between one and three 12 x 12 ft. (4 x 4 m) rooms, ranging in size from 12 x 12 ft. to 12 x 36 ft. (4 x 4 m to 4 x 11 m) (Figure 2). Most seem to have been earthfast, with wattle-and-daub walls and thatched roofs. Excavations led by Doug Armstrong at Seville and the author's recent work at Marshall's Pen have revealed that at least some Afro-creole houses had cobblestone floors. The houses at Marshall's Pen appear to have had small stone enclosures behind them, serving either as animal pens or to protect house gardens from marauding cattle. Interestingly, it appears that occasionally young men were buried in houses, although it is still unclear whether the burials would take place while the house was occupied or after it was abandoned (Armstrong and Kelly 1991; Armstrong 1995). On coffee plantations, villages consisted of a number of houses clustered together relatively close to the coffee works. Documents and maps suggest that there were relatively few houses on coffee

estates, particularly considering the size of the population. This suggests either that the houses were very crowded when inhabited, that some of the people did not spend much time in the house, or the documents and maps may not reflect the actual number of houses located in the villages (Higman 1988:244; Delle 1998).

Afro-creole houses were generally constructed of wattle and daub with thatched roofs. Entries for the first few weeks of the Radnor Plantation Book indicate that while three or four people were "making huts," one person was simultaneously cutting thatch, suggesting that the thatch was used during house construction. An undated lithograph depicting a "mountain cottage scene" (Figure 3) in Jamaica corroborates the suggestion that houses located in the mountains were constructed with thatched roofs. This illustration suggests that at least some houses contained two rooms, here indicated by a secondary roof covering an "el" attachment. Matthew Lewis

FIGURE 3. A Jamaican mountain cottage scene. (Courtesy of the National Library of Jamaica.)

(1929:197) described the slave houses on his sugar estate as being constructed of wattle and daub. Armstrong's excavations at Seville and Drax Hall, both sugar estates active in the 18th and early 19th centuries, corroborates the fact that Afro-creole houses were made of earthfast architecture, and in some cases included an overhanging roof (Figure 2). This feature created a small area in front of the house in which people could engage in domestic activities, while remaining sheltered from the rain (Armstrong 1990, 1992). In the author's own ethnoarchaeological research in the parish of St. Ann, it has been noted that modern Jamaicans living in the bush build their houses with such overhangs, orienting the house to the west. Sheltered under the overhang, it is possible for people to remain both outside and dry when the rains come, as the prevailing winds are from the east.

It is probable that, just as is the case today, in the early 19th century the most important domestic space was the yard, not the house. To this day in Jamaican creole patois the term "yard" is synonymous with "home," just as in the United States the term "house" is synonymous with "home." People worked, ate, and socialized in their yard. It was in the house yards that some cash crops, particularly fruits like coconut, papaya, and mango, were grown for sale in local markets, in garden plots of between one-eighth and one-quarter acre. Yards were also used for raising livestock, particularly pigs and chickens (Parliamentary Papers 1842:13/741).

Provision grounds were arguably the most important space to the enslaved Afro-creole population. In pre-emancipation Jamaica, planters with estates located in the interior or in mountainous areas relied on the production rather than the importation of food to feed their laborers. The laborers, in turn, were allowed access to lands to produce not only their own foodstuffs but to produce surplus for exchange in local markets. This practice was observed by William Beckford in 1790 and J. Stewart in 1823, both of whom noticed that Afro-creole farms were located in "provision grounds" on estates, each family working between a quarter acre and a full acre of land. Beckford (1790:257) observed that a quarter acre was sufficient to supply a family with both enough food for themselves and a small surplus to

carry to market (Mintz and Hall 1960; Stewart 1969:267). Afro-creoles used these provision grounds to grow their staple crops, mainly tubers including cocos, yams, cassava, varieties of sweet potatoes, and white potatoes, which have become known as "Irish potatoes." The Radnor plantation record indicates that the enslaved population attached to that estate sold these provisions, as well as fresh pork and castor oil, to the white overseers and bookkeepers employed on the estate (Delle 1998:151-155).

While provision grounds may be difficult to locate archaeologically, something can be said about how creole agriculture was organized through an examination of cartographic and documentary data. An estate plan of Green Valley, a coffee plantation located in the Blue Mountains, was drawn in 1837 specifically to measure the extent of the estate's provision grounds. The plan indicates that the provision grounds were divided into 18 pieces, ranging in size from 3 to 13 acres (Figure 4). Five years after the plan was drawn, Alexander Geddes, a Euro-creole coffee planter who owned property in the Blue Mountains, testified to a Parliamentary committee that Afro-creoles generally cultivated plots of between one-half and two acres in which people grew tubers and other staples. Within the larger plots, gardens were cultivated on a short rotational swidden system. Geddes reported that each family would cultivate a half-acre plot for two or three years, after which another would be cleared and cultivated (Parliamentary Papers 1842:13/467).

The Euro-creole Use of Space

A significant difference between Euro-creoles and Afro-creoles was their use of space. While the latter lived and operated in yards, the Euro-creoles tended to live and operate as much as was possible within their houses. In adapting to Jamaica's tropical climate, Euro-creoles devised some architectural features similar in some ways to Afro-creole features that extended the interior space of houses outward, in effect domesticating small exterior areas. These structures that Maria Nugent alternately refers to as "West India houses" or "creole houses" featured such architectural elements as galleries, piazzas or verandas, and porticoes or porches (Figures 5-8). Each of these extended the house outward,

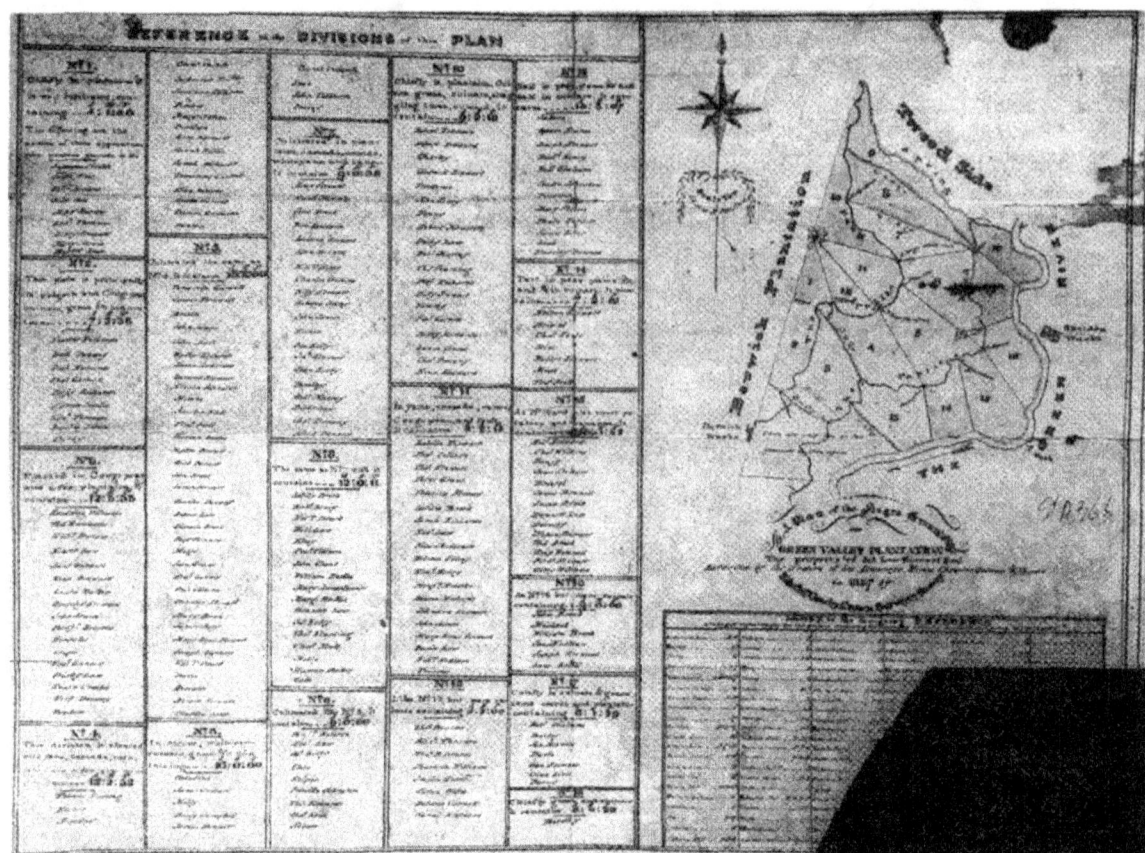

FIGURE 4. A plan of Green Valley, a coffee plantation located in the Blue Mountains. (Courtesy of the National Library of Jamaica.)

giving the Euro-creoles the opportunity to enjoy the air while not being fully exposed to the sunlight (Wright 1966:55).

Verandas become an important architectural feature of plantation buildings, providing not only comfort for the Euro-creoles, but a surveillance point from which overseers could monitor the working and domestic lives of the enslaved population. For example, the author's recent study of the design and use of architecture on coffee plantations in Jamaica's Blue Mountains (Delle 1998, 1999) suggests that verandas and balconies on overseers' houses were intentionally constructed in such a way as to maximize the overseers' ability to panoptically monitor both the domestic and work lives of the enslaved. Such features were important to Euro-creole adaptation to the social conditions of slavery as they provided a mechanism to enhance social

control. Verandas simultaneously facilitated adaptation to the ecological realities of Jamaica, extending the English world into the outside. On a veranda, the Europeans could avoid the sweltering heat of closed quarters while not exposing creoles directly to what they believed to be the very harsh effects of direct sunlight. The European fear of the outdoors is expressed in a comment made by Mrs. Nugent about her husband, the governor: "After breakfast, General [Nugent] walked out to my great annoyance and alarm . . . . He says he forgot all about the climate, and does not feel the worse for it. However, Dr. Lind had made him promise not to go out again in the heat of the day; at least not on foot" (Wright 1966:15).

To compensate for what was perceived to be a dangerous climate and extreme temperature, new types of spaces were created and used. Mrs.

FIGURE 5. Arntully great house, an early 19th-century coffee plantation house showing creole architectural elements that extended the boundaries of domesticated space as it appeared in the 19th century. (Courtesy of the National Library of Jamaica.)

Nugent repeatedly refers to West India houses that feature architectural elements through which the climate could be made more tolerable for the Euro-creoles, for example: "[Mr. Mitchell's] house is truly Creole. The wood-work Mahogany—[with] galleries, piazzas, porticoes, etc." (Wright 1966:55).

According to Mrs. Nugent, enslaved domestic servants slept in such creole houses, like the great house at Seville. After a late evening at a neighboring plantation, Mrs. Nugent returned with her hosts to Seville: "I could not help laughing, as we entered the hall at Seville, to see a dozen black heads popped up, for the negroes in the Creole houses sleep always on the floors, in the passages, galleries, etc." (Wright 1966:81).

Afro-creole Foodways

Information from the documentary record as well as archaeologically recovered material culture can provide information on the foodways developed by creoles in Jamaican. Recent excavations of African-Jamaican houses have recovered significant amounts of locally made redware vessels, usually hollow in form, and

FIGURE 6. Arntully great house, as it appeared in the mid-1990s. (Photo by James A. Delle.)

FIGURE 7. The interior of Arntully great house showing the use of mahogany and the vaulted ceilings that would have facilitated the flow of air on hot days. (Photo by James A. Delle.)

collectively known as "Yabba" or "Yabba ware" (Bonner 1974; Armstrong 1990:146-158; Reeves 1997:195-199). The Afro-creole diet was similar in many ways to the contemporary diet of African Americans in the American South. The creole diet included stews made from legumes, maize, yams, and other roots; non-indigenous fruits like breadfruit and ackee; as well as herbs like callaloo. Such vegetable foods were supplemented with pork, fresh or salt fish, salted beef, herrings, jerked pork, and chicken and other fowls. Long asserts that Afro-creoles particularly enjoyed salt fish and a kind of dish called potato-pone, made from pounded sweet potatoes and maize. Afro-creoles ate stewed dishes that were made with okra and were well seasoned with peppers. Long (1970:413-414) himself exclaimed that so-called pepper pots were "extremely relishing, and nutritive . . . ." It seems likely that much of the Afro-creole cuisine was prepared in the Yabba vessels so often recovered archaeologically.

Euro-creole Foodways

As Maria Nugent remarked, Euro-creole foodways, at least among the elite with whom she socialized, were characterized by eating an astonishing variety of foods, consumed daily during the course of four or five meals: breakfast, second breakfast, lunch, tea, and dinner. In one entry in her journal, Mrs. Nugent described what she called a "breakfast in the Creole style," which included, in her words "cassava cakes, chocolate, coffee, tea, fruits of all sorts, pigeon pies, hams, tongues, rounds of beef, and . . . turtle" (Wright 1966:55). Her journal is abundant with references to "the second breakfast," taken at about 2:00, during which people ate very rich foods, often seafood and veal in an oily sauce, followed by tarts, cakes, and fruit (Wright 1966:79). Of course, much of this food was prepared for Euro-creoles by enslaved domestic servants, many of whom were Afro-creole mulatto women; it comes as no surprise that Euro-creole cuisine was heavily influenced by Afro-creole foodways. For example, Mrs. Nugent reported that she particularly enjoyed a meal that included a course of jerked pork, and another of a stewed landcrab pepper-pot (Wright 1966:70):

> The first course was entirely of fish, excepting jerked hog. . . . There was also a black crab pepper-pot, for which I asked the receipt. . . . It is as follows; a capon stewed down, a large piece of beef and another of ham, also stewed to a jelly; then six dozen of land

crabs, picked fine, with their eggs and fat, onions, peppers, ockra [sic], sweet herbs, and other vegetables of the country, cut small; and this, well stewed, makes black crab pepper pot. . . . The second course was of turtle, mutton, beef, turkey, goose, ducks, chickens, capons, ham, tongue, crab patties, etc. . . . The third course was composed of sweets and fruits of all kinds. . . . I was really sicker than usual, at seeing such a profusion of eatables.

Afro-creole Health

Creolization involved adopting not only new forms of shelter and foodways, but adaptation to both the pathogens present in Jamaica and the sometimes dubious European remedies used to combat them. Archaeologically, there are several ways to evaluate the health of the Afro-creole population of colonial Jamaica. One can, of course, examine skeletal remains for paleopathologies, which has been done at Seville estate, where chronic anemia has been detected through osteological analysis (Fleischman 1995).

Other pathologies resulting from nutritional stress, including enamel hypoplasias and traces of lead poisoning, have been identified through the analysis of skeletal remains from Barbados (Handler and Corruccini 1983, 1986; Handler et al. 1986). Such evidence can be supplemented by documentary records which also can be used to interpret nutritional and other biological stresses experienced by the Afro-creole population. Two types of evidence are most readily available for analysis of this kind: records of slave hospitals that were located on individual plantations (Figure 9), and the records of causes of death kept by plantation managers.

The documentary record of Radnor plantation indicates that the most common disease afflicting the Afro-creole population of this estate in the 1820s was yaws, a spirochete infection symptomatically similar to syphilis. The disease often left its victims facially disfigured, as it would occasionally result in the loss of facial

FIGURE 8. A second view of the interior of Arntully great house. (Photo by James A. Delle.)

FIGURE 9. The slave hospital at Kellets Plantation, as it existed in the early 20th century. (Courtesy of the National Library of Jamaica.)

and digital extremities. The European treatment imposed on people for this disease consisted of isolation from the community, the sometimes forced application of mercurial ointment, and the ingestion of mercury pills. Although no evidence concerning the specific plants involved has yet been uncovered, Dr. James Maxwell reported that Afro-creole medical practitioners had great success treating yaws in the Caribbean using West African herbal remedies (Sheridan 1985).

Yaws is thought to be a disease indigenous to West Africa. Its presence in Jamaica suggests that the presence of the pathogen was part of the biological process of creolization. The infection was exacerbated and spread by the harsh conditions of the African slave trade. Although the incidence of yaws on Jamaica declined following the abolition of the slave trade, the disease remained prevalent in mountainous, rainy areas, the very places coffee production was most successful. The Radnor Plantation Journal (1821–1826) indicates that from 1 January 1823 until 29 September 1823, 19 people–nearly 10% of the enslaved population–were confined with yaws. Although yaws was rarely fatal, there were at least two mortal cases on Radnor

Plantation, both children. There was a West African tradition of inoculating children with yaws shortly before they were weaned, thus, it is possible that at least one of these children, at 20 months, died as a result of this inoculation.

Yaws is caused by a spirochete similar in form to syphilis; unlike syphilis, however, yaws is not classified as a sexually transmitted disease. Due to the syphilitic-like symptoms of the disease and a reluctance on the part of the African community to reveal certain conditions to the planters, there is little reliable evidence concerning venereal diseases among the slave populations of Jamaica, although venereal disease may have been a common affliction among the creole population. Thomas Thistlewood, who kept a meticulously detailed diary of his life in southwestern Jamaica, reported that gonorrhea was a fairly common disease among the enslaved population on his estate (Hall 1989). There is only one fully documented occurrence of a venereal disease in the plantation records so far investigated for this study; others are merely hinted at. While it is known that at Radnor the male slave Trim died as the result of an unnamed venereal infection, a second incident hints that at least one Radnor woman was infected with a venereal disease. The entry under "Daily Remarks" for 25 July 1823 reads: "Dr. Schroeter has verbally ordered mercurial ointment for Roseline to be rubbed into her groins, which has been done" (Radnor Plantation Journal 1821-1826). As mercurial ointment was used in the treatment of both yaws and syphilis, in this case, because the ointment was rubbed into Roseline's groin, it seems likely that it was prescribed for a venereal disease. The ambiguous phrase "which has been done" may also indicate that the treatment was performed on an unwilling patient; that Roseline may have had mercury treatment forced upon her against her will. Regardless, the use of a European treatment for syphilis on a West African disease in the Caribbean certainly reflects the creolization of an Old World medicinal practice.

Edward Long (1970:433ff) comments on the various health afflictions faced by the Afro-creole population, including yaws and venereal diseases. Long reported that unscrupulous slave traders treated Africans inflicted with yaws before the middle passage with a mixture of iron-rust, gunpowder, and lime-juice. This treatment was thought to temporarily mask the symptoms of yaws. It is likely that despite this treatment, the disease was passed on through oral transmission and the intimate contact people would endure during the middle passage. Long claimed that outbreaks of the disease were common among groups of Africans newly arrived to Jamaica. His report corroborates that yaws was treated in Jamaica by mercurial preparations, that even he believed caused dangerous side-effects, including problems in the joints and a potentially mortal infliction known as dropsy, or edema (Long 1970:433-434).

Other pathogens and biological disorders plaguing the creole population included small-pox, pleurisies, fluxes (diarrhea or dysentery), worms, and tetanus (Long 1970 [1774]:433-434; Sheridan 1985; Higman 1986). Dr. David Collins (1971) commented that the harsh working conditions on West Indian plantations took a considerable toll on the enslaved population.

Beyond the skeletal analysis undertaken by Fleischman and Handler and Corruccini, little archaeological research into the health of the Afro-creole population of the British West Indies has yet been undertaken. Should excavations ever be completed on, for example, a slave

hospital site, much more could be said about the specific pathogens and treatments that were part of the creole experience. Flotation of soil samples from privies and wells associated with a slave hospital may reveal floral evidence of the types of herbs used by Afro-creole healers in specific remedies. It would be expected that many such remedies had African antecedents; it remains to be seen archaeologically whether African plants or those indigenous to the West Indies were in common use as remedies. Wilkie (1996a, 1996b) presents African-American analogies.

Euro-creole Health

Due probably to chronic dehydration and dyspepsia from the nearly incessant over consumption of alcohol and rich foods, and exposure to various tropical mosquito-borne pathogens, particularly yellow fever and malaria, the Euro-creole population of Jamaica was not an especially healthy group. Maria Nugent recognized that certain habits injured the health of men in particular, commenting for example that she was "not astonished at the general ill health of the men of this country; for they really eat like cormorants and drink like porpoises" (Wright 1966:81). Her journal is full of passages commented on the poor habits of the Euro-creole population, habits which she was sure injured their health. She described the appearance of an unhealthy creole planter who dined with her at the governor's residence: "Mr. Wilkie . . . dined with us. He is exactly like a man who has been buried and dug up again so pale, lean, and miserable looking" (Wright 1966:55). In other passages she more specifically remarked on the cost of incessant overeating: "Mr. Mitchell's delight is to stuff his guests, and I should think it would be quite a triumph to him, to hear of a fever or apoplexy, in consequence of his good cheer" (Wright 1966:55). "I don't wonder now at the fever the people suffer from here–such eating and drinking I never saw! Such loads of all sorts of high, rich, and seasoned things, and really gallons of wine and mixed liquors as they [referring to the creoles] drink! I observed some of the party, to-day, eat of late breakfasts, as if they had never eaten before. . . it was all as astonishing as it was disgusting" (Wright 1966:57). "[I] could not help observing, although the gentlemen of our party had all eaten and drank at Fort Brunswick [earlier in the day], they did the same here, and I am sure so much eating injures the health of many of them. General N. and I touched nothing at either place" (Wright 1966:77). This last comment implies that all the eating and drinking Mrs. Nugent observed were not artifacts merely of her presence as an eminent visitor, but reflected the established culinary habits of the Euro-creole population. That the ill health of the Euro-creole population may have been caused by intemperate behavior may be supported by Mrs. Nugent's observation on widows: "Alas! How often in this country do we see these unfortunate beings! Women rarely lose their health, but men as rarely keep theirs" (Wright 1966:58-59).

Yellow fever was a mortal pathogen that afflicted the Euro-creole population throughout the 19th century. It was not recognized until the early 20th century that yellow fever was transmitted by mosquitoes. Be this as it may, Maria Nugent commented frequently on how annoying, if not recognizably deadly, these creatures were to even elite members of the Euro-creole society. Ironically, in the same passage concerning the differential health of white creole men and women, she remarked: "Annoyed sadly by musquitos [sic], and my little protégé Brooke's face is terribly disfigured by them . . ." (Wright 1966:59). In another passage she notes: " . . . among the agrémens of this climate, the innumerable musquitoes, that have almost eaten us up, and certainly spoilt our beauty. My face, neck, hands, and arms, have been martyrs . . ." (Wright 1966:22).

Conclusion: Implications for an Historical Archaeology of Creolization

The ethnohistorical evidence reviewed in this article reveals that a self-conscious process of self-identifying as "creole" was ongoing in late-18th- and early-19th-century Jamaica. Euro-creoles recognized themselves, and were recognized by others, as being a distinct society, with rules based upon English precedent, but transformed by the realities of the vast inequalities of slavery, and the exalted position that Euro-creoles enjoyed in the colonial social order. This cognitive process of self-identifying was reinforced by a distinct material culture, based

on English precedent but transformed both by African and Afro-creole influences, and the need to accommodate the climatic and ecological realities of a tropical island. The emergent Euro-creole material culture can be observed in several manifestations, including architecture and use of space, foodways, and medical realities.

Similarly, the evidence suggests that Afro-creoles also self-identified themselves in such a way as to distinguish themselves from newly arrived Africans; a syncretic Afro-creole ethnicity seems to have been established by the beginning of the 19th century. The Afro-creole population, primarily enslaved, were accorded a degrading and oppressive position in the social hierarchy of colonial slavery. Although constrained by the realities of slavery, a dynamic and creative Afro-creole ethnicity may well have emerged as part of the process of creating social solidarity among the enslaved, including not only the creation of a shared creole dialect, but a series of new material cultures. As was the case for the Euro-creoles, the process of creolization involved the evolution of new cultural elements, based in this case on African precedents, but influenced by the presence of a dominant European and Euro-creole society. This process too, is manifested in architecture, foodways, and the biocultural adaptation to the political and ecological realities of slavery in Jamaica.

As the material dimension of creolization has left traces in the archaeological record, future informed excavations of Jamaican sites should produce more evidence concerning the ways in which material culture mediated the process of negotiation inherent both in the cognitive and material elements of creolization. Though not focused specifically on the creolization process, the author's recent work on Blue Mountain coffee plantations (Delle 1998, 1999) suggests how landscape archaeology can be used to interpret the ways in which power and the process of creolization were intimately connected. The creation of new landscape forms, like coffee plantation, can itself be seen as part of the material process of creolization. Analyzing how the negotiation of such landscapes affected the lives of both enslaver and enslaved can in turn reveal some of the ways in which space was used to mediate power between Euro-creoles and Afro-creoles, an important dimension of both Euro-creole and Afro-creole identities.

More site-specific excavations, informed by research designs that consider the material dimensions of creolization, could better elucidate just how the cognitive and material worlds of Afro-creoles and Euro-creoles differed and were similar, both to each other and to their Old World precedents. The excavations of house areas, like those conducted at Seville and Drax Hall (Armstrong 1990), and the ongoing research project at Marshall's Pen, can reveal how space was defined and used within Afro-creole villages. The analysis of the artifacts, not only the locally produced Yabba wares, but English ceramics as well, might well reveal the syncretic nature of the creolization process where creolization occurs not in the production of but in the multivalent uses of the material culture.

When creolization is considered as both a cognitive and material process, it can be a concept used to accomplish what historical archaeologists have so often tried in vain to do: link the physical to the social, the material to the cognitive. If the concept can be so used, it may well provide the theoretical basis for interesting work.

ACKNOWLEDGMENTS

I would like to thank all those who provided assistance on the crafting and revision of this article, including Shannon Dawdy, Laurie Wilkie, Doug Armstrong, Ken Kelly, Samuel and Huguette Levine, and the anonymous reviewers.

REFERENCES

ARMSTRONG, DOUGLAS V.
1990 *The Old Village and the Great House: An Archaeological and Historical Examination of Drax Hall Plantation, St. Ann's Bay, Jamaica.* University of Illinois Press, Urbana.
1992 African Jamaican Housing at Seville: A Study of Spatial Transformation. *Archaeology Jamaica,* No. 6.
1995 African Jamaican Transformations at Seville: Application of a Functional Analysis. Paper presented at the 28th Annual Conference on Historical and Underwater Archaeology, Washington, DC.

ARMSTRONG, DOUGLAS V., AND KENNETH G. KELLY
1991 Processes of Change and Patterns of Meaning in a Jamaican Slave Village. Paper presented at the 24th Annual Conference on Historical and Underwater Archaeology, Richmond, VA.

BAKAN, ABIGAIL B.
1990 *Ideology and Class Conflict in Jamaica: the Politics of Rebellion.* McGill-Queen's University Press, Montreal, Quebec.

BECKFORD, WILLIAM
1790 *A Descriptive Account of the Island of Jamaica.* T. and J. Egerton, London, England.

BRATHWAITE, [EDWARD] KAMAU
1971 *The Development of Creole Society in Jamaica, 1770-1820.* Clarendon Press, Oxford, England.

BONNER, TONY
1974 Blue Mountain Expedition: Exploratory Excavations at Nanny Town by the Scientific Exploration Society. *Jamaica Journal,* 8(2-3):46-50.

BURTON, RICHARD D. E.
1997 *Afro-Creole: Power, Opposition, and Play in the Caribbean.* Cornell University Press, Ithaca, NY.

COLLINS, DAVID
1971 [1811] *Practical Rules for the Management and Medical Treatment of Negro Slaves, in the Sugar Colonies, by a Professional Planter.* Books for Libraries Press, Freeport, NY.

DELLE, JAMES A.
1998 *An Archaeology of Social Space: Analyzing Coffee Plantations in Jamaica's Blue Mountains.* Plenum Press, New York, NY
1999 The Landscapes of Class Negotiation on Coffee Plantations in the Blue Mountains of Jamaica, 1790-1850. *Historical Archaeology,* 33(1):136-158.

EDWARDS, BRYAN
1810 *The History, Civil and Commercial, of the British Colonies in the West Indies,* Vol. 2. Levis and Weaver, Philadelphia, PA.

FERGUSON, LELAND
1992 *Uncommon Ground: Archaeology and Colonial African-America.* Smithsonian Institution Press, Washington, DC.

FLEISCHMAN, MARK
1995 Anemia and Stress in Archaeological Populations of African Descent. Paper presented at the 28th Annual Conference on Historical and Underwater Archaeology, Washington, DC.

HALL, DOUGLAS
1989 *In Miserable Slavery: Thomas Thistlewood in Jamaica, 1750-86.* Macmillan, London, England.

HANDLER, JEROME S., ARTHUR C. AUFDEHEIDE, ROBERT S. CORRUNICCINI, ELIZABETH M. BRANDON, AND LORENTZ E. WITTMNERS, JR.
1986 Lead Contact and Poisoning in Barbados Slaves: Historical, Chemical, and Bioanthropological Evidence. *Social Science History,* 10:399-425.

HANDLER, JEROME S., AND ROBERT S. CORRUCCINI
  1983 Plantation Slave Life in Barbados: A Physical
        Anthropological Analysis. *Journal of Interdisciplinary
        History,* 14:65-90.
  1986 Weaning Among West Indian Slaves: Historical and
        Bioanthropological Evidence from Barbados. *William
        and Mary Quarterly,* 3rd series, 43:111-117.

HEUMAN, GAD
  1981 *Between Black and White: Race, Politics and the
        Free Coloreds in Jamaica, 1792-1865.* Greenwood
        Press, Westport, CT.

HIGMAN, BARRY
  1986 *Slave Population and Economy in Jamaica, 1807-1834.*
        Cambridge University Press, Cambridge, England.
  1988 *Jamaica Surveyed: Plantation Maps and Plans of
        the Eighteenth and Nineteenth Centuries.* Institute
        of Jamaica, Kingston.

HOLT, THOMAS
  1992 *The Problem of Freedom: Race, Labor, and Politics
        in Jamaica and Britain, 1832-1938.* Johns Hopkins
        University Press, Baltimore, MD.

LEWIS, MATTHEW
  1929 [1834] *Journal of a West Indian Proprietor, 1815-17,*
        edited with an Introduction by Mona Wilson.
        Houghton Mifflin, Boston, MA.

LONG, EDWARD
  1970 [1774] *The History of Jamaica.* Frank Cass & Co.,
        London, London.

MINTZ, SIDNEY, AND DOUGLAS HALL
  1960 *The Origins of the Jamaican Internal Marketing
        System.* Yale University, New Haven, CT.

PARLIAMENTARY PAPERS
  1842 Parliamentary Papers, 13. British Library, London,
        England.

RADNOR PLANTATION JOURNAL
  [1821-1826] Manuscript. National Library of Jamaica,
        Kingston.

REEVES, MATTHEW
  1997 *"By Their Own Labor": Enslaved Africans' Survival
        Strategies on Two Jamaican Plantations.* Ph.D.
        dissertation, Department of Anthropology, Syracuse
        University, Syracuse, NY. University Microfilms
        International, Ann Arbor, MI.

SHERIDAN, RICHARD B.
  1985 *Doctors and Slaves.* Cambridge University Press,
        Cambridge, England.

STEWART, J.
  1969 [1823] *A View of the Past and Present State of the
        Island of Jamaica.* Negro University Press, New
        York, NY.

WILKIE, LAURIE A.
  1996a Medicinal Teas and Patent Medicines: African-
        American Women's Consumer Choices and
        Ethnomedical Traditions at a Louisiana Plantation.
        Southeastern Archaeology, 15(2):119-131.
  1996b Transforming African-American Ethnomedical
        Practices: A Case Study from West Feliciana.
        Louisiana History, 37(4):457-471.

WRIGHT, PHILIP (EDITOR)
  1966 *Lady Nugent's Journal of Her Residence in Jamaica
        from 1801-05.* Institute of Jamaica, Kingston.

JAMES A. DELLE
DEPARTMENT OF ANTHROPOLOGY
FRANKLIN & MARSHALL COLLEGE
LANCASTER, PA 17604

DAVID R. WATTERS

Mortuary Patterns at the Harney Site Slave Cemetery, Montserrat, in Caribbean Perspective

ABSTRACT

Mortuary patterns discernible at the Harney site, despite its disturbed condition, include demographic, burial, and artifact information derived from 17 skeletons, 19 unmatched bones, 10 graves, and 134 artifacts. The cemetery dates to the late 18th century and provides data on the mortuary practices of enslaved persons in Montserrat at a time when sugar production dominated the economy of the British West Indies. A broader perspective on the mortuary patterns of enslaved populations within the Caribbean region is provided by comparable data from burial sites in two other British islands, Barbados and Jamaica, and a mainland South American colony, Dutch Guiana—now Suriname. Collaboration by avocational and professional archaeologists during the Harney site salvage project exemplifies the joint research efforts typical of many small islands in the eastern Caribbean.

Introduction

Salvage archaeology projects often impose limitations on field work and sometimes result in data recovery techniques that are less than optimum. Even when such projects are conducted under adverse conditions and constrained by time and personnel, they nevertheless generate significant archaeological data that otherwise would be lost. In some small islands of the eastern Caribbean, where there are no professionally trained resident archaeologists, it is the members of local archaeological and historical societies who have taken the lead in conducting salvage projects at threatened sites (e.g., Nicholson 1993). Historic and prehistoric sites are being damaged or destroyed with increasing frequency by development activities associated with the expanding economy, population, and tour-

ism industry of the West Indies. The benefits of collaboration between avocational and professional archaeologists for data recovery are exemplified by the salvage project jointly undertaken at the Harney site slave cemetery, in the small island of Montserrat in the northern Lesser Antilles (Figure 1).

Archaeological research in Montserrat is within the purview of the Montserrat National Trust, a non-governmental organization that has taken the lead in matters concerning the island's natural and cultural heritage (cf. Siegel 1983; Wheeler 1988; Crandall and Dyde 1989; Blankenship 1990). In June 1979, the Montserrat National Trust asked the author, then completing his dissertation research on the island's prehistoric archaeology (Watters 1980), to examine human skeletons unearthed at a house construction site, a request that resulted in a six-day salvage archaeology project at the unmarked and unrecorded Harney site cemetery (MS-A-H4). Montserratians had been unaware of the existence of this cemetery until its skeletons were first exposed by the construction crew. Historic artifacts indicated these were historic, not prehistoric, burials, but other contextual information useful for developing a salvage excavation strategy was lacking. Field work involved only the cemetery; broader spatial issues, such as relationships of the cemetery to a slave village or an entire plantation, could not be investigated during the six-day project.

Only the most significant of the field research constraints on this project, which have been detailed by Watters (1987:290–292), are discussed in this section. Bulldozers previously had scraped the land surface into backdirt piles, and construction workers had dug numerous trenches in a grid pattern across the house site (Figure 2), both being activities that resulted in the fragmentation of in situ skeletons and the scattering of bones in the trenches. Bones of more than one individual had been mixed together, placed in a paper sack, and then reburied in an isolated trench by construction workers. The construction crew continued digging trenches elsewhere in the site, leading to the unearthing of even more skeletons, while the archaeologists were recovering the remnants of the in situ

Historical Archaeology, 1994, 28(3):56–73.
Permission to reprint required.

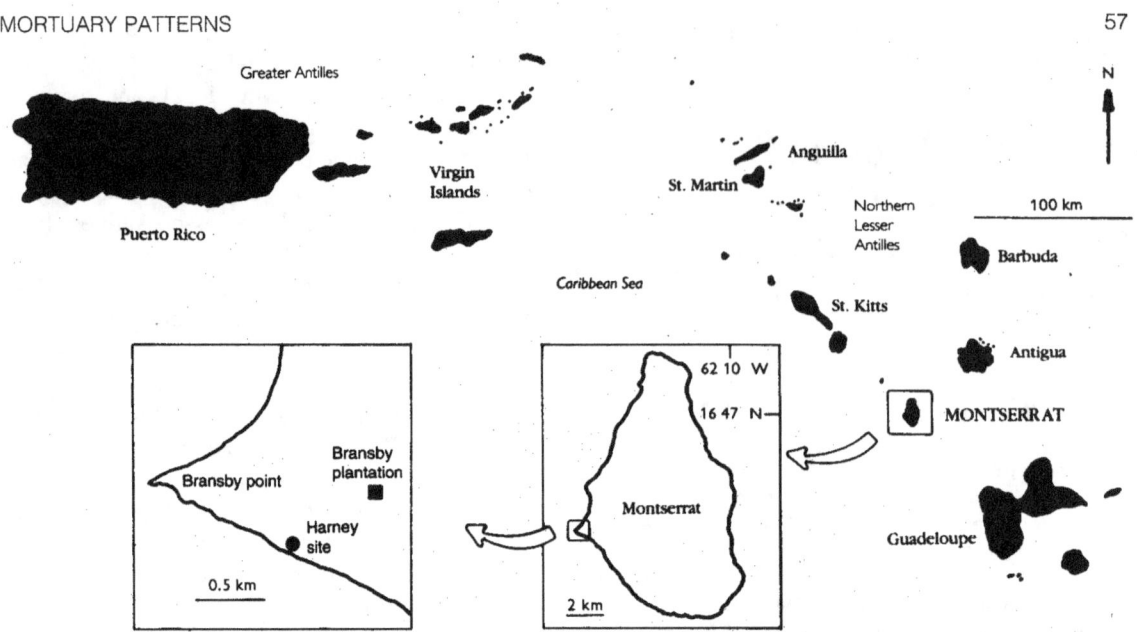

FIGURE 1. Location of the Harney site (MS-A-H4) on the west coast of Montserrat, in the northern Lesser Antilles, West Indies.

skeletons first exposed. The author and one field assistant were joined by three Montserrat National Trust volunteers, none of whom had previous archaeological field experience. The salvage project had to be terminated after six days, even though additional skeletons undoubtedly remained buried within the building site.

Mortuary patterns at the Harney cemetery were discerned only after the repetitive nature of certain elements and practices was recognized. These recurrent aspects were not recognized in three earlier articles, each of which reported on data restricted to the site excavations (Watters 1987), osteology (Mann et al. 1987), or ceramics (Petersen and Watters 1988). The mortuary patterns were first outlined in a research synopsis (Watters and Petersen 1991). Despite the field constraints noted above, the Harney site salvage archaeology project has provided valuable comparative data about the demographic, burial, and artifact patterning of a late 18th-century slave cemetery in the British West Indies.

Demographic Patterns

Seventeen individuals were identified including 10 skeletons from in situ burials (Watters 1987: 292–299) and seven more from disturbed contexts, the latter individuals being first recognized during laboratory osteological analysis (Mann et al. 1987: 320).

Skeleton 4 was the only whole skeleton among the 10 burials excavated. Nine construction-damaged skeletons consisted mainly of post-cranial elements, of which lower extremities predominated (Figure 3). Two fairly complete skulls were recovered in situ. Data for seven disturbed-context individuals, conservatively based on four left subadult and three left adult male femora, were supplemented by data on 19 other bones, none of which could be matched reliably with the other 17 skeletons (Mann et al. 1987). Table 1 provides information on the context, condition, sex, age, stature, and "race" of the 17 individual skeletons.

Demographic patterns are derived from osteo-

FIGURE 2. Construction damage at the Harney site prior to the arrival of the archaeologists. View looking northwest.

logical data for the 10 excavated skeletons, seven disturbed skeletons, and, when pertinent, the 19 unmatched bones. Females (n = 6) and males (n = 6) are equally represented among definitely sexed skeletons. Ages at death range from 7 to 60+ years for unsexed subadults and adult males and females. No infants were recovered. Watters (1987:315) and Mann et al. (1987:335) suggest that males died at younger ages than most females in the Harney skeletal sample, a hypothesis that is invalidated by statistical analysis—Wilcoxen Two-Sample test and Student's t-test—and the small sample size.

"Race" estimates were primarily based on observations of the skull, notably the shape, width, and inferior border of the nasal aperture, alveolar prognathism, dental crenulations—wrinkles, vertical subnasal corrugations, and general cranial contour (Mann et al. 1987:321). The two in situ skulls (Skeletons #4, #7) and one maxilla (Bone #19) are attributable to black individuals, while a second

maxilla (Bone #7) is a probable black but may represent admixture. The other skeletons and unmatched bones are listed as "indeterminate" because they consist almost exclusively of post-cranial elements.

Stature estimates for four Harney site skeletons (Table 1), which are derived from reconstructed long bones and therefore must be viewed cautiously, are on average slightly less than the few available stature measurements of living slaves from Montserrat (Higman 1979:Table 3).

Pathologies

Any interpretation of illnesses and health problems from skeletons is subject to a number of limitations. Most diseases do not affect the skeleton; for diseases that do affect bone, similar manifestations can result from different pathological condi-

FIGURE 3. The lower extremities of Skeleton No. 3 typify the mainly post-cranial bones recovered at the Harney site. The photographer positioned the white rock to support the distal portion of the left femur.

tions (Ubelaker 1978:77). Thus, "diagnosis of specific diseases from skeletal remains is extremely difficult because few pathological lesions are specific to a single disease" (Parrington et al. 1986: 37). Nevertheless, bone pathologies can provide important information about the general health and lifestyle of the skeletal population being studied.

Mann et al. (1987:322) based their analysis of the Harney skeletons on a three-category system—bone loss, apposition, or both—classifying the bone cell response (to disease) present in the bone. The documented pathological conditions for eight of 10 excavated skeletons, two of seven disturbed skeletons, eight of 19 unmatched bones, and many of the 92 teeth (Mann et al. 1987:323–334) are summarized below, with respect to the health of this population.

Osteoarthritic conditions include osteoporosis, eburnation, and grooved articular surfaces (n = 3 individuals), osteoarthritis in two foot phalanges and osteophytes on a distal right femur (n = 1), and ossified connective tissues, or enthesopathies (n = 2). The healed fractures are restricted to hands and legs, and they include left metacarpals (n = 2), right fibula (n = 1), and a right tibia with probable fracture, all occurring in female skeletons. Two cases of enlarged nutrient foramina—hand phalanges of one person—were observed.

The only three skulls retaining suitable eye orbit bone all displayed bilateral cribra orbitalia. Other cranial pathologies include porotic hyperostosis, enostoses, and endocranial porosity. Dental pathologies include caries (17 of 92 teeth), abscesses, enamel hypoplasias, and root hypercementosis.

Mann et al. (1987:336) conclude that pathologies identified in the Harney site skeletons, especially the frequent occurrence of fractures, cribra orbitalia, porotic hyperostosis, and enamel hy-

TABLE 1
DEMOGRAPHIC DATA FOR IN SITU AND DISTURBED SKELETONS

Skeleton	Context[a]	Condition[b]	Sex	Age	Stature (cm)	"Race"[c]
1	I	P	F	50+	157	I
2	I	P	F	20–30	—	I
3	I	P	M	35–45	163	I
4	I	C	F	60+	153	B
5	I	P	F	50+	155	I
6	I	P	F	18–35	—	I
7	I	P	M	25–35	—	B
8	I	P	F	40+	—	I
9	I	P	M	40+	—	I
10	I	P	M	35–45	—	I
11	D	F	M?	18–40	—	I
12	D	F	M	18–40	—	I
13	D	F	M	18–40	—	I
14	D	F	?	7–8	—	I
15	D	F	?	8–10	—	I
16	D	F	?	10–12	—	I
17	D	F	?	14–16	—	I

[a]I = in situ, D = disturbed
[b]P = partial, C = complete, F = fragmented (disturbed context)
[c]I = indeterminate, B = black

poplasias, are suggestive of individuals who suffered traumas and periodic severe malnutrition and, in general, experienced a harsh lifestyle.

The severity of the suffering of enslaved peoples in the British West Indies during the American Revolution is pointed out by Goveia (1965:6), who cites a 1778 report indicating Montserrat had lost nearly 1,200 slaves due to "want of provisions." Higman (1984:260–378) and Ward (1988:119–189) provide demographic and historical information on the health, mortality, and medical care of slaves in the British West Indies in the late 18th and early 19th centuries.

Burial Patterns

Burial patterns could be determined only from the 10 in situ skeletons. Five skeletons were articulated, four probably were, and one definitely was disarticulated when excavated (Table 2). Locations, sexes, and ages of the 10 skeletons are shown in Figure 4 with respect to the contractor's

grid of trenches and platforms. Spatial patterning by sex or age is dubious in this distribution, but the apparent alignment of three females (#2, #4, #5), buried in a row and at regular intervals, merits mentioning.

At least seven skeletons were interred in individual graves. Although three other skeletons (#1, female; #9, #10, males) were buried close to one another, their proximity should not be interpreted as evidence of a "multiple burial," in the sense of a single interment of three persons. Bones from one skeleton (#9), which had been interred earlier, were scattered by an intrusive burial at a later date and which resulted in the disarticulated skeleton observed during excavation (Figure 5).

The direction of the interred body was determined for eight articulated skeletons based on positioning of the legs, skull, or both (Table 2). All legs pointed eastward and the two observed crania were oriented to the west, in what has been termed a "west-headed" direction by Handler and Lange (1978:161).

Six skeletons were deposited on their backs

TABLE 2
BURIAL DATA FOR IN SITU SKELETONS

					Position		
Skeleton	Articulation[a]	Direction[b]	Orientation[c]	Deposition[d]	Legs[e]	Arms[f]	Hands[g]
1	A	WH1	243°	B	E	E	H1
2	A?	—	—	B?	—	—	—
3	A	WH1	250°	B	E?	—	—
4	A	WH3	281°	B	E	E	H2
5	A	WH1	256°	B	E	E	H1
6	A?	WH1	—	B?	—	—	—
7	A?	WH2	—	B?	—	—	—
8	A	WH1	263°	B	—	—	—
9	D	—	—	—	—	—	—
10	A?	WH1	—	B	—	—	—

[a]A = articulated, A? = probably articulated, D = disarticulated
[b]WH = "west-headed" based on legs (WH1), skull (WH2), or skull and legs (WH3)
[c]magnetic azimuth taken between femora or tibiae
[d]B = interred lying on back, B? = probably interred on back
[e]E = extended legs, E? probably extended legs
[f]E = extended arms
[g]H1 = hands on respective hips, H2 = right hand on hip and left hand centered on pelvis

(Figure 6) and three others probably were. Legs were fully extended (n = 4, one being probable); arms extended along the trunk (n = 3); and hands rested on their respective hips (n = 2) except in one case, where the right hand was on the right hip and the left was centered on the pelvis.

The corpses were interred on a rock stratum locally called "shoal," a pattern first observed by the archaeologists in the trenches dug by the construction workers, where bones protruded from the interface of the soil and shoal layers (Figure 7). The consistency of this burial pattern across the site was confirmed by subsequent excavation of the in situ skeletons, where it was evident that the grave diggers made it a practice to dig through the soil layer to the shoal stratum before they interred the body. Several skeletons were located in shallow pits dug into the top of the rock stratum. The depths of the original graves could not be determined since the ground surface had been bulldozed.

Artifact Patterns

Interpretation of artifact patterning is limited by two factors: construction damage to the graves and the improbability that these artifacts are actual grave goods. Table 3 tabulates the 134 artifacts, with 103 (77%) from burial pits and 31 (23%) from two disturbed contexts, the bulldozed backdirt piles and a reburied sack.

Most grave artifacts were recovered from soil deposits above the skeletons. Since the artifacts were not directly associated with the bones, they are regarded as merely incidental inclusions in the fill that was shoveled into the graves. Because they were inadvertently introduced into the graves, these objects cannot be interpreted as grave goods having been purposefully interred with the deceased. The distribution of eight sherds from a single Afro-Montserratian vessel, which were recovered from two graves some 10 m apart, supports their unintentional inclusion because "a single vessel could [not] have been intentionally deposited as an intact grave good in two different graves" (Petersen and Watters 1988:172). One pipe stem, some of the nails, and perhaps one bottle were the only artifacts found in close proximity to the skeletons.

Whole nails or nail fragments comprise 89 (86%) of the 103 grave artifacts. Nails were recovered from five graves, generally those being less

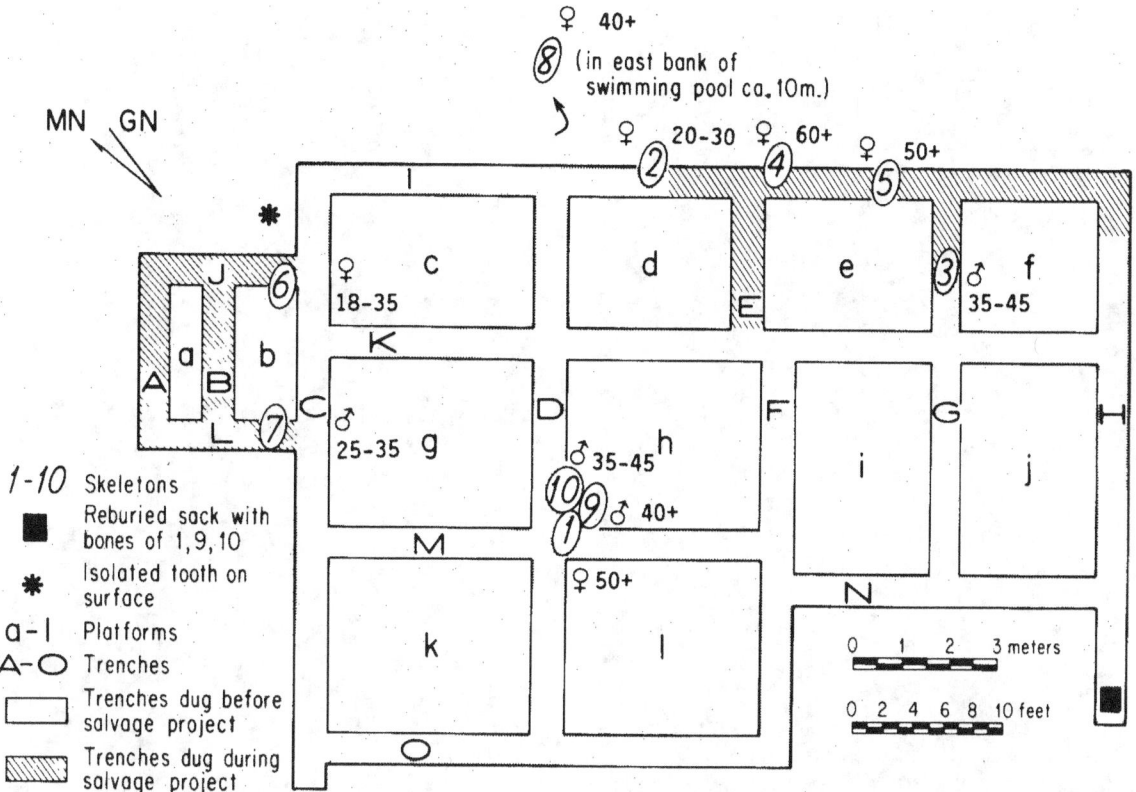

FIGURE 4. Plan view of the 10 in situ skeletons, with their ages and sexes indicated, in relation to the contractor's foundation trenches, at the Harney site.

damaged by construction and having more complete skeletons (Table 3). However, the pattern is not fully consistent because there were no nails with the only complete skeleton (#4) from an intact burial pit. The presence of nails as evidence for a possible burial pattern, coffin interment, is discussed below. Another excavated metal item is a thin (0.6 mm), roughly circular disc (Figure 8a) found in the soil above Skeletons No. 1 and 9. It definitely is not a coin.

Indirect evidence for still other metal artifacts is present in the green copper salts stains detected on three frontal bones and one right clavicle (Mann et al. 1987). The residual green stains almost certainly represent disintegrated copper alloy pins used to fasten burial shrouds at the head and upper torso (cf. Parrington and Roberts 1990:156). No buttons were recovered.

Of 26 sherds recovered, 20 are Afro-Montserratian sherds representing eight vessels (Petersen and Watters 1988), five are imported wares (tin-enameled delftware, creamware, Buckleyware, and possibly Nottingham stoneware), and one, an unglazed redware sherd, could be either imported or manufactured locally in the West Indies (Figure 8b–d).

Two kaolin pipe bowls are heelless and lack makers' marks; one has raised relief that resembles a stemmed and branching device and is present on the front and back (Figure 8e–f). Six stem fragments, two from graves, yielded five bore diameters of 4/64 in. and one of 5/64 in. Osteological evidence of smoking is found with Skeleton No. 7, an adult male having a pipe-stem groove in the left mandibular canine, and another individual exhibiting pipe wear (Mann et al. 1987:331, 334).

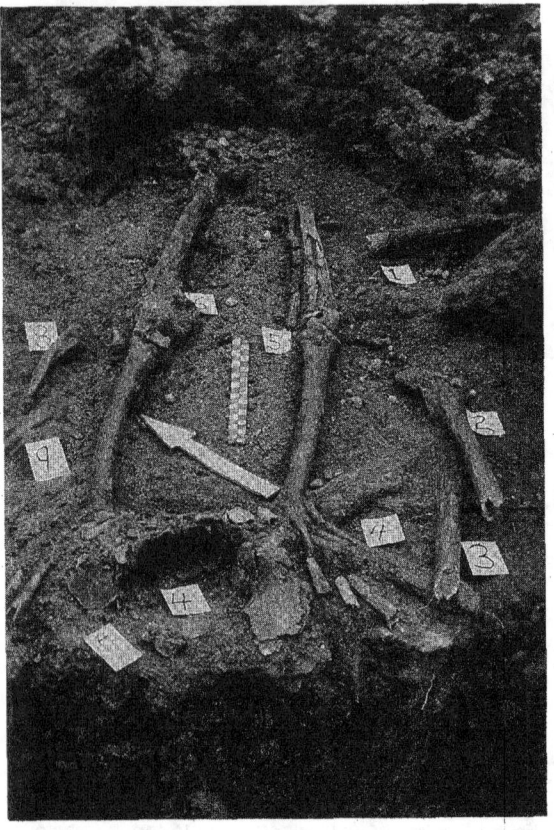

FIGURE 5. Skeleton No. 9's bones (1–4, 8–9) were scattered across the grave during the later interment of Skeleton No. 1 (bones 5–7). Leg bones of Skeleton No. 10 were later recovered from the soil in the upper left of the photograph.

FIGURE 6. The hands rested on the respective hips of Skeleton No. 5.

Of two glass artifacts recovered, the intact cello-shaped Turlington Balsam of Life phial is important because it is dated "OCT 29 1751" (Figure 9). The phial is now regarded as a genuine Robert Turlington bottle (Watters 1987:307–311, Figures 11–15), an attribution of authenticity that could not be made when the bottle was first reported (Watters 1981).

Coffins and Grave Goods

This section deals with the less definitive evidence for two other mortuary patterns, the use of coffins and the placement of selected grave goods. Coffin interment likely is a legitimate pattern; selective inclusion of grave goods remains a possibility.

Nails found in five of the 10 graves support the idea of coffin interment at the Harney site. Nails recovered adjacent to the legs of Skeleton No. 1 provide the most direct evidence of the use of some form of wooden burial device. No other coffin indicators, such as wood fragments, metal handles, or soil stains created by decomposed coffins, were observed in any grave, despite careful scrutiny by the archaeologists (Watters 1987:303–304). Moreover, the only intact grave (Skeleton #4) definitely contained neither nails nor coffin remnants. Thus, nails remain the only indicator of probable coffin use in selected graves.

A wood shortage may account for the apparent lack of coffins in some graves in the Harney cemetery. A report from the 1820s, apparently refer-

FIGURE 7. Bones at the interface of the soil and shoal layers were a consistent burial pattern observed at the Harney site.

ring to white planters, states: "Not a shingle or a board could be bought in Montserrat; the dead there were even being buried in old boxes and trunks" (Ragatz 1971[1928]:343). Goveia (1965:6) indicates that lumber was scarce in the British Leeward Islands—which included Montserrat—during the American Revolution because trade with the normal suppliers, the rebelling colonies in North America, was forbidden, and even after the war lumber prices remained high. In these circumstances, it seems unlikely that the planters would have made lumber available to the slaves for coffin construction. However, complete decomposition—without leaving soil stains—of coffins, without coffin hardware, also would account for the absence of wood remains.

The existence of nails in five graves as well as their high frequency (86%) among the total sample of excavated artifacts are incongruous with a postulated wood shortage. This inconsistency led Watters (1987:304) to conclude that, "barring a reasonable alternative explanation for the presence of nails, it seems logical to conclude that coffins, or some kind of burial apparatus (e.g., planks) requiring nails, were used in some graves at the Harney site."

Two artifacts are the best candidates for being actual grave goods intentionally buried with the deceased. The Turlington bottle was not observed in situ by the author, but his interviews with construction workers who removed the phial confirmed that its original location was in a trench from which parts of Skeletons No. 1, 9, and 10 had been dug (Watters 1987:309). Among various possible functions, the Turlington Balsam of Life phial may have contained rum for the deceased (Handler and Lange 1978:199–203) or may have soaked medicine into the grave, as Rose and Santeford (1985a:42) suggest for a later medicine bottle from the Cedar Grove cemetery in Arkansas.

A second artifact, the metal disc, may have acted as a token or fee for the return of the deceased's spirit to Africa, serving in the same manner as single coins found with eight burials at the First African Baptist Church cemetery in Philadelphia, in the interpretation of Parrington and Roberts (1990:149–150). That the disc was meant to keep the eyes closed is unlikely since it was recovered in the soil above Skeletons No. 1 and 9 rather than in the eye orbit, as reported by Rose and Santeford (1985a:61, 96) for the later Cedar Grove cemetery.

Discussion

Both internal and external correlations may be discerned in the Harney site data. These correlations are discussed below.

Internal Correlations

During the field work, the Harney site skeletons were thought to be the remains of lower-status per-

TABLE 3
DISTRIBUTION OF ARTIFACTS

Location	Metal			Glass		Kaolin Pipe		Ceramics		Total
	Nails[a]	Disc	Shim	Bottle	Fragment	Stem	Bowl	Afro-Montserratian	Imported	
Excavated Context[b]										
Skeleton #1 (+9?)	33 (17)	1	—	—	—	1	—	8	—	43
Skeleton #3	13 (9)	—	—	—	—	—	—	1	—	14
Skeleton #4	—	—	—	—	—	1	—	—	—	1
Skeleton #5	32 (12)	—	—	—	—	—	—	—	—	32
Skeleton #6	—	—	—	—	—	—	—	1	—	1
Skeleton #8	4 (0)	—	—	—	—	—	—	—	1	5
Skeleton #10	7 (2)	—	—	—	—	—	—	—	—	7
Total	89 (40)	1	0	0	0	2	0	10	1	103
Disturbed Context										
Reburied Sack	7 (3)	—	—	1	—	4[c]	1	—	—	13
Bulldozed Backdirt	—	—	1	—	1	—	1	10	5	18
Total	7 (3)	0	1	1	1	4	2	10	5	31
Total	96 (43)	1	1	1	1	6	2	20	6	134

[a]fragments; (nail heads [MNI] in parentheses)
[b]no artifacts with Burials No. 2 and 7
[c]includes one pipe stem found with "mismatched" bones

sons, based on the unmarked nature of the cemetery and the paucity of material culture (e.g., buttons and other clothing accouterments) in the graves. Further inferences about social status were unwarranted during the salvage project since field data about the skeletons and the antiquity of the cemetery were mostly lacking. The archaeologists knew these were historic burials but did not know the time period when these persons lived. There were numerous possible identities for the skeletons in view of Montserrat's lengthy colonial history since its settlement in the 1630s. They included persons with African, European, and mixed ancestries occupying a variety of positions ranging from slaves and former slaves—manumitted or emancipated; to indentured servants—often being Irish in early Montserrat, tenants, and overseers; to soldiers and militiamen.

The Harney site now is interpreted as a late 18th-century cemetery for enslaved persons of African ancestry. The cemetery most likely related to the historic Bransby Plantation, whose buildings are situated inland some 500 m from the cemetery

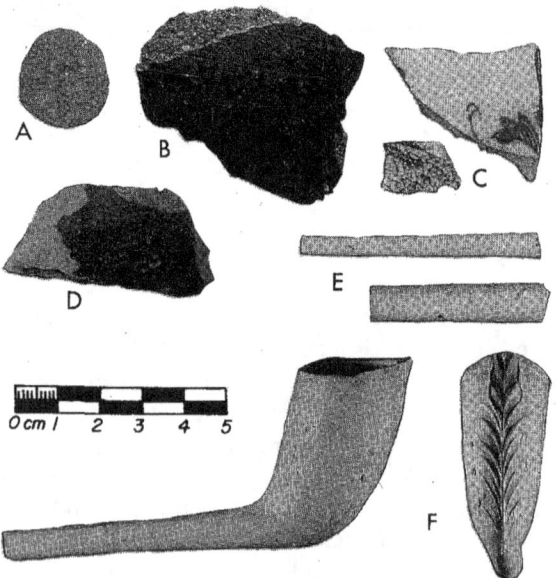

FIGURE 8. Artifacts recovered at the Harney site: *A*, metal disc; *B*, Afro-Montserratian sherd (vessel 5); *C*, two decorated delftware sherds; *D*, Buckleyware sherd; *E*, two kaolin pipe stems; *F*, side and front views of a kaolin pipe bowl exhibiting raised relief.

1 in.

3 cm.

FIGURE 9. Two views of the 1751 Turlington Balsam of Life phial.

(Figure 1). Two historic maps of Montserrat in the John Carter Brown Library at Brown University, Providence, Rhode Island, support this view. The first map (ca. 1673) shows "Bramsbis" plantation and "Bramsbis" point in their approximately correct locations. A second map (ca. 1820) depicts Bransby Point as well as Bransby Estate, the latter being the closest plantation to the Harney site.

Among the 17 individuals and the 19 unmatched bones, four were attributed to persons of black ancestry (Mann et al. 1987:Tables 1, 2). Extrapolation of African ancestry to the entire skeletal sample may seem unjustified based on the small proportion of osteologically identified black individuals. However, in all instances where appropriate cranial elements were present, the individuals were attributed to African ancestry. In no case was a bone attributed to an ancestry other than black. Also, it is very likely that some post-cranial skeletal elements can be attributed to persons of African ancestry since "the general contour of most

femora (anteroposteriorly) is flattened, further suggesting Black individuals" (Mann et al. 1987:335).

The premise that all Harney site skeletons can be attributed to African ancestry does not necessarily, by itself, correlate with these individuals having been enslaved persons. However, the osteological analysis provides evidence of a stressed population and a rigorous lifestyle that are consistent with an enslaved population (Mann et al. 1987:336; Petersen and Watters 1988:169–170; cf. Higman 1984:260–302, 339–347). They include periodic severe malnutrition and traumas, as well as developed muscle attachment areas in the phalanges and metacarpals that are suggestive of arduous grasping activities, as would be expected with tasks associated with sugar production, such as cutting cane and hoeing.

The interment timespan at the cemetery bears on the slave attribution issue. If the individuals were buried after the 1830s—emancipation in the British West Indies, they no longer would have been enslaved persons. However, a number of artifacts support a pre-emancipation use of the cemetery in the late 18th century, when slavery still existed. The most important of these is the 1751 Turlington phial. Emplacement of this bottle in the grave in the late 18th century seems reasonable, especially with the lag time from production in England, shipment to Montserrat, and interment in the grave. The pipe-stem bore diameters of 5/64 in. and 4/64 in. are mainly 18th-century sizes. Imported ceramics with known manufacturing date ranges, notably creamware and decorated delftware, were being produced in the 18th century. Pearlwares were absent at the site, and no 19th-century diagnostic artifacts were recovered. Although the Afro-Montserratian sherds, being undated, neither support nor refute the cemetery's timespan of use, their presence there is to be expected and is in accord with the slave cemetery attribution. Furthermore, it tentatively has been suggested that following emancipation, the local manufacture of hand-built ceramics largely ceased (Petersen et al. 1992). The late 18th-century use of the Harney cemetery corresponds to a disruptive period in the island's history, which resulted from the economic distress caused by the American Revolution and the capture and two-year occupation (1782–1784) of Montserrat by French military forces (Wheeler 1988:30).

These data are fully consistent with the interpretation of the Harney site as a late 18th-century slave cemetery, yet they do not "prove" that the deceased were slaves. This calls to mind the conclusion by Lange and Handler (1985:15) "that slavery cannot be identified through archaeological efforts alone." Indeed, even though the pathologies confirm a stressed population, they do not correlate exclusively with slavery. Some of the same pathologies appear in the early 19th-century free black skeletons at the First African Baptist Church cemetery (Parrington et al. 1986), and even among the late 19th- and early 20th-century free blacks at the Cedar Grove Baptist Church cemetery (Rose and Santeford 1985a, 1985b). Also, the Harney data do not contravene the possibility that the skeletons were blacks who had been manumitted in the late 18th century, before emancipation, or had been borne by freed mothers. These cautionary disclaimers merit some attention, but the weight of the archaeological evidence nevertheless supports the interpretation of the Harney site as being a late 18th-century cemetery for enslaved persons of African ancestry.

External Correlations: Cemetery and Interment Patterns

Burial orientation at the Harney site is "west-headed" in the eight observed cases. The single burial reported by Fleischman and Armstrong (1990:32) from Seville Plantation on Jamaica also is west-headed—no burials were reported from Drax Hall (Armstrong 1990). However, other Caribbean slave cemetery sites do not duplicate a solely west-headed orientation. At Newton Plantation on Barbados, Handler and Lange (1978:196–197) record orientations for 58 skeletons, with 38 (66%) being west-headed, 17 (29%) east-headed, and three (5%) north-headed. At Plantation Waterloo—initially named Grond van Lodewijcksburg—in Suriname, the former Dutch Guiana, the percentages are almost exactly the inverse of Newton Plantation. At

Waterloo, Khudabux (1991:26) found 26 (68%) east-headed skeletons and only 12 (32%) west-headed—including one oriented northwest.

Handler and Lange (1978:161–163) conclude that east-headed burials generally preceded west-headed interments at Newton Plantation, where interments occurred from about 1660 to 1820. The pattern of west-headed burials in the later portion of the Newton Plantation sequence correlates very well with a late 18th-century timespan at the Harney site and reasonably well with the inferred date (ca. 1740) for the Seville Plantation burial (Fleischman and Armstrong 1990:31). Yet, this west-headed pattern does not apply to Plantation Waterloo's cemetery where interments, ca. 1793–1861 (Khudabux 1991:17), overlap in part with the later portion of the Newton Plantation sequence. West-headed burial data are congruent for the British islands of Barbados, Montserrat, and Jamaica, yet they are incongruent with respect to the mainland Dutch colony.

Handler and Lange (1978:173–174; cf. Handler 1989:14) argue that most slaves were buried on their plantations, either within or near houses located in the slave village or in a separate cemetery situated near the village, although Christian slaves rarely were buried in church grounds. Cemetery interment took place at the Harney, Newton, and Waterloo sites; the Seville Plantation burial was in the slave village, although the skeleton probably was interred after the house-yard had been abandoned.

Single interments—one corpse in one grave—characterize all graves at Seville, Waterloo, and the Harney cemetery, and almost all burials at Newton Plantation. Handler and Lange (1978:306, fn.6) distinguish between multiple interment—"two or more people buried in the same place at the same time"—and simultaneous burial—"bodies buried in clearly distinct spaces but at the same time." They mention three probable simultaneous burials (within one pit but spatially distinct) and two positively identified paired multiple interments, each with an adult and a child in one grave (Handler and Lange 1978:119, 123, 193). Skeletons No. 1, 9, and 10 at the Harney site, being proximate to one another, might be construed as either a multiple or simultaneous interment. The "same time" criterion cannot pertain to Skeleton No. 9 since it was disturbed by the later interment of Skeleton No. 1. Skeleton No. 10 was vertically higher in the soil column than Skeleton No. 1, horizontally offset to one side from it, and seemingly oriented on a different azimuth. Therefore, the proximity of Skeletons No. 1 and 10 is simply happenstance; each skeleton was buried as a single interment.

Evidence for disturbance of earlier burials by the intrusion of subsequent interments occurs once at the Harney site but more commonly at Newton Plantation (Handler and Lange 1978:110). The causes of disarticulation for 42 (46%) of 92 skeletons at the Barbados site included subsequent burials as well as debris slumping, deep plowing, modification of plantation yards, other human and natural landscape alterations, and one case of probable intentional disarticulation (Handler and Lange 1978:51, 163). Seawater infringing on the eroding coastline contributed to the disarticulation, and poor preservation, of some skeletons at Plantation Waterloo (Khudabux 1991:18, 25). The disarticulated skeleton at the Harney site resulted from an intrusive burial. Construction damage at the Harney site may well have obliterated other cases of intrusive burials and disarticulated skeletons.

The Harney site skeletons consistently occurred atop the rock, or shoal, layer underlying the site; they occupied shallow pits dug into that stratum in several instances. The burial at Seville Plantation occurred in a rectangular pit dug at least 42 cm into limestone bedrock; the pit bisected the south wall of a house in the slave village (Fleischman and Armstrong 1990:6–7, 32). While Handler and Lange (1978:108–133) mention only one grave as being a shallow prepared subsurface pit excavated into underlying bedrock, the proximity of bedrock to the ground surface (ca. 30 cm) in some areas of Newton cemetery strongly suggests that other graves were dug to bedrock. The artificial mounds at Newton cemetery, which were formed by piling earth over the lower graves, created a situation where the later burials probably no longer reached bedrock. The Newton Plantation mounds are archaeologically unique in the West Indies, perhaps because of the greater time depth at that cemetery.

Bulldozing of the surface at the Harney cemetery precluded any investigation of the possibility of mounds at that site. Khudabux (1991:18) says the Plantation Waterloo graves were found on a "clayey beach," a coastal environment typically lacking in bedrock.

Interment of corpses on their backs, an almost universal pattern at the cemeteries, involved all 38 skeletons at Plantation Waterloo, the nine articulated skeletons at the Harney site, and 90 of 92 skeletons—exceptions being one prone and one partially flexed—at Newton Plantation (Handler and Lange 1978:162, 198). The Seville skeleton was partially on its left side when excavated, the result of the coffin having been tilted to fit in the burial pit, but the deceased originally had been placed on his back (Fleischman and Armstrong 1990:32). While full extension of the legs was typical, positions of the arms and hands were more variable, including at the sides, folded over the chest or pelvis, or each hand in a different position at Newton (n = 51) (Handler and Lange 1978:164–165); arms extended along the body (n = 4), left arm extended and right arm flexed (n = 1), right arm extended and left arm flexed (n = 4), arms crossed on the chest (n = 1) due to ankylosis of elbow joints, and arms flexed and hands crossed on the lap (n = 1) at Plantation Waterloo (Khudabux 1991:26); arms and hands at the sides (n = 1) at Seville Plantation (Fleischman and Armstrong 1990:Figure 9); and hands on respective hips (n = 2), and right hand on hip with left hand centered on pelvis (n = 1) at the Harney site.

External Correlations: Artifact Patterns

Coffin wood was preserved only in the waterlogged coastal sediments of Plantation Waterloo, where Khudabux (1991:25) was able to identify 57 graves—others had already been washed away—with coffins or remnants thereof. Of 36 intact coffins, the 19 that were examined included 15 flat and four "saddle-shaped," apparently gabled, lids (Khudabux 1991:25, Figures 9, 10). No coffin hardware was reported.

Metal coffin hardware at Newton Plantation (Handler and Lange 1978:Appendix A) provides the best non-wood evidence for coffins, with handles in 23 graves and metal plates in six graves. At this Barbados cemetery, coffin use was inferred from the presence of nails and tacks when handles were absent. By combining these data, Handler and Lange (1978:150) calculated 29 people, including one paired multiple burial, were definitely buried in coffins and 23 possibly were. At Seville Plantation, coffin use was indicated by 260 nails and the discolored soil that outlined the coffin, thereby forming a "fossil record of the wood" (Fleischman and Armstrong 1990:32–33).

Coffins, without handles, at the Harney site are inferred from more tenuous data, solely by the presence of nails in five graves. The coffinless burials in other graves could be accounted for by a postulated wood shortage or by a burial apparatus using limited wood, perhaps in the form of nailed planks somewhat similar to the burial on a door reported by Handler and Lange (1978:132).

Inadvertent introduction of artifacts into the grave fill accounted for most artifacts found with the Harney site burials. Fleischman and Armstrong (1990:31–34) also report unintentionally introduced artifacts, including imported and Afro-Jamaican sherds, in the fill at the Seville Plantation grave, as well as a large lock that they feel was purposefully emplaced. Newton Plantation yielded kaolin pipes, glass fragments, and imported and locally made pottery sherds, some of which seem to have been purposeful inclusions while others were incidental (Handler and Lange 1978:133–144, Appendix A).

The Harney site yielded only two artifacts that possibly served as grave goods, the Turlington bottle and metal disc; the Jamaica burial contained the lock; and Khudabux (1991:25) reports a single grave good, a clay pipe from Holland. The excavations by Handler and Lange (1978) at Newton Plantation provide examples of intentionally emplaced grave goods including such personal objects as rings, bracelets, earrings, beads, knives, and a short-stemmed pipe. They also found a portion of a shallow glazed redware bowl associated with

Burial No. 22, beneath its pelvis (Handler and Lange 1978:136–137).

Unlike the ceramic sherds inadvertently introduced into the grave fill at the Harney site, the Newton Plantation redware bowl was directly associated with a black skeleton, the sole example of such an association yet reported for the British Caribbean. The practice of placing a ceramic item with a corpse also is reported twice from Jamaica, but in each case with a burial thought to be a white person of British origin (Fremmer 1973). Other instances of plates or saucers being found near the abdomen or pelvic areas of black skeletons are reported from the United States, twice at the First African Baptist Church cemetery (Parrington and Roberts 1990:150) and once at Cedar Grove Baptist Church cemetery (Rose and Santeford 1985a: 96–97). An explanation for this phenomenon, beyond being simple grave goods, involves the container having held salt, to prevent the body from bloating, to keep evil spirits away from the deceased, or to prevent the deceased from harming the living. The practice of placing a salt-laden plate on a corpse seems to be a custom with origins both in West Africa (Parrington and Roberts 1990:150) and England (Fremmer 1973), although at least in the latter instance the plate apparently was meant to be removed prior to the interment of the deceased.

Clothing accouterments are present at three cemeteries. Buttons are reported from four burials at Plantation Waterloo (Khudabux 1991:25); in the Seville Plantation burial, Fleischman and Armstrong (1990:33) found nine bone buttons in the pelvic area and beside each radius, indicating the deceased was buried in a cuffed shirt and trousers with a front flap. Handler and Lange (1978:Appendix A) list two burials with buttons, one having only shell buttons and the second both bone and shell buttons, although a metal button—not associated with a specific burial—was found in another excavation; other clothing-related metal artifacts include a belt buckle, probably 11 metal fasteners—found with five burials, and possibly a pin. Clothing-related artifacts are sparsely represented in view of the number of individuals interred at these sites. The use of shrouds or some kind of cloth wrapping is inferred at the Harney site from the green copper salts stains.

Differing interpretations for intentional or unintentional inclusion of artifacts in graves, including those in the fill and those with the deceased, depend to a large degree on whether their contextual association with the corpse can be determined, or at least reasonably inferred. The argument that "placing offerings or goods inside the graves can be distinguished from placing food and goods on top of the filled-in grave during interment rites" (Handler and Lange 1978:200) is a reasonable contention and, in each instance, the placement of the goods is an intentional act (cf. Combes 1974; Thomas et al. 1977:406). Since the artifacts were purposefully emplaced, they would constitute "grave goods" in both cases. However, only the former category, those actually inside the grave, could be reasonably expected to remain in context with the deceased through time, until they ultimately were excavated as grave goods. Ceramic containers in the second category, those located on the surface of the grave, eventually would be broken and scattered across the surface of the cemetery, thereby losing their context as grave goods. The scattered items could constitute one source for the artifacts unintentionally included in graves dug subsequently. Other sources of materials for inadvertent introduction would be food or drink containers, including those used by mourners themselves in graveside rituals and those carried by workers in nearby fields (Handler and Lange 1978: 139, 167, 199–203). The eight Afro-Montserratian vessels identified at the Harney site represent already broken pottery containers whose 20 sherds were incorporated incidentally into grave fill (Petersen and Watters 1988:184).

Conclusions

One constraint of the Harney site salvage project was that the slave cemetery was the only component excavated. Because the cemetery's broader contexts, with respect to a slave village or an entire plantation, remain uncertain, the Harney site

project meets neither the standards advocated for "plantation archaeology" in general (e.g., Orser 1984, 1992), nor the combined historical and archaeological approach used effectively in the Caribbean at Newton Plantation, Barbados, by Handler and Lange (1978) and Drax Hall Plantation, Jamaica, by Armstrong (1990, 1991). Nevertheless, the Harney site salvage project has provided valuable comparative data about an enslaved population in the British West Indies in the late 18th century. These findings augment a still limited but nonetheless expanding database on mortuary patterns, health, and osteology of enslaved peoples of African ancestry in the broader Caribbean region (e.g., Rivero de la Calle 1973; Acosta Saignes 1978; Handler and Lange 1978; Handler, Coruccini et al. 1982; Corruccini, Handler et al. 1982; Handler and Corruccini 1983, 1986; Higman 1984; Corruccini, Handler, and Jacobi 1985; Handler, Aufderheide et al. 1986; Domínguez González 1986; Corruccini, Aufderheide et al. 1987; Mann et al. 1987; Fleischman and Armstrong 1990; Khudabux 1991; Crespo and Guisti 1992). The Harney site mortuary data were made available to scholars through joint field research by professional and avocational archaeologists, with the active involvement of the latter exemplifying the efforts of members of local historical and archaeological societies throughout the islands of the Caribbean.

ACKNOWLEDGMENTS

Field work in 1978–1979 was supported by a Fulbright-Hays Doctoral Dissertation Research Abroad Fellowship (DHEW:OE) and an Andrew Mellon Predoctoral Fellowship at the University of Pittsburgh. I am grateful to Cathy Watters, Gayle Baumgardner, Joan Margolin, and Marilyn Townsend for their assistance in the field; Samuel P. McChesney, then President of the Montserrat National Trust, and Percy Arthurton, then Chair of its Archaeology subcommittee, for facilitating the field work; St. Clair Harney—the contractor for whom the site is named, Jackie Dangler—the foreman, and the construction workers who assisted with the salvage project; Robert W. Mann, Lee Meadows, and William M. Bass for the osteological study; James B. Petersen for analysis of the Afro-

Montserratian pottery; Richard Scaglion for age-at-death statistical analyses; Douglas Armstrong, Edwin Crespo, Mohamed Rakieb Khudabux, Manuel Rivero de la Calle, and Daniel G. Roberts for providing pertinent publications; Mindy McNaugher, Stanley Lantz, and Bruce Manzano for photography; Charmaine Steinberg and Sylvia Keller for manuscript preparation; and Jerome Handler, James B. Petersen, Daniel G. Roberts, and three anonymous reviewers for their careful reading and insightful comments. Portions of this paper were presented at the annual meeting of the Society for Historical Archaeology Conference on Historical and Underwater Archaeology in Reno, Nevada, in 1988.

REFERENCES

ACOSTA SAIGNES, MIGUEL
1978 *Vida de los esclavos negros en Venezuela.* Ediciones Casa de las Américas, Havana.

ARMSTRONG. DOUGLAS V.
1990 *The Old Village and the Great House: An Archaeological and Historical Examination of Drax Hall Plantation, St. Ann's Bay, Jamaica.* University of Illinois Press, Urbana.
1991 The Afro-Jamaican House-Yard: An Archaeological and Ethnohistorical Perspective. *Florida Journal of Anthropology* 16:51–63.

BLANKENSHIP, JAY R.
1990 *The Wildlife of Montserrat.* Montserrat National Trust, Plymouth, West Indies.

COMBES, JOHN D.
1974 Ethnography, Archaeology, and Burial Practices Among Coastal South Carolina Blacks. *Conference on Historic Sites Archaeology Papers, 1972* 7:52–61.

CORRUCCINI, ROBERT S., ARTHUR C. AUFDERHEIDE, JEROME S. HANDLER, AND LORENTZ E. WITTMERS, JR.
1987 Patterning of Skeletal Lead Content in Barbados Slaves. *Archaeometry* 29:233–239.

CORRUCCINI, ROBERT S., JEROME S. HANDLER, AND KEITH P. JACOBI
1985 Chronological Distribution of Enamel Hypoplasias and Weaning in a Caribbean Slave Population. *Human Biology* 57:699–711.

CORRUCCINI, ROBERT S., JEROME S. HANDLER, ROBERT J. MUTAW, AND FREDERICK W. LANGE
1982 Osteology of a Slave Burial Population from Barbados, West Indies. *American Journal of Physical Anthropology* 59:443–459.

CRANDALL, DONALD R., AND BRIAN S. DYDE
1989 *The Fortification of St. George's Hill, Montserrat.* Montserrat National Trust, Plymouth, West Indies.

CRESPO, EDWIN, AND JUAN B. GUISTI
1992 Primera evidencia de mutilación dentaria en la población negroide de Puerto Rico. *Revista Salud y Cultura,* año 4, 1(1):95–105.

DOMÍNGUEZ GONZALEZ, LOURDES S.
1986 Las fuentes arqueológicas en el estudio de la esclavitud en Cuba. *Revista Cubana de Ciencias Sociales* 10:40–51.

FLEISCHMAN, MARK L., AND DOUGLAS V. ARMSTRONG
1990 Preliminary Report: Analysis of Burial SAJ–B1 Recovered from House-area 16, Seville Afro-Jamaican Settlement. *Syracuse University Archaeological Reports* 6. Syracuse, New York.

FREMMER, RAY
1973 Dishes in Colonial Graves: Evidence from Jamaica. *Historical Archaeology* 7:58–62.

GOVEIA, ELSA V.
1965 *Slave Society in the British Leeward Islands at the End of the Eighteenth Century.* Yale University Press, New Haven, Connecticut.

HANDLER, JEROME S.
1989 Searching for a Slave Cemetery in Barbados, West Indies: A Bioarchaeological and Ethnohistorical Investigation. *Research Paper* No. 59. Center for Archaeological Investigations, Southern Illinois University at Carbondale, Carbondale.

HANDLER, JEROME S., ARTHUR C. AUFDERHEIDE, ROBERT S. CORRUCCINI, ELIZABETH M. BRANDON, AND LORENTZ E. WITTMERS, JR.
1986 Lead Contact and Poisoning in Barbados Slaves: Historical, Chemical, and Biological Evidence. *Social Science History* 10:399–425.

HANDLER, JEROME S., AND ROBERT S. CORRUCCINI
1983 Plantation Slave Life in Barbados: A Physical Anthropological Analysis. *Journal of Interdisciplinary History* 14:65–90.
1986 Weaning among West Indian Slaves: Historical and Bioanthropological Evidence from Barbados. *William and Mary Quarterly,* series 3, 43:111–117.

HANDLER, JEROME S., ROBERT S. CORRUCCINI, AND ROBERT J. MUTAW
1982 Tooth Mutilation in the Caribbean: Evidence from a Slave Burial Population in Barbados. *Journal of Human Evolution* 11:297–313.

HANDLER, JEROME S., AND FREDERICK W. LANGE
1978 *Plantation Slavery in Barbados: An Archaeological and Historical Investigation.* Harvard University Press, Cambridge, Massachusetts.

HIGMAN, BARRY W.
1979 Growth in Afro-Caribbean Slave Populations. *American Journal of Physical Anthropology* 50:373–385.

1984   *Slave Populations of the British Caribbean, 1807–1834.* Johns Hopkins University Press, Baltimore, Maryland.

KHUDABUX, MOHAMED RAKIEB
1991   Effects of Life Conditions on the Health of a Negro Slave Community in Suriname. Unpublished Ph.D. dissertation, Department of Anatomy and Embryology, Leiden University, The Netherlands.

LANGE, FREDERICK W., AND JEROME S. HANDLER
1985   The Ethnohistorical Approach to Slavery. In *The Archaeology of Slavery and Plantation Life,* edited by Theresa A. Singleton, pp. 15–32. Academic Press, Orlando, Florida.

MANN, ROBERT W., LEE MEADOWS, WILLIAM M. BASS, AND DAVID R. WATTERS
1987   Description of Skeletal Remains from a Black Slave Cemetery from Montserrat, West Indies. *Annals of Carnegie Museum* 56:319–336.

NICHOLSON, DESMOND V.
1993   *Mud and Blood: Artifacts from Dredging and the Naval Hospital Site.* Museum of Antigua and Barbuda, St. John's, West Indies.

ORSER, CHARLES E., JR.
1984   The Past Ten Years of Plantation Archaeology in the Southeastern Unites States. *Southeastern Archaeology* 3:1–13.
1992   Beneath the Material Surface of Things: Commodities, Artifacts, and Slave Plantations. *Historical Archaeology* 26(3):95–104.

PARRINGTON, MICHAEL, STEPHANIE PINTER, AND THOMAS STRUTHERS
1986   Occupations and Health amongst Early Nineteenth-Century Black Philadelphians. *MASCA Journal* 4(1):37–41.

PARRINGTON, MICHAEL, AND DANIEL G. ROBERTS
1990   Demographic, Cultural, and Bioanthropological Aspects of a Nineteenth-Century Free Black Population in Philadelphia, Pennsylvania. In A Life in Science: Papers in Honor of J. Lawrence Angel, edited by Jane E. Buikstra. *Scientific Papers* No. 6:138–170. Center for American Archaeology, Kampsville, Illinois.

PETERSEN, JAMES B., AND DAVID R. WATTERS
1988   Afro-Montserratian Ceramics from the Harney Site Cemetery, Montserrat, West Indies. *Annals of Carnegie Museum* 57:167–187.

PETERSEN, JAMES B., DAVID R. WATTERS, AND DESMOND V. NICHOLSON
1992   "Afro-Caribbean" Ceramics from Antigua, Barbuda, and Montserrat: An Investigation of Ethnicity in the Northern Lesser Antilles. Paper presented at the Annual Meeting of the Society for Historical Archaeology Conference on Historical and Underwater Archaeology, Kingston, Jamaica.

RAGATZ, LOWELL JOSEPH
1971   *The Fall of the Planter Class in the British Caribbean, 1763–1833.* Reprint of 1928 edition. Octagon Books, New York.

RIVERO DE LA CALLE, MANUEL
1973   La mutilación dentaria en la población negroide de Cuba. *Ciencias Biológicas,* series 6, 38:1–21. Cuba.

ROSE, JEROME C., AND LAWRENCE GENE SANTEFORD
1985a   Burial Descriptions. In Gone to a Better Land, edited by Jerome C. Rose. *Arkansas Archaeological Survey Research Series* No. 25:39–129. Arkansas Archaeological Survey, Fayetteville, Arkansas.
1985b   Cedar Grove Burial Interpretation. In Gone to a Better Land, edited by Jerome C. Rose. *Arkansas Archaeological Survey Research Series* No. 25:130–145. Arkansas Archaeological Survey, Fayetteville, Arkansas.

SIEGEL, ALLAN
1983   *Birds of Montserrat.* Montserrat National Trust, Plymouth, West Indies.

THOMAS, DAVID HURST, STANLEY SOUTH, AND CLARK SPENCER LARSEN
1977   Rich Man, Poor Men: Observations on Three Antebellum Burials from the Georgia Coast. *Anthropological Papers of the American Museum of Natural History* 54:393–420.

UBELAKER, DOUGLAS H.
1978   Human Skeletal Remains: Excavation, Analysis, Interpretation. *Manuals on Archeology* 2. Taraxacum, Washington, D.C.

WARD, JOHN R.
1988   *British West Indies Slavery, 1750–1834: The Process of Amelioration.* Clarendon Press, Oxford.

WATTERS, DAVID R.
1980   *Transect Surveying and Prehistoric Site Locations on Barbuda and Montserrat, Leeward Islands, West Indies.* Ph.D. dissertation, Department of Anthropology, University of Pittsburgh, Pennsylvania. University Microfilms, Ann Arbor, Michigan.
1981   A Turlington Balsam Phial from Montserrat, West Indies: Genuine or Counterfeit? *Historical Archaeology* 15(1):105–108.
1987   Excavations at the Harney Site Slave Cemetery, Montserrat, West Indies. *Annals of Carnegie Museum* 56:289–318.

WATTERS, DAVID R., AND JAMES B. PETERSEN
1991   The Harney Site Slave Cemetery: Archaeological Summary. In Proceedings of the Thirteenth International Congress for Caribbean Archaeology, edited

by E. N. Ayubi and Jay B. Haviser. *Reports of the Archaeological-Anthropological Institute of the Netherlands Antilles,* 9:317–325. Willemstad, Cura-çao, Netherlands Antilles.

WHEELER, MARION M.
1988   *Montserrat, West Indies: A Chronological History.* Montserrat National Trust, Plymouth, West Indies.

DAVID R. WATTERS
SECTION OF ANTHROPOLOGY
EDWARD O'NEIL RESEARCH CENTER
CARNEGIE MUSEUM OF NATURAL HISTORY
5800 BAUM BOULEVARD
PITTSBURGH, PENNSYLVANIA 15206

JEROME S. HANDLER

A Prone Burial from a Plantation Slave Cemetery in Barbados, West Indies: Possible Evidence for an African-type Witch or Other Negatively Viewed Person

ABSTRACT

Dating to the late 1600s or early 1700s, a burial excavated from a slave cemetery at Newton Plantation in Barbados had several unique characteristics. Buried in the largest artificial earthen mound in the cemetery without grave goods or a coffin, this young adult woman was the solitary interment in the mound and the cemetery's only prone burial. Her skeleton showed no signs of unusual death although analysis of lead in her bones suggests she suffered from severe lead poisoning. Documentary evidence on Barbados slave culture in general and ethnographic/ethnohistorical evidence on West African mortuary practices suggest interpretations for this burial: She may have been a witch or some other negatively viewed person with supernatural powers who, following African custom, was feared or socially ostracized.

Introduction

The Caribbean island of Barbados was England's first American territory to depend on sugar plantations and African slave labor. From around the 1630s until emancipation in 1834 to 1838, many thousands of people, slave and free, were buried on this compact 166-sq.-mi. island. Free people were usually interred in church cemeteries, but the vast majority of the several hundred thousand slaves who perished were not baptized—baptism of slaves was infrequent in all of England's early New World colonies—and thus were not buried in consecrated grounds, particularly those of the Anglican Church, the established church of Barbados. The historical data are very strong that the great majority of these slaves were buried in unmarked plantation ceme-

Historical Archaeology, 1996, 30(3):76–86.
Permission to reprint required.

teries that were scattered throughout the island (Handler and Lange 1978:174–181; Handler 1989: 13–15). Although excavated in the early 1970s, the cemetery at Newton Plantation is still the only plantation cemetery discovered in Barbados as well as the earliest and largest undisturbed plantation slave cemetery yet reported in the New World (Handler 1989; Jamieson 1995:39, 42, 54). Archaeological research at Newton took place over an eight-week period during two field seasons in 1972 and 1973, and is described at length in Handler and Lange (1978; cf. Corruccini et al. 1982; Handler and Corruccini 1983).

Only a small portion of the cemetery was sampled, but the remains of 104 individuals, interred from about 1660 to 1820, were excavated. Some of these burials were highly distinctive relative to the cemetery population. This paper addresses one such burial, unique not only to Newton but also to early African cemetery sites in the Americas—including the hundreds of burials recently excavated from a colonial-period cemetery in New York City (e.g., Blakey et al. 1993; Harrington 1993; Handler 1994a; Mack 1994; cf. Rankin-Hill 1993; Watters 1994:68; Jamieson 1995:42).

Newton Cemetery and Mound Burials

Newton Plantation is located in Christ Church parish in southern Barbados, in one of the island's historically most fertile sugar-growing areas (Figure 1). The plantation's slave cemetery is close to the site of the former slave village, in an uncultivated field of approximately 4,500 sq. m (Figure 2). The field is covered with a thick blanket of sour grass, a common pasture grass in Barbados, and has changed very little since the early 1970s. The only major difference between then and now is that the casuarina trees which once dotted the field's surface burned down in the early 1980s (Figure 3). Surrounded by fields of sugarcane, this grassy area, which had never been cultivated or plowed because of its shallow soil cover and frequent limestone rock outcroppings, includes a rise in slope of approximately 8 m. The bottom of the slope is relatively level, and in the early 1970s most mortuary activity

FIGURE 1. Barbados parishes and the location of Newton Plantation.

was evident in this approximately 3,000 m^2 area (Figure 4). The area contained several low, formless mounds arranged in no particular pattern; before excavation these mounds appeared as slight undulations in the dense grass surface which covered the entire site. Some of the mounds turned out to be natural features of the terrain, while others were humanly created and contained burials. The Newton burial mounds are "archaeologically unique in the West Indies" (Watters 1994:68) and appear to be unique for the rest of the New World, although some prehistoric Native American mounds in the American South were reused by African Americans for burials (Jamieson 1995:48).

Mound 1, the largest and most clearly defined of the Newton mounds, was roughly circular in shape and approximately 7.5 m wide and slightly less than

1 m above ground surface. Coral limestone rubble covered the top and edges of the mound, but its core was plain earth. The size of the mound suggested that considerable effort had brought soil from elsewhere, probably a neighboring field; the amount of earth implied more labor than the requirements of simply filling a settled-in grave.

Mound 1 contained only one interment. Although the mound was only 80 percent excavated, because of a tree rooted in its southeastern portion, "related evidence from the mound suggests" that no other burials were present (Handler and Lange 1978:110–111). Reflecting the anonymity of so many early slaves, the indvidual remains nameless. Designated Burial 9 after the order in which it was excavated, the individual had been placed in a prepared sub-surface pit, a shallow excavation of about 50 cm into the underlying bedrock (Figure 5). Field notes recorded the burial as fitting "into a thin pit, which proved to be too short for the length of the body, as the head was jammed against the western edge of the pit and was slightly raised."

Burial 9 was a young adult female, around 20 years of age and perhaps of New World birth. Her possible birth area is based on an analysis of her skeletal lead content—skeletal lead content and its implications for suggesting birth in the Old or New Worlds is discussed in Corruccini et al. (1987). A trace mineral analysis method developed to measure skeletal lead content (e.g., Wittmers et al. 1981; Aufderheide et al. 1985) was applied to 52 skeletal tissue samples of the Newton slave population. The method yielded a mean bone lead content of close to 118 ppm (parts per million, or micrograms of lead per gram of bone ash). Burial 9's skeletal lead content was very high (249.7 ppm), more than twice the mean for the all-ages group as well as for her own age group (Arthur C. Aufderheide 1995, pers. comm.; Handler et al. 1986:402–403). Moreover, Burial 9 lacked modified/mutilated teeth—a virtually certain marker of African birth (Handler 1994b), and she had much higher lead levels than skeletons with this characteristic (Arthur C. Aufderheide 1995, pers. comm.).

Grave goods or associated artifacts were absent from Burial 9, and she lacked a coffin. Coffins were absent from one-third or more of Newton's burials,

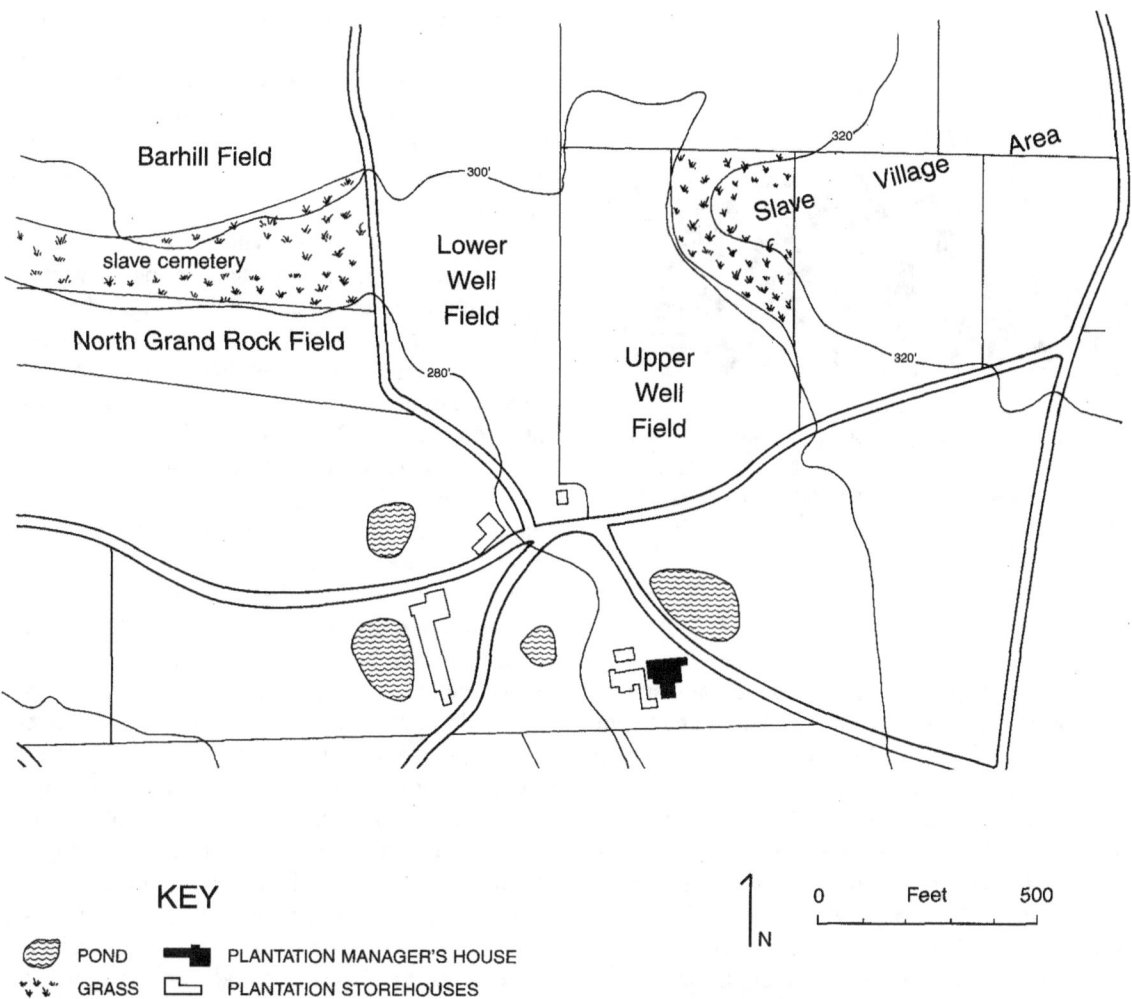

KEY

⬭ POND   ◢◣ PLANTATION MANAGER'S HOUSE
ᵛᵛ GRASS   ⊏⊐ PLANTATION STOREHOUSES

↑N   0   Feet   500

FIGURE 2. Newton Plantation. The central area of the plantation is illustrated, showing neighboring fields and the site of the slave cemetery and former slave village.

usually the earlier ones. Her skeleton was fully articulated on an east-west axis with the head facing west. Not only did Mound 1 only contain this solitary burial, but what is especially significant is that Burial 9 was also the cemetery's *only prone* burial; aside from one or two flexed burials, all others were in extended supine positions. A handful of prone burials have been reported from African-related sites in the New World, but Burial 9 is arguably the earliest and the only one known from the Caribbean (Watters 1994:68). The large African burial ground

in New York City lacked prone burials (Michael Parrington 1996, pers. comm.). Of the two reported prone burials from North America, one, from a free black cemetery in Philadelphia, dating from 1822 to 1842, is problematical—the investigators not being sure if the body shifted from the "ordinary supine position" while being lowered into the grave or "perhaps postmortem movement occurred after burial" (Parrington and Roberts 1990:154). The other prone burial, from a rural black cemetery in Arkansas, dates from around 1890 to 1927; the

FIGURE 3. Newton cemetery, 1972, facing northeast. The main burial area is along the slope bottom, lower right; the approximate location of Mound 1 after excavation is indicated by the arrow. The slave village is in the right background; the dirt road, illustrated in Figure 4, is in the foreground. The casuarina trees were gone by the early 1980s.

investigators apparently did not attach any special cultural significance to its position (Rose and Santeford 1985:59–60, 134–136). Neither of these burials were found in mounds.

Physical evidence from the fill around the skeleton and the surrounding area suggests Burial 9 was interred during the late 1600s or early 1700s, an early period in the cemetery's history and at a time when many Barbados slaves were African-born or first-generation creoles. Handler and Lange (1978: 111) provide a description of this evidence.

If Mound 1 was, indeed, constructed early, why it was not used again becomes a relevant question in interpreting Burial 9 because a smaller mound, Mound 2, approximately 3–3½ m immediately west of Mound 1 (Figure 4) contained about 45 percent of the excavated burials. Mound 2 was congested with skeletons intruding on one another at different levels (Handler and Lange 1978:112–116, Figures 11, 12). It was not a mass grave containing interments buried around the same time because of an epidemic or hurricane; rather, Mound 2 was repeatedly used over a relatively long period, apparently from the late 1600s through the early 1800s, and grew as new burials were added over the years. The people burying their dead in Mound 2 surely were

aware of the neighboring and much larger Mound 1. Yet they avoided using it. A tradition seems to have developed among Newton's slaves concerning this large mound and the individual it contained. This paper offers an explanation for why Burial 9 received different treatment than the cemetery's other burials.

The identity of Burial 9 will never be known, but questions can be raised about her status in the slave community. Burial 9's unique features as the cemetery's only prone burial and the only one interred in the cemetery's largest mound suggest that she possessed unusual characteristics or died under special circumstances. The extremely high lead level in her bones suggests that at death she would have been suffering from the effects of serious lead poisoning, and might have displayed symptoms which could have been interpreted as bizarre behavior. These symptoms might have included a "miserable, nearly daily experience" of "abdominal colic," a "paralysis of some muscles," and epileptic-like seizures or convulsions. People around her would have noticed such behavior as "sudden, abrupt episodes of clutching her abdomen, moaning or crying out in pain." These episodes could occur abruptly and unpredictably and "persist for minutes and even hours"; her "weakened and paralyzed extremity muscles would generate an erratic, grotesque gait," and the epileptic-like seizures would have varied from "uncontrollable . . . arm and/or leg movements to the whole-body convulsions followed by a variable period of disorientation, confusion, or actual coma" (Arthur C. Aufderheide 1995, pers. comm.; cf. Handler et al. 1986). One can only speculate on how these behaviors, *if they actually occurred*, would have affected her fellow slaves and the type of mortuary treatment she was accorded. Whatever the case, her skeleton displayed no physical evidence of an unusual cause of death, and Burial 9 was probably viewed as having special social characteristics. What might these have been?

Mound Burials and Prone Burials in West Africa

The relatively abundant archival sources on Newton (Handler 1971:158, 1976, 1991:60) lack

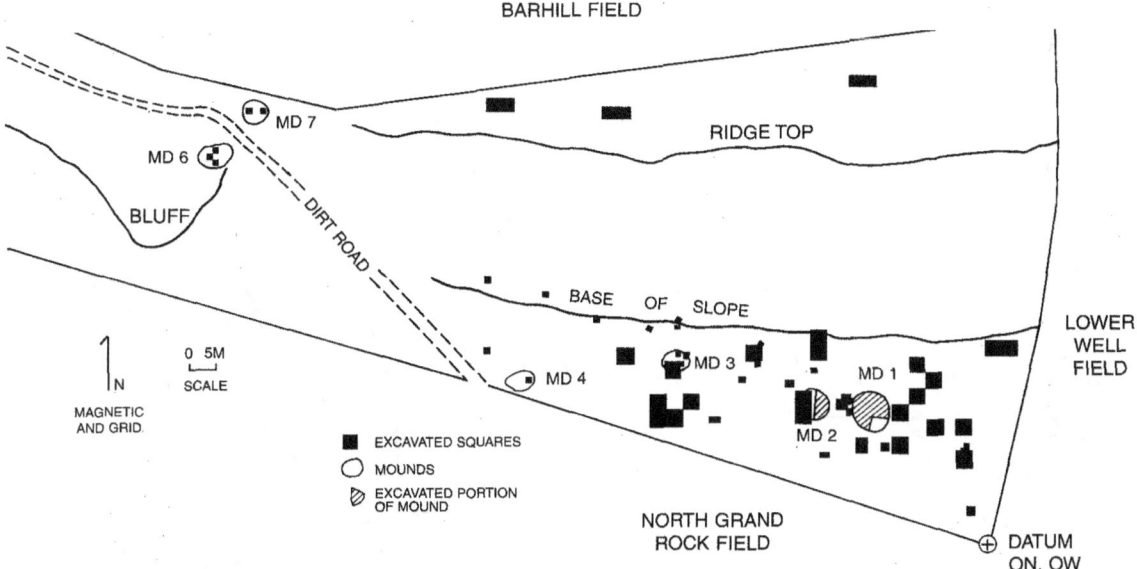

FIGURE 4. Newton cemetery area, illustrating location of excavated squares and mounds, including Mound 1, which contains Burial 9, and Mound 2.

any specific information for an interpretation of Burial 9, and there are no contemporary ethnographic or other oral data from Barbados that would help interpret the burial. For suggestive ideas one must turn to more general data on Barbadian slave culture and, lacking comparative archaeological data on colonial- or slave-period mortuary practices in West Africa (cf. Jamieson 1995:43), the ethnographic/ethnohistorical literature on West African mortuary practices. It is to be stressed that the vast majority of slaves who were transported to Barbados during the period of Burial 9's interment came from West Africa, not the Central African-Angolan region (Handler and Lange 1978:20–29).

Nothing in the Barbados documents helps to interpret the significance of Mound 1 in and of itself, and the limited information discovered on the mounding of graves in West Africa is similarly restrictive. It bears emphasis that I am specifically referring to the construction of earthen mounds, not merely covering the grave with stones, tree branches, or similar materials—an apparently common practice in West Africa. Approximately 154 published ethnographic/ethnohistorical works dealing with West African cultures were searched for information on mortuary practices, and this literature generally indicates that graves were level and not mounded. It is impractical to list all these references here; only those that yielded specific information are cited below. Only a few references to earthen or "clay" mound constructions were found in early sources and these mention or allude to diverse functions: "Big conical mounds" in an Ibibio town in southeastern Nigeria contained the bodies of horses "sacrificed to the deceased chiefs of the place" (Partridge 1905:243); a neighboring people constructed a "monument . . . of a plain and unadorned mound of hardened clay, dyed or stained black" over the graves of high-status people (Leonard 1906:183; cf. Talbot 1969[1926], 3:510). Among Akan-speakers on the Gold Coast, "traditionally a coffin-shaped mound of earth or clay is placed above a grave" (Marees 1987[1602]:181 n. 5; cf. Carnes 1969[1852]:374), while among the neighboring Ga "protective medicines" owned by medicine men were buried in special mounds of "variable size and shape made of clay [or] stone." Under these mounds there was "always . . . some

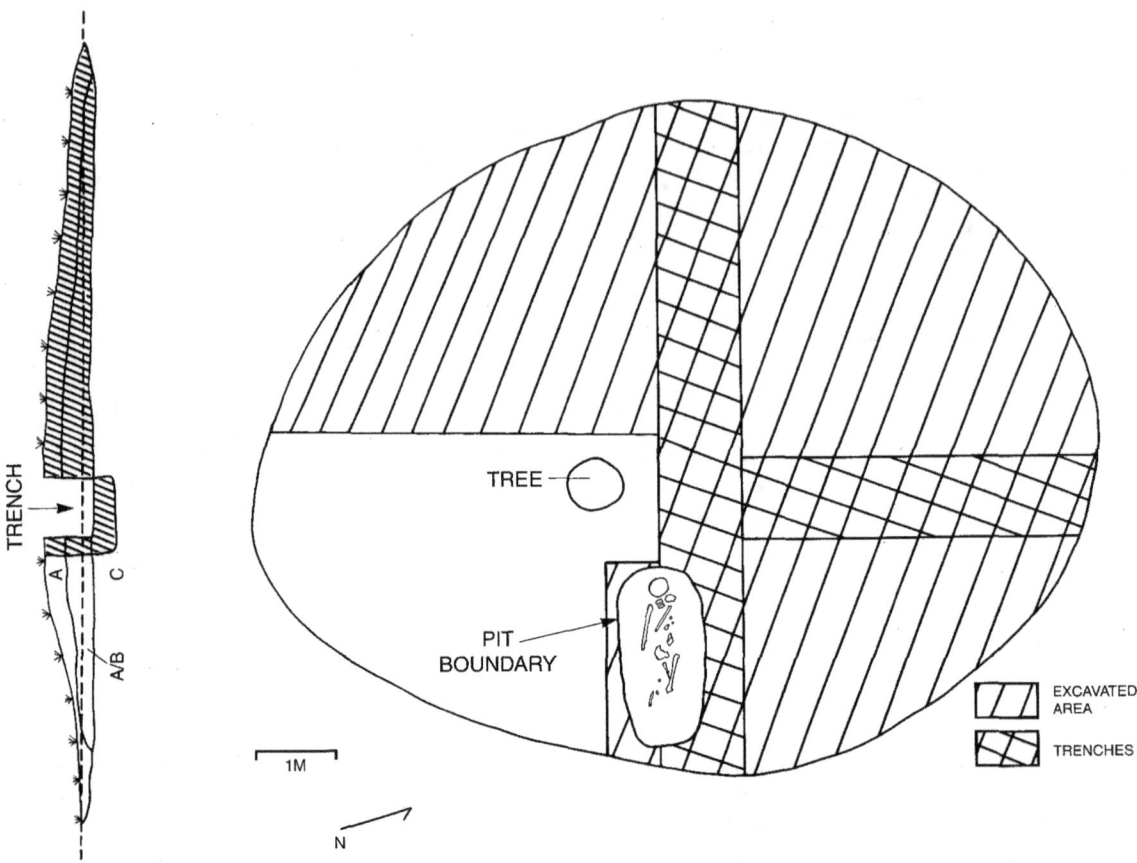

FIGURE 5. Excavation profile of Mound 1, Burial 9.

living thing buried alive''; in earlier times, the ''living thing'' was ''one or more human beings'' sacrificed to a major ''war-god'' (Field 1937:40–41, 121). Although data on earthen mounds are very sparse and sometimes vague, the few references to mounds that were located seem to link them to high-status people whose communities viewed them positively or in a favorable light. There is one exception, however, and this exception is suggestive of an interpretation for Burial 9.

Jack Goody (1962) reports that the LoDagaa of Northwestern Ghana have three main methods of ''disposing of the dead.'' The ''ordinary'' burial involves digging a new grave in the form of a ''bell-shaped chamber'' in the ''local'' cemetery or in the compound of the decedent. The other two methods are reserved for ''members of the community who are considered dangerous.'' In one method a ''trench grave'' is dug in an area removed from where normal people have been buried and without the usual funeral ceremonies. Trench grave burials can include victims of epidemics, suicides, those convicted of various crimes, and witches; the body of a witch, in fact, ''is simply disposed of as quickly as possible in an old grave, which is never again reopened.'' Another burial for ''dangerous'' persons involves the ''building of a mound above the corpse.'' This method is apparently mainly used for children ''who have not yet been weaned'' and who are thus not considered fully human; however, Goody implies this type of burial can also be used for others such as suicides and witches. Goody explains that the "principle underlying" the mound burial "appears to be the avoidance of burial within the earth itself. For the Earth is not only the custodian of corpses; she is also the guardian of the living . . . [and] is associated with the main activities of human life . . . the interment of an evil-doer below the surface of the earth might adversely affect any of these important activities"; "one way of minimizing contact with the earth is to build the grave above ground." Thus, an "evil-doer" is "buried under a pile of earth," but even persons buried in trench graves are considered to have "sinned against the Earth shrine"; witches fall well within this category, as witchcraft is considered "an offense against the earth" (Goody 1962:142, 148–155).

I am not suggesting that the mound over Burial 9 can be literally interpreted as the LoDagaa explain their mound burials, but their practices raise the possibility that mounds could be associated with persons who possessed unusual characteristics or negatively viewed traits. Such an interpretation is strongly reinforced by West African data on prone burials. As indicated above, virtually every Newton burial was in an extended supine position, a common position in West Africa as were flexed and extended lateral burials; all three positions could occur within the same geographic and cultural areas and are regularly reported in the literature (e.g., Handler and Lange 1978:198, 318 n. 28). Information on prone positions, however, is much more limited and has been far more difficult to obtain.

The many publications sampled on West African ethnography/ethnohistory yielded only a few specific references to prone burials; in each case the person was considered to have socially negative traits or had been convicted of witchcraft, a criminal offense in all West African societies. Among the Kpe and other coastal Bantu peoples in the western Cameroons, there was a "special form of witchcraft"; people convicted of this witchcraft were "buried face downward so that if they attempt to come out of their graves they will move in the wrong direction" (Ardener 1956:90, 105). Not far to the west of the Kpe, the Ibibio normally buried their dead in extended supine or flexed positions, but the bodies of "undesirables whose return is not wished are placed in the grave face downward" (Talbot (1967[1923]:144–145); among the Efik Ibibios of Old Calabar "corpses of witches were sometimes buried with the face to the ground" so that the " 'witch ghost' " would be prevented from returning to " 'wreak havoc' among the living" (Forde 1956:22).

Finally, an English resident of Sierra Leone during the late 1780s described the execution of a convicted witch among the closely related Temne, or Timne, and Bulum. He was forced to dig his own grave and stand at "the edge of the foot of it, with his face towards it"; he was then struck from behind with "a violent blow upon the nape of the neck, which causes him to fall upon his face into the grave; a little loose earth is then thrown upon him, and a sharp stake of hard wood is drove through the expiring delinquent, which pins him to the earth; the grave is then filled up, and his or her name is never after mentioned" (Matthews 1966[1788]:127–128). Little (1951:230) alludes to a similar practice among the neighboring Mende.

Interpretation of Burial 9

When specific West African evidence on prone burials is combined with broader mortuary evidence from West Africa that burial practices usually differed for people who had died in special or unusual ways, e.g., suicide, in pregnancy or childbirth, from lightning; who possessed unusual physical characteristics, e.g., albinos, twins; or negatively viewed social traits, e.g., sorcerers, witches, the case is strengthened for interpreting Burial 9 as a probable witch or some other negatively viewed person with supernatural powers. African witches were often executed for their crimes and received no interment rites. Practices regarding the disposition of their corpses varied from culture to culture, and their bodies, clothed or naked, could be burned (Nassau 1969[1904]:234; Milligan 1970[1912]:151), sometimes after being hacked to pieces (Schwab 1947:252), merely thrown into the "Bad Bush" (Talbot 1969[1926], 3:481–482), left "on the surface to rot" (Meek 1969[1904]:222), or simply placed in a grave without any ceremony (Thomas 1970[1916]:

49–51; cf. Rattray 1969[1932], 2:290; Goody 1962: 152–153); one early writer (Milligan 1970[1912]: 241) reports that women accused of having caused the death of their husbands through witchcraft were "buried alive with the dead body of the husband," and "their legs were broken before they were thrown into the grave." Further, it is important to stress that even if witch burials are not described, the sources imply or explictly indicate that their bodies were treated differently than those of other people.

Only at great personal risk could Barbadian slaves execute or murder one of their own, but, it has to be emphasized, they were relatively free to bury their dead according to their own customs (Handler and Lange 1978:171–215); relative freedom in mortuary practices was widespread in the Americas, especially during the early colonial periods (e.g., Jamieson 1995:41, 46–47). An interpretation of Burial 9 as a negatively viewed member of the slave community is further reinforced by evidence from Mound 2, the smaller mound which contained many burials interred over a relatively long period. People continued to bury their dead in Mound 2, as well as in non-mound areas of the cemetery, within plain view of Mound 1. Newton's slaves possibly avoided putting new burials in Mound 1 because a tradition was perpetuated that some person associated with evil supernatural powers was buried there.

Barbadian slaves, as West Africans in general, did not consider major illness and death as accidental; rather, such misfortunes were caused primarily by supernatural forces that acted through human agents. Thus, evil magic was a major factor in their lives, and witchcraft, in particular, was frequently invoked to explain major personal calamities. For an overview of slave beliefs concerning witchcraft/sorcery, see Handler (1996). In considering evil magic I follow a traditional anthropological distinction between sorcery and witchcraft, particularly as it relates to African societies. In sorcery, magic is consciously performed to injure, even destroy, others. Sorcerers acquire their knowledge through learning, and theoretically their techniques can be carried out by anyone with the requisite knowledge and skill. Although the witch's power might be acquired through special

ritual procedures, it is usually inborn or inherited. However acquired, this power cannot be learned; it resides within the individual and is directed against others for evil purposes. Witchcraft "is part of an individual's being, a part of his innermost self, while sorcery is merely a technique which a person utilizes" (Middleton and Winter 1963:12). Africans frequently believed that "the witch need merely wish to harm his victim and his witchcraft then does this, or it may be enough for him to merely feel annoyance or jealousy against someone for the power to set itself in operation without his being aware of the fact that it has done so" (Middleton and Winter 1963:3). Witchcraft, then, is a psychic or mental act whose believers affirm that the harmful power of the witch is unleashed merely through the activation of certain negative thoughts (e.g., Middleton and Winter 1963; Bohannan 1963:346–349; Mair 1969). Barbadian slaves, at least in the earlier periods when slave life was more directly influenced by the African-born and first-generation creoles, may have made distinctions between witchcraft and sorcery in a broadly similar manner to many West Africans. These distinctions, however, went unrecognized by the whites who reported on Barbadian slave life, and thus are difficult to isolate in the ethnohistorical record. In any event, beliefs in witchcraft and sorcery were pervasive features of the world in which slaves lived—as they were in the West African homelands, and slaves clearly subscribed to an essentially African view of witches: A witch is everything a good person should not be; witches are universally feared and despised.

A final point should be made concerning Burial 9. It was certainly not unique at Newton in its absence of grave goods, and that absence alone would not make it a very special case. In West Africa, grave goods were common and included materials ranging from food and drink to personal articles or possessions of one kind or another. The types, quality, and quantity of these goods varied by culture and, of course, according to the wealth and status of the deceased. West Africans explained grave goods in a variety of ways, but whatever the explanations, the documentary sources used for this paper yield absolutely no ethnographic/ethnohistorical evidence that grave goods were interred with persons whom their communities viewed negatively; in brief, the evidence is very clear that grave goods were only placed with persons who were positively regarded in their communities or who were considered ordinary people (cf. Jamieson 1995:48–49).

Thus, mortuary evidence on Burial 9 includes data like the burial's solitary location in Mound 1, prone position, absence of grave goods, body forced into a grave pit that was too small, possibly suggesting a disdain or lack of care for the corpse, and the possible behavior associated with severe lead poisoning. This evidence, combined with West African mortuary data on the treatment of witches or other despised/feared persons and slave beliefs concerning evil magic, leads to an interpretation of Burial 9 as that of a witch or sorceress—in any case someone who, following African custom, was feared or socially ostracized because she was a vehicle for supernatural contagion.

Conclusion

This paper has provided another possible line of evidence for the perpetuation of African mortuary practices in the New World. To date, the Newton data provide the earliest and strongest archaeological and ethnohistorical evidence for African influences on the mortuary practices of African Americans, but the evidence for African influences extends beyond Barbados into other areas of the New World—e.g., literature cited in Jamieson (1995:46–54) and Rankin-Hill (1993). However, archaeological discussions of African-American burial practices focus on the conventional mortuary treatment of "ordinary" people, or persons who were not negatively viewed, feared, or ostracized by their communities. Since African beliefs and practices were manifest in many areas of early slave sociocultural life throughout the New World, and there is ample evidence for the widespread belief in negative magic, it should not be surprising that beliefs surrounding negative magic and witchcraft should be manifest in mortuary behavior and reflected in the archaeological record.

ACKNOWLEDGMENTS

An earlier version of this paper was presented at the 1995 meeting of the Society for Historical Archaeology Conference on Historical and Underwater Archaeology, Washington, D.C.; a summary of it was published in *African-American Archaeology* (Handler 1995). The present paper was written while I was a Scholar in Residence at the Virginia Center for the Humanities, Charlottesville; preliminary versions were presented in Brown Bag talks at the Virginia Center for the Humanities and at the Department of Anthropology, University of Virginia. Archaeological research at Newton was funded by the Wenner-Gren Foundation and National Science Foundation. Frederick Lange was the principal co-investigator and played an absolutely crucial role in devising the archaeological field strategies as well as in data interpretation. Descriptions of Mounds 1 and 2 and Burial 9 are derived from Handler and Lange (1978: 110–116) and the field notes of Richard Accola, Robert Riordan, Daniel Schechter, Hilary Sio, and Frederick Lange; in 1997 these notes, and other materials pertinent to the archaeological research, will be permanently deposited in the Barbados Department of Archives. JoAnn Jacoby, Heather Wallach, and Megan Coulter helped in gathering West African mortuary data; their research assistance was aided by grants from the Office of Research and Development, Southern Illinois University at Carbondale. I am also grateful to Michael Lebovitz for his special assistance, to Arthur Aufderheide for providing data on bone lead levels, to Roy Wagner for discussing with me issues pertaining to witchcraft, to Michael Parrington for references on prone burials, and to Stephen Plog for his very helpful comments on an earlier draft. Thomas Crist, James Garman, and a third, anonymous, referee for this article provided a number of useful suggestions.

REFERENCES

ARDENER, EDWIN
　1956　Coastal Bantu of the Cameroons. *Ethnographic Survey of Africa, Western Africa, Part 4.* International African Institute, London.

AUFDERHEIDE, ARTHUR C., J. L. ANGEL, J. O. KELLEY, ET AL.
　1985　Lead in Bone III: Prediction of Social Correlates from Skeletal Lead Content in Four Colonial American Populations. *American Journal of Physical Anthropology* 66:353–361.

BLAKEY, MICHAEL L., WARREN T. D. BARBOUR, LESLEY M. RANKIN-HILL, MICHAEL PARRINGTON, ET AL.
　1993　Research Design for Archeological, Historical, and

Bioanthropological Investigations of the African Burial Ground (Broadway Block), New York, New York. Report prepared by Howard University and John Milner Associates, West Chester, Pennsylvania. Submitted to General Services Administration, Region 2, New York.

BOHANNAN, PAUL
1963   *Social Anthropology.* Holt, Rinehart, and Winston, New York.

CARNES, JOSHUA A.
1969   *Journal of a Voyage from Boston to the West Coast of Africa.* Reprint of 1852 edition. Negro Universities Press, New York.

CORRUCCINI, ROBERT S. , ARTHUR C. AUFDERHEIDE, JEROME S. HANDLER, AND L. WITTMERS
1987   Patterning of Skeletal Lead Content in Barbados Slaves. *Archaeometry* 29:233–239.

CORRUCCINI, ROBERT S., JEROME S. HANDLER, ROBERT J. MUTAW, AND FREDERICK W. LANGE
1982   Osteology of a Slave Burial Population from Barbados, West Indies. *American Journal of Physical Anthropology* 59:443–459.

FIELD, MARGARET J.
1937   *Religion and Medicine of the Ga People.* Oxford University Press, London.

FORDE, DARYLL
1956   *Efik Traders of Old Calabar.* Oxford University Press, London.

GOODY, JACK
1962   *Death, Property and the Ancestors: A Study of the Mortuary Customs of the LoDagaa of West Africa.* Tavistock, London.

HANDLER, JEROME S.
1971   *A Guide to Source Materials for the Study of Barbados History, 1627–1834.* Southern Illinois University Press, Carbondale.
1976   Sources for the Study of Preemancipation Sugar Plantations in Barbados: Manuscripts Relating to Newton and Seawell Plantations. *Caribbean Archives* 5:11–21.
1989   Searching for a Slave Cemetery in Barbados, West Indies: A Bioarchaeological and Ethnohistorical Investigation. *Research Paper* 59. Center for Archaeological Investigations, Southern Illinois University, Carbondale.
1991   *Supplement to "A Guide to Source Materials for the Study of Barbados History, 1627–1834."* John Carter Brown Library and Barbados Museum and Historical Society, Providence, Rhode Island.
1994a   Update # 4: New York's African Burial Ground. *African-American Archaeology* 12:1–2.

1994b   Determining African Birth from Skeletal Remains: A Note on Tooth Mutilation. *Historical Archaeology* 28:113–119.
1995   An African-Type Burial, Newton Plantation, Barbados. *African-American Archaeology* 15:1, 5–6.
1996   Slave Medicine and Obeah in Barbados. Manuscript on file with the author.

HANDLER, JEROME S., ARTHUR C. AUFDERHEIDE, ROBERT S. CORRUCCINI, ET AL.
1986   Lead Contact and Poisoning in Barbados Slaves: Historical, Chemical, and Bioanthropological Evidence. *Social Science History* 10:399–425.

HANDLER, JEROME S., AND ROBERT S. CORRUCCINI
1983   Plantation Slave Life in Barbados: A Physical Anthropological Analysis. *Journal of Interdisciplinary History* 14:65–90.

HANDLER, JEROME S., AND FREDERICK W. LANGE
1978   *Plantation Slavery in Barbados: An Archaeological and Historical Investigation.* Harvard University Press, Cambridge, Massachusetts.

HARRINGTON, SPENCER P. M.
1993   Bones and Bureaucrats: New York's Great Cemetery Imbroglio. *Archaeology* 46:28–38.

JAMIESON, ROSS W.
1995   Material Culture and Social Death: African-American Burial Practices. *Historical Archaeology* 29:39–58.

LEONARD, ARTHUR G.
1906   *The Lower Niger and Its Tribes.* Macmillan, London.

LITTLE, KENNETH L.
1951   *The Mende of Sierra Leone.* Routledge and Kegan Paul, London.

MACK, MARK E.
1994   New York Burial Ground from the Field to the Laboratory. *African-American Archaeology* 12:4.

MAIR, LUCY
1969   *Witchcraft.* World University Library, McGraw-Hill, New York.

MAREES, PIETER DE
1987   *Description and Historical Account of the Gold Kingdom of Guinea,* translated and edited by Albert van Dantzig and Adam Jones. Translation of 1602 Dutch edition. Oxford University Press, New York.

MATTHEWS, JOHN
1966   *A Voyage to the River Sierra-Leone.* Reprint of 1788 edition. Frank Cass, London.

MEEK, CHARLES K.
1969   *A Sudanese Kingdom: An Ethnographical Study of the Jukun-Speaking Peoples of Nigeria.* Reprint of 1904 edition. Negro Universities Press, New York.

MIDDLETON, JOHN, AND E. H. WINTER
 1963 Introduction. In *Witchcraft and Sorcery in East Africa*, edited by John Middleton and E. H. Winter, pp. 1–26. Routledge and Kegan Paul, London.

MILLIGAN, ROBERT
 1970 *The Fetish Folk of West Africa*. Reprint of 1912 edition. AMS Press, New York.

NASSAU, ROBERT H.
 1969 *Fetichism in West Africa*. Reprint of 1904 edition. Negro Universities Press, New York.

PARRINGTON, MICHAEL, AND DANIEL G. ROBERTS
 1990 Demographic, Cultural, and Bioanthropological Aspects of a Nineteenth-Century Free Black Population in Philadelphia, Pennsylvania. In A Life in Science: Papers in Honor of J. Lawrence Angel, edited by Jane E. Buikstra. *Scientific Papers* 6:138–170. Center for American Archeology, Kampsville, Illinois.

PARTRIDGE, CHARLES
 1905 *Cross River Natives*. Hutchinson, London.

RANKIN-HILL, LESLEY
 1993 Uncovering African Americans' Buried Past. *Science Year 1994*:117–131. World Book, Chicago, Illinois.

RATTRAY, ROBERT S.
 1969 *The Tribes of the Ashanti Hinterland*. Two volumes. Reprint of 1932 edition. Oxford University Press, London.

ROSE, JEROME C., AND LAWRENCE GENE SANTEFORD
 1985 Burial Descriptions [and] Cedar Grove Burial Interpretation. In Gone to a Better Land: A Biohistory of a Rural Black Cemetery in the Post-Reconstruction South, edited by Jerome C. Rose. *Arkansas Archeological Research Series* 25:38–145. Arkansas Archeological Survey, Fayetteville.

SCHWAB, GEORGE
 1947 *Tribes of the Liberian Hinterland*. Peabody Museum, Harvard University, Cambridge, Massachusetts.

TALBOT, PERCY A.
 1967 *Life in Southern Nigeria: The Magic, Beliefs, and Customs of the Ibibio Tribe*. Reprint of 1923 edition. Frank Cass, London.
 1969 *The Peoples of Southern Nigeria*. Three volumes. Reprint of 1926 edition. Frank Cass, London.

THOMAS, NORTHCOTE W.
 1970 *Anthropological Report on Sierra Leone*. Reprint of 1916 edition. Negro Universities Press, Westport, Connecticut.

WATTERS, DAVID R.
 1994 Mortuary Patterns at the Harney Site Slave Cemetery, Montserrat, in Caribbean Perspective. *Historical Archaeology* 28:56–73.

WITTMERS, LORENTZ E., A. ALICH, AND ARTHUR C. AUFDERHEIDE
 1981 Lead in Bone I: Direct Analysis for Lead in Milligram Quantities of Bone Ash by Graphite Furnace Atomic Absorption Spectroscopy. *American Journal of Clinical Pathology* 75:80–85.

JEROME S. HANDLER
CENTER FOR ARCHAEOLOGICAL INVESTIGATIONS
SOUTHERN ILLINOIS UNIVERSITY
CARBONDALE, ILLINOIS 62901

CHARLES E. ORSER, Jr.

Toward a Global Historical Archaeology: An Example from Brazil

ABSTRACT

Schuyler has recently argued that historical archaeologists can make their greatest contribution to knowledge by preparing "historic ethnographies," detailed studies of specific communities. Even though Schuyler's view has merit, no study of the modern world—including historical archaeology—can be truly complete without considering the many connections that were normally maintained by inhabitants of historical sites. Historical archaeology must be a global, broadly conceived field that looks beyond the site to the wider world. The runaway slave community of Palmares in Brazil illustrates this position.

Introduction

Historical archaeologists have been interested in defining their field's mission and scope for many years (e.g., Harrington 1952, 1955; Fontana 1965; Walker 1967; Cleland and Fitting 1968; Dollar 1968; South 1968). The discussions at the plenary session of the 1987 meeting of the Society for Historical Archaeology demonstrate that these concerns have not left historical archaeology (Honerkamp 1988). As part of this session, Robert Schuyler (1988) proposed that historical archaeologists, in order to fix their field with a clear anthropological mission, should concentrate on preparing "historic ethnographies," or anthropological studies focused on distinct communities.

Schuyler's idea initially makes a great deal of sense. Archaeologists can provide unique, detailed information about past communities. In the archaeology of the historic past, however, it becomes exceedingly difficult to define a "community" as a strictly bounded sociocultural entity. The problem of community definition arises because the historic past is partially characterized by the expanding globalization of powerful European peoples.

Historical Archaeology, 1994, 28(1):5–22.
Permission to reprint required.

The purpose of this article is to argue that Schuyler's view of historical archaeology is overly restrictive, given the social complexity and global scale of the world systems normally studied by historical archaeologists. Archaeologists conducting research at sites associated in any way with the modern world—no matter how this "world" is defined—must attempt to frame their studies in the broadest possible terms. This paper specifically shows how the study of Palmares, the great 17th-century maroon society in northeastern Brazil, must be conducted in broad terms. Palmares at first appears to present a perfect arena in which to prepare an historic ethnography. Palmares was a concrete place with a unique history and culture, though little is known about it. An historic ethnography, including a careful combination of historical and archaeological information, could provide a significant new interpretation of this important New World maroon community. The prospect of writing an archaeological ethnography loses its appeal, however, when one realizes that Palmares cannot be understood without including information about a number of locations outside the community. These locations include Portuguese sugar plantations, Dutch settlements, Native American villages, and African communities in Angola. Each of these entities played a part in creating and maintaining the Brazilian maroon community of Palmares.

Historic Ethnographies and the Modern World System

Schuyler's argument about the value of conducting archaeological research as a form of community study is not entirely new. Over a decade earlier, William H. Adams (1977) studied the town of Silcott, Washington, as a community. Confronted with the prospect of conducting archaeology within an entire town, Adams decided that the wisest approach to adopt would be to perceive the town's individual sites as activity areas within a larger, interacting community. Adams's (1977:31) study provides a view of Silcott "as it might have been, a community of people, not a collection of sites or artifacts to be viewed by and for archaeologists' own and singular enlightenment.'' Adams's overt focus is on the archaeology of socially connected people within the community of Silcott.

Schuyler does not intend to reinforce Adams's explicitly community-oriented approach; in fact, he does not even cite Adams's work. Schuyler's message is apparently a reaction to the growing trend among social scientists to conduct broad-scale studies that extend beyond an individual site, a group of sites, or even a region. Over the past two decades, a number of scholars have turned their attention toward the cultural and historical events and processes that were enacted after the commencement of European globalization, or approximately after about A.D. 1415, the date the Portuguese captured Ceuta in North Africa. The broad perspective used to examine what has since been termed the ''modern world-system,'' has been developed largely by historians (Woodruff 1967, 1981; Chaunu 1979; Marcus 1980; Scammell 1981; Braudel 1984; Curtin 1984, 1990; Phillips 1988; Abu-Lughod 1989) and historical sociologists (Wallerstein 1974, 1979, 1980; Hopkins 1982). Also conducting broad, global analyses have been economists (Frank 1978; Cameron 1989; Wallace 1990), environmentalists (Sale 1990), geographers (Genovese and Hochberg 1989; Haggett 1990), political economists (Goldfrank 1979; Martin 1990), urban sociologists (King 1984, 1989, 1990) and anthropologists (Wolf 1982; Mintz 1986). One precept of the world-system perspective is that human social interaction involves ''a totality of interconnected processes'' that cannot be understood by disassembling this totality into small, perhaps meaningless, analytical units (Wolf 1982:3).

On both methodological and epistemological levels, an important aspect of these studies has been the authors' willingness to step outside their own disciplines in order to use research materials and interpretive insights from other fields. In anthropology, Wolf (1982:ix) stresses that a true understanding of the long-term, large-scale issues that developed during the 15th century cannot be understood in any substantive manner without transcending ''the customary ways of depicting Western history.'' Similarly, Mintz (1986:xxx) proposes that ''social phenomena are by their nature historical'' (for similar comments, see Wallerstein 1979: ix–x). Wolf and Mintz continue an earlier tradition of large-scale anthropological-historical interpretation, perhaps best exemplified by Kroeber (1957, 1966), but pursued by others as well in various ways (e.g., Bourguignon and Greenbaum 1973; Murdock 1980). For such anthropologists, and for many historians (Davis 1982; Isaac 1982; Breen 1989), the difference between anthropology and history is an administrative rather than an intellectual convention.

Transcontinental and interdisciplinary studies of the modern world-system have been important in dissolving some disciplinary boundaries and in providing information about modern history and society. What is oddly lacking in these studies is the application of archaeological findings in any significant way, if at all. Even Wolf (1982:4), whose work is well-known to archaeologists (Wolf 1984) and who admits to being influenced by archaeology (Ghani 1987:357), only mentions archaeological materials in passing. Neither Wolf nor Mintz make any use of historical archaeology in their important studies of the modern world.

Schuyler (1988:37) focuses on Wolf's omission of archaeology and argues that historical archaeologists should not be surprised that historians frequently ignore their research because ''even our immediate colleagues in social anthropology'' (e.g., Wolf) have ignored it. Schuyler (1988:41) concludes that archaeologists ''do not excavate on a global level,'' but focus on only one site or community at a time. As a result, historical archaeologists should not be surprised that their studies have limited application. According to Schuyler, instead of viewing this local focus as a liability, historical archaeologists should see it as a significant strength to be used for developing historic ethnographies. These ethnographies are studies of distinct communities as ''historically integrated cultural'' units. Schuyler concedes that a broader use for historical archaeology may be found once a number of these historic ethnographies have been produced (Schuyler 1988:41).

Schuyler is correct on one obvious level: An individual archaeologist cannot excavate every site within an entire system. Anyone who attempts to excavate a complete world system will be quickly frustrated, if for no other reasons than time and funding. As geographer Peter Haggett (1990:28) observes, the "problem posed by any subject which aims to be global is simple and immediate: the earth's surface is so staggeringly large." Schuyler is also correct that archaeologists should be able to provide reasonably detailed interpretations of the sites they study. Archaeologists who study literate societies of whatever sort should be especially well equipped to present solid community studies by combining archaeological and non-archaeological information. In this sense, community studies— prepared as site reports—constitute the heart of most archaeological research. Equating sites with communities, Schuyler (1988:41) notes that "historical archaeology will always make its major contribution at the site level of analysis."

Schuyler's comments about the spatial limitations of an archaeological perspective run counter to a significant body of research. Numerous archaeologists show considerable interest in large-scale analyses of whole cultural complexes, ranging from the Ancient Near East to the American Southwest (Rowlands et al. 1987; Schortman and Urban 1987; Champion 1989).

Schuyler's call for the preparation of narrowly focused historic ethnographies is perhaps most troublesome in historical archaeology. The broad history of cultural contacts between Europeans and non-Europeans that characterizes the process of modern globalization, documented so well by Wolf (1982) and others, argues against isolationist community studies in historical archaeology. Given this well-documented history, should historical archaeologists write ethnographies of the past without adopting a global view that extends beyond the community level? Even Adams (1976, 1977:78–97), although concentrating on the concept of the "community," explores the importance of economic trade networks far beyond Silcott. Adams's (1976:110) analysis demonstrates that the "people of Silcott participated in a hierarchy of economic and social networks linking them eventually to the rest of the United States and the rest of the world." In some sense, then, it may be imagined that the people of Silcott were members of local, regional,

national, and even international "communities." A major challenge facing historical archaeologists interested in large-scale analysis and interpretation is to find ways of conducting research that is both site-specific and transcontinental in scope. Other historical archaeologists (Deetz 1977, 1991; South 1988) have made the observation that historical archaeology must develop a global perspective, noting that the field's "obvious niche as a modern, synthetic field of inquiry is in the study of the processes and interrelationships by which human social and economic organizations developed and evolved in the modern world" (Deagan 1988:8; see also Deagan 1991).

The 17th-century community of Palmares, in northeastern Brazil, provides a perfect arena in which to refute Schuyler's (1988) call for the focus of historical archaeology on community studies, or historic ethnographies. This statement seems paradoxical because Palmares initially appears to present a perfect locale for the historic ethnography. Further consideration reveals that an historic ethnography, as a community study, would be inadequate for explaining daily life at Palmares. In addition, Schuyler's cultural consensus perspective permits him to postulate that communities were "integrated" social entities. It can be doubted that consensus ever truly pervaded all levels of any sociocultural organization, especially a place like Palmares.

Palmares: A Brief Historical Account

Palmares was without doubt one of the most important maroon settlements in the history of the New World. It has been said that "all literate Brazilians . . . know of Palmares, the great slave hideaway" (Degler 1971:8), and that Palmares represents "the first dawn of independence" of an African nation (Ennes 1948:201). Palmares, the largest, longest occupied, and most tenacious runaway slave society in the New World (Moura 1987:36, 1988:205), is mentioned in some fashion in almost every book written about Brazilian history and slave resistance and rebellion in the New World (e.g., Freyre 1956:38; Bastide 1978:83–90;

Genovese 1979; Burns 1980:54; Diffie 1987:308–309; Campbell 1990:2).

Slave runaways built Palmares, probably around 1605, in the line of hills that parallel the coast of northeastern Brazil in the colonial Captaincy, or State, of Pernambuco—now the states of Alagoas and Pernambuco (Kent 1965:165). The Portuguese, who found Brazil in 1500, quickly sought to cement their presence there before the French, who were also actively exploring the coast (Diffie 1987:31). Slavery, first of Native Americans and then of Africans, was always part of the Portuguese plan for Brazil. The exact number of African slaves sent to Brazil is open to debate (Conrad 1986:25–36), but more were sent there than to any other place in the New World (Phillips 1985:192). As many as 4,400 slaves may have been sent to Pernambuco every year (Hall et al. 1987:181).

The production of sugar figured prominently in the early history of Brazil, and slaves were made to work on the sugar plantations. When Ambrósio Fernandes Brandão wrote *Dialogues of the Great Things of Brazil* in 1618, he mentioned that the production of sugar was the primary means of becoming rich in Brazil (Hall et al. 1987:132). In 1584, the Captaincy of Pernambuco contained 26 sugar mills; in 1612, the northern captaincies, including Pernambuco, had 170 mills; and 230 mills operated in Brazil in 1627–1628 (Boxer 1973a: 192). The Portuguese located these sugar mills, like all of their settlements, along the Atlantic coast. According to Brandão, the Portuguese settlement went no more than 10 leagues (about 56 km) toward the interior (Hall et al. 1987:19).

Palmares is reported to have been created by "about forty Negroes of the People of Guiné," runaways from coastal plantations (Rocha Pita 1950:294). Unfortunately, this designation is meaningless because the 17th-century Portuguese commonly referred to all Africans as "Guinean," or as having come from the Guinea Coast, a term with no clear geographical boundaries (Kent 1965: 165–166; Hall et al. 1987:57). The Portuguese called the settlement "Palmares" because of the abundance of palm trees in the area, but its inhabitants, the so-called "palmarinos," are said to have referred to the society as "Angola janga," or "Lit-

tle Angola," in honor of most of its peoples' homeland (Freitas 1984:9, 44; Schwartz 1985:342). In any case, colonial Europeans in South America were soon acquainted with Palmares, and in 1612 the Portuguese made their first, unsuccessful attack on the maroon community. The Portuguese perceived Palmares as a threat. Not only did it undermine the slave plantation economy by siphoning off slaves, it also illuminated the cracks in the power of the slavocracy by demonstrating that Africans could live free and well in the New World.

The Dutch, who had established a foothold in northeastern Brazil in 1630 (Boxer 1973b:98–100), also worried about Palmares, and in 1640 they sent a scouting party to investigate it. This reconnaissance was led by Bartholomeus Lintz, the first European to describe the Brazilian maroon society. Lintz mentions two palmarino settlements: Great Palmares, said to contain about 5,000 people who lived in valleys in dispersed cabins, and Lesser Palmares, a more nucleated settlement reported to contain about 1,000 people (Barleus 1923:315–316). Lintz describes Lesser Palmares as a village with three streets and cabins made of straw. The people, whose "business is to rob the Portuguese of their slaves," are said to subsist on "dates, beans, meal, barley, sugar-canes, tame-fowl (of which they have great plenty), and fish" (Nieuhoff 1813: 707).

In 1644, a Dutch expedition attacked Great Palmares with a force of Native South Americans and reported to have destroyed it with "iron and fire" (Barleus 1923:370). These Dutch assaults, however, had no lasting impact, and Palmares continued to grow in size and population (Drummond 1859:305; Barleus 1923:253).

The following year Jügens Reijmbach led another Dutch assault on Palmares. Reijmbach reports that the village he attacked was surrounded by a double palisade. Inside the double wall was a trench "full of pointed sticks" (Carvalho 1902:92; Carneiro 1988:256). He further reports that the village contained 220 houses, a church, four forges, and a large council house.

Between 1670 and 1694, a leader called "Ganga Zumba," or Great Lord, lived at the capital city of Macaco—presumably the village attacked by Reijm-

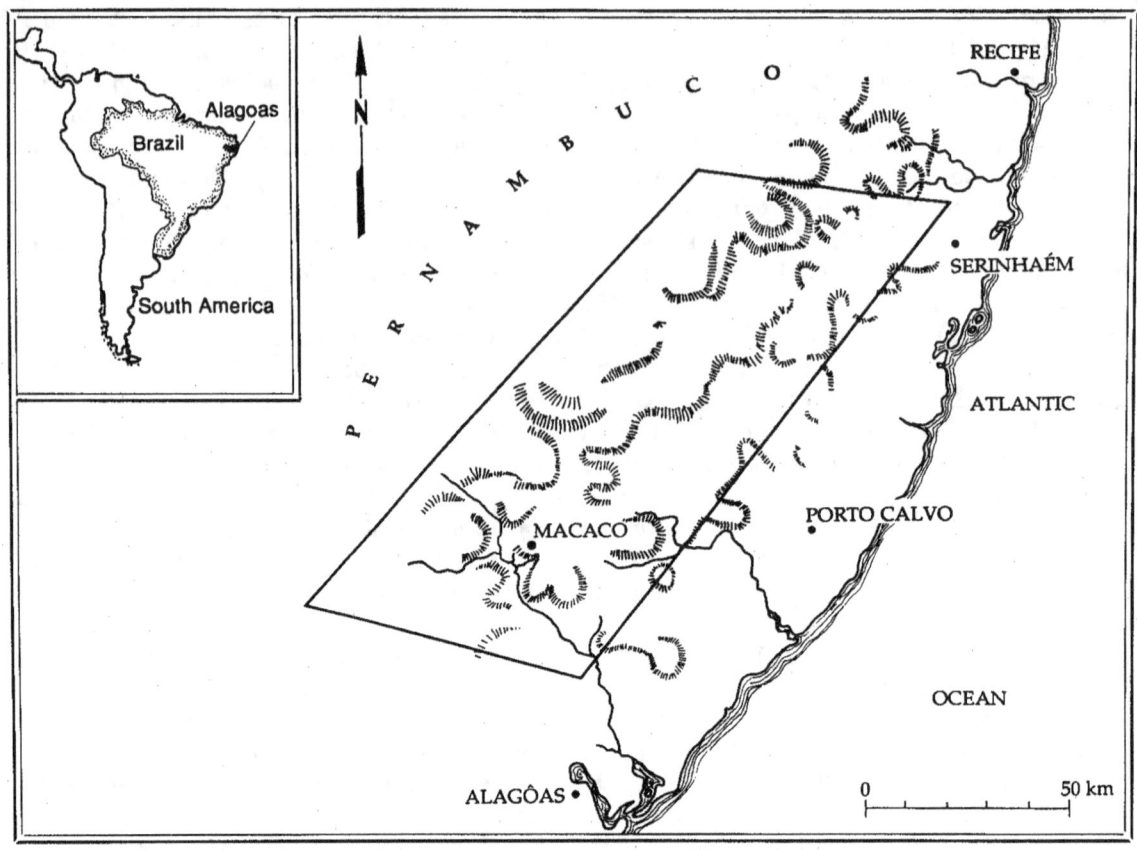

FIGURE 1. The area controlled by Palmares at the height of its development.

bach—and ruled Palmares. This village is said to have been named Macaco—Portuguese for "monkey"—because an animal of this species was supposedly killed on this site (Drummond 1859:306). Reports of this period explicitly state that Palmares housed as many as 20,000 people living in 10 separate villages: the Royal Stockade (Macaco), Osenga, Subupira, Dambrabanga, Arotirene, Tabocas (composed of two villages), Zumbi, Amaro, and Andalaquituche (Drummond 1859:304; Rodrigues 1945:131). Seventeenth-century sources indicate that the land the palmarinos controlled extended for about 170 km, or from northwest of the town of Alagôas, on the south, to northwest of Serinhaém, on the north (Drummond 1859:304). This territory extends from the Ipojuca River in the present State

of Pernambuco to the Paraiba River in the present State of Alagoas (Figure 1; Moura 1987:35).

Modern analysts have variously termed the 10 villages of Palmares a "state" (Freitas 1984; Carneiro 1988), a "republic" (Altavilla 1931; Ramos 1939; Kent 1965), a "confederation" (Moura 1987), and a "kingdom" (Curtin 1990:106). A key element of Palmares was its internal syncretic character, because its "political system did not derive from a particular central African model, but from several" (Kent 1965:175). No one knows how many cultural traditions were represented at Palmares. Most slaves in Brazil were designated by "cultural" names, based only on the port from which they had been shipped (Freitas 1984:39). Angola was the source of most Brazilian slaves during the 17th century (Conrad 1986:28–29), and Antônio Vieira's comment in 1648 that "without Angola there are no blacks" (Conrad 1986:ix) is an accurate one. Numerous distinct peoples lived in 17th-century Angola (Vansina 1963; Miller 1976; Maestri 1978; Thornton 1992), and this cultural complexity implies that Palmares was "an ethnic and cultural mosaic" (Freitas 1984:39).

The Portuguese began an energetic program of attempting to destroy Palmares around 1670, and almost every year thereafter they sent some armed force against the maroons. In 1687, Zumbi murdered his uncle, Ganga Zumba, and took control of Palmares. Tradition holds that Zumbi was more militant than his uncle and that he sought an active, armed resistance to the Portuguese rather than the uneasy peace sought by Ganga Zumba. The rise of Zumbi increased the tension between the Portuguese and the palmarinos, and in 1694, a combined force of Brazilian Indian fighters from São Paulo—the famed *bandeirantes*—and their native allies led a dramatic and successful assault on Macaco. Zumbi was captured and beheaded, and Palmares was disbanded. The palmarinos who were not captured supposedly fled into the surrounding woods. What became of these people is unknown, but the tradition of resistance continued in northeastern Brazil for several years.

The armed resistance of the palmarinos and the heroism of Zumbi are today widely commemorated in Brazil, particularly in the Northeast (Brandão 1935:66; Freitas 1984:100–165; Santos 1985: 37–47). Palmares adds an important element to today's African-Brazilian identity (Chiavenato 1980), and Zumbi is today considered to be the "first great Negro of Brazil" (Souza 1963:15). The events at Palmares have been dramatized in two full-length feature films. In 1969, a leftist group even took the name "Armed Revolutionary Vanguard—Palmares" (Dassin 1986:94).

This summary history of Palmares suggests that an historic ethnography of the sort recommended by Schuyler (1988) could be completed for Palmares. This ethnography could focus on one particular village or could view the entire 10 villages as one community. In either case, archaeology must play a prominent role in the creation of the

ethnography because the extant historical records do not provide detailed information about daily life at Palmares. The contemporary observers who wrote about Palmares were sent there to destroy it and to rob its people of their freedom. The men who wrote about the maroon society did not record precisely how the people lived, how much indigenous influence was felt in the individual palmarino villages, the nature of social stratification, or the characteristics of the palmarino language. European observers did remark on the Christian elements of the African religion practiced at Palmares, but their comments are vague enough to raise serious questions about the true nature of this syncretic religion. No one from Palmares is known to have ever written about the villages, or to have made statements that were recorded. Serious anthropological fieldwork among maroon descendants in Brazil has yet to occur, and no one knows precisely where the palmarino descendants now live. The existing written comments about Palmares cannot be considered to be impartial and unbiased. Nothing is known today about the kind of houses the palmarinos built, the varieties of pottery they used, or the size of their individual villages. The historic ethnography clearly will be an important step in understanding daily life at Palmares. The complex historical and cultural circumstances of Palmares suggest, however, that it will be impossible to construct an ethnography without adopting a wide perspective that extends well beyond the community. How could the boundaries of this community be established? Who would be considered to be its members? When is one "inside" or "outside" Palmares? These are only a few questions that a community-based perspective would bring to light. In a more concrete way, perhaps, preliminary archaeological research conducted in 1992 demonstrates the need for a broad view when considering Palmares.

Preliminary Archaeological Research at Palmares

Initial archaeological reconnaissance was conducted at Palmares in July 1992. The original intent in this survey was to locate the 10 villages that

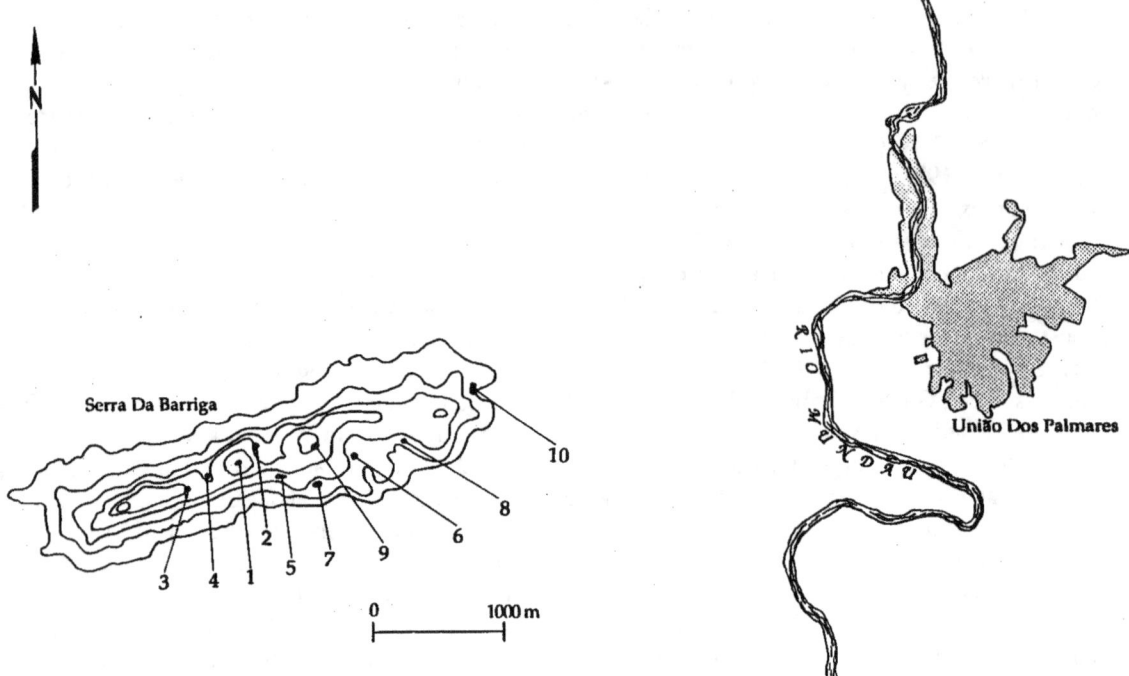

FIGURE 2. The Serra da Barriga in relation to União dos Palmares. The numbers refer to the 10 sites located during the 1992 survey.

comprised Palmares at the height of its development, from the 1670s to 1694. The abundance of surface material encountered at Macaco, the first locale examined, however, made it necessary to restrict investigations to this one area. Macaco, the former capital city of Palmares, is located on what is today called the Serra da Barriga.

The Serra da Barriga, "Potbelly Hill," is located in the municipality of União dos Palmares in the State of Alagoas. Alagoas is in the Brazilian northeast, a part of the country known today for its poverty and annual droughts. The Serra da Barriga is in a rural part of the state, about 60 km from the Atlantic coast. The hill is approximately 4,000 m east to west and from 500 to 1,000 m north to south. It ranges from 150 to 560 m above mean sea level and occurs within a region known as the Alagoan Forest (Araújo 1985:34–38). The largest nearby water source is the Mundaú River, located approximately 3,000 m to the east, but numerous small streams run to the bottom of the hill from all directions. The nearest town, União dos Palmares, is located across the river, approximately 4,500 m from the easternmost point of the Serra da Barriga (Figure 2). In the 1980s, the Serra da Barriga was declared a national monument and a commemorative statue of Zumbi was placed there.

The reconnaissance team, composed of the author, Pedro Funari, Michael Rowlands, and volunteers from Brazil and the United States, found 10 archaeological sites during the 1992 field season (Figure 2). All of these sites are significant and will eventually be the subject of further investigation. For this paper, Site 3 is perhaps the most significant because of the nature and range of material found there. The team collected 251 pieces of ceramics from this site; burned earth and charcoal were the only other materials found. The ceramics can be divided into two gross categories: unglazed wares and tin-glazed majolica. The unglazed wares can be further divided into three varieties: thin-bodied (< 1 cm), tempered wares;

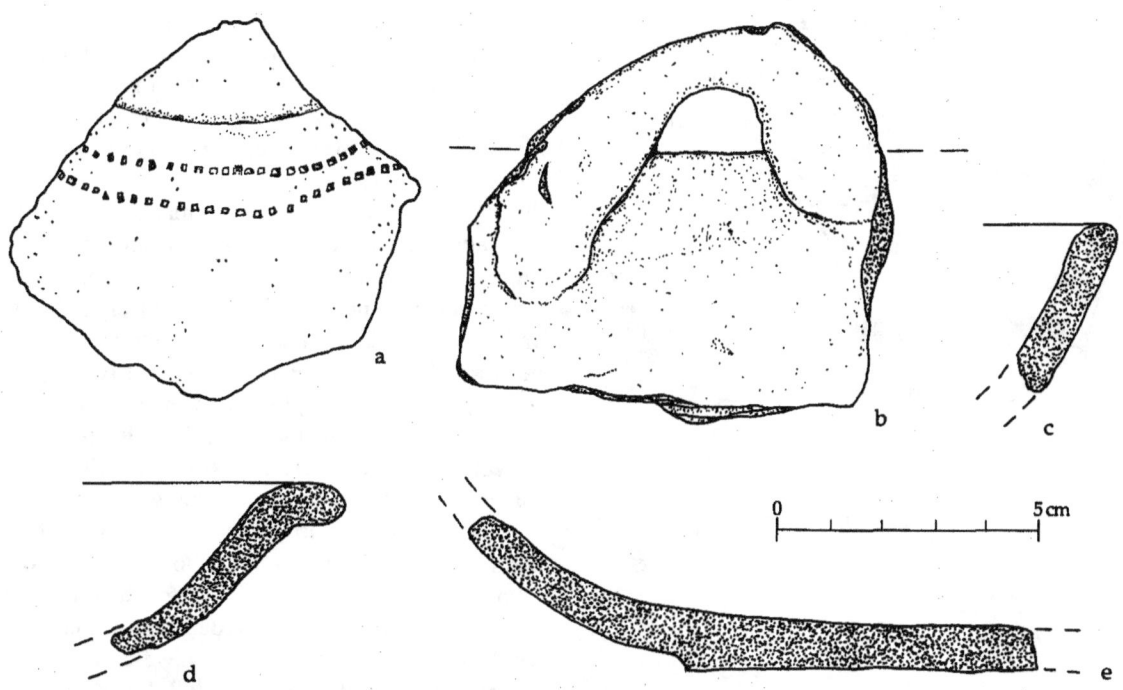

FIGURE 3. Thin-bodied, unglazed ceramics from the Serra da Barriga: a, brown, tempered ware with square punctates; b, brown, tempered ware with handle; c and d, rim profiles of thin-bodied, untempered wares; e, base profile of thin-bodied, untempered ware.

thin-bodied, untempered wares; and thick-bodied (> 1 cm), heavily tempered wares.

The thin-bodied, tempered wares are represented by a brown variety decorated with two parallel rows of small square punctates (Figure 3a), and by an undecorated brown variety that exhibits a complete handle (Figure 3b). The thin-bodied, untempered wares are light tan in color and finely made. They appear to have been formed over a mold or to have been wheel thrown. The sherds show that these vessels were made with two rim forms, one straight-sided (Figure 3c) and one with a highly angled lip (Figure 3d). These vessels also had flat standing-rims (Figure 3e). The thick-bodied wares are red in color and range in thickness from 2.45 to 2.79 cm. Although most of the sherds are undecorated and undiagnostic, one sherd has a thick collar (Figure 4).

All of the majolica was poorly made and only

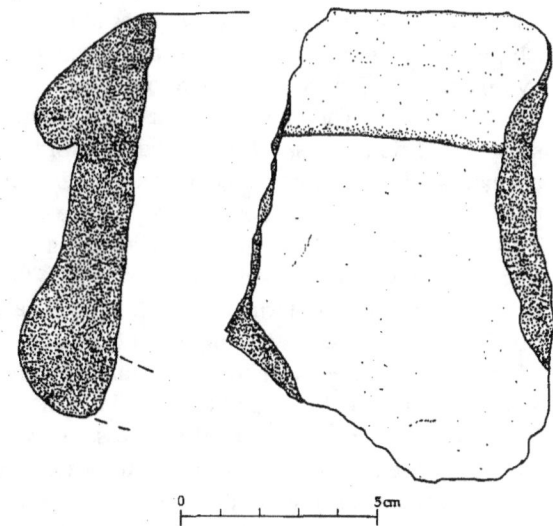

FIGURE 4. Rim sherd of a red, thick, heavily tempered ware from the Serra da Barriga.

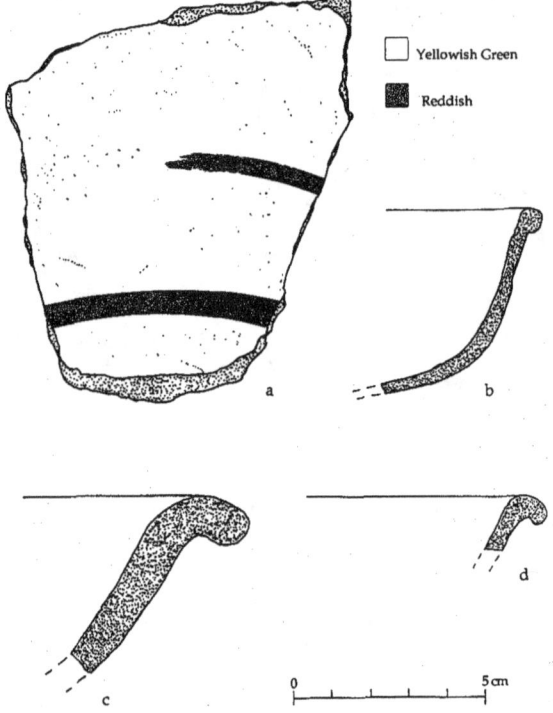

FIGURE 5. Majolica sherds from the Serra da Barriga: *a*, yellowish-green slipped ware with parallel reddish bands; *b–d*, rim profiles of majolica vessels.

one piece was decorated. This sherd has a yellowish-green slip on the interior and is decorated with two parallel reddish bands (Figure 5a). The exterior is unglazed. The other majolica sherds represent three different vessel forms. The first form is a small bowl, calculated as having had a diameter of 17 cm, with a small beaded rim (Figure 5b). This vessel has a patchy, uneven yellowish-green to pale yellow slip on both the interior and the exterior. The second form is also from a small bowl, also calculated as having had a diameter of 17 cm, with a more exaggerated rim than the first vessel (Figure 5c). The slip of this sherd is yellow, but while it extends throughout the vessel's interior, it only extends over the lip on the exterior. The third sherd is similar to the second, but the lip is even more exaggerated (Figure 5d) and the slip does not extend over the lip to the exterior. The estimated size of this vessel when whole is 34 cm.

These sherds were all located on the surface of Site 3, but a limited subsurface testing program indicated that these pieces had a firm context together. It can be assumed, therefore, that these four kinds of ceramics were used contemporaneously at Palmares. One also may assume, based on the idea that Palmares was a "cultural mosaic"—uniting Africans, Native South Americans, and even Portuguese and Dutch colonists—that these ceramics may relate in some fashion to these different groups and to the sociopolitical and economic relations between them. In essence, at this early stage of research one is willing to accept, even tentatively, that the variation in the ceramic collection may reflect the cultural differences present within Palmares. Obviously, connections between the ceramics and the society are yet to be shown, but the central question becomes, then, how can an historic ethnography of Palmares be written without considering the role that each group within the "mosaic" played in the creation, development, and maintenance of the community? Each of these groups was not necessarily a daily part of palmarino society, even though each was immensely important to it. The history of each group is complex, but even a brief consideration of each demonstrates why the understanding of Palmares must be extended beyond what might be narrowly construed as its community.

Palmares and the Colonial Portuguese in Brazil

It may seem logical at first glance to assume that the people of Palmares, as runaway slaves, and the Portuguese, as slaveowners, would have been clear and obvious enemies. Nieuhoff (1813:707) states that the chief occupation of the people of Palmares was to rob the Portuguese of their slaves, and Barleus (1974:252) mentions that all those slaves who chose to run away from their plantations were readily welcomed by the maroons. Barleus (1974:252) also notes that slaves could be captured from coastal plantations by palmarinos and taken to Palmares by force. This evidence suggests that the palmarinos represented a triple threat to the colonial Portuguese: an economic threat, because they robbed the Portuguese sugar planters of their slaves; a political threat, because they were an active enemy to the Portuguese mercantilist enterprise in Brazil; and a social threat, because they embodied a weakness in the slave regime. It may be supposed, then, that the palmarinos and the colonial Portuguese represent opposite poles of the colonial experience in the New World.

Importantly, the relations between the Portuguese and the palmarinos were not this straightforward. Portuguese colonial society was not completely united in its opposition to Palmares, and the historical evidence suggests that the palmarinos had the support of at least a segment of the colonial Portuguese population. Barleus (1974:252), for example, reports that Bartholomeus Lintz, the leader of the Dutch expedition against Palmares in 1640, "lived among them [and] after staying with them [knew] their places and mode of life." For some reason Lintz decided to betray his "ancient companions" (Barleus 1974:252) and led the first Dutch attack against Palmares. Also, in 1670, after the Dutch had left northeastern Brazil, the Portuguese colonial governor formally denounced all settlers (moradores) who continued to pass firearms to the palmarinos "in disregard of God and local laws" (Carneiro 1988:227–228). Seventeen years later, the colonial governor threatened to imprison any Portuguese settlers who were even suspected of giving support to Palmares, regardless of their social standing, or "noble birth" (Ennes 1938:240). The people of Palmares are known to have regularly bartered their "cane, bananas, and beans for such articles as utensils, arms, and ammunition" with the local moradores (Ramos 1939: 64), and these settlers are known to have passed information to Palmares about impending assaults (Kent 1965:171).

This historical information suggests that the people of Palmares maintained constant links with some segments of the local Portuguese population. The presence of these connections implies that the goals of the Portuguese colonial government and the coastal sugar planters were not necessarily those of the moradores. It seems clear that any historic ethnography of Palmares must include the morad-

ores, people of Portuguese descent who did not live in the palmarino community, but who obviously had much to do with its continued existence.

The apparent conflict between the coastal sugar planters and the more inland moradores can be better understood by a brief consideration of continental Portuguese society. Seventeenth-century Portuguese society was stratified into at least four classes: men of letters, a roughly homogeneous class of educated scholars; the nobility, composed of knights, squires, and the so-called "rich men"; the clergy; and citizens, composed of farmers, merchants, and serfs (Marques 1971:9–10). Merchants, artisans, and the "rich men" realized the greatest advantages from global exploration (Livermore 1973:69) because all three groups had opportunities to become wealthy plantation owners. The Portuguese soldiers and sailors, the "citizens," who faced the dangers of exploration were often bitter about their failure to realize any monetary rewards from exploration (Moser 1985:97–98). It can be easily imagined that the moradores would not necessarily share the vision of Brazil held by the wealthy Portuguese plantation owners, and that the moradores might be willing to assist the palmarinos, people with whom they carried on trade and acquired foodstuffs. It may have been possible that the lives of the moradores were similar to those of the palmarinos, and that the moradores had more in common with the palmarinos than with their countrymen, the plantation owners. Definitive statements cannot be made, but one may imagine that the unions between the moradores and the palmarinos had a material element. The nature of this relationship should become more clear as research progresses.

Palmares and the Native South Americans

When the Portuguese first came to Brazil in 1500, they did not find an uninhabited, empty land. Instead, they found the land inhabited by thousands of indigenous peoples who had lived in Brazil for centuries. Sixteenth-century explorers applied the name "Tupinamba" to all those peoples who spoke the Tupí-Guaraní language, and who lived along the

Brazilian coast from the mouth of the Amazon to São Paulo in the south (Métraux 1948:95). The Tupinamba represented a diverse group, but they were generally characterized by slash-and-burn horticulture mixed with hunting and gathering, huge communal houses, matrilocality, and cannibalism.

The Portuguese institutionalized the legal bondage of the indigenous cultures in Brazil in the mid-1550s (Hemming 1978:152). By the late 16th century, they had enslaved hundreds of Tupinamba for work in the sugar mills, but these native slaves were soon overworked or died from European diseases (Thornton 1992:140; see also Cardoso 1983:66–67). An observer remarked in 1583 that "no one could believe that so great a supply [of indigenous slaves] could be so quickly exhausted" (Scammell 1981:248).

The role that the indigenous peoples played at Palmares is unclear. They were employed by the Portuguese for armed assaults against Palmares, starting with Rodolfo Baro's Dutch attack in 1643 and ending with Domingos Jorge Velho's final and successful Portuguese assault in 1694 (Hemming 1978:357–359). The possible use of a native name for one of the villages of Palmares—Arotirene (Kent 1965:169)—suggests, however, that native Brazilians in the vicinity of Palmares contributed to the success and maintenance of the maroon community. The Tupinamba are known to have fought the Portuguese in the 16th century (Métraux 1948:98), and their alliance with runaway Portuguese slaves is not difficult to imagine. In addition, Barleus (1923:370) reports that Baro captured "seven Brazilians" in his attack on Palmares in 1644. From a logical standpoint alone, the continued existence of Palmares without native support in the interior is difficult to imagine, especially since the palmarinos ran away to the home country of the natives.

The research team may have found material evidence of native involvement at Palmares during the 1992 field season. The thick-bodied, heavily tempered pottery found at Site 3 may be native pottery, and its context, in association with majolica, suggests that these ceramics are contemporaneous.

The influence of indigenous people on Palmares also may be given credence by a large, intact pot-tery vessel found at Site 1. This pot, found 15 cm below the ground surface, measured 71 cm in diameter and 69 cm deep. Its body, composed of the thick-bodied redware found at Site 3, is about 3 cm thick. Inside the vessel was a smaller vessel and 31 small sherd fragments that appeared to be from the neck of the large vessel.

A functional interpretation of the large vessel is difficult to make. Large burial urns are well known in Brazilian prehistory (Meggers 1948:159), and the present inhabitants of the Serra da Barriga reported finding a similar pot containing human skeletal material and a necklace somewhere nearby (Orser 1992:25). The absence of skeletal material in the large pot does not preclude its use as a burial urn (Anna C. Roosevelt 1992, pers. comm.). Meggers and Evans (1983:316) illustrate a burial urn of the Aratu cultural tradition, dating to around A.D. 800, that bears a resemblance to the large vessel at Site 1. They note that similar vessels have been encountered in the Brazilian Northeast, including the State of Alagoas, in cemeteries "containing more than 100 urns" (Meggers and Evans 1983:317).

The presence of the small pieces of pottery at the bottom of the pot also may suggest that the pot served as a storage vessel for grain or other materials, and that the small sherds represent the depositing and removing of objects from the vessel. Pottery vessels are known to have been used for grain storage by the Mbundu, or Ovimbundu, in modern Angola for grain storage (McCulloch 1952:15). A vessel illustrated by Hambly (1934:368, Plate 14), in his ethnography of the Mbundu, has the same shape as the vessel found at Site 1, but since this shape is common throughout the world, the similarity may be coincidental.

In any case, this analysis concludes that indigenous peoples had a strong and lasting impact on Palmares. The strength and duration of this impact has yet to be determined.

Palmares and Angola

No study of Palmares could possibly be complete without considering 17th-century Angola. The cultural context of Angola at the time of the

Portuguese involvement there is exceedingly complicated and a full historical description of its complexities is outside the scope of this paper (cf. Miller 1976, 1982; Thornton 1992). Even a brief consideration will reveal its importance to Palmares.

Many distinct cultures lived in Central Africa at the time of Portuguese contact. When Diogo Cão sailed along the African coast in the early 1480s, the Kingdom of Kongo was "the undisputed leader among all the coastal states of Central Africa" (Vansina 1966:37). This kingdom allied itself with the Portuguese, its king was baptized a Christian in 1490, and Kongolese boys were sent to study in Lisbon. So linked were the colonial Portuguese and the Kingdom of Kongo that in 1512 the Portuguese were able to threaten the cessation of all trade with the Kongo unless the Africans continued to supply slaves to the Portuguese (Saunders 1982: 20–21). Within a few decades, however, attacks by the interior Jaga, or Imbangala (Vansina 1963), helped to speed the final disintegration of the Kingdom of Kongo, and the Portuguese turned their attention to the interior of what they called "Angola," after the Mbundu king known as "Ngola" (Birmingham 1965:8; Boxer 1973b: 237). So complex were the relationships forged between the Portuguese and the peoples of West Central Africa that in 1556, when the Kingdom of Kongo attacked the Kingdom of Kdongo, each side was supported by Portuguese troops (Henderson 1979:82).

The Portuguese construction of Luanda in 1575 signalled their commitment to controlling Angola. The Portuguese, however, did not seek to establish close collateral ties with the inhabitants of Angola as they had with the Kongo, but chose instead to dominate and subjugate them in what has been described as one of the most brutal regimes in colonial history (Bennett 1975:34–35).

Between 1605 and 1694, the dates that Palmares existed, the cultural situation in West Central Africa continued to be complex. Between 1605 and 1654, the Portuguese made successful efforts to stimulate the slave trade from Angola, and from 1654 to 1683, the Portuguese attempted to cement their control over Angola (Birmingham 1965:24).

In 1640, Portugal declared independence from Spain, and wealthy colonialists in Brazil were called upon to defend Angola from the inroads of the Dutch (Duffy 1962:55). The supply of slaves to the New World was briefly interrupted during this period, but not terminated.

Cultural contacts among the various peoples living in Angola was extensive (Thornton 1992:188). One of the factors that made these contacts possible, in addition to the human geography of the region, was the slave trade. Many of the slaves who were sent out of Luanda were captured in warfare, and Portuguese merchants were not above inciting a local war in order to purchase the prisoners (Duffy 1962:60). These prisoners were the people sent to Brazilian sugar plantations, and they were the people who ultimately ran away to Palmares. One must imagine that the cultures and traditions of the Angolan people consistently played a huge role in shaping the history and culture of Palmares. The way in which Angolan traditions were imprinted on the material culture of the maroon society is currently unknown.

Conclusion

Palmares appears at first glance to represent a perfect opportunity to prepare an historic ethnography of the sort promoted by Schuyler (1988). Little is known about daily life at Palmares, even though many Europeans have left accounts of the community. Archaeology, in conjunction with these accounts, will greatly enhance knowledge of Palmares and provide further information about how Africans maintained elements of their cultures in the face of slavery. At Palmares specifically, one can learn a great deal about how diverse cultures of African and American origin created a syncretic culture in the New World. Clearly, the further study of Palmares provides ample opportunity to learn about an important aspect of colonial life in the Americas, the role of runaway slaves in helping to create modern society. An historic ethnography of Palmares may be an important document in the history of this creation, even if Palmares is viewed in isolation, as a distinct community.

Even a brief consideration of the history of Palmares demonstrates that the creation of this historic ethnography is not so straightforward. Palmares was affected by many diverse peoples throughout its history. The historical record indicates that Palmares was situated between indigenous villages on the west and the colonial Portuguese on the east. At least two classes, probably with different goals and plans, existed within the colonial Portuguese settlements. These classes, *moradores* and wealthy sugar planters, each had a different impact on Palmares even though in some sense each represented Portugal. From 1630 to 1654, the Dutch also had some impact on Palmares from the northeast as they attempted to build permanent settlements in Brazil. By the same token, numerous African slaves were sent to Brazil throughout the history of Palmares and one can assume that these people continued to swell the population of Palmares until 1694. These newly arrived Africans can be expected to have kept African culture alive at Palmares, even though the palmarinos were building a syncretic culture based on African, Native South American, and European elements. Palmares was geographically situated to maintain a constant interaction with five separate groups: (1) indigenous cultures, (2) Portuguese *moradores*, (3) wealthy Portuguese sugar planters, (4) Dutch colonials (from 1630 to 1654), and (5) newly arrived African slaves (Figure 6). The importance of any one of these groups in maintaining Palmares cannot be overlooked. Each group must be considered in any historic ethnography, even though they were not palmarinos.

On a wider level, the study of Palmares should provide an alternative understanding of the growth and spread of mercantile capitalism. Palmares represents the most overt kind of resistance, and its study should provide new insights for archaeologists who wish to study the modern world from several different angles.

Schuyler's (1988) idea about the preparation of historic ethnographies in historical archaeology seems at first thought to be an important way for historical archaeologists to be widely recognized for substantive contributions to knowledge. Clearly, the historic ethnography may present a way for

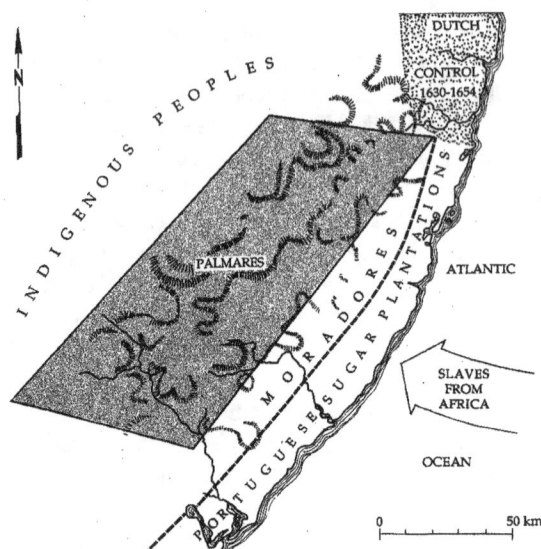

FIGURE 6. The location of Palmares in relation to other groups in northeastern Brazil.

historical archaeologists to demonstrate the interpretive power of historical archaeology to scholars outside the field. In making this contribution, however, historical archaeologists will find it difficult to define their "communities" with any clarity. The difficulty in defining communities stems from the history of the modern world as it has been documented and interpreted by Wolf (1982) and others. Historical archaeology ultimately will be harmed if its practitioners adopt a too-narrow view of the community by overlooking the larger cultural and historical environments within which all historic communities were situated. Palmares serves well to demonstrate the need for the adoption of a global perspective in historical archaeology. In addition, maroon communities may be more common in history than previously suspected, and the study of Palmares may provide insights into many issues of central concern to historical archaeology, such as racism, ethnicity, gender, and class.

ACKNOWLEDGMENTS

This paper was written after long and fruitful exchanges with Pedro Paulo Abreu Funari, of the University of Campinas, Brazil, and Michael J. J. Rowlands, of University College London, and I am grateful for their input. I am also indebted to Zezito de Araújo, Director of the Center for Afro-Brazilian Studies at the Federal University of Alagoas in Maceió, Brazil, and Clóvis Moura, President of the Brazilian Institute of African Studies in São Paulo. I have benefited from discussions with Christopher DeCorse, Robert Dirks, Mark Leone, William Marquardt, Anna C. Roosevelt, and Julie Ruiz-Sierra. I wish to thank Jerry Moore for drafting the figures and Gerlof D. Homan, Department of History, Illinois State University, for translating the Barleus material. I would like to thank the Newberry Library for making the 1647 edition of Barleus available to me. I am indebted to Janice Orser for her constant support and encouragement during this research, and for her editing skills. William Turnbaugh and the journal's reviewers provided much-appreciated advice during the preparation of this manuscript. This research was supported by grants from the National Geographic Society, Committee for Research and Exploration (Grant No. 4805–92) and the University Research Office of Illinois State University.

REFERENCES

ABU-LUGHOD, JANET L.
1989 *Before European Hegemony: The World System, A.D. 1250–1350.* Oxford University Press, New York.

ADAMS, WILLIAM H.
1976 Trade Networks and Interaction Spheres—A View from Silcott. *Historical Archaeology* 10:99–112.
1977 *Silcott, Washington: Ethnoarchaeology of a Rural American Community.* Laboratory of Anthropology, Washington State University, Pullman.

ALTAVILLA, JAYME DE
1931 *O Quilombo dos Palmares.* Companhia Melhoramentos, São Paulo.

ARAÚJO, ZEZITO DE (COMPILER)
1985 *Serra da Barriga: Exposição de Motivos para o Tombamento.* Núcleo de Estudos Afro-Brasileiros, Universidade Federal de Alagoas, Maceió.

BARLEUS, CASPAR
1923 *Nederlandsch Brazilie Onder Het Bewind van Johan Maurits, Grave van Nassau, 1637–1644.* Martinus Nijhoff, 'S-Gravenhage.
1974 *História dos Feitas Recentemente Practicados Durante Oito Anos no Brasil.* Livraria Italiaia Editora, Belo Horizonte.

BASTIDE, ROGER
1978 *The African Religions of Brazil: Toward a Sociology of the Interpretation of Civilizations,* translated by Helen Sebba. The Johns Hopkins University Press, Baltimore.

BENNETT, NORMAN R.
1975 *Africa and Europe: From Roman Times to the Present.* Africana, New York.

BIRMINGHAM, DAVID
1965 *The Portuguese Conquest of Angola.* Oxford University Press, London.

BOURGUIGNON, ERIKA, AND LENORA S. GREENBAUM
1973 *Diversity and Homogeneity in World Society.* HRAF Press, New Haven.

BOXER, C. R.
1973a *Salvador de Sá e a Luta pelo Brasil e Angola, 1602–1686,* translated by Olivério M. de Oliveira Pito. Companhia Editora Nacional, São Paulo.
1973b *The Dutch Seaborne Empire, 1600–1800.* Penguin, London.

BRANDÃO, ALFREDO
1935 Os Negros na Historia de Alagôas. *Estudos Afro-Brasileiros* 1:55–91.

BRAUDEL, FERNAND
1984 *The Perspective of the World,* translated by Siân Reynolds. Harper and Row, New York.

BREEN, T. H.
1989 *Imagining the Past: East Hampton Histories.* Addison-Wesley, Reading, Massachusetts.

BURNS, E. BRADFORD
1980 *A History of Brazil.* Second edition. Columbia University Press, New York.

CAMERON, RONDO
1989 *A Concise Economic History of the World.* Oxford University Press, New York.

CAMPBELL, MAVIS C.
1990 *The Maroons of Jamaica, 1655–1796: A History of Resistance, Collaboration, and Betrayal.* Africa World Press, Trenton, New Jersey.

CARDOSO, GERALD
1983 *Negro Slavery in the Sugar Plantations of Veracruz and Pernambuco, 1550–1680: A Comparative Study.* University Press of America, Washington, D.C.

CARNEIRO, EDISON
1988 *Os Quilombo dos Palmares.* Fourth edition. Companhia Editora Nacional, São Paulo.

CARVALHO, ALFREDO DE (TRANSLATOR)
1902 Diario da Viagem de Capitão João Blaer aos Palmares em 1645. *Revista do Instituto Arqueología e Geográfico Pernambuco* 10:87–96.

CHAMPION, TIMOTHY C. (EDITOR)
1989 *Centre and Periphery: Comparative Studies in Archaeology.* Unwin Hyman, London.

CHAUNU, PETER
1979 *European Expansion in the Later Middle Ages,* translated by Katharine Bertram. North-Holland, Amsterdam.

CHIAVENATO, JÚLIO JOSÉ
1980 Palmares: Simbolo da Capacidade de Luta do Negro Escravo. In *O Negro no Brasil: Da Senzala a Guerra do Paraguai,* pp. 158–160. Brasiliense, São Paulo.

CLELAND, CHARLES E., AND JAMES E. FITTING
1968 The Crisis of Identity: Theory in Historic Sites Archaeology. *Conference on Historic Site Archaeology Papers 1967* 2(2):124–138.

CONRAD, ROBERT EDGAR
1986 *World of Sorrow: The African Slave Trade to Brazil.* Louisiana State University Press, Baton Rouge.

CURTIN, PHILIP D.
1984 *Cross-Cultural Trade in World History.* Cambridge University Press, Cambridge.
1990 *The Rise and Fall of the Plantation Complex: Essays in Atlantic History.* Cambridge University Press, Cambridge.

DASSIN, JOAN (EDITOR)
1986 *Torture in Brazil: A Report by the Archdiocese of São Paulo,* translated by Jaime Wright. Vintage, New York.

DAVIS, NATALIE Z.
1982 The Possibilities of the Past. *Journal of Interdisciplinary History* 12:267–275.

DEAGAN, KATHLEEN
1988 Neither History Nor Prehistory: The Questions that Count in Historical Archaeology. *Historical Archaeology* 22(1):7–12.
1991 Historical Archaeology's Contribution to Our Understanding of Early America. In *Historical Archaeology in Global Perspective,* edited by Lisa Falk, pp. 97–112. Smithsonian Institution Press, Washington, D.C.

DEETZ, JAMES
1977 *In Small Things Forgotten: The Archaeology of Early American Life.* Anchor Press/Doubleday, Garden City, New York.
1991 Archaeological Evidence of Sixteenth- and Seventeenth-Century Encounters. In *Historical Archaeology in Global Perspective,* edited by Lisa Falk, pp. 1–9. Smithsonian Institution Press, Washington, D.C.

DEGLER, CARL N.
1971 *Neither Black Nor White: Slavery and Race Relations in Brazil and the United States.* Macmillan, New York.

DIFFIE, BAILEY W.
1987 *A History of Colonial Brazil, 1500–1792.* Robert E. Kreiger, Malabar, Florida.

DOLLAR, CLYDE D.
1968 Some Thoughts on Theory and Method in Historical Archaeology. *Conference on Historic Site Archaeology Papers 1967* 2(2):3–30.

DRUMMOND, CONSELHEIRO
1859 Relação das Guerras Feitas aos Palmares de Pernambuco no Tempo de Governador D. Pedro de Almeida de 1675 a 1678. *Revista do Instituto Histório e Gragráfico Brasileiro* 22:303–329.

DUFFY, JAMES
1962 *Portugal in Africa.* Harvard University Press, Cambridge, Massachusetts.

ENNES, ERNESTO
1938 *As Guerras nos Palmares (Subsídios para a sua História).* Companhia Editora Nacional, São Paulo.
1948 The Palmares "Republic" of Pernambuco: Its Final Destruction, 1697. *The Americas* 5:200–216.

FONTANA, BERNARD L.
1965 On the Meaning of Historic Sites Archaeology. *American Antiquity* 31:61–65.

FRANK, ANDRE GUNDER
1978 *World Accumulation, 1492–1789.* Monthly Review Press, New York.

FREITAS, DÉCIO
1984 *Palmares: O Guerra dos Escravos.* Fifth edition. Movimento, Porto Alegre.

FREYRE, GILBERTO
1956 *The Masters and the Slaves: A Study in the Development of Brazilian Civilization,* translated by Samuel Putnam. Second edition. Alfred A. Knopf, New York.

GENOVESE, EUGENE D.
1979 *From Rebellion to Revolution: Afro-American Slave Revolts in the Making of the Modern World.* Louisiana State University Press, Baton Rouge.

GENOVESE, EUGENE D., AND LEONARD HOCHBERG (EDITORS)
1989 *Geographic Perspectives in History.* Oxford University Press, Oxford.

GHANI, ASHRAF
1987 A Conversation with Eric Wolf. *American Ethnologist* 14:346–366.

GOLDFRANK, WALTER L. (EDITOR)
1979 *The World-System of Capitalism: Past and Present.* Sage, Beverly Hills, California.

HAGGETT, PETER
1990 *The Geographer's Art.* Basil Blackwell, Oxford.

HALL, FREDERICK HOLDEN, WILLIAM F. HARRISON,
AND DOROTHY WINTERS WELKER (EDITORS
AND TRANSLATORS)
   1987   *Dialogues of the Great Things of Brazil, Attributed
to Ambrósio Fernandes Brandão.* University of New
Mexico Press, Albuquerque.

HAMBLY, WILFRED D.
   1934   The Ovimbundu of Angola. *Field Museum of Natural History, Anthropological Series 21.* Chicago.

HARRINGTON, J. C.
   1952   Historic Site Archaeology in the United States. In
Archaeology of the Eastern United States, edited by
James B. Griffin, pp. 335–344. University of Chicago Press, Chicago.
   1955   Archaeology as an Auxiliary Science of American
History. *American Anthropologist* 7:1121–1130.

HEMMING, JOHN
   1978   *Red Gold: The Conquest of the Brazilian Indians,
1500–1760.* Harvard University Press, Cambridge,
Massachusetts.

HENDERSON, LAWRENCE W.
   1979   *Angola: Five Centuries of Conflict.* Cornell University Press, Ithaca, New York.

HONERKAMP, NICHOLAS
   1988   Questions that Count in Historical Archaeology. *Historical Archaeology* 22(1):5–6.

HOPKINS, TERENCE K.
   1982   The Study of the Capitalist World-Economy: Some
Introductory Considerations. In *World-System Anal-
ysis: Theory and Methodology,* edited by Terence K.
Hopkins and Immanuel Wallerstein, pp. 9–38. Sage,
Beverly Hills, California.

ISAAC, RHYS
   1982   *The Transformation of Virginia, 1740–1790.* University of North Carolina Press, Chapel Hill.

KENT, R. K.
   1965   Palmares: An African State in Brazil. *Journal of African History* 6:161–175.

KING, ANTHONY D.
   1984   *The Bungalow: The Production of a Global Culture.*
Routledge, London.
   1989   *Urbanism, Colonialism, and the World-Economy:
Cultural and Spatial Foundations of the World Urban System.* Routledge, London.
   1990   *Global Cities: Post-Imperialism and the Internation-
alisation of London.* Routledge, London.

KROEBER, A. L.
   1957   An Anthropologist Looks at History. *Pacific Historical Review* 26:281–287.
   1966   *An Anthropologist Looks at History.* University of
California Press, Berkeley.

LIVERMORE, H. V.
   1973   *Portugal: A Short History.* Edinburgh University
Press, Edinburgh.

MAESTRI, MARIO JOSÉ, FILHO
   1978   *A Agricultura Africana nos Séculos XVI e XVII no
Litoral Angolano.* Instituto de Filosofia e Ciências
Humanas, Universidade Federal do Rio Grande do
Sul, Porto Alegre.

MARCUS, G. J.
   1980   *The Conquest of the North Atlantic.* Boydell, Suffolk.

MARQUES, A. H. DE OLIVEIRA
   1971   *Daily Life in Portugal in the Late Middle Ages,*
translated by S. S. Wyatt. University of Wisconsin
Press, Madison.

MARTIN, WILLIAM G. (EDITOR)
   1990   *Semiperipheral States in the World-Economy.*
Greenwood, New York.

McCULLOCH, MERRAN
   1952   *The Ovimbundu of Angola.* International African Institute, London.

MEGGERS, BETTY J.
   1948   The Archaeology of the Amazon Basin. In *Handbook of South American Indians.* Vol. 3, *The Tropical Forest Tribes,* edited by Julian H. Steward, pp.
149–166. U.S. Government Printing Office, Washington, D.C.

MEGGERS, BETTY J., AND CLIFFORD EVANS
   1983   Lowland South America and the Antilles. In *Ancient
South Americans,* edited by Jesse D. Jennings, pp.
287–335. W. H. Freeman, New York.

MÉTRAUX, ALFRED
   1948   The Tupinamba. In *Handbook of South American
Indians.* Vol. 3, *The Tropical Forest Tribes,* edited
by Julian H. Steward, pp. 95–133. U.S. Government Printing Office, Washington, D.C.

MILLER, JOSEPH C.
   1976   *Kings and Kinsmen: Early Mbundu States in Angola.*
Clarendon Press, Oxford.
   1982   The Significance of Drought, Disease, and Famine
in the Agriculturally Marginal Zones of West-Central
Africa. *Journal of African History* 23:17–61.

MINTZ, SIDNEY W.
   1986   *Sweetness and Power: The Place of Sugar in Modern
History.* Penguin, New York.

MOSER, GERALD M.
   1985   Grumbling Veterans of an Empire. In *Empire in
Transition: The Portuguese World in the Time of
Camões,* edited by Alfred Hower and Richard A.
Preto-Rodas, pp. 97–105. University Presses of
Florida, Gainesville.

MOURA, CLÓVIS
    1987   *Quilombos: Resistência ao Escravismo*. Editora
            Atica, São Paulo.
    1988   *Rebeliões da Senzala: Quilombos, Insurreições,
            Guerrilhas*. Mercado Aberto, Porto Alegre.

MURDOCK, GEORGE PETER
    1980   *Themes of Illness: A World Survey*. University of
            Pittsburgh Press, Pittsburgh, Pennsylvania.

NIEUHOFF, JOHN
    1813   Voyages and Travels into Brazil. In *A General Col-
            lection of the Best and Most Interesting Voyages and
            Travels in All Parts of the World*, edited by John
            Pinkerton, pp. 697–881. Longman, Hurst, Rees,
            Orme, and Brown, London.

ORSER, CHARLES E., JR.
    1992   *In Search of Zumbi: Preliminary Archaeological Re-
            search at the Serra da Barriga, State of Alagoas,
            Brazil*. Midwestern Archaeological Research Center,
            Illinois State University, Normal.

PHILLIPS, J. R. S.
    1988   *The Medieval Expansion of Europe*. Oxford Univer-
            sity Press, Oxford.

PHILLIPS, WILLIAM D., JR.
    1985   *Slavery from Roman Times to the Early Transatlantic
            Trade*. University of Minnesota Press, Minneapolis.

RAMOS, ARTHUR
    1939   *The Negro in Brazil*, translated by Richard Pattee.
            Associated Publishers, Washington, D.C.

ROCHA PITA, SEBASTIÃO DA
    1950   *História da América Portuguesa*. Third edition.
            Livaria Progresso Editora, Salvador.

RODRIGUES, NINA
    1945   *Os Africanos no Brasil*. Third edition. Companhia
            Editora Nacional, São Paulo.

ROWLANDS, MICHAEL, MOGENS LARSEN, AND
KRISTIAN KRISTIANSEN (EDITORS)
    1987   *Centre and Periphery in the Ancient World*. Cam-
            bridge University Press, Cambridge.

SALE, KIRKPATRICK
    1990   *The Conquest of Paradise: Christopher Columbus
            and the Columbian Legacy*. Penguin, New York.

SANTOS, JOEL RUFINO DOS
    1985   *Zumbi*. Editora Moderna, São Paulo.

SAUNDERS, A. C.
    1982   *A Social History of Black Slaves and Freedmen in
            Portugal, 1441–1555*. Cambridge University Press,
            Cambridge.

SCAMMELL, G. V.
    1981   *The World Encompassed: The First European Mar-
            itime Empires, c. 800–1650*. Methuen, London.

SCHORTMAN, EDWARD M., AND PATRICIA A. URBAN
    1987   Modelling Interregional Interaction in Prehistory.
            Advances in Archaeological Methods and Theory 11:
            37–93. Michael B. Schiffer, editor. Academic Press,
            San Diego.

SCHUYLER, ROBERT L.
    1988   Archaeological Remains, Documents, and Anthro-
            pology: A Call for a New Culture History. *Historical
            Archaeology* 22(1):36–42.

SCHWARTZ, STUART A.
    1985   *Sugar Plantations in the Foundation of Brazilian So-
            ciety: Bahia, 1550–1835*. Cambridge University
            Press, Cambridge.

SOUTH, STANLEY
    1968   Comment on "Some Thoughts on Theory and
            Method in Historical Archaeology" by Clyde Dol-
            lar. *Conference on Historic Site Archaeology Pa-
            pers, 1967* 2(2):35–53.
    1988   Whither Pattern? *Historical Archaeology* 22(1):25–
            28.

SOUZA, YVONILDO DE
    1963   *Grandes Negros do Brasil*. Livraria São José, Rio de
            Janeiro.

THORNTON, JOHN
    1992   *Africa and Africans in the Making of the Atlantic
            World, 1400–1680*. Cambridge University Press,
            Cambridge.

VANSINA, JAN
    1963   The Foundation of the Kingdom of Kasanje. *Journal
            of African History* 4:355–374.
    1966   *Kingdoms of the Savanna: A History of Central Af-
            rican States Until European Occupation*. University
            of Wisconsin Press, Madison.

WALKER, IAIN C.
    1967   Historic Archaeology: Methods and Principles. *His-
            torical Archaeology* 1:23–34.

WALLACE, IAIN
    1990   *The Global Economic System*. Unwin Hyman, Lon-
            don.

WALLERSTEIN, IMMANUEL
    1974   *The Modern World-System: Capitalist Agriculture
            and the Origins of the European World-Economy in
            the Sixteenth Century*. Academic Press, New York.
    1979   *The Capitalist World-Economy*. Cambridge Univer-
            sity Press, Cambridge.
    1980   *The Modern World-System II: Mercantilism and the
            Consolidation of the European World-Economy,
            1600–1750*. Academic Press, New York.

WOLF, ERIC R.
    1982   *Europe and the People Without History*. University
            of California Press, Berkeley.

1984 Culture: Panacea or Problem? *American Antiquity* 49:393–400.

WOODRUFF, WILLIAM
1967 *Impact of Western Man: A Study of Europe's Role in the World Economy, 1750–1960*. St. Michael's Press, New York.

1981 *The Struggle for World Power, 1500–1980*. St. Michael's Press, New York.

CHARLES E. ORSER, JR.
MIDWESTERN ARCHAEOLOGICAL RESEARCH CENTER
ILLINOIS STATE UNIVERSITY
NORMAL, ILLINOIS 61790

MARIA FRANKLIN

"Power To The People": Sociopolitics and the Archaeology of Black Americans

ABSTRACT

This article is concerned with the sociopolitics of African-American archaeology. The intent here is to prompt archaeologists to think more about how our research affects black Americans today, and therefore why it is necessary that they be encouraged to take an interest in archaeological endeavors. The success or failure of our attempts to establish ties with black communities depends on us. The main emphases of this article are, therefore, focused on raising our level of awareness to the challenges we face, and increasing understanding as to the variable histories and perspectives that the diverse and knowledgeable black American public possesses and will hopefully share with archaeologists.

Introduction

The question of "Why do historical archaeology?" is often answered with the discipline's ability to give "people without a history" a "voice" (Little 1994:6; Orser and Fagan 1995:37–38). Indeed, while historical archaeology initially focused on the "rich and famous" of America's past, the discipline's growth is most notably due to the study of historically oppressed groups: Native Americans, African Americans, immigrants, and women. The emphasis on a more inclusive American history is an important goal, and this goal is often cited by archaeologists in order to substantiate the relevance of historical archaeology to today's society. Yet we seldom question our intentions in "giving a voice" to people of the past. Is it simply so that people of the present can better understand and appreciate their cultural heritage and national identity? Are we to assume that the American public is interested in the same questions that we are, and that our research both serves public interests and positively affects our society (Potter 1994:14)? Archaeologists seldom

reflect upon these questions, even though we are aware that the practice of manipulating the past to serve social, economic, and political agendas is probably as ancient and as widespread as human interest in the past itself. The addition of archaeology to the repertoire of "means to study the past" gave imperialists, nationalists, and racists one more weapon in their arsenal for re-penning histories better suited to legitimate and support their oppressive regimes (Trigger 1989). As archaeologists, we may recognize the open-ended potential for abuse through the control and subsequent distortion of historical and archaeological interpretations (Schmidt and Patterson 1995). Such an unconscionable act, we believe, could only be carried out by those politically motivated in order to further secure their privileged position in a society. We stop short of questioning our own position as guardians of the past: our inherent biases, our personal agendas (Pyburn and Wilk 1995:73), and our role in creating pasts which serve the present. It is as if we are unaware that the social and political context within which we operate has any influence on our interpretations and representations of the past. As Christopher Tilley (1989:110) warns, "an apolitical archaeology is a dangerous academic myth. The problem is not that archaeology is a political discourse, but that its politics largely take place on a tacit or unconscious level."

The unreflective practice of archaeology has had detrimental social and political effects upon people everywhere and throughout time (e.g., Hall 1984; Handsman and Leone 1989; Layton 1989; Gathercole and Lowenthal 1990; Stone and MacKenzie 1990; Potter 1991). Those who remain unwilling to reflect upon the social and political implications of their work will only escalate further alienation of archaeologists from the public. Either people will increasingly learn to live quite contentedly without archaeology (McManamon 1991:127) or, if we are not willing to change, we may eventually be forced to change (Zimmerman 1995:67). This article, then, is an attempt to challenge an uncritical

Historical Archaeology, 1997, 31(3):36-50.
Permission to reprint required.

African-American archaeology primarily through consciousness-raising.

The question I pose is, has the black archaeological past been colonized by white, middle-class specialists? I begin by briefly summarizing some of the troubling aspects of archaeological practice exposed through "critical" sociopolitical analyses which are relevant to this critique of African-American archaeology. A critical approach is necessary if African-American archaeology is to be made relevant to black Americans in particular, and American society in general. I then focus on African-American archaeology, and why it is necessary that we make more of an earnest effort to involve black Americans in research and interpretations. I discuss some of the issues that we can address as we initiate a discourse with black Americans, including the question of legitimate claims to cultural resources and dealing with a multivocal black community. The success or failure of our attempts to establish ties with black Americans will hinge upon *our* level of sensitivity, openness, and understanding of the histories and viewpoints that they bring to the exchange. For this reason, most of this discussion is meant to prompt archaeologists to reflect upon and question the current and highly problematic state of African-American archaeology. While the suggestions here are not fully developed, they can serve as a point of departure for future action in transforming our discipline.

Sociopolitics and Critical Archaeologies

> The tendency for archaeological interpretation to be influenced by society does not appear to be diminishing as archaeology becomes more theoretically sophisticated, as some archaeologists have suggested it would (Clarke 1979:154). Instead it appears to remain one of archaeology's permanent features (Trigger 1989:380).

The sociopolitical analyses of archaeology are fairly recent phenomena (Wylie 1989:95) that, while increasing in momentum and influence, cannot be labeled a unified trend (Gero 1985:342; Wylie 1985:134). As Handsman and Leone (1989:118) have observed, "the relevant literature is diverse and inconsistent in orienta-

tion." Such analyses generally involve exposing and critiquing the connections between archaeological knowledge claims and how they are "constituted" by the social and political contexts within which we practice archaeology (Wylie 1989:94). There are two ways in which this occurs, as Wylie (1983:120) further explains: "On one hand, there is a concern with the way in which contextual factors condition or control the archaeological enterprise, complemented on the other hand by a concern with the way archaeology, so conditioned, serves interests dominant in this context." The critique of sociopolitics has been carried out with varying emphases (cf. Gero 1985:342). There is, however, a unifying bond to these approaches: "They are, above all, critical" (Handsman and Leone 1989:118). Cases exist where archaeologists have been effectively critical without even referring to "sociopolitics." In these examples archaeologists have variously challenged the authority of academic knowledge claims (Klesert and Powell 1993; Zimmerman 1994), the control of cultural resources (Messenger 1995:68), and the need to actively involve descendant groups in archaeological endeavors (Spector 1993). Then there is the other end of the spectrum where lies the well-developed "philosophical" approach of the critical theorists (Wylie 1989:94). Developed by German sociologists—the Frankfurt school—in the 1920s and '30s, critical method and theory is grounded in Marxism (Leone 1984:1). Critical theorists are interested in challenging the ways in which historical interpretations are used against the dispossessed in the form of a "masking ideology;" to obscure and hence perpetuate class differences within a capitalist system where domination is assumed (Wylie 1983, 1985, 1989; Leone 1984, 1992; Handsman and Leone 1989; Tilley 1989; Potter 1994:36–39). Leone (1984:1) has observed that although critical theory is not widely used by archaeologists, "many of its insights have entered piecemeal."

By whatever means, confronting the sociopolitics of archaeology has had the effect of transforming the ways in which many of us think about, practice, and advocate our discipline (e.g., Gero et al. 1983; Gero 1985, 1989; Handsman and Leone 1989; Layton 1989; Pinsky and Wylie 1989; Tilley 1989; Wylie 1989, 1991; Gathercole and Lowenthal 1990; Stone and MacKenzie 1990; Gero and Conkey 1991; Potter 1991; Leone 1992; Spector 1993; Lynott and Wylie 1995; McDavid, this volume). This transformation owes its impetus to the initial repudiation by post-processualists of New Archaeology's unrealistic goal of a neutral, "value-free" archaeology, and an intense critique of futile attempts to achieve it (Handsman and Leone 1989:118; Tilley 1989:110–111; Trigger 1989:381; Wylie 1989:93–94). Critical archaeologists charge that interpretations and representations of the past are at all times "interest-constituted" (Handsman and Leone 1989; Wylie 1989:94). The interests served by an unreflective archaeology are of those in power who seek to tighten control of the dispossessed through history and archaeology by purchasing "an empirical substantiation of national mythology" (Leone 1973:129). An uncritical, unreflective archaeology therefore, whether we intend it or not, "sustains rather than challenges the contemporary social order" (Tilley 1989:105). In the United States, this translates to the support and legitimization of a social order permeated by racism, classism, and gender bias.

A Word on Reflection

The point of departure for critical approaches is the recognition that all forms of knowledge are interest-constituted. Next, through self-reflection, critical archaeologists attempt to demystify the relationship between sociopolitics—both within and without the discipline—and archaeological practice (Potter 1994:36). What does it mean to be "self-reflective" or "reflexive"? Reflection involves contemplation. Reflection is the means by which the archaeologist raises his or her level of awareness regarding the focus and meaning of their research: what is the subject, what are the questions, who is the intended audience, and to whom would the interpretations be most useful? An archaeology conditioned by its sociopolitical context does not readily reveal

which interest it serves. Only through reflection can we come to understand how our research could potentially serve to legitimate dominant interests at the expense of everyone else (Handsman and Leone 1989). Wylie offers this interpretation of self-reflection as a strategy employed by critical theorists:

> Critical theory is 'critical' in two senses. First, it involves critical reflection on the knowledge-producing enterprise itself. This encompasses . . . two forms of self-consciousness . . . self-consciousness about the extent to which knowledge claims are conditioned by their social context and serve interests and beliefs that comprise this context. Second, where this self-consciousness reveals the form of a dominant ideology and social order as mediated by the scientific production of knowledge, it provides a basis for reflective understanding and criticism of the social context of research; it takes the form of prospective social criticism and action (Wylie 1985:137).

Self-reflection is therefore "central" to critical theorists (Potter 1994:29), and without it, according to Potter (1994:30), "archaeologists cannot understand the relationships between their work and contemporary life." For this reason, reflection is central to all critical archaeology.

Critical, Responsible, and Accountable

Emotional confrontations between archaeologists and indigenous peoples during the last decade have prompted most of us at some time or another to reflect upon our research. Native American concerns regarding repatriation (Powell et al. 1993; Worl 1995) provoked a growing number of archaeologists to critique an archaeological enterprise "conditioned" by elitism and ethnocentrism (Klesert and Powell 1993). This line of sociopolitical analyses confronts dilemmas such as the "ownership" of cultural resources (Powell et al. 1993; Messenger 1995:68), as well as the primacy granted Anglo- or Euro-centered knowledge claims (Layton 1989; Gathercole and Lowenthal 1990; Zimmerman 1994, 1995) and archaeological knowledge claims in general. Non-archaeologists would currently find that there is little room for opposition. As academically-trained experts on the material record, our interpretations are viewed as authoritative; especially within the profession (Gero 1989). Although cultural resources are considered a "public trust" (Lynott and Wylie 1995:23), archaeologists are the self-imposed guardians of archaeological remains, and in most instances we are in the position to dictate who is allowed access to those remains. Even site reports with the requisite data tables and site information are "coded" in language often so obtuse as to be intelligible only to other archaeologists. We essentially have a monopoly on archaeological data and interpretations, which are then "packaged" and "sold" via museum exhibits or National Geographic Society articles to "passive consumers," namely, the public (Tilley 1989:107).

Sociopolitical analyses, all of which are methodologically critical, urge archaeologists to "level the playing field" (Jeppson, this volume). The general consensus among critical archaeologists is that control of archaeological resources and knowledge must be shared with descendant groups, other impacted communities, and the public at large. Critical theorists in particular contend that impacted groups must be active participants in the process of constructing histories (Handsman and Leone 1989; Potter 1994). As these insights are put into practice through public outreach and involvement, we must remain flexible, accessible, and willing to approach each situation with an open mind. To conclude, although the aforementioned issues are more often associated with the archaeology of indigenous peoples, they are increasingly entering the discourse concerning the archaeology of black Americans.

Black Americans and African-American Archaeology

> Our basic need is to reclaim our history and our identity from what must be called cultural terrorism (Carmichael and Hamilton 1970:166).

The sociopolitical climate of the 1960s and early '70s rattled the walls of academia when civil rights proponents, and most notably Black Power advocates, insisted on the institution of black studies programs nationwide (Genovese 1970:242). Black voices were the strongest in setting the agenda, which in essence insisted that American black culture and history finally be recognized as unique, valuable, and hence worthy of serious scholarship. It was no coincidence that Charles Fairbanks undertook the first anthropologically based study of an African-American site during this period of great change (Fairbanks 1984a; Ferguson 1992:xxxvi). Yet seeing as how blacks were largely responsible for igniting interest in their own histories, it is a sad irony that archaeology is perhaps the only discipline involved in the study of early black lifeways which has yet to incorporate significant contributions from any segment of black society.

The current social climate warns that the time to develop a more critical approach to African-American archaeology is past due. Our public visibility has increased as a result of the dramatic rise in the number of historical archaeologists excavating African-American sites. While the few who have made earnest efforts to communicate with black communities managed to maintain mostly positive relations (Henley et al. 1983; Leone 1992; Franklin 1996), there have been instances of conflict. Friction between white archaeologists and members of the black public over the New York African burial ground (Harrington 1993; Blakey 1995; LaRoche and Blakey, this volume) and the Venable Lane excavations (Leeds 1994; Patten, this volume) are the most notable. These examples serve to underscore the point that our research and public education efforts must be viewed within the context of contemporary American race relations. If we continue to ignore the needs and interests of descendant groups, we will foster antagonism, and our research will mean little to nothing to those segments of society whose ancestors we choose to study. If we are truly intent on using archaeology to create more meaningful histories whereby Americans of all backgrounds have the opportunity to participate in the process and, in the end, come to better understand themselves and each other, we have to start by standing in judgment of our own sociopolitics. The following observations were borne out of my initial reflective steps towards a more critical African-American archaeology. Although this critique is not fully developed, there are areas which can potentially serve as points of departure for current and future research.

Towards an Inclusive Archaeology

To start, American society remains profoundly polarized by racism. Of course most, if not all of us, realize this, but how many of us actually reflect upon how our work could potentially legitimate racism? As archaeologists, we must question how racism conditions our discipline and, in so doing, how an unreflective archaeology is fed right back into a racist society without challenging it (Potter 1991). With African-American archaeology, the potential for abuse is staggering given the uncritical state of the discipline (Potter 1991:96, 1994:15), the overwhelming number of whites excavating African-American sites, and the relatively weak efforts to involve black Americans through outreach (Fairbanks 1984b:12). This is not a statement accusing white archaeologists of racism, but to get us to think about social responsibility and ensuring that our research does not serve racist interests. This is highly likely to happen where members of descendant groups are excluded from all aspects of archaeology, including the conception of research questions, excavation, data analysis, and interpretation.

Those who have the most to gain from the current dismal state of race and class relations would continue to have only whites interpret the black archaeological past. The issue of a white majority studying and writing the histories of blacks is only beginning to be debated among historical archaeologists (Potter 1991; McKee 1994; Franklin 1996), and black Americans have generally not participated in this debate at any significant level. Yet we can look to the discourse between archaeologists and indigenous peoples to try and understand why a diverse perspective is the crucial element in the reconstruction of histories that are more relevant to

the latter (Layton 1989; Stone and MacKenzie 1990; Messenger 1995; Zimmerman 1995). Many of the concerns that blacks will have regarding the treatment of black sites will be similar to those traditionally expressed by Native Americans, as the New York African burial ground controversy demonstrated (Harrington 1993; Blakey 1995; LaRoche and Blakey, this volume). The initial lack of communication between white archaeologists and black Americans fostered mistrust, as did what was perceived to be insensitive treatment of the human remains. We are learning the hard way that archaeologists are not the only people interested in the past (Fairbanks 1984b:12), and that descendant groups have a vested interest in archaeological sites (Layton 1989; Gathercole and Lowenthal 1990; Ayau 1995; Naranjo 1995; Wylie 1996:180–183). Moreover, it is we who must bear the responsibility for bringing diverse perspectives into the discipline (Pyburn and Wilk 1995:72).

Most archaeologists agree that we have a responsibility to educate the public, but some may question the degree to which we are obligated to include the public in the research process at the level called for by critical archaeologists (McKee 1994). Fundamentally, however, our failure to establish ties with black Americans—whether they be from the local community, scholars, or members of interest groups—serves to further subjugate them, for they are in turn fully implicated in any historical interpretations concerning the black past. That is, historical and archaeological research affects *all* black Americans, not simply those whom archaeologists or others deem to be culturally, historically, or ancestrally linked to a historic site or era under study. For example, when Colonial Williamsburg's reconstructed slave quarter at Carter's Grove first opened to tourists, there were watermelons being grown in the yard, and rinds were present among the cabins' foodstuffs. Black interpreters complained that this representation of past foodways served to perpetuate negative stereotypes regarding blacks, and these items were subsequently removed (Gable et al. 1992:802). This one aspect of early black lifeways at

Carter's Grove could easily have evoked in the minds of white tourists the racist "black-face" images popularized by minstrel shows that stereotyped blacks as slow, lazy, and stupid. As this brief example demonstrates, the past does serve the present. Given this, it would not only be arrogant, but unethical, to insist that interested black Americans be able to demonstrate any sort of legitimate claim to a site before we actively involve them in a project. They are collectively impacted by our research results, and in this crucial sense, they are *all* connected to the pasts we reconstruct.

Some archaeologists might be tempted to proclaim that "history belongs to everybody" to shrug off any accountability to descendant groups, or to the general public. History belongs to everyone ideally, perhaps, but in actuality it belongs to those who have access to its material remnants, to those who control its penning, and to those who possess the power to authorize and disseminate it. History *should* belong to everyone, and that is the goal archaeologists must reach for if we are intent on archaeology being relevant to non-archaeologists.

On Relevance

Potter (1994:16) asserts that "the first responsibility of the archaeologist is not to try to make his or her research relevant but rather, it is to be conscious of how that work *is* potentially relevant, what it is relevant to, and the uses to which such work could be put." So all research is relevant, and in this case, we must determine how our research can be made relevant to black Americans. The suggestions for doing so have varied.

Much of African-American archaeology centers on the institution of slavery. Potter, a critical theorist, insists that in order for plantation archaeology to be relevant to black Americans today, it must "focus on the structures of oppression" (Potter 1991:101). That is, if through plantation archaeology we all come to "recognize contemporary vestiges of past domination," we can more effectively challenge oppression in today's society (Potter 1991:101). Potter (1991:100) further suggests that archaeologists and African Americans come together in developing research questions to ensure that the research be in the interest of the latter. Potter's method is the most direct and effective means for instituting social action through archaeology. It aims right at the system, and therefore holds the most potential for prompting people to reflect upon and challenge the system, and hopefully institute change for the better. But here I agree with McKee (1994:5) that we must be careful about confining ourselves to only certain questions. I realize that critical theory embodies a neo-Marxist critique, and therefore systems of domination and class inequalities are emphasized. A *critical archaeology*, however, need not have the same emphasis on class structure. There are other research questions which black Americans may be more interested in where the "structures of oppression" are not immediately the focus. Leone (1992:7) refers to archaeology where "local people define the questions" as archaeology through "local empowerment." I am often questioned by other blacks about the material evidence for the roots of black culture. For many, understanding where they came from is the same thing as understanding who they are, and this knowledge is the legacy that they wish to pass on to future generations (Figure 1).

In the end we must involve black Americans in archaeology. As individuals and as a people who have much to gain or lose depending on how reflective and critical we are as archaeologists, we have an obligation to ask that they be a part of any project. In so doing, we must never assume what direction their questions and concerns might take for, as Potter (1994:225) warns, "critical archaeologies are intensely local; one size does not fit all." Black Americans constitute a culturally, socially, and politically diverse and multivocal group. In working with local black communities, we must therefore be prepared for different reactions among them.

Engaging a Diverse Black Public

Ruffins (1992) observed that collections of black memorabilia assembled by black collectors during the 19th and early 20th centuries did not contain any items pertaining to slavery for a reason. Slavery was a painful and degrading memory for blacks, and its offspring Jim Crow ensured that further humiliation through racial oppression would continue. Why, then, collect the material reminders of a system so brutal? The tendency was to try and move away from this past by moving onto and up the social ladder. Although we might lament this decision by early black collectors to exclude artifacts which now would be invaluable to our understanding of American history, it is easy to sympathize with them. Slavery was a not-so-distant memory back then. But some 130 years have passed since slavery, and American society has changed. Slavery should no longer be a subject that we sweep under the rug, for that smacks of ignorance. Or does it? Scholars are discovering that there are black Americans who still feel that slavery is a shameful topic and still too sensitive to be discussed or displayed openly. Some fear that whites would only trivialize the anguish and suffering of enslaved Africans, and the brutality of slave-owning whites. Others resent how many whites continue to ignore black contributions to history by essentially "white-washing" the past by excluding blacks. Commenting on the "total plantation experience" promised by ads of Charleston, South Carolina, plantations, black tourist guide Al Miller stated: "They might tell you that blacks used to shine the brass doorknobs. Blacks built almost all the buildings in Charleston, but you don't hear that" (Wrolstad 1994). Being systematically excluded from the process of historical and archaeological research surely only exacerbates the anxiety and resentment. But not all blacks feel that the enslaved past should remain shrouded.

Black people are currently divided over what is deemed appropriate for discussion, study, and disclosure with regard to black history (Potter 1991:100; Leone 1992; McDavid, this volume). As many more black Americans move towards dealing with slavery and its prevailing social effects, confrontations between opposing black voices resound. For example, in St. Mary's County, Maryland, members of the black com-

munity debate the future of the slave quarter at Sotterley Plantation (Figure 2). George Forrest, a descendant of enslaved Africans from another St. Mary's plantation, and a trustee of the Sotterley Foundation, sums up the problem: "Some think it is a painful part of history that needs to be torn down and forgotten about. The other [approach] is to take this structure and use it as a memorial to those folks who struggled here" (Hill 1995). In another case, the Library of Congress shut down a new exhibit titled "Back of the Big House: The Cultural Landscape of the Plantation." Curated by John Michael Vlach, the exhibit was meant to show the "slaves' perspective" on the plantation (Nicholson 1995). Hours after the exhibit opened, however, a group of black employees found the exhibit offensive and demanded the exhibit's closure. David Nicholson, a black editor for the *Washington Post*, condemned the shutdown as irresponsible. Nicholson felt that slavery would remain "a psychic wound that black Americans, and only black Americans, can heal." Despite the antagonism within black society, these case studies and others demonstrate that blacks on both sides are very much emo-

FIGURE 1. "African to American," *Daily Press*, 21 August 1994:B1. (Courtesy of the *Daily Press*, Williamsburg, VA.)

FIGURE 2. "Coming to Grips With Painful Past," *Washington Post*, 2 April 1995:B3. (Courtesy of *Washington Post*,.)

tionally bound to the issue of how to deal with the legacy of slavery. These mixed emotions surfaced during the reenactment of a slave auction at Colonial Williamsburg in October 1994 (Clawson 1994; Mathews, this volume) (Figure 3). A racially mixed crowd of 2,000 supporters and protesters, including representatives from the NAACP and the Southern Christian Leadership Conference, gathered for the event (Boyd 1994; Jones 1995). Although the majority of blacks present that day supported what was deemed an educational program, the tension in the air was heavy.

Whenever black Americans have attempted to understand what it took enslaved ancestors to survive, the words "opening the wounds" and "healing," "pain," and "struggle" are invoked to describe the emotional transformation and catharsis associated with coming to terms with a slave heritage (Hill 1995; Jones 1995; Nicholson 1995). All disagreements aside, there is a

shared compassion within black society when it comes to reckoning with the experiences of their enslaved ancestors, and this is evidenced in the above examples where the debates were similarly impassioned. These emotions arise out of a shared sense of connection to the past, and with a particular sense of commitment to rising above past and present oppression.

As archaeologists, we must not take sides in these conflicts. It is important that we do not simply dismiss the voices of opposition to our work, most of which currently involves the topic of slavery, for, as I have previously argued, all black Americans are connected to the pasts we unearth. Further, most of us have not given black society much reason to feel that archaeology should be important to them. But is it our responsibility to do so? After all, archaeologists are not the only specialists involved with constructing histories, and nonprofessionals have created their own versions of the past and then

FIGURE 3. "CW auctions slaves." (Courtesy of the *Daily Press*, Williamsburg, VA.)

"imposed" them upon others. Unlike the latter, however, many archaeologists recognize that this profession exists for, and because of, the public. Along with the privilege and authority that we possess as professional archaeologists, we must bear the burden of social responsibility and set an example; for if not us, then who?

Roots, Remembrances, and Contributions

> Black scholars must remember their sources, and by this I mean no technically historical sources. I mean human sources. They are the products of their source—the great pained community of the Afro-Americans of this land. And they can forget the source only at great peril to their spirit, their work, and their souls (Harding 1986:279).

As academics we often think about how our scholarship can enrich the lives of others. Seldom do we consider how our own lives, including our research, could benefit from the knowledge and experiences of nonarchaeologists. Much of the time this occurs because we have fooled ourselves into thinking that we are in the

business of "giving" a history to the public. Instead, our discipline is but one cog in a machine that has been churning out histories long before we came along, and it will continue to do so if we are no longer around to participate in the process. I firmly believe that archaeology can be valuable and worthwhile to everyone else, but I still recognize that people would not be without history, culture, or tradition should archaeologists and anthropologists vanish from the face of the earth. Where black Americans are concerned, we have a long-standing tradition of studying ourselves, as evidenced by the pioneering work of individuals such as Zora Neale Hurston, Carter G. Woodson, and W. E. B. Du Bois. African-American archaeology must be seen as not only an extension of the disciplines of archaeology and anthropology but also of the vast body of scholarship on black American history and culture, much of it conducted by blacks themselves.

Archaeologists are in the enviable position of potentially benefiting from the exchange of information with insightful and knowledgeable black

Americans. What we must first overcome is the presumption that because we might be experts on the archaeological record, this makes us experts on black history and culture. Most practitioners of African-American archaeology do not even have a formal background in any sort of African or African-American studies. The resources that we do have within arm's reach, we often fail to call upon: black scholars and members of the black communities in which we work.

One suggestion for bridging the gap between archaeologists and black Americans has been to recruit more black archaeologists. While this goal should certainly be pursued, the diversification of archaeology will take time. At the same time, we often overlook the possibility of networking with black scholars with similar research interests in fields which largely overlap with ours: history, literature, folklore, cultural anthropology, black studies, cultural geography, museum studies, genealogy, and so on. In all of my exchanges with other black academics, I walked away with more than I arrived with. They were in turn eager to learn more about archaeology. I have also benefited greatly from the wisdom of nonacademics who were willing to share their insights and life experiences in order to enrich my research on early black culture. Archaeologists who have discovered that a "plural archaeological environment" can benefit research (Leone 1992:7; Agbe-Davies 1995; Franklin 1996; Powell 1996) are joined by other scholars who have also found enlightenment beyond the walls of academia.

Historian George McDaniel (1982) discovered an immeasurable wealth of memories and cultural traditions within the black families of

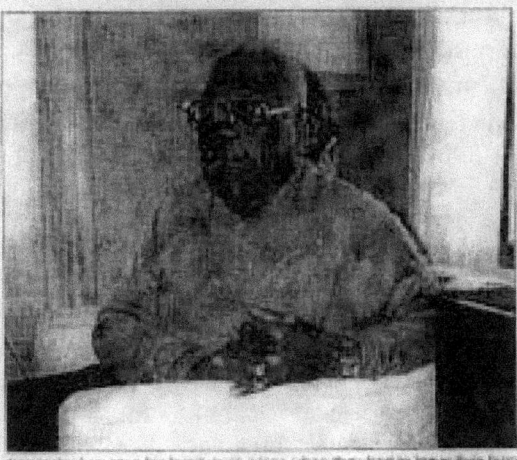

First-hand reflections

Local man source for many historians
By Jennifer Andes
Daily Press

WILLIAMSBURG
Alexander Lee was 7 when his parents learned in January 1921 that they would have to find a new home.

The Lees were among 800 or so families forced to leave an 11,433-acre area that the U.S. Navy took in the 1920s. The land, which many freedmen populated in the years after the Civil War and was known then as a reservation, is now the Yorktown Naval Weapons Station.

"My mother cried. I remember crawlin' up on my mother's lap," Lee says, recalling his mother's reaction to the government's eviction notice.

"In two to three years, my father could've sat back and smoked his pipe and sold oysters," Lee says, explaining that his father was an oysterman in the winter and farmed in the summer.

Lee's recollections of life on the land now owned by the government have been included in "Tales from James City County, Virginia Oral Histories," a 1993 pamphlet by the James City County Historical Commission.

He has also been interviewed by the Smithsonian Institution and researchers from the College of William and Mary, who recently compiled a history of people who lived on the site that is now the weapons station.

"The only thing that I ever regretted was my father never got the profit from the oysters," Lee says, thinking back on his life on the reservation.

Oysters, once planted, take three years to mature. Lee explains. His father was in the middle of a cycle and had to abandon three acres of oysters when the government came for their land.

The U.S. Navy paid $1,900 for their 86-acre farm, a meager compensation considering the family moved to a 20-acre lot in York County, which Lee's father bought from a white man for $3,000.

"He had to use his life's savings to do that," Lee says of his father. Lee, 79, and his wife, Lorestine, live in a home on the lot his father bought on Merrimac Trail in James City County, just over the York County line.

Lee lived on the reservation with his mother, father and five siblings in a wood-frame home in the upper end, where Felgate's Creek empties into the York River. "It was neatly built with plenty of room," Lee says of the house.

"The houses weren't too far apart, even though there was a lot of land," Lee says. All of his nine neighbors, and most of the other reservation families owned land, he recalls.

"After slavery, that's the biggest thing that black people did, they bought land."

Socializing was usually done on Sundays. "That's when people really met," Lee says. The Lees were members of St. John's Baptist Church, an all-black church which was moved to Penniman Road in York County after the Navy took the land.

"White went to the white church and black went to the black church," Lee says. "Nobody thought about integration."

After the family relocated to James City County, Lee and his brothers and sisters wanted to return to the reservation. "That was home down there," he says.

In retrospect, Lee says leaving the reservation was good in some ways.

"I believe we got better schools," he says. "Leaving gave us a better chance to be exposed to things going on in the world, in other parts of the county."

The weapons station hired Lee in 1936 to help build bombs. He retired as a supervisor in 1970 and now spends much of his time volunteering for St. John's Baptist Church.

Alexander Lee says his family took a loss when they had to leave their home in 1921.
Jennifer Andes/Daily Press

FIGURE 4 "First-hand reflections," *Daily Press*, 17 March 1993 (Courtesy of the *Daily Press*, Williamsburg, VA.)

Mitchellville, Maryland. When a turn-of-the-century black tenant farm house was taken down and rebuilt within the walls of the Smithsonian, McDaniel invited black families from Mitchellville to view the house. Their collective reaction? While at the Smithsonian for 10 years, the house had been displayed backwards by curators; the front of the house was supposed to be the rear, and the kitchen and living room were reversed (McDaniel 1982:26–27). McDaniel, a white historian interested in black history, found his interviews with descendants to be invaluable. With regard to his attempts to approach and talk to people he stated: "Though I have met with a few hostile receptions, the overwhelming majority of people have been cooperative because *they have been concerned about recording the history they knew* [emphasis added]" (McDaniel 1982:xv).

Individuals as well as whole communities can help to make the difference between histories viewed through a single lens, and bolder, fuller histories viewed through multiple lenses. Scholars from the Smithsonian and the College of William and Mary have interviewed Alexander Lee to help in recounting the lives of descendants of freedmen who settled in Yorktown, Virginia, after the Civil War (McDonald et al. 1992; Andes 1993) (Figure 4). When Lee was a child, the U.S. Navy used the process of "eminent domain" to seize property that had long been settled by 600 black families and as many as 200 white families (McDonald et al. 1992:43, 75). Although the government paid some compensation to landowners, unlike the whites, many blacks could not prove that the land was theirs. Some had inherited land from family members who worked the property under slavery and were then given parcels of plantation land upon emancipation without ever receiving a deed (McDonald et al. 1992:15). Their descendants therefore ended up with nothing despite the fact that they had lived on the property for years without dispute. The land is now home to the Yorktown Naval Weapons Station. Yorktown's written history and public interpretations are dominated by glorious military events such as the surrender at Yorktown during the Revolution.

The naval base serves as a constant reminder of this grand military past. In turn, Lee's memories serve to keep alive a more grim side of Yorktown's history: the disrupted lives of those who were torn from their place of birth and way of life by a system of oppression deeply rooted in American society.

Within black communities, there are living ties to the past, both historical and cultural. And while we may be the experts when it comes to the archaeological record, this does not necessarily make us experts, or the only experts, on black history and culture. Consulting with black Americans, both scholars and nonacademics, can only broaden our base of understanding of the past. This is not to say that we should privilege knowledge on the basis of skin color. Hopefully these examples simply demonstrate that black Americans possess perspectives, insights, and lifeways, the knowledge of which could benefit archaeological research.

Conclusions

The discipline of historical archaeology is not a timeless, static entity, just as the cultures that we study were and are not. The positive growth and transformation of our field depends upon the continual reexamination of our objectives. The goals of archaeologists in general have been confined to ensuring professional responsibility to other archaeologists, to protecting cultural resources, and to dictating proper field conduct. It is only recently that archaeologists have come to debate among themselves about the privileged "ownership" of archaeological knowledge and cultural resources, and the potent effects of the social and political implications of our research. The Society for American Archaeology, for example, has recently revised its ethics statements to include principles on accountability, public education and outreach, and stewardship (Lynott and Wylie 1995; Kintigh 1996:5, 17; Wylie 1996:184–187). The statement on accountability reads: "Responsible archaeological research, including all levels of professional activity, requires an acknowledgment of public accountability and a commitment to make every reasonable effort, in good faith, to consult actively with affected group(s), with the goal of establishing a working relationship that can be beneficial to all parties involved" (Kintigh 1996:7).

The World Archaeological Congress and the American Anthropological Association both have similar edicts in their bylaws. Yet, the bylaws of The Society for Historical Archaeology have no such specific clause in Article VII, its statement of "ethical positions." This is likely due to the fact that historical archaeologists have generally studied Anglo-Americans, and cases where whites are studying other whites are not perceived as a threat by most Americans who are white. For now, the study of African Americans by historical archaeologists goes virtually unnoticed by black Americans, mainly due to a lack of concerted efforts to bring this research to their attention. It is as if we are biding our time; waiting for more heated confrontations with black Americans before we are finally forced through public opinion and governmental regulations to engage them as equals in archaeological research. But why let push come to shove? No one stands to benefit through forced relations, where the long-held feelings of mistrust and resentment between blacks and whites are then further fueled by struggles to control archaeological interpretations of multiple black pasts.

In the end, it is up to archaeologists to make the initial effort of extending an open invitation to members of the black community to participate in the construction of their histories. Our interpretations of black history can potentially serve to legitimate and perpetuate racism in American society, and are more likely to do so should black Americans be excluded from the process of researching histories. We must take every measure to identify who benefits from our particular projects, and to whom our research is relevant. With an active, critical analysis of our research, and with the input from impacted groups, we are more likely to produce archaeological results which serve to uplift and empower communities which still suffer under racial and political hegemony.

For those who are still unsure about whether archaeologists should be accountable to black Americans, and whether we should have to actively involve them in archaeological endeavors, just ask ourselves why it is that we want to study black history and culture. But be warned, for there is far too much at stake to answer that one simply finds it interesting.

ACKNOWLEDGMENTS

I would like to thank Ywone D. Edwards and Marley R. Brown III for their enthusiastic support and critical feedback during the writing of this article. Carol McDavid and David Babson, I thank you for the herculean effort in getting this volume together. I owe sincere gratitude to Elizabeth Prine, Robin Sewell, Julie Endicott, Julie King, and anonymous reviewers who took the time to provide thoughtful comments which really helped to bring this article together. I also benefited greatly from exchanges with Anna Agbe-Davies, Garrett Fesler, James Deetz, Margaret W. Conkey, Michael Blakey, Cheryl La Roche, Alison Wylie, and Whitney Battle. Your passion for archaeology and your commitment to doing the right thing are inspiring. Thank you, Ronald L. Michael and James Gibb, for helping me locate sources necessary for completing this article. Any and all mistakes and oversights are, of course, my sole responsibility.

REFERENCES

AGBE-DAVIES, ANNA
1995 African American Archaeology in the Public Eye. Paper presented at the Annual Meeting of The Society for Historical Archaeology Conference on Historical and Underwater Archaeology, Washington, DC.

ANDES, JENNIFER
1993 First-Hand Reflections: Local Man Source for Many Historians. *The Daily Press*, 17 March. Williamsburg, VA.

AYAU, EDWARD HALEALOHA
1995 Rooted in Native Soil. *Federal Archaeology* 7(3):30–33. Departmental Consulting Archeologist and Archeological Assistance Program, National Park Service, Washington, DC.

BLAKEY, MICHAEL L.
1995 The Unity of Past and Present: Understanding the New York African Burial Ground Phenomenon. Paper presented at the University of California Faculty Seminar Series, Berkeley, CA.

BOYD, BENTLEY
    1994 CW Auctions Slaves: Re-enactment Provokes
          Emotional Debate. *The Daily Press*, 11 October:A1–
          2. Williamsburg, VA.

CARMICHAEL, STOKELY, AND CHARLES V. HAMILTON
    1970 Black Power: Its Need and Substance. In *What Country
          Have I?: Political Writings by Black Americans*, edited
          by Herbert J. Storing, pp. 165–181. St. Martin's Press,
          NY.

CLARKE, DAVID L.
    1979 *Analytical Archaeologist*. Academic Press, NY.

CLAWSON, MICHELLE CARR
    1994 In a Different Tongue. *Colonial Williamsburg*
          17(2):32–33.

FAIRBANKS, CHARLES H.
    1984a The Kingsley Slave Cabins in Duval County, Florida,
          1968. *Conference on Historic Sites Archaeology
          Papers, 1973* 7:62–93.
    1984b The Plantation Archaeology of the Southeastern Coast.
          Historical Archaeology 18(1):1–14.

FERGUSON, LELAND
    1992 *Uncommon Ground: Archaeology and Early African
          America, 1650–1800*. Smithsonian Institution Press,
          Washington, DC.

FRANKLIN, MARIA
    1996 Owners and Stewards, and Innocent Bystanders:
          Archaeologists and the Past as Property. Paper
          presented at the Annual Meeting of The Society for
          Historical Archaeology Conference on Historical and
          Underwater Archaeology, Cincinnati, OH.

GABLE, ERIC, RICHARD HANDLER, AND ANNA LAWSON
    1992 On the Uses of Relativism: Fact, Conjecture, and
          Black and White Histories at Colonial Williamsburg.
          American Ethnologist 19(4):791–805.

GATHERCOLE, PETER, AND DAVID LOWENTHAL (EDITORS)
    1990 *The Politics of the Past*. Unwin Hyman, London.

GENOVESE, EUGENE D.
    1970 The Influence of the Black Power Movement on
          Historical Scholarship: Reflections of a White
          Historian. In *In Red and Black: Marxian Explorations
          in Southern and Afro-American History*, edited by
          Eugene D. Genovese, pp. 230–255. Pantheon, NY.

GERO, JOAN M.
    1985 Socio-politics and the Woman-at-Home Ideology.
          American Antiquity 50(2):342–350.
    1989 Producing Prehistory, Controlling the Past: The Case

of New England Beehives. In *Critical Traditions in
          Contemporary Archaeology*, edited by Valerie Pinsky
          and Alison Wylie, pp. 96–116. Cambridge University
          Press, Cambridge, England.

GERO, JOAN M., DAVID M. LAACY, AND MICHAEL L.
BLAKEY (EDITORS)
    1983 *The Socio-Politics of Archaeology*. University of
          Massachusetts, Amherst.

GERO, JOAN M., AND MARGARET W. CONKEY (EDITORS)
    1991 *Engendering Archaeology: Women and Prehistory*.
          Basil Blackwell, Oxford.

HALL, MARTIN
    1984 The Burden of Tribalism: The Social Context of
          Southern African Iron Age Studies. *American Antiquity*
          49(3):455–467.

HANDSMAN, RUSSELL G., AND MARK P. LEONE
    1989 Living History and Critical Archaeology in the
          Reconstruction of the Past. In *Critical Traditions in
          Contemporary Archaeology*, edited by Valerie Pinsky
          and Alison Wylie, pp. 117–135. Cambridge University
          Press, Cambridge, England.

HARDING, VINCENT
    1986 Responsibilities of the Black Scholar to the
          Community. In *The State of Afro-American History:
          Past, Present, and Future*, edited by Darlene Clark
          Hine, pp. 277–291. Louisiana State University Press,
          Baton Rouge.

HARRINGTON, SPENCER P. M.
    1993 Bones and Bureaucrats: New York's Great Cemetery
          Imbroglio. *Archaeology* 46(2):28–38.

HENLEY, LAURA A., ANN M. PALKOVICH, AND JONATHAN
HAAS
    1983 The Other Side of Alexandria: Archeology in an
          Enduring Black Community. In *Approaches to
          Preserving a City's Past*, pp. 41–44. Alexandria Urban
          Archeology Program, Alexandria, VA.

HILL, RETHA
    1995 Coming to Grips with Painful Past. *Washington Post*,
          2 April:B3. Washington, DC.

JONES, CHARISSE
    1995 Bringing Slavery's Long Shadow to the Light. *New
          York Times*, 2 April:A1, A3.

KINTIGH, KEITH W.
    1996 SAA Principles of Archaeological Ethics. *Society for
          American Archaeology Bulletin* 14(3):5, 17. Mark
          Aldenderfer, Newsletter Editor. Santa Barbara, CA.

KLESERT, ANTHONY L., AND SHIRLEY POWELL
1993 A Perspective on Ethics and the Reburial Controversy. *American Antiquity* 58(2):348–354.

LAYTON, ROBERT (EDITOR)
1989 Who Needs the Past?: Indigenous Values and Archaeology. Unwin Hyman, London.

LEEDS, JEFF
1994 Blacks Protest Excavation Team. *Washington Post*, 18 January:D–4.

LEONE, MARK P.
1973 Archaeology as the Science of Technology: Mormon Town Plans and Fences. In *Research and Theory in Current Archaeology*, edited by Charles Redman, pp. 125–150. Riley and Sons, NY.
1984 Critical Theory in Archaeology. Paper presented at State University of New York, Binghamton.
1992 A Multicultural African-American Historical Archaeology: How to Place Archaeology in the Community in a State Capital. Paper presented at the Annual Meeting of the American Anthropological Association, San Francisco, CA.

LITTLE, BARBARA J.
1994 People with History: An Update on Historical Archaeology in the United States. *Journal of Archaeological Method and Theory* 1(1):5–40.

LYNOTT, MARK J., AND ALISON WYLIE (EDITORS)
1995 *Ethics in American Archaeology: Challenges for the 1990s.* Society for American Archaeology, Washington, DC.

MCDANIEL, GEORGE W.
1982 *Hearth and Home: Preserving a People's Culture.* Temple University Press, Philadelphia, PA.

MCDONALD, BRADLEY M., KENNETH E. STUCK, AND KATHLEEN J. BRAGDON
1992 "Cast Down Your Bucket Where You Are": An Ethnohistorical Study of the African-American Community on the Lands of the Yorktown Naval Weapons Station, 1865–1918. Report prepared by William and Mary Center for Archaeological Research, College of William and Mary, Williamsburg, VA. Submitted to Atlantic Division, Naval Facilities Engineering Command, Yorktown.

MCKEE, LARRY
1994 Is It Futile to Try and Be Useful?: Historical Archaeology and the African-American Experience. *Northeast Historical Archaeology* 23:1–7.

MCMANAMON, FRANCIS P.
1991 The Many Publics for Archaeology. *American Antiquity* 56(1):121–130.

MESSENGER, PHYLLIS MAUCH
1995 Public Education and Outreach. In *Ethics in American Archaeology: Challenges for the 1990s*, edited by Mark J. Lynott and Alison Wylie, pp. 68–70. Society for American Archaeology, Washington, DC.

NARANJO, TESSIE
1995 Thoughts on Two Worldviews. *Federal Archaeology* 7(3):16. Departmental Consulting Archeologist and Archeological Assistance Program, National Park Service, Washington, DC.

NICHOLSON, DAVID
1995 The Costs of Cultural Blackmail: Shutting Down the Slavery Exhibit Only Denies Our Suffering and Triumph. *Washington Post*, 24 December:C2.

ORSER, CHARLES E., JR., AND BRIAN M. FAGAN
1995 *Historical Archaeology.* HarperCollins College, NY.

PINSKY, VALERIE, AND ALISON WYLIE (EDITORS)
1989 *Critical Traditions in Contemporary Archaeology.* Cambridge University Press, Cambridge, England.

POTTER, PARKER B., JR.
1991 What Is the Use of Plantation Archaeology? *Historical Archaeology* 25(3):94–107.
1994 *Public Archaeology in Annapolis: A Critical Approach to History in Maryland's Ancient City.* Smithsonian Institution Press, Washington, DC.

POWELL, LEAH CARSON
1996 Traditional Narratives and Oral History. In *Home Herafter: An Archaeological and Bioarchaeological Analysis of an Historic African-American Cemetery (41GV125)*, edited by Helen D. Dockall, Joseph F. Powell, and D. Gentry Steele, pp. 231–219. *Reports of Investigation* 5. Center for Environmental Archaeology, Texas A&M University, College Station.

POWELL, SHIRLEY, CHRISTINE E. GARZA, AND AUBREY HENDRICKS
1993 Ethics and Ownership of the Past: The Reburial and Repatriation Controversy. In *Archaeological Method and Theory*, edited by Michael B. Schiffer, pp. 1–42. University of Arizona Press, Tucson.

PYBURN, K. ANNE, AND RICHARD R. WILK
1995 Responsible Archaeology Is Applied Anthropology. In *Ethics in American Archaeology: Challenges for the 1990s*, edited by Mark J. Lynott and Alison Wylie, pp. 71–76. Society for American Archaeology, Washington, DC.

RUFFINS, FATH DAVIS
1992 Mythos, Memory, and History: African American Preservation Efforts, 1820–1990. In *Museums and Communities: The Politics of Public Culture*, edited

by Ivan Karp, Christine Mullen Kreamer, and Steven D. Lavine, pp. 506–611. Smithsonian Institution Press, Washington, DC.

SCHMIDT, PETER R., AND THOMAS C. PATTERSON (EDITORS)
1995   *Making Alternative Histories: The Practice of Archaeology and History in Non-Western Settings.* School of American Research Press, Santa Fe, NM.

SPECTOR, JANET D.
1993   *What This Awl Means.* Historical Society Press, St. Paul, MN.

STONE, PETER, AND ROBERT MACKENZIE (EDITORS)
1990   *The Excluded Past: Archaeology in Education.* Unwin Hyman, London.

TILLEY, CHRISTOPHER
1989   Archaeology as Socio-political Action in the Present. In *Critical Traditions in Contemporary Archaeology,* edited by Valerie Pinsky and Alison Wylie, pp. 104–116. Cambridge University Press, Cambridge, England.

TRIGGER, BRUCE G.
1989   *A History of Archaeological Thought.* Cambridge University Press, Cambridge, England.

WORL, ROSITA
1995   NAGPRA: Symbol of a New Treaty. *Federal Archaeology* 7(3):34–5. Departmental Consulting Archeologist and Archeological Assistance Program. National Park Service, Washington, DC.

WROLSTAD, MARK
1994   Re-examining a Past Built on Slavery. *Atlanta Journal/ Atlanta Constitution,* 13 March:M6. Atlanta, GA.

WYLIE, ALISON
1983   Comments on the Sociopolitics of Archaeology: The Demystification of the Profession. In *The Sociopolitics of Archaeology,* edited by Joan M. Gero, David M. Lacy, and Michael L. Blakey, pp. 119–130. University of Massachusetts, Amherst.
1985   Putting Shakertown Back Together: Critical Theory in Archaeology. *Journal of Anthropological Archaeology* 4:133–147.
1989   Introduction: Socio-political Context. In *Critical Traditions in Contemporary Archaeology,* edited by Valerie Pinsky and Alison Wylie, pp. 93–95. Cambridge University Press, Cambridge, England.
1991   Gender Theory and the Archaeological Record: Why Is There No Archaeology of Gender. In *Engendering Archaeology: Women and Prehistory,* edited by Joan M. Gero and Margaret W. Conkey, pp. 31–54. Basil Blackwell, Oxford.
1996   Ethical Dilemmas in Archaeological Practice: Looting, Repatriation, Stewardship, and the (Trans)formation of Disciplinary Identity. *Perspectives on Science* 4(2):154–194.

ZIMMERMAN, LARRY
1994   Sharing Control of the Past. *Archaeology* 47(6):65, 67–68.
1995   Regaining Our Nerve: Ethics, Values, and the Transformation of Archaeology. In *Ethics in American Archaeology: Challenges for the 1990s,* edited by Mark J. Lynott and Alison Wylie, pp. 64–67. Society for American Archaeology, Washington, DC.

MARIA FRANKLIN
DEPARTMENT OF ARCHAEOLOGICAL RESEARCH
THE COLONIAL WILLIAMSBURG FOUNDATION
WILLIAMSBURG, VA 23187-1776
AND DEPARTMENT OF ANTHROPOLOGY
UNIVERSITY OF CALIFORNIA, BERKELEY
BERKELEY, CA 94720

J. W. Joseph

Resistance and Compliance: CRM and the Archaeology of the African Diaspora

ABSTRACT

Archaeological investigations carried out in compliance with the dictates of the National Historic Preservation Act have played an integral role in developing our understanding of and approach to the archaeology of the African diaspora. These cultural resource management (CRM) studies include several landmark projects that helped shape the national approach to African American archaeology. However, as with other sectors of the discipline, CRM archaeology of the African diaspora is presently suffering from a period of stagnation and lack of focus. This paper considers CRM's contribution to the archaeology of African America, past and present, and attempts to project the future place of CRM in the study of the African American past.

Introduction

> "Personal decoration, like ceramics, may be an effort among the freedmen to imitate the master class, or it may represent a significant African tradition" (Trinkley 1986:279).

African American archaeology and the archaeology of cultural resource management (CRM) have enjoyed a symbiotic relationship since the advent of CRM in the late 1960s (by CRM I refer to archaeological and historical studies undertaken in compliance with sections 106 and 110 of the National Historic Preservation Act). Established by the National Historic Preservation Act of 1966 (and subsequent amendments), CRM seeks to identify and evaluate archaeological and historical resources that would be affected by federally funded, permitted, or mandated projects, as well as those sites located on federal lands. Sites are evaluated with reference to their eligibility for listing on the National Register of Historic Places. Of the four evaluative criteria for listing, Criterion D, which states that an archaeological site may be eligible for the scientific information it has provided or can provide,

has become the standard of CRM archaeological site evaluations.

CRM has taken archaeologists, many trained as prehistorians but a growing number educated in historical archaeology, into settings that had not previously been the focus of historical or archaeological research. Highway projects, urban redevelopments, Corps of Engineers reservoirs and drainage works, and Department of Defense installation inventories all exposed a wider array of sites than had traditionally been studied, which forced archaeologists to develop historical contexts and criteria for assessing the significance of previously unevaluated resources. In concert with trends in social history, historical anthropology, and cultural geography, which recognized the significance of people on the periphery of traditional history, CRM archaeologists began to research and recognize the archaeological value in the study of small farmsteads, urban working-class house lots, tenant sites, ethnic groups, the 19th century in general, and other archaeological remains that had previously received little attention by a discipline directed, before the 1960s, more toward the study of lost Colonial towns, forts, and the house yards of the well-to-do. Prominently featured in this new focus was CRM's discovery of African America.

The history of African American archaeology can be traced to a number of landmark studies: Adelaide and P. Ripley Bullen's excavation and Vernon Baker's analysis of Black Lucy's Garden, a freedman site in Massachusetts (Bullen and Bullen 1945; Baker 1980); Robert Ascher and Charles Fairbanks's work with enslaved African American cabin sites at Ryefield and Kingsley Plantations in the late 1960s and early 1970s (Ascher and Fairbanks 1971; Fairbanks 1974); Robert Schuyler's (1974, 1980) excavations at the African American oystering village of Sandy Ground, New York; John Otto's (1975, 1980, 1984) doctoral analyses on the archaeology of Cannons Point plantation; Leland Ferguson's (1978, 1980) study of African American colono-ware; Jim Deetz's (1977) study of Parting Ways; Sarah Bridges's and Bert Salwen's (1980) excavations at Weeksville; Joan Geismar's (1980, 1982) study of Skunk Hollow; Sam Smith's (1976,

Historical Archaeology, 2004, 38(1):18–31.
Permission to reprint required.

1977) excavations at the Hermitage Plantation in Tennessee; and John Combes's (1972) ethnohistorical and archaeological study of a late-19th to 20th-century African American cemetery at the Charles Towne Landing Site, South Carolina. These studies explored themes and perspectives that would influence the development of the discipline, most notably Ascher and Fairbanks's search for African cultural retentions; Otto's analysis of status variation within the plantation community as revealed in the archaeological record; Schuyler's application of the ethnohistoric approach to African American archaeology; Combes's study of African and African American burial practices; and Deetz's, Bridges and Salwens's, Geismar's, and Schuyler's recognition of the significance of African community with settlement structure. While all of these studies were influential, CRM's approach to African American archaeology would largely be structured by the developments within CRM itself.

Three studies from the South Carolina lowcountry signal CRM's recognition of African America and are founding elements in the discipline of African American archaeology: Lesley Drucker and Ronald Anthony's investigation of the Spiers Landing enslaved African American house (Drucker and Anthony 1979; Drucker 1981), William Lees's investigation of Limerick Plantation (1980), and Thomas Wheaton, Amy Friedlander, and Patrick Garrow's (1983) excavations of Yaughan and Curiboo Plantations. The work at Yaughan and Curiboo (Wheaton et al. 1983) was particularly significant in its influence on the discipline of African American archaeology because it found the remains of earth-walled, African-style dwellings as well as conclusive evidence for the production of a low-fired earthenware ceramic—known as colonoware—by enslaved African Americans within the villages (for further discussion of colonoware, see Ferguson 1978, 1980, 1989, 1992; Lees and Kimery-Lees 1979; Wheaton and Garrow 1985; Garrow and Wheaton 1989). These discoveries showed a clear linkage between African cultural behaviors and African adaptation to the New World. However, Wheaton and colleagues (1983) also witnessed the gradual replacement of these African artifacts with European and American ceramics and house styles. As a result, they presented a model of acculturation that posited the loss of most archaeologically identifiable African

cultural traits by the early-19th century and the eventual Americanization of enslaved Africans.

This transformation from African to African American has formed the paradigm of CRM African American archaeology over the past decade and a half. As illustrated by the opening quote from Michael Trinkley's investigation of the African American freedman village of Mitchellville, CRM archaeologists have routinely debated whether the objects of African American archaeology are legacies of African cultural behaviors or evidence of African American efforts to emulate Euramerican culture, in particular concepts and markers of social status. The majority of CRM studies have concluded that so-called Africanisms ceased to exist by the 19th century. In the absence of readily recognizable African cultural attributes, CRM archaeologists have treated African American sites, artifacts, and behaviors as analogs to their Euramerican counterparts. Sites and assemblages have thus been analyzed using concepts and indices developed for Euramerican sites that are well suited to the cursory-level analysis and interpretation of many CRM studies—George Miller's (1980, 1991) socioeconomic index scaling and Stanley A. South's (1977) artifact patterning in particular. The outcome of these studies have been two-fold: emphasizing African Americans' impoverished socioeconomic status within Euramerican economy and society, and measuring African American assimilation as seen in part by the assumed acceptance by African Americans of the Euramerican socioeconomic structure and cultural ideals. What these studies have routinely failed to seek or identify are evidences of continued African behaviors and the resistance to Euramerican cultural norms, as well as indications of the formation of a creolized, African American culture with its own distinct values and behaviors. Several recent studies illustrate CRM archaeology's ability to contribute to the study of African American creolization and provide signposts for the future of African American CRM.

This paper summarizes the results of CRM African American archaeology within the broad functional contexts of plantations, freedmen villages, tenancy, urban studies, and cemeteries. The overviews provided for each of these categories are meant to provide an introduction to the general drift of African American CRM and should not be considered as comprehensive assessments of all of the CRM archaeology conducted within a given context. This summary also reflects my geographic bias and is thus weighted toward the archaeology of Georgia and South Carolina. These overviews are followed by a summary of CRM's impact on African American archaeology and recommendations for the future direction of CRM studies.

Plantation Studies

By far, the majority of African American archaeological studies conducted within a CRM context have been completed on plantation sites, a statistic that applies to academic archaeology as well. This archaeological bias in favor of plantation sites is also found in historical studies and also reflects the social condition of the majority of African Americans within the United States prior to the Civil War. Plantation studies have been conducted throughout the southeast, from the seaboard states of the original 13 colonies to the interior states such as Kentucky and Tennessee. However, coastal plantations have received significantly greater attention than plantations of the piedmont and interior. In part, this reflects differences in the agrarian economy of the coast versus the interior and the effects of varying crop economies on site formation and preservation. Coastal crops included rice, indigo, Sea Island cotton, tobacco, and sugar cane. Of these, rice cultivation in particular and sugar and indigo to lesser degrees were associated with stable plantation settlements because of the high labor investment needed to create rice, indigo, and sugar-cane fields. These fields were enriched through tidal flooding, and the profits of these crop economies financed the creation of substantial plantation homes and complexes. Village architecture was more likely to be permanent on these plantations than on upcountry plantations, and thus the locations of enslaved African American villages are more readily identifiable. In contrast, short staple cotton, the primary crop of the interior, quickly exhausted soil nutrients. Hence cotton-field locations were rotated every three to five years. Outlying upland plantation settlements were relocated with the fields to minimize transportation of enslaved African Americans from the plantation center to the fields. Cabins were routinely constructed of log, and the archaeological legacy of these

short-lived settlements is negligible. As a result, it is extremely difficult to identify outlying village locations on upland plantations (Anderson and Joseph 1988:422–424).

Coastal plantations have also received a significantly greater degree of study than upland plantations because of the nature of development and federal permitting on the coast. The past two decades have witnessed a significant amount of development in coastal areas, particularly in South Carolina. Federal permitting increases the likelihood that a coastal development will require CRM study, either through Corps of Engineers permits (where projects are situated on major waterways or will affect wetlands) or through various coastal regulatory agencies that receive federal support. Between Drucker and Anthony's excavations at Spiers Landing in 1979 and 1998, there have been more than 30 enslaved African American site excavations within coastal South Carolina alone (Drucker and Anthony 1979; Carillo 1980; Lees 1980; Wheaton et al. 1983; Zierden et al.1986; Abbott and Brockington 1989; Poplin and Brockington 1989; Trinkley 1989, 1990, 1991, 1993a, 1993b; Wayne and Dickinson 1990; Brooker 1991; Gardner and Poplin 1992; Adams 1993, 1994a, 1994b, 1995a, 1995b; Trinkley et al. 1993, 1995; Adams and Trinkley 1994; Eubanks et al. 1994; Kennedy et al. 1994; Poplin and Brooker 1994; Trinkley 1995, 1996; Wayne et al. 1996a, 1996b). This figure does not include sites identified during CRM surveys that were not recommended for excavation or thats were preserved in place.

These excavations have revealed several important aspects of African American life on the lowcountry plantations of the old South. Work at Yaughan and Curiboo, as well as subsequent excavations at Wapoo Plantation (Gardner and Poplin 1992) and elsewhere, have revealed the presence of wall trench/mud-walled domestic architecture that is likely African in style and construction (Carl Steen [1999] suggests these structures could also reflect French architectural traditions). These excavations, coupled with the recovery of enslaved African American-made colonowares at a number of lowcountry plantation sites, suggest a measure of social autonomy which enslaved African Americans in coastal South Carolina experienced during the 18th century. In combination with historical documentation, it appears that African Americans at work on lowcountry rice and indigo plantations prior to and shortly beyond the Industrial Revolution lived in villages consisting of African-style housing and ate from handmade earthenwares similar to those used in Africa, relying on traditional African cultural practices to adapt to the New World. Indeed, Africans represented a majority of the South Carolina population by 1740, and the appearance of the colony was such that by 1737 Swiss visitor Samuel Dyseli would remark, "Carolina looks more like a negro country than like a country settled by white people" (qtd. in Wood 1974:132–133).

Interpretations based on CRM archaeology have shown that during the 18th century, enslaved African Americans in coastal South Carolina functioned under minimal supervision, lived in isolated villages, and grew rice on the margin of coastal swamps. This situation changed in the last decades of the 18th century and the first decades of the 19th century as the plantation economy matured. Plantation settlement and architecture became more structured and formal, and African American villages were moved from peripheral locations to a core area comprised of the main house and its domestic and agricultural supporting facilities. Artifacts changed as well, with European-made industrial ceramics replacing African American colonoware as the dominant ceramic within the plantation villages. While the majority of CRM studies have treated this change within the African American world as a product of acculturation, it is important to recognize that this change affected plantations as a whole and not simply the material culture of slavery. Tidal rice agriculture, employing dikes and locks and the tidal surge to flood and drain rice fields, became prominent, and with it arose more stable and profitable plantation complexes. Previously planters had resided in Charleston and allowed their plantations to be run by overseers. The profits of tidal rice agriculture as well as its geography, which emphasized proximity to the coastal rivers that were the region's highways of the era, induced planters to move onto their plantations, establish large plantation homes, and create more stable plantation structures. Racial tension was clearly a factor in these changes. Planters moved outlying villages into the big-house sphere and organized these villages along streets where enslaved Africans could be more easily supervised.

I have suggested elsewhere (Joseph 1989, 1993a, 1993b, 1997a) that the ideology of the Industrial Revolution, which focused on labor management and units of production, came to dominate the mindsets of lowcountry planters and left in its wake plantation factories. Within this European-American ideology, material cultural came to reflect class and social status, not cultural identity. As a result, images of Africa had no place. Ben Sullivan recalled that

> Old man Okra he wanted a place like he had in Africa so he built himself a hut. I remember it well. It was about twelve by fourteen feet and it had a dirt floor and he built the sides like basket weave with clay plaster on it. It had a flat roof that he made from bush and palmetto and it had one door and no windows. But Master made him pull it down. He say he ain't want no African hut on his place (qtd. in Works Project Administration 1940:179–180).

As the nature of the lowcountry plantation economy shifted from an informal system in which enslaved African Americans had a degree of social and cultural autonomy to a highly structured and profitable industry in which planters displayed economic and social standing through architecture and its organization, the appearance of Africa was forcibly erased from the plantation landscape (Joseph 1993a).

Culture change, however, is not acculturation. CRM's treatment of enslaved African Americans within the Euramerican cultural system has by and large ignored the importance of African American resistance to change and the processes of creolization, applying formulas such as artifact patterning and the socioeconomic status index to show that enslaved African Americans were "acculturated" and of a lower socioeconomic status than Euramerican planters. Work outside CRM, most notably Kenneth Brown's excavations at the Levi Jordan Plantation in Texas and more recently at Frogmore Plantation in Beaufort, South Carolina, has recovered evidence of African ritual practices and beliefs through artifact caches (containing Euramerican manufactured artifacts) found in the floors of African American dwellings. Brown suggests that archaeologists working on the plantation must be more cautious in recording and recognizing the contexts of artifacts as well as being more cognizant of African belief systems and their potential material reflections (Brown and Cooper 1990; Brown 2001).

Freedmen Villages

Southern enslaved African Americans began leaving their plantations to seek Union encampments following Union General Benjamin Butler's decision to treat enslaved African Americans who had fled to the protection of the Union forces at Fort Monroe, Virginia, as contraband of war. As the numbers of enslaved African Americans reaching Union lines increased, a plan to house them was needed. The result was the establishment of freedmen villages, camps established to support the freedmen until the war's end. These villages were established primarily in coastal areas where the Union army had formed occupations supported by their superior naval resources. Most villages were of short duration, only the wartime years, although some persisted after the conclusion of the Civil War.

Two of these village sites, Mitchellville in South Carolina and James City in North Carolina, have been the focus of extensive archaeological investigations (Trinkley 1986; Wheaton et al. 1990). Union forces both planned these freedmen villages and dictated their architecture. In these respects, life within the villages was not significantly different from life on the plantations. Both towns were occupied after the war ended, and the artifacts from both archaeological excavations are predominantly from the 1870s and 1880s. Both Trinkley's and Wheaton's analyses focus on the use of artifact patterning and socioeconomic indexing to judge status. Wheaton notes that socioeconomic status among the James City sites was slightly higher than measured for enslaved African American sites, while Trinkley notes that some high-status artifacts (considered to be products of the plantation big houses) had found their way into the archaeological record of the freedmen camps. Interestingly, Wheaton and colleagues (1990: 247–248) note evidence of communal behavior within James City, as witnessed by the use of central wells within urban blocks as well as other aspects of the archaeological and historical record. They view this communal chord as the most African element of James City.

Tenancy

For many southern African Americans, agricultural tenancy was the keynote of the postbellum South. The archaeological legacy of African American tenancy is represented by a number of CRM studies (Anderson and Muse 1982, 1983; Orser et al. 1982; Trinkley 1983; Brockington et al. 1985; Orser and Nekola 1985; Joseph et al. 1991). These studies have contributed to the archaeological debate on the visibility of tenancy and the role of artifact density in tenant site evaluation and assessments of National Register eligibility (this debate is sometimes known as the Anderson-Muse/Trinkley debate). CRM archaeologists have recognized that tenant sites are difficult to identify archaeologically because of their limited material remains and impermanent architecture and because tenant site locations were frequently employed as agricultural fields following abandonment, damaging the limited archaeological integrity these sites might earlier have possessed (Joseph and Reed 1997). Charles Orser and Annette Nekola (1985) recognize the importance of continued community relationships within the tenant community as witnessed by the perseverance of Millwood Plantation's village residences into the tenant era, and the effects of kinship on tenant settlement have been recognized elsewhere (Crass and Brooks 1997).

Urban Studies

After the war, many African Americans flocked to cities, which offered the greatest potential for employment as well as community. CRM archaeological studies of urban African American houses and neighborhoods have been conducted in Mobile (Wheaton et al. 1993; Joseph et al. 1996; Gums 1998), Atlanta (The History Group 1982), Lexington (O'Malley 1990, 1996), Pittsburgh (Carlisle et al. 1991), several towns on the Delmarva Peninsula (Catts et al. 1989; Catts and Custer 1990; Catts and McCall 1991; Catts 1992), and Washington, DC (Garrow 1982; Cheek et al. 1983; Cheek and Friedlander 1990), among other cities. The majority of these studies have addressed late-19th-century occupations, with the analysis of socioeconomic social stratification as the primary theoretical approach. Analysis of the remains of the antebellum free African American community of Springfield in Augusta, Georgia, provides an important glimpse of African American culture outside the plantation and during the first half of the 19th century (Joseph and Reed 1991; Joseph 1992, 1993c, 1997b).

Excavations at Springfield revealed a post-in-ground house with associated pit features dating to the period from 1820 to 1855. The structure measured approximately 10 x 20 ft., the common dimension for Yoruba houses in West Africa, which John Vlach (1975, 1978) views as ancestral to the shotgun house, commonly found in many southern African American neighborhoods. This house thus reflects African and Afro-Caribbean building traditions and design. The house yard was pocketed by small pit features, many of which contained light to moderate quantities of refuse that appears to represent yard sweepings. The purpose of these yard pit features is unknown, although they were possibly dug to obtain dirt for house wall or floor construction. Yard pit features have been documented both ethnographically and archaeologically by Emmanuel Kofi Agorsah (1983:106–107) as a common feature of Nchumuru settlements of West Africa and were common at Yaughan and Curriboo plantations and on other plantation workers villages. Ceramic vessels recovered from Springfield indicate a preference for hollowwares, cups and bowls, supporting an observation made by Otto (1975) at Cannon's Point that the African American diet shared West Africa attributes in its preference for liquid-based soups and stews.

A single artifact, an anthropomorphic clay pipe, provides a unique insight into free African American lives as well as the complexities of interpreting material culture. This figural pipe, representing a biblical figure as indicated by the gilt cross earrings, headdress, and gold beads in the braided beard, would obviously be considered of high socioeconomic value and status (Figure 1). However, its interpretive meaning is far more complex. Various Southern laws placed prohibitions on African American's public use of clay pipes, designed to prevent African Americans from co-opting artifacts that conveyed social status (Haughton 1972:16; Cashin 1980: 63). However, pipes were integral facets of African life, where they were also used to denote rank and status. Finally, this particular pipe possesses ideological and symbolic meaning in the personage it displays. The pipe was identified in the maker's catalog as representing a Ninevien or a citizen of the Middle Eastern town of Nineveh (Figure 2). Nineveh was one of the birthplaces of Biblical archaeology and

was excavated and described by Henry Austin Layard (1849) in *Nineveh and Its Remains*. The design of the pipe may in fact be taken from the illustrations appearing in Layard's book (Figure 3). The archaeological discovery of Nineveh was seen as proving the validity of the Bible. Nineveh may have been a particularly relevant place to African Americans of the old South, as the Old Testament prophecy of Nahum depicts God's destruction of Nineveh and the freeing of the Ninevien slaves.

These are the words of the LORD:
Now I will break his yoke from your necks
and snap the cords that bind you.
Image and idol will I hew down in the house of your
    God.
This is what the LORD has ordained for you:
never again will your offspring be scattered;
and I will grant your burial, fickle though you have
    been.

FIGURE 1. Ninivien pipe recovered from archaeological excavations at the Free African American Springfield site.

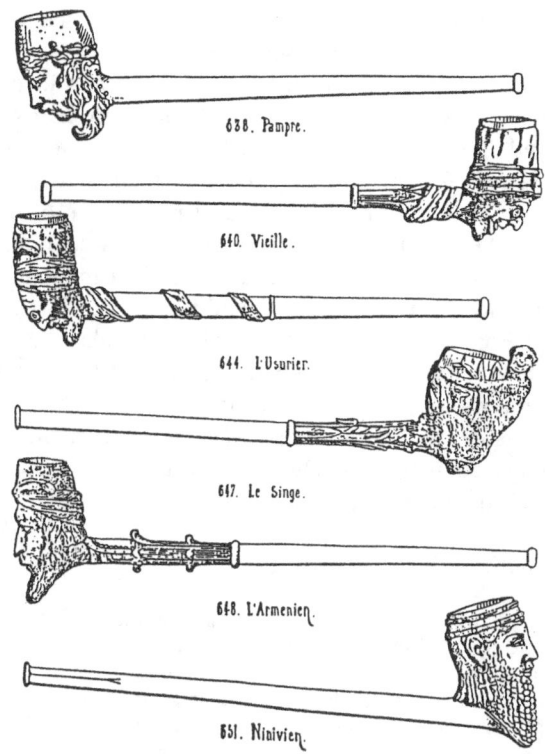

FIGURE 2. Illustration from the catalog of French pipe manufacturer Gambier (*Nomenclature des Pipes Gambier*, n.d.:46) showing the Ninivien design.

Discovery of gigantic Head

FIGURE 3. Illustration from Austen Henry Layard's (1849) *Nineveh and Its Remains* showing the discovery of statuary head which may have been the influence for Gambier's Ninivien pipe design.

Has the punishment been so great?
Yes, but it has passed away and is gone.
I have afflicted you, but I will not afflict you again.

Cemeteries

CRM has made significant contributions to the studies of African American physical anthropology, health and disease, diet, and ritual behavior through the study of African American cemeteries. Two cemetery projects in particular, the First African Baptist Cemetery (FABC) of Philadelphia and New York City's African Burial Ground, represent comprehensive, large-scale excavations that have yielded significant information concerning African American life (Parrington and Roberts 1984, 1990; Blakey 1986; Angel et al. 1987; Parrington 1987; Parrington et al. 1989; Crist et al. 1991, 1995, 1997; Harrington 1993; Crist and Roberts 1996; LaRoche 1996; Rankin-Hill 1997; Mack and Blakey, this volume).

The FABC project provided evidence of African ritual behaviors within the burial customs of Philadelphia's 19th-century African Americans. Several of the burials were placed with coins near the head. Usually this was a single penny. Michael Parrington and Daniel Roberts (1990: 150) speculate that the inclusion of a single coin in the FABC graves may reflect the West African tradition that death represents the beginning of a journey into the spirit world, and that the coins may represent the fee for traveling to the spirit world (among the Fanti of West Africa, money is interred with the corpse to help its spirit "cross the river" into the spirit world). Similarly, six burials containing a single shoe also appear to reflect the West African perception of death as a journey. Shoes are also believed to have power and can be used to keep the devil away. Two burials contained an overturned plate covering the stomach area of the deceased, which may represent a West African practice designed to contain the "essence" of the deceased within the plate from which the last meal was eaten and prevent this spirit from haunting the living. Among the African Burial Ground graves, Cheryl LaRoche (1996) notes the recovery of beads from a number of burials that are indicative of both West African dress as well as potentially ritual behavior. Beads were also recovered from burials at the Sam Goode Cemetery in southern Virginia (Crist et al. 2000). Alex Caton noted the use of beads in Ghana to provide ritual protection of the wearer, particularly infants and children. The recovery of bead necklaces from children's burials at the Sam Goode Cemetery would appear to indicate this same practice and behavior. A pierced 1854 dime recovered from another child's grave where it was worn as a necklace also appears to indicate African and African American cultural beliefs. Pierced dimes and other silver coins were reportedly worn to guard against sorcery, with the belief that if the coin turned black, then it was an indication that someone was conjuring against the wearer (Works Project Administration 1940:124–125; Crist et al. 2000).

Conclusions

CRM excavations of African American cemeteries demonstrate the persistence and continuation of African beliefs and customs into the 19th century. Similarly, the archaeology of the free African American village of Springfield shows that when left to their own resources, antebellum 19th-century African Americans drew upon their African heritage to adapt to their setting in the New World. By and large, however, CRM investigations of African American sites have been one-dimensional, emphasizing the American and neglecting the African. CRM analyses that focus on African American socioeconomic status as measured by Euramerican indices or that view cultural change using simplistic and outdated models of acculturation (for a review of acculturation studies, see Howson 1990) are meaningless at best and at worst, demeaning. CRM archaeology must study African American sites within a cultural perspective and must take into each project a knowledge of African cultural behavior as a fundamental context for understanding. While recognizing that the cultural legacy of Africa is both rich and diverse, and itself engaged in culture change from the 16th century onward (Thomas 1995), historical archaeologists working on African diaspora sites must bring an understanding of African peoples, histories, and cultures to their analysis and place less reliance on analytical techniques developed for Euramerican cultures.

By the middle of the 19th century, European and American industrial material culture dominated the world market. It should be of no surprise that these goods had also found their way into African American households. But material culture's meaning lies not in what an object is, or what it is worth, but in how it is used and in the meanings and values imposed on them (Brown and Cooper 1990; Wilkie 1995). An ornate clay pipe does not indicate simply that an individual is a smoker with some financial resources. In the case of Springfield, the pipe indicates a continuation of African traditions, a belief in Christianity and its promise of a just world, and the defiance of Euramerican laws that sought to regulate social behavior. The most promising future CRM study of African American archaeology will likewise consider sites and objects as African artifacts engaged in negotiating the passage from African to African American.

ACKNOWLEDGMENTS

I am appreciative of the efforts of Maria Franklin and Larry McKee in organizing and focusing this volume. I am also appreciative of the review comments received from other symposium participants, particularly Ann Stahl, as well as the comments offered by two anonymous reviewers. This article and author especially benefited from Franklin's thorough and engaging editorial comments. Natalie Adams, Chris Espenshade, and Tom Wheaton all provided assistance in compiling African American CRM source materials. Credit for any errors or omissions that appear in this text rests solely with me.

REFERENCES

ABBOTT, LAWRENCE E., JR., AND PAUL BROCKINGTON
    1989 Data Recovery at 38CH940 (Historic Locus), Charleston County, South Carolina. Brockington and Associates, Atlanta, GA.

ADAMS, NATALIE P.
    1993 Archaeological Investigations at 38GE377: Examinations of a Deep Creek Phase Site and a Portion of the Eighteenth-Century Midway Plantation. Chicora Foundation, Inc., *Research Series*, 37. Columbia, SC.
    1994a Management Summary of Archaeological Data Recovery at 38CH1219 and 38CH123, Kiawah Island, Charleston County, South Carolina. Chicora Foundation, Inc., *Research Contribution*, 148. Columbia, SC.
    1994b Management Summary of Archaeological Data Recovery at 38BU323 and 38BU821, Hilton Head Island, South Carolina. Chicora Foundation, Inc. *Research Contribution*, 158. Columbia, SC.
    1995a Management Summary of Archaeological Data Recovery at Freeport Plantation (38BU584), Daufuskie Island, Beaufort County, South Carolina. Chicora Foundation, Inc., *Research Contribution*, 165. Columbia, SC.

1995b Management Summary of Archaeological Data Recovery at 38BK1669 and 38BK1670, Berkeley County, South Carolina. Chicora Foundation, Inc., *Research Contribution,* 168. Columbia, SC.

ADAMS, NATALIE P., AND MICHAEL TRINKLEY
1994 In the Shadow of the Big House: Domestic Slaves at Stoney Baynard Plantation. Chicora Foundation, Inc., *Research Series,* 40.Columbia, SC.

AGORSAH, EMMANUEL KOFI
1983 *An Ethnoarcheological Study of Settlement and Behavior Patterns of a West African Traditional Society: The Nchumuru of Banda-Wiae in Ghana.* Doctoral dissertation, Department of Anthropology, University of California, Los Angeles. University Microfilms International, Ann Arbor, MI.

ANDERSON, DAVID G., AND J. W. JOSEPH
1988 Prehistory and History on the Upper Savannah River: Technical Synthesis of Cultural Resource Investigations, Richard B. Russell Multiple Resource Area. National Park Service, Atlanta, GA.

ANDERSON, DAVID G., AND JENNALEE MUSE
1982 The Archaeology of Tenancy in the Southeast: A View from the South Carolina Lowcountry. *South Carolina Antiquities,* 14:71–82.
1983 The Archaeology of Tenancy (2): A Reply to Trinkley. *Southeastern Archaeology,* 2:65–68.

ANGEL, J. LAWRENCE, JENNIFER OLSON KELLEY, MICHAEL PARRINGTON, AND STEPHANIE PINTER
1987 Life Stresses of the Free Black Community As Represented by the First African Baptist Church, 8th and Vine Streets, Philadelphia, 1824–1846. *American Journal of Physical Anthropology,* 74:213–229.

ASCHER, ROBERT, AND CHARLES FAIRBANKS
1971 Excavation of a Slave Cabin: Georgia, USA. *Historical Archaeology,* 5:3–17.

BAKER, VERNON G.
1980 Archaeological Visibility of Afro-American Culture: An Example from Black Lucy's Garden, Andover, Massachusetts. In *Archaeological Perspectives on Ethnicity in America,* Robert L. Schuyler, editor, pp. 29–37. Baywood, Farmingdale, NY.

BLAKEY, MICHAEL L.
1986 Fetal and Childhood Health in Late-Eighteenth and Early-Nineteenth-Century Afro-Americans: Enamel Hypoplasia and Hypocalcification in the FABC Skeletal Population. *American Journal of Physical Anthropology,* 72:179.

BRIDGES, SARAH T., AND BERT SALWEN
1980 Weeksville: The Archaeology of a Black Urban Community. In *Archaeological Perspectives on Ethnicity in America,* Robert L. Schuyler, editor, pp. 38–47. Baywood, Farmingdale, NY.

BROCKINGTON, PAUL, MICHAEL SCARDAVILLE, PATRICK H. GARROW, DAVID SINGER, LINDA FRANCE, AND CHERYL HOLT
1985 Rural Settlement in the Charleston Bay Area: Eighteenth- and Nineteenth-Century Sites in the Mark Clark Expressway Corridor. Report to the South Carolina Department of Highways and Public Transportation, from Garrow & Associates, Atlanta, GA.

BROOKER, COLIN
1991 Callawassie Island Sugar Works: A Tabby Building Complex. In *Further Investigations of Prehistoric and Historic Lifeways on Callawassie and Spring Islands, Beaufort County, South Carolina,* Michael Trinkley, editor, pp. 110–154. Chicora Foundation, Inc., *Research Series,* 23. Columbia, SC.

BROWN, KENNETH
2001 Archaeology of Ritual on South Carolina Plantations: Artifacts and Contexts. Paper presented at the Southeastern Archaeological Conference, Chattanooga, TN.

BROWN, KENNETH, AND DOREEN C. COOPER
1990 Structural Continuity in an African-American Slave and Tenant Community. *Historical Archaeology,* 24(4): 7–19.

BULLEN, ADELAIDE K., AND P. RIPLEY BULLEN
1945 Black Lucy's Garden. *Bulletin of the Massachusetts Archaeological Society,* 6:17–28.

CARILLO, RICHARD
1980 Green Grove Plantation: Archaeological and Historical Research at the Kinlock Site (38CH109) Charleston County. South Carolina Department of Highways and Public Transportation, Columbia.

CARLISLE, RONALD C., ARTHUR B. FOX, AND BARBARA J. GUNDY
1991 "Arthursville": An Antebellum Black Settlement in the Lower Hill District of Pittsburgh, Pennsylvania. Paper presented at the Middle Atlantic Archeological Conference, Ocean City, MD.

CASHIN, EDWARD J.
1980 *The Story of Augusta.* Richmond County Board of Education, Augusta, GA.

CATTS, WADE P.
1992 African Americans on the Upper Delmarva Peninsula: Archaeological Investigations at the Home of Thomas Cuff (c1790–1858), a "Free Negro of Chestertown." Paper presented at the Annual Meeting of The Society for Historical Archaeology, Kingston, Jamaica.

CATTS, WADE P., AND JAY F. CUSTER
1990 Tenant Farmers, Stone Masons, and Black Laborers: Final Archaeological Investigations of the Thomas Williams Site, Glasgow, New Castle, Delaware. *Delaware Department of Transportation Archaeological Series No. 82.* Dover.

CATTS, WADE P., JAY W. HODNY, AND JAY F. CUSTER
1989 "The Place at Christeen": Phase I and II Archaeological Investigations of the Patterson Lane Complex, Christiana, New Castle County, Delaware. *Delaware Department of Transportation Archaeological Series No. 74.* Dover.

CATTS, WADE P., AND DAVY McCALL
1991 A Report on the Archaeological Investigations of the House of Thomas Cuff, a Free Black Laborer, 108 Cannon Street, Chestertown, Kent County, Maryland. *North American Archaeologist,* 12(2):155–181.

CHEEK, CHARLES D., AND AMY FRIEDLANDER
1990 Pottery and Pigs Feet: Space, Ethnicity, and Neighborhood in Washington, DC., 1880–1940. *Historical Archaeology,* 24(1):34–60.

CHEEK, CHARLES D., AMY FRIEDLANDER, CHERYL A. HOLT, CHARLES E. LEEDECKER, AND TERESA E. OSSIM
1983 Archaeological Investigations at the National Photographic Interpretation Center Addition, Washington, DC, Navy Yard Annex. Report to Leo A. Daly Architects, from Soil Systems, Inc., Alexandria, VA.

COMBES, JOHN D.
1972 Ethnography, Archaeology, and Burial Practices among Coastal South Carolina Blacks. *The Conference on Historic Sites Archaeology Papers,* 7:52–61.

CRASS, DAVID COLIN, AND RICHARD D. BROOKS
1997 Settlement Patterning on an Agriculturally Marginal Landscape. In *Carolina's Historical Landscapes: Archaeological Perspectives,* Linda F. Stine, Martha Zierden, Lesley M. Drucker, and Christopher Judge, editors, pp. 71–84. University of Tennessee Press, Knoxville.

CRIST, THOMAS A. J., WILLIAM R. HENRY, J. W. JOSEPH, REGINALD H. PITTS, WADE P. CATTS, ALEX CATON, ARTHUR WASHBURN, AND SEAN NORRIS
2000 With Death Came Liberty: The Archaeology and History of the Sam Goode Cemetery, Mecklenburg County, Virginia. Report to the U.S. Army Corps of Engineers, Savannah District, from New South Associates, Inc., Stone Mountain, GA.

CRIST, THOMAS A. J., REGINALD H. PITTS, ARTHUR WASHBURN, JOHN P. McCARTHY, AND DANIEL G. ROBERTS
1995 "A Distinct Church of the Lord Jesus": The History, Archaeology, and Physical Anthropology of the Tenth Street First African Baptist Church Cemetery, Philadelphia, Pennsylvania. Report to Gaudet/O'Brien Associates and the Pennsylvania Department of Transportation, from John Milner Associates, Inc., West Chester, PA.

CRIST, THOMAS A. J., AND DANIEL G. ROBERTS
1996 Engaging the Public through Mortuary Archaeology: Philadelphia's First African Baptist Church Cemeteries. *CRM,* 10:5–8. U.S. Department of the Interior, National Park Service, Cultural Resources Division, Washington, DC.

CRIST, THOMAS A. J., DANIEL G. ROBERTS, REGINALD H. PITTS, JOHN P. McCARTHY, AND MICHAEL PARRINGTON
1997 The First African Baptist Church Cemeteries: African-American Mortality and Trauma in Antebellum Philadelphia. In *In Remembrance: Archaeology and Death,* David A. Poirier and Nicholas F. Bellantoni, editors, pp. 19–49. Bergin & Garvey, Westport, CT.

CRIST, THOMAS A. J., ARTHUR WASHBURN, AND JOHN P. McCARTHY
1991 The First African Baptist Church Revisited: Biohistorical Comparison between Two African-American Skeletal Samples from Antebellum Philadelphia. *American Journal of Physical Anthropology,* 12:63.

DEETZ, JAMES
1977 *In Small Things Forgotten.* Doubleday, New York, NY.

DRUCKER, LESLEY
1981 Socio-Economic Patterning at an Undocumented Late-Eighteenth-Century Lowcountry Site: Spiers Landing. *Historical Archaeology,* 15(2):58–68.

DRUCKER, LESLEY, AND RONALD ANTHONY
1979 The Spiers Landing Site: Archaeological Investigations in Berkeley County, South Carolina. Carolina Archaeological Services, Inc., Columbia.

EUBANKS, ELSIE, CHRISTOPHER T. ESPENSHADE, MARIAN ROBERTS, AND LINDA KENNEDY
1994 Data Recovery Investigations of 38BU791, Bonny Shore Slave Row, Spring Island, Beaufort County, South Carolina. Brockington and Associates, Atlanta, GA.

FAIRBANKS, CHARLES W.
1974 The Kingsley Slave Cabins in Duval County, Florida, 1968. *The Conference on Historic Sites Archaeology Papers 1972,* 7:62–93.

FERGUSON, LELAND G.
1978 Looking for the "Afro" in Colono-Indian Pottery. *Papers of the Conference on Historic Sites Archaeology,* 12:68–86. South Carolina Institute of Archaeology and Anthropology, University of South Carolina, Columbia.
1980 Looking for the "Afro" in Colono-Indian Pottery. In *Archaeological Perspectives on Ethnicity in America,* Robert L. Schuyler, editor, pp. 14–28. Baywood, Farmingdale, NY.
1989 Lowcountry Plantations, the Catawba Nation, and River Burnished Pottery. In *Studies in South Carolina Archaeology: Essays in Honor of Robert L. Stephenson.* Anthropological Studies 9. South Carolina Institute of Archaeology and Anthropology, University of South Carolina, Columbia.
1992 *Uncommon Ground: Archaeology and Early African America, 1660–1800.* Smithsonian Institution Press, Washington, DC.

GARDNER, JEFFREY, AND ERIC POPLIN
1992   Wappoo Plantation (38CH1199/1200): Data Recovery
        at an Eighteenth-Century Stono River Plantation in
        Charleston County, South Carolina. Brockington and
        Associates, Charleston.

GARROW, PATRICK H.
1982   Excavations at the Site of the Washington D.C. Civic
        Center. Soil Systems, Inc. Alexandria, VA.

GARROW, PATRICK H., AND THOMAS R. WHEATON
1989   Colonoware Ceramics: The Evidence from Yaughan
        and Curriboo Plantations. In Studies in South Carolina
        Archaeology: Essays in Honor of Robert L. Stephenson.
        Anthropological Studies 9. South Carolina Institute of
        Archaeology and Anthropology, University of South
        Carolina, Columbia.

GEISMAR, JOAN
1980   Skunk Hollow: A Preliminary Statement on
        Archaeological Investigations at a Nineteenth-Century
        Black Community. In Archaeological Perspectives on
        Ethnicity in America, Robert L. Schuyler, editor, pp.
        60–68. Baywood, Farmingdale, NY.
1982   The Archaeology of Social Disintegration at Skunk
        Hollow, a Nineteenth-Century Rural Black Community.
        Academic Press, New York, NY.

GUMS, BONNIE L.
1998   The Archaeology of an African-American
        Neighborhood in Mobile, Alabama. University of
        South Carolina, Center for Archaeological Studies,
        Monograph, 4. Mobile, AL.

HARRINGTON, SPENCER P. M.
1993   Bones and Bureaucrats. Archaeology, 46(2):28–39.

HAUGHTON, RICHARD H.
1972   Law and Order in Savannah, 1850–1860. Georgia
        Historical Quarterly, LVI:3–4.

THE HISTORY GROUP
1982   The Archaeology of Johnsontown. Report to the
        Metropolitan Atlanta Rapid Transit Authority, from
        The History Group, Atlanta, GA.

HOWSON, JEAN E.
1990   Social Relations and Material Culture: A Critique
        of the Archaeology of Plantation Slavery. Historical
        Archaeology, 24(4):78–91.

JOSEPH, J. W.
1989   Pattern and Process in the Plantation Archaeology
        of the Lowcountry of Georgia and South Carolina.
        Historical Archaeology, 23(1):55–68.
1992   Biblical Archaeology and the Dream: A Note from
        Springfield, Georgia. African American Archaeology,
        5:7–8.
1993a   White Columns and Black Hands: Class and
        Classification in the Plantation Archaeology of the
        Lowcountry of Georgia and South Carolina. Historical
        Archaeology, 27(3):57–73.
1993b   The Early American Period and Nineteenth Century

        in South Carolina Archaeology. In South Carolina
        Archaeology, Carl Steen, editor, pp. 63–75.
        Archaeological Society of South Carolina.
1993c   "And They Went Down Both into the Water:"
        Archeological Data Recovery of the Riverfront Augusta
        Site (9Ri165). New South Associates, Stone Mountain,
        GA.
1997a   Unwritten History, the Free African American Village
        of Springfield, Georgia. Common Ground, 2(1):41–47.
        National Park Service, Washington, DC.
1997b   Building to Grow: Agrarian Adaptations to South
        Carolina's Historic Landscapes. In Carolina's
        Historical Landscapes: Archaeological Perspectives,
        Linda F. Stine, Martha Zierden, Lesley M. Drucker,
        and Christopher Judge, editors, pp. 45–60. University
        of Tennessee Press, Knoxville.

JOSEPH, J. W., THERESA M. HAMBY, LOTTA A. C.
DANIELSSON, MARY BETH REED, LISA D. O'STEEN, LESLIE
E. RAYMER, THADDEUS MURPHY, AND NANCY PARRISH
1996   Between Conception and the Saints: Archaeological
        and Historical Studies of Late Eighteenth, Nineteenth,
        and Twentieth Century Urban Life in Mobile, Alabama.
        Report to the General Services Administration, from
        New South Associates, Stone Mountain, GA.

JOSEPH, J. W., AND MARY BETH REED
1991   Black Labor–White Land: The Archeology of Society
        and Social Change in Augusta, Georgia. Early Georgia,
        19(2):115–124.
1997   "We Were Just Dirt Farmers": The Archaeology
        of Piedmont Farmstead Landscapes. In Carolina's
        Historical Landscapes: Archaeological Perspectives,
        Linda F. Stine, Martha Zierden, Lesley M. Drucker,
        and Christopher Judge, editors, pp. 85–96. University
        of Tennessee Press, Knoxville.

JOSEPH, J. W., MARY BETH REED, AND CHARLES E.
CANTLEY
1991   Agrarian Life, Romantic Death: Archaeological and
        Historical Testing and Data Recovery for the I-85
        Northern Alternative, Spartanburg, South Carolina.
        Report to the South Carolina Department of Highways
        and Pubic Transportation from New South Associates,
        Stone Mountain, GA.

KENNEDY, LINDA, MARIAN D. ROBERTS, AND CHRISTOPHER
T. ESPENSHADE
1994   Archaeological Data Recovery at Colleton River
        Plantation (38BU647), Beaufort County, South
        Carolina: A Study of an Early Nineteenth Century
        Slave Settlement. Brockington and Associates, Atlanta,
        GA.

LAROCHE, CHERYL J.
1996   Beads from the African Burial Ground, New York
        City: A Preliminary Assessment. Beads: Journal of
        the Society of Bead Researchers, 6:3–20.

LAYARD, HENRY AUSTIN
1849   Nineveh and Its Remains. G. P. Putnam, New York,
        NY.

LEES, WILLIAM B.
1980 Limerick, Old and in the Way: Archaeological Investigations at Limerick Plantation, Berkeley County, South Carolina. South Carolina Institute of Archaeology and Anthropology, *Anthropological Studies*, 5. Columbia.

LEES, WILLIAM B., AND KATHRYN M. KIMERY-LEES
1979 The Function of Colono-Indian Ceramics: Insight from Limerick Plantation. *Historical Archaeology*, 13:1–13.

MILLER, GEORGE
1980 Classification and Economic Scaling of Nineteenth-Century Ceramics. *Historical Archaeology*, 14: 1–40.
1991 A Revised Set of CC Index Values for Classification and Economic Scaling of English Ceramics from 1787 to 1880. *Historical Archaeology*, 25(1):1–26.

O'MALLEY, NANCY
1990 A Documentary Review of the Rose Street Extension Project Area, Lexington, Kentucky. University of Kentucky Program for Cultural Resource Assessment, *Archeological Report*, 228. Report to the Lexington-Fayette Urban County Government, from University of Kentucky Program for Cultural Resource Assessment, Lexington.
1996 Kinkeadtown. University of Kentucky Program for Cultural Resource Assessment, *Archeological Report*, 377. Report to the Lexington-Fayette Urban County Government, from University of Kentucky Program for Cultural Resource Assessment, Lexington.

ORSER, CHARLES E., JR., AND ANNETTE M. NEKOLA
1985 Plantation Settlement from Slavery to Tenancy: An Example from a Piedmont Plantation in South Carolina. In *The Archaeology of Slavery and Plantation Life*, Theresa M. Singleton, editor, pp. 67–98. Academic Press, New York, NY.

ORSER, CHARLES E., JR., ANNETTE M. NEKOLA, AND JAMES L. ROARK
1982 Exploring the Rustic Life: Multi-Disciplinary Research at Millwood Plantation, a Large Piedmont Plantation in Abbeville County, South Carolina, and Elbert County, Georgia. National Park Service, Archaeological Services Branch, Atlanta, GA.

OTTO, JOHN SOLOMON
1975 *Status Differences and the Archeological Record: A Comparison of Planter, Overseer, and Slave Sites from Cannon's Point Plantation (1794–1861), St. Simons Island, Georgia*. Doctoral dissertation, Department of Anthropology, University of Florida, Gainesville. University Microfilms International, Ann Arbor, MI.
1980 Race and Class on Antebellum Plantations. In *Archaeological Perspectives on Ethnicity in America*, Robert L. Schuyler, editor, pp. 3–13. Baywood, Farmingdale, NY.
1984 *Canon's Point Plantation, 1794–1860*. Academic Press, New York, NY.

PARRINGTON, MICHAEL
1987 Cemetery Archaeology in the Urban Environment: A Case Study from Philadelphia. The Society for Historical Archaeology, *Special Publication Series*, 5:56–64. California, PA.

PARRINGTON, MICHAEL, AND DANIEL G. ROBERTS
1984 The First African Baptist Church Cemetery: An Archaeological Glimpse of Philadelphia's Early-Nineteenth-Century Black Community. *Archaeology*, 37(6):26–32.
1990 Demographic, Cultural, and Bioanthropological Aspects of a Nineteenth-Century Free Black Population in Philadelphia, Pennsylvania. In A Life in Science: Papers in Honor of J. Lawrence Angel, Jane E. Builstra, editor, pp. 138–170. *Scientific Papers of the Center for American Archaeology*, No. 6. Kampsville, IL.

PARRINGTON, MICHAEL, DANIEL G. ROBERTS, STEPHANIE PINTER, AND JANET C. WIDEMAN
1989 The First African Baptist Church Cemetery: Bioarchaeology, Demography, and Acculturation of Early-Nineteenth-Century Philadelphia Blacks. Report to the Redevelopment Authority of the City of Philadelphia.

POPLIN, ERIC, AND PAUL BROCKINGTON
1989 True Blue Plantation: Archaeological Data Recovery at a Waccamaw Neck Rice Plantation. Brockington and Associates, Charleston, SC.

POPLIN, ERIC, AND COLIN BROOKER
1994 The Historical Development of Dataw Island: Architectural and Archaeological Investigations at the Sams Plantation Complex. Brockington and Associates, Charleston and Brooker Architectural Design Consultants, Beaufort, SC.

RANKIN-HILL, LESLEY M.
1997 *A Biohistory of Nineteenth-Century Afro-Americans: The Burial Remains of a Philadelphia Cemetery*. Bergin & Garvey, Westport, CT.

SCHUYLER, ROBERT L.
1974 Sandy Ground: Archaeological Sampling in a Black Community in Metropolitan New York. In *Papers of the Conference on Historic Sites Archaeology*, Vol. 7(2), Stanley A. South, editor, pp. 13–51. SCIAA, Columbia, SC.
1980 Sandy Ground: Archaeology of a Nineteenth-Century Oystering Village. In *Archaeological Perspectives on Ethnicity in America*, Robert L. Schuyler, editor, pp. 48–59. Baywood, Farmingdale, NY.

SMITH, SAMUEL D.
1976 An Archaeological and Historical Assessment of the First Hermitage. Tennessee Department of Conservation, *Tennessee Division of Archaeology Research Series*, 2. Nashville.
1977 Plantation Archaeology at the Hermitage: Some Suggested Patterns. *Tennessee Archaeologist*, 2: 152–163.

SOUTH, STANLEY A.
  1977 *Method and Theory in Historical Archaeology.*
       Academic Press, New York.

STEEN, CARL
  1999 Stirring the Ethnic Stew in the South Carolina
       Backcountry: John de la Howe and Lethe Farm. In
       *Historical Archaeology, Identity Formation, and the
       Interpretation of Ethnicity,* Maria Franklin and Garrett
       Fesler, editors, pp. 93–120. Colonial Williamsburg
       Foundation, Williamsburg, VA.

THOMAS, BRIAN W.
  1995 Source Criticism and the Interpretation of African-
       American Sites. *Southeastern Archaeology,* 14(2):
       149–157.

TRINKLEY, MICHAEL
  1983 "Let Us Now Praise Famous Men"–If Only We Can
       Find Them. *Southeastern Archaeology,* 2:30–36.
  1986 Indian and Freedmen Occupation at the Fish Haul Site
       (38BU805), Beaufort County, South Carolina. Chicora
       Foundation, Inc., *Research Series,* 7. Columbia, SC.
  1995 Archaeological Data Recovery Excavations at
       38CH1107, Kiawah Island, South Carolina. Chicora
       Foundation, Inc., *Research Contribution,* 178.
       Columbia, SC.
  1996 Management Summary of Archaeological Data
       Recovery at a Portion of Crowfield Plantation
       (38BK103) and Its Slave Settlement (38BK1011),
       Berkeley County, South Carolina. Chicora Foundation,
       Inc., *Research Contribution,* 205. Columbia, SC.

TRINKLEY, MICHAEL (EDITOR)
  1989 Archaeological Investigations at Haig Point, Webb,
       and Oak Ridge, Daufuskie Island, Beaufort County,
       South Carolina. Chicora Foundation, Inc., *Research
       Series,* 15. Columbia, SC.
  1990 Archaeological Excavations at 38BU96, a Portion of
       Cotton Hope Plantation, Hilton Head Island, Beaufort
       County, South Carolina. Chicora Foundation, Inc.,
       Research Series 21. Columbia, SC.
  1991 Further Investigations of Prehistoric and Historic
       Lifeways on Callawassie and Spring Islands, Beaufort
       County, South Carolina. Chicora Foundation, Inc.,
       Research Series, 23. Columbia, SC.
  1993a Archaeological and Historical Examinations of Three
       Eighteenth- and Nineteenth-Century Rice Plantations
       on Waccamaw Neck. Chicora Foundation, Inc.,
       Research Series, 31. Columbia, SC.
  1993b The History and Archaeology of Kiawah Island,
       Charleston County, South Carolina. Chicora
       Foundation, Inc., *Research Series,* 30. Columbia,
       SC.

TRINKLEY, MICHAEL, DEBI HACKER, AND NATALIE ADAMS
  1993 Life in the Pee Dee: Prehistoric and Historic Research
       on the Roche Carolina Tract, Florence County, South
       Carolina. Chicora Foundation, Inc., *Research Series,*
       39. Columbia, SC.
  1995 Broom Hall Plantation: "A Good One and in a Pleasant
       Neighborhood." Chicora Foundation, Inc., *Research
       Series,* 44. Columbia, SC.

VLACH, JOHN MICHAEL
  1975 *Sources of the Shotgun House: African and Caribbean
       Antecedents for Afro-American Architecture.* Doctoral
       dissertation, Folklore, Indiana University, Bloomington.
       University Microfilms International, Ann Arbor, MI.
  1978 *The Afro-American Tradition in Decorative Arts.*
       Cleveland Museum of Arts, Cleveland, OH.

WAYNE, LUCY B., AND MARTIN F. DICKINSON
  1990 Four Mens Ramble: Archaeology in the Wando Neck.
       Southarc, Inc., Gainesville, FL.

WAYNE, LUCY B., MARTIN F. DICKINSON, AND LINDA F.
STINE
  1996a Ruins of an Old Settlement: Archaeological Data
       Recovery at 38CH1082, Dunes West, Charleston
       County, South Carolina. Southarc, Inc., Gainesville,
       FL.
  1996b Starvegut Hall Plantation: Archaeological Data
       Recovery, 38CH1398 and 38CH1400, Dunes West,
       Charleston County, South Carolina. Southarc, Inc.,
       Gainesville, FL.

WHEATON, THOMAS R., AMY FRIEDLANDER, AND PATRICK
GARROW
  1983 Yaughan and Curriboo Plantations: Studies in Afro-
       American Archaeology. Soil Systems, Inc., Marietta,
       GA.

WHEATON, THOMAS R., AND PATRICK H. GARROW
  1985 Acculturation and the Archaeological Record in the
       Carolina Lowcountry. In *The Archaeology of Slavery
       and Plantation Life,* Theresa A. Singleton, editor, pp.
       239–260. Academic Press, New York, NY.

WHEATON, THOMAS R., MARY BETH REED, RITA FOLSE
ELLIOTT, MARC S. FRANK, AND LESLIE E. RAYMER
  1990 James City, North Carolina: Archeological and
       Historical Study of an African American Urban
       Village. *New South Associates Technical Report,* 6.
       New South Associates, Stone Mountain, GA, and John
       Milner Associates, West Chester, PA.

WHEATON, THOMAS R., MARY BETH REED, AND J. W.
JOSEPH
  1993 Archeological Survey of the Beauregard Trace
       Property, Mobile, Alabama. Report to the Mobile
       Downtown Redevelopment Commission, from New
       South Associates, Stone Mountain, GA.

WILKIE, LAURIE A.
  1995 Magic and Empowerment on the Plantation: An
       Archaeological Consideration of the African American
       World View. *Southeastern Archaeology,* 14(2):136–
       148.

WOOD, PETER
  1974 *Black Majority: Negroes in Colonial South Carolina
       from 1670 through the Stono Rebellion.* W. W. Norton
       and Company, New York, NY.

WORKS PROJECT ADMINISTRATION
1940   *Drums and Shadows: Survival Studies among Georgia Coastal Negroes.* Savannah Unit, Georgia Writer's Project. Brown Thrasher Books, University of Georgia Press, Athens.

ZIERDEN, MARTHA, LESLEY DRUCKER, AND JEANNE CALHOUN
1986   Home Upriver: Rural Life on Daniel's Island, Berkeley County, South Carolina. Report to the South Carolina Department of Highways and Public Transportation, Columbia, from the Charleston Museum and Carolina Archaeological Services, SC.

J. W. JOSEPH
NEW SOUTH ASSOCIATES
6150 EAST PONCE DE LEON AVENUE
STONE MOUNTAIN, GA 30083

CHERYL J. LA ROCHE
MICHAEL L. BLAKEY

Seizing Intellectual Power: The Dialogue at the New York African Burial Ground

ABSTRACT

The New York African Burial Ground Project embodies the problems, concerns, and goals of contemporary African-American and urban archaeology. The project at once has informed and has been informed by the ever-watchful African Americans and New York public. It is a public that understands that the hypothetical and theoretical constructs that guide research are not value-free and are often, in fact, politically charged. An ongoing dialogue between the concerned community, the federal steering committee, the federal government, and the archaeological community has proved difficult but ultimately productive. The project has an Office of Public Education and Interpretation which informs the public through a newsletter, educators' conferences, and laboratory tours. The public, largely students, attends laboratory tours which often provide initial exposure to archaeology and physical anthropology. Much of this public involvement, however, was driven by angry public reaction to the excavation of a site of both historical prominence and spiritual significance.

Introduction

Excavation of the New York African Burial Ground has brought scholars, academicians, researchers, cultural resource managers, politicians, religious leaders, community activists, school children, and the general public together in a complex and often contentious philosophical and ideological relationship. The dynamics of the relationship and the shape of the project have been determined to a large extent by the relentless determination of the African-American descendant community to exercise control over the handling and disposition of the physical remains and artifacts of their ancestors. This relentless determination also ensured that the spiritual aspects of the site would not be lost in the face of scientific inquiry (Laura 1992; S&S Reporting 1993). Excavation of the African Burial Ground has global and universal implications which tran-

scend urban archaeology, physical anthropology, or the concerns of any one group.

Background

When the United States General Services Administration (GSA) contracted for the construction of a 34-story office building at Broadway, Duane, Elk, and Reade streets, New York City, on a site that historical maps indicated had been an 18th-century "Negroes Burying Ground" (Figure 1), it did not anticipate the storm of controversy that lay buried and moribund beneath nearly 30 ft. of fill. The cemetery, which was renamed the African Burial Ground in 1993 (Figure 2; Landmarks 1992), dates from before 1712 until 1794 (Howard University and John Milner Associates [HUJMA] 1993), and as the nation's earliest and largest African burial ground, holds great interest for anthropologists and historians as well as for the descendant communities. Although historians had long known of the African Burial Ground, the rediscovery was a revelation that struck a deep chord among many people of African descent in New York (Harrington 1993:33).

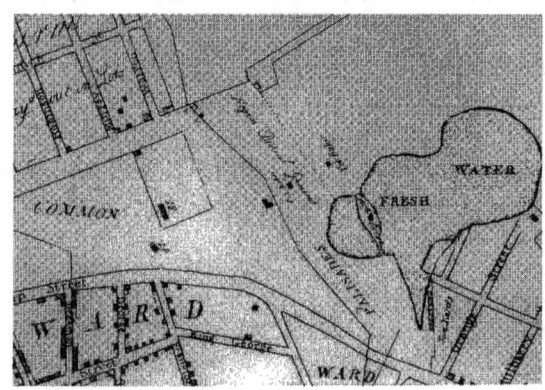

FIGURE 1. Detail of "A Plan of the City of New York from an Actual Survey," by Maerschalck, 1755. This is one of the few historic maps which specifically delineates the Burial Ground although the ravine and pertinent topography are absent. The palisades and the blockhouses for cannons are also shown. (Courtesy of the New York Historical Society, New York.)

Historical Archaeology, 1997, 31(3):84-106.
Permission to reprint required.

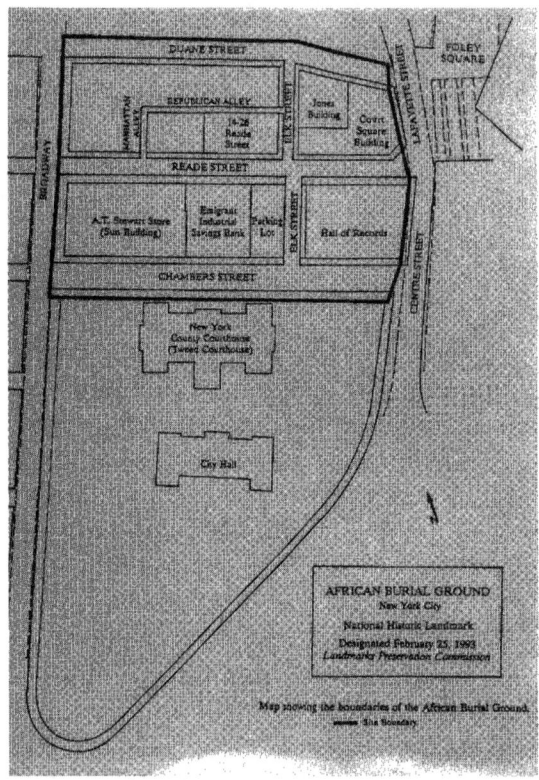

FIGURE 2. Map of lower Manhattan, outlining the original five- to six-acre boundaries of the African Burial Ground. (Reprinted with permission from National Historic Landmark Designation for the African Burial Ground, New York, February 1993.)

Excavations of the African Burial Ground began in the summer of 1991 and continued through July 1992. Early projections indicated that 50 burials would be recovered from an undisturbed area beneath Manhattan and Republican Alleys (Rutsch 1992:12). More than 400 burials were eventually disinterred from what was once the six-acre burial ground before a collaborative effort among influential and determined African Americans, and others, combined to halt excavation, take moral responsibility, and seize intellectual power.

Activism and the African Burial Ground

As chairperson of the Subcommittee on Public Buildings and Grounds, Congressman Gus Savage brought the influence and power of the U.S. Congress to challenge the GSA. Allocation of building funds for the federal government was controlled by this subcommittee, and it was Congressman Savage's gavel that signaled the end of the excavation (Finder 1992). New York City Mayor David Dinkins combined with Congressman Savage to bring considerable political weight to bear upon the project. New York State Senator David Paterson, 29th District Member, used his influence to form the Task Force for the Oversight of the African Burial Ground (Committee on Public Works and Transportation [CPWT] 1992; Paterson 1995). This task force, many members of which later served on the federal steering committee, was originally composed of concerned citizens who monitored pertinent activities and events that surrounded the site. Peggy King Jorde, Mayor Dinkins's Liaison for the Foley Square Project, and the New York City Landmarks Commission contributed municipal power and were largely responsible for alerting and updating the public about the burial ground (CPWT 1992; Jorde et al. 1993:6).

Other African Americans were also uniquely positioned for a collaborative "power play" that changed the course and direction of the project. Journalists brought the power of the press. The late jazz violinist Noel Pointer led an organization of artists. Local New York clergy members led a committee of religious leaders. Architects, lawyers, and scores of concerned citizens, many of whom represented institutions which were dedicated to taking responsibility for the spiritual, physical, and intellectual control of the site, contributed a community activism that forced the GSA to stop the excavations, alter building plans, and change the composition and direction of the professional leadership of the project (Harrington 1993:30). In the end, power was also wrested from the government by individual elderly African Americans, who understood, through life experience, the false hope of rhetoric and the emptiness of promises (Figure 3).

A team led by Michael Blakey of Howard University brought the final necessary component, intellectual power and technical expertise (HUJMA 1993). The research team based at

Howard University began presenting its proposal to direct the site's analysis in April 1992 (Blakey 1992a, 1992b). By that time, it was apparent that no contract had been let for analysis and that the research design developed by Historic Conservation and Interpretation, Inc. (HCI), the original cultural resource management firm hired to excavate the site, (revised in March of 1992) had been rejected by review agencies. The original research design of approximately 12 pages (Rutsch 1992) had devoted two pages to the site's African or African-American bioarchaeology, and it gave virtually no substantive discussion of New York's black history. The limited approach of the initial research design underestimated the enormous analytic value of the cemetery site.

In June 1992, negotiations were taking place between Blakey as Howard University's representative and Daniel G. Roberts of John Milner Associates (JMA). JMA was in the initial phases of replacing HCI, which was having difficulty administering a project of this magnitude (Cook 1993). By submitting a more appropriate research design Howard University and JMA simultaneously shared with the community and GSA the potential value of anthropological research which could at least be known, and, at best, might be retrieved.

By July 1992, after a constant barrage of petitions, angry rhetoric and community dissension, congressional hearings, professional meetings, lobbying, and political action, leadership and control of the entire project was eventually awarded to more sympathetic institutions with greater experience and which were better developed for research of this kind. The ancestral remains were subsequently sent to the Cobb Biological Anthropology Laboratory, Howard University, Washington, DC (Figure 4), and placed under the care and direction of Michael Blakey as scientific director.

Howard University has engaged a national and international team of Africanist and African-Americanist scholars for archaeological and historical analysis. JMA established an office in

FIGURE 3. Protestors gathered for one of the many rallies concerning the excavation of the African Burial Ground. The $3 million refers to monies allocated by Congress for memoralization. (Photo by Richard Brown.)

New York City and is assisting Howard University with laboratory processing and conservation of artifacts. JMA, Blakey, and Lesley Rankin-Hill had worked together on the First African Baptist Church Cemetery project in Philadelphia, in which they had facilitated reburial of 140 skeletons of African Americans (Angel et al. 1987; Parrington and Roberts 1990; Rankin-Hill 1990; Blakey et al. 1994). Each had experience in public archaeology and community consultation. Furthermore, within the American Anthropological Association (AAA) and the World Archaeological Congress, Blakey had been deeply involved in the development of position statements on repatriation issues of indigenous peoples. For several previous years he had been working with an AAA panel that would propose an anthropology of "public engagement" (Foreman 1994).

Research Questions

The research design (HUJMA 1993) specifies three major research questions about the people buried at the site: what are the origins of the population, what was their physical quality of life, and what can the site reveal about the biological and cultural transition from African to African-American identities? In 1995, the project's specialists added the examination of "modes of resistance" as a fourth major question. The methods employed to answer these questions are both anthropological and multidisciplinary. Molecular genetics, bone chemistry, skeletal biology, history and archaeology (American and African), ethnology, conservation, and African art history represent the range of fields within which this work, now underway, is concerned.

The African presence in colonial New York is approached from an African diasporic perspective, taking into account the African societies from which most of the population is derived and placing New York within the context of the broader American diaspora. The scientific approach is also biocultural and biohistorical. It examines the historical interactions of biology and culture such that data on each inform the other and, most importantly, such that human biology is interpreted within historically-specific sociocultural contexts.

The significance of the site, according to the research design, should be understood in relation to the "vindicationist" effort (Schomburg 1929) and the critical intellectual, educational, and political concerns of the African-American community. This comprehensive research plan therefore integrates the most contemporary scientific approaches and African-American intellectual traditions. The design was developed in systematic consultation with representatives of the descendant community and the anthropological community, following the African-American tradition of scholar activism as well as recent anthropological approaches to "public engagement." By acting on an interpretation of the AAA Statement on Ethics and Professional Responsibility and in consistence with the World Archaeological Congress's First Code of Ethics, the project's new leadership adhered to the right of the descendant community to accept, modify, or reject the research design. The design was approved by the federal steering committee, with some modification, and was subsequently accepted by the General Services Administration in 1993.

Professional Issues and Background

An adequate understanding of the scholarly and public concerns relating to the African Burial Ground must be informed by an awareness of long-standing debates about the politics of the past among African Americans. These debates intersect development in American anthropology and history. The theoretical precepts that guide the fields of physical anthropology, history, and archaeology converged at the African Burial Ground. But these are three areas of study which, historically and to varying degrees, have been used to either systematically victimize or alternately ignore (Fredrickson 1971:71–96;

FIGURE 4. Program from the welcoming ceremony at Howard University commemorating the transfer of the ancestral remains from New York City to the Cobb Laboratory, Howard Unversity.

Fraser and Butler 1986; Potter 1991:95; Deloria 1995; Fountain 1995) the population which scholars were now so eager to study.

Academic Anthropology and History

The skeletal population excavated from the African Burial Ground represents the remains of some of the first Africans brought to North America. These ancestral remains were of great interest to the New York Metropolitan Forensic Anthropology Team (MFAT), the original physical anthropologists working with HCI. MFAT was greatly concerned with the morphometric data (Cook 1993:26–27; GSA 1993) this baseline population contained for the development of "racing" methods. This emphasis on the application of methods of racial identification coupled with a paucity of previous African and African-American studies research characterized the approaches of the archaeologists and physical anthropologists who had excavated the site.

The potential for stereotypical, sterile, and denigrating interpretations of the site based on morphometric analysis became increasingly apparent to the African-American community. The primacy of this interest, coupled with a perceived disrespect on the part of the physical anthropologists and the GSA for the wishes of the descendant community, led to much of the conflict that has surrounded the African Burial Ground Project (CPWT 1992:34; Scarupa 1994).

Distortions of the African and African-American past by anthropologists and historians have been a prominent concern of African Americans for nearly 150 years. As early as 1854 Frederick Douglass pointed to the works of the first American physical anthropologists and Egyptologists as an effort to show blacks to be uncivilized and subhuman for the purpose of legitimating the institution of slavery (Douglass 1950[1854]). Aleš Hrdlička, the first curator of physical anthropology at the United States National Museum, Smithsonian, stated that physical anthropology was intended to have practical application through racial eugenics (Hrdlička 1918), while much of physical anthropology was being used to justify racial segregation laws which institutionalized discrimination against blacks.

Members of MFAT seemed keen on demonstrating to the public their technical knowledge by showing the cranial and post-cranial traits they used to classify the race of skeletons. Members of the New York descendant community often identified these explanations of facial and pelvic traits as troubling. Why should a grandmother have been disturbed at such demonstrations to her granddaughter? Why should an architect have asked, perplexed, how it could be possible for a femur to represent her ancestry? What has caused these negative reactions to simple biological approaches to racing? We have no certain answers to these questions, as indeed those who expressed these concerns seemed unable to explain them.

The intellectual background to the issues of racial determination may shed some light, however. There are historical precedents for objections to anthropological studies of race in the African-American community, and the Smithsonian's early racial research is representative of broader trends to which objections were made (Blakey 1987, 1996). In 1916, Hrdlička (1928) had great difficulty in obtaining cooperation from African Americans, particularly women, for his study of "The Full-Blood American Negro," whom he described as "suspicious." African Americans were generally aware of the demeaning uses of such data, which were generally used to show their inferiority and social distance, while "elite" Euroamericans clamored to be included in such research, which was generally used to demonstrate their superiority and social position. Hrdlička had a preconceived notion of full-bloods as the objective unit of biological analysis, yet most African Americans were not included in that type which he sought to measure and characterize. For African Americans today, "racing" has been associated with arguments in support of black inferiority, social and biological distance, and stereotypical images that reflected little of the range of variation that they knew of themselves.

The similarities between this historical example and the forensic approaches initially proposed for the African Burial Ground can be very informative. Forensic approaches assume the existence of a real racial biological type. While a broader range of African Americans can be captured within the black, or Negroid, classification used today, the assumption persists that there are some discrete traits that represent the features of a pure type (for example, nasal "guttering," extreme prognathism, large teeth). Morphological assessment in which MFAT was immediately involved during excavation focused on such discrete, stereotypical traits or their absence. These were the features that were being described to the public.

Furthermore, the use of inadequately tested post-cranial measurements for determining race raised both scholarly and public questioning. The MFAT method involved measures of the bones of the thigh and hip. The accuracy of this method has not been demonstrated on populations other than the Americans of the Terry Collection at the Smithsonian, with which the method had been developed (DiBennardo and Taylor 1983). The tautological nature of that test was questioned at the time of the original study. Moreover, even the more reliable cranial methods of racing that are based on African-American populations have been shown to be wholly inadequate for the study of West African populations, which are morphologically different from African Americans, different from other African populations, as well as regionally diverse. To reduce the biological identity of the African Burial Ground population to these narrow typologies was to assume, if applied, to construct a stereotype of the ancestral population. This is not far from Hrdlička's limitations at the turn of this century.

Biological race—Negroids, Caucasoids, Mongoloids—was viewed by forensics experts as the most objective or scientific means of classifica-

tion. The methodologically constructed black or "Negroid," however, is dissociated from any particular culture and history. Racing thus constructs an identity that is culture-less, history-less, and biologically shallow. Here, racing was being proposed by anthropologists who had engaged, as the community and scholars soon became aware, in very little study of Africana history and culture.

The proposed alternative combined morphological, morphometric, and molecular genetic data to assess specific breeding population affiliations (Blakey 1992a, 1992b; HUJMA 1993). Historical, archaeological, and stable isotope data would be used to interpret the cultural and ecological characteristics of the places of origin. The result should produce information about affiliated populations that have culture histories such as the Ashanti, Yoruba, Dutch, Lenape, English, and other potential origins of the people buried in the African Burial Ground. The descendant community's reaction to this biocultural approach was far more favorable than to forensic classification. Many physical anthropologists, however, objected to the rejection of MFAT's racing methods (Cook 1993; GSA 1993; Epperson 1997). In our case, it was the descendant community that would ultimately choose.

Embedded in the context of the New York African Burial Ground phenomenon is a sophisticated awareness on the part of the general African-American public regarding the demeaning abuses of anthropology and history by Euroamericans. The descendant community immediately understood the parallels between the mishandling of the bones and the racial reality of their lives (Wright and Brown 1992; Davila et al. 1994). If race follows the African descendant population beyond the grave, then racism, by definition, follows as well.

Public Engagement Through History

During the excavation phase of the project, the public was kept informed through a "grassroots," community-based newsletter, *Ground Truth*, by word of mouth, and by contacting the GSA directly for information. As leadership of the project changed, public education became a major component of the African Burial Ground project.

Sherrill D. Wilson was named director of the Office of Public Education and Interpretation (OPEI), formerly known as the Liaison Office. Prior to her work on this project, Wilson had developed an effective approach to public history through her African-American historic sites tours of New York City, "Reclaim the Memories." Her business, which she had been operating for five years, reflected the fact that African-American scholars were developing compatible resources and approaches that were informed by common understandings of the relationship of anthropology and history to the needs of their community. Her focus on public history was consistent with public engagement initiatives. The African Burial Ground Project would ultimately benefit from that preparation.

By focusing on the need to fill the gaps of omission left by Eurocentric public history in New York City, Wilson was participating in the long tradition of what St. Claire Drake termed "vindicationism." Throughout the 19th and 20th centuries, African-American and African scholars could usually be characterized as "vindicationists" because the most persistent thread running through their work was the attempt to correct the demeaning distortions of the culture, biology, and history of the Africana world (Schomburg 1929; Drake 1980). See also Rankin-Hill and Blakey (1994) for histories of anthropological contributions to the vindicationist effort; Diop (1974[1967]) and Van Sertima (1986) treat recent vindicationist efforts relating to archaeology, linguistic, and classical studies that are currently broadly read among the African and African-American public.

Eurocentric distortions of Africana history have been viewed not as accidental flaws of individual researchers but as politically motivated and systemic means of social, intellectual, and cultural control. While seminal historical works have contributed to correcting this legacy, Euroamericans rarely have had an understanding of the depth and dimension of African-American intellectual life (Hine 1986):

In virtually every area where evidence from the past is needed to support the validity of a given proposition, a historian can be found who will provide the evidence that is needed. Historians have usually been prepared to provide facile and quick explanations for the subordinate place of African Americans in American life. From the time Africans were brought as indentured servants to the mainland of English America in 1619, the enormous task of rationalizing and justifying the forced labor of peoples on the basis of racial differences was begun; and even after legal slavery was ended, the notion of racial differences persisted as a basis for maintaining segregation and discrimination (Franklin 1989[1965]:132).

Carter G. Woodson, perhaps the most important single African-American historian, founded the Association for the Study of Negro Life and History in 1915 and published the *Journal of Negro History* as the first outlet for the dissemination of black history. His efforts led to the formation of Negro History Week in 1926, which was later to become Black History Month. His most prominent book, *The Mis-education of the Negro* (Woodson 1933), speaks directly to the historiographic influences of the ideology of white supremacy.

Throughout the civil rights and black nationalist movements of the 1950s, '60s, and early '70s, "Black Studies" programs were fought for by African Americans and established at many universities (Hine 1986). During the 1980s and 1990s, an Afrocentric educational movement emerged in the black community in response to the distorted global and American history African-American children are continually taught. That history frequently presents a romantic view of European and Euroamerican identity and an omitted African and African-American presence in important societal developments, of which they were an integral part.

Indeed, New York's African Burial Ground was a vivid example of the omission of the colonial Africans' presence and contribution to the building of the city and the nation. The African-American public could at once turn to the abundant and tangible physical remains of the people omitted from the city's deficient school curricula. By omission, northern slavery and racism were denied.

The African-American public interested in the African Burial Ground was usually quite aware of bodies of "vindicationist," Africana studies and Afrocentric literature which held greater intellectual relevancy, while exposing the biases of "mainstream" or Eurocentric historiography and anthropology. Many among the New York public were influenced by extensive travel to various African countries, some of which was done with Afrocentric organizations. To quote Miriam Francis, one of the most active members of the federal steering committee, "If it was an African find, we wanted to make sure that it was interpreted from an African point of view" (Harrington 1993:34).

When vindicationist motivations were explained as part of the site's significance for the African-American community, Euroamericans, including members of the New York City Landmarks Preservation Commission and the Advisory Council for Historic Preservation, expressed fears and objections, characterizing the approach as ethnocentric bias. Yet the vindicationist tradition was posed as a corrective for persistent Eurocentric bias and misrepresentation, and as a search for truth and accuracy.

Archaeology and Cultural Resource Management

Although the impetus for the project was cultural resource management, the implications have been broad and complex. New Yorkers sought and still seek authority, defined by Kertzer (1988:110) as the right to exercise influence over behavior, with African and African-American archaeologists and anthropologists directing the research. As previously stated, there were concerns that the guiding methodologies, theories, and ideologies that govern the primary research disciplines (e.g., Hodder 1986, 1992; Leone and Potter 1988; Trigger 1989; Blakey 1990:38; Yoffee and Sherratt 1993; deMaret 1994:183; Leone and Potter 1994; Orser 1996) would be misapplied in studying the skeletal and artifactual remains from this site (Harrington 1993:36; Foster 1994:4). This concern certainly extended to archaeological theory and practices, particularly since problems that potentially have contributed to the loss of data occurred as a result of rapid excavation and inadequate stabilization of re-

mains. Although never explicitly stated, the sentiment among the descendant community was that the importance, particularly the spiritual importance that the site held, was too great to allow field excavation techniques to be the sole criterion of competence (Harrington 1993:33). The question was not whether these individuals were qualified scientists, but whether they would be qualified to direct research on an important African-American bioarchaeological site.

African Americans in and Through Archaeology

For approximately the first 75 years of the history of American archaeology, until 1946, African Americans as well as other groups without an independent income were largely excluded from the profession. During the depression it was discovered that archaeology could usefully employ large numbers of individuals to move earth. The Works Progress Administration (WPA) projects of the 1930s, and later the GI Bill, allowed a broader segment of America's social classes exposure to archaeology. Most of the first archaeologists without independent wealth were World War II veterans who benefited from the GI Bill (Barbour 1994). During the 1960s and 1970s, the Ford Foundation and other funding sources established fellowships to correct the underrepresentation of African-American scholars, which led to an increase in African-American anthropologists (Drake 1980), the vast majority of whom were cultural anthropologists.

The development of Cultural Resource Management (CRM) has fostered the growth of African-American archaeology since the 1960s (Ferguson 1992; Barbour 1996), particularly in the South. Until the excavations of the African Burial Ground, African-American archaeology in the North had concentrated on finds that reflected the interests of individual archaeologists and were largely of local interest (Barbour 1996).

Some of the early work in the North included Robert Schuyler's (1972) study of oyster fisherfolk of Sandy Ground, Staten Island; Bert Salwen's (Bridges and Salwen 1980) study at

Weeksville; James Deetz's study of black households in Massachusetts including Parting Ways (Deetz 1977) and Black Lucy's Garden (Bullen and Bullen 1945; Baker 1980); and Mark Leone's (1984) public archaeology program at Annapolis. Recently, CRM firms have added significantly to recovery of African-American history, including JMA's excavations at the two First African Baptist Church cemeteries in Philadelphia (Kelley and Angel 1989; Parrington et al. 1989; Crist et al. 1995).

CRM archaeologists have, however, been accountable to governmental and other clients who frequently are not principally interested in anthropological research, a problem which has pointed to the risk of "deskilling" (Paynter 1983) and to oftentimes inadequate resources for careful analysis (Lacy and Hasenstab 1983). The extent to which CRM archaeologists uphold disciplinary standards (Schuldenrein 1995) is also not the same as the extent to which they uphold the standards of African-American studies. The predominantly Euroamerican field of CRM archaeology and the predominantly African-American field of African-American studies remain far apart. Generally, CRM archaeologists need have little academic preparation or interest in African-American research. CRM archaeologists rarely seek academic preparation in African-American studies departments and very few faculty of African-American studies departments have been contracted by archaeologists. Is the view of African-American history and culture so deficient, so simple, that one need have no specialized training to conduct research in that culture area?

Philosophical Divergence

Philosophical divergence occurs in several areas including methods of analysis and interpretation, semantics, and social interpretation. Each is addressed more fully below.

Analysis and Interpretation

In the informally segregated United States, archaeology and African-American Studies have developed as ethnically distinct disciplines, the former mainly white and the latter mainly black, with little interaction. Theresa Singleton, the Smithsonian's leading historical archaeologist, and Ronald Bailey, chair of Northeastern University's African-American Studies Department, attempted to bring the two fields together in Oxford, Mississippi, in 1989. Singleton (1994) and Singleton and Bograd (1995) recognize that the ethnic and black studies movement of the 1960s and '70s spurred initial interest in African-American archaeology, along with historic preservation legislation and bicentennial interests. They find that "the problem [of African-American archaeology] is that the field is theory poor, not data poor" (Singleton and Bograd 1995). Samford (1996:113) has also observed, "In the two decades that archaeologists have been excavating African American slave sites, they have accumulated a substantial body of data. Unfortunately data recovery has outpaced both analysis and the reformulation of research goals."

While several important studies have certainly been done, year after year, archaeologists and physical anthropologists, some with a superficial understanding of African-American history and culture, profit from the conduct of research on archaeological sites that influence how African Americans are defined. This was clearly the case, and a major source of contention, surrounding the original excavation team at the New York African Burial Ground project.

Understandably, New Yorkers feared that the cultural significance often hidden from the boundaries of social contact and daily interaction would be unrecognized and overlooked (McGuire and Paynter 1991) and that obvious interpretations would become problematic in terms of recognition. This is particularly so since far fewer African descendant sites have been excavated or identified in the North as compared to the frequency with which southern plantation sites are excavated. Comparatively little archaeological evidence exists for 17th- and 18th-century New York Africans, suggesting that much groundwork will have to be laid in the study of this population.

Seizing intellectual control has meant that the criteria for competency have been expanded to include an affinity for African-American culture, past and *present*, and comfort with and knowledge of the politics of African descendant populations, their cultures, and their histories (CPWT 1992:34–41; Harrington 1993:33; Wilson 1995:3). As was sometimes the case at the African Burial Ground excavations, there was evidence of discomfort and uneasiness with African Americans among some excavators and archaeologists (McGowan and Brighton 1995, pers. comm.), further contributing to concerns that current racial attitudes would influence interpretations of the historical population being studied.

Furthermore, questions which reflect the general sentiment "should white people study black people?" (Nobile 1993; Wayne 1994:6; Curtin 1995) and an insistence on "racing skeletons" (GSA 1993; Epperson 1997) give the impression that simplistic questions are being asked rather than complex, insightful queries that also acknowledge the entangled philosophical and theoretical dilemmas archaeology must resolve with respect to the demands of descendant communities (Robertshaw 1995).

As Jamieson (1995:39) correctly observes regarding study of the remains from the African Burial Ground: "The developments in New York City . . . have demonstrated that contract archaeologists are required to deal with such remains, and that a solid understanding of the historical and anthropological aspects of African-American mortuary practices is necessary before interpreting them." In a field where African Americans have been largely invisible and the documentary evidence unsupportive, methodologies that uncover the archaeological visibility of African Americans are sorely needed (Barbour 1996).

According to Hodder (1986:7), "It is only when we make assumptions about the subjective meanings in the minds of people long dead that we can begin to do archaeology." This view of archaeological interpretation again would have left the New York descendant community dependent upon the largely Euroamerican researchers who would consider themselves qualified for such an interpretation (Klima 1992:20). As a result, New Yorkers insisted on African-American leadership and involvement in all aspects of this project.

Yet, Larry McKee (1995:4) argues in "Commentary: Is It Futile to Try and Be Useful? Historical Archaeology and the African American Experience" that "studying African-American life from just an African-American perspective would end up one-sided and ultimately sterile." Presumably, then, the dearth of African-American archaeologists, which he also acknowledges, implies that archaeological interpretation of African-American sites to date must be one-sided and ultimately sterile since primarily Euroamericans interpret these sites. After 125 years of American archaeology as an organized discipline, there are fewer than six African Americans who hold Ph.D.s in the field (Barbour 1994), with an equal number currently in graduate programs around the country.

There was a concern among African Americans that what would be deemed the important avenues of inquiry would be hollow and irrelevant for the African-descendant community (Muhammad et al. 1993:3). Entrenched, long-held philosophical positions of power are not easily relinquished, and new perspectives are often difficult for scholars to develop or embrace without dialogue or outside influence. As the changing archaeological perspective weds archaeological findings with interdisciplinary research and oral history, perhaps scholars and others outside the discipline may begin to access and find relevance in the body of work produced by our efforts. African-American historians, in particular, can be informed by accurate archaeological research and interpretation.

Semantics

Semantics and the use of descriptive language has been a constant theme in New York. Insistence on the use of the word African in the renaming of the "Negroes Burying Ground" demonstrates the descendant community's understanding of the power and influence of language as well as the need to eschew European descriptive terminology. These African Americans chose to call the Africans what they chose to call themselves—African Mutual Relief Society, African Free School, African Methodist Episcopal Church, for example (Stuckey 1987:199–200; Wilson 1995:11). The descendant community has insisted that "slaves" not be identified by their condition of servitude but rather by the conditions imposed upon them (S&S Reporting 1993). It is particularly telling that the term slave is never specifically defined in dictionaries to refer to enslaved Africans, although this is the most pervasive use of the word in the United States. The term "enslaved African" is perhaps more accurate than servant, bondspersons, bond chattel laborers, or slave and conveys the involuntary aspect of enslavement.

Not all linguistic restructuring is so easily accomplished, however. In many instances, the English language is limiting when one attempts to accurately convey the African-American experience. The continued use of the term "master" in anthropological (e.g., Blassingame 1972; Stuckey 1987; Meillassoux 1991; Holloway 1991) and historical (e.g., McManus 1966; Johnson 1969; Franklin 1989) writings is a clear example of the romantic use of language which reflects a Eurocentric approach indicative of a reluctance to divest of euphemistic language. The term "master" is defined as "one with the ability or power or authority to control; one who is highly skilled, superior; a victor, a conqueror; to rule or direct; an individual having predominance over another; having all others subordinate to oneself" (*Illustrated Heritage* 1967; *Oxford English Dictionary* 1971; Webster's 1971, 1991, 1994; *Scribner-Bantam English Dictionary* 1979; *World Book Dictionary* 1984; Merriam-Webster 1994). Jesus Christ is often referred to as *"the* Master" (Webster's 1983). Nowhere within the various definitions is the word "master" ever defined to accurately reflect the specific, traditional colloquial usage of the word. Never is "the master" defined as enslaver, or as one who enslaves, principally African descendant populations, or one who deprives Africans of their humanity, or one who coerces the labor and social actions, most specifically of African descendant populations.

Recently, scholars have attempted to avoid the use of the term master by using the term "slave

FIGURE 5. Burial 101 had tack heads arranged on a coffin in a shape that has been interpreted to be either a heart or to represent an Adinkra symbol. (Photo by Dennis Seckler; courtesy of U.S. General Services Administration.)

holder" (cf. Blassingame 1972; Meier and Rudwick 1986; Stuckey 1987; White 1991) or "planter" rather than enslaver as the descriptive which encompasses the slave-owning aspects inherent in the plantation system (e.g., Moore 1985; Singleton 1985; Ferguson 1992; Mintz and Price 1992). This term, however, lacks accuracy or visceral, emotive power and in no way conveys the hideousness of the institution of slavery or the function and actions of its principal perpetrator. Moreover, the term is misleading, since "the planter" might rarely plant. Intellectual empowerment equips African Americans with the ability to confront ideological justifications and rationalizations pertaining to use of traditional language.

Similar to language usage, analysis of material culture within archaeology is also an area that can be subjective and open to interpretation.

The interpreter's specialized knowledge and familiarity with the culture being studied should and does affect analysis in obvious ways. At the African Burial Ground, for example, a pattern of nail heads formed a symbol on a coffin which was widely recognized as a heart (Figure 5). An African-American scientist, while not at all a specialist in African symbolic systems, recognized the ornate heart shape as closely resembling one of the Asanti *Adinkra* symbols whose use was growing in popularity in African-American culture. When a Ghanaian historian of African art looked at this same symbol, he too saw *Sankofa*, one of the *Adinkra* symbols, and could explain the appropriateness of its temporal, cultural, and mortuary context: "The symbol expresses the Akan social thought that espouses the essence of tying the past with the present in order to prepare for the future" (Ofori-Ansa 1995:3).

While it is difficult to interpret or extrapolate meaning from a culturally ambiguous symbol within the archaeological context, *Adinkra* symbolism is more appropriate to the population buried in the African Burial Ground and demonstrates the divergent perspectives which shape interpretation. The introduction of relevant African systems of thought provides evidence of why African and African-American scholars felt compelled to broaden the prospective of this project. Myopic interpretation of the comparatively few diagnostic artifacts excavated from the site would contribute to a superficial understanding of New York's African colonial population.

Social Politics of the African Burial Ground

The African Burial Ground is often seen as an example of whites and blacks perceiving issues so differently as to merely exist together in physical space while operating in very different worlds of thought and action. African Americans succeeded as they did because their critical view of the issues was more accurate, relative to most Euroamericans involved with the project. While some Euroamericans directly involved with the controversy, and who were closely aligned with the African-American community,

did have a fundamental understanding of issues, and while many others empathized with the issue of desecration, most sought only to contain the inconveniences being fostered by black protest, a protest whose justifications they could scarcely have comprehended.

Equally significant for African Americans were the metaphorical and symptomatological meanings of the conflicts in which they were embroiled. Here were the historical and the current, day-to-day problems of racial discrimination being played out on a small scale. Audible racial epithets were not being slung, but that has not been the dominant or accepted mode of racist social relations in the United States for some time now. Instead, the federal government and its previous consultants were seen as pursuing a course of obstruction that reflected a dismissive attitude toward blacks whom they sought to control by denying access to substantive power. Both the consultants and the GSA underestimated the African-American community's resolve to establish authority over the disposition of the site and its analysis. When African-American community leaders and scientists repeatedly asserted those intentions, glaring attempts were made to ignore them or to placate them with shallow offerings.

Most of the Euroamerican government officials and their consultants acted without apparent recognition that blacks understood exactly what was being attempted and had effective strategies for surmounting those obstacles. Exclusion, dismissive attitudes, tokenism, and claims of unfairness and "reverse racism" when African Americans seek full access to resources are commonplace interactions with white Americans. The effectiveness of the sophisticated African-American lobby at the city, state, and national levels demonstrates a lack of realism on their opponents' part. Where in other aspects of daily life individual African-American citizens would be limited in their ability to roundly address such circumstances, here in the important moment and symbolism of their ancestor's dignity, white racism would be addressed in microcosm. The United States government's role as antagonist, along with that of the discipline that defined racial differences and African culture, could not have been more appropriate foils for African-American empowerment.

Despite the longer track record and established credentials of Howard University's program of research in African-American bioanthropology, members of the original excavation team characterized Howard's efforts as "reverse racism," a characterization that immediately eliminated the multitude of intellectual issues. Many of the whites who had represented anthropological and preservation concerns in New York City and who had supported greater participation by African-American scholars at the site began to object to Howard University's plan to remove the remains from New York City to its Washington laboratory. These New Yorkers thus attempted to stand in the way of African-American intellectual control, in the interests of their own access to a prominent historical resource.

Since New Yorkers can be extremely provincial (Muhammad et al. 1993), the choice on the part of the descendant community to remove what must have been viewed as "their" cultural resource to an environment where their interests could be understood, respected, and empowered is a dramatic indictment of the status quo. The need to place the remains at Howard University also speaks to the dearth of local options and the lack of investment in African-American bioarchaeology in New York City.

The Federal Steering Committee

In response to provisions set forth in Section 106 of the National Historic Preservation Act (36 CFR 800) requiring the consultation of interested parties, a federal steering committee composed of concerned community activists and various experts and professionals was formed to foster the dialogue between the GSA, archaeologists, and community members (Jorde et al. 1993). The New York descendant community was given an official voice in the project; future archaeological requirements were explained, and the government was seemingly accountable. The wishes of the descendant community could be directly articulated. Unlike their ancestors,

today's African Americans have been able to speak for themselves (Wall 1995).

The federal steering committee meetings were among the most virulent encounters associated with the African Burial Ground project (S&S Reporting 1992–1994; Schomburg Center 1992–1994). Many of the Euroamericans originally in control of the project were unaccustomed to or uncomfortable with emotional displays, and demonstrated a dismissive attitude when unable to contend with the emotionally charged, angry responses of a descendant community whose earlier moderaton was met only with betrayal.

More often, however, it was the need for "sensitivity" toward African Americans that whites recognized, but did not understand. While the issue of sensitivity toward the sacred was apparently shared by Euroamericans and African Americans alike, it was unclear whether the meanings of the concept were the same for both. African Americans were insisting on "respect" for the dead and the living. In a society imbued with racist stereotypes of blacks as overly emotional, irrational, and hyperpolitical, however, even liberal white concerns for "sensitivity" easily can be based upon a patronizing attitude whose assumptions are racist, further adding to an atmosphere of mistrust (Kutz 1994). African Americans sought control, not sympathy.

The charter of the federal steering committee was not renewed once the newly constructed federal office building was occupied in November 1994, leaving many with the impression that the federal government's only interest in addressing community concerns was expediency and that clearly no lasting changes had occurred. There are several specific issues which were never resolved by the steering committee. The areas of concern beyond the direction of the research included the establishment of a world-class museum, an appropriate memorial, and reinterment on the site (Jorde et al. 1993). This last issue, reinterment, could prove as onerous as the excavation of the cemetery if the GSA again misjudges the gravity and depth of importance African Americans attach to this final phase (Cohen 1992:21). There are a number of engineering constraints associated with site stabilization that render reburial on-site a major problem, requiring careful planning and strategy, professional expertise, and a timetable.

By disbanding the steering committee, expressed interests of the descendant community and issues which require time to resolve have been left unanswered. These unresolved issues are of continuing concern, although the force with which they are currently being addressed has diminished. Senator Paterson has convened a committee to address the issue of the museum (Paterson 1995), but progress has been slow. Although major concessions have been won on the part of the African descendant community, several unresolved issues such as reburial, memorialization, and the level of funding for scientific and historical research specified in the research design, in conjunction with unfulfilled commitments, leave the question of ultimate success unanswered.

Although the ancestral remains have been moved to Howard University and the federal steering committee is no longer in existence, New Yorkers have not relinquished stewardship of nor their desire to be closely involved in every aspect of the project (Muhammad et al. 1993:3). To quote Senator David Paterson, "The descendant community of African Americans has been left spellbound by the discovery, and impatient for results" (Assael 1993:18). Through ceremonies, symposia, lectures, demonstrations, and meetings, they have been relentless and diligent in their devotion, as have researchers in their commitment to public engagement. This is the scope and magnitude of activism that excavation of this archaeological resource has engendered.

Current Status

Today, New York no longer has a black mayor (Willen and Moses 1996), Gus Savage is no longer chair of the Subcommittee on Public Buildings and Grounds, and Congress is contemplating a decrease in funding and support for CRM (Craib and Johnson 1995). Since the federal steering committee no longer exists, much of the responsibility for fulfilling the descendant community's mandate now rests in the hands of the researchers and scientists in conjunction with the GSA. The struggle for control of the African Burial Ground site was a struggle to have the voice of the community heeded. Exclusion of direct community involvement as the project progresses removes ethical, moral, spiritual, and social issues and obligations from community control. The work of holding the GSA accountable to previous agreements with the community has been largely assumed by the anthropologists directing the project.

The Office of Public Education and Interpretation

The Office of Public Education and Interpretation (OPEI) opened in March 1993 for the express purpose of informing the New York and national communities about the ongoing status of the African Burial Ground project. Although the future of this office is unclear (Strickland-Abuwi 1996), it has provided information through its monthly reports to more than 40,000 interested persons from around the world (OPEI 1995–1996).

The OPEI conducts on-site and off-site historical slide presentations about the African Burial Ground project and the complementary history of Africans in colonial New York, archaeological laboratory tours, and educators' symposia for teachers, researchers, and other interested persons. The OPEI has trained more than 80 volunteers to help inform local communities of issues and current events relating to the project. The office also accepts high school and college students as semester interns in exchange for academic credit. Howard University also conducts laboratory tours in Washington, DC, and has trained a team of more than 25 volunteers in its efforts to make the research accessible to the public.

The OPEI publishes *Update*, a quarterly newsletter that has a readership of more than 10,000 persons per issue. As a direct result of the excavations, the African Burial Ground project has introduced the topics of archaeology, physical anthropology, and conservation to scores of children and adults who otherwise would not have been exposed to these disciplines.

The OPEI has supported Richard Brown, former steering committee member, in a community-engineered campaign to have the U.S. Postal Service issue an African Burial Ground commemorative stamp (Devieux 1995). As of August 1997, more than 104,000 signatures had been collected from 40 states and 16 countries (OPEI 1995–1996; Devieux 1997, pers. comm.). The goal of this commemorative stamp campaign was to collect 100,000 signatures for submission to the Citizens Stamp Advisory Committee in April 1996 (OPEI 1995–1996). This petition has been denied for the second time by the committee and will not be eligible for consideration again until late 1997. Such defeats only strengthen the resolve of the New York community and of the stamp campaign workers who understand the political and bureaucratic obstacles as well as the economic concerns of the committee associated with the stamp approval process (McAllister 1996a, 1996b).

Media Coverage

Media coverage of the African Burial Ground project has been extensive in documenting this unique colonial-era archaeological site. *The African Burial Ground: An American Discovery* (Kutz 1994) is an award-winning film produced by GSA; *Unearthing the Slave Trade* aired in 1993 on the Learning Channel; and *Slavery's Buried Past* aired in 1996 on the Public Broadcasting System. More than 500 newspaper and magazine articles have been published in media attempts to fill the historical voids relating to an African presence in colonial New York, and to tell the story of the New York African-American descendant community's struggle to preserve the site and disseminate its history (Citations 1995; Pearce 1995).

The African Burial Ground has also been included in at least two recent historical publications, *The Encyclopedia of New York City* (Jackson 1995) and *The Historical Atlas of New York City* (Homberger 1994). This new inclusion,

however, has not eliminated misinterpretation or misrepresentation. Bucolic depictions of the African Burial Ground in the *New York Times* (Dunlap 1992) and in the *Historical Atlas of New York City* (Homberger 1994:44–45) each misrepresent the visual imagery of the location by depicting a lush, flat pastoral landscape rather than the hilly, ravined location near New York's noxious industries. Situated on undesirable land and originally located outside the city limits, the cemetery was, by mid-18th century, beyond a gated, 14-ft.-high palisades; the hills and deep ravine described in Stokes (1915–1928:591), the National Historic Landmark Designation (Landmarks 1992:5), and other historical documents are not in evidence. Presenting such incorrect images negates the power of the African Burial Ground and the hardships faced by New York's early African community. This type of distortion reinforces the notion that African-American New Yorkers must be relentless in their insistence on accuracy in all aspects pertaining to the site.

The image (Figure 6) from *The Historical Atlas of New York City* (Homberger 1994) was approved by cartographic consultant Alice Hudson, head of the Map Division of the New York Public Library. When the inaccuracies were referenced during a lecture, Hudson stated that this bucolic scene was drawn by modern English artists and that the drawing does indeed look more like the English countryside than 18th-century New York City (Hudson 1995, pers. comm.).

Furthermore, most cartographers of the period also misrepresented the African Burial Ground by eliminating specific identification of the six-acre cemetery from the majority of the historical maps, further contributing to the geographical and topographical misinterpretation that has plagued the site (Edwards and Kelcey 1990,1, 3:147; Jorde et al. 1993:6). Since historical archaeology relies on documentary evidence as well as archaeological data for interpretation of sites, current visual misrepresentations and omissions of the past have implications for the discipline and reveal the continual problems of cultural bias.

Diversity and Divergence

Intellectual sophistication beyond the narrow limits of customary Eurocentrism requires the participation of people of diverse ethnicities in the practice of anthropology in general (Blakey 1989) and of archaeology and museology in particular (Blakey 1990:45). Thus, the intellectual evolution of the field; non-white participation; anti-Eurocentrism; and community engagement and empowerment are mutually reinforcing. As the situation in New York evolved, the African Burial Ground became apparent as a practical and dramatic case for the development of the theory and practice of inclusion and engagement. In the case of the African Burial Ground, engagement was also powerfully informed by the long tradition of African-American vindicationist critique (Foster 1994), as discussed previously, and by scholarly activism, the latter being a somewhat more assertive version of the engaged scholar or public intellectual. The interests of

the Howard University initiative and those of the African-American public seemed to largely correspond, but these could not be realized until the public took control of the situation.

While spirituality is an issue that was at the core of the African-American struggle for control (S&S Reporting 1993), there are several other issues of concern that African-American New Yorkers brought to this site. Foremost among them is the philosophical divergence among African Americans. Although there is general unity surrounding the major issues, the African descendant community speaks with many voices (*Update* 1993–1996). The Muslim community, for example, is constant in their reminders that Muslims were also enslaved and could have been buried at the cemetery (Hatim 1995).

Various religious communities approach the site from divergent philosophical as well as divergent political perspectives. The political forces active within the African-American community also have been diverse, ranging from

FIGURE 6. Idyllic modern depiction of the African Burial Ground, which was located southwest of the Collect Pond (after Homberger 1994).

black nationalists and Afrocentric organizations to individuals with strong personal beliefs. It is particularly interesting that older African Americans, some of whom have retired from professional and scientific careers, have been among the most persistent. Additionally, divergent religious, political, and scientific perspectives and philosophies in approaching the problems relating to the African Burial Ground have, at times, been the most threatening to the cohesion and resolve of the African-American community.

Conclusion

For African-American New Yorkers, the excavation of our ancestors has been a cathartic and wrenching experience. The anxiety caused by the excavations and post-excavation project management provoked anger, outrage, and cynicism. The descendant community is still highly pained and deeply offended by the desecration of this ancestral site (Daughtry 1992; Scarupa 1994).

Outraged by the fact that this population, mistreated in life, was continuing to be mistreated beyond death (Dunlap 1992), New York's African Americans were driven by a sense of responsibility for the protection of ancestral heritage and a desire to ensure that the dead were honored and memorialized (Wright and Brown 1992; Jorde et al. 1993; Wilson 1995; Devieux 1995). This sense of responsibility and descendancy rapidly spread to the national African-American communities, and to African communities as well. A royal Ghanaian delegation visited the site and Howard University in 1995, and a briefing was held for the United Nation's Human Rights Commission in Geneva in 1996.

Realization of the global importance and of the overwhelming spiritual, historical, anthropological, and scientific importance of the site has led the African descendant community to take extraordinary measures to seize intellectual control of the project. It sought power and control, not the afterthought of inclusion. With many important issues still unresolved, perhaps the true test of that power is yet to come.

Archaeology is not an end in itself. For many African Americans, it is a conduit, an avenue leading to spiritual rebirth and renewal of our history. Our history is in the bones and in the artifacts excavated from the African Burial Ground. It is tangible, it is real, and it lives through the dead: "Black people see those remains from the Burial Ground as life and death and as part of the continuum of our experience rather than a data pool to be objectified" (Nelson 1993). According to former Mayor David Dinkins:

> Millions of Americans celebrate Ellis Island as the symbol of their communal identity in this land. Others celebrate Plymouth Rock. Until a few years ago, African-American New Yorkers had no site to call our own. There was no place which said, we were here, we contributed, we played a significant role in New York's history right from the beginning . . . . Now we—their descendants—have the symbol of our heritage embodied in lower Manhattan's African Burial Ground. The African Burial Ground is the irrefutable testimony to the contributions and suffering of our ancestors (Dinkins 1994).

Noted historian John Henrik Clarke characterizes the African Burial Ground as a holistic space that touches the lives of African people in this country and might touch the lives of African people all over the world (CPWT 1992:34). The African Burial Ground project has benefited from the participation and interest of people from around the world, from all walks of life, and from many ethnic backgrounds. The project's OPEI and the archaeological and bioanthropology laboratories have been visited by scholars from Japan, East Germany, Korea, the Caribbean, Canada, England, and Ireland, as well as from a multitude of African nations and other countries.

While all African Americans are culturally affiliated, New Yorkers have an immediate and special relationship with the African Burial Ground. No one person or group, however, can speak for the dead. This project and the historical and anthropological resource it represents, can only be enhanced when people with different agendas and ideologies enter into a deeper dialogue as they raise their voices in chorus. The African Burial Ground was designated a National Historic Landmark in February 1993.

ACKNOWLEDGMENTS

We would like to thank Dr. Sherrill D. Wilson, Director of the Office of Public Education and Interpretation for the African Burial Ground, for her contribution to and critique of this work. The contributions of Dr. Warren T. D. Barbour, Dr. Warren R. Perry, and Daniel G. Roberts are also greatly appreciated. We acknowledge the financial support of the U.S. General Services Administration. Noel Pointer and Edmund Francis, two active and dedicated members of the African-American community, have both gone on to join the Ancestors during the course of the African Burial Ground project; may they rest in peace.

REFERENCES

ANGEL, J. LAWRENCE, JENNIFER OLSEN KELLEY, MICHAEL PARRINGTON, AND STEPHANIE PINTER
1987 Life Stresses of the Free Black Community as Represented by the First African Baptist Church, 8th and Vine Streets, Philadelphia, 1824–1846. *American Journal of Physical Anthropology* 74:213–229.

ASSAEL, SHAUN
1993 Warring Archaeologists Scrape Graveyard Booty: No Indiana Jones or King Tut as PhDs ID Slavery's Moldy Bones. *New York Observer*, 7 June:1, 18.

BAKER, VERNON G.
1980 Archaeological Visibility of Afro-American Culture: An Example from Black Lucy's Garden, Andover, Massachusetts. In *Archaeological Perspectives on Ethnicity in America: Afro-American and Asian American Culture History*, edited by Robert Schuyler, pp. 29–36. Baywood, Farmingdale, NY.

BARBOUR, WARREN
1994 The Hidden Heritage of Africa's Descendants. *Federal Archeology Report* 7:1.
1996 African-American Archaeology: Its Past, Present and Future. Invited paper for Conference *Opening Doors*, February 16–17. South Carolina African American Heritage Council and South Carolina Department of Archives and History, Charleston.

BLAKEY, MICHAEL L.
1987 Skull Doctors: Intrinsic Social and Political Bias in the History of American Physical Anthropology. *Critique of Anthropology* 7(2):7–35.
1989 The Future of Anthropology. *Anthropology Newsletter* 30(7):8. David Givens, Newsletter Editor. American Anthropological Association, Washington, DC.
1990 American Nationality and Ethnicity in the Depicted Past. In *Politics of the Past*, edited by Peter Gathercole and David Lowenthal, pp. 38–48. Unwin Hyman, London.
1992a Testimony Before the City Council of New York Concerning the Role of the Howard University Laboratory for Biological Anthropology in the Negro Burying Ground Archaeological Project, 12 April.
1992b Research Design for Temporary Curation and Anthropological Analysis of the "Negro Burying Ground" (Foley Square) Archaeological Population

at Howard University, 11 June. On file with the author.
1996 Skull Doctors Revisited: Intrinsic Social and Political Bias in the History of American Physical Anthropology, with special reference to the work of Aleš Hrdlička. In *Race and Other Misadventures: Essays in Honor of Ashley Montagu in His Ninetieth Year*, edited by Larry T. Reynolds and Leonard Lieberman, pp. 64–95. General Hall, Dix Hills, NY.

BLAKEY, MICHAEL L., TERESA E. LESLIE, AND JOSEPH P. REIDY
1994 Frequency and Chronological Distribution of Dental Enamel Hypoplasia in Enslaved African Americans: A Test of the Weaning Hypothesis. *American Journal of Physical Anthropology* 95(4):371–383.

BLASSINGAME, JOHN W.
1972 *The Slave Community: Plantation Life in the Antebellum South*. Oxford University Press, New York, NY.

BRIDGES, SARA T., AND BERT SALWEN
1980 Weeksville: The Archaeology of Black Community. In *Archaeological Perspectives on Ethnicity in America*, edited by Robert L. Schuyler, pp. 38–47. Baywood, Farmingdale, NY.

BULLEN, ADELAIDE K., AND RIPLEY P. BULLEN
1945 Black Lucy's Garden. *Bulletin of the Massachusetts Archaeological Society* 6(2):17–28.

CITATIONS
1995 Citations on the New York African Burial Ground, 1991–1995. Compiled by the Office of Public Education and Interpretation of The African Burial Ground, New York, NY.

COHEN, PATRICIA
1992 Feds Won't Rebury Remains at Site. *Newsday*, 15 May:21.

COMMITTEE ON PUBLIC WORKS AND TRANSPORTATION (CPWT)
1992 Foley Square Construction Project and the Historic African Burial Ground, New York, NY. *Hearings Before the Subcommittee on Public Buildings and Grounds of the Committee on Public Works and Transportation, House of Representatives*. New York, 27 July. 102nd Congress, second session, Document 102–80. Washington, DC.

COOK, KAREN
1993 Black Bones, White Science: The Battle Over New York's African Burial Ground. *The Village Voice*, 4 May:23–27.

CRAIB, DONALD, AND RALPH JOHNSON
1995 The First Session of the 104th Congress: Examining National Priorities for Archaeology. *Society for American Archaeology Bulletin* 13(4):18.

CRIST, THOMAS A. J., REGINALD H. PITTS, ARTHUR
WASHBURN, JOHN P. MCCARTHY, AND DANIEL G. ROBERTS
    1995 "A Distinct Church of the Lord Jesus": The History,
          Archeology, and Physical Anthropology of the Tenth
          Street First African Baptist Church Cemetery,
          Philadelphia, Pennsylvania. Report prepared by John
          Milner Associates, Inc., West Chester, PA. Submitted
          to Caudet/O'Brien Associates and the Pennsylvania
          Department of Transportation, Philadelphia.

CURTIN, PHILIP D.
    1995 Ghettoizing African History. *Chronicle of Higher
          Education,* 3 March.

DAUGHTRY, REV. HERBERT
    1992 Remarks at an Ecumenical Service for the African-
          American Burial Ground. *Ground Truth* 1(1), 3 April.

DAVILA, YVETTE, KEVIN FOSTER, AND D. PERRY
    1994 Twelve Voices. In *Update: Newsletter of the African
          Burial Ground and Five Points Archaeological
          Projects* 1(3):4–5, 11–12. Sherrill D. Wilson,
          Newsletter Editor. OPEI, New York, NY.

DEETZ, JAMES
    1977 *In Small Things Forgotten: The Archeology of Early
          American Life.* Anchor Press/Doubleday, New York,
          NY.

DELORIA, VINE, JR.
    1995 *Red Earth, White Lies, Native Americans, and the
          Myth of Scientific Fact.* Scribner, New York, NY.

deMARET, PIERRE
    1994 Archaeological and Other Prehistoric Evidence of
          Traditional African Religious Expression. In *Religion
          in Africa,* edited by Thomas D. Blakely, Walter E. A.
          van Beek, and Dennis L. Thomson, pp. 182–195.
          Heinemann, Portsmouth, NH.

DEVIEUX, MARIE-ALICE
    1995 Stamping Grounds. *Update: Newsletter of the African
          Burial Ground and Five Points Archaeological
          Projects* 1(8):6, 13. Sherrill D. Wilson, Newsletter
          Editor. OPEI, New York, NY.

DiBENNARDO R., AND J. V. TAYLOR
    1983 Multiple Discriminant Function Analysis of Sex and
          Race in the Postcranial Skeleton. *American Journal
          of Physical Anthropology* 61:305–314.

DINKINS, DAVID
    1994 Preface. In *Reclaiming Our Past, Honoring Our
          Ancestors: New York's 18th-Century African Burial
          Ground and the Memorial Competition,* edited by
          Edward Kaufman. African Burial Ground Competition
          Coalition, NY.

DIOP, CHEIKH ANTA
    1974 *The African Origin of Civilization: Myth or Reality.*
          Reprint of 1967 edition. Lawrence Hill, Chicago, IL.

DOUGLASS, FREDERICK
    1950 The Claims of the Negro Ethnologically Considered.
          Reprint of 1854 edition. In *The Life and Writings of
          Frederick Douglass,* edited by P. S. Foner, pp. 289–
          309. International, NY.

DRAKE, ST. CLAIRE
    1980 Anthropology and the Black Experience. *The Black
          Scholar* 11:2–31.

DUNLAP, DAVID W.
    1992 Mistake Disturbs Graves at Black Burial Ground:
          Despite Promises, Workers Unearth Bones. *New
          York Times,* 21 February:B3, 5.

EDWARDS AND KELCEY
    1990 *Draft Environmental Impact Statement.* Foley Square
          Proposed Federal Courthouse and Federal/Municipal
          Office Building. Edwards and Kelcey Engineers,
          Inc., New York, NY.

EPPERSON, TERRENCE W.
    1997 The Politics of "Race" and Cultural Identity at the
          African Burial Ground Excavations, New York City.
          World Archaeological Bulletin 7:108–117.

FERGUSON, LELAND
    1992 *Uncommon Ground: Archaeology and Early African
          America, 1650–1800.* Smithsonian Institution Press,
          Washington, DC.

FINDER, ALAN
    1992 U.S. Permanently Halts Digging at Cemetery Site.
          New York Times, 31 July:B3.

FOREMAN, SHEPARD (EDITOR)
    1994 *Diagnosing America: Anthropology and Public
          Engagement.* University of Michigan Press, Ann
          Arbor.

FOSTER, KEVIN
    1994 Dry Bones Gonna' Rise: Black Thought and the
          African Burial Ground of New York. Unpublished
          M.A. thesis, Department of Anthropology, University
          of Texas, Austin.

FOUNTAIN, DANIEL L.
    1995 Historians and Historical Archaeology: Slave Sites.
          The Journal of Interdisciplinary History 26(1).

FRANKLIN, JOHN HOPE
    1989 *Race and History: Selected Essays 1938–1988.*
          Louisiana State University Press, Baton Rouge.

FRASER, GERTRUDE, AND REGINALD BUTLER
1986   Anatomy of a Disinterment: The Unmaking of Afro-American History. In *Presenting the Past Essays on History and the Public,* edited by Susan Porter Benson, Stephen Brier, and Roy Rosenzweig, pp. 121–132. Temple University Press, Philadelphia, PA.

FREDRICKSON, GEORGE M.
1971   *The Black Image in the White Mind: The Debate on Afro-American Character and Destiny, 1817–1914.* Wesleyan University Press, Hanover, NH.

GENERAL SERVICES ADMINISTRATION (GSA)
1993   *Comments of the Draft Research Design for Archaeological, Historical, and Bioanthropological Investigations of the African Burial Ground and Five Points Sites, New York, NY.* General Services Administration, Region 2, 26 Federal Plaza, New York, NY 10013.

HARRINGTON, SPENCER P. M.
1993   Bones and Bureaucrats: New York's Great Cemetery Imbroglio. *Archaeology* 16(2):28–38.

HATIM, IMAM MUHAMMAD
1995   Comments by Imam Muhammad Hatim, UN/NGO Representative, Admiral Family Circle Islamic Community. *Fall Educators Symposium on the New York African Burial Ground,* 4 November, New York, NY.

HINE, DARLENE CLARK (EDITOR)
1986   *The State of Afro-American History: Past, Present, and Future.* Louisiana State University Press, Baton Rouge, LA.

HODDER, IAN
1986   *Reading the Past: Current Approaches to Interpretation in Archaeology.* University of Cambridge, Cambridge, UK.
1992   *Theory and Practice in Archaeology.* Routledge, London, UK.

HOLLOWAY, JOSEPH E. (EDITOR)
1991   *Africanisms in American Culture.* Indiana University Press, Bloomington and Indianapolis.

HOMBERGER, ERIC
1994   *The Historical Atlas of New York City: A Visual Celebration of Nearly 400 Years of New York City's History.* Alice Hudson, Cartographic Consultant. Henry Holt, NY.

HOWARD UNIVERSITY AND JOHN MILNER ASSOCIATES INC. (HUJMA)
1993   *Research Design for Archeological, Historical, and Bioanthropological Investigations of the African Burial Ground (Broadway Block) New York, NY.* 14 December. Howard University, Washington, DC, and John Milner Associates, Inc., New York, NY.

HRDLIČKA, ALEŠ
1918   Physical Anthropology: Its Scope and Aims, Its History and Present Status in America. *American Journal of Physical Anthropology* 1:3–34.
1928   The Full-Blood American Negro. *American Journal of Physical Anthropology* 12:15–30.

ILLUSTRATED HERITAGE
1967   *The Illustrated Heritage Dictionary and Information Book.* Houghton Mifflin, NY.

JACKSON, KENNETH T. (EDITOR)
1995   *The Encyclopedia of New York City.* Yale University Press, New Haven, CT, and The New York Historical Society, NY.

JAMIESON, ROSS W.
1995   Material Culture and Social Death: African-American Burial Practices. *Historical Archaeology* 29:4.

JOHNSON, JAMES WELDON
1969   *Black Manhattan.* Atheneum, NY.

JORDE, PEGGY KING, MARSHA SIMMS, AND FEDERAL STEERING COMMITTEE
1993   *Final Recommendations Report to the U.S. Congress on the Memorialization of the African Burial Ground.* 6 August. On file with the Federal Steering Committee.

KELLEY, JENNIFER OLSON, AND J. LAWRENCE ANGEL
1989   The First African Baptist Church Cemetery: Bioarcheology, Demography, and Acculturation of Early Nineteenth-Century Philadelphia Blacks. Vol. 3, Osteological Analysis. Report prepared by Smithsonian Institution, Washington, DC. Submitted to Redevelopment Authority of the City of Philadelphia, PA.

KERTZER, DAVID I.
1988   *Ritual, Politics and Power.* Yale University Press, New Haven, CT.

KLIMA, DON L.
1992   Construction of Federal Courthouse and Federal Office Building at Foley Square, New York, NY (excerpted letter). *Ground Truth* 1:3.

KUTZ, DAVID (DIRECTOR)
1994   *The African Burial Ground: An American Discovery.* Film, written by Christopher Moore. On file with the Office of Public Education and Interpretation, NY. Also available from National Technical Information Services, National Audio Visual Center, 5285 Port Royal Road, Springfield, VA 22161, (703) 487-4650. Reference Number AVA 19619-VNB1.

LACY, DAVID, AND ROBERT HASENSTAB
1983   The Development of Least Effort Strategies in CRM: Competition for Scarce Resources In Massachusetts. In *The Sociopolitics of Archaeology,* edited by J.

Gero, D. Lacy, and M. Blakey, pp. 31–50. University of Massachusetts, Department of Anthropology, Amherst.

LANDMARKS
1992   National Historic Landmark Designation. Landmarks Preservation Commission, 100 Old Slip, New York, NY.

LAURA, EMILY [EMILYN L. BROWN]
1992   Honoring the Dead: A Bridge Between Two Worlds. *Ground Truth* 1(1).

LEONE, MARK P.
1984   Interpreting Ideology in Historical Archaeology: The William Paca Garden in Annapolis, Maryland. In *Ideology, Power, and Prehistory*, edited by Daniel Miller and Christopher Tilley, pp. 25–35. Cambridge University Press, Cambridge, UK.

LEONE, MARK P., AND PARKER B. POTTER, JR.
1994   Historical Archaeology of Capitalism. *Society for American Archaeology Bulletin* 12(4):14–15. Mark Aldenderfer, Editor. Washington, DC.

LEONE, MARK P., AND PARKER B. POTTER, JR. (EDITORS)
1988   *The Recovery of Meaning*. Smithsonian Institution Press, Washington, DC.

McALLISTER, BILL
1996a   Post Office Jumps at Help from Bugs. *The Washington Post*, 17 May:A21.
1996b   Georgia on Their Minds. *The Washington Post*, 17 May:Weekend 70.

McGUIRE, RANDALL H., AND ROBERT PAYNTER (EDITORS)
1991   *The Archaeology of Inequality*. Blackwell, Oxford, UK.

McKEE, LARRY
1995   Commentary: Is It Futile to Try and Be Useful? Historical Archaeology and the African American Experience. *Northeast Historical Archaeology* 23:1–7.

McMANUS, EDGAR J.
1966   *A History of Negro Slavery in New York*. Syracuse University Press, Syracuse, NY.

MEIER, AUGUST, AND ELLIOTT RUDWICK
1986   *Black History and Historical Profession, 1915-1980*. University of Illinois Press, Urbana, IL.

MEILLASSOUX, CLAUDE
1991   *The Anthropology of Slavery*. The University of Chicago Press, Chicago, IL.

MERRIAM-WEBSTER
1994   *The Merriam-Webster Dictionary*. Merriam-Webster, Springfield, MA.

MINTZ, SIDNEY, AND RICHARD PRICE
1992   *The Birth of African-American Culture: An Anthropological Perspective*. Beacon Press, Boston, MA.

MOORE, SUE MULLINS
1985   Social and Economic Status on the Coastal Plantation: An Archaeological Perspective. In *The Archaeology of Slave and Plantation Life*, edited by Theresa A. Singleton, pp. 141–162. Academic Press, Orlando, FL.

MUHAMMAD, AMAL, ESTER DAWSON, CLAUDIA MILNE, AND CHRIS MOORE
1993   Twelve Voices. *Update: Newsletter of the African Burial Ground and Five Points Archaeological Projects* 1(2):3. Sherrill D. Wilson, Newsletter Editor. OPEI, New York, NY.

NELSON, DOVILLE
1993   Twelve Voices. *Update: Newsletter of the African Burial Ground and Five Points Archaeological Projects* 1(2):4. Sherrill D. Wilson, Newsletter Editor. OPEI, New York, NY.

NOBILE, VINCE
1993   White Professors, Black History: Forays into the Multicultural Classroom, in Teaching Innovations Forum. *Perspectives, American Historical Association Newsletter* 31:6.

OFFICE OF PUBLIC EDUCATION AND INTERPRETATION (OPEI)
1995–   Monthly Reports. Reports on file, OPEI, 6 World
1996   Trade Center, New York, NY.

OFORI-ANSA, KWAKU
1995   Identification and Validation of the Sankofa Symbol. *Update: Newsletter of the African Burial Ground and Five Points Archaeological Projects* 1(8):3. Sherrill D. Wilson, Newsletter Editor. OPEI, New York, NY.

ORSER, CHARLES E., JR.
1996   *A Historical Archaeology of the Modern World*. Plenum, NY.

OXFORD ENGLISH DICTIONARY
1971   *Oxford English Dictionary*. Compact edition. Two volumes. Oxford University Press, Oxford, UK.

PARRINGTON, MICHAEL, AND DANIEL G. ROBERTS
1990   Demographic, Cultural, and Bioanthropological Aspects of a Nineteenth-Century Free Black Population in Philadelphia, Pennsylvania. In A Life of Science: Papers in Honor of J. Lawrence Angel, edited by Jane E. Buikstra. *Scientific Papers of the Center for American Archeology* 6:138–170. Kampsville, IL.

PARRINGTON, MICHAEL, DANIEL G. ROBERTS, STEPHANIE A. PINTER, AND JANET C. WIDEMAN
1989   The First African Baptist Church Cemetery:

Bioarcheology, Demography, and Acculturation of Early Nineteenth-Century Philadelphia Blacks. Vol. 1, Historical and Archeological Documentation; Vol. 2, Artifact Catalog/Faunal Analysis. Report prepared by John Milner Associates, Inc., Philadelphia, PA. Submitted to Redevelopment Authority of the City of Philadelphia, PA.

PATERSON, DAVID A.
1995   Letter to LaRoche, regarding reinstatement of the Task Force for the Oversight of the African Burial Ground, 31 October. Letter on file with Cheryl J. LaRoche.

PAYNTER, ROBERT
1983   Field or Factory?: Concerning the Degradation of Archaeological Labor. In *The Socio-Politics of Archaeology*, edited by J. Gero, D. Lacy, and M. Blakey, pp. 31–50. University of Massachusetts, Department of Anthropology, Amherst, MA.

PEARCE, SUSAN
1995   Collective Amnesia, Knowledge Recovery: The Significance of the African Burial Ground for the Descendant Community. Paper presented at the Annual Meeting of the American Association of Anthropology, Washington, DC.

POTTER, PARKER B., JR.
1991   What Is the Use of Plantation Archaeology? *Historical Archaeology* 25(3):94–107.

RANKIN-HILL, LESLEY M.
1990   Afro-American Biohistory: Theoretical and Methodological Considerations. Unpublished Ph.D. dissertation, Department of Anthropology, University of Massachusetts, Amherst, MA.

RANKIN-HILL, LESLEY M., AND MICHAEL BLAKEY
1994   W. Montague Cobb (1904–1990); Physical Anthropologist, Anatomist, and Activist. *American Anthropologist* 96:74–96.

ROBERTSHAW, PETER
1995   *Knowledge and Power.* Department of Anthropology, California State University, San Bernardino, CA.

RUTSCH, EDWARD S., AND STAFF
1992   *A Research Design for the Broadway Block Including an In-Progress Field Work Summary Report.* Historic Conservation and Interpretation, Inc. Newton, NJ.

S&S REPORTING
1992– Minutes of the Steering Committee on the African
1994   Burial Ground of the City of New York. S&S Reporting, 132 Nassau Street, New York, NY.

1993   *A Public Forum on the Draft Proposal to the U.S. Congress for Commemorating the African Burial*

Ground. City Hall, Public Hearing Chambers, 14 June. S&S Reporting, 132 Nassau Street, New York, NY.

SAMFORD, PATRICIA
1996   The Archaeology of African-American Slavery and Material Culture. *The William and Mary Quarterly,* third series, 53(1):87–114.

SCARUPA, HARRIET JACKSON
1994   Learning from Ancestral Bones. *American Visions* 9:1.

SCHOMBURG, ARTHUR A.
1929   The Negro Digs Up His Past. In *Anthology of American Negro Literature*, edited by V. F. Calverton, pp. 299–323. Modern Library, New York City, NY.

SCHOMBURG CENTER
1992– Minutes. Sound recordings of Federal Steering
1994   Committee Meetings, NY. Schomburg Center for Research in Black Culture, New York, NY.

SCHULDENREIN, JOSEPH
1995   The Care and Feeding of Archaeologists: A Plea for Pragmatic Training in the 21st Century. *Society for American Archaeology Bulletin* 13(3):22.

SCHUYLER, ROBERT L.
1972   Sandy Ground: Archaeological Sampling in a Black Community in Metropolitan New York. *Conference on Historic Sites Archaeology Paper* 7:13–51.

SCRIBNER-BANTAM ENGLISH DICTIONARY
1979   *The Scribner-Bantam English Dictionary.* Revised edition. Bantam, NY.

SINGLETON, THERESA A.
1994   The African-American Legacy Beneath Our Feet. In *African-American Historical Places*, edited by Beth Savage, pp. 33–40. Preservation Press, Washington, DC.

SINGLETON, THERESA A. (EDITOR)
1985   *The Archaeology of Slavery and Plantation Life.* Academic Press, Orlando, FL.

SINGLETON, THERESA A., AND MARK D. BOGRAD
1995   The Archaeology of the African Diaspora in the Americas. *Guides to the Archaeological Literature of the Immigrant Experience in America* 2. The Society for Historical Archaeology, California, PA.

STOKES, I. PHELPS
1915– *Iconography of Manhattan Island, 1498–1909,* Vol. 4.
1928   Robert H. Dodd, NY.

STRICKLAND-ABUWI, LULA
1996   Raise Some Dust: Oppose Burial Ground Office Ousters. *The City Sun*, 3–9 July, 12(25):4, 7.

STUCKEY, STERLING
    1987 *Slave Culture: Nationalist Theory and The Foundations of Black America.* Oxford University Press, NY.

TRIGGER, BRUCE G.
    1989 *A History of Archaeological Thought.* Cambridge University Press, NY.

UPDATE
    1993– *Update: Newsletter of the African Burial Ground and*
    1996   *Five Points Archaeological Projects.* Sherrill D. Wilson, Newsletter Editor. OPEI, New York, NY.

VAN SERTIMA, IVAN
    1986 *Great African Thinkers.* Transaction, New Brunswick, NJ.

WALL, DIANA DIZEREGA
    1995 Silent Witnesses. *Seaport: New York's History Magazine* 29:3.

WAYNE, LUCY B.
    1994 Letters. *African-American Archaeology: Newsletter of the African-American Archaeology Network* (summer) 11:6–7. Thomas R. Wheaton, Newsletter Editor. New South Associates, Stone Mountain, GA.

WEBSTER'S
    1971 *Webster's Third New International Dictionary of the English Language, Unabridged.* G. and C. Merriam, Springfield, MA.
    1983 *Webster's New Universal Unabridged Dictionary.* Second edition. Simon and Schuster, NY.
    1991 *Webster's College Dictionary.* Random House, NY.
    1994 *Webster's New World Dictionary of American English.* Third college edition. Prentice Hall, NY.

WHITE, SHANE
    1991 *Somewhat More Independent: The End of Slavery in New York City, 1770–1810.* University of Georgia Press, Athens, GA.

WILLEN, LIZ, AND PAUL MOSES
    1996 At Top, Blacks Scarce: Few Hold Key Jobs on Rudy's Staff. *Newsday*, 29 April:A2–3.

WILSON, SHERRILL D.
    1995 African American Beginnings. *Update: Newsletter of the African Burial Ground and Five Points Archaeological Projects* 1(7):11–12. Sherill D. Wilson, Newsletter Editor. OPEI, New York, NY.

WOODSON, CARTER G.
    1933 *The Mis-education of the Negro.* Associated Publishers, Washington, DC.

WORLD BOOK DICTIONARY
    1984 *World Book Dictionary.* World Book/Scott Fetzer, Chicago, IL.

WRIGHT, HOWARD D., AND EMILYN L. BROWN (EDITORS)
    1992 *Ground Truth.* Concerned Citizens for the Preservation of African-American Heritage, NY.

YOFFEE, NORMAN, AND ANDREW SHERRATT (EDITORS)
    1993 *Archaeological Theory: Who Sets the Agenda?* Cambridge University Press, Cambridge, UK.

CHERYL J. LAROCHE
JOHN MILNER ASSOCIATES
6 WORLD TRADE CENTER B-26A
NEW YORK, NY 10048

MICHAEL L. BLAKEY
NEW YORK AFRICAN BURIAL GROUND PROJECT
COBB LABORATORY
DEPARTMENT OF SOCIOLOGY AND ANTHROPOLOGY
HOWARD UNIVERSITY
WASHINGTON, DC 20059

Mark E. Mack
Michael L. Blakey

The New York African Burial Ground Project: Past Biases, Current Dilemmas, and Future Research Opportunities

ABSTRACT

The recent excavation of skeletal remains from the African Burial Ground in New York City and their current bioanthropological study and analysis at Howard University is contributing to our understanding of the conditions faced by Africans and their descendants in colonial North America. The complex nature of African enslavement points to the need for interdisciplinary and comparative research on African origins, as well as the biocultural interaction of members of the African Diaspora in the context of European enslavement practices. Research on variation in the biological health status of African-descent communities in the Americas is shown to contribute to knowledge of their social and cultural histories. Through public approval and support, our research team has been able to pursue a more sophisticated and extensive research plan than is usually allowed. The identities thus constructed are complex and compel novel questions. Additionally, our methodological approach empowers the descendant community to engage in its own cultural and historical construction.

Introduction

Approximately five years have passed since the arrival of the New York African Burial Ground skeletal remains at Howard University's Cobb Laboratory for curation and analysis. During this time, cleaning, reconstruction, and recordation of the remains have largely been completed. Historical and archaeological analyses are well advanced, and specialized invasive studies, such as bone and dental chemistry and DNA analysis, have begun. The total research effort contributes to a comprehensive understanding of the conditions faced by Africans and their descendants in colonial North America.

The purpose of this paper is twofold. First of all, based on our scientific findings and the present opportunity to reflect and think beyond the tasks at hand, discussion is focused on the particular areas of skeletal biological research that need to be explored more extensively in the bioarchaeology of the African Diaspora. Secondly, we address the scientific value of public engagement for this particular research project. Special emphasis will be placed on the benefits and challenges of these methodological approaches. Lessons learned along the course of the project might be usefully applied to future bioarchaeological investigations of the African Diaspora.

Areas of Further Research

The African Burial Ground Project's Research Design (Howard University and John Milner Associates 1993) originally pointed to three major research questions regarding those interred at the site: (1) What were their populational and geographical origins; (2) what was the physical quality of life for these largely enslaved Africans; and (3) what can be uncovered about the biocultural transformations of these people from African to African American identities. A fourth question, that of possible modes of resistance, was added in 1995. A wide range of anthropological and interdisciplinary methods is being used to answer these questions. Osteological and dental radiology and chemistry, molecular genetics, history, archaeology, botany, and African art history are but a few of the fields represented in this endeavor. This paper will not address this ongoing interdisciplinary effort in detail but will mainly provide examples of emergent challenges and prospects for biological anthropology that result from the project's biocultural, nonracial, diasporic, and publicly engaged emphases.

An African diasporic perspective locates colonial New York City in relationship to Africa, the American Diaspora, and the Atlantic World. Within this context, the political economy of slavery becomes more apparent, and the identities of African New Yorkers are informed

Historical Archaeology, 2004, 38(1):10–17.
Permission to reprint required.

by histories that extend both to and beyond their enslavement experiences. The scientific approach is also biocultural and biohistorical. It examines the historical interactions of biology and culture such that data on each inform the other and, most importantly, such that human biology is interpreted within historically specific, sociocultural contexts. These specifications defy the use of simplistic, static, biological classifications. Finally, the research design was developed through systematic consultation among representatives of the descendant African American community and scholars, following the African American tradition of scholar activism (Hansberry 1923:8; Drake 1980), as well as recent anthropological approaches to "public engagement" (Forman 1994).

Concerning the issue of population origins, initial studies of mitochondrial DNA sequences extracted from bones of 32 individuals show a high probability of maternal ancestors shared with specific living populations in Benin, Nigeria, Senegal, Niger, and elsewhere. Measurements of 26 intact crania are more similar to the Akan-speaking peoples of Ghana and the Ivory Coast than to 36 other worldwide comparative samples (Howells 1973). Dental morphometric data have been collected for the entire population, many of whom exhibit similar morphometric frequencies to those dentitions from sub-Saharan Africa investigated by Joel Irish (1997). Twenty-three adults exhibit dental modifications (deliberate filing or chipping) with at least eight different styles displayed, ranging from a wedge pattern (Burial 23) to an hourglass pattern (Burial 194). Archaeological and historical data further point to a broad range of specific African origins of New York's population.

Far more research needs to be conducted on comparative populations in order to provide clearer genetic and cultural relationships. The dearth of appropriate West and Central African comparative databases has made it more obvious that we are asking quite different questions of our data than those on which most skeletal biologists and geneticists have previously focused, i.e., the cultural origins of the African Diaspora in America. The traditional anthropological focus on race has led to the lumping of diverse groups within single categories for comparison. For example, had we not been able to collect our own comparative craniometric data

on Asante individuals from the collections of the American Museum of Natural History, the population affiliations would have been with some other group with similar morphology or would have been generically "West African." Anthropological questions regarding human origins focus on East and Southern African populations and hunter-gatherers who were peripheral to the Atlantic trade in human captives.

Dental morphological studies are used to ascertain genetic relationships; however, these studies rarely include references to specific African populations. Instead they are lumped into racial or large regional groupings into which populational and cultural identities dissolve (Irish 1997). Available dental morphology reference casts for comparability are based on Asian and Native American populations (Turner et al. 1991), which might not be representative of African and European variations of dental cusp morphology that would be of interest to us. Several previously unreported cusp patterns have already been observed in the African Burial Ground population that are not associated with known Native American and Asian dental samples. Additionally, identifying individual dental modifications with specific African populations is problematic due to a dearth of published comparative data (Handler 1994), and the observation by Donald Ortner (1966) that identical dental modification patterns can be found in a number of different regional populations. Our extensive survey of the literature supports those views. We are proceeding with the use of dental chemistry to establish the childhood ecosystem relationships of African Burial Ground individuals in combination with genetic, cultural, and historical data in an attempt to pin down population origins. However, in the dynamism of African and diasporic history, we expect that maternal genetic lines, phenotypic similarities, locales, and culture may also often be discordant. Clearly, the use of more diverse data sets enhances our ability to get at the complexity of life and culture histories, yet their use may expand the boundaries of interpretation as easily as they can narrow them.

Problems also emerge for the study of the physical quality of life. Those buried at the site showed skeletal evidence of intense labor, high rates of systemic infection, poor dental health, varying degrees of healthy dental development, a high rate of infant mortality, and relatively early adult mortality.

Historical evidence of Africans engaged in strenuous labor activities is abundantly supported by the analysis of the skeletal remains. Nearly 82% (n = 87) of men and 60% (n = 72) of women with reliable age and sex estimates exhibit changes in bony muscle attachments associated with muscle and ligament tears or persistent excessive strain associated with heavy lifting and moving. Many men sustained spinal injuries as a result of arduous labor, including 11 affected by fractures to the cervical and thoracic vertebrae (Hill et al. 1995). Eight others exhibited fractures to the bones of the feet, which might have resulted from work-related trauma.

Comparisons with Europeans and continental Africans are impeded by the dearth of similar work on archaeological populations representing those groups. Anthropologists have traditionally taken little interest in the bioarchaeology of colonial Africa or of European America, whose remains are seldom excavated. Collections that we might ourselves assess are few and small. Comparisons with the more abundant (yet often crude) mortality and fertility data from church and census documents on colonial Europeans have different biases than skeletal populations and cannot be easily compared. Cemetery returns may provide for the most useful comparisons, but an excavation of historic European cemeteries, such as New York's Trinity Church Yard, would give the most scientifically defensible (and perhaps ethically indefensible) means of knowing the difference between the physical quality of life for colonial Africans and Europeans.

Within-group comparisons are also raising questions that require nonanthropological data sets to adequately answer. We recently found that the skeletal distribution of moderate to severe hypertrophy is similar between men and women; indices of muscle groups being used (that is, aspects of elements that tend to be hypertrophic) are similar between the sexes. Although it is uncertain that women were doing the same work as men, a majority of women's bodies were definitely being exerted and stressed by the labor activities they were performing to the same extent as the bodies of men.

While both genders used neck muscles extensively, women's use of the neck and shoulders are distinctive. Men, however, are more involved in work that uses the muscles and bones of the middle and lower back. We need to better understand how lifting took place differently in men and women as well as other work-related behaviors that may have used culturally specific techniques that have influenced the distribution patterns of spinal degenerative disease. Historical and ethnographic research in conjunction with anatomical information might be required to reveal the significance of these differences much beyond mere statistical quantification.

At least five women sustained cranial base ring fractures, which we believe to be the result of carrying loads on the head (axial loading) that were either too heavy or which led to fracturing of the occipital bone because of a misstep (Hill et al. 1995). Other forms of deliberate and accidental trauma are also being explored.

Heavy labor and general exploitation also affected maternal health and consequently impacted neonatal health as well. Intriguing evidence of this can be found in the mother-infant burial of 12/14. Aged at 35–40 years, the woman's skeletal remains reveal evidence of enlarged muscles of the arms and legs. Additionally, as the result of lifting or pushing a load too heavy for her physical capabilities, she suffered a fracture of her 12th thoracic vertebra that split the spinous process down the middle. The fracture healed, but there was nonunion of the spinous process, exposing the spinal cord to further possible injury.

Burial 12 also suffered from a number of dental pathologies. Many of her teeth were affected by severe caries. Periapical abscessing (tissue and possible alveolar inflammation around the tooth root) resulting in the spread of infection would have been likely, lowering her body's immunoresponse system to environmental insults. Reduced dietary intake due to masticatory pain would also contribute to disease risk.

Finally, her skeleton is riddled with sclerotic periostitis (inflammation of the tissue surrounding bone, ultimately causing dense changes on the bone surface) affecting her clavicles, humeri, ribs, vertebrae, and pelvic bones, indicative of a systemic infection. Her poor overall health should have negatively affected her child (Burial 14) both in utero and early life. Poor mineralization of the neonate's deciduous dentition and the simple but sad fact that both the mother and newborn appear to have died shortly after childbirth is consistent with such effects. Our demographic studies show, moreover, that neonates and 30–35 year old females are in the highest risk categories for mortality for this population.

Skeletal analysis of some of the child burials suggests that children suffered the traumatic effects of heavy labor as well. Burial 39, a six year old (+/- 24 months), has dental developmental defects showing that he/she was ill at birth, implying poor maternal health as well. The eye orbits exhibit pitting characteristic of active anemia at the time of death. Periosteal lesions (mild to moderate inflammations of the tissue surrounding bone) indicate generalized infection, and pitting on the inner corpus of the mandible indicates vitamin C deficiency. The child's humeri exhibit a rugose morphology of the deltoid tuberosities (bony buildup at the muscle attachment as a response to prolonged use of those muscles) and enthesopathies (muscle and/or tendon tears, tearing away bone fragments at the muscle attachment site as well) are present at the insertion of the brachialis muscle on both ulnae (both the deltoid and brachialis muscles are used in lifting). Additionally, the first and second vertebrae exhibit asymmetrical, delayed fusion, possibly due to force or axial loading trauma to the top of the skull. Finally, this child exhibits premature sagittal suture closure (craniosynostosis), which may have congenital, nutritional, and/or mechanical causes (Turvey et al. 1996). Our historical data show that older children were actively involved in the labor activities of the colony; however, the pathologies affecting this child suggest that younger children may have labored as well.

Subadults had 24 occurrences of perimortem fractures probably caused by trauma around the time of death. The remaining fractures (four) were comminuted (the affected bone is broken into many places), partial or greenstick (incomplete fracture with the bending of the bone), or unspecified. All fractures occurred in the humerus, ulna, femur, tibia, and fibula. These perimortem fractures to the arms and legs are most suggestive of accidents, some possibly involving work, or they may be the results of abuse. These traumatic injuries may be better indicators of children's exposure to hazardous work environments than the various degenerative changes of adults who lived long enough to show

such changes that require many years of exposure to repetitive tasks. Interestingly, there is little involvement of the vertebral column in subadult trauma when compared with adults, probably relating to greater spinal involvement in adult work, accidents, and other possible violence.

Concerning the biocultural transformation of Africans into African Americans, further research is needed concerning West and Central African burial practices and mortuary patterns, as well as those of the African Diaspora. For instance, how common is Adinkra symbolism, suggested by the heart-shaped symbol on the coffin of Burial 101, within Akan-derived populations in the diaspora? To what extent are heart-shaped symbols used in non-Akan-speaking African burial practices? The genetic evidence of Akan or other West African origin compelled us to begin our investigation there. We are also examining the site for possible Islamic mortuary patterns as well as possible syncretisms of African traditional and Christian burial practices, all of which reflect on the complex interactions of the various cultural origins of these enslaved Africans. Biologically, Burial 101 may be both related to Akan and nearby Islamic populations. Where does this observation lead us? The more we know, the more we need to know.

The skeletal analysis and research questions of the African Burial Ground have opened areas of future research opportunities that have heretofore been neglected, of gaps in comparative data that must be filled, of historical and cultural complexities that must be explained.

Benefits and Challenges of Public Engagement

The gaps in the comparative databases of anthropology which point to new research opportunities result from the unusual nature of our research questions that are strongly influenced by public engagement. Questions from the descendant community needed responses for the justification of research on the African Burial Ground Project.

Cheryl LaRoche and Michael Blakey (1997) detail the level of awareness and feeling that the African American public had for the African Burial Ground. The descendant community demanded respect in handling the remains, a comprehensive scientific analysis of the site, timely reports on the findings, and general progress of the investigation. The community demanded authority in the decision to ultimately reinter the remains. The African American community was uniquely responsible for altering the course of the U.S. General Services Administration's (GSA) plans for the excavation and use of the site and skeletal remains. Journalists brought the glaring attention of the media. Artists, religious leaders, and other concerned individuals formed commit-tees and coalitions in order to take responsibility for the spiritual, physical, and intellectual aspects of the site. That same awareness and depth of feeling for the skeletal remains is still felt and influences the course of the project, whose final disposition remains uncertain.

Acknowledging GSA as our "business client," we also recognize the descendant community as our "ethical client"; we work for them. The descendant community is not a monolithic entity but is comprised of individuals and groups with widely divergent ideologies, cultural backgrounds, and belief systems as well as various age and socioeconomic groups. Visitors to the Cobb Lab-oratory have included delegates from the Ghana-ian National House of Chiefs, delegations from the Nation of Islam and the American Muslim Council, numerous Christian groups, various gov-ernment officials, interested scholars, university to elementary students, and diverse individuals of the lay public, representing many ethnicities. Those of us who conduct tours must necessarily relate to these various groups from the standpoint of our own sociocultural specificity as we convey knowledge of the site. In this capacity, one takes on a variety of roles from teacher, to tour guide, to "custodian of the ancestors" as some visitors describe our collective role. We are truly both participants and observers of cultural con-struction, engaged in an interactive process that contributes to a more democratic and ethnically plural production of knowledge. In the end, this knowledge contributes to a broadening of identity and ethnic empowerment.

Many individuals and groups who engage this project come with hidden, and sometimes overt, political and social agendas. The extremes range from those African American cultural nationalists claiming the remains as exclusively their own (not to be touched by whites) to some Euramericans who question our ability to conduct scientifically competent research due to racist beliefs about white objectivity and intelligence that renders the notion of black scientists as oxymoronic. However, most visitors, young and old, leave feeling enlightened and moved by so intimate an experience as interpreting slavery from the physical remains and associated burial artifacts of the enslaved. Some seem pleasantly surprised also by the juxtaposition of technical and ethical principles. We do influence politics by being generators of social knowledge and are influenced in turn, yet we seek greater awareness and choice about how we are being influenced. All anthropologists belong to communities with specific political, cultural, and psychological relationships to the people studied. Such constraints and/or opportunities can be denied or recognized and negotiated.

One avenue towards successfully negotiat-ing this political bias is to endeavor to pres-ent evidence, collected and analyzed based on rigorous scientific methods, and to protect the scientific integrity and honesty of the research project. Still, this effort does not exist in a social, political, or cultural vacuum. This does not achieve neutrality. For example, differences simply in the geographical and cultural scope of research (localizing to New York vs. broadening to the diaspora) can alter a population's character, identity, and humanity substantially.

The desire by members of the descendant community for a detailed understanding of the African cultural backgrounds and, therefore, the basic humanity of those who were enslaved, dis-tinguishes these very Africans as people with his-tories and social lives of their own. The terrible experience of being forcefully taken from their homelands, surviving the horrors of the Middle Passage, and being treated as chattel and forced to labor may take on a different significance depending on whether their previous human experiences are or are not also part of the story. The construction of their humanity becomes clear when one presents them as cultural beings upon whom enslavement is thrust. It is from this understanding that the term "enslaved African" arises as preferred over "slave" by descendants. Diasporic studies of colonial America, Africa, the Caribbean, and South and Central America might also enlarge and enrich the understanding and identity of any local population that lived within the diasporic context. More geographical and cultural areas should be studied in order to compare and contrast the experiences of enslaved and free Africans, their varied interactions with other populations, and their place in the creation of the global economy and "Western" society. If one views those interred in the African Burial Ground simply as slaves, as isolated characters in a local colonial American setting, one would ask different kinds of questions and get different answers regarding local artifacts and skeletal remains. The more we understand about Africa and the Caribbean, the more we can see their influences on the people in New York.

The heart-shaped symbol on the coffin lid of Burial 101, only imagined in the local colonial American context, might be assumed as evidence of acculturation. On the other hand, a present understanding of the historical use of such symbols in West Africa suggests an interpretation of African continuity and resistance (Ofori-Ansa 1995; Willis 1998). Alternatively, it is representative of the "dualism" of W.E.B. DuBois (1903), a possibility requiring familiarity with African American scholarship that archaeologists rarely demonstrate. The difference of this story is the result of inclusion, dialogue, and conscious agreement of scientists and the descendant community who recommended that we pay greater attention to their African origins.

The descendant community also expressed the need for the research project to focus on local outreach and public education; the existence of the African Burial Ground and the African contribution to the development of New York was completely absent in local curricula. Thus, our cooperation with the ethical client in disseminating information, or "spreading the word," to very young audiences is a political choice meant to modify identities, social perceptions, and potentially, behavior (a major goal of the descendant community, especially the elders). As a result, the Office of Public Education and Interpretation (OPEI) was established with Dr. Sherrill Wilson, a cultural anthropologist, as its director. Since its creation, OPEI has provided information through its monthly reports to more than 80,000 people worldwide, conducted archaeological lab tours, and held educators' symposia on how the African Burial Ground phenomenon can be utilized in the classroom (Office of Public Education and Interpretation 1995–1998).

We are also activist scholars by taking the African Burial Ground Project internationally to the United Nations Human Rights Commission, when asked by representatives of our ethical client who were seeking "moral compensation" for descendants of the enslaved.

We constantly have to remind the public that more than likely we will never know the names and the exact identities of those buried at the site. Yet, from our research we are providing a comprehensive body of knowledge on some of the earliest Africans brought to these shores unwillingly. Still, their interest in individual identities, not necessarily of great value for modern skeletal biology, is being accommodated by the most complete individual descriptions we can make. Below we provide two examples.

The first example: Burial 101 was a male aged between 30 to 35 years; his healthy dental development and above-average height (5 ft. 10 in. to 6 ft.) indicated a healthy childhood. He was afflicted with a treponemal infection (probably yaws) during early adulthood, suggesting an early life spent in a tropical environment. This infection might have been syphilis, a scourge of the colonial era, sometimes called "French Pox" by the British. Burial 101 led a strenuously active life from his teens to his relatively early death. Skeletal indicators of heavy labor included robust muscle attachments, nonfusion of the tip of the acromion, and a fracture of the spinous process of the 12th thoracic vertebra. Populational and cultural affiliation evidence points to West African origins. In fact, dental modifications of his maxillary central incisors strongly suggest that he was born in Africa and lived there at least until adolescence. Mitochondrial DNA analysis demonstrates affinity with modern West African people, and craniometric analysis indicates a close affinity to the Asante of Ghana. Importantly, the English noted the involvement of the Asante in New York and Caribbean rebellions. The heart-shaped symbol on his coffin lid, if indeed Asante, represents the Adinkra symbol "Sankofa." We might proceed from this individual description to related historical, biological, and archaeological observations of the population.

The second example: Burial 25 was a female aged in her early twenties who was 5 ft. 1 in. tall (during tours we cradle her skull to show our audience her "face"); she was the victim of a violent death by the hands of a person or persons with access to firearms. During excavation a lead musket ball was found lodged in her ribs. The young woman had been shot from behind; the musket ball entered through and shattered her left scapula and third rib, probably injuring her left lung. Additionally, she sustained an oblique fracture to the proximal end of her right radius as the result of someone violently twisting her right arm. Remodeled bone at the margins of the fracture indicates that she might have lived for several days following the assault. Finally, the woman sustained multiple perimortem blunt-force fractures of the lower face. Archaeologists believe she was buried with an elderly African man who had such extensive osteomyelitis as to suggest grave infirmity and debility. What happened to her and what was their relationship are questions to which future research might add clues, while much will remain unanswered.

These simple yet powerful personalizations of otherwise anonymous remains offer a type of data representation that is both desired and valued by the community. Although contrary to the populational approach, it does not conflict with scientific requirements. Interestingly, this sort of human identification does differ from forensic science (which also emphasizes the individual) in important ways. For instance, the forensic anthropologist, whose business clients are frequently law enforcement units or the courts, usually focuses on reporting height, weight, approximate age, race, and cause of death. There is little emphasis on cultural background, and the details of their reports are not presented to elementary school children! In contrast, with the African Burial Ground Project, the descendant community is interested in where each individual comes from, what their lives were like, whether or not they received enough to eat, how many mothers were buried with their children, and so on. These are questions that go to the heart of the cultural and spiritual connection between these skeletal remains and the descendant community. This connection, as evidenced by the personal stories, is strengthened by the populational and statistical approaches that we are also taking.

Concluding Remarks

Many of the lessons we have learned through our experience with the African Burial Ground Project can be applied to other research efforts. The major lesson is that the descendant community has to be an integral part of any research effort, both to address its concerns and sensitivities and to empower the community to engage in its own cultural and historical construction. Further, with the support of the descendant community, the research effort becomes more diverse, requires more time for public interaction, and is therefore better received and supported. In our case, more extensive research can be conducted than is usually allowed. The project's directions have led to methodological problems that have exposed gaps in the comparative database as a result of past biases in physical anthropology and bioarchaeology.

It is questionable whether the project would have had the same level of visibility and significance were another approach taken, marked by both less community involvement and conflict with the biases of bioarchaeology. The project has greatly contributed to a broadened public knowledge of anthropology and increased public concern for previously neglected African and African American sites. Paying lip service to or providing token involvement of the descendant community is not enough and often is counter-productive (Blakey 1997).

Prior to our involvement and utilization of the approach presented here, immediate reburial appeared to be imminent due to antagonisms among excavators, the government, and the descendant community. The earlier scope of research was both local and narrow rather than diasporic and interdisciplinary. The methodological focus had been on human identification involving racial typology rather than on the culture, history, and specific genetics of the people interred. Anthropologists did not seek out community involvement and direction. In essence, the earlier approach led to public dismay and, ultimately, outrage. Until the discipline views descendant communities as integral participants in the comprehensive research effort, there will always be the real risk of lost research opportunities and scientifically and humanistically problematic and ineffective investigations of the African Diaspora.

ACKNOWLEDGMENTS

The authors wish to acknowledge the dedication and contributions of the scholars who have participated in the multidisciplinary research efforts of the New York African Burial Ground Project: Edna G. Medford, Linda Heywood, and Selwyn Carrington (history); Warren Perry, Jean Howson, Leonard Bianchi, Christopher DeCorse, Kofi Agorsah, and Augustin Holl (archaeology); Kwaku Ofori-Ansa (art history); Fatimah L. C. Jackson and Shomarka O. Y. Keita (biological anthropology).

REFERENCES

BLAKEY, MICHAEL L.
1997 Past Is Present: Comments on "In the Realm of Politics: Prospects for Public Participation in African-American Plantation Archaeology." *Historical Archaeology,* 31(3):140–145.

DRAKE, ST. CLAIR
1980 Anthropology and the Black Experience. *The Black Scholar,* 11:2–31.

DUBOIS, W.E.B.
1903 *The Souls of Black Folk.* Reprinted in 1997 by Bedford Books, Boston, MA.

FORMAN, SHEPARD (EDITOR)
1994 *Diagnosing America: Anthropology and Public Engagement.* University of Michigan Press, Ann Arbor.

HANDLER, JEROME S.
1994 Determining African Birth from Skeletal Remains: A Note on Tooth Mutilation. *Historical Archaeology,* 28(3):113–119.

HANSBERRY, WILLIAM L.
1923 *Howard University Record,* 17:8.

HILL, MARY C., MARK E. MACK, AND MICHAEL L. BLAKEY
1995 Women, Endurance, Enslavement: Exceeding the Physiological Limits. Skeletal Biology IV: Women's Bodies, Women's Lives: Biological Indicators of Labor and Occupation. Abstract, *American Journal of Physical Anthropology, Supplement,* 20:110–111.

HOWARD UNIVERSITY AND JOHN MILNER ASSOCIATES, INC.
1993 Research Design for Archeological, Historical, and Bioanthropological Investigations of the African Burial Ground (Broadway Block) New York, NY. 14 December. Howard University, Washington, DC, and John Milner Associates, Inc., New York, NY.

HOWELLS, W. W.
1973 Cranial Variation in Man. *Peabody Museum of Archaeology and Ethnology Papers,* Vol. 67. Cambridge, MA.

IRISH, JOEL D.
1997 Characteristic High- and Low-Frequency Dental Traits in Sub-Saharan African Populations. *American Journal of Physical Anthropology,* 102:455–467.

LAROCHE, CHERYL J., AND MICHAEL L. BLAKEY
1997 Seizing Intellectual Power: The Dialogue at the New York African Burial Ground. *Historical Archaeology,* 31(3):84–106.

OFFICE OF PUBLIC EDUCATION AND INTERPRETATION
1995–1998 Monthly Reports. Office of Public Education and Interpretation, 6 World Trade Center, New York, NY. [Interim mailing address for OPEI offices is 201 Varick St., Room 1021, New York, NY 10014.]

OFORI-ANSA, KWAKU
1995 Identification and Validation of the Sankofa Symbol. *Update: Newsletter of the African Burial Ground and Five Points Archaeological Projects,* 1(8):3. (Office of Public Education and Interpretation, 6 World Trade Center, New York, NY.) [Interim mailing address for OPEI offices is 201 Varick St., Room 1021, New York, NY 10014.]

ORTNER, DONALD J.
1966 A Recent Occurrence of an African Tooth Type Mutilation in Florida. *American Journal of Physical Anthropology,* 25:177–180.

TURNER, CHRISTY G., II, CHRISTIAN R. NICHOL, AND G. RICHARD SCOTT
1991 Scoring Procedures for Key Morphological Traits of the Permanent Dentition: The Arizona State University Dental Anthropology System. In *Advances in Dental Anthropology,* Marc A. Kelley and Clark S. Larsen, editors, pp. 13–32. Wiley-Liss, New York, NY.

TURVEY, TIMOTHY A., KATHERINE W. L. VIG, AND RAYMOND J. FONSECA (EDITORS)
1996 *Facial Clefts and Craniosynostosis: Principles and Management.* W.B. Saunders, Philadelphia, PA.

WILLIS, W. BRUCE
1998 *The Adinkra Dictionary: A Visual Primer on the Language of Adinkra.* The Pyramid Complex, Washington, DC.

MARK E. MACK
DEPARTMENT OF ANTHROPOLOGY AND SOCIOLOGY
W. MONTAGUE COBB BIOLOGICAL ANTHROPOLOGY
LABORATORY
ROOM 230, DOUGLASS HALL
2441 SIXTH ST. NW
HOWARD UNIVERSITY
WASHINGTON, DC 20059

MICHAEL L. BLAKEY
DEPARTMENT OF ANTHROPOLOGY
WASHINGTON HALL 103
THE COLLEGE OF WILLIAM AND MARY
WILLIAMSBURG, VA 23187

ROBERT K. FITTS

The Landscapes of Northern Bondage

ABSTRACT

In his 1988 book, *Black Yankees*, William Piersen argued that quartering slaves within their owners' homes led to a mild and paternalistic form of slavery in New England. This article challenges this position by arguing that in Narragansett, Rhode Island, shared domestic space was an important aspect of slave control. Quartering slaves within the main house allowed planters to monitor their actions and led to a form of racial segregation at meals, church, and in burials designed to mark slaves as aliens and teach them "their place." Slaves responded by circumventing monitored space and turning segregated space to their advantage by using this unsupervised time to socialize among themselves. This conflict between the masters' desire to monitor their bondsmen—the term used in historical accounts and documents—and the slaves' attempts to escape this surveillance typified Narragansett master/slave relations. In this manner, slavery in Narragansett, Rhode Island, was strikingly similar to southern slavery.

Introduction

Soon after its publication, William Piersen's (1988) *Black Yankees* was hailed as a "superior piece of scholarship," and, indeed, it is an important contribution to African-American history (Jacobs 1989:397). Piersen, a folklorist, examined the formation of African-American culture in the New England colonies and was the first to show how northern slaves kept alive African traditions and symbols to "resist the constant onslaught of demeaning Euroamerican prejudices" (Piersen 1988: 146). Yet, strangely, Piersen did not see northern master/slave relations as characterized by conflict. Instead, he concluded that paternalism typified most New England master/slave relationships. He wrote, "in its paternalism, Yankee bondage followed an already established regional pattern of treating white servants as part of their masters' patriarchal families" (Piersen 1988:146). Piersen's

Historical Archaeology, 1996, 30(2):54–73.
Permission to reprint required.

conclusion partly rests on the argument that "most Yankee masters and their slaves shared a common residence and daily activities. This led to a necessary intimacy, fostering both a relatively mild form of servitude and a kind of household kinship" (Piersen 1988:146). This paper takes a contrary position regarding slaveholders and their bondsmen—the term used in historical accounts and thus retained in this study. It argues that on the plantations of Narragansett, Rhode Island, shared domestic space led to conflict between the slave-holders' methods of spatial control and the bondsmen's efforts to resist them. This position, in turn, highlights the similarities between northern and southern slavery.

The Narragansett Plantations

Narragansett is a 19-×-14-mi. area in southeastern Rhode Island bordering on Narragansett Bay and Block Island Sound. Presently, it contains the towns of North and South Kingstown, Charlestown, and Narragansett (Figure 1). For most of the 18th century, Narragansett was dominated by mixed-crop and cattle-raising plantations and contained the highest black to white population ratio in New England. In this article, "slave plantation" is defined as an agricultural enterprise where slaves produced goods for the world market while their owners controlled all profits, but rarely participated in agricultural labor (Mintz 1959; Padilla 1959; Thompson 1959; Singleton 1985; Curtin 1990). Thus, slave plantations differ in structure, not just size, from farms. Farms are best defined as "a settlement for which a family supplies most of the labor with little help from the outside and where goods are produced" first for subsistence and secondly for the market (Singleton 1985:2). In Narragansett, plantations were characteristically smaller than in the South. Most contained 1,000–2,000 acres, but several exceeded 4,000 acres (Fitts 1995). These plantations did not produce a cash crop; instead, cereals, dairy products, and livestock were raised for export to the Caribbean and American South. Probates indicate that during the 18th century, the average planter owned 43 head of cattle and 126 sheep,

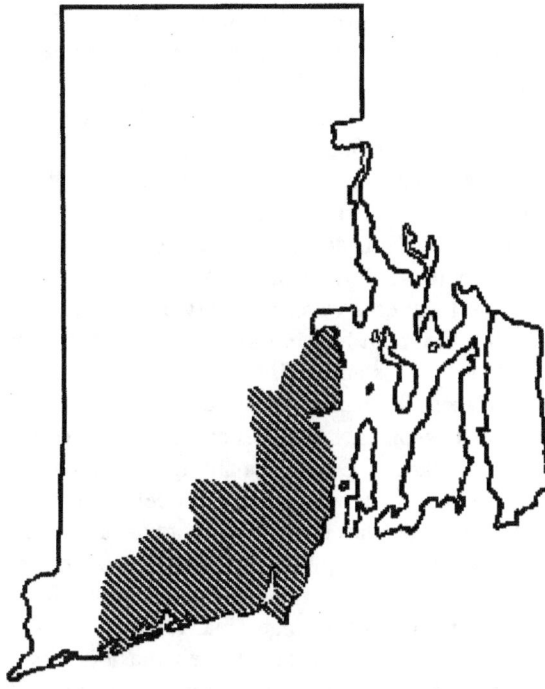

FIGURE 1. Map of Rhode Island showing, in grey, the location of Narragansett.

although more prosperous planters often owned over 150 head of cattle, 40 horses, and 500 sheep (South Kingstown Probates 1704–1789).

For labor, planters relied on African slaves, supplemented by Native American slaves and indentured servants and English free laborers. Oral tradition states that the wealthiest planters owned between 40 and 60 slaves (e.g., Updike 1847; Bicknell 1920; Greene 1942:321; McLoughlin 1978: 65); however, no documentary evidence supports this view. A review of probate inventories, wills, and census data suggests that wealthy planters actually owned between 10 and 20 slaves, while the average slave-holder owned four (South Kingstown Probates 1704–1789). From 1730 to 1770, at the plantation economy's height, roughly 13 percent of Narragansett's population was enslaved (Douglass 1753; Bartlett 1858; Bicknell 1920; Greene 1942). Yet, in South Kingstown, where most of the plantations were concentrated, one out of every four people was a black slave (McBurney 1981:96). For comparison, during the same period, slaves made up roughly 3 percent of New England's population and about 34 percent of the population in the antebellum South (Patterson 1982:483; Piersen 1988).

The Narragansett plantations' prosperity was short-lived. The region's plantation economy developed in the first two decades of the 18th century and was already in decline by the 1760s (McBurney 1981). Although Narragansett's original settlers purchased large tracts of land, these were gradually subdivided as each generation disbursed their holdings among their offspring. McBurney (1981:200) notes that planters needed 300–1,000 acres to create sufficient surplus to make exporting profitable. By the 1760s, many planters left their children just over the 300-acre minimum; a generation later, plots were proportionally smaller (McBurney 1981:202–203). Smaller land holdings led to overworked soil, which further decreased the agricultural output. This decreased production, combined with the economic problems stemming from the Seven Years' War (1756–1763) and the British occupation of Newport (1776–1779), forced many small planters to abandon exporting agricultural goods as their main source of income. The emancipation act of 1784, which freed all slaves born after 1 March, and the many subsequent manumissions, pushed planters to rely more on indentured servants and wage laborers. As a result, by the early 19th century, only a handful of plantations continued to produce for the overseas market. Despite the plantations' demise, slavery in Rhode Island continued until the death of its last slave in 1859 (McLoughlin 1986:106–107).

Domestic Space in Narragansett

Although William Piersen did not empirically analyze slave housing, he correctly states that most northern slaves lived within their owners' houses. In Narragansett, oral tradition stated that most masters housed their slaves in the main house or other existing structures, rather than building them separate quarters. For example, Wilkins Updike (1847: 175) wrote, "some of the large mansion houses of the slave-holders, with spacious gable roofs, are now standing, the garret rooms in which, with their outhouses, were the sleeping places of the slaves.'' Other oral traditions noted that slaves sometimes lived in wings of the planters' houses. For example, a 1879 description of the Rowland Robinson house states, "originally, the house including the negro quarters was one hundred and five feet in length, the stone foundation of the whole being now visible; but the present structure measures but fifty-four feet front" (Hazard 1879:9). George Rome, who owned the most elaborate estate in Narragansett, also housed his slaves in an attached wing: "In the basement of the Rome mansion, on one side of the kitchen, with its vast fire-place, where his famous dinners were wont to be roasted, baked and boiled, there were to be seen, until the recent demolishment [*sic*] of the house, a group of tiny white-washed bedrooms where a part of his numerous retinue of slaves was lodged" (MacSparran 1899:79).

South and North Kingstown probate inventories also show that planters kept their slaves in, or near, the main house. All surviving probate inventories from South Kingstown dating between 1704 and 1789 were examined to locate slave sleeping/living quarters. Ninety-two of the 195 surveyed inventories listed slaves among the probated property. Of these 92, only 19 (21%) noted slave sleeping areas. These were usually identified by the location of the slaves' beds. The paucity of probates listing slave bedding is a direct result of the inventorers' methods. In South Kingstown, inventorers rarely recorded items in a room-by-room format. Instead, most inventories merely listed the deceased's valuables by type. Thus, bedding from the entire house was often recorded consecutively, while slaves were usually listed with cattle. This convention has made it impossible to reconstruct where the slaves were quartered for 79 percent of South Kingstown's probated slave-holders.

The 19 probates which listed where the slaves slept are representative of South Kingstown's slaveholders. This group contains both wealthy planters, who owned over 10 slaves, and less wealthy slaveholders, who owned only one or two bondsmen. Table 1 lists the probated individual, date, number of slaves, and their sleeping place. Note that one inventory from North Kingstown was added to this sample. Some inventories did not state the precise location of slave bedding; therefore, some interpretation is necessary. In Table 1, the phrase "on farm" refers to entries where slave bedding was listed between farm animals and produce, which suggests that they lived in an outbuilding, though this cannot be firmly established. The phrase "in storage area" means that slave bedding was listed along with tools and dry goods, but no animals. These locations were probably in a back room within the main house, but this interpretation also cannot be substantiated.

Of these 20 planters, four definitely housed their slaves in separate structures and three housed them "on the farm." Of the remaining 13 planters, two housed their slaves in the attic or cellar, two in the kitchen, one placed them in storage areas, seven placed their slaves in the central part of the main house, and one planter quartered his slaves in both the kitchen and a storage area. Records show that slaves slept on all stories of their masters' houses. Of the 13 planters who quartered their slaves in the main house, five put them on the ground floor, six put them on the second floor, one put them in the cellar, and one put them in the garret. Thus, the limited evidence from Narragansett supports Piersen's assertion that most northern slaves shared domestic space with their owners.

Nevertheless, there is little evidence from Narragansett that shared space "led to a necessary intimacy, fostering both a relatively mild form of servitude and a kind of household kinship" (Piersen 1988:146). Piersen offered no evidence in *Black Yankees* to support this conclusion but, instead, seemed to rely on the belief that increased knowledge about other races leads to mutual understanding and compassion. Recent studies, however, show that living in the main house may have given slaves certain material privileges, but life in this house could also resemble a prison (e.g., Webber 1978:66; Jones 1990). Former slaves remembered always being at their masters' beck and call and having no time for themselves, always being scrutinized and often punished for minor mistakes, and not being able to slip away during the nights to visit slaves on other plantations (Webber 1978:66; Jones 1990).

In Narragansett, quartering slaves within the

TABLE 1
LOCATIONS OF SLAVE SLEEPING QUARTERS

Name	Date	No. of Slaves	Location
R. Smith	1692	8	Stone house
R. Robinson	1710	9	Old house chamber
R. Helm	1712	2	Master's chamber
S. Hazard	1727	3 (+ 4 servants)	On farm
T. Potter	1728	5 (+ 1 servant)	In storage area
W. Gardner	1732	13	Cellar
R. Hannah	1736	4	Barn
I. Potter	1739	2	West lower room
J. Case	1739	4	Lower bedroom
J. Wilson	1740	3 (+ 1 servant)	Garret
A. Shearman	1742	4	Kitchen chamber
R. Wilcox	1742/3	2	On farm
H. Gardner	1744	7	West chamber
G. Hazard	1746	10	On farm
J. Hazard	1746/7	12	Kitchen and storage area
R. Hazard	1752	5	Kitchen
B. Holway	1761	2	North chamber
W. Congdon	1762	1	East chamber
R. Robinson	1762	2	Separate quarters
R. Hazard	1771	3 (+ 1 servant)	Kitchen

Sources: R. Smith (1692); South Kingstown Probates (1704–1789).

main house helped planters control their bondsmen's movement. For example, Jeremiah Wilson's and William Gardner's slaves were quartered in the easily locked garret and cellar. Few, however, were able to monitor their slaves' behavior like Rowse Helm. Helm quartered his adult slaves, Jack and Nan, in his own bedroom (South Kingstown Probates 1704–1789, 1:50–53). Even slaves who lived on different floors than their masters found it difficult to escape their owners' surveillance. For example, Reverend MacSparran's slave Hannibal discovered the difficulty of slipping out of his Narragansett master's house during the night. For the next morning MacSparran got up early, noticed the transgression, and promptly punished Hannibal (MacSparran 1899:52). In this manner, quartering slaves within the main house, or in nearby buildings, allowed planters more easily to detect absences and other transgressions of discipline, for which the slaves were quickly punished.

Although it was probably only an unintentional by-product of living in the master's house, shared domestic space also helped control slaves by denying them their own space and, thus, part of their cultural autonomy. In many West African societies, space "had a psychological, familial, and religious significance . . . beyond its economic meaning" (Jones 1981:2, cf. 1986, 1993). As a result, "most Africans built houses according to ritual requirements, and their location and structure had spiritual significance" (Sobel 1987:72). The creation of symbolic space was thus an important part of many West Africans' worldview, yet those enslaved in Narragansett had little chance to alter their physical surroundings. This acted as yet another reminder that planters controlled most aspects of their daily lives.

The lack of their own space also hampered slaves' ability to practice African traditions openly and build a culture of resistance. In the South, slave quarters were the site of activities and rituals that kept alive ties with an African past. In the privacy of the quarters, slaves practiced West African religious ceremonies (e.g., Brown and Cooper 1990) and created symbols of their African past through material culture (e.g., Vlach 1991; Ferguson 1992). Furthermore, southern quarters also gave slaves the privacy to keep contraband material culture. Some of these goods were used in rituals (e.g., Brown and Cooper 1990), but most were secular objects stolen from whites or tools such as firearms or writing implements forbidden to slaves (Fairbanks 1984). Often these objects were hidden in pits dug into the quarters' floors (Kelso 1984). These pits are common on southern slave sites, suggesting that they were an important part of African-Americans' strategies of resistance. With their beds stuck in the corners of the main house, Narragansett slaves did not have their southern counterparts' limited privacy to keep alive many African-derived rituals and material culture or to store forbidden goods.

The southern quarters also provided slaves with a relatively safe area to speak openly. In the quarters, slaves instructed their children, and each other, on how best to handle their masters and on the methods and problems of escape and resistance (Webber 1978). They shared news from outside the plantation, they told jokes at their masters' expense, and they created a form of Christianity which inverted the social structure by promising them salvation and their masters eternal hell (Rawick 1972; Raboteau 1978; Jones 1990). This discourse allowed slaves to maintain a hold over their lives both by resisting degradation and by giving them the knowledge to mitigate their masters' dominance. By boarding their slaves in the main house, Narragansett planters gave their slaves fewer opportunities to speak openly. This made it difficult for slaves in Narragansett to practice traditions and exchange information to help them resist their masters' domination.

Therefore, contrary to Piersen's (1988:146) statement, the boarding of slaves within the main house did not foster closer relations between master and slave but, instead, gave planters fuller control over their bondsmen. Piersen mistakes the lack of open conflict caused by the masters' tight control over their households' space for the lack of slave resistance. He does not consider that this proximity denied northern slaves the same freedom of movement and security to create a subordinate culture

that southern slaves had. This proximity undercut the Narragansett slaves' ability to resist domination and, as a result, was one of the more successful strategies of control within the planters' arsenal. The proximity of the planters' and slaves' living quarters also fostered another form of spatial control: ritual segregation.

Segregation and the Ideology of Alienation

Although Narragansett slaves lived within the main house, spatial segregation was imposed during rituals, such as meals, church services, and burials. Cross-cultural studies show that in nearly all societies where masters and slaves share physical space, slaves are symbolically marked as inferior outsiders (Park 1937; Finley 1980; Donley 1982; Patterson 1982; Epperson 1990; Meillassoux 1991). This line was drawn, in part, because slaves who lived in the main house saw their masters and their families during intimate moments. In some households, slaves had access to their masters' bedrooms to tend fires and wake their masters each morning. Some slaves even helped their masters bathe and dress (Owens 1976). To maintain a feeling of privacy during these intimate moments, whites viewed slaves more as things than as full human beings: "Sometimes contacts were close, but impersonal, bordering on intimate burlesque. The slave Henry Bruce remembered being called as a boy to the side of his unclad mistress in her bathroom merely to pour additional water for a bath. She seemed, he recalled, aloof, almost unaware of his presence, though he clearly was not of hers" (Owens 1976: 115).

Robert Park (1937:xix) argued, "it was quite possible, on the plantation, and particularly in the case of the house servants and the master's family, to maintain the most intimate relationships between master and slave provided the social ritual defining and maintaining the caste relationship was maintained in its integrity." Planters used the ideology of alienation to maintain this social distance. French anthropologist Claude Meillassoux (1991) first developed the concept of alienation better to understand African slavery. He concluded that the fundamental characteristic of the institution was that slaves were incorporated into society as aliens. Aliens, according to Meillassoux, were people who lacked kinship ties within their society. In most societies, this view precluded the individual from becoming a full social being with rights to property, political power, and a legitimate family. It also provided the legal and ethical basis for exploitation. Orlando Patterson (1982), who studied slavery cross-culturally, and M. I. Finley (1980), who examined classical slavery, found that most slave-holding societies developed ideologies for treating their bondsmen as aliens. Since most societies do not enslave members of their own society, the ideology of alienation provided a rationale for classifying slaves as outsiders. Furthermore, the ideology helped rationalize owning fellow humans by depicting slaves as inferior, thus suggesting that they either deserved their fate or benefited by serving a superior race. To insure their alien status, most cultures bestowed slaves with exotic or animal-like characteristics and developed racist ideologies to justify their exploitation. To begin with, slaves were taken from distant, unrelated societies but were all called by a common name. This group was assigned physical and mental traits that made them inferior, but hardy slaves (Meillassoux 1991:67, 74–75). Further, "because of their alien origin, slaves were permanently relegated to the category of beings of a different and naturally inferior species: tolerated if they kept their distance, rejected if they showed the slightest desire to identify themselves with 'humans'" (Meillassoux 1991:75).

In Anglo-America, the ideology of alienation manifested itself in racist attitudes towards Africans. As the enslavement of Africans progressed, Europeans increasingly saw Africans as inferior and even animal-like. Whites associated negroid features with ugliness and claimed that Africans had lower intelligence than other races. A myth developed that Africans were ideal for physical labor but lacked the mental capacity to engage in intellectual pursuits. As a result, many Europeans concluded that God had created Africans to serve them. By the mid-18th century, racism against Africans and African Americans was so entrenched that most Anglo-Americans unquestionably accepted the ideology.

Once slaves were integrated into their new society, the process of alienation continued. The ideology was reinforced by symbolically separating slaves from the rest of society and marking them as inferior. Common markers included special clothes, special names, branding, tattoos, shaved heads, racial characteristics, and specific rules of etiquette (Patterson 1982:58–62). This step reinforced their alien status by making it obvious to both captives and others that they were slaves. Some slave-holders intentionally used these symbols of alienation. For example, one Texas planter was aware of the symbolic power of etiquette and wrote, "in a well regulated community, a negro takes off his hat in addressing a white man. . . . Where this is not enforced, we may always look for impudent and rebellious negroes" (in Stampp 1956:145–146). These masters hoped that ritual degradation would undermine the slaves' self-esteem and cause them to internalize their alien status, thus making them easier to control, since they would accept their position as the natural outcome of their inferiority. If this did not occur, planters hoped that at least the process of alienation would teach slaves "to know and keep their places, [and] to feel the difference between master and slave" (in Stampp 1956:145).

Other slave-holders, however, were not as conscious of the role of these symbols in slave control. Instead, this knowledge was part of these slave-holders' "practical consciousness." Anthony Giddens (1984:xxiii) defined practical consciousness as "all the things which actors know tacitly about how to 'go on' in the contexts of social life without being able to give them direct discursive expression." This knowledge stems from the routines of daily life and enables people to accomplish daily tasks and participate in social encounters without expending undo energy on consciously thinking through each act. Giddens (1984:375) noted, however, that practical consciousness differs from the subconscious because, if pressed, actors can explain the reasons behind their behavior. Thus, masters followed their practical consciousness and marked slaves with symbols of alienation because it "felt right." This process was recursive. Marking slaves with symbols of alienation "felt right" because it followed social norms, and using the symbols perpetuated these norms. In this manner, these slave-holders followed the same patterns of symbolic control that other masters consciously employed. It is important to note that slave-holders may have consciously employed some symbols of alienation, and only followed the prevailing norms with other symbols. Thus, slave-holders cannot be neatly classified into those who consciously used symbolic control and those who did not.

The symbols of alienation also had an unintended effect. They reinforced the slaves' alien status in the masters' minds. This helped masters view slaves as not quite human, thus removing some of the moral objections to slavery. Denying the slaves' intrinsic humanity was especially important when masters and slaves shared intimate space, as it allowed planters to view slaves as aliens to whom the etiquette of privacy and personal space did not apply. Through symbolically separating and degrading them, planters made it clear that sharing intimate space and time did not alter their status as slaves. Although Narragansett planters used a variety of symbols to mark their slaves as aliens (Fitts 1995), this article focuses exclusively on how planters alienated their slaves by segregating them during rituals, such as meals, church services, and burials.

Segregation in Narragansett

In the early modern period, Europeans, and consequently many Americans, attached great importance to seating during meals, making them appropriate rituals for alienating slaves (Braudel 1973; Collomp 1989:514–515; Fischer 1989:74; Flandrin 1989:270–271). In Narragansett, slaves were physically and symbolically separated from the rest of the family during meals. Oral tradition states that the house was divided into the planters' relations, known as the ''parlor'' family, and the ''kitchen'' family, which consisted of the slaves (Hazard 1879: 12). The two parts of the family were named after where they ate. In most households throughout New England, slaves were not allowed to eat at their masters' table and were often served their masters' leftovers (Piersen 1988:31–32). The stories of Thomas Hazard (1879, 1915) show that this pattern

was followed in Narragansett. For example, one evening a planter served both mutton and duck for dinner: ''The mutton, however, had proved so delicious, that none of the great-room folks did more than taste a morsel of the game ducks, and the whole of one and more than half of the other went to the kitchen table'' (Hazard 1915:71). By segregating slaves and relegating them to inferior stations, masters reinforced their status as aliens and their low position in the social hierarchy.

Although this separation was probably meant to teach slaves ''their place,'' its effect is unclear. Some slaves may have internalized their inferior status. For example, in nearby Massachusetts, when Lucy Prince, a freed slave ''visited a white family . . . she . . . refused a place at the table, saying, 'No Missy, no. I know my place' '' (Piersen 1988:31–32). Although it is unclear if Prince internalized her alien status, or was just acting deferentially, evidence suggests that other slaves relished this separation at dinner time. One of the difficulties of Narragansett slave life was escaping the masters' constant surveillance. Some slaves manipulated the strategy of alienation to their advantage by using this time to talk freely among themselves. Thomas Hazard (1915:83–85) remembered how, in the early 19th century, his grandfather's black slaves and servants told stories about Africa and sang African songs in the privacy of the kitchen. Scholars have shown that African stories and songs were an important part of slave culture (e.g., Webber 1978; Stuckey 1987; Robinson 1990). These oral traditions kept alive ties to a free past in Africa and emphasized pride in their African heritage. This was especially important to counter their masters' degradation of everything African. Often these traditions contained a lesson or moral which taught slaves how to interact with whites and survive under slavery. Thus, these stories and songs were a significant part of the slaves' resistance to the planters' ideologies of control. These segregated meals, instead of instilling slaves with an inferiority complex, gave slaves the opportunity to keep alive African traditions which combated white racist ideologies.

No matter how segregated meals affected slaves, there is no doubt that it affected whites. Many whites were so convinced by their own racist ideologies that they found sharing their tables with blacks to be repulsive. These whites saw a breakdown in the segregated space as a calamity. For example, in the 1690s, John Saffin chastised his tenant Thomas Shepard for allowing his slave Adam to eat at the family's table, because it contributed to a breakdown in discipline (Saffin 1701). Approximately 20 years later, Sarah Knight, a wealthy Bostonian traveling through eastern Connecticut, disapprovingly reported that farmers were "too indulgent . . . to their slaves: suffering too great familiarity from them, permitting them to sit at [the] table and eat with them, (as they say to save time,) and into the dish goes the black hoof as freely as the white hand" (Winship 1935:37–38). The separation of whites and blacks during meals resulted from the slaves' status as inferior aliens, but it also reinforced their lowly status in the eyes of elite whites. This distinction helped planters view slaves as social nonbeings to whom the rules of white society did not apply.

Segregation continued at Sunday church services. In 18th-century Narragansett, the majority of planters belonged to St. Paul's Anglican Church (Woodward 1971:65). According to folklore, planters attended these services in their best clothes, riding their favorite horses, and attended by their personal slaves (Carpenter 1924:77–91). The morning began with Reverend MacSparran (1899:6) "instructing the negro's [sic], in preaching, praying and praising." Then, white church members entered and sat in their assigned pews, while slaves climbed the staircase to their seats in the balcony (Figure 2). St. Paul's slave balcony was approximately 5 ft. wide and stretched along three sides of the church. It was reached by a staircase located on the right-hand side in the back of the church. Slaves sat on wooden bleacher-style benches which raised them high enough to see the pulpit. The gallery's position suggests that slaves were also forced to take communion after whites, thus segregating even this aspect of the service. Once seated, northern ministers, like their southern brethren, introduced slaves to the aspects of Christianity that upheld their bondage (Parish 1989). Sermons often emphasized the virtues of loyalty, honesty, and chastity and stressed the acceptance of authority and the importance of

FIGURE 2. View of the interior of St. Paul's Church in Wickford, Rhode Island, as seen from the slave gallery.

the next world over the sufferings of life (Greene 1942:286–288; Piersen 1988:55–56).

Similar to mealtimes, segregated space in church upheld the ideology of alienation. By placing the slaves in the balcony, planters were once again reinforcing their status as outsiders and at the same time degrading them by giving them lesser accommodations. This symbolism, however, was stronger in the church than in the household, because planters were symbolically stating that God also recognized them as aliens. In this manner, the form of Christianity taught to the slaves, which emphasized the sanctity of the master/slave relationship, was reinforced though space. The Narragansett slaves' reaction to this segregation is unknown, but in nearby Boston, Chloe Spear did not seem traumatized by it. Bored with the sermons, she took advantage of the secluded seats by spending the time

TABLE 2
KNOWN SLAVE BURIAL GROUNDS IN NARRAGANSETT

Planter	No. of Burials	Location
Updike	80+	Cocumscussoc, N. Kingstown
Gardiner/Stanton	many	Stony Fort Rd., N. Kingstown
Gardiner/Robinson	75–80	Unknown S. Kingstown
Phillips	17	Tower Hill Rd., N. Kingstown
Willet/Carpenter	unknown	Carroll Rd., N. Kingstown
Hall/Carpenter	unknown	Post Rd., N. Kingstown
Browning	7	Boston Neck Rd., N. Kingstown
Fones	28	Austin Rd., N. Kingstown
Unknown	25	Walmsley Hill, N. Kingstown
Col. R. Brown	unknown	Unknown S. Kingstown

Sources: Arnold (1909); McBurney (1981:134); McAleer et al. (1992); Brayton ([ca. 1950–1970:v]).

"playing, eating nuts, and enjoying other diversions" with her friends (Piersen 1988:51).

Nevertheless, as with most ideologies, this strategy was most effective among its creators. The slaves' alienation within the church helped planters believe in the morality of slavery. Carefully chosen scriptures upheld their right to own slaves, while the segregation of space within church had two functions. First, through reinforcing the slaves' alien status, it helped planters justify their ownership. As they believed slaves were mentally and morally inferior, many whites deluded themselves into thinking that blacks were better off as slaves in a Christian country than free in heathen Africa (Updike 1847:173–177). Second, segregated space kept slaves out of sight during sermons on Christian virtues which might undermine the sanctity of slavery.

The Narragansett slaves' spatial alienation continued after their deaths. Just as slaves were segregated and degraded during meals and at church, they were buried separately from whites. Cemeteries in 18th-century Narragansett followed a pattern similar to the American South. Common burial grounds were rare and only associated with particular churches. Instead, most whites and blacks were buried in family plots on the homestead farm or plantation. Although African-American slaves and servants were buried on their masters' plantations, they were rarely interred within the family graveyards. Planters' cemeteries were usually set off from the surrounding landscape by walls, hedges, or fencing. Outside of these barriers, but nearby, lie the slaves. Few slave burial grounds survive in Narragansett, but 19th-century cemetery surveys note a number (Table 2).

The Platform Cemetery, one of Narragansett's few common burial grounds, located at the original site of St. Paul's Church, was also segregated. The graveyard lies on a slope to the east of the church's foundation and was used between 1720 and the early 19th century (Figure 3). At the higher elevations are the graves of the planters and other freewhites. At the bottom of the slope, marked with fieldstones, lie the slaves (MacSparran 1899:85). Slaves buried here were actual members of the congregation or were those whose masters never established separate graveyards on their plantations. For example, the church's minister, Reverend MacSparran, buried most of his slaves here. His diary entry for 4 May 1745 reads, "I preached his [MacSparran's slave, Stepney] Funeral Sermon to a great Assembly of negro's [sic] in the ch[urch] & interred him in ye ch[urch] yard" (MacSparran 1899:24).

Within cemeteries different styles of tombstones symbolically reinforced the slaves' alienation. Planters' graves were usually marked with stones carved by the famous Newport stonecutters Henry Bull and John Stevens & Sons. These expensive, and often large, stones declared the interred's status. Slaves, on the other hand, were almost always given

FIGURE 3. The Platform Cemetery in North Kingstown, Rhode Island. Fieldstones marking slave burials are in the foreground, while the planters' more elaborate gravemarkers are visible uphill.

plain fieldstone markers. Notably absent are the elaborately carved gravestones for slaves found in Newport's Common Burying Ground (e.g., Kruger-Kahloula 1989; Garman 1994). This is not surprising, as carved gravestones were expensive. The graves of poor whites, and even some members of planter families, were also marked by fieldstones. Thus, the primary reason for the slaves' fieldstone markers was undoubtedly economic. Nevertheless, in opposition to planters' ornate stones, slaves' fieldstones further marked them as separate and unequal to their masters.

The spatial layout of the Narragansett burial grounds sent several symbolic messages. The separate burial plots, outside planters' walled cemeteries, marked slaves as outside white society, thus reinforcing their alien status in the same manner as seating during meals and at church. Like spatial alienation in church, the segregated cemeteries had special meaning because of the religious importance of burials. In both these places, the spatial segregation suggested that slaves were aliens in God's eyes, as well as in their masters'. This symbolic statement upheld the planters' right to keep blacks in bondage, since even God saw them as different and inferior.

The Effects of Segregation

Segregated space during meals, in church services, and in cemeteries reflected the planters' belief that slaves were outside white society, and was a strategy designed to teach slaves their alien status. Nevertheless, the most important audience for these symbols was the planters themselves. For planters, at a subconscious level, segregated space reinforced the slaves' alienation by constantly reminding them that slaves were inferior outsiders, which had two consequences. First, segregated space, like other symbols of alienation, helped maintain the social distance needed for slaves to live within the main house. Alienation helped planters dehumanize slaves and view them as just helping hands, thereby allowing slaves to share intimate space without disturbing the planters' sensibilities of privacy or undermining the social hierarchy. Second, on a more general level, by reinforcing the slaves' alienation, segregation upheld the planters' racist ideologies which supported the institution of slavery. These ideologies, which depicted Africans as inferior beings destined to serve Europeans, also justified the use of force to control bondsmen.

At the conscious level, planters hoped that slaves would learn ''to know and keep their places'' (in Stampp 1956:145). One southern planter, B. Mc-Bride, wrote in 1830, ''to moralize and induce the slave to assimilate with the master and his interest has been and is the great desideratum aimed at'' (McBride in Breeden 1980:79). Although Narragansett planters did not leave explicit statements like these, the slaves' systematic segregation at meals, at church services, and in cemeteries suggests that these northern planters also hoped that slaves would internalize the ideology of alienation and accept their lowly position without resistance. Unfortunately, the paucity of slave narratives and oral traditions from Narragansett precludes the knowledge of how slaves reacted to this symbolic degradation. The little evidence that does exist suggests that segregated space may have offered slaves a temporary escape from their masters' surveillance rather than causing them to internalize their alien status.

Circumventing Monitored Space

As the previous sections showed, shared domestic space increased the Narragansett planters' con-

trol over their slaves. Slaves tried to resist these methods of control by circumventing the plantation landscapes to find unmonitored space. Out of their masters' view, slaves exchanged information, renewed ties to loved ones and friends, and occasionally kept alive African traditions through rituals. To reestablish their control, planters attempted to identify and then monitor, or eliminate, these places, while slaves continually changed these sites' locations to prevent their discovery. James Scott (1990:119) argues that creating these unmonitored places is, by itself, ''an achievement of resistance''; thus, conflict between dominants and subordinates always surrounds these sites (Walker 1985; Scott 1990:118–122). This conflict over the control of space contradicts Piersen's argument that shared domestic space led to harmonious master/ slave relations.

Since they were closely guarded secrets, the locations of the slaves' meeting places are difficult to ascertain, but oral tradition and local laws suggest the types of places used (e.g., Pearce 1842; Hazard 1879, 1915; Brown 1883). After the workday was over, slaves sometimes left their plantations and congregated at houses owned by free blacks. In these houses, safe from their masters' surveillance, slaves and free blacks exchanged information and discussed events. Planters tried to prevent these meetings. In December of 1724, the South Kingstown Town Meeting passed a law against slaves visiting free blacks:

> Voted that from after this time that if any negro slave or other slave be found at any negroes house or cottage in this town and be duly convicted there of either by their own confession or the testimony of one creditable person or other [illegible word] that shall be thought sufficient before any constable or justice of the peace of this town that the said slave or slaves with the owner of the house in which they are found if he be found there present with the slave or slaves shall then each of them be publicly whipt at discretion of said justice or justices not exceeding thirty-one lashes (South Kingstown Town Meeting Records 1723–1785, 1:10).

The 1708 Rhode Island ''Act to Prevent the Entertainment of Negroes & C.,'' passed by the Assembly, suggests that slaves were congregating at free peoples' houses and perhaps taverns throughout the colony. The act noted, ''whereas, there is a law in this colony to suppress any persons from entertaining of negro slaves or Indian servants that are not their own, in their houses, or unlawfully letting them have strong drink . . .'' (Bartlett 1859: 50).

Slaves also used errands for their masters as excuses to visit other slaves outside of the planters' surveillance. Narragansett planters often sent their slaves to other plantations or to the towns of Wickford and Newport to deliver messages, pick up goods, and move livestock (MacSparran 1899). These slaves were given a pass and told to return by a certain time. Many slaves extended this unsupervised time as long as possible. For example, on 24 May 1745, Reverend MacSparran (1899:26) complained, ''Harry is gone this morning for Molasses but stays long. Stepney, poor boy, is dead and I have no servant I can now so well depend upon to go and come quick and [do] his errands well.'' On these trips, slaves were able to converse with each other in private.

Throughout the New World, slaves slipped into wooded areas surrounding their plantations to escape their masters' surveillance. Most slaves stayed for only a few hours, but sometimes runaways lived in nearby woods for days. Bondsmen slipped into the woods for a variety of reasons; some went to find solitude, some to escape an ensuing punishment, while others congregated to discuss events and enact rituals (Webber 1978:184–185; Isaac 1982; Upton 1988:367). The paucity of slave narratives and planter diaries from Narragansett makes it difficult to understand the woods' importance in circumventing the planters' surveillance, but Cato Pearce's remembrances suggest one way it was used. Pearce was born in 1790 to North Kingstown slaves. By the act of 1784, he was born free, but was indentured to his mother's master until the age of 21. Throughout his life in Narragansett, Pearce left the plantations and wandered into nearby woods when he needed solitary time to think or pray (Pearce 1842). In retreating to the woods, Pearce was following a strategy probably used by many Narragansett slaves who wished momentarily to escape their masters' constant surveillance.

Slaves also met each other in the woods to exchange information and keep alive African-based

traditions. Once a year in June, Narragansett's slaves met on Rose Hill in Potter's Woods to hold a fair (Hazard 1879:121; South Kingstown Town Meeting Records 1723–1785, 1:13). As early as 1726, slaves used these fairs as relief from their masters' control (South Kingstown Town Meeting Records 1723– 1785, 1:13). At these meetings, slaves kept alive African traditions by telling stories, dancing, and enacting rituals (Reidy 1978; Piersen 1988:119– 134; Wade 1988). Some historians note that this celebration's form closely resembled certain African rituals (Aimes 1905; Reidy 1978:108). In this manner, slaves created a subordinate culture that helped them adapt to bondage. During the first half of the 18th century, planters tried to stop these fairs, since they slowed down plantation production and gave slaves the chance to congregate (South Kingstown Town Meeting Records 1723–1785, 1:13, 87; Wade 1988). Yet, their attempts were unsuccessful, and the fairs continued (Greene 1942; South Kingstown Town Meeting Records 1723–1785, 1:87).

In the second half of the 18th century, planters gave up trying to stamp out the fairs and instead tried to control them, at which they were more successful. The fairs began to be held in open areas and featured the famous Negro election. In this ritual, the local slaves and free blacks elected a leader, known as the governor (Brown 1883:12–17; Greene 1942; Piersen 1988:119–134; Wade 1988). The popularity and extravagance of the Narragansett Negro Elections reached their zenith around the time of the Revolution and gradually declined as the slave population diminished: ''In 1975, elections were held in North and South Kingstown, but in a few years, one was held in South Kingstown only'' (Updike 1847:178). The Updike account books show that blacks still attended the elections at the turn of the century. A 20 June 1800 entry reads, ''by one day lost Negro [E]Le . . . ion'' (Updike 1800). Yet, the event died out during the next 20 years (Updike 1847:178).

Although the account may be romanticized and is written from the planters' perspective, Wilkins Updike described the festival as it was practiced in the late 18th and early 19th centuries. Note the planters' strong involvement in the ritual through supporting their favorite slaves:

The negroes held an annual election on the third Saturday in June, when they elected their Governor. . . . This annual festivity was looked for with great anxiety. Party was as violent and acrimonious with them as among the whites. The slaves assumed the power and pride and took the relative rank of their masters, and it was degrading to the reputation of the owner if his slave appeared in inferior apparel, or with less money than the slave of another master of equal wealth. The horses of the wealthy land-holders were on this day all surrendered to the use of the slaves, and with cues, real or false, head pomatumed and powdered, cocked hat, mounted on the best Narragansett pacers, sometimes with their masters' sword, with their ladies on pillions, they pranced to election, which commenced generally, at 10 o'clock. The canvass for votes soon commenced, the tables with refreshments were spread, and all friends of the respective candidates were solicited to partake, and as much anxiety and interest would manifest itself, and as much family pride and influence was exercised and interest created, as in other elections, and preceded by weeks of parmaterring (parliamenteering), about one o'clock the vote would be taken, by ranging the friends of the respective candidates in two lines under the directions of a chief marshall, . . . with assistants. This was generally a tumultuous crisis until the count commenced, when silence was proclaimed, and after that no man could change sides or go from one rank to the other. The chief marshall announced the number of votes for each candidate, and in an audible voice proclaimed the name of the Governor elected for the ensuing year. The election treat corresponded in extravagance in proportion to the wealth of his master. The defeated candidate was, according to custom, introduced by the chief marshall, and drank the first toast after the inauguration, and all animosities were forgotten. At dinner, the Governor was seated at the head of the long table, under trees or an arbor, with the unsuccessful candidate at his right, and his lady on the left. The afternoon was spent in dancing, game of quoits, athletic exercises, & c. (Updike 1847:177–178).

By providing their slaves with clothes, horses, and other goods for the election, planters became an important part of these festivals (Updike 1847:177–179; Reidy 1978; Wade 1988), which had several consequences. First, planters now attended the fairs, thus extending the area they monitored. As a result, slaves could no longer express themselves openly. Second, many slaves, seeking their masters' support in the elections, probably tried to remain in their masters' favor, which helped planters maintain control in the weeks prior to the fairs. Third, planters gave governors the power to punish other slaves for minor transgressions (Greene 1942; Wade 1988). In nearby Newport, the sentencings were open to the public and ''the 'sneers and contempt' of the black

community accompanied the punishment, usually administered with abastinado—a board used to strike the feet or buttocks of the offender'' (Reidy 1978:105). Thus, the planters' involvement helped turn an event designed to escape their surveillance into a further extension of their control. Therefore, even though the fairs helped keep alive African traditions, once they were held away from the woods and under the planters' supervision, they were no longer a threat to ruling whites.

Although the Narragansett planters manipulated landscapes to help control their bondsmen, the slaves' efforts to circumvent these landscapes show that their control was not absolute. By congregating in the houses of free blacks, during errands, in wooded areas, and at festivals, slaves were able to escape their masters' surveillance and speak openly among themselves. This respite enabled them to share the information needed to mitigate the planters' dominance and survive under slavery.

Conclusion

By quartering slaves within their own houses, the Narragansett planters were able to monitor much of their slaves' behavior. This control may have discouraged acts of resistance and minor transgressions of discipline and helped planters discover these acts when they occurred. It also denied slaves a place to speak openly among themselves and practice African-American rituals. To gain the privacy needed for such acts, slaves had to circumvent the plantation landscapes. They did this by meeting in private homes, on their masters' errands, and during large festivals. Yet, these attempts did not go unchallenged. Planters searched for these unmonitored places and tried to extend their control over them.

The conflict between the masters' desire to monitor their bondsmen and the slaves' attempts to escape this surveillance typified Narragansett master/slave relations. This interpretation contradicts William Piersen's conclusion in *Black Yankees,* that shared space fostered a ''mild form of servitude and a kind of household kinship'' (Piersen 1988:146). Piersen argued that working and living side by side fostered close ties and mutual respect between masters and their slaves. He provided no evidence, however, to support this conclusion. This study shows that rather than fostering close relations, the Narragansett plantation landscapes were important to the planters' strategies of slave control. Not only were slaves subject to close monitoring and denied the freedom to speak openly, but shared domestic space led to their symbolic marking as aliens. Planters used segregation during meals, in church services, and in cemeteries to mark slaves as aliens in an attempt to reinforce their lowly status and "teach them their place." In this fashion, the Narragansett planters used space as a symbol to instill their ideology of alienation. By circumventing the planters' landscapes, however, slaves were able to undermine the symbols of alienation and resist this dominant ideology. Nevertheless, the process of segregating slaves during rituals had a profound affect on the slaves' lives. It reinforced the planters' already-held racist beliefs, which supported the institution of slavery and justified the use of force to uphold it.

Although this article relies on documentary rather than archaeological evidence, it has several ramifications for archaeologists. Slavery rests on the ability of one person to control another person's actions; thus, power relations should be at the center of plantation studies. Too many historical archaeologists focus on planter and slave lifeways but ignore this fundamental aspect of plantation life. In the past few years, however, a handful of archaeologists have begun to examine how slave-holders used space to control their bondsmen. Studies of American and Jamaican plantations (e.g., Orser 1988; Michie 1990; Armstrong and Kelly 1992; McKee 1992; Joseph 1993), and Frankish villas (Samson 1992), show that slave-owners manipulated their landscapes to help monitor their slaves' behavior. By placing slave housing in orderly formations, and surrounding areas with walls, masters were able to control their slaves' movements and quickly note transgressions of discipline. These studies have greatly increased researchers' understanding of spatial control, but the topic is far from exhausted. For example, the consequences of subdividing plantations with walls and fences into concise, easily manageable areas is still poorly under-

stood. Both Anthony Giddens (1985) and Michel Foucault (1979) argue that placing laborers in specific areas is essential for surveillance in the workplace. This strategy allows management to easily supervise workers; if a worker is not in his assigned place, or if his station is not accomplishing the assigned goals, then the worker is at fault and the transgression is clearly visible. Some preliminary research suggests that segmenting plantation landscapes may have affected slaves similarly (Isaac 1992:410–418; Fitts 1995). By assigning exact areas for slaves to work in, masters or overseers could, at a glance, note the absence of certain slaves, which decreased the slaves' chances of escape or slipping off for a short time. Furthermore, by estimating the time needed to accomplish specific tasks, planters could gauge how hard slaves were working. In 1833, one unknown southern planter explicitly stated, "in the different departments on the plantation as much distinction and separation are kept up as possible with a view to create responsibility" (in Breeden 1980:51). This situation allowed planters to detect strategies of nonviolent resistance such as work slowdowns and tool breakage. It is unknown if planters purposely segmented plantation space to achieve this end, and, if they did, how often this method of spatial control was employed. Further research could help archaeologists illuminate how methods of spatial control helped shape plantation landscapes.

Although gaps exist in the understanding of how planters manipulated landscapes to monitor slaves, the use of space to support dominant ideologies is even less understood. This study shows that planters attempted to use space to reinforce their ideology of alienation. Yet, evidence suggests that while the ideology of alienation was an important method of control it did not necessarily convince slaves of their own inferiority. Archaeological studies of the American South (Deetz 1988; Epperson 1990, 1991; McKee 1992; Joseph 1993; Vlach 1993; Stewart-Abernathy 1995), South Africa (Hall 1992), and the island of Lamu off Kenya (Donley 1982) demonstrate that owners used space to mark their slaves as different and inferior to free people. This suggests space was commonly used to reinforce the dominant ideology of alienation. Nevertheless, most of these scholars avoid using the term ideology when discussing this phenomenon. Furthermore, in most other studies of plantation archaeology, the topic is avoided altogether.

This avoidance of ideological control probably stems from the criticism Mark Leone received on his examination of gardens in Annapolis, Maryland (e.g., Beaudry et al. 1991; Hall 1992; Kelso 1992). Leone (1984, 1988a, 1988b, 1989) argued that 18th-century Maryland elites successfully used landscape symbolism to support the social hierarchy by making it seem natural. This conclusion, however, rests on the theory of false consciousness which has been shown to have serious theoretical flaws (e.g., Abercrombie et al. 1980, 1990; Scott 1985, 1990). Recent studies of power relations suggest that dominant ideologies rarely, if ever, convince subordinates of their own inferiority or the naturalness of their position. Instead, the most important consumers of these ideologies are the dominants themselves. The ideologies, and the symbols which uphold them, help convince dominants of their right to rule and help them justify the use of force to stay in power (e.g., Scott 1985, 1990; Hill 1990; Turner 1990; Bell 1992).

Although these studies show that subordinates rarely internalize dominant ideologies, they also demonstrate that dominants attempt to use ideological control. Dominant ideologies, therefore, are not figments of Marxist scholars' imaginations. Of particular interest to archaeologists should be how space and material culture were used as symbols to reinforce these ideologies. Analyses of this nature would help make power relations the central theme of plantation archaeology. Scholars, however, should not rely on the theory of false consciousness. Instead, archaeologists must determine the ideology's affect by examining both the dominants' and subordinates' reactions to the symbols which support the ideology. As this article shows, subordinates can undermine spatial control by circumventing dominant-planned space. To determine the effectiveness of spatial control, scholars need to remember the element of time and ask themselves if subordinates were always present, or did they meet in unmonitored space to escape the dominant group's power. Methods of spatial control are not static. A landscape's influence changes according to the subordinates' ability to circumvent it and the dominants' ability to extend their surveillance into new areas. This dynamic is a topic which more archaeological studies of plantations need to address.

This discussion of Narragansett plantation landscapes and recent research in the field of historical archaeology show that cross-culturally slave owners used landscapes similarly to help control their bondsmen. Studies of southern and Jamaican plantations (e.g., Orser 1988; Michie 1990; Armstrong and Kelly 1992; McKee 1992) and Frankish villas (Samson 1992) show that planters manipulated their landscapes to help monitor their slaves' behavior, while works on the American South (Deetz 1988; Epperson 1990, 1991; McKee 1992; Joseph 1993; Vlach 1993; Stewart-Abernathy 1995) and Africa (Donley 1982; Hall 1992) demonstrate that owners used space to mark their slaves as different and inferior to free people. The similarities between these authors' conclusions and those of this study suggest that Narragansett planters followed commonly practiced methods of spatial control. This conclusion contradicts the accepted view that northern and southern slavery were fundamentally different.

Historians have long argued that northern slavery was milder than the southern institution (e.g., Updike 1847; Potter 1851; Hazard 1879, 1915; C. Hazard 1893; Bicknell 1920; Miller 1933; Woodward 1971). This interpretation derived from 19th-century northern historians' conscious and unconscious efforts to excuse their ancestors' involvement with slavery and to differentiate the North from the rebellious South (White 1989; Fitts 1995). Some 20th-century historians kept alive this interpretation by uncritically accepting these early conclusions (e.g., Woodward 1971; Piersen 1988; Rosivach 1993), while others demonstrated that the legal status of African-American slaves in New England was, in fact, better than in most southern colonies (e.g., Jordan 1968; Meier and Rudwick 1970; Higginbotham 1978; Twombly and Moore 1982[1967]). Yet, by focusing on accessible legal documents, these scholars missed how slaves were treated at the everyday level.

This study of spatial control supports recent conclusions that northern master/slave relations were marked by the same conflict that characterized the southern institution (McManus 1973; White 1989; Fitts 1995). These studies show that both northern and southern slave-holders tried to control their bondsmen with violent punishments, the threat of sale, symbolical degradation, and self-serving ideologies, while slaves attempted to resist their owners' domination through running away, violently striking back, and creating a culture based on African identity to maintain their self-worth in the face of their masters' symbolic degradation. This last point has ramifications for archaeologists. As both the northern and southern slaves created symbols of African identity, it follows that a distinctive African-American material culture also may have been present in colonial New England. A few preliminary studies have found colonoware sherds and distinctive African-American architectural and dining patterns (Deetz 1977; Baker 1980; Smith 1995), which suggests that the demographic differences between northern and southern slavery did not significantly alter the slaves' strategies of resistance. Nevertheless, without the excavation of northern slave quarters the extent of these similarities will remain obscure.

Some scholars have openly questioned historical archaeology's ability to make significant contributions to the understanding of the past (Burke 1991). Yet, by examining spatial control, historical archaeologists have the potential to elucidate the intricacies of master/slave relations. This approach provides a new perspective to an old topic by showing that to understand fully the planters' strategies of control and the slaves' responses, one must look beyond well-documented revolts and legislation and examine how often unrecorded methods of control and resistance were played out at a daily level.

ACKNOWLEDGMENTS

I would like to thank Patricia Rubertone, Shepard Krech III, Rhett Jones, Douglas Anderson, Rebecca Yamin, Jesse Ponz, and Julia King for commenting on previous drafts of this paper. Discussions with Joanne Melish, Lauren Cook, Jim Garman, Mark Harding, and John Sweet also helped solidify aspects of my argument. I take full responsibility for any errors and misinterpretations which may appear.

REFERENCES

ABERCROMBIE, NICHOLAS, STEPHEN HILL, AND
BRYAN TURNER
1980   *The Dominant Ideology Thesis.* George Allen and Unwin, London.
1990   *Dominant Ideologies.* Unwin Hyman, Boston, Massachusetts.

AIMES, HUBERT
1905   African Institutions in America. *Journal of American Folklore* 18:15–32.

ARMSTRONG, DOUGLAS V., AND KENNETH KELLY
1992   Spatial Transformations in African Jamaican Housing at Seville Plantation. Paper presented at the Annual Meeting of the Society for Historical Archaeology Conference on Historical and Underwater Archaeology, Kingston, Jamaica.

ARNOLD, JAMES
1909   *Inscriptions on the Gravestones on the Old Churchyard of Saint Paul's, Narragansett, North Kingstown, Rhode Island.* Merrymount Press, Boston, Massachusetts.

BAKER, VERNON
1980   Archaeological Visibility of Afro-American Culture: An Example from Black Lucy's Garden, Andover, Massachusetts. In *Archaeological Perspectives on Ethnicity in America,* edited by Robert L. Schuyler, pp. 29–37. Baywood, Farmingdale, New York.

BARTLETT, JOHN (EDITOR)
1858   *Census of the Inhabitants of the Colony of Rhode Island and Providence Plantations, Taken by Order of the General Assembly, in the Year 1774.* Knowles, Anthony & Co., Providence, Rhode Island.
1859   *Records of the Colony of Rhode Island and Providence Plantations in New England.* Vol. 4, 1707–1740. Knowles, Anthony & Co., Providence, Rhode Island.

BEAUDRY, MARY, LAUREN COOK, AND
STEPHEN MROZOWSKI
1991   Artifacts and Active Voices: Material Culture as Social Discourse. In *The Archaeology of Inequality,* edited by Randall McGuire and Robert Paynter, pp. 150–191. Basil Blackwell, Cambridge, Massachusetts.

BELL, CATHERINE
1992   *Ritual Theory, Ritual Practice.* Oxford University Press, New York.

BICKNELL, THOMAS
    1920   *The History of the State of Rhode Island and Provi-
            dence Plantations.* American Historical Society, New
            York.

BRAUDEL, FERNAND
    1973   *Capitalism and Material Life, 1400–1800.* Harper and
            Row, New York.

BRAYTON, SUSAN
    [ca.   Henry Marchant: A Rhode Island Patriot, 1741–1796.
    1950–   Manuscript on file, Rhode Island Historical Society
    1970]   Library, Providence, Rhode Island.

BREEDEN, JAMES
    1980   *Advice Among Masters: The Ideal in Slave Manage-
            ment in the Old South.* Greenwood Press, Westport,
            Connecticut.

BROWN, KENNETH, AND DOREEN COOPER
    1990   Structural Continuity in an African-American Slave
            and Tenant Community. *Historical Archaeology*
            24(4):7–19.

BROWN, WILLIAM
    1883   *The Life of William J. Brown of Providence, R.I.*
            Angell, Providence, Rhode Island.

BURKE, PETER
    1991   Overture: The New History, Its Past and Its Future. In
            New Perspectives on Historical Writing, edited by
            Peter Burke, pp. 1–23. Pennsylvania State University
            Press, University Park, Pennsylvania.

CARPENTER, ESTHER
    1924   *South County Studies.* Merrymount Press, Boston,
            Massachusetts.

COLLOMP, ALAIN
    1989   Families: Habitations and Cohabitations. In *A History
            of Private Life: Passions of the Renaissance,* edited by
            Philippe Aries and Georges Duby, pp. 493–529. Har-
            vard University Press, Cambridge, Massachusetts.

CURTIN, PHILIP
    1990   *The Rise and Fall of the Plantation Complex.* Cam-
            bridge University Press, New York.

DEETZ, JAMES
    1977   *In Small Things Forgotten: The Archaeology of Early
            American Life.* Anchor Press/Doubleday, New York.
    1988   American Historical Archaeology: Methods and Re-
            sults. *Science* 239:362–367.

DONLEY, LINDA
    1982   House Power: Swahili Space and Symbolic Markers.
            In *Symbolic and Structural Archaeology,* edited by
            Ian Hodder, pp. 63–73. Cambridge University Press,
            Cambridge.

DOUGLASS, WILLIAM
    1753   *A Summary, Historical and Political, of the First

Planting, Progressive Improvements, and Present
            State of the British Settlements in North America,* Vol.
            2. D. Fowle, Boston, Massachusetts.

EPPERSON, TERRENCE
    1990   Race and the Disciplines of the Plantation. *Historical
            Archaeology* 24(4):29–37.
    1991   *"To Fix a Perpetual Brand": The Social Construc-
            tion of Race in Virginia, 1675–1750.* Ph.D. disser-
            tation, Department of Anthropology, Temple Uni-
            versity, Philadelphia, Pennsylvania. University
            Microfilms, Ann Arbor, Michigan.

FAIRBANKS, CHARLES
    1984   The Plantation Archaeology of the Southeastern
            Coast. *Historical Archaeology* 18(1):1–14.

FERGUSON, LELAND
    1992   *Uncommon Ground: Archaeology and Early African
            America, 1650–1800.* Smithsonian Institution Press,
            Washington, D.C.

FINLEY, MOSES I.
    1980   *Ancient Slavery and Modern Ideology.* Penguin, New
            York.

FISCHER, DAVID
    1989   *Albion's Seed.* Oxford University Press, New York.

FITTS, ROBERT
    1995   *Inventing New England's Slave Paradise: Master/
            Slave Relations in 18th-Century Narragansett, Rhode
            Island.* Ph.D. dissertation, Department of Anthropol-
            ogy, Brown University, Providence, Rhode Island.
            University Microfilms, Ann Arbor, Michigan.

FLANDRIN, JEAN-LOUIS
    1989   Distinction Through Taste. In *A History of Private
            Life: Passions of the Renaissance,* edited by Philippe
            Aries and Georges Duby, pp. 265–307. Harvard Uni-
            versity Press, Cambridge, Massachusetts.

FOUCAULT, MICHEL
    1979   *Discipline and Punish: The Birth of the Prison.* Ran-
            dom House, New York.

GARMAN, JAMES
    1994   Viewing the Color Line Through the Material Culture
            of Death. *Historical Archaeology* 28(3):74–93.

GIDDENS, ANTHONY
    1984   *The Constitution of Society.* University of California
            Press, Berkeley.
    1985   Time, Space, and Regionalisation. In *Social Relations
            and Spatial Structures,* edited by Derek Gregory and
            John Urry, pp. 265–295. St. Martin's Press, New
            York.

GREENE, LORENZO
    1942   *The Negro in Colonial New England, 1620–1776.*
            Columbia University Press, New York.

HALL, MARTIN
1992   Small Things, and the Mobile, Conflictual Fusion of Power, Fear, and Desire. In *The Art and Mystery of Historical Archaeology: Essays in Honor of James Deetz*, edited by Anne Yentsch and Mary Beaudry, pp. 373–399. CRC Press, Boca Raton, Florida.

HAZARD, CAROLINE
1893   *College Tom.* Houghton, Mifflin, Boston, Massachusetts.

HAZARD, THOMAS ROBINSON
1879   *Recollections of Olden Times.* John Sanborn, Newport, Rhode Island.
1915   *The Jonny-Cake Papers of "Shepherd Tom."* Merrymount Press, Boston, Massachusetts.

HIGGINBOTHAM, A. LEON
1978   *In the Matter of Color.* Oxford University Press, New York.

HILL, STEPHEN
1990   Britain: The Dominant Ideology Thesis after a Decade. In *Dominant Ideologies*, edited by Nicholas Abercrombie, Stephen Hill, and Bryan Turner, pp. 1–37. Unwin Hyman, Boston, Massachusetts.

ISAAC, RHYS
1982   *The Transformation of Virginia.* University of North Carolina Press, Chapel Hill.
1992   Imagination and Material Culture: The Enlightenment on a Mid-18th-Century Virginia Plantation. In *The Art and Mystery of Historical Archaeology: Essays in Honor of James Deetz*, edited by Anne Yentsch and Mary Beaudry, pp. 401–423. CRC Press, Boca Raton, Florida.

JACOBS, DONALD
1989   Review of *Black Yankees*, by William Piersen. *William and Mary Quarterly* 46(2):396–397.

JONES, NORRECE
1990   *Born a Child of Freedom Yet a Slave.* University Press of New England, Hanover, New Hampshire.

JONES, RHETT
1981   Place and People: Working Paper #1 on the Environment Project. Manuscript on file with the author.
1986   Plantation Society in the Narragansett Country of Rhode Island, 1690–1790: A Preliminary Study. *Plantation Society* 2(2):157–170.
1993   Afrocentricity: An Environmental Perspective. *Afrocentric Scholar* 2(1):1–22.

JORDAN, WINTHROP
1968   *White over Black: American Attitudes Toward the Negro, 1550–1812.* Penguin, Baltimore, Maryland.

JOSEPH, J. W.
1993   White Columns and Black Hands: Class and Classification in the Plantation Ideology of the Georgia and South Carolina Lowcountry. *Historical Archaeology* 27(3):57–73.

KELSO, WILLIAM
1984   *Kingsmill Plantations, 1619–1800.* Academic Press, New York.
1992   Big Things Remembered: Anglo-Virginian Houses, Armorial Devices, and the Impact of Common Sense. In *The Art and Mystery of Historical Archaeology: Essays in Honor of James Deetz*, edited by Anne Yentsch and Mary Beaudry, pp. 127–148. CRC Press, Boca Raton, Florida.

KRUGER-KAHLOULA, ANGELIKA
1989   Tributes in Stone and Lapidary Lapses: Commemorating Black People in Eighteenth- and Nineteenth-Century America. *Markers* 6:33–100.

LEONE, MARK
1984   Interpreting Ideology in Historical Archaeology: Using the Rules of Perspective in the William Paca Garden in Annapolis, Maryland. In *Ideology, Power and Prehistory*, edited by Daniel Miller and C. Tilley, pp. 25–35. Cambridge University Press, Cambridge.
1988a   The Relationship Between Archaeological Data and the Documentary Record: 18th-Century Gardens in Annapolis, Maryland. *Historical Archaeology* 22(1):29–36.
1988b   The Georgian Order as the Order of Merchant Capitalism in Annapolis, Maryland. In *The Recovery of Meaning*, edited by Mark Leone, pp. 235–263. Smithsonian Institution Press, Washington, D.C.
1989   Issues in Historic Landscapes and Gardens. *Historical Archaeology* 23(1):45–47.

MACSPARRAN, JAMES
1899   *A Letterbook and Abstract of Out Services, 1743–1751.* Merrymount Press, Boston, Massachusetts.

MCALEER, ALTHEA, BEATRIX HOFFIUS, AND DEBY NUNES
1992   *Graveyards of North Kingstown, Rhode Island.* Privately printed, North Kingstown, Rhode Island.

MCBURNEY, CHRISTIAN
1981   The Rise and Decline of the South Kingstown Planters, 1660–1783. Unpublished B.A. honors thesis, Department of History, Brown University, Providence, Rhode Island.

MCKEE, LARRY
1992   The Ideals and Realities Behind the Design and Use of 19th-Century Virginia Slave Cabins. In *The Art and Mystery of Historical Archaeology: Essays in Honor of James Deetz*, edited by Anne Yentsch and Mary Beaudry, pp. 195–214. CRC Press, Boca Raton, Florida.

MCLOUGHLIN, WILLIAM
1978   *Rhode Island.* W. W. Norton, New York.

McMANUS, EDGAR
1973   *Black Bondage in the North.* Syracuse University Press, Syracuse, New York.

MEIER, AUGUST, AND ELLIOT RUDWICK
1970   *From Plantation to Ghetto.* Hill and Wang, New York.

MEILLASSOUX, CLAUDE
1991   *The Anthropology of Slavery.* University of Chicago Press, Chicago, Illinois.

MICHIE, JAMES
1990   *Richmond Hill Plantation, 1810–1868.* Reprint Company, Spartanburg, South Carolina.

MILLER, WILLIAM
1933   The Narragansett Planters. *Proceedings of the American Antiquarian Society* 43.

MINTZ, SIDNEY
1959   The Plantation as a Socio-Cultural Type. In *Plantation Systems of the New World,* edited by Vera Rubin, pp. 42–49. Pan American Union, Washington, D.C.

ORSER, CHARLES E., JR.
1988   Toward a Theory of Power for Historical Archaeology. In *The Recovery of Meaning,* edited by Mark Leone, pp. 313–343. Smithsonian Institution Press, Washington, D.C.

OWENS, LESLIE
1976   *This Species of Property.* Oxford University Press, New York.

PADILLA, ELENA
1959   Colonization and Development of Plantations. In *Plantation Systems of the New World,* edited by Vera Rubin, pp. 54–58. Pan American Union, Washington, D.C.

PARISH, PETER
1989   *Slavery: History and Historians.* Harper and Row, New York.

PARK, ROBERT
1937   Introduction. In *The Etiquette of Race Relations in the South,* by Bertram Doyle, pp. xi–xxiv. University of Chicago Press, Chicago, Illinois.

PATTERSON, ORLANDO
1982   *Slavery and Social Death.* Harvard University Press, Cambridge, Massachusetts.

PEARCE, CATO
1842   *Brief Memoir of the Life and Religious Experience of Cato Pearce a Man of Color.* Cato Pearce, Pawtucket, Rhode Island.

PIERSEN, WILLIAM
1988   *Black Yankees.* University of Massachusetts Press, Amherst.

POTTER, ELISHA R., JR.
1851   *An Address Delivered Before the Rhode Island Historical Society, on the Evening of February Nineteenth, 1851.* George H. Whitney, Providence, Rhode Island.

RABOTEAU, ALBERT
1978   *Slave Religion.* Oxford University Press, New York.

RAWICK, GEORGE
1972   *From Sundown to Sunup.* Greenwood, Westport, Connecticut.

REIDY, JOSEPH
1978   "Negro Election Day" and Black Community Life in New England, 1750–1860. *Marxist Perspectives* 3:102–117.

ROBINSON, BEVERLY
1990   Africanisms and the Study of Folklore. In *Africanisms in American Culture,* edited by Joseph Holloway, pp. 211–224. Indiana University Press, Bloomington.

ROSIVACH, VINCENT
1993   Agricultural Slavery in the Northern Colonies and in Classical Athens: Some Comparisons. *Comparative Studies in Society and History* 35(3):551–567.

SAFFIN, JOHN
1701   *A Brief and Candid Answer to a Late Printed Sheet, Entitled, the Selling of Joseph.* Privately printed, Boston, Massachusetts.

SAMSON, ROSS
1992   Knowledge, Constraint, and Power in Inaction: The Defenseless Medieval Wall. *Historical Archaeology* 26(3):26–44.

SCOTT, JAMES
1985   *Weapons of the Weak.* Yale University Press, New Haven, Connecticut.
1990   *Domination and the Arts of Resistance.* Yale University Press, New Haven, Connecticut.

SINGLETON, THERESA
1985   Introduction. In *The Archaeology of Slavery and Plantation Life,* edited by Theresa A. Singleton, pp. 1–14. Academic Press, New York.

SMITH, J. N. LEITH
1995   Preliminary Analysis of African-American Colono Wares from the Central Artery/Tunnel Project in Boston. Paper presented at the Annual Meeting of the Society for Historical Archaeology Conference on Historical and Underwater Archaeology, Washington, D.C.

SMITH, RICHARD, JR.
1692   Estate Inventory. *Updike Papers,* Case 14:7, 9. Rhode Island Historical Society Library, Providence, Rhode Island.

SOBEL, MECHAL
1987   *The World They Made Together.* Princeton University Press, Princeton, New Jersey.

SOUTH KINGSTOWN PROBATES
1704–   *South Kingstown Town Council and Probates.* Town
1789   Hall, South Kingstown, Rhode Island.

SOUTH KINGSTOWN TOWN MEETING RECORDS
1723–   *South Kingstown Town Meeting Records,* Vol. 1.
1785   Town Hall, South Kingstown, Rhode Island.

STAMPP, KENNETH
1956   *The Peculiar Institution.* Vintage, New York.

STEWART-ABERNATHY, LESLIE
1995   *Separate Kitchens and Intimate Archaeology: Constructing Urban Slavery on the Antebellum Cotton Frontier.* Paper presented at the Annual Meeting of the Society for Historical Archaeology Conference on Historical and Underwater Archaeology, Washington, D.C.

STUCKEY, STERLING
1987   *Slave Culture.* Oxford University Press, New York.

THOMPSON, EDGAR
1959   The Plantation as a Social System. In *Plantation Systems of the New World,* edited by Vera Rubin, pp. 26–36. Pan American Union, Washington, D.C.

TURNER, BRYAN
1990   Conclusion: Peroration on Ideology. In *Dominant Ideologies,* edited by Nicholas Abercrombie, Stephen Hill, and Bryan Turner, pp. 229–256. Unwin Hyman, Boston, Massachusetts.

TWOMBLY, ROBERT, AND ROBERT MOORE
1982   Black Puritan: The Negro in Seventeenth-Century Massachusetts. Reprint of 1967 publication. In *Race Relations in British North America, 1607–1783,* edited by Bruce Glasrud and Alan Smith, pp. 145–163. Nelson-Hall, Chicago, Illinois.

UPDIKE, DANIEL
1800   Ledger Book B: May 1800 to January 2nd, 1801. Manuscript on file, Rhode Island Historical Society Library, Providence, Rhode Island.

UPDIKE, WILKINS
1847   *A History of the Episcopal Church in Narragansett, Rhode Island.* Henry Onderdonk, New York.

UPTON, DELL
1988   White and Black Landscapes in Eighteenth-Century Virginia. In *Material Life in America, 1600–1860,* edited by Robert St. George, pp. 357–369. Northeastern University Press, Boston, Massachusetts.

VLACH, JOHN
1991   *By the Work of Their Hands.* University Press of Virginia, Charlottesville.
1993   *Back of the Big House.* University of North Carolina Press, Chapel Hill.

WADE, MELVIN
1988   "Shining in Borrowed Plumage": Affirmation of Community in the Black Coronation Festivals of New England, ca. 1750–1850. In *Material Life in America, 1600–1860,* edited by Robert St. George, pp. 171–182. Northeastern University Press, Boston, Massachusetts.

WALKER, RICHARD
1985   Class, Division of Labour, and Employment in Space. In *Social Relations and Spatial Structures,* edited by Derek Gregory and John Urry, pp. 164–189. St. Martin's Press, New York.

WEBBER, THOMAS
1978   *Deep Like the Rivers.* W. W. Norton, New York.

WHITE, SHANE
1989   Slavery on the Periphery, New York. Paper presented at "Cultivation and Culture: Labor and the Shaping of Slave Life in the Americas," University of Maryland, College Park.

WINSHIP, GEORGE (EDITOR)
1935   *The Journal of Madam Knight.* Peter Smith, New York.

WOODWARD, CARL R.
1971   *Plantation in Yankeeland.* Pequot Press, Chester, Connecticut.

ROBERT K. FITTS
JOHN MILNER ASSOCIATES
6 WORLD TRADE CENTER B-26-A
NEW YORK, NEW YORK 10048

LU ANN DE CUNZO

A Future after Freedom

ABSTRACT

Just after the Civil War, two African-American families left
Maryland to build new lives in northern Delaware. Sidney
and Rachel Stump and David and Sarah Walmsley probably
did not know each other in Maryland, but they settled in
nearby communities in Delaware. There work, family, church,
and community connections may have introduced them. Both
men labored on area farms, when they could get work, until
they were at least 70 years old. Both women did laundry
and sewing for neighbors in town. Both families raised their
children to work hard and to value education, their faith, and
"joyous play." The Stumps and Walmsleys drew on their
pasts and looked to the future as they created a distinctive
cultural style framed by racism and constrained opportunities. Archaeology prompted by the Delaware Department
of Transportation's road-building activities has brought us
closer to these families' stories. In this paper, readers visit
them in their homes on the edge of town, as they prepare
for a most important event in their annual festive calendar,
the Big Quarterly.

Introduction

I began my apprenticeship in Delaware historical archaeology at the end of a hot summer in
1989. A few years before, Delaware archaeologists had entered a race with the highway builders intent on paving the state. The archaeologists
have left in their wake a state inventory enhanced by hundreds of newly-identified historical-
period sites, a warehouse of recovered material
remains, and a veritable mountain of reports. I
struggled through those reports trying to get my
bearings. To my chagrin, my colleagues produced them at an alarmingly rapid rate. I read
and reread them, and my guide in this endeavor,
Wade Catts, quizzed me subtly but regularly. I
failed miserably, always confusing the details of
places, buildings, landscapes, people, objects, and
histories.

Each time I returned to the ever-growing
mound of reports, two unfailingly intrigued me.
When I first discovered these sites in the litera-

ture a few years ago, they were virtually unique
in the annals of Delaware historical archaeology,
and our colleagues in the Midatlantic and Northeast had completed few comparable studies.
Although I did not realize the reasons for some
time, I now see that it was my own personal and
professional stereotypes that kept leading me
back to these sites. They just did not "fit" my
naive, uncritical expectations; they did not "fit,"
dare I say it, the "pattern."

The sites comprised three houselots where two
African-American families lived on the margins
of two northern Delaware towns from the mid-
1870s until the early 1920s. Sidney Stump and
David Walmsley and their sons labored long,
hard hours, weeks, years on others' farms for
little pay. Neither continuity nor certainty characterized their work, as competition, machinery,
and crop failures left them without work or income for days or months at a time. Their wives,
Rachel Stump and Sarah Walmsley, and their
daughters contributed more regularly to their
families' income, taking in mounds of other
people's dirty laundry to wash, iron, and fold,
and meeting their neighbors' diverse sewing
needs.

The image historians and archaeologists had
constructed of families like the Stumps and
Walmsleys, and that I had uncritically accepted,
embodied an impoverished material life on the
edge of subsistence. But the archaeological evidence conjured another image—of a life shaped
by a diverse, extensive, captivating array of objects—sparkling glassware, shining gilded china
plates, silvered jewelry, pantries full of canned
fruits and vegetables, ice skates, toy watches, and
homes the families owned. The material attests
to other stories, other histories.

Telling these stories is far from easy. Any
archaeologist who has questioned storytelling as
an appropriate mode of discourse has never tried
to tell a story. The key to good stories, as to
good scholarship, is details—an object, an action,
a thought, a look. The stories I tell and the
images I present here negotiate a difficult path.

Historical Archaeology, 1998, 32(1):42–54.
Permission to reprint required.

My imagination should paint in few of the details while allowing the stories to communicate the messages and meanings I intend. These messages center around two African-American families shaping and valuing their material world as it shaped them. The stories also highlight ambivalence toward identities grounded in materialism, and to a lesser extent, racism—lesser not because it did not define these families' lives in important ways, but because its influences and injustices have received heightened attention in archaeologists' stories about African Americans in recent years. These stories of racism had in part shaped my own inaccurate image of families like the Stumps and Walmsleys. I wanted to highlight other images. Illustrating these new stories has also posed special problems, and I have had to cast a broader net than the people and communities about which I speak in order to help readers imagine the past I seek to represent.

Work Time, Family Time, Festive Time, and Material Representations of Time

Afternoon turned slowly to evening on a Saturday in late August, and Rachel Stump looked up from the supper dishes she washed to let the light breeze cool her warm, damp face. The breeze warned of a coming storm, and she groaned softly as she thought of the work awaiting her before sunset. Then she smiled to herself, for though work was work, these preparations were special. Tomorrow she and Sidney would rise before dawn to travel the 10 miles to Wilmington for the annual Big Quarterly. Since their sons, George and Jacob, and daughter Lydia, had married, they no longer traveled to the city for the whole weekend celebration. But they never missed the love feast early Sunday morning and the hours of festival, dancing, singing, eating, worshipping, and remembering that followed. This year they would have to leave extra early, for the first Big Quarterly of the new century—yes, it was 1900 already—would doubtless draw thousands. Last year, Rachel remem-

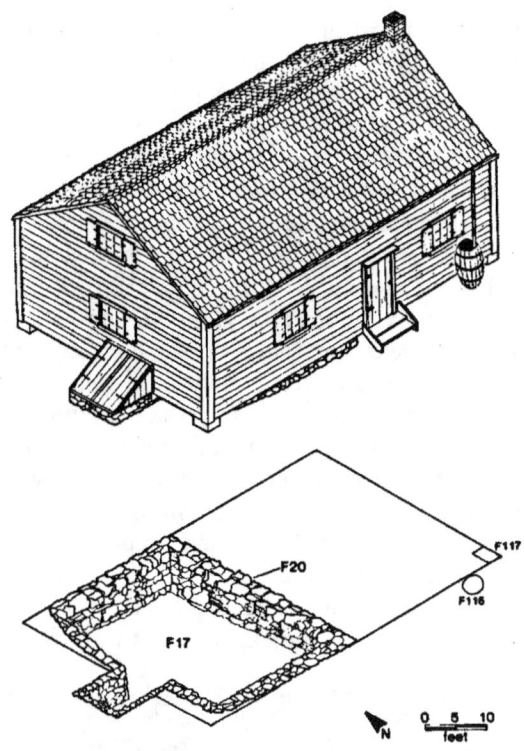

FIGURE 1. Artist's rendering of the Stump house and the archaeological basis of the reconstruction (Catts and Custer 1990:214).

bered, friends at church claimed the newspapers reported 10,000 celebrants had jammed the city.

A low rumble of thunder reminded Rachel she might not have much time. She stacked the dishes to dry, and concentrated on the work at hand. And, by the way, where did Sidney get to, and with all these preparations unfinished. Just like him to disappear when she had a list in mind of a hundred things for him to do. As usual, she would just have to take care of everything herself.

Their church, the St. Thomas African Union Methodist Protestant Church of Glasgow, Delaware, celebrated a community Little Quarterly the weekend before Big Quarterly each year, yet the women still always contributed to the church's love feast at Wilmington. Rachel hurried out of the kitchen and around the house to the cellar entrance (Figure 1). Thank the Lord that Thomas Williams, the stonemason who once owned the house, had dug a deep cellar below the parlor and carefully lined it with stone. With the bulkhead door opened wide so she could see, she climbed down the steep steps, grabbed a basket from the stack on the floor, and turned to the shelves of canned produce (Figure 2). Coming as it did at the end of summer harvest, Big Quarterly celebrants gave thanks for the earth's fruitfulness with offerings from their own bounty. Scanning the shelves of early summer fruits and vegetables already put up for winter, Rachel selected several jars of her widely renowned strawberry preserves. Back outside, she headed around behind the house and across the yard, down toward the garden.

Even in her hurry, Rachel pulled the garden gate shut behind her, an automatic gesture to close out marauding rabbits and the spirits of the damp, wild woods and marsh. Setting her laden basket down on an old table in the shed, she retrieved her special garden basket from its hook on the wall and headed toward the corner melon patch. There she swiftly and expertly inspected the rows of vines, and chose a half dozen melons whose size, color, and firmness she knew meant they were perfectly ripe. Back in the garden shed, she retrieved her basket of preserves and, with the wind at her back, hurried out the garden gate toward the cooler shed (Figure 3).

Inside, she struggled with the wooden door over the small, round storage pit that never failed to keep fresh the root crops, milk, butter, and fruits she stacked around its walls. This time she wanted a few carefully sealed tubs of butter and the small baskets of wild blackberries she had collected early that morning. As she rearranged her basket, she heard the rain start

FIGURE 2. Photograph of Features 17 and 20, the stone-lined cellar underlying the west end of the Stump house, after excavation. View looks south. The cellar figures in the story as Rachel Stump's storage area for the garden produce she canned each year (Catts and Custer 1990:114).

pattering and soon pounding on the tin roof. Well, the rain would at least give her a minute to catch her breath before her next challenge—summoning up Sidney to load the wagon before dark. Thinking of him as she set the door back in place over the hole, she remembered that spring back in 1876—almost a quarter century ago now, when they had built their cooler.

They had lived in Delaware for 10 years before they could buy that house. They both wanted their own home so badly, and they had worked *hard* during those years to afford one. After the Great War for Freedom, they *had* to leave Maryland. Home there held too many painful memories. They had friends who had gone north to work for the big grain and peach farmers in Delaware, and they joined them with their new baby, George. Sidney, bless him, was young and strong in those days, and he worked hard. All the best farmers would hire him—Mr.

Cazier, Mr. Black, Mr. Frazer, Mr. Cann, and Mr. Clark—although none would pay what they paid those dirty, worthless Irish men. Rachel wanted to be close to her baby, and the two others she bore in those years, but she had skills and knew the meaning of work too. Fortunately for her, those Irish women did no better than their men, and before long Mrs. Cazier, Mrs. Black, and the others refused to hire them as servants. They would rather *she* and her friends take their laundry and sewing work and do it at home. That suited her fine, and so for the next 10 years that's what they did—work and save every penny they could.

It surprised Rachel that she could no longer remember how she and Sidney learned of this Glasgow property or why the widow Williams and her children had decided to sell it. Mr. Williams had died years before, and the family hadn't kept the house and grounds very well.

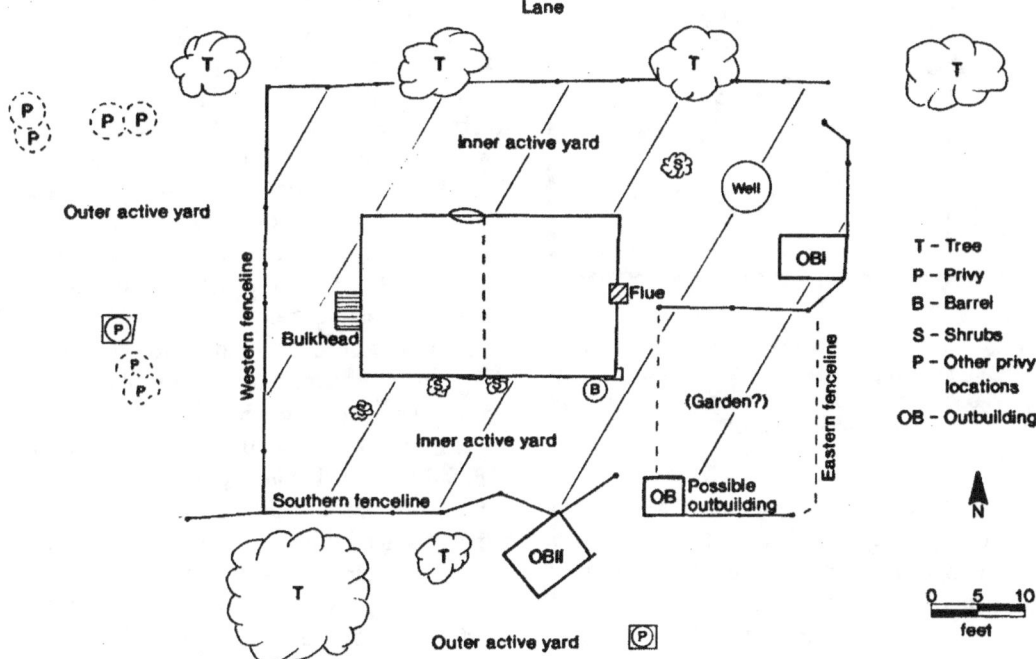

FIGURE 3. Plan of the landscape of the Stump houselot, based on archaeological evidence. The "Possible outbuilding" in the southwest corner of the garden is the garden shed in the story, and "OBI" is the cooler. The bulkhead provided access to the stone-lined cellar (Catts and Custer 1990:219).

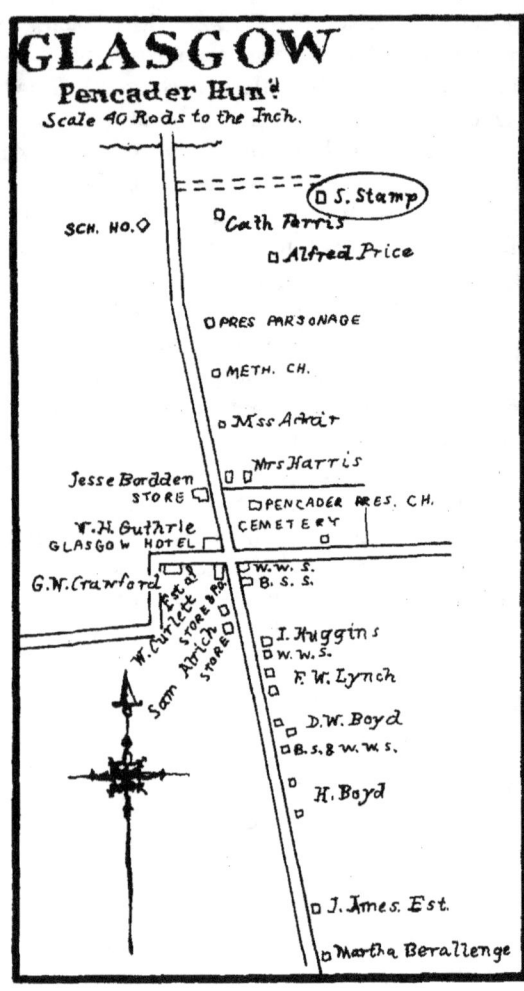

FIGURE 4. Redrawn detail of *Atlas of the State of Delaware* (Baist 1893), showing the Stump houselot on the north edge of Glasgow, set well back from the main road through the village (Catts and Custer 1990:26).

They knew that white folks didn't sell to the likes of them if they could help it. But this lot lay on the *edge* of town, near the river and rims of woods and marsh, and the house stood way back from the road (Figure 4). Nobody even knew it was there, or seemed to care too much when the Williamses agreed to the $250 they offered. The nearness to the water, the woods,

the marsh, the house set on a bit of a hill, cleared all around with a fenced yard and garden above the field (so what that the fence was falling down)—well, Rachel and Sidney surely could make this their home.

Sidney and George first fixed the fences to keep out, well, everything and everybody that didn't *belong*—the pigs they let feed out in the woods, the raccoons and deer and possum—all those wild, dirty animals that rooted around in the yard Rachel swept clean each day, and that ate anything and everything they tried to grow in their garden. Between that garden and the well, on the high ground east of the house, toward the ancestors' homes in Africa and the dawn, Sidney dug the cooler pit and raised its shed house. When he finished, Rachel dug a small hole in the bottom of the pit, and in it she placed an ax head of iron. Her mother and grandmother had taught her about the power of iron, ideas from a homeland that Rachel never knew. But she knew the iron would protect the foods she grew and gathered from the threatening spirits that lurked beyond the fence.

The thought of such spiritual power made Rachel stop and listen. She heard nothing, and then realized it meant the storm had passed. Outside, the rain had made the dirt yard a bit slick, but Rachel didn't notice. She smiled at the wet leaves on the maple trees beyond the house sparkling in the setting sun, and turned toward the stable below the houseyard. Sidney stood inside the door, tending to the wagon. She called to him to pick up her baskets of food, and headed back to the house to pack up the corn breads and cakes she baked that morning.

Finally, Rachel could climb the stairs to their small bedroom and prepare their best clothes for the day's festivities. For many years after they moved to their new house, they had scarcely any money to spend on store-bought clothes. The mortgage, books and school supplies for the children, and toys that would teach them valuable lessons—these were more important, so Rachel relied on the sewing skills and sense of style the

No. 23496 Lace and Hair Braid Mixed, a shape that is bound to be a success in '97. This is a new stylish straw hat. (See cut.) Each.............. 50c

a

b

23526

No. 23528 American Beauty Rose with foliage. A very pretty and popular flower, (see illustration). Pink and Jack shades. Each....18c

c

FIGURE 5. The hat Rachel Stump created to wear to Big Quarterly may have resembled *a*, this one available from Sears, Roebuck and Company; *b*, straw hats; and *c*, silk flower trimmings were also available from Sears, Roebuck and Company (Israel 1968:301–303).

good Lord had given her (and these were considerable, if she did say so herself).

Now she could do so much more with all the choices available at Boulden's and Alrich's stores in town and through those mail-order houses. Rachel still made her own best summer dress each year of a light-colored cotton. Cool and comfortable, it had other meanings, too, when worn to Big Quarterly. Cotton for remembering her enslaved ancestors down South, and their sufferings in the fields. Homemade to display their skill, style, and pride in doing and making for themselves. She had also carefully selected the straw hat and trimmings at Boulden's. From these she designed a colorful, fanciful creation of flowers, feathers, and bows held in place by a sparkling, jeweled hat pin (Figure 5). It fairly shouted her personal style and announced her identity—as a person's head and its appearance should—as a woman, a successful seamstress, a gardener, a provider for her family. And it showed proper reverence to the Lord when she entered His sanctuary.

Sidney would wear his summer church suit and straw Canton hat with its wide white ribbon that matched the silk ribbon of his watch fob. It, too, held special meaning at Big Quarterly (Figure 6). The silk fob resembled military medals and other badges of honor and heroism (Figure 7). Sidney and the other men wore them to memorialize the bravery of their ancestors that the other world denied. The watch was *time* in a form you could hold in your hand and pin on your chest and give to your son. Remembering time past. Looking to the future. Living in today's world, with American conceptions of minutes, hours, days, work time, a new century. A measure of wealth. An heirloom.

Rachel caught her mind wandering again. It was getting dark, and she could no longer see the matches to light the lamp on the table next to the bed. She reached out to feel for the matches, brushed something on the table, and heard the smashing of glass before realizing what she had done. Sidney's watch. She took another step toward the table. Oh no! The watch had skidded further across the floor than she'd figured, and now it gave way under her. Footsteps downstairs. Sidney. She panicked and froze for an instant. But then something in her mind clicked. Tomorrow was Big Quarterly, a time to remember a past when her people were owned like this very watch. A time to give thanks and praise the Lord. A joyful time. A spiritual time. And here she was fussing over this broken thing. Why, she was behaving just like one of those women she worked for who spilled tea on a new dress. What does it matter, she always chided, when they had a dozen more in the closet? Good Lord, what had happened to her? Who had she become?

Glittering Goods, Shattered Ideals?

David Walmsley stooped over the shattered glass vase. The sharp pieces glinted in the sun-

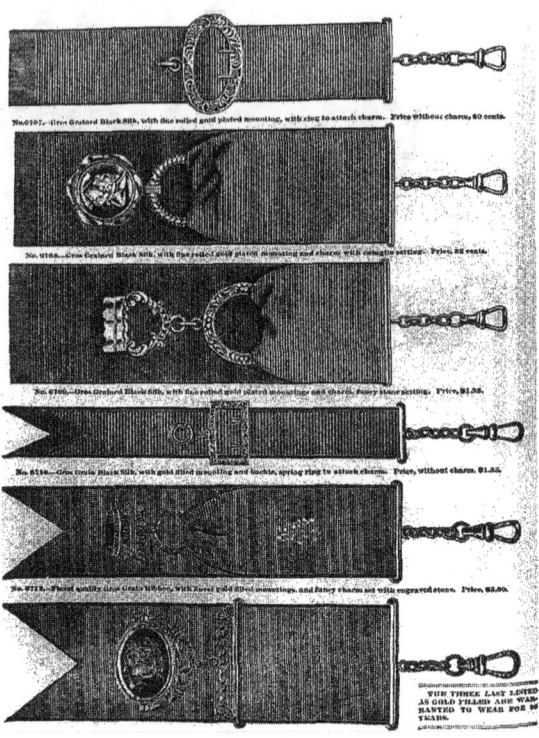

FIGURE 7. Archaeologists excavating the cellar of the Stumps' house found watch fob fittings similar to those on these silk fobs advertised by Sears, Roebuck and Company in 1897 (Israel 1968:408).

FIGURE 6. Archaeologists excavating the cellar of the Stumps' house found watch parts from a watch similar to these advertised by Sears, Roebuck and Company in 1897 (Israel 1968:373).

light streaming through the dining room window as he stiffly swept them into the dustpan. He mumbled under his breath as he heard his wife Sarah slamming the pots behind him in the kitchen. That woman was sputtering mad, and it just didn't make sense to him. She might have known better than to ask him to stretch up and reach that vase on the top shelf of the cupboard. He was an old man—80 years this Lord's year of 1900—and sometimes he just couldn't feel his hands anymore. He'd grasped that vase and slid it off the shelf, but before he could turn and set it on the table, it slipped out of his gnarled fingers. Now it lay in little pieces on the floor. The children *had* given it to them in celebration of 50 years of marriage, and this *was* the annual family dinner after Big Quarterly, and those molded diamonds *did* glitter in the light, and draw your attention to the flowers Sarah always carefully arranged in the vase set in the center of the table. But for David it still remained a vase. It didn't deserve all that fussing. They could buy another one, and many things mattered more (Figure 8).

The banging of pots grew even louder from the kitchen, and David finished his sweeping, grabbed the waste bucket and headed for the door. Outside, the sweaty heat of midday engulfed him, and he walked slowly across the small yard to the back fence. He dumped the bucket over the fence (Figure 9). The fragmented glass clattered as it hit the soft earth. David stared for a moment at the pieces lying amidst the discarded remains of all Sarah's preparations for this dinner—husks and shells and chicken innards—then took out his white-clay tobacco pipe and lit it.

As he smoked, he looked out over the fence, beyond the dump, down the hill, and across marsh toward the Christina River. Just when had Sarah changed? How? Why? After the Great War, they, like many others, had left Maryland. They wanted a kind of freedom and independence the old white folks back home could never, or would never, give them. So they'd come here, to a small commercial town named Christiana Bridge near Wilmington, where the men could get field work in season and in the city or on the water other times, and the women could hire out to the big farmers' and merchants' wives. Those years took their toll, David thought as the pain shot down his back, but they had done it for themselves, and more importantly, for the children and their future. True, they'd wandered about unsettled those first years, but then the African Methodist Episcopal (A.M.E.) Church established itself on the hill at the north end of town. The revived church just drew people like the Walmsleys. So they'd rented a place way down behind the church, in the lowland along Eagle Run, and there they raised six children (Figure 10).

David chuckled as he remembered the first time Bartholomew trapped a muskrat, and the

FIGURE 8. Fragments of a pressed glass vase similar to this "celery vase" (Lee 1985:38) figure prominently in the story of the Walmsley family. Archaeologists recovered them from a midden excavated on the houselot.

first fish George caught. With Sarah and the girls' gardening and their hunting, trapping, gathering, and fishing, they could feed the whole family, and eat well too. His wages covered the rent most months, and they saved much of Sarah's earnings to buy a house—a dream they shared. During those same years, though, they began to argue over the children. The church stressed the importance of schooling and hard work; these he and Sarah valued too and encouraged in the children. For him, the rewards were good health, a full stomach, a home of your own, a caring family, a close-knit community of the faithful, and a little left over to help those in need. But Sarah spent a lot of time in the homes of white neighbors who could afford her services as laundress and seamstress as well as many other *things*. She valued those things more and more, until she was buying the children toy watches, dolls, marbles and jacks, iron horses and wagons, whistles, kazoos, and even ice skates. Good Lord, did she get mad if he said a word!

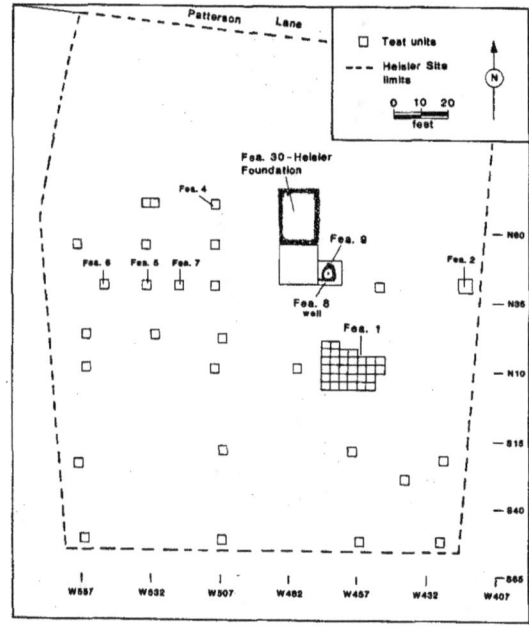

FIGURE 9. Archaeological site plan showing excavations at the home of the Walmsley family. Features 8, 9, and 30 represent the house, and Feature 1 designates the midden that extended south down the slope away from the house (Catts et al. 1989:227).

Fully 20 years passed, and most of the children had grown and married, before David and Sarah saved enough to buy the house up the hill from their tenant house, nearer the church and the main road into town. David was already 67 years old and, although he spent less time in the woods and marsh and on the water, he wished he didn't have to climb up and down the steep slope to reach them. And the house sat on a lot so small they could hardly plant a garden. But Sarah didn't care. To her mind, they moved up in the world when they moved up that hill into a house a full two stories tall and featuring a fancy stone gate post out front. And of course, the old furniture and dishes and glasses and, well almost everything, would not do. So the money he'd rather they spent on some land went instead into an array of fancy store-bought things. Worst of all, he frowned, most of the children seemed to share their mother's new ideas about what mattered. They marked special days in their parents' lives not by joining them for a day of worship at church, but with a glass vase or some other trifling thing.

Sarah's call urged him to hurry up, open the oysters, and get changed before the children arrived. As he hobbled back toward the kitchen, he could smell the mingling aromas of the roast chicken, breads, pies, and stewing squash. Flies buzzed around the bushel of oysters Sarah had just hauled up from the cooler. He found his shucking knife and headed toward a shady spot behind the kitchen. Inside, he heard the familiar tinkling of china, glass, and silverware. He could easily imagine Sarah carefully setting out the delicate china plates and bowls decorated with flowers like those she *usually* displayed so proudly in her glittering glass vase. Each place also received an immaculately ironed and folded linen napkin, polished silvered knife, spoon, and fork, and a drinking glass. On the cupboard server stood the line of china and glass platters and the gilded dessert wares, and a large mirror hung on the opposite wall. Even David had to admit the table shimmered and sparkled, and he

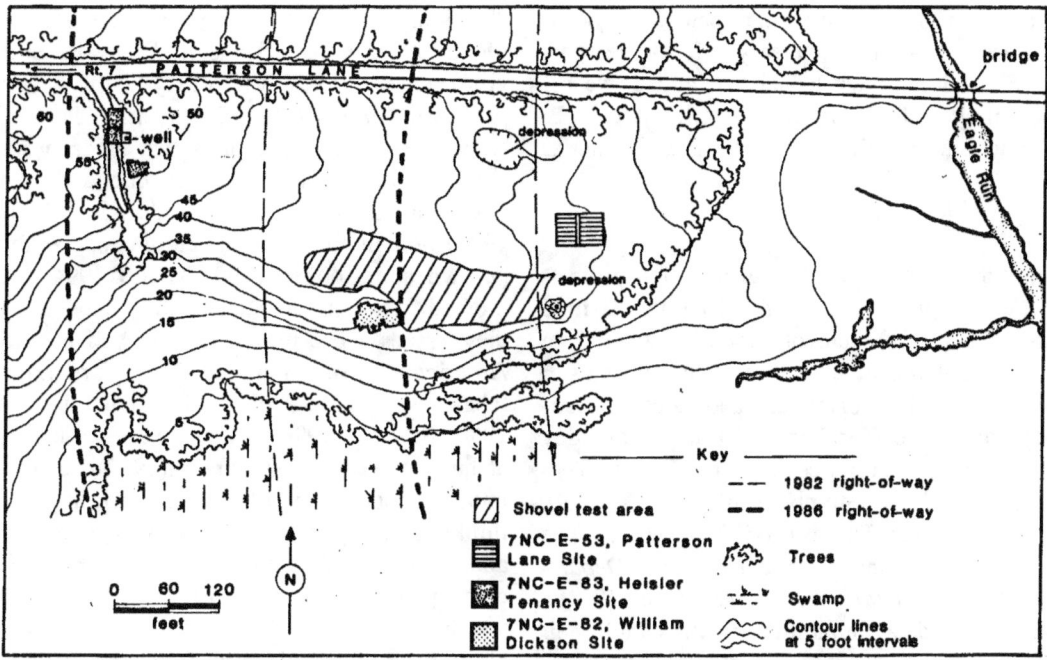

FIGURE 10. Map showing the environmental and topographical setting of the Walmsley houselot (7NC-E-83, Heisler Tenancy site). Note the proximity to Patterson Lane, Eagle Run, and the wood-edged marshes at the base of the slope falling away from the houselot to the south. The Walmsleys moved to this house in 1887 from a house they rented down the slope, nearer the marshes and the Christina River beyond (7NC-E-82, William Dickson site) (Catts et al. 1989:3).

did understand the power of shining, reflecting objects. In African beliefs that his father taught him as far back as he could remember, such things allowed a view into the world of the spirits, catching and holding them for at least a moment. Maybe he was beginning to understand; maybe she had *not* forgotten what their life was all about, what the Big Quarterly ensured they remembered and celebrated. The ancestors; their African home; their salvation from slavery; their children; food blessed and shared—the symbol of life itself.

David would have given almost anything to go to Big Quarterly, but his rheumatism had gotten too bad this past year. Instead, he'd have to settle for reliving it through the stories his children and grandchildren would tell round Sarah's finely dressed table later that day. And those of Big Quarterlies past that he would tell them one last time.

Stories of Connection, Past and Present

David Walmsley did not live to celebrate Big Quarterly in 1901.

A lifetime later, atop the hill on the edge of the old port town, developers built a temple to sparkling, shimmering consumerism and tax-free shopping—the Christiana Mall. A maze of roads fed into the temple from all directions, and plans slated one to pass over the Walmsleys' former house and yard. One fine spring day in 1986, an archaeologist stooped over a test unit trowelling intently. The trowel caught the edge of a large piece of molded glass, and it popped out of the soil, sparkling in the sunlight. Less than a mile away in the mall, a woman paid for a beautiful glass vase—an anniversary gift for her parents. She hurried back to her car, and drove off to Wilmington for a meeting at the A.U.M.P. church to plan for that summer's Big Quarterly.

Bibliographic Essay

Delaware Department of Transportation projects on Route 7 just outside of Christiana Bridge (Catts et al. 1989), and on State Route 896 in Glasgow (Lothrop et al. 1987; Catts and Custer 1990), prompted historical archaeological investigations at the former homes of the Walmsley family (7NC-E-83, referred to as the Heisler Tenancy site) and the Stump family (7NC-D-130, referred to as the Thomas Williams site). The site reports, published in the *Delaware Department of Transportation Archaeological Series*, provided the data about the families and their material world that I translated into the stories presented in this article. My interest in these sites predated the opportunity to participate in the "Archaeologists as Storytellers" session. Historical (Munroe 1957; Hancock 1968; Livesay 1968; Gutman 1976) and historical archaeological (Geismar 1982; Orser 1988) scholarship on African Americans and the ravages of racism had shaped my expectations of the material signatures I would find inscribed in the archaeological sites of families like the Stumps and the Walmsleys. Prompted by the dramatic disparity between my expectations and the archaeological remains, I had reexamined parts of the sites' collections, conducted additional research on issues that intrigued me, and drafted narratives—not stories—about the families and their worlds (De Cunzo 1997).

My concern for historical archaeologists' general failure to attend to the power of religion in the lives of people we study (De Cunzo 1995) led me to center religious belief and action in these stories. Wade Catts' discussion of the Big Quarterly in the site report on the Thomas Williams site (Catts and Custer 1990:68–69) intro-

duced me to this central event in the religious life of African Americans in Delaware and beyond in the 19th and early 20th centuries (Baldwin 1980, 1981). Discovering the spiritual and other cultural meanings that African Americans in postbellum Delaware encoded in their environment and cultural landscape (Gundaker 1993) and in the material culture of family life (Brown and Cooper 1990; Martin 1994) proved more difficult, as few researchers have explored these issues. The presentation of self in African-American culture has received more attention (Genovese 1972; Jones and Holloman 1990; Kerr 1990; Simkins 1990; Starke 1993). That scholarship, coupled with Levine's (1977) treatment of multiple conceptions of time in African-American thinking and Busch's (1983) work on watches and the commodification of time in the late 19th century, informed the story of Sidney Stump's watch.

W. E. B. Du Bois was an important African-American spokesperson, strident reformer, prolific writer, and contemporary of the Stumps and Walmsleys. His eloquent yet conflicted descriptions of African Americans living in two worlds in late 19th- and early 20th-century America (Du Bois 1899, 1961), and other scholars' work on the ways that the ideology of consumption increasingly shaped these worlds (McDaniel 1982; Fox and Lears 1983; Miller 1987; McCracken 1988; Bronner 1989; Brown and Cooper 1990; Stewart-Abernathy 1992), helped me to understand the material world of the Stumps and the Walmsleys. It is this understanding that I endeavored to share in these stories, inspired by the pioneering storytelling of archaeologist Janet Spector (1993).

ACKNOWLEDGMENTS

Historical archaeological investigations sponsored by the Delaware Department of Transportation have shaped our understanding of the history and cultures of Delaware in profound ways, and I am thankful for the department's continuing commitment to the state's heritage. These stories build on the work of Wade

Catts in several ways. He participated in all components of the archaeological investigations at both sites and coauthored both reports; he generously served as my guide to Delaware historical archaeology when I first began work in the state; his training as historian and archaeologist has influenced my thinking through both his writing and our joint work on several projects. Jay Custer graciously provided access to the collections recovered by University of Delaware Center for Archaeological Research archaeologists at the house sites of the Stumps and Walmsleys and to the site records the archaeological team created. Mary Beaudry, Ann Smart Martin, and Anne Yentsch especially influenced my thinking and my approach as I attended increasingly to context and narrative in my initial work with these two families. Bernard Herman's thoughts on stories as parables and Janet Spector's exemplary storytelling inspired my own novice attempt at writing stories. I am also grateful to Mary Praetzellis and Adrian Praetzellis for giving me the opportunity to experiment with storytelling as a mode of archaeological discourse. My thinking about what I do and about how to present my work have been irrevocably shaped by the experience. While I acknowledge these debts to my colleagues, I must also note that the perspectives and views expressed in these stories, and the responsibility for any misinterpretations, are mine.

REFERENCES

BAIST, G. WILLIAM
  1893 *Atlas of the State of Delaware.* G. William Baist, Philadelphia, PA.

BALDWIN, LEWIS V.
  1980 *"Invisible" Strands in African Methodism: A History of the African Union MethodistProtestant and Union American Methodist Episcopal Churches, 1805–1980.* Ph.D. dissertation, Northwestern University, Evanston, IL. University Microfilms International, Ann Arbor, MI.
  1981 Festivity and Celebration: A Profile of Wilmington's Big Quarterly. *Delaware History* 19(4):197–211.

BRONNER, SIMON J.
  1989 Object Lessons: The Work of Ethnological Museums and Collections. In *Consuming Visions: Accumulation and Display of Goods in America, 1880–1920*, pp. 217–254. Winterthur Museum, Winterthur, DE.

BROWN, KENNETH L., AND DOREEN C. COOPER
  1990 Structural Continuity in an African-American Slave and Tenant Community. *Historical Archaeology* 24(4):7–19.

BUSCH, JANE C.
  1983 *The Throwaway Ethic in America.* Ph.D. dissertation, University of Pennsylvania, Philadelphia. University Microfilms International, Ann Arbor, MI.

CATTS, WADE P., AND JAY F. CUSTER
  1990 Tenant Farmers, Stone Masons, and Black Laborers: Final Archaeological Investigations of the Thomas Williams Site, Glasgow, New Castle County, Delaware. *Delaware Department of Transportation Archaeology Series* 82. Dover.

CATTS, WADE P., JAY HODNY, AND JAY F. CUSTER
  1989 "The Place at Christeen": Final Archaeological Investigations of the Patterson Lane Site Complex, Christiana, New Castle County, Delaware. *Delaware Department of Transportation Archaeology Series* 74. Dover.

DE CUNZO, LU ANN
  1995 Reform, Respite, Ritual: An Archaeology of Institutions; the Magdalen Society of Philadelphia, 1800–1850. (Special Issue.) *Historical Archaeology* 29(3).
  1997 *People and Places, Cultures and Histories: The Contexts of Historical Archaeology in Delaware.* University of Delaware Press, Newark, in press.

DU BOIS, W. E. B.
  1899 The Philadelphia Negro: A Social Study. *Publications of the University of Pennsylvania Series in Political Economy and Public Law* 14. University of Pennsylvania, Philadelphia.
  1961 *The Souls of Black Folk: Essays and Sketches by W. E. Burghardt Du Bois.* Dodd, Mead, New York.

FOX, RICHARD W., AND T. J. JACKSON LEARS
  1983 Introduction. In *The Culture of Consumption: Critical Essays in American History, 1880–1980*, edited by Richard W. Fox and T. J. J. Lears, pp. ix–xvii. Pantheon, New York.

GEISMAR, JOAN H.
  1982 *The Archaeology of Social Disintegration in Skunk Hollow: A Nineteenth-Century Rural Black Community.* Academic Press, New York.

GENOVESE, EUGENE D.
  1972 *Roll, Jordan, Roll: The World the Slaves Made.* Vintage, New York.

GUNDAKER, GREY
1993 Tradition and Innovation in African-American Yards. *African Arts* 26(2):58–71.

GUTMAN, HERBERT G.
1976 *The Black Family in Slavery and Freedom, 1750– 1925.* Pantheon, New York.

HANCOCK, HAROLD B.
1968 The Status of the Negro in Delaware after the Civil War, 1865–1875. *Delaware History* 10(2):115–151.

ISRAEL, FRED L. (EDITOR)
1968 *1897 Sears Roebuck Catalogue.* Chelsea House, New York.

JONES, ISABEL, AND LILLIAN O. HOLLOMAN
1990 The Role of Clothing in the African American Church. In *African American Dress and Adornment: A Cultural Perspective,* edited by Barbara Starke, Lillian Holloman, and Barbara Nordquist, pp. 156–165. Kendall/Hunt, Dubuque, IA.

KERR, JANE BUCHWALD
1990 Dress as a Status Symbol. In *African American Dress and Adornment: A Cultural Perspective,* edited by Barbara Starke, Lillian Holloman, and Barbara Nordquist, pp. 93–105. Kendall/Hunt, Dubuque, IA.

LEE, RUTH WEBB
1985 *Early American Pressed Glass.* New edition. Charles E. Tuttle, Rutland, VT.

LEVINE, LAWRENCE W.
1977 *Black Culture and Black Consciousness: Afro- American Thought from Slavery to Freedom.* Oxford University Press, New York.

LIVESAY, HAROLD C.
1968 Delaware Negroes, 1865–1915. *Delaware History* 13(2):87–123.

LOTHROP, JONATHAN C., JAY F. CUSTER, AND COLLEEN DeSANTIS
1987 Phase I and II Archaeological Investigations of the Route 896 Corridor, Route 4–West Chestnut Hill Road to Summit Bridge Approach, New Castle County, Delaware. *Delaware Department of Transportation Archaeology Series 52.* Dover.

MARTIN, ANN SMART
1994 Boundaries in the World of Shopping: Race, Class, and Gender in the Eighteenth-Century Virginia Store Trade.

Paper presented at the Annual Meeting of the American Studies Association, Nashville, TN.

McCRACKEN, GRANT
1988 *Culture and Consumption: New Approaches to the Symbolic Character of Consumer Goods and Activities.* Indiana University Press, Bloomington.

McDANIEL, GEORGE W.
1982 *Hearth and Home: Preserving a People's Culture.* Temple University Press, Philadelphia.

MILLER, DANIEL
1987 *Material Culture and Mass Consumption.* Basil Blackwell, Oxford, UK.

MUNROE, JOHN A.
1957 The Negro in Delaware. *South Atlantic Quarterly* 56:428–444.

ORSER, CHARLES E., JR.
1988 *The Material Basis of the Postbellum Tenant Plantation: Historical Archaeology in the South Carolina Piedmont.* University of Georgia Press, Athens.

SIMKINS, ANNA ATKINS
1990 Function and Symbol in Hair and Headgear among African American Women. In *African American Dress and Adornment: A Cultural Perspective,* edited by Barbara Starke, Lillian Holloman, and Barbara Nordquist, pp. 166–172. Kendall/Hunt, Dubuque, IA.

SPECTOR, JANET D.
1993 *What this Awl Means: Feminist Archaeology at a Wahpeton Dakota Village.* Minnesota Historical Society Press, St. Paul.

STARKE, BARBARA M.
1993 Nineteenth-Century African-American Dress. In *Dress in American Culture,* edited by Patricia Cunningham and Susan V. Lab, pp. 66–79. Bowling Green State University Popular Press, Bowling Green, OH.

STEWART-ABERNATHY, LESLIE C.
1992 Industrial Goods in the Service of Tradition: Consumption and Cognition on an Ozark Farmstead before the Great War. In *The Art and Mystery of Historical Archaeology: Essays in Honor of James Deetz,* edited by Anne Elizabeth Yentsch and Mary C. Beaudry, pp. 101–126. CRC Press, Boca Raton, FL.

LU ANN DE CUNZO
DEPARTMENT OF ANTHROPOLOGY
UNIVERSITY OF DELAWARE
NEWARK, DE 19716

PAUL R. MULLINS

Race and the Genteel Consumer: Class and African-American Consumption, 1850-1930

ABSTRACT

Between the Civil War and the 1920s, a consumer culture emerged which attempted to evade class tension by focusing on contrived racial differences. The vast majority of American-born whites and European immigrants alike embraced the illusion of a classless consumer culture in which opportunity was available to white citizens alone. African Americans were caricatured as being racially unsuited to those citizen privileges in consumption and labor space. Archaeological assemblages from Annapolis, Maryland demonstrate, however, that African-American consumers actively sought the opportunities consumer culture promised and articulated an anti-racist class struggle in consumer space.

Introduction

In the wake of the Civil War, Americans faced a society profoundly transformed by European immigration, mass marketing, working-class formation, and the eradication of slavery (Susman 1984; Agnew 1990; Kasson 1990:34). Historically, the moment potentially could have realized the erosion of racism as African Americans were transformed into free laborers with the privileges of citizenship (Du Bois 1935; Foner 1988:xxv). Instead, the post-Civil War period witnessed a dramatic expansion of anti-black racism which pitted racial groups against each other and condemned the plausibility of an interracial sociopolitical order.

Racism certainly did not first spring into Western life in the middle of the 19th century (Morgan 1977). Racial identities varied significantly over time, between classes, and across regions, but by the mid-19th century race was a central feature of American class identity and material consumption (Roediger 1991). In the urban Northeast, race structured social identity through complex differentiations between groups such as Irish, Anglos, African Americans, and native-born rural newcomers to the cities. In the South, on the other hand, popular discourse tended to distill racial differences into a stark black/white divide. Regardless of region, though, race lay at the heart of American social structure.

For mannered, well-born, and affluent genteel whites, the Civil War's wake posed a deeply troubling rabble of European immigrants, native-born white working classes, and newly freed African Americans. Genteel white Anglo-Saxon Protestants were ambivalent about the rise of "uncouth" newly moneyed whites, apprehensive of European immigrants, and distressed by the possibilities of African-American freedom. In 1875, newspaperman Edward King was one of many voices who sent shudders into genteel white society when he concluded that the Civil War and Emancipation had a "genuine leveling influence" on Southern social structure. King recognized that

> there were but two classes in the South under the old [antebellum] system, the high up and the low down . . . . The negro did not count; he was a commodity . . . . Now-a-days a middle class is gradually springing into existence . . . and some of the more intelligent and respectable negroes are taking rank in this class (King 1875:773-774).

For his WASP readers, King prophesied the most distressing prospects of post-war America. He acknowledged the emergence of an African-American "middle class," a moniker which in King's usage had as much to do with genteel performance as material standing. This African-American "middle class" was a somewhat distressing possibility, but it was not particularly unsettling because of the dearth of affluent post-war African Americans (Foner 1988:398). King's more troubling implication was that social and material "leveling" could produce a mobile, interracial class structure which inevitably would reach outside the South and unsettle WASP

Historical Archaeology, 1999, 33(1):22–38.
Permission to reprint required.

domination throughout the resurrected nation (King 1875:776).

For aspiring white and European working-class laborers, African America's ascension to freedom was equally troubling, albeit for quite different reasons. After the Civil War, formerly enslaved laborers ostensibly could aspire to and even assume a footing alongside "free" American white laborers. For many white working-class laborers, this was not the makings of interracial class empowerment; it was instead a profound reduction in status, because "free" labor dominated by whites meant nothing without the polarized guise of unfree black labor. The notion of unfree black labor was a critical structuring mechanism which aspired to make race, labor, and class inseparable phenomena.

The authors and audiences of popular discourses as disparate as etiquette books, blackface minstrelsy, and advertising constructed a white ideal by fashioning a store of racial caricatures which monolithically defined and universally degraded African Americans (Roediger 1991; Lott 1995). This tacit white backdrop simultaneously restricted African-American freedoms and petitioned the non-black masses to envision racial difference, particularly distance from an idealized whiteness, as the fundamental structuring element of American society. Popular assumptions about African Americans provided a clear contrast to "white" behavior, material consumption, and social rights: for white Americans (and immigrants like the Irish who aspired to white privilege), black racial caricatures were the inverse of the white racial ideal they strove to reproduce (Ignatiev 1995).

W. E. B. Du Bois (1935:727) argued that this public demeaning of African Americans "compensated" white workers because it provided social status in the absence of material affluence. Du Bois contended that racial caricatures provided the white working class "a public and psychological wage." Despite the material subordination they shared with many African Americans, most white and European laborers assumed they were of higher social status than African Americans and enjoyed exclusive privileges by virtue of being white (Roediger 1991:12-13).

Class rarely figured in popular discourses after the Civil War. Instead, those discourses fixated on race and recast pervasive class turmoil as the inevitable product of various non-white racial groups, especially blacks. In the face of a rapidly emerging consumer culture, genteel WASPs faced a thorny dilemma of simultaneously rationalizing elite control of labor, legitimizing unequal resource distribution, and reproducing the labor of subordinated groups, which included European immigrants, working-class whites, and African Americans. Racists attempted to defuse class consciousness by forging a contrived white racial consensus which was far more significant than class interests. This maneuver fabricated an ostensibly classless mass consumer culture which promised racially exclusive privileges to all white citizens. The glaring material disparities among those citizens were inelegantly rationalized as evidence of the uncommon merit of individuals in pursuit of an ideal which was presumably attainable by all white people (Cohen 1993:136).

This work examines the complex union of racial discourse, labor structure, and class in African-American material consumption. Archaeological data from African-American homes in Annapolis, Maryland, illuminate how race shaped and reflected labor relations, community consumption patterns, and class structure in the mid-Atlantic. In an effort to defuse racism, a rich cross-section of elite, upwardly mobile, and marginalized African Americans aggressively pursued civil privileges, developed consumption tactics which minimized community racism, and subverted racist caricatures. Archaeological material culture reflects that African Americans simultaneously aspired to the genteel privileges of consumer space and tactically undermined its anti-black racism through consumption. Archaeological and documentary data demonstrate the complex relationship between racism and African-American material consumption and the repercussions of race on class structure between the mid-19th century and the New Deal.

Class Structure and Consumption Relations

Class analyses typically focus on the determining weight of production and economic realms and ignore or minimize consumption (Williams 1977:75-82). In most such formulations, class conflict fundamentally looms as friction between groups with differential relations to the means of production. Even theorists who see consumption as part of a production system tend to reduce consumption to a logical end-product of production. Ultimately, though, this tends to fetishize consumption as instrumental shopping behavior, focusing on purchase itself and evading how goods assume social meanings (Miller 1995:53).

It would be naive to discard the recognition that class tension reflects differential positioning in labor structure. Nevertheless, it makes sense to assertively probe how consumption itself was a mechanism which structured class. Posing class as differential relations to consumption challenges the assumption that the most fundamental social relations are fashioned by a group's position within the labor structure (Miller 1987:48). Since consumer culture began to emerge in the late-19th century, a fundamental dimension of class structure and conflict has been between consumers differentiated by various social and state mechanisms, not simply (or even primarily) by their unequal control of labor and production. Americans' widespread social and material investment in consumption risked minimizing the profound sway of production, but most consumers saw the struggle waged in consumer space as one which inevitably involved the material opportunities provided (or denied) by labor structure. Americans clearly began to believe that their social and material ambitions could be realized by commodity consumption which required privileges in both workplaces and public consumer space.

For African America, citizen privilege lay in securing consumer rights as much as labor and production rights. In their association of citizenship and consumption, African America was not alone: in late-19th century America, material goods provided idealized opportunities, worlds of novel symbolic objects with which myriad individuals imagined new experiences and fresh identities (Susman 1984; Campbell 1995). It would be rash to reduce class analysis simply to this idiosyncratic and highly individualized consumer desire, because a focus on consumption symbolism alone would produce a highly fragmented vision of class and social structure. Nevertheless, any analysis of African-American class must consider the positioning of African Americans within a racist mode of production as well as position within—and resistance against—an equally racist consumer space. In that culture of resistance is a critical dimension of African-American class struggle: material goods and attendant genteel social behaviors reflect African America's class struggle within and against dominant racist labor relations, communities, state interests, and other consumers.

Community and National Marketing

Consumer goods displayed late-19th century Americans' investment in national affluence, showcased their gentility, and provided the symbolic means to entertain myriad individual desires and aspirations. Among the flood of new consumers were many African Americans who were eager to demonstrate their American identity, celebrate their freedom from servitude, and test the possibilities of an ostensibly equitable consumer marketplace. In Annapolis, African Americans developed a relatively consistent body of consumer tactics. For instance, Annapolitan archaeological materials indicate an African-American focus on brand consumption during the late-19th century. The largest African-American bottle assemblage in Annapolis came from the Maynard-Burgess House (Mullins and Warner 1993). The free African-American household of John and Maria Spencer Maynard built a house at 163 Duke of Gloucester Street between 1850 and 1858. The home was occupied by three generations of Maynards between the 1850s and 1914, when relative Willis Burgess purchased it (Mullins 1996a:164). Burgesses lived in the home until the 1980s, and archaeological collections span the whole range of the home's occupation. Among those deposits was a subsurface cellar accessed through an external bulkhead entrance at the rear of the house. The four-foot deep, earthen-walled cellar was filled with domestic debris which had a *terminus post quem* of 1889. Among a rich assemblage of household refuse, the cellar contained 87 glass vessels (79 bottles and 8 table vessels) (Mullins 1996b:4-5). Every one of the 26 embossed vessels in the deposit was from a nationally advertised brand (Mullins and Warner 1993:1:103-105). Several brands were used recurrently, and no bottles had the embossments of local pharmacists or bottlers. The mean production date for the bottle assemblage was 1882.52; this date is relatively close to the assemblage's 1889 *terminus post quem*, indicating that most of the vessels were produced, sold, and discarded relatively quickly.

The same pattern of national brand predominance was identified at two other African-American sites in Annapolis. Gott's Court was an alley community located on the interior of a city block. The Court was a 24 apartment frame complex which was home exclusively to African-American renters from 1907 until its demolition in 1952. Only one locally bottled beverage in an assemblage of 54 glass vessels (42 bottles and 12 table vessels) was recovered from Gott's Court. The Gott's Court assemblage can be dated tentatively to early in the Court's occupation, but because it came from sheet refuse the dating is somewhat more provisional than that of the other African-American assemblages, which were all sealed features.

The Courthouse site was a neighborhood which was home to African Americans of all socioeconomic stations from the 1830s into the 1960s. The block contained an alley community known as Bellis Court, which was built in 1897 and razed in 1939 (Aiello and Seidel 1995:1:48).

Unlike the 24-household Gott's Court, Bellis Court had only 6 units, but both complexes were dominated by service laborers (e.g., domestics, porters, laundresses, waiters, etc.). Other addresses in the Courthouse block were home to local African-American elite, several groceries and small businesses, and Annapolis' African-Methodist-Episcopal congregation. Of these contexts within the Courthouse block, Bellis Court contained the best-preserved bottle assemblage. A privy containing 66 glass vessels (56 bottles and 10 table vessels) with a mean production date of 1905.68 included only 2 locally bottled goods (Mullins 1996a:184-185).

Consistent national brand consumption among materially stable home owners at Maynard-Burgess and marginalized tenants at Gott's Court and Bellis Court suggests that the pattern is not class related. If bottle consumption followed some class pattern among African-American Annapolitans, it would be reasonable to expect differences between the Maynard-Burgess assemblage and that of renters at the two alley communities. Instead, all of these sites were overwhelmingly dominated by nationally produced brands, whose distribution mushroomed in the 1870s (Schlereth 1991:162). Brand consumption patterns from non-African American sites is irrelevant to an understanding of African-American brand preference; besides assuming a dubious "norm" for brand consumption patterns, the desire for a pattern comparison implies that African-American consumption can only be understood when that implicitly white consumer norm is itself defined.

The favor for brands certainly was not fueled by economizing: whether bottled, bagged, wrapped in paper, or canned, brands were significantly more expensive than loose goods (Edwards 1969 [1932]:58). Instead, brand consumption was a tactic which circumvented local marketers' racism and reflected African Americans' aspiration to the consumer privileges trumpeted in brand advertising (Lears 1994). Legions of African Americans served white households as domestics, cooks, and service laborers, so they accumulated "a wealth of knowledge regarding brands and qualities and varieties" (Edwards 1969 [1932]:168). In a 1932 study of African-American consumption in the urban South, Paul Edwards (1969 [1932]:52-53) found that the vast majority of African-American consumers favored brand goods. Edwards' study indicated that the difference in brand consumption between African-American laborers and professionals was negligible, a class consistency which is also suggested by Annapolitan archaeology. Edwards argued convincingly that the consistent favor for brands was an effort to circumvent racist marketers. In the South (if not elsewhere), African Americans were constantly cheated by community merchants who bottled their own products, sold dry goods from barrels, and marketed goods loose. Nationally produced goods, in contrast, assured the same quality in every container, and because they were sealed outside the local market neighborhood retailers had no opportunity to adulterate the ingredients. Canned foods offered the same advantage and the Maynard-Burgess cellar contained nearly 800 corroded metal fragments which could be conclusively identified as cans.

Lizabeth Cohen's (1990, 1993) research on Chicago between the World Wars reveals that European immigrants, unlike African Americans, tended to continue buying loose goods from community merchants. In Chicago, though, these merchants were usually from the same ethnic group as consumers, creating a consumer venue which reproduced many distinctive cultural conventions (Cohen 1993:137-138). In contrast, she found that African Americans tended to heavily favor brand goods and chain stores, which offered lower prices and large stocks of nationally produced goods (Cohen 1990:152). Shopping at African-American stores was not a particularly viable option in Annapolis or Chicago, because cash-strapped African-American entrepreneurs tended to run sparsely stocked, expensive, and short-lived ventures (Cohen 1990:151-154). An African-American Annapolitan remembered that during the 1930s "we did have a few black people who had stores, but they were smaller . .

. they were mostly, well, a few canned goods like beans and sugar and, maybe, a small amount of meat, pork chops, maybe bologna and cheese, a few eggs and stuff like that. Their volume was very small" (Maryland State Archives 1990).

The lower costs of the chains certainly was attractive, but for African-American consumers it was also critical that chains lay outside the control of local marketers. The racism of community merchants was a tangible lived experience, and many African Americans placed comparatively more hope in a national market which displayed less clearly defined racism. For African-American Annapolitans, though, the paucity of pre-Depression chain stores minimized the chain patronage favored by African Americans in Chicago. In 1930, Annapolis' 220 retail stores included 192 single store independents, 20 stores in a regional chain, and just 8 units of a national chain (U. S. Department of Commerce 1930:1). This predominance of independently owned corner stores was typical of most Maryland markets at the outset of the Depression (U. S. Department of Commerce 1937:85). Not strategically organized or limited to one class, brand consumption negotiated the persistent racism of these Annapolis corner marketers and reflects African Americans' rapid attachment to a nationally based consumer culture (Mullins 1996a:308-316).

Class and Materialism in African-American Annapolis

Bottle consumption similarities among African-American Annapolitans do not suggest marked class differences, but the appearance of class homogenization is misleading. Wealth and material display often were less crucial to African-American elite status than they were among white elite (Gatewood 1990:206-207). Willard Gatewood (1990:343-345) demonstrates that African-American elite throughout the country were distinguished by long-term family prestige, often descended from free African Americans; education; material wealth, albeit usually modest by white standards; and light skin complexion, which reflected the mixed ethnic ancestry of many African-American elite (Foner 1988:397-398). In Annapolis, African-American status was most clearly vested in social circles whose espoused values—education, self-control, rational morality, material denial—mirrored white genteel ideology.

Rather than embrace pretentious material display, African-American elite focused on genteel social performance, education, and status of established families. Elite and upwardly mobile African Americans often viewed working-class African Americans with ambivalence, but "respectable" African Americans labored to school the African-American masses in genteel social behavior and often were vocal advocates for African-American civil rights. This desire to "uplift" all African Americans was not wholly altruistic: racism cast African Americans as one monolithic lot, so African-American elite were distressed that their genteel identity was undermined by the social behavior of "coarse" African Americans (Gatewood 1990:343). In Maryland, for example, resistance to segregated rail car laws was spearheaded by the Baltimore and Annapolis elite, including William Bishop of the region's prestigious Bishop family (*Afro American Ledger*, 22 February 1902:4). The resistance to "Jim Crow" car laws, though, was not without self-interest: many elite African Americans were convinced that separate car laws were a white scheme to force "respectable" African Americans to consort with "uncouth" African Americans (Gatewood 1990:309).

Many upper-class African Americans positioned themselves as voices for African America in visible public positions, such as entrepreneurs, journalists, and ministers. Annapolis had a circle of such figures who spoke to whites as well as African Americans on a variety of social and material issues. Among the most prominent African-American voices in Annapolis was that of Wiley Bates. Born enslaved in 1859, Bates shucked oysters, huckstered, and waited tables in order to rent a modest Annapolis grocery which he opened in 1879. By 1897, Washington's

African-American newspaper *The Bee* concluded that Bates' Annapolis grocery "takes rank among the leading grocery houses of the city" (*The Bee* 9 January 1897b:1). Like many other African Americans, Bates was a testament to the power of Booker T. Washington's quest to instill genteel "middle class" aspiration among self-made African Americans. Bates mirrored Washington's call for African-American material solidarity, labor discipline, and cultural and educational refinement. Much like Washington, Bates decried racism, but he embraced the bourgeois notion of a *laissez faire* free market. Indeed, Bates was among the African Americans who viewed racism simply as an obstacle to participation in an otherwise equitable labor and economic system (Mullins 1996a:328-332).

In Annapolis, African-American elite were dominated by modest entrepreneurs like Bates who were active in fraternal organizations and the church. They championed social refinement and were eager to display their good graces. In 1897, for instance, (*The Bee* 1 January 1897a:8) reported that "Wm. H. Bates, our popular grocery-man, gave a reception to Universal Lodge No 14, A. F. & A. M. . . . Four courses were served in excellent style, consisting of everything eatable. No wines or liquors were served." It was evident to any genteel reader that Bates' Mason's Lodge reception embraced dominant social canons, serving a diverse meal in a series of "stylish" courses and spurning alcohol. These good graces extended to cultural refinement as well. In 1900, for example, Bates was among a group of African-American entrepreneurs and professionals who formed the "Bamuke Literary and Musical Association, (colored)" to "develop a taste for classical literature. To attain success the organization will invite acknowledged exponents and prominent educators of both races to deliver lectures, addresses, &c." (*Anne Arundel Examiner*, 11 October 1900:5). The link between African-American social status and education was evident in the group's membership: the association included graduates of Howard, Wilberforce, Lincoln, Oberlin, and Morgan.

Annapolitan elite were energetic champions of African-American economic organization, ranging from small business to modest cooperative ventures. That economic organization was centered in fraternal organizations, a pattern typical throughout African America (Frazier 1924:293). In Annapolis these fraternals included an African-American Elks Lodge which was organized in 1910 by J. Albert Adams, a City Council member who also ran a funeral parlor and a liquor store (Brown 1994:110; Mullins 1996a:560). The most prestigious African-American fraternal group was the Masons, who established an Annapolis lodge in 1864 and included Wiley Bates among their number (Brown 1994:112). The Masons, though, were among the most exclusive and class-conscious of all African-American fraternals: throughout the country, their number included a disproportionate volume of well-educated, moneyed, and light-complexioned African Americans (Gatewood 1990:212).

This Annapolitan circle of African-American elite primarily distinguished themselves by genteel behavior, rather than conspicuous materialism. Genteel African America's puritanical focus on behavior, lineage, and education was comparable to an anti-materialist bent in WASP discourse, which routinely divorced status from material affluence as a means to curb social ascent (Horowitz 1985). Despite their professed anti-materialism, though, Annapolis' African-American elite did have some material distinctions, and a handful of African-American Annapolitans achieved the material trappings of an idealized genteel household. In 1860, for instance, William Bishop owned 11 properties in Annapolis as well as a house in Albany, New York worth a total of more than $12,000 (Calderhead 1977:18). Born enslaved in 1802 of a European-born white father and African-American mother, Bishop was the wealthiest African American in Annapolis and Anne Arundel County in 1860, and he ranked among Annapolis' 12 richest families (Calderhead 1977:18). The Bishops' African-American neighbors on Duke of Gloucester Street included William H.

Butler, a businessman who owned 33 homes and 4 vacant lots worth over $24,000 by the mid-1870s (Ives 1979:147). In 1873 Butler became the first African-American elected official in Maryland when he won a seat on the Annapolis City Council, and in 1876 he was the largest private landowner in Annapolis (*Maryland Pendulum* 1987:10).

Less affluent African Americans like the Maynards aspired to genteel standing and accumulated more modest, albeit distinctive material assemblages. The Maynards' tax and property values and social associations suggest the household was materially stable, and they were at least familiar with prominent African Americans in the city. Born free in 1810, John Maynard waited tables, probably at Annapolis' renowned City Hotel, and he and wife Maria purchased the $400 Duke of Gloucester Street lot in 1847 (Mullins 1996a:159). The Maynard's pre-Emancipation neighborhood included several prominent free African Americans, such as William Bishop and Main Street merchant Henry Price (Hurst 1981:244). An 1849 book of 344 Annapolis tax valuations provides suggestive evidence for the standing of Maynard and 19 other free African-American Annapolitans at mid-century. Maynard was assessed an amount of $525, a value higher than 103 of the white taxpayers and 10 of the 19 African Americans (Sullivan 1849). It is unclear how these 19 African-American households compared to the city's 533 free blacks, 642 enslaved blacks, or 1,826 whites recorded in the following year's census (Ives 1979:133). These 19 free African-Americans, however, like the whites recorded in the 1849 tax book, likely were among the city's most affluent residents at mid-century.

In February 1876, James C. Bishop and William H. Butler inventoried the material possessions of their neighbor John Maynard, who died in July 1875. James C. Bishop was a sugar manufacturer who lived on Church Circle, as the elder William Bishop had, so James likely was one of William's older sons (Gatewood 1990:74). Bishop and Butler's inventory of the Maynards' household reveals a distinctly genteel living space

(Maryland State Archives 1876:553-554). The home's "front room" contained a sideboard, mahogany chairs, a sofa, a carpet, six "pictures" (i.e., chromolithographs), cane chairs, side tables, curtains, and mass-produced bric-a-brac and "china": over half of the probate's value was invested in the goods in this single room. As in any showpiece Victorian social space, the concentrated assemblage of material goods stressed a social and material investment in American consumer affluence. Household manuals argued that such genteel living environments and material assemblages were essential to impart cultural refinement, morality, and intellectual development (Mullins 1996a:84-97).

Relatively inexpensive chromolithographs like those in the Maynards' house were typical of the many consumer goods laden with moral and social symbolism. An 1873 household guide advised consumers that "the subjects of the pictures must be such as we can truly sympathize with, something to awaken our admiration, reverence, or love" (Ellett 1873:21). Many African Americans like the Maynards followed such genteel decorative dictates. In 1901, for instance, William Taylor Thom (1901a:91) reported that in the homes of Sandy Spring, Maryland's African Americans "many of the rooms are carpeted and adorned with prints and pictures on the wall." Marginalized African Americans also included illustrations as a central element of household aesthetics. In 1880 a *Harper's Weekly* correspondent touring Georgia noted that it was common to find African-Americans' cabin "walls covered with newspapers. *Harper's Weekly* was a great favorite for this purpose . . . it served the double purpose of wall-paper and pictures" (*Harper's Weekly* 1880:733). In 1913 Robert Park (1969 [1913]:160) even suggested that only one other item of household material culture was more important to African Americans than pictures: "after he [i.e., an African American] gets a bathroom he will probably want to have some pictures." The designs and sources of prints differed between African-American consumers, and the symbolism of such decorative goods likely differed between households, but the consumption of prints clearly appeared to be a widespread phenomenon across classes.

Fish and Genteel Identity

Neglected by the inventory yet symptomatic of the household's genteel aspirations are archaeological fish remains. The earliest sealed archaeological deposit at Maynard-Burgess dates from 1874 to1877, when a rear addition was built onto the back of the house, sealing a dense assemblage of faunal discards scattered around the home's original back door. This rear assemblage indicates that from the 1850s until the mid-1870s the household was consuming a diverse range of fish from Annapolis area waters. In contrast, later deposits from both the 1889 cellar and a 1905 barrel privy contain considerably lower quantities of fish. The gradual decline of fish consumption in this household suggests a distancing from racist caricatures and the mid-Atlantic fish market, both of which had a direct influence on regional class structure and consumption.

Most antebellum Southern rivers, streams, and ocean fronts were communal fishing spaces, and in the Annapolis area African Americans and whites fished in the Chesapeake Bay and its network of tributaries surrounding the city (McDaniel 1982:145). Yet as mass consumption expanded after the Civil War fishing began to be viewed as a rustic or African-American consumer pattern. Racist ideologues disparaged fishing by associating it with caricatured black traits. In 1860, for instance, D. R. Hundley (1973 [1860]:342-343) observed that the "genuine" African American "dotes on fishing. . . . Angling requires little exertion, and your genuine Cuffee most cordially hates exertion." Fishing was essential to the subsistence of many Southerners, but Hundley's caricature of African Americans dismissively denigrated it through racist hyperbole.

Archaeology does not indicate that legions of African Americans congregated by water's edge in Annapolis. Annapolitan evidence instead sug-

TABLE 1
MAYNARD-BURGESS 1870-1874 REAR ADDITION FISH ASSEMBLAGE

Fish	NISP	MNI
striped bass	16	3
white perch	19	4
croaker	13	3
genus catfish	13	
pike	9	2
yellow perch	9	5
white catfish	7	2
menhaden	7	4
black sea bass	6	3
brown bullhead	6	2
shad	6	3
herring	5	3
genus bass	4	
genus crappie	4	
drum	4	4
spot	2	1
bluegill	1	1
pumpkinseed	1	1
white crappie	1	1
mullet	1	1
weakfish	1	1
unidentified fish	543	
scale	229	
TOTAL	907	44

Note. Only elements identified to species level were included in MNI count. Wet screen artifacts are not included in NISP or MNI. (From Warner 1998.)

gests decreased African-American fish consumption after Reconstruction, and archaeological assemblages do not reflect any direct relationship between fish consumption and economic standing. Fish accounted for 17.45% of the 1874-1877 Maynard-Burgess rear addition bone count (678 fish bones excluding scales and wet screen)(Mullins and Warner 1993:121, Warner 1998). Mark Warner's (1998) analysis of the Maynard-Burgess fish remains identified considerable species diversity dominated by freshwater, estuarine, and marine species from Annapolis waters. Warner generated a Number of Individual Specimens (NISP) count of 907 fish elements, excluding 209 fish bones and 1322 scales

recovered through wet screening. A Minimum Number of Individuals (MNI) count was produced using all bones identified to species, producing a count of 44 individual fish from the rear assemblage. Eighteen different fish species were included in the assemblage, with white perch, striped bass, catfish and croaker most common (Table 1). With the exception of sea bass, all of the fish in the assemblage could be caught from the Annapolis shoreline or in modest boats. Warner concludes that species diversity and the relatively modest local fish market after the Civil War argue that the vast majority of the household's fish was caught by local hucksters and household members, rather than commercial fisheries. Of the four most common fish in the rear assemblage, only perch was commonly marketed by commercial fishers after the Civil War (Bayliff 1971:296). In contrast, the 1889 *tpq* cellar had an MNI of 14 fish (total MNI of 39) and NISP of 68 (7.11% of assemblage NISP), a considerably lower percentage of

TABLE 2
MAYNARD-BURGESS 1889 *TPQ* CELLAR FISH ASSEMBLAGE

Fish	NISP	MNI
striped bass	7	2
white perch	3	2
croaker	2	1
yellow perch	2	1
black sea bass	2	2
genus bass	1	
drum	1	1
weakfish	1	1
blueback herring	2	1
shark/dogfish	1	1
unidentified panfish (lepomis)	2	1
unidentified fish	43	1
scale	1	
TOTAL	68	14

Note. Only elements identified to species level were included in MNI count. Wet screen artifacts are not included in NISP or MNI. (From Warner 1998.)

TABLE 3
MAYNARD-BURGESS 1905 *TPQ* PRIVY FISH ASSEMBLAGE

Fish	NISP	MNI
striped bass	3	2
white perch	6	2
croaker	2	1
yellow perch	1	1
black sea bass	1	1
weakfish	1	1
blueback herring	1	1
genus herring	1	
menhaden	1	1
bluegill	3	2
brown bullhead	1	1
white catfish	1	1
genus catfish	1	
unidentified fish	54	
TOTAL	79	14

Note. Only elements identified to species level were included in MNI count. Wet screen artifacts are not included in NISP or MNI. (From Warner 1998.)

fish than from the rear assemblage, and it contained only 10 different species (Table 2) (Warner 1998). The 1905 *tpq* barrel privy was comparable to the cellar, containing an NISP of 79 fish (7.61% of privy NISP), an MNI of 14 (34.14% privy MNI), and 11 different species (Tables 3, 4).

Trowel and wet screen excavation recovered 1,780 fish scales in the rear assemblage. Most were recovered around the back door, hence it

seems clear that fish were being cleaned and the scales discarded in the yard directly around the kitchen door. In contrast, the 1889 cellar assemblage included few scales (1 from trowel excavation and 80 in wet screen). The privy likewise contained only 15 fish scales, all recovered from wet screen samples. The scarcity of scales in the 1889 deposit may reflect formation differences between the rear addition and the cellar and privy deposits, but it likely also reveals that the household purchased cleaned fish from hucksters after the mid-1870s. Many African Americans who caught fish for their household exchanged their surplus around Annapolis, selling to African Americans and whites. A white Annapolitan who grew up at the turn of the century, Evangeline Kaiser White remembered that African-American hucksters sold fresh fish at her Annapolis home each morning. After her mother "bargain[ed] for the fish she wished," they "would be scaled and cleaned right from the cart in a bucket hanging underneath" (White and White 1957:58). Fish which were cleaned through this technique clearly would decrease the amount of scales recovered archaeologically.

Fish remains from other African-American Annapolitan sites reflect low consumption of fish after Reconstruction (Warner 1992; Goodwin, et al. 1993; Warner and Mullins 1993; Aiello and Seidel 1995:1:226-227). For instance, the Bellis Court privy contained a small faunal assemblage of 355 bones, but no fish were included (Aiello and Seidel 1995:1:226-228). The Bellis Court

TABLE 4
PERCENTAGE OF FISH IN MAYNARD-BURGESS DEPOSITS

Deposit	NISP (% of deposit NISP)	MNI (% of deposit MNI)
circa 1870-1874 addition	907 (17.45%)	44 (47.31%)
1889 tpq cellar	68 (7.11%)	14 (38.46%)
1905 tpq privy	79 (7.61%)	14 (34.14%)

Note. NISP and MNI counts do not include wet screen artifacts. (From Warner 1998.)

residents were tenants of relatively modest means, so if consumption were economically determined the Bellis Court families would seem most likely to consume inexpensive goods and minimize their consumption expenses. Any assumption that marginalization would be reflected in fishing was also undermined by the Gott's Court assemblage, where only 18 fish bones were recovered from an assemblage of 678 bones (Warner 1992:Appendix 3).

African-American Annapolitans apparently decreased their fish consumption at the very moment the regional fishing industry flooded regional markets with Chesapeake Bay seafood. After 1870, new net and oyster dredging technologies fueled the expansion of the Chesapeake seafood industry (Bayliff 1971:297). Vast quantities of shad, white perch, herring, and pike were hawked in Annapolis markets, and the overwhelming glut of herring induced many local fish dealers to pickle and can herrings for sale to markets in the western United States. By 1873 Annapolis' *Maryland Republican State Capital Advertiser* (27 September 1873:3) already was proclaiming "the progress of the oyster business for the past few years in our city. At the present time, no less than eleven oyster packing establishments are in successful operation." Chesapeake oyster canneries, fishing fleets, and myriad market positions were dominated by a mobile seasonal labor force of African Americans, and some African Americans employed in fisheries even took their pay in fish, reselling some and using the remainder to feed their families (Frissell and Bevier 1899:33). The fishing industry contracted somewhat in the early twentieth century, because over-harvesting dampened seafood prices and triggered the Bay's ecological decline after the early 1880s (Thom 1901b:1122; Bayliff 1971:294). Nevertheless, Annapolis markets had abundant supplies of inexpensive fish in the late-19th and early 20th centuries.

The gradual decline in Annapolitan fish consumption may reflect the stigmatization of African-American hucksters and the caricature of fishing as a black and "rustic" consumer pattern

(Mullins 1996a:440-445). Critique of hucksters clearly was fueled by racial apprehension in the Northeast as well, where hucksters were almost all newly arrived Europeans (Heinze 1990:196). African-American hucksters usually were reduced to standard racial stereotypes. Touring Washington, D. C.'s market in 1910, Katherine Busbey observed that a "semi-rural element" of African Americans would regularly "appear outside the big market in the city's heart on market-days, offering the products of their tiny garden patch" (Busbey 1910:217). She rhapsodized that in the winter, when African American marketers could be found outside the market "squatting about their little charcoal fires in the midst of their wares, the flickering light playing over their shining black faces and glistening the whites of their up-turned eyes, they make, to me, one of the most picturesque details of Washington life." Busbey's travelogue applauded Washington's storefront consumer spaces and department stores, but she facilely reduced African-American marketers to humorous racial ornamentation and disparaged open-air marketers and their consumers.

Despite such stigmatization, African-American hucksters continued to sell goods in Annapolis streets into the 1940s, and public markets and retailers always had a sufficient supply of fish. Consequently, African America's effort to be seen as genteel consumers certainly is not the sole explanation for the decline in African-American fish consumption. In post-Emancipation cities like Annapolis—which had a sizable, socially aspiring African-American community since the early 19th century—many African Americans may have willingly shifted to genteel foods and market venues, eager to play out the possibilities of their new consumer citizenship. African-Americans' modest fish consumption in Annapolis may also reflect that genteel consumer ambitions were more seriously pursued in urban settings, a suggestion which casts fish consumption as an urban rather than class pattern. In the rural mid-Atlantic, fish consumption continued to be central to many rural African Americans' diets well into the 20th century. Budget studies

TABLE 3
MAYNARD-BURGESS 1905 *TPQ* PRIVY FISH ASSEMBLAGE

Fish	NISP	MNI
striped bass	3	2
white perch	6	2
croaker	2	1
yellow perch	1	1
black sea bass	1	1
weakfish	1	1
blueback herring	1	1
genus herring	1	
menhaden	1	1
bluegill	3	2
brown bullhead	1	1
white catfish	1	1
genus catfish	1	
unidentified fish	54	
TOTAL	79	14

Note. Only elements identified to species level were included in MNI count. Wet screen artifacts are not included in NISP or MNI. (From Warner 1998.)

fish than from the rear assemblage, and it contained only 10 different species (Table 2) (Warner 1998). The 1905 *tpq* barrel privy was comparable to the cellar, containing an NISP of 79 fish (7.61% of privy NISP), an MNI of 14 (34.14% privy MNI), and 11 different species (Tables 3, 4).

Trowel and wet screen excavation recovered 1,780 fish scales in the rear assemblage. Most were recovered around the back door, hence it

seems clear that fish were being cleaned and the scales discarded in the yard directly around the kitchen door. In contrast, the 1889 cellar assemblage included few scales (1 from trowel excavation and 80 in wet screen). The privy likewise contained only 15 fish scales, all recovered from wet screen samples. The scarcity of scales in the 1889 deposit may reflect formation differences between the rear addition and the cellar and privy deposits, but it likely also reveals that the household purchased cleaned fish from hucksters after the mid-1870s. Many African Americans who caught fish for their household exchanged their surplus around Annapolis, selling to African Americans and whites. A white Annapolitan who grew up at the turn of the century, Evangeline Kaiser White remembered that African-American hucksters sold fresh fish at her Annapolis home each morning. After her mother "bargain[ed] for the fish she wished," they "would be scaled and cleaned right from the cart in a bucket hanging underneath" (White and White 1957:58). Fish which were cleaned through this technique clearly would decrease the amount of scales recovered archaeologically.

Fish remains from other African-American Annapolitan sites reflect low consumption of fish after Reconstruction (Warner 1992; Goodwin, et al. 1993; Warner and Mullins 1993; Aiello and Seidel 1995:1:226-227). For instance, the Bellis Court privy contained a small faunal assemblage of 355 bones, but no fish were included (Aiello and Seidel 1995:1:226-228). The Bellis Court

TABLE 4
PERCENTAGE OF FISH IN MAYNARD-BURGESS DEPOSITS

Deposit	NISP (% of deposit NISP)	MNI (% of deposit MNI)
circa 1870-1874 addition	907 (17.45%)	44 (47.31%)
1889 tpq cellar	68 (7.11%)	14 (38.46%)
1905 tpq privy	79 (7.61%)	14 (34.14%)

Note. NISP and MNI counts do not include wet screen artifacts. (From Warner 1998.)

of the African-American sites in Annapolis contains significant quantities of coarse stoneware or glass preserving jars: the 1889 Maynard-Burgess cellar contained just two glass preserving jars (in an assemblage of 71 bottles) and a single stoneware jar lid (in a ceramic minimum vessel count of 42) (Mullins 1996a:505). Cheek and Friedlander (1990:53-54) identified the same paucity of preserving vessels in Washington. They found that street front white assemblages contained twice as much stoneware as those of African Americans in adjoining alleys. Consequently, the preservation of fruits and vegetables which was common in rural southern Maryland was apparently quite rare in Annapolis and nearby Washington. The availability of professionally canned foods in urban markets like Annapolis and Washington likely influenced home food preservation, a possibility strengthened by the presence of almost 800 metal cans in the Maynard-Burgess cellar. Rural households' preservation patterns likely reflected less stringent domestic labor structure and more modest community stores.

Class, Race, and Mass Consumer Culture

Consumer culture is often seen as a "mass culture": i.e., it replaced significant class distinctions with mass standards of living and social conventions shared by virtually all citizens (Agnew 1990). In the face of racial ideology—which restricted privileges and opportunities in consumer space—this clearly is, at best, an overstatement, and a steady stream of labor disputes throughout America demonstrate that workers' class struggle never disappeared in favor of shopping. Historians including Warren Susman (1984), Ronald Edsforth (1987), and Lizabeth Cohen (1990) argue that labor militancy in the 1920s and 1930s actually should be seen as embedded in (if not emanating from) a clearly articulated class struggle for consumer rights in the preceding decades. By the early 20th century, an increasingly broad swath of Americans began to envision their fundamental citizen rights and aspirations in material consumption. Jean-

Christophe Agnew (1990) argues that this definition of citizenship placed mass material standards at the heart of American identity and turned away from previous touchstones such as labor identities, nationalism, and religion.

Examining African-American consumption as evidence of a long-simmering class struggle centered on consumption rights unsettles the assumption that class is best studied in workplaces or labor relations. Envisioning African-American class struggle in post-Emancipation consumer space has paradoxically conservative and radical implications on archaeological interpretations of class in emergent consumer culture. On one hand, the gradual mass homogenization of consumer culture is suggested by African-American archaeological materials, since Annapolitan evidence argues that African Americans shared many consistent consumption patterns across classes. It seems clear that resistance to racism spurred similar consumption tactics among African Americans of different material standings. Material similarities did not create a monolithic African-American Annapolis, though, because affluent households inevitably fulfilled genteel material ideals more seamlessly than others. Most significantly, class structuring principles like family heritage, education, and skin complexion ensured that many African Americans did not assume a footing among the African-American aristocracy (Gatewood 1990:95). In this defense of social distinctions, African-American consumers refrained from a radical critique of consumer culture's class underpinnings. Few African Americans actually anticipated or even desired a classless consumer culture: they simply desired individual and group rights which were unhindered by systemic inequalities like racism. This conservative desire to equitably participate in consumer space was a fundamental element of African-American class struggle against racially exclusive civil privileges. It may seem somewhat disarming and even politically misguided to critique consumer culture using consumption itself; nevertheless, the notion that American political rights are vested in material consumption clearly took hold of mass imagination after World War II, and that idea remains a central feature of contemporary consumer culture (Agnew 1990:14).

Yet, on the other hand, African-American consumption was not utterly conservative, because African America's class struggle never ignored racism. Indeed, African-American consumers attempted to purge emergent consumer culture of anti-black racism. This was a radical critique because racism and white privilege lay at the heart of consumer culture. During the early 20th century, African-American thinkers became increasingly critical of the racist ideology embedded in consumer culture and American society. For instance, African-American labor organizer Asa Philip Randolph (1919:10) argued that capitalist inequality "does not apply to Negroes only. It is the common fate of the servant class, black and white. But they must not understand that their interests are common. Hence race prejudice is cultivated." Randolph recognized that consumer culture's racist restrictions were deeply implicated in dominant class interests. However he failed to understand that African Americans' powerful desire for consumer goods was a political and class struggle against anti-black racism, not simply instrumental elite abuse of African American and white laborers alike. Ultimately Randolph and many subsequent observers failed to consider that African-American class structure may have been as clearly focused on racism's restrictions on consumer privilege as on unequal relations to the means of production.

The eventual erosion of genteel African-American social conventions reflects African America's shifting perception of class and consumption after World War I. In 1928, the 69-year old Wiley Bates penned an autobiography in which he struggled to reproduce conventions separating genteel and "uncouth" African Americans (Bates 1928). Bates clung to his status as a social and moral voice for African-American Annapolis, defending aspiration, stressing that material wealth did not inevitably impart character, and reducing racism to a superficial obstacle. By the 1920s, though, this evasion of racism and stringent call to discipline was an untenable position for most African Americans (Gatewood 1990:313-319). Dismayed by resurgent racism, vexed by over 50 years of material marginalization, and faced by discourses transparently trumpeting a classless mass culture, African Americans were hard-pressed to see racism as something utterly separate from consumer culture.

Even when it passed unspoken, racism structured class struggle in all American consumers' experience. By articulating class difference as a "natural" by-product of race, late-19th century class loomed as a conglomeration of racial categories, behavioral conventions, and material wealth. That definition evaded the anti-black social marginalization and white privilege which was the backdrop against which consumer culture emerged. African Americans maneuvered between mass culture and class society, seeking the equity mass consumer culture promised and forging evidence that African America could reproduce dominant social and material symbolism. Like most Americans, African Americans were deeply attracted to the material self-determination and attendant citizen privileges promised by consumer culture, and increasingly more African Americans saw consumer culture as a space to articulate social aspirations and class struggle. Inevitably African-American consumers were compelled to confront racism in consumer space and probe its implication in broader social structure.

Racism was essential to consumer culture's evasion of class structure and the increasing acceptability of race as a basis for dispensing social privilege. To truly understand class in emergent consumer culture, it is essential to acknowledge that labor, consumer space, and social and material privileges were—and in many ways still remain—fundamentally structured by race.

ACKNOWLEDGEMENTS

Bob Paynter, Mark Warner, and Marlys Pearson focused my thinking on various elements of this paper.

Mark Warner graciously provided his dissertation data and ideas on fish consumption. John McCarthy, Rob Fitts, and LouAnn Wurst provided suggestions to revise a late draft. Elements of this research were conducted through grants from the Wenner-Gren Foundation, Sigma Xi, the Scientific Research Society, and a Winterthur Museum Fellowship. Other ideas were planted by Helan Page and Daniel Horowitz. None of these folks bears any responsibility for the shortcomings of the paper.

REFERENCES

AFRO AMERICAN LEDGER
   1902   Protest Against "Jim Crow" Cars: A Strong Delegation of Business and Professional Men Visit Annapolis. *Afro American Ledger*, 22 February 1902:4. Baltimore, MD.

AGNEW, JEAN-CHRISTOPHE
   1990   Coming Up for Air: Consumer Culture in Historical Perspective. *Intellectual History Newsletter* 12:3-21.

AIELLO, ELIZABETH A. AND JOHN L. SEIDEL
   1995   Three Hundred Years in Annapolis: Phase III Archaeological Investigations of the Anne Arundel County Courthouse Site (18AP63), Annapolis Maryland, 2 vols. Report submitted to Spillis Candela/ Warnecke, Washington, from Archaeology in Annapolis, Annapolis, MD.

ANNE ARUNDEL EXAMINER
   1900   Officers Elected. *Anne Arundel Examiner*, 11 October 1900:5. Annapolis, MD.

BATES, WILEY H.
   1928   *Researches, Sayings and Life of Wiley H. Bates*. City Printing Company, Annapolis, MD.

BAYLIFF, WILLIAM H.
   1971   Natural Resources. In *The Old Line State: A History of Maryland*, edited by Morris L. Radoff, pp. 267-307. Hall of Records, Annapolis, MD.

THE BEE
   1897a Annapolis Notes. *The Bee*, 1 January 1897:8. Washington.
   1897b W. H. Bates, Grocer. *The Bee*, 9 January 1897:1. Washington.

BROWN, PHILIP L.
   1994   *The Other Annapolis, 1900-1950*. Annapolis Printing Company, Annapolis, MD.

BUSBEY, KATHERINE G.
   1910   *Home Life in America*. Methuen, London.

CALDERHEAD, WILLIAM L.
   1977   Anne Arundel Blacks: Three Centuries of Change. In *Anne Arundel County Maryland: A Bicentennial History, 1649-1977*, edited by James C. Bradford, pp.11-25. Anne Arundel County and Annapolis Bicentennial Committee, Annapolis, MD.

CAMPBELL, COLIN
   1996   The Sociology of Consumption. In *Acknowledging Consumption: A Review of New Studies*, edited by Daniel Miller, pp.96-126. Routledge, London.

CHEEK, CHARLES D. AND AMY FRIEDLANDER
   1990   Pottery and Pig's Feet: Space, Ethnicity, and Neighborhood in Washington, D.C., 1880-1940. *Historical Archaeology* 24(1):34-60.

COHEN, LIZABETH
   1990   *Making a New Deal: Industrial Workers in Chicago, 1919-1939*. Cambridge University Press, New York.
   1993   The Class Experience of Mass Consumption: Workers as Consumers in Interwar America. In *The Power of Culture: Critical Essays in American History*, edited by Richard Wightman Fox and T. J. Jackson Lears, pp.135-160. University of Chicago Press, Chicago.

DU BOIS, W. E. B.
   1935   *Black Reconstruction in America*. Harcourt Brace, Cleveland, OH.

EDSFORTH, RONALD
   1987   *Class Conflict and Cultural Consensus: The Making of a Consumer Society in Flint, Michigan*. Rutgers University Press, Brunswick, NJ.

EDWARDS, PAUL K.
   1969   *The Southern Urban Negro as a Consumer*, reprint of 1932 edition. Negro Universities Press, New York.

ELLETT, MRS. E. F.
   1873   *The New Cyclopaedia of Domestic Economy and Practical Housekeeping*. Henry Bill Publishing, Norwich, CT.

FONER, ERIC
   1988   *Reconstruction: America's Unfinished Revolution, 1863-1877*. Harper and Row, New York.

FRAZIER, E. FRANKLIN
   1924   Some Aspects of Negro Business. *Opportunity* 2(22):293-297.

FRISSELL, H. B. AND ISABEL BEVIER
1899   Dietary Studies of Negroes in Eastern Virginia in 1897 and 1898. *U. S. Department of Agriculture Bulletin* 71:1-45. Washington.

GATEWOOD, WILLARD B.
1990   *Aristocrats of Color: The Black Elite, 1880-1920.* Indiana University Press, Bloomington.

GOODWIN, R. CHRISTOPHER, SUZANNE L. C. SANDERS, MICHELLE T. MORAN, AND DAVID LANDON
1993   Phase II/III Archaeological Investigations of the Gott's Court Parking Facility, Annapolis, Maryland. Report prepared by R. Christopher Goodwin and Associates, Frederick, Maryland. Submitted to City of Annapolis, Annapolis, MD.

HARPER'S WEEKLY
1880   Inside Southern Cabins. *Harper's Weekly* 27 November:765-766.

HEINZE, ANDREW R
1990   *Adapting to Abundance: Jewish Immigrants, Mass Consumption, and the Search for American identity.* Columbia University Press, New York.

HOROWITZ, DANIEL
1985   *The Morality of Spending: Attitudes Toward the Consumer Society in America, 1875-1940.* Johns Hopkins University Press, Baltimore, MD.

HUNDLEY, D. R.
1973   *Social Relations in our Southern States,* reprint of 1860 edition. Arno, New York.

HURST, HAROLD W.
1981   The Northernmost Southern Town: A Sketch of Pre-Civil War Annapolis. *Maryland Historical Magazine* 76:240-249.

IGNATIEV, NOEL
1995   *How the Irish Became White.* Routledge, London.

IVES, SALLIE
1979   Black Community Development in Annapolis, Maryland, 1870-1885. In *Geographical Perspectives on Maryland's Past,* edited by Robert D. Mitchell and Edward K. Muller, pp.129-149. University of Maryland Department of Geography, College Park, MD.

KASSON, JOHN F.
1990   *Rudeness and Civility: Manners in Nineteenth-Century America.* Hill and Wang, New York.

KEITH, RUTH
1977   Social Life. In *Anne Arundel County Maryland: A Bicentennial History, 1649-1977,* edited by James C. Bradford, pp.152-170. Anne Arundel County and Annapolis Bicentennial Committee, Annapolis, MD.

KING, EDWARD
1875   *The Great South: A Record of Journeys.* American Publishing Company, Hartford, CT.

LEARS, JACKSON
1994   *Fables of Abundance: A Cultural History of Advertising in America.* Basic Books, New York.

LOTT, ERIC
1995   *Love and Theft: Blackface Minstrelsy and the American Working Class.* Oxford University Press, Oxford, England.

MARYLAND PENDULUM
1987   William H. Butler Sr., another Black Political Pioneer. *Maryland Pendulum* 5(1):10.

MARYLAND REPUBLICAN STATE CAPITAL ADVERTISER
1873   Our Oyster Trade. *Maryland Republican State Capital Advertiser* 27 September 1873:3. Annapolis, MD.

MARYLAND STATE ARCHIVES
1876   Inventory of the Estate of John T. Maynard. Anne Arundel County Inventories, folio 553. Maryland Hall of Records, Annapolis, MD.
1990   Oral History Interview Transcripts. Annapolis I Remember Collection, Maryland Hall of Records, Annapolis, MD.

McDANIEL, GEORGE W.
1982   *Hearth and Home: Preserving a People's Culture.* Temple University Press, Philadelphia, PA.

MILLER, DANIEL
1987   *Material Culture and Mass Consumption.* Basil Blackwell, Oxford, England.
1995   Consumption as the Vanguard of History. In *Acknowledging Consumption: A Review of New Studies,* edited by Daniel Miller, pp. 1-57. Routledge, London.

MORGAN, EDMUND S.
1977   *American Slavery, American Freedom: The Ordeal of Colonial Virginia.* Norton, New York.

MULLINS, PAUL R.
1996a *The Contradictions of Consumption: An Archaeology of African America and Consumer Culture, 1850-1930.* Ph.D. dissertation, Department of Anthropology,

University of Massachusetts, Amherst. University Microfilms International, Ann Arbor, MI.

1996b An Archeology of Race and Consumption: African-American Bottled Good Consumption in Annapolis, Maryland, 1850-1930. *Maryland Archeology* 32(1):1-10.

MULLINS, PAUL R. AND MARK S. WARNER
1993 Final Archaeological Investigations at the Maynard-Burgess House (18AP64), An 1850-1980 African-American Household in Annapolis, Maryland. Report submitted to Port of Annapolis, Annapolis, MD, from Archaeology in Annapolis, Annapolis, MD.

PARK, ROBERT E.
1969 Negro Home Life and Standards of Living, reprint of 1913 edition. In *The Negro's Progress in Fifty Years*, edited by Emory R. Johnson, pp.147-163. Negro Universities Press, New York.

RANDOLPH, A. PHILIP
1919 Lynching: Capitalism Its Cause; Socialism Its Cure. *The Messenger* 2(7):9-12.

ROEDIGER, DAVID R.
1991 *The Wages of Whiteness: Race and the Making of the American Working Class.* Verso, New York.

SCHLERETH, THOMAS J.
1991 *Victorian America: Transformations in Everyday Life, 1876-1915.* Harper Perennial, New York.

SULLIVAN, JAMES W.
1849 James W. Sullivan's Collector's Tax Book for the Year 1849. Davis Collection, Maryland Hall of Records, Annapolis, MD.

SUSMAN, WARREN I.
1984 *Culture as History: The Transformation of American Society in the Twentieth Century.* Pantheon, New York.

THOM, WILLIAM TAYLOR
1901a The Negroes of Sandy Spring, Maryland: A Social Study. *U. S. Department of Labor Bulletin* 32:43-102. Washington.

1901b The Negroes of Litwalton, Virginia: A Study of the "Oyster Negro." *U. S. Department of Labor Bulletin* 37:1115-1170. Washington.

UNITED STATES DEPARTMENT OF COMMERCE
1930 *Statistical Abstract of the United States, 1930, 52nd number.* United States Department of Commerce, Washington.

1937 *Census of Business, 1935. Vol.4, Retail Distribution.* United States Department of Commerce, Washington.

WARNER, MARK S.
1992 Test Excavations at Gott's Court, Annapolis, Maryland (18AP52). Report submitted to Historic Annapolis Foundation, Annapolis, MD, from Archaeology in Annapolis, Annapolis, MD.

1998 *Food and the Negotiation of African American Identities in Annapolis, Maryland and the Chesapeake.* Ph.D. dissertation, Department of Anthropology, University of Virginia, Charlottesville. University Microfilms International, Ann Arbor, MI.

WARNER, MARK S. AND PAUL R. MULLINS
1993 Phase I-II Archaeological Investigations on the Courthouse Site (18AP63), An African-American Neighborhood in Annapolis, Maryland. Report submitted to Historic Annapolis Foundation, Annapolis, MD, from Archaeology in Annapolis, Annapolis, MD..

WHITE, CLARENCE MARBURY, SR. AND EVANGELINE KAISER WHITE
1957 *The Years Between: A Chronicle of Annapolis, Maryland, 1800-1900.* Exposition Press, New York.

WILLIAMS, RAYMOND
1977 *Marxism and Literature.* Oxford University Press, Oxford, England.

PAUL R. MULLINS
DEPARTMENT OF SOCIOLOGY
AND ANTHROPOLOGY
GEORGE MASON UNIVERSITY
FAIRFAX, VA 22030

THERESA A. SINGLETON

The Archaeology of the Plantation South: A Review of Approaches and Goals

Introduction

Perhaps the earliest known effort to study a plantation through archaeology dates from 1931 at Mount Vernon, George Washington's plantation home. Morley Jeffers Williams, a trained landscape architect, conducted archaeological studies at Mount Vernon as part of a larger study of southern colonial plantations and gardens. From 1936 to 1939, as Mount Vernon's Director of Research and Restoration, Williams systematically tested for the location of structural remains (Pogue 1988:3). The beginning of historic preservation in the United States is often linked with the restoration of Mount Vernon, and the archaeology undertaken there coincided with the emergence of historical archaeology as a recognized field of endeavor in the historic preservation movement (Deagan 1982:155). Today, plantation archaeology has greatly advanced beyond merely being a tool for restoration and preservation activities. Archaeologists are now attempting to understand the cultural, economic, and political milieu in which plantation societies operated as expressed in archaeological resources.

As the title suggests, this essay is a review of how archaeologists have studied plantations in the American South and for what purpose. This is an evaluation of research in plantation archaeology through time as it discusses both the promises and problems of past and current studies. The profound impact of plantation archaeology on the development of historical archaeology as a whole is also considered. Because plantations operated within a complex world, archaeologists engaged in plantation research find themselves in situations where they must examine a number of interrelated issues

such as class, race, ethnicity, economics, and relations of domination. These investigators are pioneers, and their research in plantation archaeology has either shaped or contributed to the structuring of many concepts in historical archaeology—for example, the archaeology of the "inarticulate," "status patterning," "artifact patterns," and more recently, "power and economics." Additionally, the burgeoning field of African-American archaeology developed largely from archaeological studies of slavery. While much of plantation archaeology has addressed questions that are now viewed as poorly conceived with findings that are often descriptive, this research presents an unrealized potential to reshape significantly the interpretation of plantation life and labor.

The Beginnings (1931–1974)

Archaeologists often place the origin of plantation archaeology with James A. Ford's work in the 1930s at the Elizafield Plantation located along the Altamaha River Drainage in Georgia (Orser 1984; Joseph 1989). Ford launched a six-week investigation to determine the function and data of the tabby ruins local historians had thought to be the site of a Spanish mission (Cate 1930:34). Ford (1937) concluded that the ruins were those of a 19th-century sugar processing mill once part of the Elizafield Plantation.

A more thorough examination of early studies in historical archaeology reveals that several sporadic investigations took place at plantations as early as 1931 at Mount Vernon and continued into the late 1950s and early 1960s when more systematic, historically oriented and anthropological studies in plantation archaeology began to emerge. This early archaeological research was initiated in most cases to assist in architectural reconstruction and was consistent with a primary goal of historical archaeology at the time—the restoration and preservation of former historic settlements such as Williamsburg, Plymouth, and Jamestown.

Investigators of this early plantation research included both trained archaeologists and interested amateurs. Unfortunately, these researchers often failed to write reports, publish their results, or communicate their findings to other interested professionals; thus, it is impossible to know just how much work was actually undertaken. Examples of plantations known to have been investigated during what might be called the exploratory phase of plantation archaeology include: Mount Vernon, Monticello, Gunston Hall, Stratford, and Woodlawn in Virginia (Pogue 1988:4); Somerset Plantation, North Carolina (Christopher Hughes 1989, pers. comm.); and Mound Plantation or Mount Locust, Mississippi (Phelps 1941). Unlike Ford's study of the Elizafield ruins—referred to as a "classic example of disproving a traditional site" (Harrington 1965:17) and correctly described as "archaeology at a plantation rather than plantation archaeology" (Orser 1984:2), the plantation research of the exploratory phase addressed questions similar to those addressed in plantation archaeology today. Excavations were undertaken to determine the general layout and configuration of the plantation, the location and identity of structures, and the delineation of special activity areas. Thus, the antecedents for present-day plantation archaeology are found in these archaeological studies of the exploratory phase and not in Ford's work at Elizafield.

The first historically oriented studies in plantation archaeology developed out of this exploratory research. Historically oriented studies in historical archaeology are those designed to supplement the written record of a site with the goal of deriving a narrative account of what happened there. Moreover, historically oriented studies often lack explicitly stated research questions and are not concerned with anthropological problems. In plantation archaeology these studies integrate exhaustive historical research with archaeological data, describing in great detail the material culture associated with plantations. The first of these studies (Caywood 1955; Noël Hume 1962b; Watkins 1968) focused on the planter's household in the "Big House" and only incidentally upon slaves (Noël Hume 1966). This historically oriented approach to plantation archaeology continues today, but now its advocates view sites once occupied by slaves and other agricultural laborers as essential components to understanding plantation life (Kelso 1984, 1986; Reinhart 1984).

These largely descriptive studies in plantation archaeology, as Charles Orser (1984:4) has pointed out, supply valuable information on artifacts which form the foundation for the development of analytical techniques used in historical archaeology. For example, at Cannon's Point Plantation, the identification and attribution of "status" objects associated with horse equipment and vehicles (Otto 1975:282) was based upon C. Malcolm Watkins' (1968:169–170) description of horse and vehicle gear recovered from the Mercer Plantation in Virginia. The Mercer Plantation study also contains valuable information on structural and nonstructural features associated with a colonial Virginia plantation (Watkins 1968:71–114). A great deal can be learned from these first systematic historical studies in plantation archaeology. When appropriate these data should be incorporated into current research, and it may be necessary to restudy these collections to obtain information on topics that did not interest the investigators at the time, such as objects made by African Americans. Enslaved African Americans possibly manufactured some of the hardware recovered from plantation structures, such as hand-wrought nails, hinges, and pintles. Additionally, recent studies suggest that African Americans produced locally made colonoware ceramics (Deetz 1988) and some clay pipes (Emerson 1989) found at colonial plantations in Virginia. As new interpretations in plantation archaeology and material culture arise, these earlier studies offer a significant resource for the examination of new questions (e.g., Klingelhofer 1987; Crass 1988).

An anthropological approach to plantation archaeology emerged with the initial testing of plantation sites by Charles Fairbanks in the 1960s. Anthropological studies in plantation archaeology are frequently narrative in scope just as are the historically oriented studies, but they are generally directed toward anthropological problems. For example, the extent to which an African heritage was transplanted, modified, and replaced in slave material culture was one of the initial goals of anthropological plantation archaeology, and this objective remains a major focus of present research.

Fairbanks conducted his first study in plantation archaeology at the Von Bulow Plantation near Daytona Beach, Florida. A brief survey and limited testing revealed the location of the former slave cabins, but limited funds did not permit the excavation of the cabins (Fairbanks 1983:22–23). This inital work, however, set in motion Fairbanks' interest in the archaeological study of slavery, an interest he successfully pursued at the Kingsley Plantation (Fairbanks 1974) and at the Rayfield Plantation (Ascher and Fairbanks 1971). From the excavation results at Kingsley and Rayfield, Fairbanks (1983:23) concluded that "enough had been done in the archaeology of non-big-house-plantation remains to allow us to formulate some problems that could be systematically tested by further excavations and by more detailed examination of the documents." This statement characterizes Fairbanks' enduring influence upon plantation archaeology—the shift away from the study of slaveholders to plantation archaeology is almost synonymous with the study of slavery (Singleton 1985b).

In general the shift from the study of the big house to the study of slaves grew out of social and political changes in the 1960s that altered the direction of scholarship in the social sciences. The new scholarship, variously referred to as the "new social history," the "new ethnicity," or the "history of the inarticulate," emphasized the richness and diversity of America's heritage and departed from the "melting pot" thesis (McKee 1987:31). Fairbanks was certainly influenced by these new trends in social science research, but his interest in undertaking archaeology at African-American sites may have stemmed from an earlier interest in race relations. Inspired by the work of Melville Herskovits (1941), Fairbanks set out to dispel myths concerning the biological and cultural inferiority of black Americans used to justify legalized segregation in the South (Fairbanks and Smith 1958). His research on slave sites built upon this pre-existing interest in African Americans established at least a decade before he conducted excavations. Given this context, Fairbanks' test excavations of slave quarters at Kingsley and Rayfield Plantations marked simultaneously the beginnings of both an anthropological approach to plantation archaeology and African-American archaeology.

The Development of Plantation Archaeology: The Past Fifteen Years (1974–1989)

John Otto's study of Cannon's Point Plantation, completed in 1975, ushered in a new direction for the study of plantations. This approach viewed the plantation as a microcosm of southern society in which "status and caste" or "class and race" differences—as manifested in the differential material culture of planters, overseers, and slaves—could be studied and compared (Otto 1975, 1977, 1980, 1984). Otto's analytical techniques helped structure the concept of "status patterning" as a determination of potential socioeconomic status or class based upon archaeological indices, such as the frequency of certain ceramic types, shapes, and forms (Otto 1977) or the kinds and diversity of foods consumed (Otto 1984:45–60, 105–112, 139–150). Status patterning at plantations as defined by Otto and refined by Moore (1981, 1985) has been correctly criticized as an oversimplification of the southern plantation (Orser 1988a). Despite its limitations, status patterning has had a far-reaching impact in historical archaeology as both historically oriented and anthropological historical archaeologists rely upon the concept of "status patterning" to establish indices for known site occupants, to compare these patterns with other sites, and to interpret archaeological data recovered from sites of unknown occupants. Perhaps the best example of the use of status patterning to identify the socioeconomic status of unknown occupants at a plantation site was at Spiers Landing, South Carolina. The archaeological data strongly suggested that the site had been occupied by a slave or some other type of agricultural worker (Drucker and Anthony 1979; Drucker 1981). On the other hand, the identification of status or class from purely archaeological sources runs the risk of misrepresenting how the material correlates of a particular plantation society may have been manifested. For example, in the upland antebellum cotton belt in Mississippi, an area that has not been investigated archaeologically, planters originally lived in log dwellings only slightly larger than the slave houses around them. This was due to the transitory nature of antebellum agriculture and to the preference of many upland cotton growers to spend their money on slaves and land instead of houses and grounds (J. Moore 1958:41). Thus, because plantation houses apparently were not an accurate gauge of wealth or the social position of their owners, the archaeology of status and class may have limited applications in this area of the Old South (Singleton 1989).

The archaeology of "status and caste," however, has inspired new ways of looking at the emergence of racism, class struggle, and the relations of domination which characterized plantation society. The new archaeology of race and class, what Orser (1988a) has termed "economics and power," utilizes varied Marxist and non-Marxist approaches to identify the material elements of domination, power, and ideology particularly in plantation landscapes. This contextual approach to archaeology, sometimes referred to as post-processual (Hodder 1985b) or radical (Earle and Preucel 1987) archaeology, combines historical materialism, structural Marxism, and social critical theory. It brings an orientation to plantation archaeology that can address broader theoretical issues. A major weakness of plantation archaeology is that it has lacked an explicitly stated theoretical foundation specifically applicable to understanding the complexities of plantation society.

The archaeology of "economics and power" is an embryonic approach to plantation archaeology. Yet, its application to plantation studies, as seen in the work of Orser (1987, 1988a, 1988b, 1988c) and Epperson (1987, 1988a, 1989), has already resulted in provocative new insights. Orser identifies evidence of power relations in the size and spatial arrangement of plantation housing at Millwood, a postbellum tenant plantation located in the South Carolina Piedmont. His findings show that house size was dependent upon the inhabitants' tenure group—landlord, millwright, tenant, servant, wage hand—which corresponded with the

political and economic power a tenure group occupied within the plantation hierarchy. He further suggests that distances between buildings occupied by each major tenure group may be a reflection of "the power relations enacted within the dominant mode of production at the plantation" (Orser 1988c:329). Epperson, in turn, sees colonial slavery in the Chesapeake as a system of domination characterized by a fundamental contradiction between incorporation of the oppressed and the need to create distance, difference, and otherness (exclusion). Incorporation is perhaps best represented by the Christian baptism of slaves while exclusion is at least archaeologically manifested in the definition of spatial relationships on a plantation. Epperson suggests that a planter's power of domination is reflected in the landscape and architectural space that he controlled and that evidence of both class formation and the racism in the Chesapeake is indicated by the exclusion of slave dwellings from the formal landscape of the plantation. It is interesting to note that while both scholars share similar theoretical positions and apply these frameworks better to understand spatial arrangements on plantations, they reach different conclusions in their interpretation of race and class. Orser (1987: 131) sees the postbellum plantation in South Carolina as essentially an economic institution which exhibits class differences that are not necessarily related to race, while Epperson (1988a) sees the development of plantation spatial patterns in colonial Virginia as evidence of class formation based upon racist ideology. These differences in interpretations suggest that an archaeology of "power and economics" or an archaeology of "domination" may be a sensitive device for discerning the special character of race and class relationships in a particular plantation society. If so, it offers numerous possibilities for future research. At this juncture, however, this framework appears to be only applicable to studies of plantation housing and settlement and mute to other forms of archaeological data.

More often than questions of race and class, plantation archaeology of the past 15 years has concentrated upon the reconstruction of everyday lives of plantation occupants. As discussed earlier, a major emphasis set in motion by Fairbanks was the examination of slave life. Archaeological studies of slavery have more or less developed along three lines: (1) the search for material correlates of ethnicity or what might be better termed cultural studies of the slave community; (2) examinations of slave material life with emphasis upon housing, diet, food procurement techniques, culinary practices, and household equipment; and (3) interpretation of class and race. These lines of inquiry are not mutually exclusive, and most studies consider all three. Because the third topic already has been considered, the following discussion summarizes the research of the first two lines of inquiry.

Fairbanks was unsuccessful in his efforts to identify African elements in slave material culture, but he did maintain an interest during the remainder of his career in devising strategies that would show when and how an African-American material cultural tradition arose (Fairbanks 1984:2). The search for archaeological evidence of ethnicity indicative of either an African heritage or a newly created African-American tradition has met with a great deal more success in recent years. Suggestions of African-American material culture inferred from the archaeological record of slaves include: slave-made ceramics recovered from plantations in South Carolina (Ferguson 1980, 1985) and in Virginia (Deetz 1988:365–366), building technologies (Wheaton and Garrow 1985), foodways (McKee 1987), locally made clay pipes decorated with motifs suggestive of African origins (Emerson 1989), artifacts suggestive of ritual or healing practices (Brown and Cooper 1989), or artifacts that perhaps served an unknown aesthetic or functional need (Klingelhofer 1987). A few African objects have also been recovered from slave sites, such as cowrie shells (Garlid 1979:22; Kelso 1986:30) and an ebony ring (Katie Parker 1989, pers. comm.). Some of these interpretations are based upon compelling evidence while others appear to be more speculative and need more verification before they are accepted as conclusive. Yet, these tentative suggestions represent significant threads of evidence that support the widely held view in the scholarship of slavery that enslaved Africans and their descendants nurtured and

sustained cultural traditions in spite of the oppressive, dehumanizing conditions of slavery.

Slavery studies directed toward questions of ethnicity also have the potential to study cultural interchange or "mutual acculturation" between blacks and whites (Otto 1984:177) and blacks and Native Americans (Kelso 1984:184). One of the best examples of a study in the acculturation of a slave community was undertaken at the Yaughan and Curriboo Plantations located in Berkeley County, South Carolina (Wheaton et al. 1983; Wheaton and Garrow 1985). This study demonstrated that changes from African-style housing to European house forms and from decreasing use of colonoware ceramics to imported European wares corresponded with changing black to white demographic patterns. The ratio of blacks to whites dropped from 11 blacks to 1 white person in 1790 to 6.6:1 in 1800 (Friedlander 1985:354). These changing demographic patterns, coupled with the changes in artifact patterns, may have been an indication that fewer African-born slaves with firsthand knowledge of African building designs and ceramic manufacturing techniques were entering the area.

Another example of acculturation is the recent suggestion that the enslaved Africans made the colonoware ceramics found in the Virginia Tidewater (Deetz 1988:365–366). Unlike the colonoware found in South Carolina, which appears to be comparable to African forms and perhaps represents a persistence of African foodways in South Carolina (Ferguson 1985), colonoware found in the Chesapeake was made in a wide variety of forms, closely copying English prototypes (Deetz 1988:239). The presence of colonoware in the Chesapeake appears to correspond to changes in residential patterns, further suggesting that blacks began making this pottery as a consequence of their contact with whites. Black slaves and white indentured servants shared living spaces with planters prior to 1680, and after that date, when race became the basis for slavery, blacks were placed in separate living areas on the plantation. When settled in separate living areas, enslaved blacks lacking household utensils may have been forced to make pottery in forms that they previously used (Deetz 1988:239). The production of slave-made colonoware in colonial Virginia most likely resulted from black-white interaction and black-Native American interaction.

All archaeological studies of slavery regardless of their research orientation contribute to an understanding of the material conditions associated with slavery. The recovery of detailed information on the everyday life of slaves in their quarters supplies the empirical data that are essential to writing historical ethnographies of slave communities and to generating new questions in the archaeological study of slavery. These data not only embellish the historical record of slavery, but offer new and provocative insights as to how slaves survived the rigors of everyday life. In this area of research, archaeological studies of slave subsistence, derived largely from the study of faunal remains, offer a significant contribution and are key to understanding how slave dietary needs were met (Gibbs et al. 1980; Reitz et al. 1985; McKee 1987). These findings are beginning to make their way into general discussions of slave diet and nutrition (Kiple 1987: 12, 13–14) and are likely to have a profound impact upon that area of research.

Artifacts recovered from slave quarters provide specific details that illuminate descriptions of slave housing and household objects obtained from other sources. At the same time, these objects present interpretative problems regarding what these objects reflect. For example, does the presence of graphite fragments and an eyeglass lens imply a level of literacy or enumeracy among slaves? While this interpretation will always be subject to question, it is supported by the recovery of both graphite pencils and spectacles from the house site of Benjamin Banneker, a free black person living in Maryland in the 18th century, whose literacy and enumeracy skills are well documented (Hurry 1989). Artifact pattern recognition, a technique which quantifies artifacts into functional categories—e.g., kitchen, architecture, furniture, arms, clothing, personal, tobacco, and activities, can assist in the analysis of interpretative problems. Although South (1988:27) criticizes the use of artifact pattern recognition in particularistic analysis, its application to slave studies suggests that it can

be used to discern differences in slave assemblages that may be related to cultural, economic, and temporal differences as well as differences resulting from excavation strategies (Joseph 1989).

Another potential avenue to artifact interpretation is to understand what objects meant to the enslaved black community as compared to the free white community. Historical archaeologists have increasingly incorporated the concept of *mentalité*, coined by the *Annales* historians, to understand the native meanings of objects (Leone and Potter 1988). Archaeological evidence that can provide some insights into the world view of enslaved African Americans is difficult to ascertain because so much of slave material culture was imposed upon slaves by owners (Singleton 1988:358). Subtle possibilities, however, are suggested in foodways (Ferguson 1985; McKee 1987), housing, and the use of space (Vlach 1978:125; Wheaton and Garrow 1985). Even the use of mass-produced objects may have special meanings. The recovery of blue, faceted glass beads from slave cabins that were of European manufacture may be related to the Moslem belief that a single blue bead will ward off evil spirits (Adams 1989).

Investigations of sites occupied by owners and managers are generally approached within the larger framework of race and class studies or status patterning (Zierden et al. 1986; Adams 1987; Adams and Boling 1989). Studies directed exclusively toward the investigation of the planter household are designed to understand the material life and world view of the planter class and general information on the economic functioning of the plantations (L. Lewis 1978, 1985; Haskell 1981; K. Lewis 1985). Data generated from these studies are particularly important for comparison with other sites and in determining to what extent the actual wealth of planters is evident in material resources. Even these studies inadvertently supply information on slave activities associated with the big house, kitchen, and other service buildings.

The one area of plantation archaeology that has advanced little since Ford's work at the Elizafield ruins is the study of plantation industrial sites. Industrial sites are frequently excavated on plantations but analyses are usually restricted to how these industrial works operated (e.g., Crook and O'Grady 1977; Orser 1985). The significance of this technology within the plantation economy and its effect upon plantation life and labor are not discussed. A notable exception in southern plantation studies is an archaeological study of a sugar processing mill at the John H. McIntosh Plantation in Camden County, Georgia (Eubanks 1985). In this study an analytical framework based in cultural materialism was utilized to understand the relationships between modes of production and reproduction, domestic economy, and political economy. This approach was found to explain why the sugar mill was built, why it took the form it did, why it was abandoned, and how it fit into a surplus production of the plantation. Eubanks' study and a similar study of a sugar mill at the Galways Plantation in Montserrat, West Indies (Pulsipher and Goodwin 1982), propose a new direction for the study of industrial sites at plantations.

The research in plantation archaeology of the past 15 years is best characterized in a word—*proliferation*. There has been a proliferation of sites, data, approaches, and interpretations. These advancements have been good not only for the development of plantation archaeology but for historical archaeology in general. The modes of analysis and interpretation for the study of plantations have broad applications to the archaeological study of other complex societies.

The Future

What does the future hold for plantation archaeology? For the immediate future the developments of the most recent past are likely to continue into the 1990s and beyond. However, if plantation archaeology is to have an enduring role in the interpretation of southern agricultural history, its goals and approaches need strengthening to broaden the scope of this research. Space limitations do not permit a lengthy discussion of potential avenues for future research. The closing comments offered here are suggestions of where plantation archaeology appears to be and where it should be headed.

Future approaches to plantation archaeology should take into consideration "questions that count," that is, questions specifically geared toward archaeological analysis (Deagan 1988:10). For plantation archaeology this approach will entail the development of methodologies that utilize and maximize the multiple categories of evidence in historical archaeology. Frequently, the archaeological record is given secondary attention to the written record or the spoken word in plantation research. Much of the analysis of plantation landscapes, for example, is derived from historical plats, written descriptions, and geographic models rather than from archaeology. Some examples of "questions that count" which currently are emerging include: (1) How are differences from region to region manifested in the archaeological records, from the formative years of a plantation society to its more mature years, or from labor system to labor system? (2) What is the archaeological evidence of a social hierarchy within the slave community? and (3) Do the recovered food remains from slave cabins represent regular meals, or are these the remains from occasional efforts to satisfy hunger?

The determination of "questions that count" should consider where present gaps exist in the data base. A neglected area of research in the archaeological study of southern agriculture is the Upland Cotton or Short-staple Cotton Belt. This crop region embraces most of the interior portions of the Lower South, especially in South Carolina, Georgia, Alabama, and Mississippi. Pioneering work conducted on the postbellum tenant plantations has been undertaken in the Upland South (Adams 1980; Orser 1988b), but the antebellum short-staple cotton plantation has been virtually unexplored. This absence represents a significant gap in archaeologists' understanding of plantation societies, as the vast majority of slaves in the antebellum South labored on short-staple cotton plantations located in the interior areas of the South, not on the long-staple cotton plantations along coastal South Carolina and Georgia. The spread of slavery beginning in the 19th century resulted in the main from the invention of the Whitney saw gin which facilitated the processing of short-staple cotton in the southern United States. If it were not for the spread of cotton cultivation throughout the interior portions of the antebellum South, slavery would most likely have been a minor institution confined to the tobacco, rice, and long-staple cotton plantations of the eastern seaboard states and to the sugar plantations of Louisiana. In 1850, nearly 75% of all plantations in the South were engaged in cotton cultivation (Gray 1933:529), and the legacy of cotton plantations continued into the postbellum South. Certainly this example is only one gap in the archaeological study of southern plantations, and numerous areal and topical themes need to be considered in developing research "questions that count" in future studies.

A final comment on the future of plantation research touches upon the debate of whether historical archaeology is particularistic (historical), scientific (generalizing), or humanistic (an aesthetic appreciation of the human condition) (Deagan 1982:157). This argument, which has had a profound impact upon the development and direction of research in historical archaeology, is discussed in numerous other places (e.g., South 1977:5–17; Schuyler 1979; Deagan 1982; Deetz 1983). Plantation archaeology has been approached with all three paradigms, used either singly or sometimes in a combined form. Because of the orientation toward restoration and historical supplementation, many early studies were characterized by particularism. Fairbanks introduced humanism to plantation research through his interest in the search for material evidence of an African heritage and in describing slaves through the archaeological record. Status patterning studies proposed generalizations on plantation societies through the examination of artifact patterns attributable to socioeconomic class. These scientific studies contributed to both humanistic and particularistic research because of their concern with identifying ethnicity and reconstructing life at a specific plantation.

The archaeology of "power and economics" examines the processes that resulted in relations of domination in particular plantation societies with the goal of developing a general theoretical approach through which all plantation societies could be studied. For the immediate future, the formulation of generalizations from plantation archaeology appears to be unlikely. The data base is still too small, and the frameworks needed to understand the complexity of plantation society through archaeology are too novel at this stage of research. Scientific methods will continue to provide the basis for archaeological analysis. A more appropriate goal for plantation archaeology lies in understanding how a particular plantation society operated within an historical frame of reference. This goal will hopefully be realized in an approach that combines historical particularism and humanism with scientific analysis in order to understand the nature of plantation life and labor.

JEAN E. HOWSON

Social Relations and Material Culture: A Critique of the Archaeology of Plantation Slavery

Introduction

The archaeology of southern plantations promises to provide new data about slave life. This is most welcome, but like all sets of data—whether historical, anthropological, or archaeological, archaeological data require analysis and interpretation before becoming important or even useful. It is well to pause periodically and assess the links between methods of analysis and the theories which shape archaeological interpretations.

The way archaeologists think about the relationship of material remains to slave societies will—and should—shift in response to changing ideas about slave culture and about culture change in general. Plantation archaeology is currently undergoing a shift: (1) like historians, archaeologists are coming to view the culture of slaves as a key to understanding social structure and its transformation in the plantation South; (2) the meaning of the African heritage is being explored critically; (3) material culture studies are beginning to help in addressing questions about meaningful cultural categories and social change; and (4) a social action approach is replacing a status model of plantation social relations. All of these reflect, perhaps belatedly, the development of social theory in which culture is viewed in terms of a dynamic relationship between structure and practice, and symbols are analyzed in contexts of action. A critical approach to the relevant theoretical issues hopefully will be part of the new direction in which plantation archaeology is beginning to move.

This brief examination of the archaeology of plantation slavery reviews some of the dangers into which archaeologists have already fallen and offers suggestions for enhancing the theoretical underpinnings of archaeological work. First, a look at the use of cultural markers points up the need for a more sophisticated approach to the issue of culture change. Next is an exploration of the ways in which interpretations of material culture can be enriched through a more dynamic understanding of context. Finally, the usefulness of status definitions for modeling plantation social relations is assessed. To begin, a discussion of the relation between historical archaeology and the discipline of history brings out a curious fact: most archaeologists' notions about the purpose of history have hindered the participation of historical archaeology in some of the most interesting debates in the historiography of American slavery, centering on the meaning of slave culture.

History and Historical Archaeology: The Search for Africa in Slave Culture and the Problem of Acculturation

As historians of slavery have turned their attention to questions of culture, providing an important bridge to anthropological archaeology, archaeologists must be aware of historiographic issues and develop a critical approach to the broader arguments. Critical reading of the work of historians over the past 15 years (e.g., Genovese 1974; Gutman 1976; Mintz and Price 1976; Levine 1977; Blassingame 1979; Joyner 1984; Sobel 1987; Stuckey 1987; Fox-Genovese 1988) points out both how fruitful the cultural approach to history can be and the variation in orientation possible within the culturalist framework. Archaeologists for the most part still tend to turn to history for "the facts," confining their historiographic critique to a discussion of how "good" the documents are for specific purposes. History is often seen as a set of givens which provide background for archaeological research; at best, documentary research provides a complementary body of data which can promote constructive feedback between the disciplines (Deetz 1988:363; Salwen 1988; Schuyler 1988). But the historiography of slavery surely stands as one of the outstanding examples of how complex theoretical issues underlie scholarly historical research (e.g., Fox-Genovese and Genovese 1983a:136–171). History is not an established sequence of events, nor is it an existing explanatory structure just waiting to be filled in with more data, some documentary, some archaeological. Many archaeologists—especially those in public archaeology—applaud the interdisciplinary approach of historical archaeology, but what they are really extolling is the benefit they derive from having trained historians on the job to supply the facts about people, places, and things. If "the gap between history and anthropology appears to be closing in plantation archaeology" (Orser 1984: 3), it is more a by-product of the fact that people trained in anthropology are being forced to draw on historical research methods than a move toward interdisciplinary theory-building.

Turning to a concrete example, a potentially wasteful direction for archaeological research may be avoided by adopting a more sophisticated approach to the place of African roots in slave society. Just as social anthropologists went through a period of searching for tangible remnants of true African culture—or "survivals" or "retentions"—in African-Caribbean and African-American culture (Herskovits 1941; Mintz and Price 1976), historical archaeologists were for a time concerned with finding a visibly African style in the material remains they unearthed. Because archaeologists did not find many clear stylistic markers, they have had to be more subtle in their analyses in order to *make* materially visible the African component in the material remains of slaves. The focus recently among many researchers has been on finding an African-American "pattern" in the material record (e.g., Singleton 1980; Wheaton et al. 1983; Armstrong 1985), but others still seek tangible evidence of stylistic continuity. Leland Ferguson's (1989) study of pottery marks and Matthew Emerson's (1988) work on clay pipes are perhaps the best examples of the latter approach and demonstrate that African stylistic elements could survive in material culture as submerged indicators of belief systems or in a syncretic alliance with European style.

What is not always explicitly recognized by archaeologists is that the study of "Africanisms" is a politically significant and highly charged issue; for a brief review see Watson (1978). Important debates in linguistics, folklore, art and architecture, family and kinship studies, sociology, economics, and every other field relating to black America have centered on the question of cultural roots. But while it is beyond doubt that African culture did survive in many important ways under slavery and played an immense role in the forging of a new and viable society among slaves, sorting this sense of an African tradition out from the equally important constraints of slavery is no simple matter. For one thing, the very diversity of African societies from which slaves came needs to be taken into account from the start (Posnansky 1989). This diversity had a profound affect on the cultural transformation that took place in the plantation societies of the Western hemisphere.

A seminal essay argues that, given the diversity of African cultures and the process of adaptation necessary in the New World setting, archaeologists need to look for continuities at the level of underlying assumptions and structure:

> Those deep-level cultural principles, assumptions and understandings which were shared by the Africans in any New World Colony—who tended to be a tribally heterogeneous aggregate of individuals—would have represented a limited though crucial resource. For they could have served as a catalyst in the processes by which individuals from diverse societies forged new institutions, and could have provided certain frameworks within which new forms could have developed (Mintz and Price 1976:7).

The notion of transformational principles which lay beneath the "creolization" process has proven useful to historians, as well:

> Changes in other aspects of culture were akin to the transformation in [Gullah] language. Implicit but pervasive grammatical principles of culture lay behind the transformation of slave folklife in all its various manifestations. It is axiomatic that any people must build their response to the challenges and demands of a new environment out of the materials at hand. But those materials are put together in the manner they perceive to be most appropriate to the situation. The response may be in itself innovative—the creation of a new language, a new house-type, or new folktales—but the perception of appropriateness is cultural. Traditional notions of appropriateness in work and worship,

in feeling, thinking, and living—notions . . . influence the cultural choices forced by new conditions (Joyner 1984: 237).

Care should be taken in such an approach, however, not to imply a uniform understanding of "appropriateness" among African Americans. Culture is not a uniform thing in the first place, and the diversity of African origins meant that variation was a particularly essential aspect of culture in slave societies. The relation between *variation* and *change* has been central in analyses of creole language, and the extension of a creolization model to all of culture should incorporate a concept of variation as a locus of change (Drummond 1980; Le-Page and Tabouret-Keller 1985). Mintz and Price (1976:7) themselves are actually cautious about just how much weight can be given to a shared cultural "grammar" given a context of rapid change, stating that, "The probable importance of such generalized principles notwithstanding, the Africans in any New World colony in fact became a community and began to share a culture only insofar as, and as fast as, they themselves created them."

Although others would consider them overly cautious about tangible African "survivals" (e.g., Braithwaite 1971; Sobel 1987), Mintz and Price are certainly correct in pointing out that *traits do not equal culture,* and that even the act of reconstituting African cultural forms in the New World plantation setting implied creative transformation. Herbert Gutman (1976:260), who was influenced by Mintz, also argues in his study of the black family that African-American beliefs, even given African roots, had to be sustained by cultural forms and institutional arrangements which developed over time within slavery. But the "problem" of slave culture remains: The building of an African-American community with its own culture involved the development of traditions of practice within a day-to-day existence conditioned unavoidably by the fact of enslavement itself. Eugene Genovese (1974) thus chooses a model of class conflict and focuses on the role of the master-slave relationship in the development of black culture under slavery. All of these authors recognize the political significance of slave culture.

Given the foregoing, plantation archaeologists address some fairly central social and historical issues whenever they explore issues of "Africanism" and "acculturation." Simplistic notions of culture change will not work when applied to material culture any more than to belief systems or social structure. Reliance on cultural markers— specific material traits which archaeologists can discern—in reconstructing so-called "acculturation" sequences not only is dangerous in terms of over-simplifying the role of "Africanisms," but also is naive about the role of material culture. Material evidence about slave life on the plantations should be analyzed within a theoretical framework in which *both* change and continuity, at various times and in various contexts, embodied the process of cultural and political struggle of African Americans.

The study of slave-produced ceramics provides a good example of the "cultural marker" approach. A great deal has been said about these artifacts (Ferguson 1978; Lees and Kimery-Lees 1979; Anthony 1979; Deetz 1988), and no review is attempted here; however, a study published by Wheaton, Friedlander, and Garrow (1983)—see also Friedlander (1985) and Wheaton and Garrow (1985)—on South Carolina plantation sites points out the complexities in the interpretation of "Africanisms" and their relation to "acculturation." These authors are sensitive to the fact that slaves' material culture was restricted by slaveholders, and they have chosen to study foodways because this intimate aspect of slave life is less likely to reflect direct coercion from above. They present "a chain of data . . . which tends to link Colono with colonowares in other regions of the east coast, and to the Caribbean Islands and possibly to Africa" and conclude that "Colono and colonoware may be the most African 'Africanism' to appear on slave sites and as such the single most useful artifact for studying slave acculturation" (Wheaton et al. 1983:335). (As an aside, Wheaton, Friedlander, and Garrow mis-cite Handler and Lange as stating "that as Barbadian slaves became more acculturated the African attributes in their pottery disappeared" [Wheaton et al. 1983:335]. No such sequence was revealed for Barbados, nor is "acculturation'' mentioned. Rather, and importantly, Handler and Lange [1978:144] discuss specific historical, geographic, and ''industrial'' factors which affected the slave manufacture of ceramics.)

The acculturation model posits a gradual process of adapting to European-American ways with concurrent loss of African traits. The hypothesis of these researchers (Wheaton et al. 1983) is that the observed decrease in Colono ceramics was due not simply to availability of European wares but to the changing attitude of slaves toward those items—in other words, the cultural identity of slaves was being transformed. But the development of their argument involves a specific historical sequence:

> [The] data . . . showed a clear increase in the nonlocal ceramics and a decrease in Colono from 1740 to 1825. . . . Reasons for this trend were hypothesized to have been an increase in the slave population, a resident owner at Yaughan, and intensification of agricultural activity which caused greater regimentation to be imposed on the slaves and allowed them less free time to pursue individual craft activities. Perhaps the most important reason for this trend was acculturation of the slaves themselves (Wheaton et al. 1983:343).

The ''most important'' reason for the decline of Colono ceramics may never be known. Significantly, these authors have chosen to see the decline in terms of cultural change rather than as a function of the trans-Atlantic trade and economic conditions in the Old South (see Lees and Kimery-Lees 1979). But by abstracting this change from the context of power within which it occurred, they have obscured rather than clarified the nature of the process. Acculturation is an inaccurate, passive model for a dynamic process: the creation of a community and shared culture among slaves in the context of their struggle against an oppressive system, a system with styles of domination and resistance shaped by specific relations of production. The whole concept of acculturation rests on an inadequate definition of culture, one which emphasizes complexes of traits rather than peoples' ongoing interpretation, evaluation, and creative response, the strategies and symbolic revaluing that form the basis of cultural process. The acculturation model was developed in the context of the anthropological study of Native American groups,

and some of the best criticism of the model comes from Americanists; see especially Fowler (1987).

Wheaton, Friedlander, and Garrow adopt an interdisciplinary approach at the outset of their research (Friedlander 1985:217). The ahistorical model which they develop is not a function of any lack of historical information, which is amply provided, but rather the result of the kinds of a priori assumptions about culture change which most archaeologists adopt. Their argument rests on the idea that slave-owner interaction is a *demographic* issue (Friedlander 1985), that somehow the degree of contact between the two is the crux of the matter and has determined the course of culture change. This position is a troubling notion akin to the idea that social structure in itself determines the meaningful content of social action. The approach corresponds to the mistaken archaeological notion that the meaning of things somehow can be construed directly from frequency distributions (Wheaton and Garrow 1985:253). As these authors are no doubt aware, the forces behind culture change were not demographic but had to do with the kinds of social interaction—among slaves and between slaves and free whites—that developed in slave societies.

Others also are aware that master-slave relations played a part in determining African cultural continuity:

> Despite the apparent persistence of certain African architectural traits, most planters openly discouraged African style huts on their plantations. . . . Thus, the more intimate expressions of tidewater slave life—which were either overlooked by plantation whites *or were hidden from their view*—often contained vestiges of the African cultural past: these included cookery, speech, stories, sorcery, basketry, quilting, the carving of figurines and walking sticks, and dance forms . . . intangible words, behaviors, or artifacts that were fashioned from perishable wood and fiber [emphasis added] (Otto 1984:43,87).

Like Wheaton, Friedlander, and Garrow, Otto recognizes that power was exercised over slaves in terms of cultural style. What kind of power was this, and how did it operate? *Why* did slaves have to hide their cultural expression? Otto addresses this question for workplace contexts:

> The plantation whites were most concerned that slaves acquire the appropriate standards of speech and behavior

that would allow them to perform their agricultural, skilled, and service roles. In the work context, there was much interaction between blacks and white supervisors, and the domestic servants, in particular, were under the close scrutiny of whites. Therefore, the slave operating cultures in the white-dominated work contexts would have shown conformity to white American standards (Otto 1984:86).

The "more intimate" lives of slaves, it can be argued, also were subject to pressure from above, all the more reason for slaves to hide as much as they could. That pressure stemmed from the masters' fear, from their understanding that cultural expressions are not harmless, and from their ideology of paternalism. As Genovese (1974) has so well understood, paternalism was an invasive policy. The problem of cultural hegemony and the debate over the "paternalistic compromise" needs to be addressed in examining the significance of African style—if only because Genovese has brought Gramsci's concept to bear on slave studies and created heated controversy in so doing (see criticisms by Anderson 1976; Wilson 1976; Johnson 1978:91). But in each specific case the question remains as to whether, how, and to what extent pressures on slave culture penetrated and were resisted—surely a pertinent question in the study of material culture.

Historical archaeologists have a tendency to confuse behavior with culture. Particularly disturbing are comments such as J. W. Joseph's (1989:64) suggestion that "more diligent supervision may have inspired more rapid acculturation" on the part of slaves housed along orderly streets. "Acculturation" is not an appropriate or accurate way to describe slave response to "diligent supervision." Culture change is rarely a simple response to coercion; behavior can be coerced, not culture. Cultural continuity is not simply the residue surviving in the interstices of imposed change. Change and continuity characterize all cultural systems and can be evaluated only insofar as archaeologists understand specific historical contexts and the social relations that obtained in those contexts. It is the political content of cultural style that is lost when archaeologists adopt an acculturation model.

The search for African style misses a crucial point about the nature of slavery, having to do with relations between classes, not with forms of culture contact or the contact of cultural forms. What has been called "acculturation" was a question of power in the broadest sense. Thus, resistance, rather than mere conservatism or continuity, may be the relevant context within which to view expressions of separate cultural style on the part of slaves. Perhaps "separatism" is a better concept than "persistence" or "continuity," because it does not exclude transformations, is interactive, and has more political force than "boundary maintenance." At the same time, culture change within the slave community which can be "demonstrated" archaeologically or otherwise is not necessarily an indicator of acculturation, except insofar as the material idiom of the political battle had shifted.

Wheaton, Friedlander, and Garrow (1983) are not alone in neglecting the political aspects of culture change, and the conceptual muddiness inherent in an acculturation model has not cleared. The model continues to lead to rather unfortunate interpretations and has been misapplied in an approach which sees change as bidirectional. In a recent example, Joseph (1989) has written an otherwise useful article which picks up on the contrast between plantations studied in South Carolina and Georgia first pointed out by Theresa Singleton (1985a:7). Differences in agricultural region, research design, and excavation strategy can account for some of the variations in "artifact pattern" that have been discerned, but time period is also shown to determine which pattern applies. Joseph suggests this reflects real culture change between the 18th and 19th centuries. Instead of seeing this change as one way, he argues that slaves and masters alike "acculturated" on the plantations. Other archaeologists probably will be attracted to a bidirectional model, even though it represents an incorrect use of the term acculturation and is a potential way of sidestepping the important issues. (Acculturation, in its classic formulation, meant the gradual loss of indigenous culture traits and assimilation to white European-American culture [see Linton 1940; Spicer 1961]. Archaeologists subsequently adapted the concept for use in classifying material culture in terms of degrees of acculturation. The model is unidirectional in any case.)

Joseph (1989:64–65) suggests that whites realized "by the 19th century" that slaves were humans, became concerned with slave health when the slave trade was cut off, came to view their chattels differently, and thus were "acculturated." There can be little doubt that masters recognized the humanity of their slaves all along, and it also seems clear that the strongest racist ideologies developed alongside 19th-century paternalist policies, while mutual cultural exchange was particularly marked in the 18th century (Sobel 1987). The argument that acculturation on the part of masters "fostered an improved, and also more Anglo American, material culture for 19th-century slaves" (Joseph 1989:65) cannot stand close scrutiny. An argument for the changing perceptions of slaveholders, however, can in fact be made, not on the basis of their recognition of slaves' humanity and the need for a self-reproducing labor force, but on entirely different grounds: Slaves had so staunchly fought for and defended their customary rights, and through slaves' efforts, the patterns of material exchanges between them and their masters had become so entrenched, that the perceptions of the masters came to include many "taken-for-granteds" brought about through this interaction. Whether this is labeled a "paternalistic compromise"—after Genovese (1979)—or not, at its core is the struggle between slaves and masters, *not* a shift between cultural models.

Attitudes toward time and work rhythms are another good example of the dialectic within which slave culture affected slaveowners' relations with their labor force—and hence the whole character of the southern economy—as well as vice versa (Genovese 1974:283–324; Joyner 1984:41–89; Sobel 1987:21–67). While plantation owners forced slaves to do specific kinds of harsh labor necessary to keep profits up, slaves took advantage of agricultural, season-, and crop-oriented rhythms, as well as community forms of labor, to create distinctive work patterns. This in turn reinforced the essentially rural and preindustrial character of a system highly resistant—in terms of culture as well as economics—to the type of change associated with capitalist production.

In rejecting the idea of slaves as passively acculturated, archaeologists must not merely rely on a simplistic argument that acculturation was a two-way street; the nature of the relationship between the two groups involved must remain central. In contact situations both cultures change, but surely New World slavery is a special case of "contact." The plantation clearly provided a special environment for intimate contact between bearers of African and white European-American culture, but at the same time it was the locus of profound class antagonisms between enslaved and free. Recent historical treatments reflect this dualism, and archaeologists can benefit from insights gained through different approaches. Mechal Sobel presents the Virginia masters' and slaves' "world they made together" as a product of cultural interaction, and often convergence, over the course of the 18th century. If Sobel seems to overlook too much of the political content of cultural interaction, she nevertheless provides an important addition to the history of plantation life and the necessary historical foundation for studies of the 19th century when "the social and emotional distance between whites and blacks grew" (Sobel 1987:240). From Joyner's (1984) point of view, the distinctive life of the quarters underpinned a viable creolized slave culture which can be studied as a coherent whole on its own terms. To understand how slaves used the cultural space which they carved out for themselves is crucially important, but Joyner downplays the political, contested aspects of culture and the class-consciousness behind cultural distinctiveness. Focusing on the 19th century, Elizabeth Fox-Genovese (1988) sees the plantation "household" as a context for surface intimacy between mistresses and slaves, underlain by deep divisions and racist oppression. Like Genovese (1979), Fox-Genovese sees class and cultural identity as inextricably intertwined and conflict as the motor force behind social and cultural change on the plantations.

Archaeologists may find one of these approaches more appropriate to their data than the others, depending on the important variables of time and place, but change within the dominant class culture and within slave culture cannot be subsumed within a model of mutual acculturation. The imposed conjunction of class and race tended to over-determine all social relations, and the struggles within which African-American culture developed must be placed with this context of unequal interaction. At the same time, the fundamentally separatist aspect of slave culture is not obviated because slaves eventually lived in, used, wore, and ate European material goods. All cultures change as people actively create and respond to historical realities. What archaeologists should want to know is how the institution of slavery and the African heritage alike shaped the process by which African Americans made their world.

In sum, when historical archaeologists set out to "build a case for acculturation" (Wheaton and Garrow 1985:243), it is not clear whether they view it as an active *response* to oppression or as a *by-product* of culture contact. In any case, neither approach to culture change in the slave community is appropriate. These authors insist that material culture can be an index of change, but their notion of change is far too simplistic:

> The acculturation of the Afro-American slaves from an Afro-Caribbean (or West African, or Afro-Caribbean-American Colonial) cultural model within Yaughan and Curriboo plantations to a more Euro-American cultural model can be demonstrated through a study of architectural evidence, recovered artifacts, and subsistence data (Wheaton and Garrow 1985:243).

People do not shift from Cultural Model A to Cultural Model B, and if "acculturation" is to be used by plantation archaeologists in this way, the term should be discarded. Moreover, it would be difficult for material culture to "demonstrate" any such shift, for material things are imbedded in multiple contexts of behavior and meaning.

The Contexts of Material Culture

From the point of view of archaeology, material culture is at least quadruply imbedded—its past

involved contexts of production, distribution (including procurement, acquisition, exchange), use, and discard. Archaeologists working at plantation slave sites have too often erred in focusing on only one or at most two of these contexts. The interpretation of cultural remains depends upon the ability not only to reconstruct individual contexts, but to discern multiple and often ambiguous ones. Furthermore, archaeologists need to consider relationships between the relevant contexts for particular classes of artifacts.

A concentration on either distribution context or use context characterizes much plantation archaeology, including both Handler and Lange's (1978) study of a Barbadian cemetery and Otto's (1984) work at Cannon's Point Plantation. These researchers have advanced the interpretation of material remains, and their analyses make it abundantly clear that information about social life potentially can be gleaned from archaeological data. Their work also points to a next step in the analysis of material culture, however, which relates distribution to use in attempting to derive meaning. If the treatment of one specific artifact, clay pipes, is examined, the problem can be highlighted.

As an illustration of their ethnohistorical approach, Handler and Lange discuss their research into the reward/incentive system on the plantation. Documents were reexamined for information on artifacts recovered archaeologically, including clay pipes. Pipes and tobacco were among the material items used as "rewards" to slaves, and Handler and Lange

> began to suspect that the occurrence of particular artifacts . . . with interments may have been a manifestation of plantation rewards or incentives. As a result, the notes were more intensively reexamined, the presence of a reward-incentive system was established to a degree not previously understood, and the function of various archaeological materials as remnants of the system was inferred (Handler and Lange 1978:218).

If, however, the use context of clay tobacco pipes on slave plantations is examined, the interpretation can be richer and more pertinent to the study of slave life. As noted by archaeologists, pipe smoking was a very important "recreation" among slaves (Handler and Lange 1978; Otto 1984:91). The use of tobacco marked their leisure hours, their Sundays off, "their" time as opposed to their master's time (Genovese 1974:556; Joyner 1984:127–140). Smoking could also be a social activity, and social life within the quarter was the crucible of slaves' resistance, central to their survival and humanity. This means that even if the white owners on Barbados thought that the reward/ incentive system created compliance, obedience, and status hierarchy among slaves—as well as social distance between slaves and paternalistic masters, the material and behavioral results of that system also may have furthered the social and cultural distinctiveness of slaves and made more obvious the existence of an alternative society to that envisioned by planters.

So when Handler and Lange find burials containing clay pipes, are they seeing evidence of a system meant to foster obedience through status-striving, or are they actually seeing evidence for a system of values among slaves that resulted in people being buried with the items that they enjoyed in daily life among their fellows and that represented membership in a community? It should be obvious that both are represented; the ambiguity is real. Lange and Handler (1985:26) in fact do suggest that the pipes buried with some Newton slaves had symbolic significance. The question is, from what social contexts did that significance derive? Many archaeologists have limited their interpretations by choosing to focus on factors of distribution, such as the common categories "imported" versus "local," and to neglect use context. Care should be taken not to assign social meaning to material remains without taking into account the ambiguous contexts which produced that meaning, because:

> Material symbols can be used covertly to disrupt established relations of dominance. . . . The 'power' of material symbols . . . resides also in the ambiguous meanings of material items. Unlike spoken language, the meanings of material symbols can remain undiscussed and implicit. Their meanings can be reinterpreted and manipulated covertly (Hodder 1983:10).

Otto's (1984:168–169) analysis of plantation material culture sets slaves' clay pipes against the cigars which were used by white owners and over-

seers, a material pattern related to one kind of status difference between blacks and whites. This difference is said to reflect the "white dominance" pattern, a material reflection of the fact that whites of any bracket held higher racial-legal status than slaves. Otto focuses on the use context of pipes to derive this pattern but points out that slaves *acquired* these goods through purchase or trade in garden produce or livestock (Otto 1984: 71–80). (The subject of slaves' "internal economy" has received a great deal of recent attention among historians of the plantation South, though its importance has long been recognized in the Caribbean [Mintz and Hall 1960; McDonald 1981; Morgan 1982, 1983].) Distribution context is therefore at least as relevant as use context in this case. The ability of slaves to purchase and trade for "luxury" items places such goods firmly within a separate category. The pipes can hardly be said to "reflect" slaves' given subordinate status when they are the result of a clear bid for a degree of autonomy and an independent livelihood. Once again the struggle between slaves and owners, not their structural position, must be centralized. It can be argued that the internal economy was just another aspect of the slaves' exploitation to the extent that they were merely providing their own subsistence. The meaning of the system for its participants, however, could never have been determined solely through such an objective analysis. As Otto (1984:79–80) notes, planters fought to restrict slaves' trading activity; evidence that this was an area of contention should draw attention to the possible implications for the meaning of material goods at slave sites.

It would probably be possible to incorporate an analysis of acquisition context within Otto's formulation of status patterning since the boundary between slaves and whites was maintained, the line of "white dominance" drawn from above. But in identifying such a "pattern" it is necessary to focus on the *contrast* between the smoking habits of slaves and whites, thus obscuring the internal meaning of pipe smoking within slave culture. Likewise, overseers' material culture had an internal social meaning: The smoking habits of overseers would be more similar to planters than to slaves because it is the planters with whom they wished to identify socially, not because they were legally dominant over blacks. Here again, material culture theorists have urged caution against over-simplifying the processes of cultural categorization of the material world. Hodder (1983:9) notes that "the meaning of an object resides not merely in its contrast to others within a set. Meaning also derives from the associations and use of an object, which itself becomes, through the associations, the node of a network of references and implications. There is an interplay between structure and content," and Miller (1987:129) states, "The physicality of the artifact lends itself to the work of praxis—that is, cultural construction through action rather than just conceptualization." In other words, material objects are more than just a language of distinction between social groups. The contrast between cigars and clay pipes has to do with the meaningful contexts of their acquisition and use, not just with the structural relationship between whites and slaves. Just as the context of pipe acquisition was the struggle for a measure of autonomy, the social context of pipe smoking among slaves was the internal life of the slave quarter. The abstraction of a pattern has in this case meant the reduction of meaning.

If archaeologists have tended to isolate either use or distribution context, they have also failed to look for relationships between contexts. The study of slave diet illustrates this problem. It has been suggested that "one of the most promising areas of study" in regard to understanding "the archaeological nature of plantation slavery in concrete, material terms" is the study of slave diet (Orser 1984:4). Many have shared this optimism, as an examination of the sections on diet in most studies of plantation sites demonstrates—see, however, a review of the evidence by Reitz (1987). But archaeologists should also be interested in viewing food in less "concrete" and "material" terms.

Twenty years ago, Robert Ascher and Charles Fairbanks stated:

> People classify the food they eat in many ways. . . . From the point of view of the slave, a fundamental division was food distributed by the owner and food the slave supplied for himself. . . . With this knowledge, we abandon our usual categories and replace them with those meaningful to the people who interest us (Ascher and Fairbanks 1971:11).

Accepting this position, historical archaeologists classify food remains accordingly. This classification by production and procurement/acquisition contexts is an appropriate one, and analyses of diet that follow from it are equally so. But analysis of context should not stop here. It should be possible, with historical research, to relate use context—that is, consumption—to these other contexts when analyzing archaeological remains. Did consumption of slave-raised stock and produce or slave-collected wild foods take place at different times and on different social occasions than that of planter-provided fare? And what about stolen food? Were consumption patterns related solely to supply and the dictates of hunger and nutrition, or did the preparation, serving, and consumption of food have additional cultural significance in part *derived from* its means of acquisition?

A pattern is emerging regarding the co-option by slaves of items associated with or produced by their masters, to be given new meaning and new context within their own society. Much more research is required, perhaps, concerning the adoption by subordinate classes of the cultural property of elites. This forms a part of the larger problem of culture change and the role of material culture in that process. The problem is particularly relevant in situations of culture contact, colonialism, and slavery. It can be argued that what has recently been labeled "recontextualization" (D. Miller 1987) in fact has long been the central interpretive issue addressed by all American historical archaeology.

The role of material goods in maintaining and articulating social categories and relations—with consumption serving to establish, mark, or transform people's perceptions of themselves especially in relation to others—has been explored in detail (Douglas and Isherwood 1979), to which has been added a cross-cultural perspective (Appadurai 1986) which may be more attuned to the realities of slave society. The crossing of a cultural boundary between slaves and slaveholders by commodities may involve very shallow sets of shared values (Appadurai 1986:14) yet result in considerable overlap in material goods. Moreover, it seems possible that different values nonetheless might be deliberately expressed through very similar, even identical, things, especially if one group perceives a commodity as having been diverted and hence its value enhanced or transformed. The flouting of implicit sumptuary laws on the part of slaves caused continual annoyance to white southerners, for instance. The supposed preference of slaves for stolen meat was, if anything, an example of this conscious revaluing. Arjun Appadurai (1986:26), in referring to theft as a form of commodity-diversion, illuminates its political implications. It does seem obvious that ''theft'' by slaves of their masters' goods was a political act. The pertinent question becomes, then, in what ways did the ''paths'' of commodities—in Appadurai's sense—determine their meanings to consumers?

What all of this means is that archaeologists must contextualize their data more fully. Hodder (1987) has conceived the method of ''contextual analysis'' as threefold: (1) to examine functional-environmental context; (2) to analyze material things structurally-semiotically, as in reading a text; and (3) to examine particular situations to derive historical meaning. The first task traditionally has been most archaeologists' strong suit, and the second has been enjoying primacy among structuralist-oriented researchers. The third task is most basic if archaeologists wish to incorporate a view of culture as constituted through praxis, a view too often lacking in historical archaeologists' treatment of slave material culture. Marshall Sahlins (1976:22) has contrasted ''praxis theory''—which holds that ''the specific construction of culture is the product of a concrete activity which transcends the system to appropriate the novelty and actuality of the material world—with structuralism, in which the focus is on the system itself. Writing on material culture, Christopher Tilley (1983) uses the ''notion of praxis as mediation between activity and consciousness'' to argue that material things, as foci of social action, embody ideational systems. The assignment of artifacts to particular classes within overall distribution patterns cannot continue based on partial understandings of context. The derivation of meaningful patterns can only rest on meaningful and thickly conceived historical and anthropological interpretations.

Status Patterning

Handler and Lange (1978:226) note that a central problem in the study of plantation sites is that the sources of material goods were available to free whites, free nonwhites, and slaves, and that patterns of lateral cycling through ''purchase, trade, exchange, or gift giving would have tended to blur absolute artifactual distinctions between the non-slave and slave segments'' of a population. Otto (1984) has taken as his starting point the elucidation of a pattern that at first simply appears ''blurred.'' By holding status constant, he can look at how variously defined status differences produced patterning in the archaeological remains. Classes of artifacts were found to reflect one of three patterns: (1) ''white dominance,'' based on racial/legal status (housing construction, housing amenities, liquor bottles, pipes, and glass beads); (2) ''hierarchical,'' based on social/occupational status (housing living space, ceramic shape and form); and (3) ''wealth-poverty,'' based on economic status (wild food, domestic food, and ceramic decorative type). The classification depends upon whether each item is most similarly distributed between overseers and planters versus slaves (white dominance), overseers and slaves versus planters (wealth-poverty), or graded between the three (hierarchical).

Otto's work has been criticized for oversimplifying plantation social organization in terms of planter/overseer/slave, when in fact social distance between overseers and planters varied greatly (Orser 1984:5–6). The importance of Otto's work, however, is not in showing how to recognize these three groups archaeologically (Drucker 1981), but in demonstrating that different kinds of status may be manifested materially by different kinds of remains; in other words, that status and its material correlates are too complex to be inferred directly. Nevertheless, archaeologists persist in applying a status model, concentrating on explaining deviations from Otto's original formulation. There is less need for a continued refinement of the artifact assignments (e.g., Adams and Boling 1989) than for an examination of the underlying reason for inconsistencies, namely the limitations of the model itself.

The problem Otto faces—along with many others—stems from conceiving of society in terms of differing levels of status in the first place, rather than in terms of social relations (Orser 1988a). Slaves had lower status than their owners because they were owned—clearly the power relations are primary, and status is simply a static way of describing the product of social action.

Dominance is not a status term, it is a relation, one in which the dominant group always has an effect on the dominated, and in which the autonomy of the dominated is restricted in order to be consistent with the interests of the dominant group. The response of one group to domination by another takes certain forms. What archaeologists should study is how domination operates and how responses to it are enacted, which means that differences in material remains should be examined in terms of their function within a context of social action, rather than as status markers. Furthermore, material culture must be understood not as merely reflecting social relations, but as participating actively in their creation, operation, and maintenance. Regardless of the nature and degree of elite penetration of slaves' cultural identity, the material contexts of daily life certainly played a role. The resistance of slaves was largely acted out daily in the assertion of a degree of cultural autonomy, which necessarily had to make use of material "givens" and their manipulation. Again, the work of Douglas and Isherwood, Hodder, Daniel Miller, and Appadurai on material culture can be useful for historical archaeologists.

Through co-opting items of material culture, slaves created material contexts for the internal social life of their community. Clay pipes suggest that Otto's pattern of "white dominance" in material remains was at best ambiguous. Beads and liquor bottles fall into the same category of "white dominance," but these objects, too—regardless of their distribution among slaves, overseers, and owners, speak to slaves' private and/or communal lives, not to the structure of subordination.

What about the "wealth-poverty" and "hierarchical" patterns? The first is problematical because Otto fails to consider fully the relationship between planters and specific overseers—some of whom were planters' sons—at Cannon's Point. Once again, social relations have been overlooked in the desire to establish status. If overseers look "poor" in terms of food and ceramic patterns, it may be because they actually participated in the domestic life of the great house to a greater extent than assumed by Otto. But the fact remains that many poor overseers lived on southern plantations. This situation does not mean, however, that the relevant contrast is between poor slaves and overseers on the one hand and wealthy planters on the other. Ideologically speaking, poor whites were participants in the same social caste as wealthy ones, whereas slaves were a separate caste. To consider slaves and poor whites as members of the same economic class is to overlook the caste aspect of slavery. Put another way, it is to see class as fully definable in terms of its economic determinants, without its social and ideological correlates.

In a critique of the analyses of both Otto (1984) and Sue Mullins Moore (1985), Charles Orser (1988a) argues that their caste model of plantation society links race and class but gives race primacy. He prefers to focus on the power the class of slaveowners held over their slaves, a power that included control over material items slaves possessed. Orser is right to bring economics and power more prominently into the archaeological analysis of plantation social relations, but these factors cannot "replace" caste and status. The imposed conjunction of race and class is precisely what gave planter hegemony its strongest tool.

"Hierarchy" is equally problematical. To use the concept of hierarchy is to assume the existence—either actual or ideal—of a continuous series of social statuses. No such continuous series—either actual or ideal—existed in southern society. The series was discontinuous at the point where some groups of people owned others and at the point where racial lines were drawn. Orser (1988a) rightly calls attention to the occupational ranking system on plantations, but his argument that "occupation can be looked upon by archaeologists as the most important social characteristic" within the plantation hierarchy (Orser 1988a:741) is disquieting; occupation may have been the *second* most important criterion of social rank, but surely the slave/free dichotomy came first. This is part of a wider issue which continues to have relevance today, the question of cultural evaluation of social situations. Groups and individuals *interpret* their inequality differently: Where some see occupation and wealth as the primary determinants of status, others see discrimination and racism as key, reflecting real differences in experience as well as "objective" analysis. This is a good example of how structural relations are subject to varying interpretation as well as ideological manipulation. Diane Austin (1984) analyzes the ideology of education in Jamaica as the modern outgrowth of an earlier ideology of occupational ranking that had its roots in the slave plantation. She argues that this dominant-class ideology is refuted by the poor, who interpret inequality in terms of discrimination.

Given the fact that legal and racist barriers do exist in societies such as the plantation South under slavery, the expression of hierarchy in material culture nevertheless may serve a very real social end. The pretense of a status hierarchy can function in society toward fostering the acceptance of inequality. Slaves were clearly not simply on the bottom rung of some social ladder. The interest of the elite was to create an illusion of such a social order to promote a sense of "naturalness" in inequality, which they possibly accomplished partially through overt material signs.

If Otto's classification of material remains relating to housing is examined, an interesting "pattern of patterns" can be discerned. In terms of how well built the structures are and the amenities they contain, "white dominance" is indicated. But in terms of sheer space, hierarchy is represented. Bernard Herman (1984:276) also notes that in the South dwelling size was not necessarily correlated with quality, comfort, or expense of furnishings and concludes somehow that this situation contradicts Genovese's (1974) contention that planter he-

gemony was expressed in housing. What may be expressed is the creation of an environment—the material context of life on the plantation—in which external signs illustrate and promote the false and artificial concept of social hierarchy, only to be belied by the evidence for actual quality of life.

Whether or not planters were attempting to express and create the cultural hegemony of their class—based on the idea of a patriarchal order—in this way becomes an historical question. Of particular interest to some historical archaeologists is the role of material culture in relation to ideology, used here in the sense of the establishment of taken-for-granteds which serve to obscure power relations (Leone 1982). At first glance, a Marxist definition of ideology may seem inappropriate for slave societies. After all, here is a case where dominance and coercion were overt, where status was assigned by law, and where the need for promoting a false consciousness on the part of the oppressed was surely obviated by their legal enslavement. The question of motivation is complicated: Planters needed an ethical justification for the basic inequality on which they depended and may have sought it in the "natural order," while conscious misdirection of observers' perceptions of plantation life may have motivated others. These "internal" and "external" factors motivating plantation planning need to be explored through research into the historical records relating to plantation housing. It is hardly necessary to point out here that the use of material symbols by planters to establish a naturalness in the patriarchal order does not at all mean that slaves were "taken in." Slaves knew all too intimately what occurred within planters' and overseers' houses. Likewise, poor whites, especially plantation dependents, may have been well aware of the political nature of their subordination and may have seen it as anything but natural. It is a grave mistake to assume that what planters told themselves about plantation life ever convinced anyone else who had to experience it.

Other archaeologists have looked at status patterning in the material record in their attempts to apply or add to Otto's formulation. William Adams and Sarah Boling (1989:94), for example, point out that slaves on three coastal plantations in

Georgia had higher priced ceramic wares in some forms than their owners. They argue that the task system allowed these slaves time to earn income of their own. Given that many of their material goods were obtained through purchase, Adams and Boling conclude that these slaves were using ceramics, much as did whites, as status markers within their *own* community. But this interpretation begs the question: *Why* would these items have held status value for slaves? If such goods were indeed high-status possessions for slaves, their meaning derives at least as much from their context of acquisition as from their association with white European-American culture. Care must be exercised when interpreting material goods in the same way for slaves as for plantation whites precisely because slaves did *not* "participate freely within the Southern market economy" (Adams and Boling 1989:94). To conclude that "on [task-labor] plantations slaves may be better understood within the context of being peasants or serfs, regarding their economic status" (Adams and Boling 1989:94) is to overlook a host of economic, political, social, and cultural realities for the sake of retaining status-markers as analytical tools. Historical archaeologists need to examine historically how slaves' interpretations, reinterpretations, and contested interpretations of material things were worked out.

Conclusions

Otto has done historical archaeologists an important service. He has shown that status cannot possibly be inferred directly from material remains. He and many others nonetheless have retained this concept, simply assigning independent status definitions to various data as they seem to fit. The analytical weakness of a concept of status has been demonstrated, but plantation archaeologists do not seem to realize the implications, choosing instead to refine the heuristic device in order to apply it more closely without noticing that this approach only takes the discipline further from society conceived as a whole. Human social relations are not reducible to sets of status variables,

any more than historical change is reducible to models of acculturation.

What is needed is a contextual description of material culture that is conscious of both plantation class relations and historical processes of culture change—an ambitious goal. The study of slave culture can liberate historians—and slaves—as historical actors from the bare analysis of exploitation and oppression. On the other hand, a focus on the class structure of plantation society and the master-slave relationship, always keeping in view the issue of power and the political fact of enslavement, prevents researchers from *neglecting* the bare realities of exploitation and oppression. This essay has attempted to show that given an adequate conception of culture and social action, contexts of both power/resistance and cultural separatism are relevant to the interpretation of material remains at slave sites. The exercise of power affects the material idiom of cultural expression and the political interpretation of material symbols. Cultural separatism allows meanings to be articulated and contested by individuals and groups within the black community, but also constitutes a form of resistance to slaveholder power. Throughout, archaeologists need to recall that meaning is generally negotiable and that material things are susceptible to various or contested meanings through contexts of action. As Sahlins (1985:ix) notes, "If culture is as anthropologists claim a meaningful order, still, in action meanings are always at risk."

Artifacts, then, do not work well either as cultural markers or as status markers. Their distributions do not "map" culture change or social relations in a direct way. An interpretive step must be taken in the archaeological study of slave culture and plantation society, a step which should incorporate: (1) an analysis of whether material change reflects the structure of power relations or social strategies and cultural recontextualization within that structure; (2) an understanding of how material things come to have meaning through specific and historically definable contexts of action; and (3) an exploration of how manipulation of material symbols helps to create and maintain particular interpretations of social reality. Culture itself must be defined in a way that reflects the acknowledgment of contested interpretations of symbols and experience. A more sophisticated understanding of culture in turn will allow archaeologists to approach the historical issues from a new perspective, with new means for using material culture to address key questions.

Acknowledgments

This essay is a substantially revised version of a paper delivered at the 1987 Northeastern Anthropological Association meeting, Amherst. I would like to thank Randall White for his helpful comments on the original essay. The present version benefitted substantially from the careful reading and suggestions of Marjorie Ingle and Diana Wall. Charles Orser also commented on an early draft, and I thank him for his help in preparing the final version for publication. I cannot fully measure the late Bert Salwen's influence on the development of the ideas that have gone into this paper. Even though the opinions expressed are my own, I do hope that the result at least reflects his commitment to interdisciplinary research goals.

38

Barbara J. Heath
Amber Bennett

"The little Spots allow'd them": The Archaeological Study of African-American Yards

ABSTRACT

Yards, like buildings and more portable artifacts, are significant expressions of culture. Yet within African-American archaeology, yards have not been the focus of serious discussions addressing questions of work and leisure activities, community interactions, aesthetics, and culture change. The authors review archaeological, ethnographic, and historical evidence of yards associated with New World slave quarters and present a framework for analysis. Results of recent excavations at a slave quarter at Poplar Forest in central Virginia, occupied from ca. 1790 to 1812, are presented within the context of this framework. The archaeological study of yard spaces provides significant information about cultural meanings and uses of space.

Introduction

Early archaeological studies of plantation slavery attempted to define the material conditions of life common to enslaved men and women and to trace the persistence of African cultural retentions through time. More recent studies have addressed questions of status and hierarchy within plantation communities, the negotiation of relationships between planters and enslaved people, the creation of an African-American ethnic identity, and the symbolic representations of belief systems (Singleton and Bograd 1993:14-29). Nearly all of these studies of plantation slavery are based on the analysis of individual households; indeed, most have focused on the physical remains of quarters and the artifacts associated with them.

In the preface to Richard Westmacott's *African American Gardens and Yards in the Rural South*, Theresa Singleton referred to the use of space as "the most monumental aspect of material culture" (Singleton 1992:x). Studies of the use of architectural space have been of enormous benefit in understanding symbolic and functional aspects of daily life in the past (Upton 1985; Vlach 1991;

Deetz 1996). Similarly, investigations focusing on the ways in which people appropriated external space, or crafted and used the spaces allotted to them, define the emerging subdiscipline of landscape archaeology. Like the structures they surround, yards and gardens have the ability to instruct scholars about the lives of their inhabitants.

The yard is defined here as the area of land, bounded and usually enclosed, which immediately surrounds a domestic structure and is considered an extension of that dwelling. A yard is set aside for particular personal or group uses, including, but not limited to, food production and preparation, care and maintenance of animals, domestic chores, storage, recreation, and aesthetic enjoyment. It is at once a part of the domestic compound and a mediating space between the natural, public world and the constructed, private world of the dwelling.

This definition includes garden areas, which are used for small-scale, personal production of useful and ornamental plants, but excludes larger provision grounds, which were often located some distance from the quarters. This broad definition of yard allows for the acknowledgment of regional differences in yard construction and use. Particular examples of yard spaces must be understood both within this broad framework and as individual products of time and place.

As modern ethnographers have demonstrated, the shaping of one's yard is an action laden with meaning. Through their yards, enslaved African Americans spoke to many audiences: ancestors, family members, neighbors, overseers, planters, and outsiders. While yards cannot be studied independently of the houses they surround, the authors believe it is time to develop tools and to frame questions that take advantage of the unique perspective these external spaces have to offer. Archaeologists must learn to read the multiple messages enslaved men and women sought to express in their yards since the study of these spaces provides information about past lives which can be obtained nowhere else. The focus of this work, thus, is on both the construction of a broadly useful archaeological perspective of African-American yards and its application

Historical Archaeology, 2000, 34(2):38—55.
Permission to reprint required.

to a specific site located in Bedford County, Virginia.

Historical Evidence of Yards

The evidence of the nature of yard spaces includes historical, ethnographic, and archaeological information drawn from Africa, the Caribbean, and the United States. While each of these sources has particular biases, taken together, this body of evidence provides a starting point for a contextualized understanding of slave yards in the American South.

In general, historical documents offer few detailed descriptions of West African yards or of the yards of bondsmen in the Caribbean and the American South. This may be the result of a number of factors: authors may have overlooked yards in favor of house descriptions; they may have deliberately ignored aspects of the day-to-day lives of the enslaved; or they may have seen few distinctions between African-American yards and those of poor whites. The primary descriptions are few in number and are seldom free of bias. Still, available contemporary descriptions offer valuable clues regarding the appearance, use, and development of African and African-American yard spaces over time.

West Africa

Traveler's accounts of West Africa were consulted for historic descriptions of yards. These include Mungo Park's search for the source of the Niger in 1795, Rene Caillie's travels to Timbuktu and Hugh Clapperton's expedition to Soccatoo in the 1820s, and Paul du Challu's explorations of equatorial Africa in the 1850s and 1860s. From the late-18th through the mid-19th centuries, these travelers described domestic architecture and yard spaces in areas encompassing what is today The Gambia through Senegal to Mali and Nigeria.

Broad patterns can be identified despite regional variation in house styles and yard layouts. Free people often lived in compounds consisting of several individual buildings enclosed within a fence. While some enslaved people were housed within these compounds, others lived in individual structures at the edges of villages or in villages of their own. "The houses consist of circular huts, or coozies, built of clay and thatched: a number

of these, enclosed in a square fence of matting, generally form but one house," commented one observer (Clapperton 1829:73). Connected by a wall, the structures enclosed an open and airy courtyard. Here, amidst their flocks of fowl, men sat to exchange news and greet neighbors and friends, and women performed daily chores, including cooking and spinning (Clapperton 1829:92, 141, 214; Caillie 1968:202-203, 205, 302-304; Miller 1969:138). The courtyards, as well as the houses, were routinely kept clean and sprinkled with water every morning (Clapperton 1829:142). This treatment was so customary that special note was taken by Clapperton (1829:162) in the town of Roma, where the chief's courts "were overgrown with weeds and grass." Adjacent to houses, free women and children and enslaved people planted gardens in which they cultivated fruit and nutbearing trees, herbs, and vegetables (Caillee 1968:196-197, 202-203, 212, 224, 278, 282, 308).

Houses and courtyards served the needs of the dead as well as the living. Parks (Miller 1969:212) noted that the Mandingoes "frequently dig the grave in the floor of the deceased's hut, or in the shade of a favorite tree." Near the market town of Koolfie, Clapperton noted the Negro custom of burying the dead "in a round hole like a well, about six feet deep, sometimes in the house, sometimes in the threshold of the door, and sometimes in the woods . . .", while at Soccatoo, he learned that the Fellatas "always bury their dead behind the house which the deceased occupied while living" (Clapperton 1829:141-142; 213).

The primary accounts thus reveal that historically in West Africa, yards were used for work, for the raising of poultry, for gardening, for socializing, and sometimes as repositories for the dead. Such patterns are seen to have continued as West Africans were brought to the Caribbean and the American South in bondage.

The Caribbean

To understand slave yards in the Caribbean, descriptions by travelers and residents and commentary by modern scholars were surveyed. Most authors writing from the late-18th century through Emancipation based their observations on experiences in the British West Indies, particularly Jamaica and Barbados. Though varying in importance from island to island, the yards of enslaved men and women fulfilled several common needs. Following West African traditions, enslaved people used their yards to cook, to grow fruits and vegetables (often raising surplus for market), to perform domestic chores, and, less frequently, to bury their dead.

On mountainous islands like Jamaica, planters initially provided enslaved workers with grounds adjacent to their dwellings which they were encouraged to cultivate. As plantations grew and land was needed for additional cane cultivation, owners bribed, coerced, or otherwise persuaded them to give up this land in favor of provision grounds located on less desirable pieces of land some distance from the quarters (McDonald 1993:19-20). A two-tiered self-provisioning system emerged in which enslaved residents undertook relatively large scale agriculture at grounds some distance from their home and cultivated foodstuffs for domestic consumption in the yards immediately surrounding their dwellings. They sold surplus food raised at the provision grounds or in house yards at weekly markets, using the profits to buy additional food, livestock, and a range of material goods.

On Barbados, Antigua, and other relatively flat islands, planters chose to use all available land to raise cash crops and purchased most of the food provisions for their workforce (Mintz and Hall 1960:10). As a result, yards became the only locations where enslaved families could produce foodstuffs and raise small livestock. This land management policy resulted in a more intensive use of yard space and, consequently, a greater dependence on the planter for the necessities of life. West Indian historian Hilary Beckles argues, however, that, "All these slaves had was the little house spot, generally no more than 15 square yards, on which to base their autonomous production and marketing activity . . . and yet the vibrancy of their huckstering business was no less developed than that in Jamaica where slaves cultivated acres of land" (Beckles 1989:78). Indeed, visitors to Barbados noted enslaved women "travelling . . . for several miles to market with a few roots, or fruits, or canes, sometimes a fowl or a kid, or a pig [from] their little spots of ground . . ."(Dickson 1789:11).

Late 18th- and 19th-century accounts from both Jamaica and Barbados describe slave houses and their accompanying yards on several occasions, recording the practice of growing groves of fruit trees and tending plots of vegetables close to the house. Gardens contained herbs, edible plants, ornamentals, and plants used for preparing medicines and cosmetics, fulfilling household chores, or making household items (Pulsipher 1994:215). Enslaved residents also raised and penned small livestock in house yards (Beckford 1788:91, 1790:[1]229; McNeill 1788:3-4; Pinkard 1806:[2]116-117; Barclay 1826:315, 317; Bayley 1833:92-93; Kelly 1838; Phillippo 1843:217). Regarding Jamaica, Bryan Edwards noted, "The cottages of the Negroes usually compose a small village. . . . They are seldom placed with much regard to order, but being always intermingled with fruit-trees, particularly the banana, the avocado pear and the orange (the Negroes own planting and property) they sometimes exhibit a pleasing and picturesque appearance" (Edwards 1793:[2]163). A visitor to Barbados in 1806 remarked "At the negro yards it is common for the slaves to plant fruit and vegetables, and to raise stocks. Some of them keep a pig, some a goat, some Guinea fowls, ducks, chickens, pigeons, or the like; and at one of the huts of Spendlove [estate], we saw a pig, a goat, a young kid, some pigeons, and some chickens, all the property of an individual slave . . ." (Pinkard 1806:[1]368). A Jamaican account notes that enslaved people raised poultry, pigs, and goats in their yards, and kept larger livestock in the plantation pen (McNeill 1788:3-4). Enslaved Jamaicans constructed "inclosures of pales or sticks . . . placed near their houses to confine their stock at night," roofing them with sticks or thatch. Pens for hogs were positioned on hillsides to facilitate drainage, while chickens were placed in hanging baskets at night to safeguard them from rats (Columbian Magazine or Monthly Miscellany 1797; Barclay 1826:315, 317).

Enslaved West Indians also used their yards for cooking. On Jamaica they built small sheds or kitchens behind the house, and constructed outdoor barbecues "made of sticks and bark cordage raised on four posts" (Columbian Magazine or Monthly Miscellany 1797; Phillippo 1843:221). The practice of cooking in a detached kitchen continued into the 20th century (Gardner 1873:181; Livingstone 1899:51; Davenport 1961:435-437).

The West African tradition of burying family members in the house or yard appears to have continued to at least a limited extent in the Caribbean. A visitor to Jamaica in 1823 noted such a burial. "Adjoining to the house is usually a small spot of ground, laid out into a sort of garden and shaded by various fruit-trees. Here the family deposit their dead, to whose memory they invariably, if they can afford it, erect a rude tomb" (Stewart 1823:267). Such practices also persisted in Barbados into the late 18th century, although common burial grounds determined by plantation managers appear to have been more prevalent by this time (Council of Barbados 1789; Parry 1789:17; Handler and Lange 1978:174; Watters 1994).

Comparison of African and Caribbean yard use shows much continuity. Slavery in the Caribbean, however, forced men and women to change traditional African uses of yard spaces, altering both the arrangement and the scale of activities. While the strictures of institutionalized slavery probably dictated many of the transformations from African practices, environmental and technological factors also contributed to changing patterns of domestic activities. Enslaved Africans brought to the Americas encountered unfamiliar animal and plant life, learned new work patterns, and became accustomed to using new tools and to building in new ways. These new plants, work patterns, and tools became incorporated into and transformed traditional African uses of yards.

The American South

Like many of their West Indian contemporaries, Southern planters allotted to enslaved persons patches or provisioning grounds within the plantation on which they could cultivate a variety of crops (Vlach 1991:220). Philip Fithian reported on the actions of enslaved men and women in Westmoreland County, Virginia on a Sunday in the spring of 1774, noting that "in several parts of the plantation they are digging up their small Lots of ground allow'd by their Master for Potatoes, peas &c. . . ." Later that year, Fithian added that "Sundays they commonly spend in fishing making potatoes &c, building & patching their Quarters or rather Cabins" (Farish 1957:96, 202-203).

Provision grounds were widely documented in the 19th century throughout the Southeast (Ball 1837:128; Thomas Jefferson's Poplar Forest 1844-1854; Stowe 1853:9; Silva 1914; Rawick 1972:7, 38, 53, 57; Hundley 1973:340-355; Morgan 1982:571-573; McDonald 1993:51-52; Schlotterbeck 1995:173-174).

Enslaved African Americans also located smaller kitchen gardens close to their cabins. Edward Kimber, an Englishman who visited Maryland and Virginia in the 1740s, described the quarters he saw as "a Number of Huts . . . where the Negroes reside with their Wives and Families, and cultivate, at vacant Times, the little Spots allow'd them" (Kimber 1907:6). In urban areas, garden patches might be set aside for the use of enslaved workers within the larger estate garden. Such was the case at Druid Hill in Baltimore, where an 1801 plat shows a 36 x 82 ft. (11 x 25 m) vegetable patch "for servants" adjacent to a quarter and a hog pen (Sarudy 1998:54-55). In the rural antebellum South, Frederick Law Olmsted reported that the slave households he observed had an area set aside where residents "could always grow as many vegetables as they wanted" (Hawke 1971:36). Observing quarters in South Carolina, Olmsted noted that "in the rear of the yards were gardens—a half-acre to each family" (Hawke 1971:74).

Gardens were located close to the quarters, thus enslaved residents could work in them during breaks in the daily work routine or in the evenings. This location also meant that the aged, retired from field work, could tend the family's crop of vegetables and herbs as well (McDonald 1993:51). Enslaved women, as well as men, appear to have been active gardeners (Ware 1997:156-157).

Evidence from the post-Emancipation era indicates that gardens were designed to be ornamental as well as useful. In an early 20th-century interview of a freed slave from South Carolina, social reformer Mark Hicks noted: "Encircling her house are lilacs, althea, and flowering trees that soften the bleak outlines of unpainted out-buildings. A varied collection of old-fashioned plants and flowers crowd the neatly swept dooryard" (Ware 1997:157). Hicks went on to describe the house of two African-American sisters. "their front yard is full of flowers. Vegetables are at the side in the same inclosure with the flowers" (Rawick 1972:59) (Figure 1).

Figure 1. Uncle Daniel's Cabin, Bon Air, Virginia, 1888. Note the clumps of irises along the snake fence. (Courtesy of Valentine Museum, Richmond, Virginia.)

Women and men recalled their yards in first-hand accounts of their experience during slavery. "When farm work was not pressing, we got all of Saturday to clean up 'round de houses . . ." (Adeline Jackson [Westmacott 1992:18]). One woman who was freed from slavery in South Carolina noted that "All de people would make dey own gardens in dem days" (Agnes James [Westmacott 1992:18]), while a freed woman from Virginia recalled, "people used to raise goard fer dippers, an' de goards grew on vines in ev'ybody's garden" (Mrs. Patience Avery [Perdue 1976:16]). Former enslaved men and women also made note of socializing and playing in their yards. In relating a story, one freedman from Virginia began, "One day all de little chillun wuz in the yard playing—running 'roun. An de gal's husband wuz settin' near de do' wid de baby in his arms-rockin' away—looking in child's face an' at de chillun play' in de yard . . ." (Rev. Ishrael Massie [Perdue 1976:207]). Another recalled that on evenings spent in the yard, "we would spin on the old spinning wheel, quilt, make clothes, talk, tell jokes. . . . We would have candy pulls, from cooked molasses, and sing in the moonlight by the tune of an old banjo picker" (Mrs. Marriah Hines [Perdue 1976:141]).

Beyond gardening, socializing, and relaxing out-of-doors, enslaved African Americans living in the South used the spaces around their cabins for performing household chores such as cooking, laundering, butchering, and raising animals (Figure 2). Poultry-keeping appears to have been most common, but sometimes they kept

pigs as well. In Virginia, owners purchased eggs, chickens, ducks, and turkeys from the men and women they held in bondage (Morgan 1988:468; Vlach 1991:220; Stanton 1993:165-166; Thompson 1993:15-16; Schlotterbeck 1995:174; Heath 1999:50). Olmsted (1861:442) noted that "eggs constitute[d] a circulating medium" on one South Carolina plantation, observing that the spaces to the sides of quarters were enclosed with palings to contain chickens and pigs. William Howard Russell, describing Louisiana African-American dwellings in 1863, noted that "the negroes rear domestic birds of all kinds" and that "behind each hut are rude poultry hutches, which, with geese, turkeys and a few pigs form the perquisites of the slaves" (Russell 1863:371, 396). The marketing of surplus garden produce and livestock provided an important source of economic autonomy for the Louisiana enslaved community (McDonald 1993:50-54, 56). In the Upper South, it appears that gardens were less economically significant, although there is good evidence that enslaved men and women sold their produce to their owners, at market, and at local stores (Martin 1993:308-309; Schlotterbeck 1995:175-176; Heath 1997).

Ethnographic Studies of Houses and Yards

While documents preserve glimpses of slave yards, modern ethnographers can provide important information about contemporary practices and attitudes that may have historic roots. Anthropologist Sidney Mintz (1974:225-250) pioneered the study of yards in the West Indies during the 1950s, detailing the importance of the house-yard

Figure 2. Yard scene, Southern Pines, North Carolina, 1914. (Photo by E. C. Eddy, courtesy of Prints and Photographs Division, Library of Congress, Washington.)

pattern in understanding the Caribbean peasantry. In the house yard, he observed, "decisions are made, food is prepared and eaten, the household group—whatever its composition—sleeps and socializes, children are conceived and born, death is ceremonialized. . . . Together, house and yard form a nucleus within which the culture expresses itself, is perpetuated, changed and reintegrated" (Mintz 1974:231-232). Since that time, anthropologists, folklorists, geographers, and landscape architects have studied African-American yards in the Caribbean and in the American South (McDaniel 1982; Westmacott 1992; Gundaker 1993; Ware 1997).

Ethnographic studies have confirmed that many of the practices noted during the era of slavery continue in contemporary communities, including the use of yards for subsistence activities, such as gardening and livestock rearing, for household work, for storage, and for socializing and recreation (McDaniel 1982:168; Westmacott 1992; Ware 1997:159-170). Additionally, they suggest modern activities and attitudes about yard spaces that may have roots in the past. These include the use of yards for storage (McDaniel 1982:168), keeping the yard clean by sweeping, and the creation and maintenance of spiritually and socially meaningful yard ornamentation (Thompson 1990:164-167; Westmacott 1992:45-50; Gundaker 1993).

Today, African, Caribbean, and African-American yards serve as locations for spiritual and artistic expression (Thompson 1984:142-158; Gundaker 1993). Swept yards are common features of West and Central African domestic compounds. There, the practice of sweeping carries spiritual as well as social dimensions (Thompson 1990:164). Among the Bakongo of Central Africa, "sweeping is an ordinary ritual gesture for ridding a place of undesirable spirits" in a landscape populated by day with the ghosts of witches and others who have not been accepted into the villages of the dead, and by night with the ancestors (MacGaffey 1986:45-56).

This African practice of yard sweeping has continued into the 20th century among African Americans from rural Maryland to the hills of Jamaica (Davenport 1961:435-437; Welty 1971:156; McDaniel 1982:158-160, 213; Jones-Jackson 1987:8; Westmacott 1992:76, 80, 99, 111, 126). Sweeping is explained as a way to keep the yard free from insects and provide a comfortable

area for social activities (Jones-Jackson 1987:8), but may preserve spiritual meaning as well.

Much like swept yards, bottle trees—comprised of bottles, containers, and a variety of other spiritually meaningful elements arranged on or imitating trees—serve aesthetic and protective roles. The trees protect houses and yards from evil spirits by "luring them inside the colored bottles, where they cannot get out again" (Welty 1971:156). The presence of these trees in the New World may be traced to the Kongo custom of placing branches capped with bottles or pots around the house, a practice first recorded in the late 18th century (Thompson 1990:165). Bottle trees persist in both the American South and the Caribbean (Thompson 1990:164-164).

Yards have given rise to other forms of aesthetic expression as well. Grey Gundaker has studied the "dressed yards" of modern African Americans, spaces characterized by the recycling of castoff objects into works of sculptural art symbolic to their creator and perhaps to his or her community. In Gundaker's words, these yards use "a flexible visual vocabulary that creolizes and revitalizes American, European and African traditions through everyday materials. . . . The makers of these special yards work to please themselves and to instruct visitors in appropriate behavior, sometimes in the broadest spiritual sense" (Gundaker 1993:59). The history of contemporary yard art remains a mystery. The tradition of shaping one's yard in an effort to create an aesthetically pleasing or spiritually meaningful space, however, can be glimpsed in historic African and Caribbean descriptions of bottle trees, in the inclusion of ornamental plants in slave gardens, and in the burial of the dead in slave yards.

Finally, it is important to note that as extensions of the house, yards are seen as private spaces. In her novel *To Kill a Mockingbird*, set in a small Depression-era Southern town, Harper Lee used Southern views of proper and improper behavior to construct a defense for Tom, a black man accused of rape. "He seemed to be a respectable Negro, and a respectable Negro would never go up into somebody's yard of his own volition" (Lee 1974:196). People "went inside the fence" by invitation only.

This brief survey of documentary and ethnographic data suggests both some continuities between yards in West Africa and in the New

World, as well as some distinct differences. Yards appear to function across time and space as workspaces and as economic units, providing families with fruits, vegetables, meat, and eggs that could be sold or consumed. The extent of yard cultivation and livestock rearing is unclear, however, as much of the evidence presented here is anecdotal, and focuses on the late 18th and 19th centuries. By its site-specific approach, archaeology can help to trace the economic role of yards backwards in time and space. Ethnographic evidence has suggested the social dimensions of yards as private places that create both social barriers and convey social and symbolic messages. Did people in the past have such control over their environs, or were yards shared work spaces available to all within the quarter? Were spaces defined by the owner, by individual slave families, or by some process of negotiation? Contemporary sources also suggest that yard uses were divided along gender and age lines. Can we see evidence of such divisions within the slave household? Finally, West and Central African spiritual beliefs, reflected in yard sweeping, in the progenitors of bottle trees, and in the use of house-yard spaces for burials, appear to have been transplanted to the New World. How widespread were these practices? Did they change over time? Were house-yard burial practices ever used in the American South? When burials themselves ceased to occur in the house-yard complex, did enslaved people adopt other symbols to communicate the spiritual dimensions of their domestic spaces, or did the meanings of their houses and yards change? While archaeologists cannot perhaps answer all of these questions, they have some powerful tools at their disposal to study the changing use of yard spaces through time and space.

The Archaeology of Yards

Unlike historical archaeologists in general, who have made the study of yards integral to their research (Gibb and King 1991; Beaudry 1993; Cummings 1994; Rovner 1994), archaeologists working on African-American sites have seldom widened their frame of reference beyond dwellings. For the most part, attention has focused on the analysis of artifactual and structural data in an effort to reconstruct sites and lifestyles. These analyses have often neglected yards as an important part of the environment in which

people lived. Landscape archaeology has in recent years begun to focus attention on yards and gardens, seeing landscapes as expressions of the "relationships among people in their physical environment" (Gleason 1994:20). Even with explicit attention to these relationships, little attention has been paid to the landscapes formed and experienced by African Americans. This is perhaps best exemplified by Yentsch and Kratzer's (1994:198) attention to "great gardens," those belonging to persons with "wealth, power, prestige and knowledge," rather than to the gardens of "ordinary folk."

Archaeologists, however, have recently focused their attention on understanding yards often associated with African-American tenants on postbellum farms throughout the South. Randall Moir has developed a model of yard usage based on the study of sheet refuse distributions across domestic farms on rural sites (Moir 1987:229-237). The active yard, of one-half to two-thirds of an acre immediately around the farmhouse, incorporates an immediate active yard extending in a circle of up to 20 ft. (6 m) from the house, and an outer active yard, which contains storage sheds, smokehouses and other dependencies, and extends to a distance of approximately 60 ft. (18 m) from the dwelling. Beyond these inner yard spaces lies the peripheral yard, which, at some distance from the house, provides the setting for major outbuildings such as barns. Moir argues that these zones are gender specific, with women's activities tending to cluster in the inner active yard and men's most often undertaken in the outer active yard (Moir 1987:234-235). The recognition of artifact patterning which corresponds to this division of space has allowed others to use Moir's work as a research tool (Crass and Brooks 1995).

The applicability of this model to antebellum slave yards has not been tested. Indeed, yards have not yet received much attention from those studying the archaeological record of slavery. A few notable exceptions include the work of Douglas Armstrong in Jamaica and Garrett Fesler at the Utopia Quarter in Virginia. Armstrong, working at the Drax Hall plantation, drew on Mintz's model to design his excavation strategy for areas associated with the slave village and post-emancipation housing. By exploring areas outside of identified house remains, he uncovered evidence of cooking sheds and identified a slave yard where "significant activities" took place (Armstrong 1990:104, 109, 121). These discoveries underscored the importance of the yard and associated garden to the house-yard complex (Armstrong 1990:268-269).

At the Utopia Quarter, archaeologists discovered the remains of 11 buildings and associated yard features, including fence lines, ditches, trash pits, a well, and an adjoining burial ground dating from 1670 to 1780 (Fesler 1997b:4). During the early 18th century, the enslaved residents constructed three houses and a storehouse, arranged to form a square compound with a central courtyard. Fesler argues that this house-yard complex, occupied by newly enslaved West African men and women, carried contrasting social meanings. Designed to reinforce the owner's philosophy of the management of his enslaved population, the space was perceived by its inhabitants as a familiar echo of home, and ultimately helped to strengthen their cultural identity (Fesler 1997a). By extending his analysis to the house yard, or domestic compound level, Fesler arrived at a richer and more complex interpretation of the site.

Slave yards have also been sampled at the Andrew Jackson's Hermitage quarters in Tennessee, and at several quarters in Virginia, including those at Monticello, Rich Neck, and Utopia (Kelso, et al. 1984, 1985; Agbe-Davies 1994; Thomas, et al. 1995:14-22; Fesler 1997a, 1997b; McKee 1997).

Methodological Concerns

There have been few efforts within African-American archaeology to create a methodology or a framework for analysis useful to the investigation of yard spaces. Landscape archaeology has attempted to define the parameters of the investigation of space, but in general has not led investigators to focus on what went on within those spaces. Absent are tools for understanding functional, community, and individual uses of yards. More broadly, space serves to define class, religious beliefs, personal and group identity, and the relationships among different communities and individuals. Investigative and interpretive methods must recognize all of these potential uses if they are to serve as a means for understanding past cultures.

One of the main goals in looking at slave yards is to first understand the differential uses of space at domestic sites over time, and then to assess the meaning of such differences. A major component of this process is the need to understand patterns of activities or "activity systems." Expanding on the model introduced by Edward Hall (1966), Amos Rapoport (1993:13) has outlined three arenas in which activity systems can be observed in the environment: fixed-feature elements, defined as architectural components; semi-fixed feature elements or "furnishings;" and non-fixed-feature elements, defined as people and their behavior at a given point in time. While individual activities cannot usually be detected in the archaeological record, evidence of activity systems are preserved in Rapoport's fixed and semi-fixed elements. For the purposes of yard analysis, fixed elements include permanent yard features such as fences, sheds, pens, or trees. Semi-fixed feature elements, or yard furnishings, might include rain barrels, wood piles, benches, and other semi-permanent artifacts, as well as cooking pits, trash pits, or middens, whose locations may shift around the yard over time. Past people and behaviors can only be observed indirectly, thus it is essential to look at both fixed and semi-fixed feature elements to understand past activity systems. For the most part, and for obvious reasons, archaeologists have concentrated on the recovery of fixed elements (architectural remains and fences), which tend to be most visible archaeologically. Others have suggested that refuse disposal areas are rich sources of data (Fairbanks 1976, 1977; Otto 1980:4-5).

On plantation sites, where stratigraphic layers and shallow features often have been erased by plowing, semi-fixed elements are difficult to locate and understand. The work of King, Miller, Pogue, and Riordan on 17th-century sites in Maryland. however, has demonstrated that spatial relationships are discernible on plowed sites, allowing for reconstructions of houselot layouts and domestic use patterns over time (King and Miller 1987:37-59; King 1988:23-37; Pogue 1988:43-55; Riordan 1988; Miller 1994:73-81). Even middens, though mixed vertically, remain visible within the plowzone, preserving many of their depositional relationships. On sites of short occupation, plowzone data can yield important information about semi-fixed elements of the

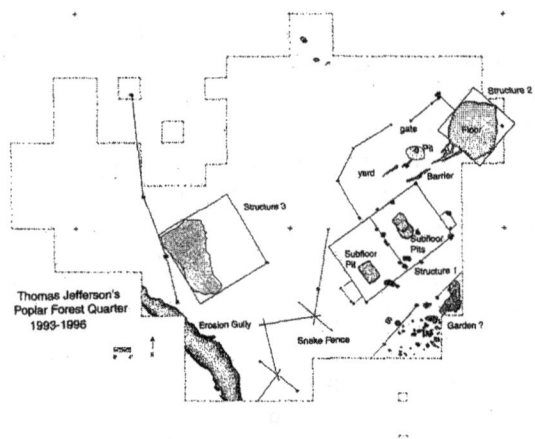

Figure 3. Map of Thomas Jefferson's Poplar Forest Quarter Site.

site. In short, ignoring the plowzone on African-American sites may mean throwing away most or all of the information concerning occupation of that site. An example of the combined use of feature and plowzone data to understand yard spaces is seen in the study of the Poplar Forest slave quarter.

The Poplar Forest Quarter Site

Between 1993 and 1996 archaeologists working at Poplar Forest, Thomas Jefferson's plantation in Bedford County, Virginia, discovered a complex of features associated with an early quarter. The site, known as the Quarter Site, dates ca. 1790-1812 (Figure 3). Although the quarter does not appear on any contemporary maps or letters, early 19th-century maps do provide some clues about the landscape of the property during this period. The site lay within the 45-acre "mansion house field" which contained the "mansion house" or overseer's house situated several hundred feet farther to the south and east. To the north, the maps locate a narrow stretch of land referred to as "the lane." Excavations undertaken from 1996 to 1998 explored an earlier quarter farther north within the lane.

By the summer of 1996, archaeologists had completed a block excavation measuring some 80 ft. (24 m) north-south by 100 ft. (30 m) east-west. Although the site was located on the side of a hill, its eastern half had been plowed in the 19th or early 20th century, while the western half,

downslope, consisted of occupation and destruction layers sealed by thick layers of wash. The hill ranged from 10% to 15% slope. Excavators removed all plowzone and cultural layers in 5 x 5 ft. (1.5 x 1.5 m) units and screened them through ¼ in. (6 mm) mesh to ensure high rates of artifact recovery. In addition, soil chemical samples were collected from plowzone and cultural layers at 10 ft. (3 m) intervals. Flotation samples were also collected from soils contained within features associated with structures.

Excavations unearthed the remains of three buildings, referred to in this discussion as Structures 1, 2, and 3. Structure 1, interpreted as a duplex cabin, measured approximately 15 x 25 ft. (4.5 x 7.6 m) and was divided into two equal sized rooms of 12.5 x 15 ft (3.8 x 4.5 m). Indicated only by the presence of postholes and quantities of daub, wood, and clay chimneys may have been located on the gable ends of the building, with a single fireplace heating each room. Three subfloor pits were contained within the building; one in the west room and two in the east.

Structure 2 was discovered by archaeologists, 13 ft. (4 m) northeast of the duplex cabin. This building measured approximately 13 ft. (4 m) square, and faced north, with a door opening along that wall. No evidence of a chimney survived. Large fragments of daub recovered from the fill within the building and from the adjoining yard suggest that the building was constructed of logs. Structure 2 may have been originally intended for use as a service room or storage space rather than a house. The lack of evidence for a chimney or subfloor pits are at odds with features of contemporary cabins. Numerous domestic artifacts found within the fill of the building and around the structure suggest that for part of its lifespan, the building served as a dwelling.

Structure 3 was located 14 ft. (4 m) northwest of Structure 1. It had been built on one of the steepest parts of the hillside, directly on top of a backfilled erosion gully. A posthole defined the location of the southeast corner. The building must have been raised on piers along its northern face to provide a level floor. Structure 3 measured 18.5 ft. (5.6 m) to a side. The presence of high levels of potassium and magnesium suggest that a chimney stood along the northeastern wall, while artifact concentrations suggest that the door faced north (Fischer 1996:19). Based on the number

TABLE 1
CERAMIC SHERD AND MINIMUM VESSEL COUNTS, QUARTER SITE MIDDENS

Ceramics	MIDDEN 1 Count	MNV	MIDDEN 2 Count	MNV	MIDDEN 3 Count	MNV
Black basalt	4	1	1	-	4	1
Bone china	1	1	-	-	-	-
Chinese porcelain	2	1	1	1	1	1
Creamware	300	11	29	1	217	12
Delft	-	-	-	1	1	-
Pearlware	202	16	28	1	210	12
Redware	42	10	8	-	49	11
Stoneware	34	6	6	1	14	3
TOTAL	585	46	73	4	496	41

and variety of domestic artifacts found in the crawl space beneath the building, along its western wall, and in a midden to the north, Structure 3 clearly served as a dwelling.

The excavation of this site was designed with the intent to recover as much information as possible about the size, orientation and use of associated yard spaces. The remains of five contemporary fences were uncovered at the site. The first fence enclosed a space beginning at the northwest wall of Structure 1 and extending to the northwest wall of Structure 2 (Figure 3). Small diameter posts set at approximately 10 ft. (3 m) intervals anchored panels of wooden pickets, forming the outside line of this fence. The line was interrupted by a 4.5 ft.(1.4 m) wide gate located midway between Structures 1 and 2.

This space was bounded to the south by a second barrier defined by a series of narrow trenches cutting through subsoil (Figure 3). Significant differences in artifact densities and soil chemical levels from one side of the trenches to the other indicate that some type of physical barrier divided this space (Fischer 1996:24).

The yard defined within these limits measured approximately 12 x 30 ft. (3.7 x 9 m). Soil chemical analysis provided clues for understanding the physical layout and use of the space within and adjacent to the yard. Four principal chemicals were investigated: phosphorus, calcium, potassium, and magnesium. Phosphorus is found in human and animal tissues and waste, and high levels can be associated with animal pens, trash dumps, or privies. Calcium is a component of bone and shell. In the acidic soils of central Virginia, these substances often decompose rapidly, leaving behind only their chemical signatures. High concentrations of calcium may mark the locations of middens or processing areas for meat. Potassium, found in wood and wood ash, can suggest the placement of hearths or ash deposits.

TABLE 2
GLASS SHERD AND MINIMUM VESSEL COUNTS, QUARTER SITE MIDDENS

Glass Type	MIDDEN 1 Count	MNV	MIDDEN 2 Count	MNV	MIDDEN 3 Count	MNV
Undecorated bottle						
Clear	15	1	6	-	9	2
Dk. green	268	13	29	1	166	13
Pattern molded bottle						
Blue-Aqua	6	-	4	-	9	1
Green-Aqua	1	-	-	-	1	-
Pharmaceutical	4	1	-	-	-	-
Tableware	5	1	-	-	1	1
TOTAL	299	16	39	1	186	17

Note: For vessels with counts but no minimum number assigned, the majority of sherds
associated with this vessel were found elsewhere on the site

Some archaeologists studying soil chemicals have tentatively linked high magnesium levels in soil to activities associated with burning (Fischer 1996).

Elevated levels of phosphorus and calcium within the plowzone corresponded with areas of high artifact density and helped to confirm the location and formation of middens along the inner and outer edges of the yard fence. These middens may have contained refuse similar to the "heaps of . . . broken crockery, old shoes, rags, and feathers" reported by Russell to be "found near each hut" (Russell 1863 [1954:77]). Chemicals suggest that the enslaved residents may have deposited certain types of organic waste away from the larger middens where animal bones and household trash were dumped. A small concentration of artifacts and an elevated level of phosphorus was detected adjacent to the cabin, hinting at the location of a doorway along the north wall of the structure. For the most part, however, the yard between the structures contained lower densities of ceramics, bottle glass, and other domestic trash, suggesting that this area was considered a clean space.

Ceramic and glass (Tables 1 and 2) distributions from the area around Structure 1 were plotted to test the hypothesis that residents of the Quarter regularly swept the yard. Adams (1987:47) posited that yard sweeping should be detectable in the archaeological record by differences in sherd densities, with lesser densities in the swept areas, and greater densities in the outlying middens. He observed such a distribution, based on differential sherd weights, at the Mabry site at Kings Bay. At Poplar Forest, distributions were determined based on an analysis of size rather than weight. Sherds of both ceramics and bottle glass were divided into two size categories (those less than ½ in. [13 mm] diameter, and those greater than ½ in.), and the distribution of each was plotted. Over 80% of ceramic sherds and 56% of the bottle glass from the site were smaller than ½ in., thus results were inconclusive (Brooks 1996:2, 35-36). The fragmentary nature of the assemblage is probably a result of trampling during occupation of the site and post-occupation plowing. Analyses of distributions at sites benefiting from better preservation may, however, allow for the detection of this yard treatment.

The yard could have been entered directly from a door located on the northern wall of Structure 1. Non-residents could access the yard through the gate located along its northern boundary. The placement of the fence provides a spatial connection between at least the eastern half of that building and Structure 2, suggesting that the residents of these two housing units shared a common social bond. A letter between an overseer and Jefferson confirms that at least some extended enslaved families shared duplex cabins at Poplar Forest (University of Virginia 1814). Such family ties may be preserved in the evidence of a shared yard between dwellings at this quarter.

Historic maps suggest that the overseer's house (the "mansion house" referred to earlier) sat some distance south of the duplex cabin. It is interesting to note that residents of this cabin sited the enclosed yard on the north side of the dwelling. This plan allowed space, air, and light to work in, while at the same time effectively shielding residents working or socializing in the yard from the overseer's surveillance.

Evidence of a "worm" or "snake" fence was uncovered west of the Structure 1, separating that building from Structure 3 (Figure 3). Fences of this type sat on the surface of the ground, and could easily be disassembled and moved (Betts 1944:492-493). While many snake fences sat entirely on the surface, some were stabilized by opposing pairs of wooden stakes driven into the ground (Figure 1). Small diameter postholes, found in pairs separated by 10 ft. (3 m) intervals, provide evidence of such a fence treatment at the Quarter.

Four postholes located south of Structure 1 suggest the location of a fourth, gated fence (Figure 3). Limited access to this area precluded further excavations to define its limits. This section of the site was almost devoid of artifacts, but numerous irregular soil disturbances created by plants of varying sizes were discovered beneath the plowzone. Surrounding these planting features was soil rich in potassium and phosphorus, chemicals associated with burned wood and decaying organic matter. Such a chemical signature might be left by repeated applications of fertilizing agents such as wood ash and animal dung (Spurrier 1793:35, 41; Miller 1994; Fischer 1996:24-25). Together, these clues suggest that this space was cultivated. Whether it served as the site of the enslaved residents' vegetable patch or the edge of a garden associated with the overseer's house located further to the southeast is not known.

The analysis of macroplant remains recovered from subfloor pits and floor surfaces within each structure sheds light on plants consumed by the residents, some of which were possibly grown around the cabins. Archaeologists recovered fruit seeds and pits, including raspberry, cherry, peach, huckleberry, persimmon, and grape; vegetable remains including beans, sunflowers, and grains such as corn and wheat; and nut shells from walnuts and hickory trees. Besides harvesting nuts, the residents of the site may have used walnut bark as a dye for textiles. Weed seeds from goosefoot, smartweed, and pokeweed may represent the remains of plants that were consumed for food or for medicine, while a burned fragment of bedstraw may represent bedding material or may have been used medicinally (Raymer 1996:13-17).

Charred fragments of hickory were recovered from three of the postholes associated with Structure 1, suggesting its use as a construction material (Raymer 1996:18). Fragments of charcoal found in the fill of subfloor pits and associated with the floor surface in Structure 2 indicate that pine and oak constituted the primary fuel woods at the site, while smaller quantities of hickory and elm were also recovered (Raymer 1996:18).

A large part of the yard to the south and west of Structure 3 appears to have been roughly paved with local quartz cobbles. Additionally, numerous pieces of blacksmithing slag, material commonly used for paving, were found intermixed with the quartz cobbles. This surface may indicate a narrow, paved yard laid down to lessen the effects of erosion. The western edge of this yard is roughly defined by the site's fifth fence line, marked by the presence of four postholes set on 12 ft. (3.7 m) centers.

Most artifacts recovered from the site resulted from secondary deposition in one of three major middens associated with each of the structures (Tables 1 and 2). As such, they reflect residents' attitudes towards the appropriate disposal of trash rather than the location of individual activities such as dining, sewing, or socializing. An analysis, however, of the distribution patterns of specific

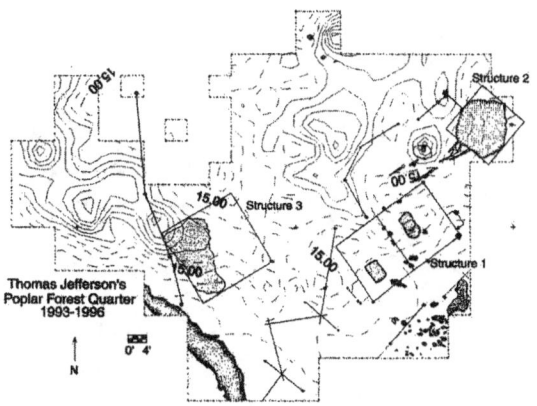

Figure 4. Distribution of ceramics recovered from the Thomas Jefferson's Poplar Forest Quarter Site.

artifact types within these middens and of the location of individual artifacts recovered from contexts other than the middens has offered some suggestions for yard use and raised some questions.

Midden 1 extended along the external line of the fence connecting Structures 1 and 2. Midden 2, a significantly smaller concentration of artifacts associated with Structure 2, appeared at the northeast corner of that building. Roughly half of that structure lay on land not owned by Poplar Forest, thus it was not possible to fully explore its associated yard. Based on crossmends between Structures 1 and 2 and the enclosed yard between them, it seems likely that trash from Structure 2 was deposited within Midden 1 as well.

The placement of Midden 3, associated with Structure 3, varied through time. The earliest phase of deposition overlay a backfilled erosion gully that cut the slope in this area. It is likely that historically a shallow depression marked the location of the gully as its backfill settled, and that trash generated by the residents of Structure 3 accumulated there. Over time, the depression was filled in, and the midden shifted to the south and east, drawing nearer to the northwest corner of the building.

Ceramic and glass distributions were plotted using SURFER, a commercially available software that can be used to create contour and isometric maps based on artifact densities (Figures 4 and 5). The main ceramic concentrations on the site were associated with Structures 1 and 3. The former is contained within the boundaries of Midden 1

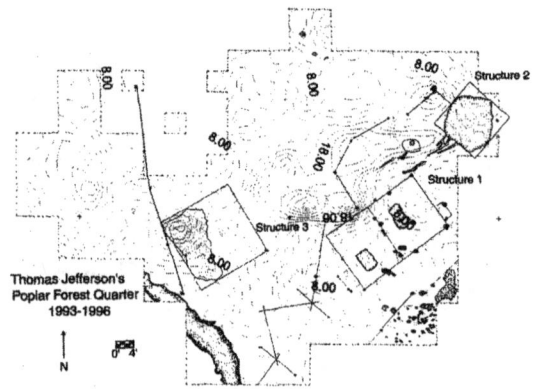

Figure 5. Distribution of glass recovered from the Thomas Jefferson's Poplar Forest Quarter Site.

and appears to indicate an intentional effort to keep ceramics and other forms of domestic refuse outside of the fenced yard (Brooks 1996:21). The latter, contained within Midden 3, runs downslope from Structure 3 in a northwesterly direction. By comparison, the distribution of green wine bottle glass runs parallel to the north wall line of Structure 1 and appears unaffected by the placement of the fence. Although the meaning of this glass distribution is far from clear, it is possible that it reflects glass usage as well as disposal. Perhaps some empty bottles were reused or stored within the yard and later broken in-situ, while other bottles joined ceramic waste and were disposed of outside of the fence.

Distribution patterns for other artifact types provide additional clues concerning the use of the yard. Most counts by type are too small to yield statistically significant findings; however they do suggest some interesting spatial relationships. Fragments of clay and stone tobacco pipes (n=66) clustered within each of the three cabins, the yard between Structures 1 and 2, and Midden 1, suggest that smoking and socializing took place both within and in close proximity to the cabins. Buttons (n=115), whose deposition archaeologically may reflect sewing, laundering, or accidental loss, clustered within each of the structures, in the northwest corner of the enclosed yard between Structures 1 and 2, in the middens, and along the line of the worm fence running southwest from Structure 1 (n=80). The association of buttons with fencelines may indicate the practice of hanging clothing on fences to air or to dry following laundering.

Conclusions

A survey of the historic, ethnographic and archaeological literature has provided some guidelines and provoked some important questions for those wishing to explore, through archaeology, the use and meaning of yard spaces shared by enslaved African Americans. For yards to contribute to our understanding of slavery, they must first be recognized as important sources of data. This brief survey has demonstrated that yard spaces have the potential to comment upon the economic, social, and spiritual lives of their occupants. Archaeologists must now seek methods of excavation and interpretation to fully realize this potential. Appropriate for the spatial and temporal contexts in which archaeologists work, research strategies must be designed which anticipate the recovery of features associated with gardens and small orchards, structures such as sheds, hen houses, pigsties, middens, and workspaces that provide information about the independent economic lives of residents. Equally important are attempts to recover subtle clues, preserved in the distributions of soil chemicals and artifacts, that allow yards to be seen as their creators saw them: spaces defined by clean swept surfaces and jumbled trash, by workbenches and fruit trees, through which people expressed a variety of messages to the living and the dead.

Many of these messages have been clouded through the passage of time and by subsequent disturbances to the site, often by plowing. Yet excavations at the Poplar Forest Quarter Site provide strong evidence that even in the face of sustained plowing and erosion, artifact distributions retain much of their horizontal integrity. Through a strategy which combined large area excavation with total plowzone recovery of artifacts and systematic soil sampling for chemical testing and flotation, the fixed remains of the yard's architecture and the artifactual and chemical signatures of its changing landscape were recovered.

Perhaps the most obvious problem with this approach is that it is extremely time-consuming and, consequently, costly. In the end, large areas of the "yard" remain undefined. What happened outside of the enclosures? Where are the conceptual boundaries of the house-yard complex, and how might they be found archaeologically? Clearly, standard shovel test intervals of 50 to 100 ft. (15 to 30 m) fail to provide firm site boundaries, or to distinguish accurately between one house yard and the next.

In spite of these problems, the study of yards at the Poplar Forest quarter provided important, and in some cases, unique insights into the lives of its occupants. The yards preserved evidence of communal activities and of time spent gardening, performing chores, and building and maintaining friendships. The yards also reflect messages sent by the African Americans to the plantation's white occupants. Yard spaces placed limits on the intrusions of outsiders into the quarter, limits which were mutually understood. They signaled a point of mediation across which black and white could meet, often through economic exchange, to define and maintain the delicate balance which was the plantation system.

Contained within the archaeological remains of African-American yards are the world views of those who created and used them. Archaeologists have much to learn by extending their perspective beyond the traditional limits to cover the broader landscape of sites occupied by enslaved people. As has been seen at Poplar Forest, there lie in yard scatters and fencelines expressions of individual identity and community structure waiting to be read and understood.

ACKNOWLEDGEMENTS

An earlier version of this paper was presented at the 1997 meeting of the Society for Historical Archaeology Conference on Historical and Underwater Archaeology, Corpus Christi, Texas. The authors would like to thank The Henry Luce Foundation for support of excavation and analysis of the Quarter Site; Thomas Jefferson's Poplar Forest for continuing support of archaeological research; Lisa Fischer for analysis and interpretation of soil chemical content; Alasdair Brooks and Heather Olson for artifact analysis; Leslie Raymer for macrobotanical analysis; Anna Agbe-Davies, Garrett Fesler, Maria Franklin, and Larry McKee for supplying unpublished data; and the reviewers, Leslie Stewart-Abernathy, Amy Young, and Sue Moore, for their helpful comments. Interpretations in this analysis are those of the authors alone.

REFERENCES

ADAMS, WILLIAM H. (EDITOR)
1987   Historical Archaeology of Plantations at Kings Bay, Camden County, Georgia. Report to Naval Submarine Base, U.S. Navy from Department of Anthropology, University of Florida, Gainesville.

AGBE-DAVIES, ANNA
1994   Preliminary Findings from the Rich Neck Slave Quarter Excavations. Paper presented at the Annual Meeting of the Council for Northeast Historical Archaeology, Williamsburg, VA.

ARMSTRONG, DOUGLAS V.
1990   *The Old Village and the Great House: An Archaeological and Historical Examination of Drax Hall Plantation at St. Ann's Bay, Jamaica.* University of Illinois Press, Urbana.

BALL, CHARLES
1837   *Slavery in the United States: A Narrative of the Life and Adventures of Charles Ball, a Black Man.* J. S. Taylor, New York, NY.

BARCLAY, ALEXANDER
1826   *A Practical View of the Present State of Slavery in the West Indies.* Smith Elder, & Co., London, England.

BAYLEY, F. W. N.
1833   *Four Years Residence in the West Indies.* William Kidd, London, England.

BEAUDRY, MARY C.
1993   Public Aesthetics versus Personal Experience: Worker Health and Well-Being in 19th-Century Lowell, Massachusetts. *Historical Archaeology* 27(2):90-105.

BECKFORD, WILLIAM
1788   *Remarks upon the Situation of Negroes in Jamaica.* London, England.
1790   *A Descriptive Account of the Island of Jamaica.* T. J. Egerton, London, England.

BECKLES, HILARY M.
1989   *Natural Rebels, A Social History of Enslaved Black Women in Barbados.* Rutgers University Press, New Brunswick, NJ.

BETTS, EDWIN M.
1944   *Thomas Jefferson's Garden Book.* American Philosophical Society, Philadelphia, PA.

BROOKS, ALASDAIR M.
1996   Analysis of Ceramics and Glass from the Quarter Site. Manuscript, Department of Archaeology, Thomas Jefferson's Poplar Forest, Forest, VA.

CAILLIE, RENE
1968   *Travels through Central Africa to Timbuctoo and Across the great Desert, To Morocco, performed in the years 1824-1828,* Vol. 1. Reprint of 1830 edition, Frank Cass, London, England.

CLAPPERTON, HUGH
1829   *Journal of a Second Expedition into the Interior of Africa, from the Bight of Benin to Soccatoo.* John Murray, London, England.

COLUMBIAN MAGAZINE OR MONTHLY MISCELLANY
    1797   Characteristic traits of the Creolian and African
            Negroes in this Island, etc., etc. *Columbian
            Magazine or Monthly Miscellany*, April.

COUNCIL OF BARBADOS
    1789   Replies to queries 6, 15, 22, 23, 24 and 25 of the
            Report of the Lords of the committee of Council
            . . . concerning the present state of the trade to
            Africa . . . and the effects and consequences of this
            trade . . . in Africa and in the West Indies, Part 3.
            Parliamentary Papers, 26. London, England.

CRASS, DAVID COLIN, AND MARK J. BROOKS (EDITORS)
    1995   Cotton and Black Draught: Consumer Behavior
            on a Postbellum Farm. South Carolina Institute
            of Archaeology and Anthropology, University of
            South Carolina, *Savannah River Archaeological
            Research Papers 5*. Columbia.

CUMMINGS, LINDA SCOTT
    1994   Diet and Prehistoric Landscape During the Nineteenth
            and Early Twentieth Centuries at Harpers Ferry,
            West Virginia: A View from the Old Master
            Armorer's Complex. *Historical Archaeology*
            28(4):94-105.

DAVENPORT, WILLIAM H.
    1961   The Family System in Jamaica. *Social and Economic
            Studies* 10:420-454.

DEETZ, JAMES
    1996   *In Small Things Forgotten: An Archaeology of
            Early American Life*. Anchor Books, New York,
            NY.

DICKSON, WILLIAM
    1789   *Letters on Slavery*. J. Phillips, London, England.
            Reprinted 1970, Negro University Press, Westport,
            CT.

EDWARDS, BRYAN
    1793   *The History, Civil and Commercial, of the British
            Colonies in the West Indies*. J. Stockdale, London,
            England.

FAIRBANKS, CHARLES
    1976   Spaniards, Planters, Ships, and Slaves: Historical
            Archaeology on Florida and Georgia. *Archaeology*
            29:165-172.
    1977   Backyard Archaeology as Research Strategy. *The
            Conference of Historic Site Archaeology Papers*,
            11. Columbia, SC.

FARISH, HUNTER DICKENSON (EDITOR)
    1957   *Journal and Letters of Philip Vickers Fithian
            1773-1774: A Plantation Tutor of the Old Dominion*.
            University Press of Virginia, Charlottesville.

FESLER, GARRETT
    1997a   Expressions of Power and Gender at an Early
            18th-Century African-American Chesapeake Slave
            Quarter. Paper presented at The Society for
            Historical Archaeology Conference on Historical and
            Underwater Archaeology, Corpus Christi, TX.
    1997b   Landscapes of Control and Autonomy: The
            Spatial Contestation of the Utopia Slave Quarter.
            Manuscript, Department of Archaeology, Thomas
            Jefferson's Poplar Forest, Forest, VA.

FISCHER, LISA
    1996   Report on the Chemical Analysis of Soils at the
            Poplar Forest Quarter Site. Manuscript, Department
            of Archaeology, Thomas Jefferson's Poplar Forest,
            Forest, VA.

GARDNER, W. J.
    1873   *A History of Jamaica*. F. Cass, London, England.

GIBB, JAMES G., AND JULIA A. KING
    1991   Gender, Activity Areas, and Homelots in the 17th-
            Century Chesapeake Region. *Historical Archaeology*
            25(4):109-131.

GLEASON, KATHRYN L.
    1994   To Bound and to Cultivate: An Introduction to
            the Archaeology of Gardens and Fields. In *The
            Archaeology of Garden and Field*, Naomi Miller
            and Kathryn Gleason, editors, pp. 1-24. University
            of Pennsylvania Press, Philadelphia.

GUNDAKER, GREY
    1993   Tradition and Innovation in African-American
            Yards. *African Arts* 26:58-71.

HALL, EDWARD
    1966   *The Hidden Dimension*. Doubleday, Garden City,
            NY.

HANDLER, JEROME S, AND FREDERICK W. LANGE
    1978   *Plantation Slavery in Barbados: An Archaeological
            and Historical Investigation*. Harvard University
            Press, Cambridge, MA.

HAWKE, DAVID (EDITOR)
    1971   *The Cotton Kingdom: A Selection*. Bobbs-Merrill,
            Indianapolis, IN.

HEATH, BARBARA J.
    1997   Slavery and Consumerism: A Case Study from
            Central Virginia. *African-American Archaeology*
            19:1-8.
    1999   *Hidden Lives: The Archaeology of Slave Life at
            Thomas Jefferson's Poplar Forest*. University
            Press of Virginia, Charlottesville.

HUNDLEY, DANIEL R.
    1973   *Social Relations in Our Southern States*. Reprint of
            1860 edition, Arno Press, New York, NY.

JONES-JACKSON, PATRICIA
    1987   *When Roots Die, Endangered Traditions on the Sea
            Islands*. University of Georgia Press, Athens.

KELLY, JAMES
1838   *Jamaica in 1831*. James Wilson, Belfast, Northern Ireland.

KELSO WILLIAM M., DOUGLAS W. SANFORD, DINAH CRADER JOHNSON, SONDY SANFORD, AND ANNA GRUBER
1984   A Report on the Archaeological Excavations at Monticello, Charlottesville, VA, 1982-1983. Manuscript, Thomas Jefferson Memorial Foundation, Charlottesville, VA.

KELSO, WILLIAM M., DOUGLAS W. SANFORD, ANNA GRUBER, DINAH CRADER JOHNSON, AND ANN MORGAN SMART
1985   Monticello Black History/Craftlife Archaeology Project 1984-85 Progress Report. Manuscript, Thomas Jefferson Memorial Foundation, Charlottesville, VA.

KIMBER, EDWARD
1907   Observations in Several Voyages and Travels in America. *William and Mary Quarterly*, 1st Series, 14:1-17, 15:215-225. Reprint of 1746 edition.

KING, JULIA A.
1988   A Comparative Midden Analysis of a Household and Inn in St. Mary's City, Maryland. *Historical Archaeology* 22(2):17-39.

KING, JULIA A., AND HENRY M. MILLER
1987   The View from the Midden: An Analysis of Midden Distribution and Composition at the van Sweringen Site, St. Mary's City, Maryland. *Historical Archaeology* 21(2):37-59.

LEE, HARPER
1974   *To Kill a Mockingbird*. Pan Books, London, England.

LIVINGSTONE, WILLIAM PRINGLE
1899   *Black Jamaica: A Study of Evolution*. S. Law, Marstan, London, England.

MACGAFFEY, WYATT
1986   *Religion and Society in Central Africa: The BaKongo of Lower Zaire*. University of Chicago Press, Chicago, IL.

MARTIN, ANN SMART
1993   *Buying into the World of Goods: Eighteenth-Century Consumerism and the Retail Trade from London to the Virginia Frontier*. Ph.D. dissertation, Department of History, College of William and Mary, Williamsburg, VA. University Microfilms International, Ann Arbor, MI.

MCDANIEL, GEORGE W.
1982   *Hearth and Home: Preserving a People's Culture*. Temple University Press, Philadelphia, PA.

MCDONALD, RODERICK A.
1993   *The Economy and Material Culture of Slaves, Goods and Chattels on the Sugar Plantations of Jamaica and Louisiana*. Louisiana State University Press, Baton Rouge.

MCKEE, LARRY
1997   Summary Report on the 1994 Excavation at Alfred's Cabin. Manuscript, The Hermitage, Hermitage, TN.

MCNEILL, HECTOR
1788   *Observations on the Treatment of Negroes in the Island of Jamaica*. G. G. J. and J. Robinson, London, England.

MILLER, NAOMI F.
1994   Fertilizer and the Indentification and Analysis of Cultivated Soil. In *The Archaeology of Garden and Field*, Naomi Miller and Kathryn Gleason, editors, pp. 25-43. University of Pennsylvania Press, Philadelphia.

MILLER, RONALD (EDITOR)
1969   *Mungo Park's Travels in Africa*. Dent, London, England.

MINTZ, SIDNEY
1974   *Caribbean Transformations*. Johns Hopkins University Press, Baltimore, MD.

MINTZ, SIDNEY, AND DOUGLAS HALL
1960   The Origins of the Jamaican Internal Marketing System. *Yale University Publications in Anthropology* 57. New Haven, CT.

MOIR, RANDALL W.
1987   Farmstead Proxemics and Intrasite Patterning. In *Pioneer Settlers, Tenant Farmers and Communities: Objectives, Historical Background, and Excavations*, Randall W. Moir and David H. Jurney, editors, Archaeology Research Program, Institute for the Study of Earth and Man, Southern Methodist University, *Richland Creek Technical Series* 4, Dallas, TX.

MORGAN, PHILIP
1982   Work and Culture: The Task System and the World of Lowcountry Blacks, 1700-1880. *William and Mary Quarterly*, 3rd Series, 39(4):563-599.
1988   Slave Life in Piedmont Virginia, 1720-1800. In *Colonial Chesapeake Society*, Lois Green Carr, Philip D. Morgan, and Jean B. Russo, editors, pp. 433-484. University Press of North Carolina, Chapel Hill.

OLMSTED, FREDERICK LAW
1861   *A Journey in the Seaboard Slave States, with Remarks on their Economy*. Mason Brothers, New York, NY.

OTTO, JOHN S.
1980   Race and Class on Antebellum Plantations. In *Archaeological Perspectives on Ethnicity in America*, Robert L. Schuyler, editor, pp. 3-13. Baywood, Farmingdale, NY.

PARRY, DAVID
1789   Extract of a letter from Governor Parry to the Right Honourable Lord Sydney, 18 August 1788. *Parliamentary Papers*, 26:13-24. London, England.

PERDUE, CHARLES L. (EDITOR)
1976   *Weevils in the Wheat: Interviews with Virginia Ex-Slaves*. University Press of Virginia, Charlottesville.

PHILLIPPO, JAMES M.
1843   *Jamaica: Its Past and Present State*. J. Snow, London, England.

PINKARD, GEORGE
1806   *Notes on the West Indies*. Longman, Hurst, Rees, and Orme, London, England.

POGUE, DENNIS J.
1988   Spatial Analysis of the King's Reach Plantation Homelot, ca. 1690-1715. *Historical Archaeology* 22(2):40-56.

PULSIPHER, LYDIA MIHELIC
1994   The Landscapes and Ideational Roles of Caribbean Slave Gardens. In *The Archaeology of Garden and Field*, Naomi Miller and Kathryn Gleason, editors, pp. 202-221. University of Pennsylvania Press, Philadelphia.

RAPOPORT, AMOS
1993   Systems of Activities and Systems of Settings. In *Domestic Architecture and the Use of Space, an Interdisciplinary Cross-Cultural Study*, Susan Kent, editor, pp. 9-20. Cambridge University Press, Cambridge, England.

RAWICK, GEORGE (EDITOR)
1972   *Kansas, Kentucky, Maryland, Ohio, Virginia and Tennessee Narratives*. Greenwood, Westport, CT.

RAYMER, LESLIE
1996   Macroplant Remains from the Jefferson's Poplar Forest Slave Quarter: A Study in African-American Subsistence Practices. Report to Thomas Jefferson's Poplar Forest, Forest, VA, from New South Associates.

RIORDAN, TIMOTHY B.
1988   The Interpretation of 17th-Century Sites through Plow Zone Surface Collections: Examples from St. Mary's City, Maryland. *Historical Archaeology* 22(2):2-16.

ROVNER, IRWIN
1994   Floral History by the Back Door: A Test of Phytolith Analysis in Residential Yards at Harpers Ferry. *Historical Archaeology* 28(4):37-48.

RUSSELL, WILLIAM HOWARD
1863   *My Diary North and South*. Bradbury and Evans, London, England. Reprinted 1954, Harper, New York, NY.

SARUDY, BARBARA WELLS
1998   *Gardens and Gardening in the Chesapeake 1700-1805*. Johns Hopkins University Press, Baltimore, MD.

SCHLOTTERBECK, JOHN T.
1995   The Internal Economy of Slavery in Rural Piedmont Virginia. In *The Slaves' Economy: Independent Production by Slaves in the Americas*, Ira Berlin and Philip D. Morgan, editors, pp.170-181. Frank Cass, London, England.

SILVA, JAMES S.
1914   *Early Reminiscences of an Old St. Marys Boy now in His 82nd year*. Southeast Georgian, Kingsland, GA.

SINGLETON, THERESA A.
1992   Preface to *African-American Gardens and Yards in the Rural South*, by Richard Westmacott. University of Tennessee Press, Knoxville.

SINGLETON, THERESA A., AND MARK D. BOGRAD
1993   The Archaeology of the African Diaspora in the Americas. *Guides to the Archaeological Literature of the Immigrant Experience in America*, 2. The Society for Historical Archaeology, California, PA.

SPURRIER, JOHN
1793   *The Practical Farmer*. Brynberg and Andrews, Wilmington, DE.

STANTON, LUCIA
1993   Those Who Labor for My Happiness. In *Jeffersonian Legacies*, Peter S. Onuf, editor, pp. 147-180. University Press of Virginia, Charlottesville.

STEWART, JOHN
1823   *A View of the Past and Present State of the Island of Jamaica*. Oliver & Boyd, Edinburgh, Scotland.

STOWE, HARRIET BEECHER
1853   *A Key to Uncle Tom's Cabin*. John P. Jewett, Boston, MA.

THOMAS, BRIAN W., LARRY MCKEE, AND JENNIFER BARTLETT
1995   Summary Report on the 1995 Hermitage Field Quarter Excavation. Manuscript, The Hermitage, Hermitage, TN.

THOMAS JEFFERSON'S POPLAR FOREST
1844-   Hutter Farm Journal. Thomas Jefferson's Poplar
1854   Forest, Forest, VA.

THOMPSON, MARY V.
1993   "Better . . . Fed than Negroes Generally Are?":
        Diet of the Mount Vernon Slaves. Manuscript,
        Mount Vernon Ladies' Association, Mount Vernon,
        VA.

THOMPSON, ROBERT FARRIS
1984   *Flash of the Spirit, African and Afro-American
        Art and Philosophy.* Vintage Press, New York,
        NY.
1990   Kongo Influences on African-American Artistic
        Culture. In *Africanisms in American Culture,*
        Joseph E. Holloway, editor, pp. 148-184. Indiana
        University Press, Bloomington.

UNIVERSITY OF VIRGINIA
1814   Letter from Jeremiah Goodman to Thomas Jefferson,
        30 December. University of Virginia Special
        Collections, Charlottesville.

UPTON, DELL
1985   White and Black Landscapes in Eighteenth-Century
        Virginia. *Places* 2(2):59-72.

VLACH, JOHN MICHAEL
1991   *By the Work of Their Hands: Studies in Afro-
        American Folklife.* University Press of Virginia,
        Charlottesville.

WARE, SUE ANNE
1997   The Sisterhood of Gardens: African-American
        Women's Gardens, from the Backwoods to the Cul-
        de-Sac. In *The Influence of Women on the Southern
        Landscape, Proceedings of the Tenth Conference
        on Restoring Southern Gardens and Landscapes*
        1995:154-171. Winston-Salem, NC.

WATTERS, DAVID R.
1994   Mortuary Patterns at the Harney Site Slave Cemetery,
        Montserrat, in Caribbean Perspective. *Historical
        Archaeology* 28(3):56-73.

WELTY, EUDORA
1971   *The Wide Net and Other Stories.* Harcourt, Brace,
        Jovanovich, New York, NY.

WESTMACOTT, RICHARD
1992   *African-American Gardens and Yards in the Rural
        South.* University of Tennessee Press, Knoxville.

YENTSCH, ANNE E., AND JUDSON M. KRATZER
1994   Techniques for Excavating and Analyzing Buried
        Eighteenth-Century Garden Landscapes. In *The
        Archaeology of Garden and Field,* Naomi Miller and
        Kathryn Gleason, editors, pp. 168-201. University
        of Pennsylvania Press, Philadelphia.

BARBARA J. HEATH
THOMAS JEFFERSON'S POPLAR FOREST
PO BOX 419
FOREST, VA 24551-0419

AMBER BENNETT
DEPARTMENT OF ANTHROPOLOGY
SWEET BRIAR COLLEGE
SWEET BRIAR, VA 24595-9999

KENNETH L. BROWN
DOREEN C. COOPER

Structural Continuity in an African-American Slave and Tenant Community

Introduction

Cary Carson (1978:42) once stated, "No matter what standard objective scholars use they can hardly avoid the conclusion that the study of artifacts has contributed to developing the *main themes* of American history almost not at all" (emphasis in original). This quote illustrates a problem in conducting an archaeological investigation within historic contexts in the United States. While this sentiment is not surprising from an historian, it also appears to be a widely held opinion among historical archaeologists (I. Walker 1968; Noël Hume 1969b, 1978b; Adams 1979). During the past three decades, American archaeologists have developed a number of techniques designed to improve their ability to study human behavior in more than an historical fashion. Studies of the structure of past cultures as well as the processes behind culture change have taken over the literature of prehistoric archaeology. Conversely, such studies are not central to the goals expressed by some historical archaeologists (Noël Hume 1969b), because historical archaeologists have access to documents which outline the broad processes and structures of their study populations. Archaeology, it is argued, provides interesting details not otherwise available to historians; history provides whatever else might be needed (Noël Hume 1969b).

This concept is most clearly observed in the use of the functional classification systems employed by historical archaeologists. Artifacts recovered from an historically defined context somehow have a meaning very different from that which would be assigned to them if they had come from a prehistoric context. One of the main classification systems employed by historical archaeologists is that proposed by Roderick Sprague. His system is intended to be one based upon assumed function: "Any classification, especially a functional one, imposes the culture of the researcher upon that body of data. However, in most 19th- and 20th-century sites, I have found this to be far less of a problem than utilizing a material based classification" (R. Sprague 1981:252).

This methodology rests upon the assumption that historical archaeologists have access to a wide variety of documents which give both function and meaning to the artifacts recovered. In the final analysis, however, it is the historical archaeologist's knowledge of modern material culture—its uses and meanings—which is employed to determine an artifact's function and, therefore, to produce behavioral interpretations. Within Sprague's (1981: 256–257) classificatory scheme, for instance, horseshoes are listed in three places: "domestic ritual," "household pastimes," and "agriculture and husbandry." This list of potential functions for horseshoes might logically be enlarged well beyond Sprague's simply on the basis of an individual interpreter's knowledge of how others employ horseshoes. Thus, for example, a horseshoe can function in the "culinary" category (as a trivet), in "home education, information, and business" (as a paper weight), or in "domestic safety" (as a weapon). The point here is that the functions of the artifacts recovered should, whenever possible, be based upon the associational context of the artifacts—a generally held belief in prehistoric archaeology. However, for Sprague and others, any individual artifact's function is based upon the totality of assumed "functions" for the associated artifacts. It is the assumed function for each of the artifacts that is based upon the prior knowledge of the archaeologist—the archaeologist's "cultural baggage." The assignment of artifact function based on a priori knowledge is a questionable practice even in the archaeology of European-Americans since it precludes discovery of cultural changes or adaptations. This practice is clearly inappropriate in the study of non-European-Americans—even those who operate within a European-American-defined cultural setting—because their use of European-American technology will not necessarily be subject to the same cultural baggage as that carried either by members of the dominant culture or by the archaeologist. Prehistorians, by definition, lack historical documents and, therefore, must rely solely on the associational contexts of artifacts within the archaeological record in order to assign function and use. Historical archaeologists may not have to rely solely on the context within the archaeological record. If they choose to investigate African-American cultural contexts, however, they must employ a more "value-free" approach.

The issues involved in this debate are not trivial. In the case of "Plantation Archaeology," this issue directly affects one's future success in contributing to an increased understanding of the rural South, its agricultural system, and what might be called the "African-American past." While it may be easy and convenient to assign function and use to artifacts based on a supposed knowledge of historical documents, a major disservice to the past will occur if the analysis is stopped there. If the goal is to increase understanding of plantation communities, then archaeologists must look at the function, use, and meaning of artifacts within a context that is not totally dependent upon the dominant European-American behavioral system. Africans became African-Americans; during the acculturation process, they adapted European-American material culture into some of their African behavioral systems.

The goal of this paper is to illustrate the acculturation of an antebellum and postbellum slave and tenant community—the Levi Jordan Plantation—from the Gulf Coastal Plains of Texas. Through the use of a methodology which employs ethnographic analogies derived from African and African-American contexts, this essay demonstrates how the study of artifacts can contribute to the main themes of American history by focusing on one plantation site in east Texas.

Potential Historical Archaeological Data

Within this overall conception of historical archaeology, the methodological approach advocated here is viewed as an important mechanism designed to incorporate more "insider" data into the study of the African-American past. That is, archaeologists have the potential to develop descriptions of and interpretations from the artifacts left behind by the individuals who used them in a past behavioral system. These "documents," studied by historical archaeologists and rarely employed by historians, were deposited as a result of the patterned behavior of the human beings who actually existed within the cultural systems under study. Obviously, not all deposited artifacts yield the same level of behavioral information due to the context of the artifacts and the formation processes which occurred in the production of that archaeological context (Schiffer 1976, 1987). The potential for more accurate "insider" information from these artifacts, however, is actually greater than that derived from the "outsider" historical documents. In this sense, "outsider" means that many of the documentary sources were produced by individuals who were not members of the slave or tenant communities about which they wrote. In the study of the agricultural systems of the rural South prior to 1920, for example, the available written documents generally include plantation records, agricultural journals, census and tax records, diaries, and travelers' journals. These sources were composed by individuals who clearly were outsiders to the slave or tenant communities they observed. They may be sources which are "emic" to the study of the elite patriarchy, e.g., the European-American component, of the plantation society, but they are "etic" with regard to the slave and later tenant portions of the society. Thus, from the viewpoint of the actual material remains, historical archaeologists working on plantation sites have an ideal opportunity to investigate a slave or tenant community employing a very different data set than that used in traditional history. This data set has the potential to be derived from the past activities of the people who lived within the behavioral system under investigation.

Unfortunately, archaeological studies of slave and tenant farmer systems conducted to date have generally not produced many new insights into the evolution of African-American culture. Much of this research has concentrated on tests for the determination of ethnicity of slaves and tenants (Handler and Lange 1978; Schuyler 1980; Otto 1984; Singleton 1985a, 1985b). Historians, on the other hand, clearly acknowledge that slaves and slave descendants were blacks abducted from Africa. In order for historical archaeologists to begin to produce new insights into the functioning of the behavioral systems of plantation communities, they must begin to test for specific African and African-American behavioral patterns within the material remains encountered during excavations of slave and tenant sites. For this type of study, the traditionally employed historical documents will actually be of little help. Like prehistorians, historical archaeologists will have to begin their analyses with a lack of knowledge as to artifact function and use by the people who used and deposited the remains.

In order to answer questions about "African holdovers," acculturation, and plantation community organization, historical archaeologists must alter their approach both to history and to the application of models about historical artifact use. Artifacts indicative of ethnicity or ethnic retentions probably represent African or African-American behaviors which, for the most part, utilized the available European-American material culture. Artifacts traditionally used to define ethnicity—carved bone, hand-made musical instruments, toys, effigies, and carved and drilled shell—would have been highly curated items. Within the plantation community, such items probably would not have entered the archaeological record in large numbers. Importantly, however, other items may have been produced by European-Americans but which had their patterned use altered to permit and define meaning for the African-American population employing them. An example of this type of artifact might be a shell button which has an African or African-American symbol carved onto one of its surfaces. Colored glass beads and drilled coins can be other items whose traditional or primary functions within the dominant culture were altered (Adams 1987).

Levi Jordan Plantation Quarters

The Levi Jordan Plantation was founded in 1848 on 2,222 acres of rich river bottomland on the Gulf Coastal Plains of Brazoria County, Texas, approximately 60 miles south of Houston and 15 miles inland from the Gulf of Mexico. During the antebellum period, the major cash crops produced on the plantation were sugar and cotton. Jordan's sugar mill generated additional cash by processing sugar cane for a number of the surrounding plantations (Strobel 1926; Platter 1961). Creighton (1975) and W. Johnson (1961) also provide detailed descriptions of the sugar industry in Brazoria County. For a period of time after the Civil War, Jordan attempted to continue producing sugar, although the main focus of his agricultural activities appears to have shifted to cotton and cattle ranching (Platter 1961). After his death in 1873, the northern half of the plantation was run by his grandsons until 1876 (West Publishing Company 1892), when it was then leased until 1885. Throughout this time of transition, the activities initiated by Jordan continued, although an emphasis on cattle ranching began to assume an increasingly larger proportion of the cash basis of the plantation (U.S. Bureau of Census 1870, 1880a; Platter 1961:162). Around 1890 or 1891, after acrimonious litigation between two grandsons and four great-grandsons, the northern half of the plantation, including the house and the former slave quarters, was divided among the four great-grandsons.

Interestingly, the main house—a major portion of which is still standing, the original plantation hospital and house slave residence, and a few small outbuildings were built of wood. The bulk of the buildings constructed on the plantation, especially those having to do with the slaves and the plantation's production, were made of brick. Of the major brick buildings, only the sugar house currently has above-ground walls.

The slave and tenant quarters were located approximately 400 feet northwest of the main house (Figure 1–1). The quarters were occupied from their construction beginning late in 1848 through their forced abandonment around 1891. Thus, the archaeological deposits were produced over a 42-year time span that encompasses both slavery and early tenancy. The quarters consisted of eight long, barracks-like structures built in groups of two.

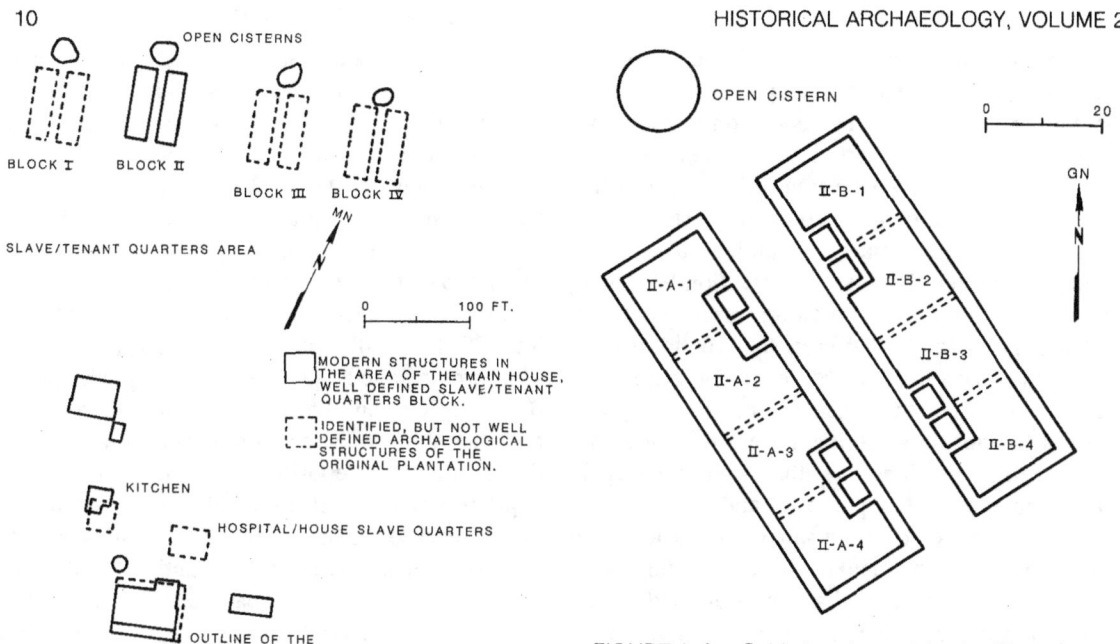

FIGURE 1–1. Location of Jordan Plantation quarters.

FIGURE 1–2. Cabin locations at Jordan Plantation.

Each of these sets of structures shared a common central hallway probably with a single roof. Entrances into the individual cabins were located in this central hallway. Archaeological evidence demonstrates that from three to four individual cabins were built within each of the long buildings (Figure 1–2). The 1860 population census lists the plantation as having 29 slave cabins for the 141 slaves (U.S. Bureau of Census 1860). This configuration would fit within the defined area noted above. Archaeological evidence also supports the hypothesis that several of the so-called cabins may have been larger and served as dormitories. At its height, approximately 150 slaves lived on the plantation (Brazoria County 1862). Unfortunately, records do not exist to indicate the number of wage labor tenants who lived on the plantation. Excavation within the individual cabins demonstrates a reduction in the number of cabins occupied. The archaeological evidence suggests that this change occurred after the Civil War, and thus that the number of tenants might have been lower than the number of slaves.

From an archaeological point of view, possibly the single most important event in the history of the quarters is that their occupants were forced to leave. A large percentage of the artifacts thus far recovered represents the preserved remains of possessions abandoned by the occupants as they were forced to leave. The historical documents do not indicate exactly when this abandonment occurred. Several lines of evidence—including family oral history and two civil court cases, however, suggest that it happened sometime late in 1890 or early in 1891. This forced removal has resulted in the preservation of an important set of artifacts representing items that were hastily abandoned by their owners. Further, the materials have been recovered in positions relatively close to the place of their use.

Four other factors are of great importance in the assessment of the nature of the archaeological data set from these quarters. First, the exterior walls of the quarters were made of brick set into a shallow foundation trench. This trench had been excavated about 1 ft. into the subsoil around the entire perimeter of each structure. This construction method had the effect of sealing the archaeological deposits from outside intrusions; for example, artifacts could not be deposited under the floors from outside the cabins. Second, the "crawl space" between the floor and the soil within the area defined by the wall trench was too narrow to permit the retrieval of a large quantity of materials which might have fallen through the floor boards. Construction evidence supports the idea that the floor was constructed within approximately 4–6 in. of the ground surface inside the structures. Third, archaeological evidence has shown that each of the quarters was padlocked after the inhabitants were removed and not reopened until long after the cabins had begun to deteriorate. Closed padlocks and door hinges have been recovered in the same general location within the three individual cabins under study. The closed padlocks suggest that the doors had either fallen or were knocked into the cabins at some point. Fourth, the area of the plantation occupied by the quarters has never been plowed.

Oral history and archaeological data both suggest that for a time the cabins were allowed to deteriorate naturally. The wooden floors of the cabins decomposed and collapsed onto the ground below, while soil, brick fragments, and organic refuse built up over the deposits dating from their forced abandonment (1890–1891) until 1913. Based upon the family's oral history, in 1913 the owner of the quarters area contracted with a developer to remove the bricks from the walls of the quarters. Bricks were salvaged to the base of the foundation trench in some areas, but usually the removal process stopped at or just below the original floor level. This action added to the pile of debris that accumulated on the old floor area—as much as a foot of brick rubble was present in some areas tested—and further protected the floor area and the artifacts. In August 1913, and again just over a year later (Creighton 1975), the area of the quarters was flooded, depositing from 3 to 6 in. of silt over the area. This silt effectively sealed the remaining deposit. As a result of these site formation processes, the actual floor areas of individual cabins within the structures could be defined.

The excavations into the slave and tenant farmer community at the Jordan Plantation have been de-veloped both to excavate intensively a number of the individual cabins and to test systematically the area around the quarters. In both sampling strategies, the standard excavation unit was 5 × 5 ft. in size. All units excavated at the quarters, however, began at this size, but usually were enlarged. That is, once a unit in the quarters had been excavated to the top of the brick layer that immediately over-laid the cabin deposits, each unit was segmented into 25 1- × -1-ft. sub-units. Further, once this level was reached—generally at a depth of 0.3 to 0.5 ft. below surface, a system of both arbitrary and "natural" levels was employed in the excavation of the cabin deposits. The basic arbitrary level depth was 0.1 ft., unless a soil change was noted. Within each of these 0.1 ft. levels, however, artifacts were generally pedestaled until all of the sub-units of the level were excavated. This procedure has permitted the relatively rapid excavation of the deposits, while still providing extensive point plotting of the artifacts. This methodology has proven to be extremely important, especially within the "abandonment zone." Through this methodology, areas of differential use of cabin floor space can be identified, and the original internal cabin walls can be defined. The external walls were made of brick, but those on the inside were made of a more perishable material, probably wood. Thus, the walls were defined on the basis of "shadows" in the artifact distribution.

To date, excavations have been conducted in nine of the individual slave cabins within the community. Based upon the present interpretation of the data, this would translate into six tenant cabins; two other structures became two-room cabins, while another may not have been employed as a residence after the Civil War. In terms of economic, social, and political organization, the excavations have provided clear evidence that both economic and political hierarchies existed within the community during both the slave and tenant occupations. In fact, the data suggest that a great deal of continuity existed within this community over these time periods.

From a behavioral perspective, the social, political, economic, and in a slightly more tentative manner, some of the ideological structure of the

Jordan Plantation slave and tenant community can also be defined. As would be predicted, the deposits around the cabins demonstrate a very general and rather uniform distribution of the various major artifact types. Much of this material relates to the domestic activities of the cabins. The differences noted in the distribution of these materials likely relate to differential activity use in the area of the quarters, e.g., internal plantation roads, outdoor work areas, outdoor social areas, and so on. The internal cabin deposits demonstrate something very different. The internal deposits provide evidence of occupational specialization, political and economic status, and ethnicity. The best evidence for African behavioral holdovers and behavioral change also derives from the internal cabin deposits. Given the large number of Africans by birth found in Brazoria County, e.g., 133 according to the 1870 population census, some of this culture change is conceivably the result of acculturation and behavioral adaptation—the development of "African-American culture"—as well as the changes brought about by the emancipation of the slaves.

The Interpretation of Social Hierarchies and Social Change

The definition of status hierarchies within historical archaeological research has presented many formidable problems. These problems include the computing of costs for items found in the archaeological record; the determination of gifts versus purchases, especially when dealing with slaves; the often expressed belief that the plantation's owner or agent, e.g., the overseer, conferred status (Frazier 1930), thus making status and material possessions dependent variables (Adams 1987); and that status on a plantation is somehow relative to the plantation's status within the region (Rawick 1972; Kelso 1984; S. Moore 1985; Adams 1987). These factors do indeed represent problems in the interpretation of the archaeological remains. Within the context of the materials from the Jordan Plantation, however, these problems in the demonstration of status hierarchies can be addressed.

The slave and tenant community hierarchy and the plantation owner's established hierarchy may or may not have been the same. Certainly, the positions defined by the archaeological evidence do not all coincide with those normally attributed to a plantation's hierarchy. For example, as will be demonstrated below, evidence exists for a traditional African religious practitioner, a specialized metal worker, and a craftsman producing carved bone and shell objects. Jordan would not likely have established or assigned these positions to members of the community. While each person may also have had some formal position within Jordan's assigned plantation hierarchy, the archaeological evidence suggests that the community hierarchy was at least somewhat independent of Jordan's. However, the important hierarchy here is the one that would have been internal to the slave and tenant community itself, the social order that was internally defined and sanctioned, and effectively controlled the lives of the members of the community. One of the primary functions of this internal hierarchy would be to "cushion" the impact of slavery and tenancy on the members of the community, functioning to control and direct behavior within the community, as well as to provide aid and support to its members. Thus, this hierarchy would provide its members with a sense of continuity and support despite the oppressive nature of the system of which it was a part. This internal hierarchy is the one which has continuity through time and for which archaeological evidence remains. Even after slavery gave way to wage labor tenancy on the Jordan Plantation, the community and its hierarchy remained essentially intact and functioning.

The major changes that have so far appeared in the archaeological record of the quarters occur in the areas of settlement patterning, diet, occupation, and the internal economic system. To date, no major changes have been discovered in the retention of African behavioral patterns. Patterns within the abandonment data are essentially identical to those representing the accumulation of debris during the occupation of the cabins. This absence of change should not be taken, however, to imply that the system was static. Rather, the ar-

TABLE 1–1
TOTAL ARTIFACT COUNTS PER CABIN

Artifact Type	II-A-2	II-A-3	II-B-1	II-B-2	II-B-3
Bone fragment	3,789	2,598	5,874	5,993	6,390
Ceramic fragment	187	91	289	242	414
Porcelain	5	0	54	16	11
Glass fragment	481	190	908	877	733
Cutlery	5	4	32	33	20
Pipes	7	6	14	40	24
Munitions	7	23	44	43	59
Melted lead	6	7	17	74	4
Beads	8	8	26	13	25
Store-bought jewelry	7	6	31	26	23
Sewing equipment	1	0	18	10	10
Buttons	42	46	404	248	340
Coins	1	1	5	5	7
Shell artifact	5	17	37	13	42
Carved bone	0	0	0	1	2
Pocket knife	1	0	4	8	6
Total	4,552	2,997	7,757	7,642	8,110

Cabin Number	Number of Excavation Units	Square footage Excavated	Weight Amount
II-A-2	3	75	2.08
II-A-3	3	75	2.08
II-B-1	6.2	156	1.00
II-B-2	4.8	119	1.24
II-B-3	6	150	1.04

chaeological evidence analyzed to date suggests that the positions continued, even though the beliefs and meanings may have changed somewhat.

The definition of this hierarchy is based on differential distributions of artifact classes among the various cabins thus far analyzed. As can be seen from the tables, significant differences appear in the artifact class frequencies recorded for five of the slave cabins. Table 1–1 depicts the artifact class counts from the excavation units into these cabins. Table 1–2 presents the weighted average counts and percentages of these same artifact classes. To obtain these weighted averages, excavation units—or portions of excavation units—contained within each cabin were determined. A

square footage for each cabin, based on excavated and analyzed units, was then calculated. The cabin with the largest square footage excavated, II-B-1, was assigned a weight of "1." All other cabins were then weighted according to the percentage of their excavated square footage to that of Cabin II-B-1 (shown in Table 1–1), and the weighted artifact totals and percentages in Table 1–2 were computed.

Settlement Change

In terms of the settlement patterning of the quarters area, two major changes have been identified.

TABLE 1–2
WEIGHTED ARTIFACT AVERAGES
(% in parentheses)

Artifact Type	II-A-2	II-A-3	II-B-1	II-B-2	II-B-3
Bone	7,881 (24)	5,404 (16)	5,874 (18)	7,431 (22)	6,901 (21)
Ceramic	389 (24)	189 (12)	289 (18)	300 (19)	447 (28)
Porcelain	10 (10)	0 (0)	54 (56)	20 (21)	12 (13)
Glass	1,000 (24)	395 (9)	908 (22)	1,087 (26)	792 (19)
Cutlery	10 (9)	8 (7)	32 (28)	41 (36)	22 (19)
Pipes	15 (13)	12 (10)	14 (12)	50 (43)	26 (22)
Munitions	15 (7)	48 (21)	44 (20)	53 (24)	64 (29)
Melted lead	12 (9)	15 (11)	17 (12)	92 (66)	4 (3)
Beads	17 (17)	17 (17)	26 (25)	16 (16)	27 (26)
Store-bought jewelry	15 (13)	12 (10)	31 (27)	32 (28)	25 (22)
Sewing equipment	2 (5)	0 (0)	18 (42)	12 (28)	11 (26)
Buttons	87 (7)	96 (8)	404 (32)	308 (24)	367 (29)
Coins	2 (9)	2 (9)	5 (22)	6 (26)	8 (35)
Shell artifact	10 (7)	35 (24)	37 (26)	16 (11)	45 (31)
Carved bone	0 (0)	0 (0)	0 (0)	1 (33)	2 (67)
Pocket knife	2 (9)	0 (0)	4 (17)	10 (43)	7 (30)

The first is that some of the residents converted their cabins into two-room structures, which is best seen in the set of cabins designated II-B-1 through II-B-4 (Figure 1–2). Artifact distributions within structure II-B appear to identify four cabins utilized during the slave occupation: three functioned as residences, while the fourth may have had a specialized function. At some point in time after the Civil War, this set of cabins was converted to only two residential units and two special purpose units each connected to one of the residences.

The second apparent shift in the settlement of the quarters was the abandonment of the dormitories as residences. During the occupation of the quarters by slaves, at least one of the cabins tested archaeologically, Cabin III-A-1, appears to have functioned as a dormitory. It also lacks an obvious abandonment deposit. The presence of dormitories is suggested by the 1860 population census data, in which Jordan listed a total of 132 slaves. Of these slaves, 59 were over the age of 20 (34 males, 25 females), while 73 were below the age of 20 (37 males, 36 females) (Figure 1–3); these data suggest that nine adult males may have lacked spouses in residence on the plantation. These single males may have occupied the larger cabins. Further,

given the interesting decrease in the number of slaves aged 20 to 34 between 1850 and 1860 (34 down to 19; a decrease of 9 males and 6 females), and the corresponding increase of children below the age of 20 (47 up to 73; an increase of 20 males and 6 females) as illustrated in Figure 1–3 (U.S. Bureau of Census 1850, 1860), dormitories for older children might also have been necessary.

Dietary Change

Little can be conclusively stated concerning the changes in diet for the residents of the quarters. Although detailed study has yet to be undertaken on the nearly 40,000 faunal elements excavated, a shift does seem to occur in animal types as one moves upward in the stratigraphy below the cabin floors. Specifically, the amount of wild animal bone decreases upward through the deposit. That is, bones and other parts of deer, reptiles, fish, various rodents, and other wild animals decrease in number over time, while those of animals such as chickens, pigs, and cattle increase. This trend may simply be a function of the size of the bones—the smaller animal bones falling through the flooring and being deposited, while the larger ones would

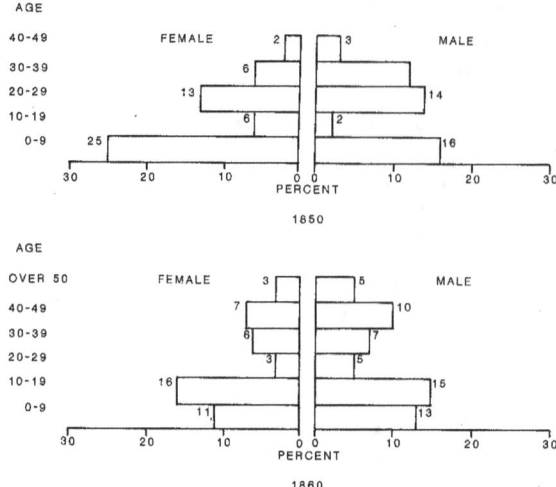

FIGURE 1–3.   Age-sex profile for Jordan Plantation.

have been discarded outside of the cabin itself. Chicken eggshell, however, appears throughout the sequence, while fish scales, fish bones, and turtle shell fragments appear to decrease over time. While analysis of this material is necessary, at this time it appears that the wage labor tenants may have had a diet consisting of a higher quantity of domesticated animals than their slave counterparts.

Occupational Change

The archaeological evidence for occupation and occupational differences among the residents of the quarters must be examined in two ways: the occupations necessary for the plantation's economic system and the occupations which functioned within the internal economic system of the slave and tenant community. While these are not mutually exclusive economies, the different items produced play very different roles within the combined economic system of the plantation. The primary economic activities within the slave and tenant community were those related to the production of two cash crops, sugar and cotton, as well as to making the plantation as self sufficient as possible. Archaeological data currently support the following part-time, if not full-time, occupations practiced by both the slave and tenant occu-

pants: seamstress (at least three slave and two tenant), carpenter (possibly two for each time period), hunter (at least three slave and three tenant), and a blacksmith or someone who repaired metal objects. While this list fails to include specialized agricultural workers, e.g., the actual field hands and sugar mill workers, these exclusions are more likely a factor of tool storage—away from the cabins—and of the archaeological record than the structure of the plantation, and should not be taken to mean there were none. Fragments of agricultural tools, especially hoes, were recovered from several of the cabins. The tools associated with occupations such as seamstress, blacksmith, carpenter, or hunter, however, are more distinctive of these specialized activities, and possibly more often stored in a residence, than are the tools connected with agricultural activities. Further, agricultural activities may have been carried out for the plantation as well as for the individual slave or tenant households. Thus, the presence of agricultural tools in the archaeological record of a cabin does not necessarily indicate the plantation occupation of the cabin's resident. Specialized tools are also more likely than agricultural tools to be used and stored within the cabins, especially after the Civil War, as craftsmen became more nearly "self-employed." Therefore, it should be expected that such tools would enter the archaeological record of the cabins more often than agricultural ones. This hypothesis is supported by the abandonment deposit, where a large percentage of the craft tools and related items has been located.

Internal Economic System

Of equal importance for the successful functioning of the slave and tenant community, however, was the internal economic system. Evidence from the excavations to date suggests that a number of important occupations fall into this category, including: hunters (three for both the slave and tenant occupations), a political leader, a healer/magician, a "metalsmith or shot maker," and an "African craftsman." Given the importance of meat protein in the diet of the various members of the plantation community, the hunters probably functioned in both the plantation and the internal slave/tenant community economic systems. Their importance in the internal system would center on their ability to provide the community with additional foodstuffs without the overseer or owner necessarily interfering. Such an activity might provide a mechanism for within-community status enhancement. In these cases, hunting may have served as an additional mechanism for social control and status maintenance. Further, the occupants of Cabin II-B-2 appear to have provided the lead shot which may have been used by the hunters. As can be seen in Table 1–2, this cabin accounts for fully 66% of the sheet lead and melted lead "refuse" by artifact count. By weight, however, Cabin II-B-2 accounts for an even larger percentage of these artifact classes. Further, the majority of "Munitions" recovered from this cabin (59%) consists of unfinished or unfired lead shot. Finally, a shot-making tool was also recovered. In light of the clear connection between metalsmithing and religion in both African and African-American cultures, the location of this cabin is interesting. While additional analysis is necessary, the apparent incorporation of Cabin II-B-2 into II-B-1 might suggest that the healer/magician and the metalsmith may have been or become the same individual.

The so-called African craftsman's cabin (II-A-3) produced a variety of items which form the "ethnic identifiers" discovered within the slave and tenant cabins. The tools for manufacture of the drilled shell artifacts and a number of blank shells of a variety of fresh and salt water types came from this cabin. Given the large number of fresh water mussel shells located within this cabin (an item not found in other cabins), this individual may have worked shell for other artifacts, such as buttons. In fact, a number of shell and bone buttons from the quarters appear to be "homemade." In addition, at least one apparent "store-bought" button, recovered within the deposits of the quarters, was found to have had a six-sided star carved into one of its surfaces. Such a symbol is found on African and African-American ritual objects (Thompson 1983). Evidence for this craft production is found from the base of the below-floor deposit through the abandonment level.

African Retentions and Symbolism

One of the interesting aspects of the data so far generated concerns the manipulation of African-derived objects and symbols. While all of the cabins thus far tested have yielded a number of drilled shell artifacts, two cabins had occupants who manipulated a wider variety of African and European-American symbols. Both of these cabins' occupants were extremely important in the functioning of the community of slaves and tenants. Cabin II-B-3/4 was occupied by an individual who probably functioned in a social control capacity. This hypothesis is supported by the discovery of a shackle chain bricked into the west wall of Cabin II-B-3, a high number of weapon-related artifacts, as well as a very high number of African and European-American status items, e.g., carved bone, drilled shells, store-bought jewelry, and coins of high denomination. Most of these items were recovered from the abandonment level of II-B-3/4, while the occupational deposits of II-B-3 contained a very low frequency of artifacts, possibly indicating that II-B-3 was utilized as a "jail" for some portion of its use, later becoming part of a larger, two-room cabin.

The community-wide function of another cabin's occupants provides an important test of "African" retentions through the differential manipulation of European-American material culture. This cabin was occupied by a traditional healer/magician. Similar to the political leader's cabin (II-B-3/4), the evidence here supports the hypothesis that the healer/magician occupied a single cabin during slavery and expanded it into two rooms sometime after 1865. The added space served as an "office" or ritual room. A vast majority of the artifacts that formed part of the healer's ritual paraphernalia date to the rapid abandonment of the cabin. For whatever reasons, the artifacts remained behind and in a condition fairly similar to the way they were left.

The main data come from a restricted area of a single cabin. Of primary importance here are five cast-iron kettle bases, several pieces of utilized chalk, fragments of a small scale, bird skulls, an animal's paw, medicine bottles, bullet casings put together to form a sealed tube, ocean shells, small doll parts, a high frequency of nails and spikes, several tablespoons, metal knives—both real and "fake," a chert projectile point, and two chert scrapers. The so-called "fake" knives are long pieces of metal made in the general shape of a knife; they are, however, much thicker than a normal knife and have a wedge-shaped cross-section. In most cases, these fake knives have an uneven "cutting edge." These objects probably all relate to the ritual "tool kit" of a traditional West African and African-American healer/magician. Clearly, a very large percentage of these artifacts would have functioned in other activities—and likely did at various points in their use-lives. In fact, in a number of currently employed artifact cataloguing schemes, these artifacts would be subsumed in household and architectural categories and their significance in ritual activities missed. When these artifacts are taken together in an explicit test of the healer/magician model, however, this pattern of co-occurrence becomes significant in the study of African retentions in an African-American rural farming community.

Research conducted by other scholars (Bascom 1952; Janzen and MacGaffey 1974; MacGaffey 1977; Thompson 1983; Janzen 1986) can be employed to construct a behavioral analogy which can be tested against the data from the healer/magician's cabin. For example, William Bascom (1952) has demonstrated that in Cuba many of the divination rituals and equipment found within the modern black and creole populations originated in West Africa. Equipment regularly employed in these ritual activities included, among other items, wooden or metal trays, white chalk or powder, metal staffs, and bird symbolism. The trays and chalk or white powder were often used together. The powder/chalk was spread across the surface of the tray with the divination proceeding with the marking of symbols into the powder on the surface of the tray. The chalk could also be used to make the symbols not only on the tray but on other surfaces as well. Bascom further notes the close association of divination and healing knowledge and ritual with birds and bird symbolism in both Africa and the New World. Sealed, hollow metal staffs or

smaller cylindrical metal objects are important symbols of the healer/magician's power. Finally, Richard Thompson (1983:56) notes the following description of the beginning of a charm ritual: "On the island of Cuba, when Kongo ritual leaders wish to make important Zarabanda charm . . . they begin by tracing, in white chalk, a cruciform pattern on the bottom of an iron kettle."

These behavioral descriptions clearly help to tie a number of the artifacts discovered in the archaeological record of the tenant quarters of the Jordan Plantation into a "functional set." This functional set concerns both curing and magic ritual and ritual objects. However, the ritual objects are not the elaborate and symbolically decorated items generally noted within the ethnographic descriptions. In the case of the Jordan Plantation artifacts, they are simply adaptations of existing European-American material culture. Given the differences in the cultural settings described, e.g., a free community composed of and controlled by its black or creole inhabitants versus a community of free blacks within a larger community controlled by whites in a generally antagonistic setting, one might predict some simplification of the material culture involved. Slave and tenant communities might not be expected to produce the highly decorated artifacts given their status and the need to "go underground" in order to carry out these traditional practices. Thus, the symbolic meanings of the items would be clear within the context of the black community, and generally learned orally, rather than being expressed openly on the objects. If members of the dominant society happened to discover the objects, the general form and even the association might not be understood by the "foreign" discoverer. Thus, the lack of symbolic expression on the artifacts and their general "domestic" nature would aid in keeping the likelihood of discovery low, further helping to keep the behavior operating within the adapting community of African-Americans.

Other artifacts associated with the ritual objects and a nearby plastered area of the cabin's floor may well be all that remains within the archaeological record of another item within this general ritual tool kit—the anthropomorphic wooden figures called *Nkisi*. As John Janzen and Reinhild Janzen (1988:38) note, such figures are "power objects" in a community and/or public context. They also serve in the treatment of sickness, the protection of individuals and communities, and for the initiation of novices into the ritual order common to the *Nkisi*. These authors also state that usually when these figures are employed in ritual activities, then:

> At this time they are combined with other objects or ritually treated to achieve a particular end. Nails or wedges driven into the wooden figure represent the oaths that bind the word of the spell. "Injuring" the nkisi, thus provoking it, compels it to act in the desired manner (Janzen and Janzen 1988:38).

While the actual carved object is missing archaeologically, a variety of artifacts in very close association with ritual objects, items employed in the production of charms and curing, do appear. Within an 8-sq.-ft. area around the plastered surface were recovered 11 spikes, approximately 254 nails, at least 2 broken knife blades, a number of wedge-shaped metal pieces, and a large number of other metal objects. The amount of metal from this small portion of the unit is from 12 to 15 times the average amount of metal from a similar-sized area of the quarters. Again, these artifacts all might have had different functions and uses at some point in their history, but within the testing of a nonhistorically documented and non-European-American behavioral model, they help to support the hypothesis that they were ultimately used in an African or African-American ritual context. By simply placing these artifacts into European-American behavioral sets—e.g., culinary, gustatory, architectural sets—as is common in historical archaeology, their importance in the definition and reconstruction of African and African-American behavior would have been totally lost. A vast majority of these items are typical of those found within the average slave or tenant household—even within the average plantation owner's household, a fact which may have allowed some of the behavioral patterns to have survived within the context of the plantation community.

Conclusion

A couple of issues raised at the beginning of this paper can now be readdressed. Specifically, some of the issues related to the archaeological definition of ethnicity, "African retentions," and African-American acculturation and adaptation within the context of the agricultural system of the South can be explored. First, the discovery of ethnicity and African retentions will come from historical archaeologists systematically investigating artifact context without a priori definitions of artifact function and use. The associational context of that portion of the Jordan Plantation discussed here has been highly preserved. While such a situation may be rare—indeed some reviewers have stated "unique," it can still be employed to demonstrate an important issue within historical archaeology. This issue is that of assigning function and meaning to artifacts. The pronounced tendency among historical archaeologists is to make such assignments from the viewpoint of "cultural descendants." In such a situation, documents and acquired "knowledge" of artifact function and historical context define both the function and meaning of items recovered in the archaeological record. Such a view is static at best and unscientific at worst. For all archaeologists, the assignment of function and meaning requires the excavation of sites in which the associational context has been preserved on some or all of the sites. It may well be that such contexts are rare on extant plantation sites. If so, then historical archaeologists will be limited in their ability to reconstruct behavior in slave and tenant farmer communities independent of historical documents. Associational context provides the data necessary for the reconstruction of individual, small group, and community activities, statuses, roles, and changes within each of these. Open community deposits, e.g., general site middens, trash dumps, and under-house deposits, and so forth, do not permit these types of questions to be researched. Such community deposits are the result of the activities of use and disposal for all of the inhabitants of the site, human as well as nonhuman. Archaeologists have no effective method to "control" these deposits and factor out the actual depositional agents.

Second, the question of the definition of function and meaning directly affects the way historical archaeologists understand the development of culture. As the artifactual evidence from the Jordan Plantation demonstrates, the material culture employed and deposited at the plantation was almost solely of European-American origin and had function and meaning within that context. When the material culture was employed within the slave and tenant farming community contexts, however, some portion of it acquired distinctly different meanings and uses. Questions raised by archaeologists concerning ethnicity and the definition of acculturation and adaptational patterns and processes involves sets of behaviors, not single artifactual differences. The point here is that individuals and groups can, and do, select material items and invest them with certain beliefs and symbols. The cultural origin of the material items represents only one part in a group's consideration of function and meaning. Within American slavery and tenancy, the differential use and manipulation of certain of the dominant culture's material objects may likely have been the rule rather than the exception, in which case such behavior might aid in the explanation of some of the variation noted in African-American and European-American "culture" within the United States. Definition and meaning of objects of material culture, as well as acceptance, rejection, and modification of ideas, behavioral patterns, and material items, are processes subject to variation depending upon the background and interaction of those involved. Traditionally, historians and historical archaeologists

have looked at the development of African-American culture as a process of acceptance, modification, or rejection of European-American culture. However, just as clearly, this has not been an entirely "one way street." In order to investigate this interaction more fully, archaeologists must look for and extensively excavate associational contexts within slave and tenant farmer communities throughout the South. Only through the comparisons of such data can one begin to talk about acculturation processes, the retention of so-called African behavioral patterns, and the definition of ethnicity. Further, such comparisons should help to define the amount of interplay between aspects of European-American and African-American culture in the evolution of both.

Finally, if historical archaeologists wish to utilize archaeology to provide new insights into the cultural evolution of Africans into African-Americans, detailed, fine-scale artifact analyses must be employed. Such analyses may lead to the discovery of ethnicity, African retentions, and the acculturation and adaptational processes. These analyses must include the testing of ethnographic analogies derived from African and African-American sources. European-American sources for behavioral interpretation should be expected to be somewhat different from African and African-American ones, at least until they can be demonstrated to explain more of the data derived from historical archaeological research. Africans and African-Americans may often be "invisible" in written history, but through carefully constructed archaeological research, they do not have to remain that way.

LINDA FRANCE STINE
MELANIE A. CABAK
MARK D. GROOVER

Blue Beads as African-American Cultural Symbols

ABSTRACT

Blue beads are consistent finds at African-American sites. Archaeologists acknowledge these artifacts were used for adornment, yet some researchers also propose beads possessed additional cultural meaning among African Americans. For this study bead data from African-American sites in the South are analyzed. The results indicate blue is the predominant bead color. The prevalence of these items suggests they may indeed have been an important yet unrecognized aspect of African-American culture. The multiple underlying meanings assigned to blue beads are considered through reference to ethnographic information, folklore, and oral history associated with West and Central Africa and the Southeast.

Introduction

Although almost always recovered in small quantities, historical archaeologists have nevertheless noted that glass beads, especially blue beads, are typical finds at African-American sites. These artifacts have been interpreted in several ways. At a minimal level, beads are considered to be merely clothing or personal artifacts. Several archaeologists suggest beads were primarily used by women (Smith 1977:160–161; Drucker and Anthony 1979: 79; Otto 1984:73, 174–175; Yentsch 1994a, 1994b) and reflect cultural practices derived from West Africa (Handler et al. 1979:15–18; Armstrong 1990:272; Yentsch 1994a, 1994b). Concerning blue beads, Ascher and Fairbanks (1971:8) suggest they are similar to trade beads highly valued in Africa. Smith (1977:161) and Otto (1984:75) propose they are ethnic markers for sites occupied by African Americans. Adams (1987:14) argues blue beads were symbolically meaningful artifacts for slaves between the 18th and 19th centuries. An alternative

interpretation is that the cultural meaning assigned to blue beads is a creation of archaeologists and has had little historic validity among African Americans in the past (e.g., Wheaton 1993:80).

The following essay evaluates the assumptions that blue is the most common bead color on slave sites and that these objects were symbolically laden artifacts for African Americans. *Interpretation is based upon five interrelated facts:* (1) between the 16th and 19th centuries Central and West African cultural groups used beads, in addition to other items, for adornment and as personal charms for protection from misfortune and illness; (2) these African-derived practices were in turn transplanted and reinterpreted by African Americans in the South; (3) enslaved African Americans participated in informal economies that provided limited access to material goods such as beads; (4) belief in the evil eye was present among slaves in the study region; and (5) the color blue, a recurring and abundantly documented motif in African-American folklore along the Sea Islands, is considered to be a potent form of spiritual protection. The role of blue beads considered in this essay is anthropologically relevant because these items provide insight concerning the African-American worldview they embodied. Hence, these artifacts and their related meanings offer an emic perspective regarding African-American material culture during the slavery era.

The results of archaeological data analysis are first presented followed by a brief overview of bead use in Africa. A discussion of how African Americans may have obtained beads is then offered. This study then considers the multiple functions of beads among slaves. This paper concludes with a discussion of the worldview and cultural processes illustrated by the use of blue beads by African Americans.

Archaeological Data

In plantation archaeology a systematic or synthetic study of beads from African-American sites has yet to be conducted. A data set based on the distribution of beads at African-American sites was

Historical Archaeology, 1996, 30(3):49–75.
Permission to reprint required.

therefore assembled to determine if blue was indeed the most common bead color at these sites. Artifact analysis was conducted at both national and regional levels. Data from North American sites illustrate general trends of bead use. To provide finer grained analytical resolution and a regional perspective, beads from South Carolina and Georgia sites are in turn considered in greater detail. Archaeological data incontrovertibly demonstrate blue beads are consistently represented more often than any other bead color on African-American sites.

Preliminary data were collected by placing a bead survey form in the spring 1994 issue of *African-American Archaeology* (No. 10). The survey form listed frequency of beads found by color, probable date range, and context. Beads were recovered from rural and urban sites, and the contexts consisted of burials, middens, and structural features. Information provided in the survey responses was supplemented with published testing and excavation reports. The survey responses were from Alabama, California, Georgia, Kentucky, Louisiana, North Carolina, South Carolina, Tennessee, Virginia, Montserrat, and Barbados. These data are from a total of 51 temporal components and 26 sites. As illustrated in Table 1, considerable variety exists within this sample. Blue beads comprise 27 percent of the total site sample (n = 1,676). Blue is the most prevalent bead color and blue beads are present in 63 percent of the components. No other color is as uniformly represented. The difference in the distribution of beads by color at these sites proved to be statistically significant ($X^2 = 1,462.29$, $df = 10$, $p = <.001$). The unidentified bead category was removed before calculating this statistic for glass beads. The assembled information clearly illustrates that although blue is not always the most prevalent bead color at each African-American site across the country, blue nevertheless is the most consistent bead color present at each African-American site. No other bead color is as uniformly represented in the national site sample.

To provide finer grained analytical resolution, a data set based on beads from a specific geographic region was assembled. Beads from African-American sites in South Carolina and Georgia were ex-

TABLE 1
BEAD COLOR DISTRIBUTIONS FOR AFRICAN-AMERICAN SITES

Bead Color	Bead		Components	
	N	%	N	%
Blue	448	26.73	32	62.75
Black	64	3.82	6	11.76
Green	50	2.98	5	9.80
Clear	343	20.46	14	27.45
White	139	8.29	16	31.37
Multicolor	200	11.93	9	17.65
Red	79	4.71	10	19.61
Purple/Pink	17	1.01	3	5.88
Amber	12	0.72	3	5.88
Yellow	15	0.89	6	11.76
Brown	232	13.84	4	7.84
Stone	4	0.24	4	7.84
Shell	11	0.66	4	7.84
Unidentified	62	3.70	12	25.53
Total	1,676	99.98		

Sources: Survey responses supplemented by Ascher and Fairbanks (1971); Smith (1975, 1977); Good (1976); Handler and Lange (1978); Drucker and Anthony (1979); Wheaton et al. (1983); Carnes (1984); Zierden et al. (1986); Gardner (1987); Watters (1987); Babson (1989); Shogren et al. (1989); Wayne and Dickinson (1990); Pogue and White (1991); Norrell and Meyer (1992); Praetzellis and Praetzellis (1992); Stine (1993); Heath (1994); Stine et al. (1994); O'Malley (1995); Steen (1995).

amined in greater depth due to the larger number of African-American sites that have been investigated in these states. The geographic setting of the majority of the study sites was the lower coastal plain and coastal areas in South Carolina. The level of investigation for the site sample was either intensive testing or excavation. Archaeological investigations that relied only on survey methods were not considered since survey methods usually result in low recovery rates for small artifacts. Data were obtained primarily from published books and compliance reports. Information concerning the geographic setting, site function, excavation methods, temporal periods, bead colors, bead types, counts, and authors' interpretations of the beads was tabulated. Frequency and color were the most consistently recorded attributes of analysis. Bead type and size were not always recorded or comparable. The

TABLE 2
BEAD COLOR BY SITE FUNCTION ON AFRICAN-AMERICAN SITES IN
SOUTH CAROLINA AND GEORGIA

Bead Color	Domestic		Kitchen		General		Total	
	%	(N)	%	(N)	%	(N)	%	(N)
Blue	47.6	(101)	24.4	(10)	20.9	(29)	35.7	(140)
Black	15.6	(33)	2.4	(1)	10.8	(15)	12.5	(49)
Green	9.0	(19)	4.9	(2)	3.6	(5)	6.6	(26)
Clear	6.6	(14)	12.2	(5)	2.2	(3)	5.6	(22)
White	4.2	(9)	36.6	(15)	45.3	(63)	22.2	(87)
Multicolor	3.8	(8)	7.3	(3)	7.2	(10)	5.4	(21)
Red	2.8	(6)			2.9	(4)	2.6	(10)
Unidentified	3.3	(7)	7.3	(3)	3.6	(5)	3.8	(15)
Purple/Pink	2.8	(6)					1.5	(6)
Amber	1.4	(3)	4.9	(2)			1.3	(5)
Yellow	1.4	(3)					0.8	(3)
Stone	0.9	(2)			0.7	(1)	0.8	(3)
Gray	0.5	(1)					0.3	(1)
Gold					0.7	(1)	0.3	(1)
Brown					0.7	(1)	0.3	(1)
Shell					1.4	(2)	0.5	(2)
Total	99.9	(212)	100	(41)	100	(139)	100.2	(392)

Sources: Rayfield Plantation (Ascher and Fairbanks 1971); 38BK160 (Drucker and Anthony 1979); 38CH109 (Carrillo 1980); 38BK75, 38BK76, and 38BK245 (Wheaton et al. 1983); Cannon Plantation (Otto 1984); 38CH322 (Brockington et al. 1985); 38DR38 (Zierden et al. 1985); Midway Plantation (Smith 1986); 38BK202 (Zierden et al. 1986); 38BU805 (Trinkley 1986); 9CM172, 9CM183, and 9CM194 (Adams 1987); 38GE267 (Michie 1987); 38AB9 (Orser et al. 1987); 38GE306 (Michie and Mills 1988); 38BU96 (Trinkley 1990); 38CH1081, 38CH1083, and 38CH1086 (Wayne and Dickinson 1990); 38GE410 (Weeks 1990); 38BU805 (Espenshade and Grunden 1991); 38BU966 and 38BU967 (Kennedy et al. 1991); 38BU1214 (Trinkley 1991); 38CH1100 and 38CH1101 (Wood 1991); 38CH1098 (Gardner 1992); 38CH1199/38CH1200 (Gardner and Poplin 1992); 38RD397 (Groover 1992); 38BK1608 (Steen 1992); 38LU323 (Trinkley et al. 1992); 38GE377 (Adams 1993); 38BU880 (Kennedy et al. 1993); Bowers Housesite (Paonessa et al. 1993); 38CH127 (Trinkley 1993a); 38GE294, 38GE297, and 38GE340 (Trinkley 1993b); 38FL240 (Trinkley et al. 1993); 38CH812 and 38CH1214 (Wheaton 1993); 38BU791 (Eubanks et al. 1994); 38BU890 (Garrow 1994); 38BU647 (Kennedy et al. 1994); 38BR522, 38BR619, and 38BR629 (Crass and Brooks 1995); 38BK38 (unpublished).

bead data were placed in three broad temporal periods: the colonial period—18th century; the antebellum period—19th century, pre-Civil War; and the postbellum-modern period—post Civil War to 1950. Recovery locations and contexts were separated according to the categories of African-American residences—slave quarters, tenant and yeoman farms; plantation kitchens; and plantation complexes. The plantation complex category refers to excavations around the main house or excavations that did not firmly determine the specific functional context yet contained a large proportion of Colono Ware. It is assumed this distinctive ware indicates an African-American presence (Ferguson 1992).

The South Carolina and Georgia study sample is composed of 392 beads recovered from 50 sites that possessed 58 temporal components (Table 2). Within this site sample, beads were recovered at 42 sites, and blue beads were found at 34 sites representing 81 percent of the sites that contained beads. Glass is the primary material type but plastic, shell, and stone beads were also recovered. The sample contained a wide range of bead colors including red, green, yellow, pink, blue, gray, and white. There were also several polychrome beads—i.e., two-toned, striped, and floral—within the sample. The results clearly indicate blue is the predominant color of beads found on sites inhabited by African Amer-

TABLE 3

BEAD COLOR BY TEMPORAL PERIOD ON AFRICAN-AMERICAN DOMESTIC SITES IN SOUTH
CAROLINA AND GEORGIA

Bead Color	Period					
	Colonial		Antebellum		Postbellum	
	%	(N)	%	(N)	%	(N)
Blue	51.1	(24)	52.2	(60)	34.0	(17)
Black	2.1	(1)	15.7	(18)	28.0	(14)
Green	6.4	(3)	7.0	(8)	16.0	(8)
Clear	6.4	(3)	8.7	(10)	2.0	(1)
White	4.3	(2)	2.6	(3)	8.0	(4)
Multicolor	12.8	(6)			4.0	(2)
Red	2.1	(1)	2.6	(3)	4.0	(2)
Unidentified	12.8	(6)	0.9	(1)		
Purple/Pink			3.5	(4)	4.0	(2)
Amber			2.6	(3)		
Yellow			2.6	(3)		
Stone	2.1	(1)	0.9	(1)		
Gray			0.9	(1)		
Total	100.1	(47)	100.2	(115)	100.0	(50)

Sources: Rayfield Plantation (Ascher and Fairbanks 1971); 38BK160 (Drucker and Anthony 1979); 38BK75, 38BK76, and 38BK245 (Wheaton et al. 1983); Cannon Plantation (Otto 1984); 38CH322 (Brockington et al. 1985); 38BK202 (Zierden et al. 1986); 38BU805 (Trinkley 1986); 9CM172, 9CM183, and 9CM194 (Adams 1987); 38GE267 (Michie 1987); 38AB9 (Orser et al. 1987); 38GE306 (Michie and Mills 1988); 38BU96 (Trinkley 1990); 38CH1081, 38CH1083, and 38CH1086 (Wayne and Dickinson 1990); 38GE410 (Weeks 1990); 38BU805 (Espenshade and Grunden 1991); 38BU966 and 38BU967 (Kennedy et al. 1991); 38BU1214 (Trinkley 1991); 38CH1100 and 38CH1101 (Wood 1991); 38BK1608 (Steen 1992); 38GE377 (Adams 1993); 38BU880 (Kennedy et al. 1993); Bowers Housesite (Paonessa et al. 1993); 38GE297 and 38GE340 (Trinkley 1993b); 38FL240 (Trinkley et al. 1993); 38BU791 (Eubanks et al. 1994); 38BU890 (Garrow 1994); 38BU647 (Kennedy et al. 1994); 38BR522, 38BR619, and 38BR629 (Crass and Brooks 1995); 38BK38 (unpublished).

icans in the South Carolina and Georgia region. Blue beads comprise 36 percent (n = 140) of the total sample. For the analysis category of location, blue beads comprise 48 percent of the sample from African-American residences, 24 percent of the sample from plantation kitchens, and 21 percent of the sample from general plantation contexts (Table 2). A chi-square test of association indicates the difference in the distribution of blue beads between African-American domestic components and other plantation areas is significant (X^2 = 28.7784998, df = 1, p = < 0.01). This comparison indicates while blue beads were typically lost in a variety of locations on plantations, these beads were predominantly lost or intentionally discarded in and around African-American residences.

Consideration of African-American sites, con-sisting of slave, tenant, and yeoman domestic components, by temporal period, indicates blue beads were much more prevalent during the colonial and antebellum periods than after the Civil War (Table 3). Blue beads represent 51 percent of the sample during the colonial period and 52 percent during the antebellum period. During the postbellum period both blue (34%) and black (28%) are the predominant bead colors. A chi-square test demonstrated the difference in the distribution of blue beads between the colonial-antebellum and postbellum periods is statistically significant (X^2 = 4.88138515, df = 1, p = < 0.05).

Analysis results firmly demonstrate that blue beads were deposited most often in African-American domestic areas, particularly during the colonial and antebellum periods in South Carolina and Georgia. If the distribution of blue beads was only a result of availability and not cultural preference, blue beads should have been found equally in all areas of the plantation.

West and Central African Antecedents

In order to achieve an enhanced understanding of bead use among African Americans in the South, the African antecedents of this practice must first be considered. Among the estimated 10 million Africans brought to the New World between the 16th and mid-19th centuries (Blassingame 1974:3), approximately 40 percent originated in Kongo and Angola (Thompson 1993:56). These areas of Africa included many different tribes such as the Ibo, Ewe, Biafada, Bakongo, Wolof, Bambara, Ibibio, Serer, and Arada (Blassingame 1974:2). Since African-American slaves originated from such a wide range of cultural groups, it is difficult to associate specific African cultural groups with specific regions in the South. Also, slave traders and holders were aware of ethnic differences (Littlefield 1981:115–173) and therefore often intentionally broke up ethnic groups and families (Genovese 1974). Consequently, specific, as opposed to regional, origins for individual plantation inhabitants are very difficult, if not impossible, to reconstruct.

Many South Carolina slaves, a regional focus of this study, originated from the Kongo-Angola region and the rice growing areas of Gambia and the Windward coast. A study of slaves imported to Charleston from 1733 to 1807 records six major source areas for slaves: Senegambia (19.7%); the Windward Coast (23.3%); Gold Coast (13.4%); Whydah-Behhin-Calabar area (3.7%); Congo (16.9%); and Angola (23%) (Pollitzer 1975:268; cf. Littlefield 1981:109–114; Creel 1988:16–44; Ferguson 1992:61; Kernan 1993:30; Thompson 1993: 56). Africans from Gambia were desired by South Carolina planters because they already had specialized knowledge needed for the successful cultivation of rice and indigo, which were important regional cash crops (Creel 1988:34–36; Ferguson 1992:61).

Due to the demographic realities of the African slave trade, discussed above, African-American culture in the South during the era of slavery should therefore be regarded as a fusion of African-inspired cultural forms and practices. Hence, it is expected that bead use among enslaved African-Americans represents a pan-cultural phenomenon derived from African origins. It is not only difficult but counterproductive to attempt to identify direct, one-to-one correspondences between artifact patterning and artifact types at specific plantation sites and specific ethnic groups in Africa. However, it is not unreasonable to anticipate that broadly based practices and beliefs associated with beads and personal ornamentation, in addition to other aspects of the material domain, both survived the middle passage and were eventually transformed into new cultural traits by enslaved African Americans in the South.

Long before the arrival of Europeans, beads were an important aspect of West and Central African material culture. Beads had many religious and secular uses in Africa. Lois Dubin (1987:122), who has collected and studied beads from around the world, notes that "beads are central to the lives of all Africans" and have a wide variety of functions. Historic travelers to West Africa recorded that people used beads to adorn their body, as jewelry, to adorn ceremonial costumes, and to decorate everyday clothes. Today, and in the past, West Africans wear beads in their hair, on clothing, and as necklaces, bracelets, waistbands, and anklets. Beads were a form of personal adornment and perhaps more importantly, they conveyed social meaning and denoted information concerning wealth, age grade, marital status, artistic attitudes, and political, religious, and cultural affiliation. Beads were also important trade items often used as currency. These items were also associated with myths, with ceremonies such as rites of passage, and with religious cults, and were made into sculptural beadwork and worn as amulets and charms (Rattray 1923:147, 187, 1927:22, 46, 62, 66, 171; Ellis 1964:232, 235, 237, 240; Farrow 1969:47; MacDonald 1969:58–61; Courlander 1975:120–123; Fisher 1984:67–106; de Marees 1987; Dubin 1987:119–151). Furthermore, different regions or cultural groups had particular preferences for certain bead types and colors (Erikson 1969:59; de Marees 1987:56; Nourisson 1992:29). In contemporary West Africa, beads manufactured in the 19th century are often curated and highly valued (DeCorse 1989:44; Steiner 1990:59). For example, although Côte d'Ivoire women of West Africa wear modern European-style jewelry manufactured from gold, silver, and plastic, glass trade beads are nevertheless still valued and purchased for their spiritual potency (Steiner 1990:59).

The manner in which West and Central Africans incorporated beads into charms, amulets, and fetishes is particularly relevant to this study. Charms, considered to have spiritual power, are used to insure success in all aspects of life, including journeys, hunting, farming, and romance, as well as to ward off evil, sickness, and misfortune, and to gain material goods (Kingsley 1897:448; Nassau 1904: 78, 83; Lowie 1924:269–270; Wallis 1939:33–34; Farrow 1969:122–124). Some charms are used to avert witchcraft, particularly as manifested through illness and misfortune. Amulets therefore have an important function in health care among West and Central African groups. For example, among various West African groups, where infant mortality is high, it is thought that mothers and children particularly require the protection provided by charms and amulets (Rattray 1927:22; Ellis 1964:232; Janzen 1982:55–56; de Marees 1987:25, 75). Farrow (1969:84) notes that among the Yoruba *Abiku* cult, to prevent harm from the vengeful spirits of children that died in infancy, "iron rings, waist belts, anklets, and wristlets of beads and other charms are put upon young children from their earliest days." A string tied around the waist of a child is also a widespread West African charm (Milligan 1912: 220). American writer Era Bell Thompson (1954: 26) observed a Liberian infant encircled by a string of blue beads (cf. DeCorse [1997]). This amulet is worn throughout childhood for good health. In Kongo terms, this practice keeps the child's soul round, or rich, with life's possibilities. A mother would "fashion a small round disk from wood or a seed, perforate it, and attach it to a string to hang over his heart or tie around her neck, waist, or ankle. This would become a guide and charm to the child's soul, guarding its round boundaries, charting the

child's safe circuit to maturity and old age" (Thompson 1993:57).

Charms were expressed verbally, through ceremony or as material objects (Milligan 1912:220; Farrow 1969:121). Amulets, charms, and fetishes are any material object that is thought to contain spiritual power (Lowie 1924:268–270; Wallis 1939:33–34; Hoebel 1966:487). Many items are used for charms including beads, animal bones or teeth, stones, iron, broken pottery, feathers, bits of skin, leaves, hair, and fingernails (Nassau 1904:76, 84–85; Puckett 1975:172, 217–218). There are principally two types of charms, consisting of personal and household amulets (Burton 1864:361; Baudin 1885:83; Ellis 1894:118; Parrinder 1957:114–115, 1961:160–161; Farrow 1969:123; Awolalu 1979: 79). Personal amulets are worn around the neck, arm, wrist, or ankle. These objects protect the wearer. Household amulets are placed on the house or on household property to protect the actual structure, its contents, and residents (Parrinder 1957: 114–115, 1961:160–161; Nassau 1969:85; Ellis 1970:92).

Beads were, and still are, typically used for making amulets and charms among many African cultures (Baudin 1885:83; Rattray 1927:22; Nassau 1969:82). However, within some regions, such as southern Togo, beads are rarely used in charms (Nourisson 1992:32). Among the people of the Gold Coast, bead charms were often worn by pregnant women on their wrists, ankles, and neck to avert harm (Ellis 1964:232). Among the Ewe, a Popo bead and human tooth worn around the neck prevented sickness (Ellis 1970:93). In 17th-century Guinea, the traveler de Marees (1987) recorded that shirts fashioned like nets were worn by small children. The children's parents would:

> drape the Net extensively with their Fetissos, such as little golden crosses, tie strings of beads around the children's hands, feet and neck, and fill their hair with little shells, which they greatly esteem; for they say that as long as the young child is draped with this Net, the Devil cannot catch the child or carry it away; but without it would be carried away by the Devil. They highly esteem the Fetisso of the Beads which they hang around the neck of the little child and they consider it protection against vomiting, falling, bleeding, harmful animals, unhealthiness, and for sleeping well (de Marees 1987:25).

In contemporary Guinea, this custom persists and parents still adorn and protect their infants with various amulets, beads, cowrie shells, and bangles (de Marees 1987:25).

The above review illustrates that in West Africa beads were often used in amulets for protection from harm and illness. The archaeological data gathered for this study indicate blue beads are associated with African-American sites. To understand the role of these artifacts in the lives of African Americans it is, in turn, necessary to consider the meaning and uses of blue beads in West Africa.

European visitors to West Africa between the 15th and 19th centuries observed that certain blue beads were highly valued. The most well-known bead is the aggri or akori bead, which was possibly blue (Fage 1962; Landewijk 1970; Davison et al. 1971; Kalous 1979). Magical and mythical qualities were associated with this bead. Aggri beads were incorporated into jewelry, but they were also used in ritual and placed in burials. Among the Ashanti aggri beads were often placed in containers during offerings and divination (Parrinder 1961:67). Along the Gold Coast this bead was worth its weight in gold, and a person's wealth could be determined by the number of aggri beads they owned (MacDonald 1969:58–61).

Upon initial consideration the aggri appears to be an appropriate example of blue bead use in West Africa that could demonstrate continuity with African-American practices. However, as a caveat it should be emphasized that West and Central African groups exhibited tremendous cultural variation. DeCorse ([1997]) also emphasizes that beads had numerous uses and meanings among cultural groups involved in the Atlantic slave trade, and likewise slaves may have had a range of uses and meanings for blue beads. In summary, this section has attempted to illustrate that beads in West and Central Africa were important social, economic, and religious items that were used for a wide range of purposes.

Bead Sources and Availability of Goods

Archaeological data indicate the distribution of beads at South Carolina and Georgia sites is sta-tistically significant in terms of differences in color, context, and time periods. This section considers the crucial element of acquisition—or how enslaved African Americans, tenants, and freed persons may have obtained beads. Archaeological interpretation of personal artifacts such as beads is usually based on the assumption that they were bought by planters for African Americans, were hand-me-downs from the planter family, or were stolen (e.g., Kelso 1984: 190, 201). A few reports indicate that some personal items may have been curated heirlooms or were produced by slaves for their own use (e.g., Drucker and Anthony 1979; Wheaton et al. 1983; Otto 1984: 73, 174–175; Zierden et al. 1986). If slaves indeed had little or no influence in the items they used in daily life, then the distribution of beads identified in this study may merely reflect the tastes or economies of planters and overseers. If slaves were able to make decisions concerning their material life, then bead color preferences should be viewed as an aspect of African-American consumerism within the informal slave economy.

Conversely, beads from African-American sites may merely reflect availability and manufacturing trends rather than slave or planter choices or cultural preferences. In order to explore these issues, the color distributions of glass beads that were produced, sold, and traded between the 17th and 19th centuries were investigated. This proved a daunting task, since published reports detailing production types and numbers are not readily available. Numerous glassmakers produced beads throughout Europe, Asia, and the Middle East and most kept information about processes, amounts, and other manufacturing arts secret (e.g., Moore 1924:48–50; Robertson 1969:38; Kidd 1970; Smith and Good 1982:12–15; Harris 1984; DeCorse 1989:41–44). Two published bead catalogs suggest that manufacturers offered more varieties of blues, blue-greens, and greens than other colors (Karklins 1985: 12, 43). This trend could be the result of consumers purchasing more shades of blue and green, or merely bead manufacturing technology. In discussing glass production, Jones and Sullivan (1989:14) state that "cobalt is one of the strongest colorants available to glass manufacturers." Nonetheless, if bead consumers refused to purchase, trade, or use blue beads, it is doubtful that so many varieties would have been available in bead catalogs.

Concerning bead sources, colonial merchants and planters often participated in both the African and Indian trade. Deeply involved in the mercantile system, merchants and planters ordered goods on credit from factors in colonial ports such as Charleston, or directly from factors in London (Rawley 1981; Stine 1990; Braund 1993). During the 17th century, Amsterdam was the ''. . . great entrepôt for western Europe. To it came the products needed in the slave trade: cloths from many nations, beads, copper, iron, brandy, and tobacco, and numerous other commodities. Slave ships from foreign nations, notably England, often put into Amsterdam to acquire wares for the African trade'' (Rawley 1981: 81). Traders and planters often purchased goods from the same London merchants (Stine 1990:27). Late 18th-century Bristol slave trader James Rogers mentions his captain buying trade goods at ''the bead store'' in London. There he ''found beads plentiful, but he had not determined the price for cowries'' (Rawley 1981:186).

Bristol slave ships carried numerous slaves to Virginia and the Carolinas. Some local traders waited and purchased leftover goods from African slave dealers in Virginia ports. Travelers and traders, in the words of John Lawson, ''came often to a good Market, at the Return of the *Guinea*-Ships for Negro's, and the Remnant of their Stores, which is very commodious for the *Indian*-Trade'' (Lefler 1967:94). Their merchandise likely included beads. This information suggests that a variety of goods were available in the colonies for the Indian trade as well as for resale to plantation owners, local storekeepers, and the general population.

Lists of trade goods, account books, and published histories of some of the great trading houses were consulted to gain a sense of the amounts and types of beads shipped to North America (e.g., Crane 1928; Coker 1976; Coker and Watson 1986; Wright 1986; Weisman 1989; Stine 1990; Merrell 1991; Braund 1993). Unfortunately, most trade lists merely record the price of strings of beads in number or weight of deerskins without mentioning color (e.g., Crane 1928:331–332). Occasionally a record with a little more detail is encountered, such as a listing that enumerated ''5 strings barley seeds, 5

strings common beads, 10 strings white enameled beads'' (Weisman 1989:67, Table 4).

Consumer Choice

The above discussion illustrates that primary and secondary information concerning the range and types of beads produced in the Old World and shipped to North America is not abundantly available. However, a substantial amount of information regarding the types of items preferred by traders and merchants, and perhaps more importantly, the influence exerted by consumers, has been recorded since the 17th century. The influence of local demand on the types of goods offered by European traders is illustrated in Senegal, West Africa (Opper and Opper 1989:5–6). In 1678 French voyager Jean Barbot noted that specific beads were preferred by certain African buyers. Some trade goods were purchased by inhabitants and remade into items that conformed to local taste (Opper and Opper 1989:7). West Africans in Senegal were willing to pay more for certain types of beads and often refused to purchase goods made in unpopular colors or shapes (Opper and Opper 1989:5–8).

In North America there are numerous examples of the effect of consumer choice on the types and varieties of colonial and antebellum trade goods, particularly for Native American contexts. Traders and factors often complained of kettles that were too large or of receiving shipments of beads and blankets that were the wrong colors—items that Native Americans, in turn, adamantly refused to purchase (e.g., Peake 1954:70; Stine 1990; Braund 1993: 121). William Byrd (in Tingling 1977:63–64) wrote to merchants Perry and Lane in 1686 complaining, ''Your duffeilds this year proved indifferent onely narrow & some too light a blew . . . beads you sent me [were] large white instead of small. I can by no means put them of, pray (if it's not too late) send me none but small white this year.'' Braund (1993: 121) writes that ''Creek spokesmen were very specific about what they needed and wanted in exchange for their deerskins.'' Thus, among Native Americans during the colonial period there existed a clear pattern of consumer choice that affected the quality, range, and types of goods that were traded, including beads. For example, in a recent study of Plains Indian bead use and ethnicity, researchers discovered that many tribal groups used similar colors and types of beads. The selection of design elements, however, was directly related to the ethnicity of the maker and the time period of manufacture (Logan and Schmittou 1995). Archaeological data likewise substantiate this interpretation. Beads from trading posts across North America illustrate the extent of variation in consumer demand that existed among Native Americans. Consequently, the distribution of beads recovered at individual posts was undoubtedly influenced by the cultural preferences of the native groups that were trading at specific posts (DeVore 1992:61). For example, 72 percent of the beads recovered from Fort Michilimackinac, Michigan, for contexts dating between 1714 and 1781, were white (Stone 1974). At Fort Vancouver, British Columbia, for contexts dating between 1829 and 1860, 57 percent of the beads found in the fort and 74 percent of the beads from the Indian trade store were white (Ross 1990). The most prevalent bead color from Fort Union, North Dakota, occupied between 1829 and 1865, was blue, comprising 43 percent of the bead assemblage (DeVore 1992).

Archaeological studies of Native American groups in the Eastern Woodlands indicate a similar pattern. The same bead types were traded throughout the area, but Native American groups firmly preferred specific colors and bead types (Smith 1983:151). For example, in the Northeast, red beads predominate at archaeological sites (Hamell 1983; Kenyon and Kenyon 1983:69; Smith 1983:151). Conversely, in the Chesapeake, blue beads and blue and white striped glass beads are by far the most prevalent on 17th-century Native American and trader-planter sites (Miller et al. 1983:133, Table 3). In Jamestown, between 1607 and 1608, Captain John Smith traded 4 lb. of beads for 600 bu. of corn, since he had convinced local leaders that blue beads were used by only the most high-status chiefs (Miller et al. 1983:127). Fourteen years and a rebellion later, "20,000 blue beads were paid for some mats," indicating blue beads were no longer viewed as scarce, high-status items (Miller et al. 1983:127). As the period of intense Indian trade

declined, so too did the number of blue and other beads in regional sites (Miller et al. 1983:130–132).

In a study that compared 19th- and 20th-century Upper Creek towns in Alabama and Georgia to Creek towns in Oklahoma, Good discovered a contrasting pattern in bead use. In Oklahoma Creek artifact assemblages "anything other than blue and 'white' faceted beads is in limited quantities; and of the faceted beads, there are always a greater number of blue ones." Varieties of blue beads were also the most prevalent in the Alabama and Georgia study sites (Good 1983:160, 162). Seminole sites dating to the 1830s also often contain large proportions of blue beads (Piper and Piper 1982; Piper et al. 1982; Weisman 1989:69–76).

The North Carolina Occaneechi, who were middlepersons in the southern piedmont trade between 1680 and 1710 (Stine 1990), did not prefer blue or even red beads, but white (Carnes 1987:151). Sissipahaw villagers between 1660 and 1680 preferred blue and white seed beads (Carnes 1987:151; Ward and Davis 1993:109, 141). In the village of Upper Saratown along the Dan River, the Sara also decorated their clothes with sewn white and blue seed beads, and occasionally wore necklaces and bracelets of large white, blue, and blue and white striped beads (Ward and Davis 1993:423–428).

Although blue was a common bead color used by Native Americans and Euroamericans, it is not the most prevalent color at all non-African-American sites. Native Americans displayed pronounced variation in bead use and preferences, especially during periods of culture contact and change. If Native Americans and Euroamericans could significantly influence the types of beads obtained from traders, then it is not unreasonable to infer that the distribution of beads characteristic of African-American sites is likewise quite possibly the result of cultural preferences and consumer choice rather than mere market availability. Consideration of the informal slave economy reinforces this interpretation.

The Informal Slave Economy

The idea that enslaved peoples had some control over their symbolic and material world has been discussed in recent archaeological studies (Single-ton 1991; Orser 1994). However, the notion of slaves as consumers appears contradictory. Archaeologists typically think about enslaved African Americans as producers, but seldom as consumers. One can infer that if slaves were also consumers, they may have influenced the types of goods made available for sale. In order to resolve this issue, archaeologists must first determine if slaves exercised decision-making in the acquisition of material goods such as beads. What were their opportunities to purchase them, and did they have the means to do so?

Although planters provisioned slaves, the quality and quantity of goods differed by individual inclination and wealth. On many plantations slaves were expected to contribute towards their own provisioning—from garden plots and wild foodstuffs (Berlin and Morgan 1990:3–4; McDonald 1990:187; Gasper 1991:134–135). As a consequence of this practice, an informal barter economy quickly developed in which slaves exchanged surpluses with each other, with plantation owners, and with local storekeepers (Berlin and Morgan 1990:12). In many regions slaves, and later tenants, excelled at poultry production, selling eggs and fowls both on and off the plantation (Schlotterbeck 1990:170, 189; Pulsipher 1991:150–155). Sunday markets were also commonplace, where slaves sold poultry, garden produce, fish, and handcrafts (Mintz and Hall 1960; Price 1966; Berlin and Morgan 1990:9–11, 13; Pulsipher 1990, 1991; Schlotterbeck 1990:173; 189). In the early 19th century, South Carolina slaves often personally sold goods at public markets (Campbell 1990:147).

Many slaves also labored extra hours during official rest periods, such as holidays, during the evening, on Saturday afternoons, and Sundays. They worked in their gardens or at their crafts, but some also toiled additional hours both on their own and on the planter's cash crops. Through these efforts they earned cash, either by direct wages or selling bales of cotton, cords of lumber, or other commodities. Some planters arranged for slaves to work for other planters as skilled laborers. In some cases, slaves received a portion of the wages. Over time occasional work privileges were viewed as

entitlements (Berlin and Morgan 1990:4; Campbell 1990:134, 141; McDonald 1990:187).

Several laws were passed in various regions to stop or control these practices but had little success (Berlin and Morgan 1990:10; Campbell 1990: 143–144; Schlotterbeck 1990:171). Slaves sold their legal—and illegal—goods to yeomen, to local storekeepers, to itinerant peddlers, and to planters (Berlin and Morgan 1990:12; Campbell 1990:140; McDonald 1990:195–197; Schlotterbeck 1990:173, 175, 190–191). During the later antebellum period some planters regained more control over their slaves' purchasing activities by issuing credit instead of cash. Planters also became factors for their slaves' goods (Campbell 1990:151). This modification of the informal economy in turn reduced direct access to markets.

Slaves rarely accumulated large sums of cash or credit. They could only marginally participate in personal enterprises outside the heavy demands of plantation labor. For example, Guignard Plantation slaves in upcountry South Carolina made about three dollars a year between 1802 and 1804. Campbell (1990:135) estimates the typical field hand earned between $3 and $8 annually. At the Gay Plantation in Louisiana, slaves in 1844 earned between $1 and $82. Between 1858 and 1859 slaves at Tureaud's Plantation earned between $1 and $170 (McDonald 1990:191, 199).

Slaves purchased a great variety of items, especially "tobacco, alcohol, cloth, clothing, bowls, pots, and other utensils" as well as jewelry, watches, and other personal goods (Berlin and Morgan 1990:13; McDonald 1990:135–136, 200–201; Schlotterbeck 1990:177). Larger commodities such as stock animals and furniture were also purchased, but less frequently (Berlin and Morgan 1990:13). When comparing Georgia and South Carolina plantation task labor systems, Joseph (1987) discovered a generalized pattern of slave purchases. The three general categories of purchased goods were improved subsistence items, high-status objects, and luxury consumables. He states, "Items which reflect personal/individual status, such as finer quality clothing, beads, elaborate buttons, eyeglasses, . . . or [artifacts which demonstrate] the success of entire households and families, such as wagon and buggies, decorative ceramics, mirrors, more elaborate furniture, and perhaps window glass, would be another means of expressing financial accomplishments through a material medium'' (Joseph 1987: 5). These items may have been multifunctional, communicating more than economic information within slave society.

Historical studies of the informal slave economy do not list the entire range of items that were purchased or traded. They do, however, mention many primary sources that list these goods. For example, *Negro Account Books* maintained by merchants and plantation records offer a wealth of information for future research. Besides urban merchant houses and stores, colonists could purchase goods from local stores. These stores became more plentiful in the antebellum period.

In the postbellum period, local stores gained an important role in the economic system, replacing many of the large urban factors (Stine 1989). Some of the larger landowners also operated commissaries for laborers (Campbell 1990:147). The store ledgers for Oakley Plantation, Louisiana ''demonstrate that African-American tenants bought 'lace,' 'trim,' 'beads,' and 'buttons' to ornament their clothing'' (Wilkie 1994:4; cf. Bell 1994:9). Likewise, an 1871 account book lists items purchased by an African-American servant from a Pike County, Georgia, store. She purchased a number of items on credit, including ''one string of beads'' worth $0.25 (Fincher 1871).

Extant information therefore underscores the fact that many enslaved individuals participated in local, informal economies. During the last four centuries, people of African descent have therefore had access, albeit differential and circumscribed, to material goods. These men and women often maintained exchange relations with individuals on other plantations, as well as traders, peddlers, and storekeepers. It is not far-fetched to consider they may have exercised influence on the varieties of items sold and bartered, such as beads. Since people of African descent were able to pick and choose *some* of the things in their lives—certain material items like beads, other objects for personal adornment, and perishable or curated luxury goods—then it follows that slaves could also influence the types

and varieties of goods stocked by merchants. Also, due to the autonomy represented by purchasing decisions, the personal artifacts encountered at slave sites may possess social and symbolic significance not usually recognized by archaeologists.

Beads and African Americans in the South

African-American culture developed and was transformed from West and Central African antecedents within the rural South, and beads illustrate one aspect of this historical process. Beads and their related meanings offer an emic understanding of rural African-American culture. In order to explore the role of beads among slaves, African-American belief systems must first be considered. While many slaves embraced Christianity and Islam, the forms of worship, organization of churches, tenets, and symbolic systems were often translated into a specifically African-American worldview (Herskovits 1962:207–260; Thompson 1993:74–95).

An appreciable degree of consistency existed with the rural, African-American worldview. This level of consistency suggests that the development of African-American culture from West and Central African antecedents and influences from European and Native American elements was a process characterized by selection and amplification (Herskovits 1962). This same cultural process has been documented by Joyner (1984:14) concerning the way a distinctive form of Christianity emerged from diverse West African belief systems and European influences among African Americans along the South Carolina and Georgia coast. Ferguson (1992) has likewise explored the fusion of cultural forms within African-American material culture during the colonial period. Thompson has also examined how this process is expressed in African-American art (Thompson 1993).

African and rural African-American belief systems were characterized by an animistic orientation in which the world was inhabited by both benign and malign spirits (Folklore Project [1930s]; Works Progress Administration [WPA] 1974[1940]; Puckett 1975; Joyner 1984). Individuals could both benefit and suffer from the whims of these forces, and conjurers were seen as powerful people who could control the supernatural. Illness and misfortune were typically explained through the actions of malevolent spirits.

Ex-slave interviews, compiled during the 1930s by the Works Progress Administration, convincingly demonstrate the persistence of West and Central African inspired animism in the South. The interviews were conducted among rural African Americans in a number of southern states. Although researchers using these collections have to be aware of the cultural context and biases in the oral history data, certain common themes emerge from these sources. As illustrated in the interviews, concern with good and bad spiritual forces was a central element in the rural African-American worldview. The mediator between the human and spiritual world was the minister and the conjurer. Besides prayer, one of the most efficient means for influencing the spiritual world was through the use of charms and amulets obtained from conjurers (WPA 1974[1940]:7, 20–21, 92, 124–125). The role of these individuals figured prominently in the culture of rural African Americans in the South. Blassingame (1974:45) notes, "Often the most powerful and significant individual on the plantation was the conjurer." For example, in 1822, Gullah Jack drew some of his charisma as a leading rebellion figure for Lowcountry slaves from his use of powerful charms (Herskovits 1962:138).

Like their West and Central African predecessors, conjurers claimed they could influence all aspects of life, such as causing and preventing sickness and death and influencing romance and success. Healers also had extensive knowledge of the medicinal qualities of roots and herbs which were used to cure the sick. Reliance upon conjurers, their spiritual knowledge, and the charms they manufactured extended to all practical affairs of life within southern African-American culture. Charms and amulets were manufactured from a wide range of materials, represented by bluestone, blue glass, lodestone, red pepper, graveyard dirt, horseshoes, red flannel, hairpins, copper, silver, human hair and nails, nutmeg, buckeyes, *beads*, finger rings, wrist or ankle bands of various materials, and perforated

coins (Botkin 1966:630–632; WPA 1974[1940]:74; Puckett 1975:235, 237, 240–241).

Personal charms in the South were typically worn on the neck, finger, wrist, waist, or ankle, tied or sewn to garments, and carried in the pockets, shoes, or hats (WPA 1974[1940]; Puckett 1975). Household charms were also distributed about the house, under or around the doorstep, placed under the bed or pillow, placed on a gatesill or doorsill, or over the door (Botkin 1966; WPA 1974[1940]). Personal charms, as noted in the ex-slave narratives, were used to prevent illness, ward away evil, and bring good luck in all aspects of life. Examples of personal charms consist of metal wire, heavy cord, or a leather strap worn on the ankle, wrist, or neck (WPA 1974[1940]:20–21; Rawick 1972a:235; Puckett 1975:314), nutmeg worn on a string around the neck to cure headaches (Rawick 1972b:244–245), and a silver coin worn around the ankle, neck, or in the shoe (WPA 1974[1940]:92, 125; Rawick 1972b:245, 1972c:31; Puckett 1975:288, 314; Escott 1979:109). In recent years archaeological examples of personal charms have been identified at numerous African-American sites (e.g., Adams 1987; McKee 1992; Patten 1992; Samford 1994; Young 1994; Singleton and Bograd 1995:23; Wilkie 1995; Russell 1996). Examples of likely house charms have likewise been documented at the Eno Quarter and Stagville Plantation, both near Durham, North Carolina, and at Prestwould Plantation in Mecklenburg County, Virginia (Samford 1996: 107–109).

The above information suggests that charms were a fundamental element of African-American material culture and belief systems. For example, Liza, a former slave from Harris Neck, Georgia, remembered that "most of the folks carry something for protection" (WPA 1974[1940]:125). Further, given their significance in West Africa, beads were probably a typical item used for charms in the South. African-American slaves, like their African predecessors, wore beads in jewelry or affixed to clothing. Although the role of beads among African Americans in the South was poorly documented, a few observations were recorded in the Caribbean. Griffin Hughes, a Caribbean planter, remarked in

1750 that his slaves adorned their bodies with beads, but he did not offer an explanation for their purpose (Handler and Lange 1978:147; Karklins and Barka 1989:75). Europeans in Barbados and Jamaica also observed plant material, such as seeds, that were used for beads (Handler and Lange 1978:147). Eighteenth-, 19th-, and 20th-century engravings, portraits, and photographs depict African Americans adorned with beads. Beads have likewise been worn by African-American women, and some men, since the colonial period, and are still worn today. Illustrations may be found in Hughes and Meltzer (1968), Wesley (1968), Johnson and Dunn (1986), Welty (1989), Gasper (1991: 134–135), Singleton (1991:163), and White (1991: 102).

Ex-slaves in Georgia during the 1930s recalled that beads were worn for adornment (Rawick 1972c:217, 312, 1972d:71). Callie Elder, an ex-slave from Athens, Georgia, stated that "them blue and white beads what the grown woman wore was just to look pretty. They never meant nothing else" (in Rawick 1972c:312). The response provided by Callie Elder is interesting, since it implies that the interviewer thought blue and white beads had symbolic meaning. As Callie Elder noted in the 1930s, beads were often used for adornment. However, it is clear from ethnographic information that beads were more than mere ornaments in Africa. The role of beads as socially meaningful objects probably continued in the South, particularly among African Americans along coastal South Carolina and Georgia. This inference is supported by several examples which suggest that bead charms were often used by African Americans to avert misfortune and illness. Beads were also used during prayer by Muslim and Catholic African Americans.

Botkin (1966:630), a folklorist, recorded that beads were worn as charms in the South. Further, blue beads on African-American sites have been interpreted to be indicative of the evil eye belief (Adams 1987). Blue beads are considered to be particularly effective in warding away the evil eye in many cultures (Maloney 1976). The persistence of the evil eye belief in the study region is confirmed by the presence of practicing Muslim slaves, his-

torical references to the evil eye, and archaeological evidence.

Ex-slave narratives collected during the Depression contain several direct references to Muslim religious practices (WPA 1974[1940]:76), including the use of prayer beads by Muslim African Americans. A former slave recalled that people would "pray on duh bead" (WPA 1974[1940]:166) and that "duh beads is on a long string. Belali he pull bead" as he prayed (WPA 1974[1940]:161). Former slave Charles Ball also spoke of Muslim practices on the plantation where he resided. Ball recalled that one slave prayed five times a day to the east (Frazier 1930:202). The presence of Muslim religious practices in the Southeast may have included the use of blue beads to ward away the evil eye. Christian tradition is also another source for the evil eye concept. Both the books of Proverbs and Ecclesiastes contain references to the evil eye (Dundes 1981:41–43).

Laura Towne, a reconstruction-era schoolteacher on St. Helena Island, South Carolina, recorded in her diary that the Gullah "believe in the evil eye, and also in the power of a good eye for healing" (Creel 1988:315). Likewise, C. R. Tredman, a writer for the WPA Folklore Project in South Carolina, recorded from an informant in the 1930s that, among African-American residents of Edisto Island,

> some would rather encounter the devil himself than the [witches] known as hags, for if one of them should cast her eye in their direction bad luck would overtake them. Some believe that a hag can bewitch a person by merely looking at them. This is known as the "evil eye" and is very much feared (Folklore Project [1930s]:1655, D-4-27A:2).

Puckett (1975:188) also recorded that African Americans used charms and amulets to avert the Judas eye, another name for the evil eye. Beads, then, were probably a typical element of charms that were worn and used for the prevention of illness and misfortune. The firmest archaeological evidence to date for the presence of the evil eye belief at a single plantation has perhaps been recovered from the Hermitage in Nashville. In addition to a predominance of blue beads—25 of 71 beads, comprising 33 percent of the total bead sample—three brass *figas*, which figure prominently in the evil eye complex (Distasi 1981), have been recovered from slave residences (Smith 1976; McKee 1992; Russell 1996).

In addition possibly to being used to avert the evil eye, beads were also used to bring good luck and prevent illness. Former slave Mollie Dawson recalled, "Most all de young girls had what we called a charm string. Dey was a lot pettier den dese beads we buys at de store now. Dis charm string was suppose ter bring good luck ter de owner of it" (Singleton 1991:163). As late as the 1930s, African Americans continued to wear beads to prevent illness. This practice is illustrated by an elderly African-American woman photographed by a fieldworker with the Farm Services Administration. The photograph's caption states that the woman wore "black beads to prevent heart trouble" (Nixon 1938). Mrs. Holmes, from Amite County, Mississippi, remembers her grandfather praying on a long string of beads. He would then put one of the beads in a cup of tea which he said would cure rheumatism (Rawick 1972d:254).

Besides the use of beads in daily life, archaeologists have discovered beads in African-American interments. These mortuary contexts provide additional information concerning symbolic bead use. During the excavations at Parris Island, South Carolina, an African-American graveyard was encountered (South et al. 1988:163–165). This cemetery, called the Means Graveyard, was part of the Means Plantation which was occupied during the 18th and 19th centuries. Within the graveyard, a pit containing charcoal and 3,481 glass beads, predominately blue and polychrome—blue, white, and coral—was found. Archaeologists found two more cremated, bead-filled pits located some distance from the African-American graveyard, but in the Means Plantation. These pits date between the late 17th and 19th centuries. By conducting interviews with members of the nearby African-modeled Yoruba ceremonial center, South was informed that West African inspired funerals involve two ceremonies, one in which the physical body is buried and another in which material possessions are cremated. South suggests these pits may represent the "practice of cremating material possessions" and offer firm evidence of African beliefs regarding the burial of the dead in the past (South et al. 1988:165).

In contrast to the Means Graveyard, most excavated African-American cemeteries do not contain very many beads. For example, excavation at seven cemeteries demonstrates burials containing beads average less than 5 percent of the total excavated burials (Handler and Lange 1978; Handler et al. 1979; Rose 1985; Parrington 1987; Watters 1987; Shogren et al. 1989; Cotter et al. 1992; LaRoche 1994). A good example of the mortuary distribution of beads is Elko Switch Cemetery which was in use between 1850 and 1920. This cemetery contained relatively few graves with beads (4% or two of 56 excavated burials). A middle-aged African-American woman over 50 years old (Burial 3), interred between 1850 and 1870, was buried with a necklace composed of 33 black wire-wound beads and one blue glass bead. Interestingly, the faceted blue bead was located in the center of the strand (Shogren et al. 1989:46–49, 143). Burial 24, an infant interred in 1895, contained 300 clear glass beads. Twenty-four of the beads are large necklace beads, and the rest are seed beads. This burial contained an ornately decorated coffin (Shogren et al. 1989:91–93).

Recently recovered information from the African Burial Ground in New York city also illustrates the persistence of African-derived cultural practices and bead use. Seven interments out of a sample of over 400 individuals contained beads. Interestingly, the burials containing beads were the remains of three women and two infants—the sex of the other two individuals was not determined. One woman exhibited dental mutilation, an African form of body decoration, and was buried with a waist strand composed of over 100 beads. One of the infants also possessed a waistlet. The beads associated with the other infant appear to have been worn in a necklace. The functional context of the beads interred with the other four individuals was not determined. Interestingly, blue and turquoise beads comprise 58 percent of the total sample (LaRoche 1994:3–20).

Mortuary information therefore illustrates beads were not typically an aspect of African-American burial practices. However, interments that do have beads appear to be associated more often with the graves of children, women, and conjurers (Handler et al. 1979; Rose 1985; Shogren et al. 1989; La-Roche 1994). Finally, although only quantifiable at the African Burial Ground, Newton, and Elko Switch cemeteries, blue beads in interments represent less than 30 percent of the beads by color. This distribution differs significantly with the number of blue beads (48%) from African-American domestic contexts ($X^2 = 14.34$, $df = 1$, $p = < 0.01$). More detailed analysis of burial data could refine these insights, but in general it appears that different colors of beads may have been used in daily life and burial practices by African Americans.

Future archaeological research pertaining to bead use in both mortuary and daily life contexts should be conducted. This study examined only beads contained in published reports and books. In these reports the only consistently recorded bead attribute is color. Additional research should encompass the variables of manufacturing techniques, shape, diaphaneity, color, and size. A detailed comparison of bead data from cemeteries may reveal that age, gender, and status are important variables related to bead use.

Color Symbolism

Color symbolism is a central aspect of Central and West African religious beliefs (Farrow 1969; Janzen 1977, 1982; Gleason 1987). Concern with the spiritual qualities attributed to specific colors was also reestablished in the New World, in both South (Sturm 1977; Gleason 1987; Omari 1994) and North America. In North America, colors are often imbued with meaning in African-American traditions. Florida author Zora Neal Hurston (1978) writes in *Mules and Men* that 20th-century candle colors had symbolic meaning as follows: blue provided protection and success, or in an inversion could cause death. White was used for peace, weddings, or ''to uncross''; red represented victory; pink, love and drawing away success; green aided success, or helped to ''drive off'' [haints]; yellow and brown brought money; lavender ''caused harm''; and black ''always [represented] evil or death'' (Wahlman 1993:113). Color continues to be a key element in the modern novels of African-

American writers such as Toni Morrison. Baby Suggs in *Beloved* contemplates blue and yellow, because ''that don't hurt nobody'' (Morrison 1988: 179).

In studies of quilts made by African Americans in North Carolina, researchers found that strong, contrasting color choice was an important aesthetic (McDonald 1986:36, Roberson 1988:5). Twentieth-century quilter Pecolia Warner used blue to symbolize truth, red for blood, white or silver for peace, yellow or gold for love, and brass for trouble. Black, although representing mourning in clothes, was used more for aesthetics by Warner as a contrast color in her quilts (Wahlman 1993:113). Various sources suggest that combined colors, such as red and white, in clothing and other textiles were often worn to ward away spirits (Wahlman 1993:113). In her folklore study of the Sea Islands, Twining (Wahlman 1993:113; 129 fn. 51) states that four colors—blue, black, red, and white—are ''linked to a deeper set of values and meanings in culture.'' These colors are often used by African Americans in combinations that express binary oppositions such as good and bad or safe and dangerous. Color choice is important in African-American aesthetics, and certain colors used in specific contexts carry specific symbolic meaning.

The archaeological data compiled for this study clearly indicate that blue beads are the predominant bead color associated with African-American residences in the study area between the 18th and 19th centuries. It is, in turn, proposed that the predominance of blue beads at African-American slave sites was due to intentional selection. Their meaning reflects both aesthetics and religious beliefs. Blue beads were used as adornment and probably worn, in part, as amulets for protection from illness and misfortune. This interpretation is supported through consideration of the meaning attributed to the color blue in rural African-American belief systems. These belief systems are particularly apparent within folklore and art.

A wide array of items were used to make charms in the Southeast, and the color blue was commonly used for items incorporated into personal charms. Concerning the qualities attributed to the colors used in charms, a sheriff in the Beaufort area of

South Carolina in the late 1960s wrote that root doctors "deal in tokens or charms of varying colors, and powders. A token of one color may cast a spell while another color is reputed to take it off" (McTeer 1970:72). Further, the Beaufort sheriff noted that blue charms are used for protection against evil and misfortune (McTeer 1970:24). In the South, powdered blue glass and bluestones were used in charms (Botkin 1966[1949]:632; Rawick 1972e:34; Puckett 1975:237, 240), blue ribbons are used in love charms (Hughes and Bontemps 1958: 194; Hurston 1978:283), and according to McTeer (1970:24) blue amulets are often used for romance. Jay Mills (1991, pers. comm.) has collected similar African-American oral histories about the importance of blue for protection and blessings in the Carolina Lowcountry.

In addition to personal charms, household charms and furnishings that contained the color blue were also used to protect the residences of rural African Americans. For example, in South Carolina and Georgia, African Americans in the past and present sometimes paint the attic louvers, gables, doors, and window molding blue for protection from spirits and witches (Folklore Project [1930s]: 1655, D-4–27A(1), D-4–27B(1); 1885, D-4–27A, F-2–18A; Crum 1968:85; Joyner 1984:153; Creel 1988:321; Conroy 1990:29; Wahlman 1993:113). During the 1930s, C. S. Murray, a Folklore Project writer, recorded that

> The color blue is a sure charm against both ghosts and lightning, the Sea Island negroes hold. This is one reason why the doors and windows of almost every negro cabin are painted bright blue . . . ghosts are afraid of this particular color because it reminds them of heaven. . . . They cannot face the sunlight, and neither can their eyes bear the sight of the color blue, for blue is the color of heavens. . . . Lightning too is an evil spirit. Holy blue has the power to divert it from harm, if the bolt should enter the cabin while the doors and windows are open and the blue charm is temporarily hidden. In fact the color blue is a charm against almost any kind of evil, for the negroes like to think God himself prefers blue. (Folklore Project [1930s]:1655, D-4-27A).

Concerning this practice, Creel likewise states that

> interviewers for the Federal Writers Project observed that nearly all the doors and windows of Gullah cabins were painted blue, the color of the heavens. One theory was that the custom of painting doors and windows blue was an

unconscious holdover from the early days of slavery in the Sea Islands when Gullahs were given the residue from indigo vats to use on the doors and windows of their cabins. However, this does not explain the fact that Gullah conjurers concocted pills for their patients, the color of which was usually blue also. Perhaps then, the shade blue was effective in keeping out spirits (Creel 1988:321).

A resident of Georgia recently stated he still trims his house in this color to honor his elders' beliefs that they warded their homes from spirits by "painting the shadows" (Joel Jones 1994, pers. comm.). Mrs. Elizabeth Porcher Mahoney, a native of Porcher's Bluff near Mt. Pleasant, South Carolina, also indicated that the blue trim around many local residences was to "keep out the hags" or witches (Elizabeth Porcher Mahoney 1995, pers. comm.). Mailboxes painted blue are also thought to keep away bad news (Steen 1992:53). Within the house, blue candles for furnishings are thought to provide success and protection (Hurston 1978:287). Similarly, when houses are cleaned, blue-colored scrub water is sometimes used to protect the residents (Hurston 1978:284, 286).

Bottle trees can be seen in Alabama, Georgia, Louisiana, and Mississippi. Brightly colored bottles, often blue, serve as protection from spirits (Melissa Beasley and John Cottier 1994, pers. comm.). Bottle trees, mirrors, and other objects could bless the person of good heart, or drive away those of evil intent (Thompson 1993:82–83; Vernon 1993:158). On a recent trip through Cleveland, Alabama, a decorated bottle tree placed in an African-American man's backyard was observed. Blue painted Clorox bottles were hung on a tree close to the property's boundary with a cemetery (Stine 1994, pers. observation). In a number of illustrations of African-American yards and graves blue is likewise a prevalent color (Thompson 1993:79, 86 Plates 70, 71, 72; 91 Plates 62, 83; 94 Plate 93).

Conclusion

Through consideration of archaeological, ethnographic, and historical information, the preceding study attempted to demonstrate that blue beads served as both jewelry for personal adornment and charms among African Americans. Concerning general trends, several observations are apparent. Analysis of archaeological data demonstrated that blue is the predominant color of beads recovered from African-American domestic sites occupied during the colonial and antebellum periods in South Carolina and Georgia. Archaeological data clearly indicate that while only a few beads are typically recovered at African-American sites and cemeteries, the differences in color distributions are significant. For the entire South Carolina and Georgia site sample, blue beads comprise 36 percent, or represent on average eight beads per site. Mortuary data indicate beads are usually associated with women and infants, which parallel the preventive role of beads in West and Central Africa. Ethnographic information and folklore studies also demonstrate a strong degree of continuity existed between African Americans and their West and Central African predecessors in both their general animistic belief systems and the use of charms to influence the world they perceived. Archaeologically derived interpretations are supported by historical observations and folklore.

Our interpretation described the distribution of a specific artifact type and the beliefs, or emic worldview, possibly expressed by these artifacts. However, information presented in this essay has archaeological and anthropological relevance concerning historical processes of cultural continuity and change that extend beyond an artifact study. Diverse Central and West African groups exhibited staggering variation in material culture related to ornamentation and associated belief systems. Within the colonial and antebellum South an amalgam of West and Central African groups were forced to survive in a new and often hostile setting. A consequence of this experience was that previous and specific cultural elements were selected, rejected, modified, and magnified by African Americans and a largely uniform African-American culture emerged, particularly along coastal South Carolina and Georgia.

The pervasive aspect of blue within the African-American worldview and material domain illustrates this process. From a multitude of cultural traditions and possibilities, African Americans along the Sea Islands of South Carolina and Georgia apparently selected blue as a socially meaningful cultural element. The symbolic role of this color, in the absence of clear African parallels, possibly represents the development of a uniquely African-American practice. The underlying reasons why this color was specifically selected are unknown, yet research conducted by psychologists indicates blue exhibits beneficial, curative qualities and has been used around the world to prevent illness and cure diseases (Birren 1961[1950]:37, 57, 109, 260, 1978:95; Mahnke and Mahnke 1987:13). These qualities parallel the role of blue as a form of protection from misfortune and sickness documented in the South. The selection of this culturally meaningful element was in turn amplified and expressed within the material domain of rural African Americans between the 18th and 20th centuries. This folk belief also persisted differentially to the present. Ex-slave Callie Elder stated that blue beads had no particular meaning but were merely for decoration. Conversely, former slave Mollie Dawson recalled that beads were worn for good luck. The elderly African-American woman photographed in the 1930s stated that black beads were worn to prevent heart trouble. These examples illustrate that the folk beliefs considered in this essay persisted among some African-American people and not others in the South. The meaning attributed to blue survived in several material domains, yet was lost or forgotten in others, such as the realm of personal ornamentation. Oral history and folklore reveal that quilts, window trim, scrub water, mailboxes, and candles were imbued with the beneficial quality attributed to blue. The prevalence of blue beads at African-American sites offers compelling evidence these items were likewise vested with this characteristic during the colonial and antebellum periods.

ACKNOWLEDGMENTS

Earlier versions of this paper were presented in 1994 at the annual meetings of the Southeastern Archaeological Conference in Lexington, Kentucky, and the American Anthropological Association in Atlanta, Georgia. The authors thank Christopher De-

Corse, Leland Ferguson, and Jay Mills for constructive suggestions on the subject. We also thank Thomas Wheaton for including the bead survey form in *African-American Archaeology* and appreciate the response from the newsletter's readers. Keith Derting of the South Carolina Institute of Archaeology and Anthropology was instrumental in helping locate reports and site information that formed the basis of the data set. Support for this study was provided by the Savannah River Archaeological Research Program. The authors assume responsibility for any errors in the essay.

REFERENCES

ADAMS, NATALIE
    1993   Archaeological Investigations at 38GE377: Examination of a Deep Creek Phase Site and a Portion of the Eighteenth-Century Midway Plantation. *Research Series* 37. Chicora Foundation, Columbia, South Carolina

ADAMS, WILLIAM H. (EDITOR)
    1987   Historical Archaeology of Plantations at Kings Bay, Camden County, Georgia. *Reports of Investigations* 5. Prepared by the Department of Anthropology, University of Florida, Gainesville. Submitted to the Naval Submarine Base, Kings Bay, Georgia.

ARMSTRONG, DOUGLAS
    1990   *The Old Village and the Great House: An Archaeological and Historical Examination of Drax Hall Plantation, St. Ann's Bay, Jamaica.* University of Illinois Press, Chicago.

ASCHER, ROBERT, AND CHARLES H. FAIRBANKS
    1971   Excavations of a Slave Cabin: Georgia, U.S.A. *Historical Archaeology* 5:3–17.

AWOLALU, J. O.
    1979   *Yoruba Beliefs and Sacrificial Rites.* Longman Group Limited, Burnt Mill, United Kingdom.

BABSON, DAVID W.
    1989   Pillars on the Levee: Archaeological Investigations at Ashland-Belle. Helene Plantation, Geismar, Ascension Parish, Louisiana. Report prepared by Midwestern Archaeological Research Center, Normal, Illinois. Submitted to Division of Archaeology, Louisiana Department of Culture, Recreation, and Tourism, Baton Rouge.

BAUDIN, REV. P
    1885   *Fetichism and Fetich Worshipers.* Benziger Brothers, New York.

BELL, ELIZABETH Y.
    1994   Buttons as Reflections of Plantation Culture. Paper presented at the Annual Meeting of the Southeastern and Midwestern Archaeological Conference, Lexington, Kentucky.

BERLIN, IRA, AND PHILLIPS A. MORGAN (EDITORS)
    1990   *The Slaves' Economy: Independent Production by Slaves in the Americas.* Frank Cass, London.

BIRREN, FABER
    1961   *Color and Psychology and Color Therapy: A Factual Study of the Influence of Color on Human Life.* Reprint of 1950 edition. University Books, Secaucus, New Jersey.
    1978   *Color and Human Response.* Van Nostrand Reinhold, New York.

BLASSINGAME, JOHN W.
    1974   *The Slave Community: Plantation Life in the Antebellum South.* Reprint of 1972 edition. Oxford University Press, New York.

BOTKIN, B. A.
    1966   *A Treasury of Southern Folklore: Stories, Ballads, Traditions, and Folkways of the People of the South.* Reprint of 1949 edition. Crown, New York.

BRAUND, KATHRYN E. HOLLAND
    1993   *Deerskins and Duffels: The Creek Indian Trade with Anglo-America, 1685–1815.* University of Nebraska Press, Lincoln.

BROCKINGTON, P., M. SCARDAVILLE, P. GARROW, D. SINGER, L. FRANCE, AND C. HOLT
    1985   Rural Settlement in the Charleston Bay Area: Eighteenth- and Nineteenth-Century Sites in the Mark Clark Expressway Corridor. Report prepared by Garrow and Associates, Atlanta, Georgia. Submitted to South Carolina Department of Highways and Public Transportation, Columbia.

BURTON, RICHARD F.
    1864   *A Mission to Gelele, King of Dahome.* Tinsley Brothers, London.

CAMPBELL, JOHN
    1990   As "A Kind of Freeman"?: Slaves' Market-Related Activities in the South Carolina Upcountry, 1800–1860. In *The Slaves' Economy: Independent Production by Slaves in the Americas,* edited by Ira Berlin and Phillips A. Morgan, pp. 131–169. Frank Cass, London.

CARNES, LINDA F.
    1984   Archaeological Investigations of Third Halifax Jail, Historic Halifax. North Carolina Historic Sites Division, Department of Cultural Resources, Raleigh.
    1987   Euroamerican Artifacts from the Fredricks, Wall, and Mitchum Sites. In The Siouan Project: Seasons I and II, edited by Roy S. Dickens, Jr., H. Trawick Ward,

and R. P. Steven Davis, Jr. *Research Laboratories of Anthropology Monograph* 1:141–165. University of North Carolina, Chapel Hill.

CARRILLO, RICHARD F.
1980   Green Grove Plantation: Archaeological and Historical Research at the Kinlock Site (38CH109), Charleston County. Report submitted to South Carolina Department of Highways and Public Transportation, Columbia.

COKER, WILLIAM S.
1976   Entrepreneurs in the British and Spanish Floridas, 1775–1821. In *Eighteenth-Century Florida and the Caribbean*, edited by Samuel Proctor, pp. 15–39. University Presses of Florida, Gainesville.

COKER, WILLIAM S., AND THOMAS D. WATSON
1986   *Indian Trader of the Southeastern Spanish Borderlands: Panton, Leslie and Company and John Forbes and Company, 1783–1847*. University of West Florida Press, Pensacola.

CONROY, PAT
1990   *The Water Is Wide*. Reprint of 1972 edition. Old New York Book Shop Press, Atlanta, Georgia.

COTTER, JOHN L., DANIEL G. ROBERTS, AND MICHAEL PARRINGTON
1992   *The Buried Past: Archaeological History of Philadelphia*. University of Pennsylvania Press, Philadelphia.

COURLANDER, HAROLD
1975   *A Treasury of African Folklore: The Oral Literature, Traditions, Myths, Legends, Epics, Tales, Recollections, Wisdoms, Sayings, and Humor of Africa*. Crown, New York.

CRANE, VERON W.
1928   *The Southern Frontier, 1670–1732*. Duke University Press, Durham, North Carolina.

CRASS, DAVID C., AND MARK J. BROOKS (EDITORS)
1995   Cotton and Black Draught: Consumer Behavior on a Postbellum Farm. *Savannah River Archaeological Research Papers* 4. South Carolina Institute of Archaeology and Anthropology, University of South Carolina, Columbia.

CREEL, MARGARET WASHINGTON
1988   *"A Peculiar People": Slave Religion and Community-Culture Among the Gullahs*. New York University Press, New York.

CRUM, MASON
1968   *Gullah: Negro Life in the Carolina Sea Islands*. Negro Universities Press, New York.

DAVISON, CLAIRE, ROBERT GIAUQUE, AND DESMOND CLARK
1971   Two Chemical Groups of Diachronic Glass Beads from West Africa. *Man* 6(4):645–659.

DeCORSE, CHRISTOPHER
1989   Beads as Chronological Indicators in West African Archaeology: A Reexamination. *Beads: Journal of the Society of Bead Researchers* 1:41–54.
[1997] Oceans Apart: African Perspectives on New World Archaeology. In *"I, too, Am America": Studies in African American Archaeology*, edited by Theresa A. Singleton. University Press of Virginia, Charlottesville, forthcoming.

DE MAREES, PIETER
1987   *Description and Historical Account of the Gold Kingdom of Guinea (1602)*, translated by Albert van Dantzig and Adams Jones. Oxford University Press, New York.

DeVORE, STEPHEN LEROY
1992   *Beads of the Bison Robe Trade: The Fort Union Trading Post Collection*. Friends of Fort Union Trading Post, Williston, North Dakota.

DISTASI, LAWRENCE
1981   *Mal Occhio [evil eye]: The Underside of Vision*. North Point Press, San Francisco, California.

DRUCKER, LESLEY M., AND RONALD W. ANTHONY
1979   The Spiers Landing Site: Archaeological Investigations in Berkeley County, South Carolina. Report prepared by Carolina Archaeological Services, Columbia, South Carolina. Submitted to U.S. Department of Interior, Heritage Conservation and Recreation Services, Interagency Archaeological Service, Atlanta, Georgia.

DUBIN, LOIS
1987   *The History of Beads: From 30,000 B.C. to the Present*. Harry N. Abrams, New York.

DUNDES, ALAN (EDITOR)
1981   *The Evil Eye: A Folklore Casebook*. Garland, New York.

ELLIS, A. B.
1894   *The Yoruba-Speaking Peoples of the Slave Coast of West Africa*. Chapman and Hall, London.
1964   *The Tshi-Speaking Peoples of the Gold Coast of West Africa*. Reprint of 1897 edition. Benin Press, Chicago, Illinois.
1970   *The Ewe-Speaking Peoples of the Slave Coast of West Africa*. Reprint of 1890 edition. Anthropological Publications, The Netherlands.

ERIKSON, JOAN M.
1969   *The Universal Bead*. W. W. Norton, New York.

ESCOTT, PAUL D.
1979   *Slavery Remembered; A Record of Twentieth-Century Slave Narratives*. University of North Carolina Press, Chapel Hill.

ESPENSHADE, CHRISTOPHER, AND RAMONA GRUNDEN
1991   Contraband, Refuge, and Freedman: Archaeological

and Historical Investigations of the Western Fringe of Mitchelville, Hilton Head Island, South Carolina. Report prepared by Brockington and Associates, Atlanta, Georgia. Submitted to Greenwood Development Corporation, Hilton Head Island, South Carolina.

EUBANKS, ELISE, CHRISTOPHER ESPENSHADE,
MARION ROBERTS, AND LINDA KENNEDY
1994   Data Recovery Investigations of 38BU791, Bonny Shore Slave Row, Spring Island, Beaufort County, South Carolina. Report on file, Brockington and Associates, Atlanta, Georgia.

FAGE, J. D.
1962   Some Remarks on Beads and Trade in Lower Guinea in the Sixteenth and Seventeenth Centuries. *Journal of African History* 3(2):343–347.

FARROW, STEPHEN S.
1969   *Faith, Fancies and Fetich or Yoruba Paganism.* Reprint of 1926 edition. Negro Universities Press, New York.

FERGUSON, LELAND
1992   *Uncommon Ground: Archaeology and Early African America, 1650–1900.* Smithsonian Institution Press, Washington, D.C.

FINCHER, JOSEPH TRAVIS
1871   Account Book of Mr. Joseph Travis Fincher of Pike County, Georgia. On file with Fincher's great-granddaughter, Linda Fincher Wood, Birmingham, Alabama.

FISHER, ANGELA
1984   *Africa Adorned.* Harry N. Abrams, New York.

FOLKLORE PROJECT
[1930s] Folklore Project, Works Progress Administration, No. 1655, D-4-27A(1), D-4-27B(1); No. 1885, D-4-27A, F-2-18A. Manuscripts Division, South Caroliniana Library, University of South Carolina, Columbia.

FRAZIER, E. FRANKLIN
1930   The Negro Slave Family. *Journal of Negro History* 15(2):198–259.

GARDNER, JEFFREY W.
1987   The Hunter's Hill Project: Historical and Archaeological Research at the Shute-Turner Farm, Davidson County, Tennessee. Ladies Hermitage Association, The Hermitage, Hermitage, Tennessee.
1992   Historic Adaptations Through Time: Archaeological Testing of Five Sites, Francis Marion National Forest, Berkeley and Charleston Counties, South Carolina. Report prepared by Brockington and Associates, Charleston, South Carolina. Submitted to the U.S.D.A. Forest Service, Francis Marion National Forest, Columbia, South Carolina.

GARDNER, JEFFREY W., AND ERIC POPLIN
1992   Wappo Plantation (38CH1199/1200): Data Recovery at an Eighteenth-Century Stono River Plantation in Charleston County, South Carolina. Report prepared by Brockington and Associates, Charleston, South Carolina. Submitted to the U.S.D.A., Agriculture Research Service, South Atlantic Area, and U.S. Vegetable Laboratory, Charleston, South Carolina.

GARROW, PATRICK
1994   Postbellum Life on Hilton Head Island: The Frazier Cabin Site. Paper presented at the Annual Meetings of Southeastern Archaeological Conference and Midwest Archaeological Conference, Lexington, Kentucky.

GASPER, DAVID BARRY
1991   Antiqua Slaves and Their Struggle to Survive. In *Seeds of Change: A Quincentennial Commemoration,* edited by Herman J. Viola and Carolyn Margolis, pp. 130–138. Smithsonian Institution Press, Washington, D.C.

GENOVESE, EUGENE D.
1974   *Roll, Jordan, Roll: The World the Slaves Made.* Vintage Books, New York.

GLEASON, JUDITH
1987   *Oya: In Praise of the Goddess.* Shambhala, Boston, Massachusetts.

GOOD, MARY E.
1976   Glass Beads from the First Hermitage. In An Archaeological and Historical Assessment of the First Hermitage, edited by Samuel D. Smith. *Research Series* 2:237–248. Division of Archaeology, Tennessee Department of Conservation, Nashville, and Ladies Hermitage Association, The Hermitage, Hermitage, Tennessee.
1983   A Comparison of Glass Beads from Upper Creek Indian Towns in the Southeast and in Oklahoma. *Proceedings of the 1982 Glass Trade Bead Conference, Rochester Museum and Science Center Research Records* 16:159–166. Charles F. Hayes III, editor. Rochester, New York.

GROOVER, MARK D.
1992   Of Mindset and Material Culture: An Archaeological View of Continuity and Change in the 18th-Century South Carolina Backcountry. *Volumes in Historical Archaeology* 20, edited by Stanley South. South Carolina Institute of Archaeology and Anthropology, University of South Carolina, Columbia.

HAMELL, GEORGE R.
1983   Trading in Metaphors: The Magic of Beads. *Proceedings of the 1982 Glass Trade Bead Conference, Rochester Museum and Science Center Research Records* 16:5–28. Charles F. Hayes III, editor. Rochester, New York.

HANDLER, JEROME S., AND FREDERICK W. LANGE
 1978 *Plantation Slavery in Barbados: An Archaeological and Historical Investigation.* Harvard University Press, Cambridge, Massachusetts.

HANDLER, JEROME S., FREDERICK W. LANGE, AND CHARLES E. ORSER
 1979 Carnelian Beads in Necklaces from a Slave Cemetery in Barbados, West Indies. *Ornament* 4(2):15–18.

HARRIS, ELIZABETH
 1984 Late Beads in the African Trade. *Archaeological Research Booklets* 19. Center for Books on Beads, G. B. Fenstermaker, Lancaster, Pennsylvania.

HEATH, BARBARA J.
 1994 An Interim Report on the 1993 Excavations: The Quarter Site at Poplar Forest, Forest, Virginia. Manuscript on file, Poplar Forest State Historic Site, Poplar Forest, Virginia.

HERSKOVITS, MELVILLE J.
 1962 *The Myth of the Negro Past.* Reprint of 1941 edition. Beacon Press, Beacon Hill, Boston, Massachusetts.

HOEBEL, E. ADAMSON
 1966 *Anthropology: The Study of Man.* McGraw-Hill, New York.

HUGHES, LANGSTON, AND ARNA BONTEMPS
 1958 *The Book of Negro Folklore.* Dodd, Mead, New York.

HUGHES, LANGSTON, AND MILTON MELTZER (EDITORS)
 1968 *A Pictorial History of the Negro in America.* Third edition, revised by C. Eric Lincoln and Milton Meltzer. Crown, New York.

HURSTON, ZORA NEALE
 1978 *Mules and Men.* Indiana University Press, Bloomington.

JANZEN, JOHN M.
 1977 The Tradition of Renewal in Kongo Religion. In *African Religions: A Symposium,* edited by Newell S. Booth, Jr., pp. 69–116. NOK, New York.
 1982 *Lemba, 1650–1930: A Drum of Affliction in Africa and the New World.* Garland, New York.

JOHNSON, THOMAS L., AND PHILLIPS C. DUNN (COMPILERS)
 1986 *A True Likeness: The Black South of Richard Samuel Roberts; 1920–1936.* Bruccoli Clark, Columbia, and Algonquin Books, Chapel Hill, South Carolina.

JONES, OLIVE, AND CATHERINE SULLIVAN
 1989 *The Parks Canada Glass Glossary for the Description of Containers, Tableware, Flat Glass, and Closures.* Studies in Archaeology, Architecture, and History. Environment Canada-Parks, Ottawa, Ontario.

JOSEPH, J. W.
 1987 Highway 17 Revisited: The Archaeology of Task Labor in the Lowcountry of Georgia and South Carolina.

Paper presented at the Annual Meeting of the Society for Historical Archaeology Conference on Historical and Underwater Archaeology, Savannah, Georgia.

JOYNER, CHARLES
 1984 *Down by the Riverside: A South Carolina Slave Community.* University of Illinois Press, Chicago.

KALOUS, MILAN
 1979 Akorite? *Journal of African History* 20:203–217.

KARKLINS, KARLIS
 1985 *Glass Beads: The 19th-Century Levin Catalogue and Venetian Bead Book and Guide to Description of Glass Beads.* Studies in Archaeology, Architecture, and History. Environment Canada-Parks, Ottawa, Ontario.

KARKLINS, KARLIS, AND NORMAN BARKA
 1989 The Beads of St. Eustatius, Netherlands Antilles. *Beads: Journal of the Society of Bead Researchers* 1:55–80.

KELSO, WILLIAM M.
 1984 *Kingsmill Plantations, 1619–1800; Archaeology of Country Life in Colonial Virginia.* Academic Press, New York.

KENNEDY, LINDA, CHRISTOPHER T. ESPENSHADE, AND RAMONA GRUNDEN
 1991 Archaeological Investigations of Two Turn-of-the-Century Farmsteads (38BU966 and 38BU967), Hilton Head Island, South Carolina. Report prepared by Brockington and Associates, Atlanta, Georgia. Submitted to the Greenwood Development Corporation, Hilton Head Island, South Carolina.

KENNEDY, LINDA, MARION D. ROBERTS, AND CHRISTOPHER T. ESPENSHADE
 1993 Archaeological Data Recovery at River Club (38BU880), Hilton Head Island. Beaufort County: A Study in Late Eighteenth-/Early Nineteenth-Century African-American Lifeways. Report on file, Brockington and Associates, Atlanta, Georgia.
 1994 Archaeological Data Recovery at Colleton River Plantation (38BU647), Hilton Head Island, Beaufort County, South Carolina: A Study of an Early 19th-Century Slave Settlement. Report on file, Brockington and Associates, Atlanta, Georgia.

KENYON, IAN, AND THOMAS KENYON
 1983 Comments on Seventeenth-Century Glass Trade Beads from Ontario. *Proceedings of the 1982 Glass Trade Bead Conference, Rochester Museum and Science Center Research Records* 16:59–74. Charles F. Hayes III, editor. Rochester, New York.

KERNAN, MICHAEL
 1993 The Object at Hand. *Smithsonian* 20:30–32.

KIDD, KENNETH E.
1970   Glass Bead-making from the Middle Ages to the Early 19th Century. *History and Archaeology* 30. Ottawa.

KINGSLEY, MARY H.
1897   *Travels in West Africa*. Macmillan, New York.

LANDEWIJK, J. E. J. M. VAN
1970   What Was the Original Aggrey Bead (a New Aggrey Bead Hypothesis)? *Ghana Journal of Sociology* 6(2): 89–99.

LANGE, FREDERICK W., AND JEROME S. HANDLER
1985   The Ethnohistorical Approach to Slavery. In *The Archaeology of Slavery and Plantation Life*, edited by Theresa Singleton, pp. 15–32. Academic Press, New York.

LAROCHE, CHERYL J.
1994   Beads from the African Burial Ground, New York City: A Preliminary Assessment. *Beads: Journal of the Society of Bead Researchers* 6:3–20.

LEFLER, HUGH TALMAGE (EDITOR)
1967   *A New Voyage to Carolina by John Lawson*. University of North Carolina Press, Chapel Hill.

LITTLEFIELD, DANIEL C.
1981   *Rice and Slaves: Ethnicity and the Slave Trade in Colonial South Carolina*. Louisiana State University Press, Baton Rouge.

LOGAN, MICHAEL H., AND DOUGLAS A. SCHMITTOU
1995   With Pride They Made These: Tribal Styles in Plains Indian Art. *Occasional Paper* 12. Frank H. McClung Museum, University of Tennessee, Knoxville.

LOWIE, ROBERT H.
1924   *Primitive Religion*. Boni and Liveright, New York.

MACDONALD, GEORGE
1969   *The Gold Coast, Past and Present: A Short Description of the Country and Its People*. Negro Universities Press, New York.

MAHNKE, FRANK H., AND RUDOLF H. MAHNKE
1987   *Color and Light in Man-Made Environments*. Van Nostrand Reinhold, New York.

MALONEY, CLARENCE (EDITOR)
1976   *The Evil Eye*. Columbia University Press, New York.

MCDONALD, MARY ANNE
1986   Jennie Burnett: Afro-American Quilt Maker. In *Five North Carolina Folk Artists*, edited by Charles G. Zug III, pp. 27–39. Ackland Art Museum, University of North Carolina Press, Chapel Hill.

MCDONALD, RODERICK A.
1990   Independent Economic Production by Slaves on Antebellum Louisiana Sugar Plantation. In *The Slaves' Economy: Independent Production by Slaves in the Americas*, edited by Ira Berlin and Phillips A. Morgan, pp. 182–208. Frank Cass, London.

MCKEE, LARRY
1992   Summary Report on the 1991 Hermitage Field Quarter Excavation. *Tennessee Anthropological Association Newsletter* 18(1):1–17.

MCTEER, J. E.
1970   *High Sheriff of the Low Country*. Beaufort Books, Beaufort, South Carolina.

MERRELL, JAMES H.
1991   *The Indians' New World: Catawbas and Their Neighbors from European Contact Through the Era of Removal*. Second edition. W. W. Norton, New York and London.

MICHIE, JAMES L.
1987   Richmond Hill and Wachesaw: An Archaeological Study of Two Rice Plantations on the Waccamaw River, Georgetown County, South Carolina. *Research Manuscript Series* 203. South Carolina Institute of Archaeology and Anthropology, University of South Carolina, Columbia.

MICHIE, JAMES L., AND JAY MILLS
1988   The Search for Architectural Remains at the Planter's House and the Slave Settlement, Richmond Hill Plantation, Georgetown County, South Carolina. *Research Manuscript Series* 205. South Carolina Institute of Archaeology and Anthropology, University of South Carolina, Columbia.

MILLER, HENRY, DENNIS POGUE, AND
MICHAEL SMOLEK
1983   Beads from the Seventeenth-Century Chesapeake. *Proceedings of the 1982 Glass Trade Bead Conference, Rochester Museum and Science Center Research Records* 16:127–144. Charles F. Hayes III, editor. Rochester, New York.

MILLIGAN, ROBERT H.
1912   *The Fetish Folk of West Africa*. Fleming H. Revell, New York.

MINTZ, SIDNEY W., AND DOUGLAS HALL
1960   The Origins of the Jamaican Internal Marketing System. In *Papers in Caribbean Anthropology* 57, edited by Sidney W. Mintz. Yale University Publications in Anthropology, New Haven.

MOORE, N. HUDSON
1924   *Old Glass: European and American*. Tudor, New York.

MORRISON, TONI
1988   *Beloved*. Plume Contemporary Fiction, New York.

NASSAU, ROBERT H.
1904   *Fetishism in West Africa*. Charles Scribner's Sons, New York.
1969   *Fetishism in West Africa*. Negro Universities Press, New York.

NIXON, HERMAN CLARENCE
1938   *Forty Acres and Steel Mules.* University of North Carolina Press, Chapel Hill.

NORRELL, ROBERT J., AND CATHERINE C. MEYER
1992   History and Archaeology of Nineteenth-Century Alabama. *Report of Investigations* 64. Report prepared by Division of Archaeology, University of Alabama, Alabama Museum of Natural History. Submitted to Transcontinental Gas Pipe Line Corporation of Houston, Texas.

NOURISSON, PASCALE
1992   Beads in the Lives of the People of Southern Togo, West Africa. *Beads: Journal of the Society of Bead Researchers* 4:29–38.

O'MALLEY, NANCY
1995   Archaeological Investigations in Kinkeadtown, a Post-Civil War African-American Neighborhood in Lexington, Kentucky. Department of Anthropology, University of Kentucky, Lexington.

OMARI, MIKELLE SMITH
1994   Candomlé: A Socio-Political Examination of African Religion and Art in Brazil. In *Religion in African Experience and Expression*, edited by Thomas D. Blakely, Walter E. A. van Beek, and Dennis L. Thomson, pp. 135–159. Heinemann, Portsmouth, New Hampshire.

OPPER, MARIE-JOSE, AND HOWARD OPPER
1989   Diakhite: A Study of the Beads from an 18th- to 19th-Century Burial Site in Senegal, West Africa. *Beads: Journal of the Society of Bead Researchers* 1:5–20.

ORSER, CHARLES E., JR.
1994   The Archaeology of African-American Slave Religion in the Antebellum South. *Cambridge Archaeological Journal* 4(1):33–45.

ORSER, CHARLES E., JR., ANNETTE M. NEKOLA, AND JAMES L. ROARK
1987   Exploring the Rustic Life, Multidisciplinary Research at Millwood Plantation, a Large Piedmont Plantation in Abbeville County, South Carolina, and Elbert County, Georgia. Report prepared by Mid-American Research Center, Loyola University, Chicago, Illinois. Submitted to U.S. Army Corps of Engineers, National Park Service, Atlanta, Georgia.

OTTO, JOHN SOLOMON
1984   *Cannon's Point Plantation, 1794–1860: Living Conditions and Status Patterns in the Old South.* Academic Press, New York.

PAONESSA, LAURIE J., SCOTT K. PARKER, AND LYNNE G. LEWIS
1993   "I Was Born and Raised Here": Investigations at the Bowens House Site, Drayton Hall, Spring 1992. *National Trust Archaeological Research Center, Monograph Series* 6. Montpelier Station, Virginia.

PARRINDER, GEOFFREY
1957   *African Traditional Religion.* Hutchinson House, New York.
1961   *West African Religion: A Study of the Beliefs and Practices of Akan, Ewe, Yoruba, Ibo, and Kindred Peoples.* Epworth Press, London.

PARRINGTON, MICHAEL
1987   Cemetery Archaeology in the Urban Environment: A Case Study from Philadelphia. In Living in Cities: Current Research in Urban Archaeology, edited by Edward Staski. *Special Publication Series* 5:48–55. The Society for Historical Archaeology, California, Pennsylvania.

PATTEN, M. DRAKE
1992   Mankala and Minkisi: Possible Evidence of African American Folk Beliefs and Practices. *African American Archaeology* 6:5–7.

PEAKE, ORA BROOKS
1954   *A History of the United States Indian Factory System, 1795–1822.* Sage, Denver, Colorado.

PIPER, HARRY M., KENNETH W. HARDIN, AND JACQUELYN G. PIPER
1982   Cultural Responses to Stress: Patterns Observed in American Indian Burials of the Second Seminole War. *Southeastern Archaeology* 1(2):122–137.

PIPER, HARRY M., AND JACQUELYN G. PIPER
1982   Archaeological Excavations at the Quad Block Site, 8-Hi-998; Located at the Site of the Old Fort Brooke Municipal Parking Garage, Tampa, Florida. Report on file, Piper Archaeological Research, St. Petersburg, Florida.

POGUE, DENNIS J., AND ESTHER C. WHITE
1991   Summary Report on the "House of Families" Slave Quarter Site (44 Fx162/40–47). File Report 2. Report on file, Mount Vernon Ladies' Association, Mount Vernon Plantation, Mount Vernon, Virginia.

POLLITZER, W. S.
1975   The Negroes of Charleston (S.C.): A Study of Hemoglobin Types, Serology, and Morphology. In *Man and Nature, Studies in the Evolution of the Human Species*, edited by Frederick S. Hulse, pp. 266–283. American Book-Stratford Press, Brattleboro, Vermont.

PRAETZELLIS, MARY, AND ADRIAN PRAETZELLIS
1992   "We were there too": Archaeology of an African-American Family in Sacramento, California. Report on file, Anthropological Studies Center, Sonoma State University, Rohnert, California.

PRICE, RICHARD
    1966   Caribbean Fishing and Fishermen: A Historical Sketch. *American Anthropologist* 68:1363–1383.

PUCKETT, NEWBELL NILES
    1975   *Folk Beliefs of the Southern Negro.* Reprint of 1926 edition. Negro Universities Press, New York.

PULSIPHER, LYDIA M.
    1990   They Have Saturdays and Sundays to Feed Themselves: Slave Gardens in the Caribbean. *Expedition* 32(2):24–33.
    1991   Galways Plantation, Montserrat. In *Seeds of Change: A Quincentennial Commemoration,* edited by Herman J. Viola and Carolyn Margolis, pp. 139–159. Smithsonian Institution Press, Washington, D.C.

RATTRAY, R. S.
    1923   *Ashanti.* Clarendon Press, Oxford.
    1927   *Religion and Art in Ashanti.* Clarendon Press, Oxford.

RAWICK, GEORGE P.
    1972a   *The American Slave: A Composite Autobiography.* Vol. 6, *Alabama and Indiana Narratives.* Greenwood, Westport, Connecticut.
    1972b   *The American Slave: A Composite Autobiography.* Vol. 4, *Texas Narratives, Parts 1 and 2.* Greenwood, Westport, Connecticut.
    1972c   *The American Slave: A Composite Autobiography.* Vol. 12, *Georgia Narratives, Parts 1 and 2.* Greenwood, Westport, Connecticut.
    1972d   *The American Slave: A Composite Autobiography, Supplement Series 1.* Vol. 6, *Mississippi Narratives, Part 1.* Greenwood, Westport, Connecticut.
    1972e   *The American Slave: A Composite Autobiography.* Vol. 4, *Georgia Narratives, Part 1.* Greenwood, Westport, Connecticut.

RAWLEY, JAMES A.
    1981   *The Transatlantic Slave Trade: A History.* W. W. Norton, New York and London.

ROBERSON, RUTH HAISLIP (EDITOR)
    1988   *North Carolina Quilts.* North Carolina Quilt Project, University of North Carolina Press, Chapel Hill.

ROBERTSON, ROBERT ALEXANDER
    1969   *Chats on Old Glass.* Dover, New York.

ROSE, JEROME C. (EDITOR)
    1985   Gone to a Better Land: A Biohistory of a Rural Black Cemetery in the Post-Reconstruction South. *Arkansas Archeological Survey Research Series* 25. Arkansas Archeological Survey, Fayetteville.

ROSS, LESTER A.
    1990   Trade Beads from Hudson's Bay Company, Fort Vancouver (1829–1860), Vancouver, Washington. *Beads: Journal of the Society of Bead Researchers* 2:29–68.

RUSSELL, AARON E.
    1996   "Spiritual" Artifacts from Hermitage Slave Dwellings. Paper presented at the Annual Meeting of the Society for Historical Archaeology Conference on Historical and Underwater Archaeology, Cincinnati, Ohio.

SAMFORD, PATRICIA
    1994   West African Cultural Traditions in the Archaeological Record. Paper presented at the Annual Meetings of the Southeastern Archaeological Conference and Midwest Archaeological Conference, Lexington, Kentucky.
    1996   The Archaeology of African-American Slavery and Material Culture. *William and Mary Quarterly,* third series, 53(1):87–113.

SCHLOTTERBECK, JOHN T.
    1990   The Internal Economy of Slavery in Rural Piedmont Virginia. In *The Slaves' Economy: Independent Production by Slaves in the Americas,* edited by Ira Berlin and Phillips A. Morgan, pp. 170–181. Frank Cass, London.

SHOGREN, MICHAEL G., KENNETH R. TURNER, AND JODY C. PERRONI
    1989   Elko Switch Cemetery: An Archaeological Perspective. *Report of Investigations* 58. Division of Archaeology, Alabama State Museum of Natural History, Moundville.

SINGLETON, THERESA A.
    1991   The Archeology of Slave Life. In *Before Freedom Came: African-American Life in the Antebellum South,* edited by Edward D. C. Campbell, Jr., with Kym S. Rice, pp. 155–175. Museum of the Confederacy, Richmond, and University Press of Virginia, Charlottesville.

SINGLETON, THERESA A., AND MARK D. BOGRAD (COMPILERS)
    1995   The Archaeology of the African Diaspora in the Americas. *Guides to the Archaeological Literature of the Immigrant Experience in America* 2. The Society for Historical Archaeology, California, Pennsylvania.

SMITH, MARVIN T.
    1983   Chronology from Glass Beads: The Spanish Period in the Southeast, 1513–1670. *Proceedings of the 1982 Glass Trade Bead Conference, Rochester Museum and Science Center Research Records* 16:147–158. Charles F. Hayes III, editor. Rochester, New York.
    1986   Archaeological Testing of Sites 2 and 3, Heritage Plantation, Georgetown County, South Carolina. Report prepared by Garrow and Associates, Atlanta, Georgia. Submitted to Heritage Plantation, Pawleys Island, South Carolina.

SMITH, MARVIN, AND MARY ELIZABETH GOOD
    1982   *Early Sixteenth-Century Glass Beads in the Spanish Colonial Trade.* Cottonlandia Museum, Greenwood, Mississippi.

SMITH, SAMUEL D.
1975   Archaeological Explorations at the Castalian Springs, Tennessee, Historic Site. Tennessee Historical Commission, Nashville.
1976   An Archaeological and Historical Assessment of the First Hermitage. *Research Series* 2. Tennessee Division of Archaeology, Nashville.
1977   Plantation Archaeology at the Hermitage: Some Suggested Patterns. *Tennessee Anthropologist* 2(2):152–163.

SOUTH, STANLEY, RUSSELL K. SKOWRONEK, AND RICHARD E. JOHNSON
1988   Spanish Artifacts from Santa Elena. *Anthropological Studies* 7. Occasional Papers of South Carolina Institute of Archaeology and Anthropology, University of South Carolina, Columbia.

STEEN, CARL
1992   A Preliminary Report on the 1992 Excavations at Pine Grove Plantation, Berkeley County, South Carolina. Report on file, Diachronic Research Foundation, Columbia, South Carolina.
1995   Archaeological Investigations at Somerset Plantation, Washington County, North Carolina. Report prepared by Diachronic Research Foundation, Columbia, South Carolina. Submitted to the North Carolina Historic Sites Division, Department of Cultural Resources, Raleigh, North Carolina.

STEINER, CHRISTOPHER
1990   West African Trade Beads: Symbols of Tradition. *Ornament* 14(1):58–61.

STINE, LINDA FRANCE
1989   Raised Up in Hard Times: Factors Affecting Material Culture on Upland Piedmont Farmsteads, circa 1900–1940s. Unpublished Ph.D. dissertation, Department of Anthropology, University of North Carolina, Chapel Hill.
1990   Mercantilism and Piedmont Peltry: Colonial Perceptions of the Southern Fur Trade, circa 1640–1740. *Volumes in Historical Archaeology* 14, edited by Stanley South. South Carolina Institute of Archaeology and Anthropology, Columbia.
1993   Archaeological Testing at the Saddlebag Cabin, Forks of Cypress Plantation, Lauderdale County, Alabama. Report prepared by RUST International, GIS Labs, Samford University, Birmingham, Alabama. Submitted to Heritage Preservation, Florence, Alabama.

STINE, LINDA F., PAUL BROCKINGTON, JR., AND CONNIE HUDDLESTON
1994   Searching for the Slave Village at Snee Farm Plantation: The 1987 Archaeological Investigations. Report prepared by Brockington and Associates, Atlanta, Georgia. Submitted to the Southeastern Regional Offices, National Park Service, Atlanta, Georgia.

STONE, LYLE M.
1974   *Fort Michilmackinac, 1515–1781: An Archaeological Perspective on the Revolutionary Frontier.* Publications of the Museum, Michigan State University, East Lansing.

STURM, FRED GILLETTE
1977   Afro-Brazilian Cults. In *African Religions: A Symposium,* edited by Newell S. Booth, Jr., pp. 217–240. NOK, New York.

THOMPSON, ERA BELL
1954   *Africa: Land of My Fathers.* Doubleday, New York.

THOMPSON, ROBERT FARRIS
1993   *Face of the Gods: Art and Altars of Africa and the African Americas.* Museum for African Art, New York, and Prestel, Munich.

TINGLING, MARION (EDITOR)
1977   *The Correspondence of the Three William Byrds of Westover, Virginia, 1684–1776.* Virginia Historical Society, University Press of Virginia, Charlottesville.

TRINKLEY, MICHAEL (EDITOR)
1986   Indian and Freedmen Occupation at the Fish Haul Site (38BU805), Beaufort County, South Carolina. *Research Series* 7. Chicora Foundation, Columbia, South Carolina.
1990   Archaeological Excavations at 38BU96, a Portion of Cotton Hope Plantation, Hilton Head Island, Beaufort County, South Carolina. Chicora Foundation, Columbia, South Carolina.
1991   Further Investigations of Prehistoric and Historic Lifeways on Callawassie and Spring Islands, Beaufort County, South Carolina. *Research Series* 23. Chicora Foundation, Columbia, South Carolina.
1993a The History and Archaeology of Kiawah Island, Charleston County, South Carolina. *Research Series* 30. Chicora Foundation, Columbia, South Carolina.
1993b Archaeological and Historical Examinations of Three Eighteenth- and Nineteenth-Century Rice Plantations on the Waccamaw Neck. *Research Series* 31. Chicora Foundation, Columbia, South Carolina.

TRINKLEY, MICHAEL, NATALIE ADAMS, AND DEBI HACKER
1992   Plantation Life in the Piedmont: A Preliminary Examination of Rosemont Plantation, Laurens County, South Carolina. *Research Series* 29. Chicora Foundation, Columbia, South Carolina.

TRINKLEY, MICHAEL, DEBI HACKER, AND NATALIE ADAMS
1993   Life in the Pee Dee: Prehistoric and Historic Research on the Roche Carolina Tract, Florence County, South Carolina. *Research Series* 39. Chicora Foundation, Columbia, South Carolina.

VERNON, AMELIA WALLACE
1993 *African Americans at Mars Bluff, South Carolina.* Louisiana State University Press, Baton Rouge.

WAHLMAN, MAUDE SOUTHWELL
1993 *Signs and Symbols: African Images in African-American Quilts.* Studio Books, Museum of American Folk Art, New York.

WALLIS, WILSON
1939 *Religion in Primitive Society.* F. S. Crofts, New York.

WARD, H. TRAWICK, AND R. P. STEPHENS DAVIS, JR.
1993 *Indian Communities on the North Carolina Piedmont, A.D. 1000 to 1700.* Reprint of 1978 edition. Cleveland Museum of Art, Cleveland, Ohio.

WATTERS, DAVID R.
1987 Excavations at the Harney Site Slave Cemetery, Montserrat, West Indies. *Annals of Carnegie Museum* 56:289–318.

WAYNE, LUCY B., AND MARTIN F. DICKINSON
1990 Four Men's Ramble: Archaeology in the Wando Neck, Charleston County, South Carolina. Report prepared by SouthArc, Gainesville, Florida. Submitted to Dunes West Development Corporation, Mount Pleasant, South Carolina.

WEEKS, WILLIAM M.
1990 The John H. Allston House Site: An Initial Occupation of Richmond Hill Plantation, Georgetown County, South Carolina. *Volumes in Historical Archaeology* 10, edited by Stanley South. South Carolina Institute of Archaeology and Anthropology, University of South Carolina, Columbia.

WEISMAN, BRENT RICHARDS
1989 *Like Beads on a String: A Culture History of the Seminole Indians in North Peninsular Florida.* University of Alabama Press, Tuscaloosa.

WELTY, EUDORA
1989 *Eudora Welty Photographs,* forward by Reynolds Price. University Press of Mississippi, Jackson.

WESLEY, CHARLES HARRIS
1968 *In Freedom's Footsteps: From the African Background to the Civil War.* International Library of Negro Life and History. Publishers Company, New York.

WHEATON, THOMAS R.
1993 Archaeological Testing of Willow Hall and Walnut Grove Plantations, Francis Marion National Forest. Report prepared by New South Associates, Stone Mountain, Georgia. Submitted to U.S.D.A. Forest Service, Francis Marion National Forest, Columbia, South Carolina.

WHEATON, THOMAS R., AMY FRIEDLANDER, AND PATRICK GARROW
1983 Yaughan and Curriboo Plantations: Studies in Afro-American Archaeology. Report prepared by Soil Systems, Marietta, Georgia. Submitted to U.S. Army Corps of Engineers, Charleston District.

WHITE, DEBORAH GRAY
1991 Female Slaves in the Plantation South. In *Before Freedom Came: African-American Life in the Antebellum South,* edited by Edward D. C. Campbell, Jr., with Kym S. Rice, pp. 101–121. Museum of the Confederacy, Richmond, and the University Press of Virginia, Charlottesville.

WILKIE, LAURIE A.
1994 Archaeological Evidence of an African-American Aesthetic. *African-American Archaeology* 10:1, 4.
1995 Magic and Empowerment on the Plantation: An Archaeological Consideration of African-American Worldview. *Southeastern Archaeology* 14(2):136–148.

WOOD, KAREN G.
1991 Site Evaluation on Three Sites at Historic Clayfield Plantation, Wambaw Ranger District, Francis Marion National Forest, South Carolina. Report prepared by Southeastern Archaeological Services, Athens, Georgia. Submitted to U.S.D.A, Forest Service, Francis Marion and Sumter National Forest, Columbia, South Carolina.

WORKS PROGRESS ADMINISTRATION (WPA)
1974 *Drums and Shadows: Survival Studies among the Georgia Coastal Negroes.* Savannah Unit, Georgia Writers' Project, Work Projects Administration. Reprint of 1940 edition. Reprint Company, Spartanburg, South Carolina.

WRIGHT, J. LEITCH, JR.
1986 *Creeks and Seminoles: The Destruction and Regeneration of the Muscogulge People.* University of Nebraska Press, Lincoln.

YENTSCH, ANNE E.
1994a *A Chesapeake Family and Their Slaves: A Study in Historical Archaeology.* Cambridge University Press, Cambridge.
1994b Beads as Silent Witnesses of an African-American Past: Social Identity and the Artifacts of Slavery in Annapolis, Maryland. Paper presented at the Annual Meeting of the Society for Historical Archaeology Conference on Historical and Underwater Archaeology, Vancouver, British Columbia.

YOUNG, AMY L.
  1994   Change and Continuity in African-Derived Religious
         Practices on an Upland South Plantation. Paper pre-
         sented at the 51st Southeastern Archaeological Con-
         ference, Lexington, Kentucky.

ZIERDEN, MARTHA A., JEANNE CALHOUN, AND DEBI
HACKER-NORTON
  1985   Archdale Hall: Investigations of a Low Country Plan-
         tation. *Archaeological Contributions* 10. Charleston
         Museum, Charleston, South Carolina.

ZIERDEN, MARTHA A., LESLEY M. DRUCKER, AND
JEANNE CALHOUN
  1986   Rural Life on Daniel's Island, Berkeley County,
         South Carolina. Report prepared by Carolina Archae-
         ological Services, Columbia, and Charleston Mu-
         seum, Charleston. Submitted to South Carolina De-
         partment of Highways and Public Transportation,
         Columbia.

LINDA FRANCE STINE
1801 15TH STREET
SILER CITY, NORTH CAROLINA 27344-2131

MELANIE A. CABAK
SAVANNAH RIVER ARCHAEOLOGICAL RESEARCH
   PROGRAM
P. O. DRAWER 600
NEW ELLENTON, SOUTH CAROLINA 29809-0600

MARK D. GROOVER
UNIVERSITY OF TENNESSEE
DEPARTMENT OF ANTHROPOLOGY
252 SOUTH STADIUM HALL
KNOXVILLE, TENNESSEE 37996-0720

LAURIE A. WILKIE

Secret and Sacred: Contextualizing the Artifacts of African-American Magic and Religion

ABSTRACT

Although historical archaeologists have accumulated a large amount of data regarding African-American magical and religious systems, researchers still underestimate the importance of magical and religious systems within African-American communities. In addition, archaeologists seem reluctant to interpret these data in a diachronic manner. Spiritual beliefs affected all arenas of the African-American experience including medicine, childcare, gender, family, and community relations. To properly understand African-American daily life, attention must be paid to spiritual traditions. This paper addresses the role of magical practices within African-American society and the importance of recognizing the role of gender ideologies within magical and religious practice, and proposes a diachronic model for understanding the changing relationship between magic and religion. The model, consisting of three stages of cultural change, Formative, Persisting, and Transformative, provides a means of linking the archaeological and documentary databases. Application of the model to three archaeologically well-studied regions demonstrates that, despite growing interest in the archaeological study of African-American spiritual traditions, archaeological evidence for these traditions is sparse when analyzed diachronically.

Introduction

In the last 10 years, archaeologists have made important strides in recognizing material culture associated with African-American magical and religious practices from the earliest time of enslavement through the early 20th century (e.g., Adams 1987; Klingelhofer 1987; Ferguson 1992; Patten 1992; Orser 1994; Santorio 1994; Wilkie 1994, 1995; Yakubik and Mendéz [1995]; Yakubik et al. 1994; Leone 1995; Handler 1996; Stine et al. 1996). The abundance and breadth of material leaves no doubt that enslaved African, then African-American, families and communities created secret and sacred landscapes, separated and internally constructed, but still sometimes

Historical Archaeology, 1997, 31(4):81–106.
Permission to reprint required.

influenced by the spiritual lives of European and Native Americans.

Archaeologists continue to accumulate a broad array of material evidence associated with this spiritual and magical realm of African-American life, drawing upon oral histories, ethnographies, and documentary evidence to shed light on the meanings of specific types of artifacts (e.g., Patten 1992; Pearce 1993; Santorio 1994; Wilkie 1994a, 1994b, 1995; Samford 1996; Stine et al. 1996; Young 1996, 1997). While we may successfully identify uses and meanings of individual artifacts, we have been hesitant to understand the broader cultural tapestry in which these artifacts derived meaning. Unless archaeologists begin to study magical-religious artifacts in their broader cultural, geographic, and temporal context, we will not contribute any greater knowledge about African-American spiritual life to the social sciences.

In this article, a summary of the ways that magical and religious practice shaped and influenced African-American life, and how we as archaeologists can strive to more fully recognize and interpret material cultural reflections of this facet of the African-American experience, both during and after enslavement, will be provided. The discussion will focus on the following issues:

1) the role of magical practice within African-American society, magical practitioners, and the uses of magic; 2) the importance of recognizing the role of gender ideologies within magical and religious practice; 3) the changing relationship between magic and religion through time, and how we might employ a diachronic approach in our interpretations which recognizes the cultural processes of syncretism and creolization.

While archaeologists have begun to discuss African-American religious practices, we have not attempted, in any clear way, to understand the changing relationship between the broad range of magical and religious practice in any diachronic way. To this end, I propose the adoption of a three-stage model of religious change employed by George Brandon (1993) in his study of

Santeria. Brandon's model recognizes three stages of religious transformation: Formative, Persisting, and Transformative. The Formative period represents the initial changes that take place in a religion or belief system as a result of contact or internal culture change, and is represented by the development of numerous religious alternatives. As one alternative becomes the norm, the religion has entered a stage of religious Persistance. The Transformative stage represents a new series of innovation that affects a religion, as seen in the Formative period. I will be discussing this model and its potential applications in the diaspora, below.

While always linked, magic and religion represent and fulfill different needs within African and African-American society through time. Religion is a set of rituals, symbols, and sacred histories that explain a culture's origin and regulate the interaction between humans and culturally postulated extra-humans. Magical practices represent a means of manipulating supernatural forces, be they deities, ancestral spirits, witches, or ghosts. Magical practices can be a means of manipulating or interacting with deities, and therefore are inherently entwined in religious practice (Marwick 1970; Mbiti 1970).

In this article, a summary of the ways that magical and religious practice shaped and influenced African-American everyday life will be provided. Further, the potential for recognizing artifacts that represent African continuities in organized religious practice versus syncretised magical-medical practices, the range of magical practice recorded historically and ethnographically, the gender constructs that shape African-American magical practice, and the importance of archaeological provenience in the recognition of magical and religious artifacts will be discussed.

The Societal Role of African-American Magic and Religion

Magical practices within the African-American community do not represent merely a single facet of the African-American experience. Magic, ideas about divinity, spirituality, the nature of life

and death, and control of natural and supernatural elements are all intertwined to create an African-American worldview that is distinct and unique from that of Chinese Americans, Hispanic Americans, Euroamericans, and Native Americans. Just as archaeologists studying overseas Chinese populations have come to recognize that Chinese Taoist, Confuscionist, and Buddhist philosophies shape every facet of overseas Chinese culture (e.g., Langenwalter 1987; Mueller 1987; Wegars 1993), so African Americanists must recognize that African-American philosophies shaped gender relations, family life, food preparation, medicinal practice, religion, and work.

Scholars have been tempted to dismiss magic as an important element of African-American life. In ex-slave narratives, many African Americans deny knowledge of hoodoo or magic. Likewise, anthropologists working in the American South during the 1920s and 1930s also portray magical beliefs as declining (e.g., Puckett 1968[1926]; Powdermaker 1993[1937]). Before dismissing the importance of magic within African-American communities, it is important to consider the following experience of Zora Neale Hurston:

> I was once talking to Mrs. Rachel Silas of Sanford, Florida, so I asked her where I could find a good hoodoo doctor. "Do you believe in dat ole fogeyism, chile? Ah don't see how nobody could do none of dat work, do you?" She laughed unnecessarily. "Ah been hearin' about dat mess ever since Ah been big enough tuh know mahself, but shucks! Ah don't believe nobody kin do me harm lessen they git somethin' in mah mouth."
>
> "Don't fool yourself," I answered with assurance. "People can do things to you. I done seen things happen."
>
> "Sho nuff? Well, well, well! Maybe thing *kin* be done tuh harm yuh, cause Ah done heard *good* folks— folks dat ought to know—say dat it sho is a fact. Anyhow, Ah figger it pays tuh be keerful" (Hurston 1990b[1935]:185–186).

By the end of her conversation with Mrs. Silas and another neighbor, Hurston established not only that both women believed in hoodoo, but actively sought magical protection from specialists, and were able to direct Hurston where to find a "two-headed doctor." Hurston's experience illustrates not only the prevalence of magical practice but the secret nature of these beliefs.

That African-influenced magical religious traditions exist in the New World is now clear from archaeological, ethnographic, and documentary evidence (e.g., Ferguson 1992; Wilkie 1995; Stine et al. 1996). The question that must be more clearly addressed is why these continuities persist and how their meanings may change through time. Dollard, writing in 1937, had the following observations to make about the role of African-American supernatural beliefs:

> There is another means of accommodating to life when it is not arranged according to one's wishes. This is the use of magic. Of course, one can think of magical practices among the Negroes as lagging culture patterns, which they are, but one can also think of them as forms of action in reference to current social life. Magic accepts the *status quo* [original emphasis]; it takes the place of political activity, agitation, organization, solidarity, or any real moves to change status. It is interesting and harmless from the standpoint of the caste system and it probably has great private value for those who practice it. These psychological satisfactions are important, even if they do not alter the social structure and are mere substitutes for more effective efforts to alter it (Dollard 1957[1937]:263).

Although written over 60 years ago, Dollard's argument that the use of magic had psychological merits for the African-American community is relevant for contemporary consideration. Although rarely discussed in a forthright manner by historical archaeologists, violence and the threat of violence, in both physical and psychological forms, were an ongoing aspect of the African-American experience during the period of enslavement and beyond (Farnsworth 1996).

Magic, particularly magic to harm, provided African Americans with a means of retaliating against Euroamerican violence with a supernatural violence of their own. In the 19th century, African Cubans were reported to have used magic to attack slaveholders (Thompson 1983:125). Likewise, Young (1997) has explored the role of magic as a means of combating planter violence. Just as planters threatened and used violence to attempt to control enslaved, and

later freed, African Americans, magic provided a potential threat wielded by African Americans.

While early historians and anthropologists of the American South often portray European culture as "advanced" or based in "reason," whereas the African-American population was "primitive," "superstitious," or "heathen" (e.g., Dollard 1957[1937]; Puckett 1968[1926]; Saxon et al. 1989[1945]; Powdermaker 1993[1937]), such descriptions are not only racist but also misrepresentative of both groups' cultural beliefs. The European-descended population of the American South had its own complex cosmology regarding the use of magic and the existence of supernatural beings (e.g., Hand 1980). The magical/supernatural beliefs of Europeans and Africans were complementary, and undoubtedly influenced one another. The use of fetishes, for instance, was common to each group, as were beliefs in witches and ghosts. Ethnohistorical data clearly demonstrate that many Euroamericans consulted African-American conjurers for magical assistance (e.g., Hurston 1990a[1938], 1990b[1935]; Powdermaker 1993[1937]).

Likewise, Euroamericans were known to have peddled magical charms. One African American interviewed by the North Carolina Federal Writer's Project in the 1930s stated:

> White folks comes round sometimes, not much now as dey use to, tryin' to sell stones and roots and one thing after another, to keep off bad luck, dey claims. I always told 'em I didn't mind buyin' nothin' dat would bring me good luck, but wa'nt (worth) while to talk to me' dey wa'n't no money for good luck at our place. I don't worry much about dey bad lucks (Terrill and Hirsch 1978:93).

Puckett (1968[1926]) demonstrated that many magical practices among the African-American populations he studied in Mississippi were similar to magical beliefs he found in Europe. While Puckett interpreted these similarities as evidence that black folk traditions only represented holdovers of extinct European beliefs, it seems more likely that the similarities represent a form of syncretism or creolization on both ethnic groups' part. As new magical tools were encountered, they were added to the magical tool kit. Just as people of European descent came to consult African and African-American magical practitioners, European magic was incorporated into the African-based magical and religious arsenal. That there are similarities between the coexisting magical systems is potentially significant and meaningful when considering race relations. If a common magical language was shared between the black and white populations of the diaspora, then the implied threat of magical use would be understood as such by both parties.

The idea that continuities of African-based belief systems served as a means of resistance is often advanced in historical archaeological arguments attempt to explain its existence (e.g., Orser 1994; Leone 1995; Wilkie 1995). As yet, however, archaeologists have been slow to recognize magical systems as more elemental expressions of an African-American cultural reality. The secret maintenance of magical practices was not merely a means of exerting control over circumstances of life or of resisting planter authority, beliefs in magic and magical practices also persisted because they were intrinsic to the ways in which enslaved Africans defined themselves, their families, and their relationship to life, death, and the world around them (Herskovits 1962[1941]; Thompson 1981, 1983). Magical and religious beliefs within enslaved African and, then, African-American cultures served as an explanatory system for the workings of the world. Magic and religion provided not only information regarding the inhabitants of the natural and supernatural worlds, but also how these players related to and impacted one another. To completely abandon one's cosmology would be to completely abandon one's original image of oneself.

Magical and Medical Practitioners of the African-American Community

Three predominant types of professional practitioners offered magical and magico-medical services to the African-American community: midwives, root doctors, and conjurers. While these types of practitioners will be discussed as independent and distinct from one another, it is important to note that in some communities, a midwife may act as a root doctor, or a root doctor may also serve as a conjurer. Root doctors and midwives used a combination of spiritual and physical techniques to treat illness or attend a delivery (Campbell 1946; Laguerre 1978), while conjurers (often referred to as Hoodoos or Hoodoo Doctors in the American South or Obeahs in the Caribbean) provided a range of magical services that typically were related to social control of some kind, be it a love charm or a spell to kill or sicken. Each of these practitioners came to their trade as a result of a vocation. While the infamous Marie Laveau received her vocation to conjuring from a rattlesnake (Hurston 1990b[1935]:193), many later conjurers attributed their vocation to God. Powdermaker described one conjurer who gave the following account of his calling:

> His first experience came to him when he was a young man, walking along a country road after church. The moon was full, and looking up he saw in it a face he had never seen before. Then he heard a voice telling him how to cure his ailing wife. He followed instructions, and his wife became better. Ever since then he sees spirits and hears voices. He knows the past and can foretell the future (Powdermaker 1993[1937]:293).

Another conjurer gave an account of his calling:

> Chile, I could always see things. God Almighty fixed me so I could. No, chile, I didn't study no books to learn, that is a gift just handed down from my forefathers. You know even before we was brought here from Africa by the white folks, and heathens as they say we was, there was that gift shown in many ways. I'se still traveling 'cause I got faith in God (Terrill and Hirsch 1978:23).

African-American healers often attributed their strength and skill not only to God and the training they received, but often credited their forebears in a spiritual way. For instance, a midwife recounts her experiences while attending a difficult birth:

My feelings were all mixed up with praying and wishing Aunt Jeanie [the woman who trained her to be a midwife] was there to help. Then, like a sudden swift witness, a new strength and wisdom came into me and steadied my heart and mind and holded my hands to do the right thing. And after that Ludy birthed her baby . . . .Then I knew what had happened to me. Aunt Jeanie had been there in the spirit to lend me her help and strength. Not no ghost nor no vision from heaven . . . . And knowing that, my mind picked up the last words Aunt Jeanie said to me, 'After a little rest, I'll be right back there to take hold and help out with sick folks and babies' (Campbell 1946:244–245).

After receiving their vocation, a person would become an apprentice to an expert in the field of their calling. Often, the person training them would be a close relative or friend, who would pass along their practice to the younger person once the training was complete.

Magical specialists did not seem to be gender-exclusive roles, although midwives were likely to be women who had already raised their own children, and were beyond their childbearing years. I have found one instance of a male African-American midwife (Logan as told to Clark 1989). There is some debate concerning whether or not conjurers are more likely to be men than women, and whether women are more likely than men to be root doctors. While claims have been made on both accounts (e.g., Herskovits 1962[1941]; Puckett 1968[1926]; Powdermaker 1993[1937]), my survey has found no clear correlation between gender and the form of magical practice.

Root doctors, while also employing a range of magical techniques, mainly specialized in the production and use of herbal and animal product pharmaceuticals to combat diseases that were perceived as being caused by natural agents of illness (Wilkie 1996a, 1996b). Teas, brewed from medicinal herbs or substances, salves, or whiskey-based "home-made bitters" were made and found in the medical kits of midwives, root doctors, and sometimes, conjurers (Campbell 1946; Logan as told to Clark 1989; Clayton 1990; Mathews 1992). Conjurers were more likely to use magical means to treat diseases that were perceived as being caused by supernatural agents or to create magical means of control—be it in matters of love, hate, or luck—and used a combination of charms and spells to exert magical influence. As Powdermaker (1993[1937]) observed, conjurers were varied in their chosen magical styles. Four conjurers provided magical services to the community studied by Powdermaker. "Reverend" D. used the state pharmaceutical regulation to write legal prescriptions. He also created medicines after going into a trance and wrote charms on pieces of paper. "Reverend" R., another conjurer, used a steel rod he called an "electreat" on his patients and consulted with spirits. He did not use charms. Mr. T., of mixed Cherokee and African descent, used herbal potions that can attract luck and repel danger. Finally, Dr. A. wrote charms on papers, but relied upon published magical volumes for his inspirations (Powdermaker 1993[1937]:292–294).

Archaeologically, the distinctive magical specialists of the African diaspora should be identifiable to some degree. I have analyzed artifacts associated with an African-American midwife's housesite in Mobile, Alabama (Wilkie and Shorter [1997]) and found a range of artifacts that seem to be associated with midwifery, including large numbers of medicine bottles once containing patent medicines sold broadly throughout the United States to treat illnesses related to children and infants; large numbers of whiskey containers, likely to be related to the preparation of home-made bitters; zooarchaeological remains related to the preparation of calf's foot jelly (a medicine-food for invalids, children, and mothers recovering from childbirth); and objects of potential magical significance, including yellow sulfur, a glass crystal, and flaked stones.

Kenneth Brown (Brown and Cooper 1990), in his excavations at Levi-Jordan plantation, discovered an assemblage of artifacts that he has interpreted as representing a "traditional healer/magician." This assemblage included "five cast iron kettle bases, pieces of utilized chalk, fragments of a small scale, bird skulls, and animal's paw, medicine bottles, bullet casings put together to form a sealed tube, ocean shells, small doll parts, a high frequency of nails and spikes, several tablespoons, metal knives—both real and 'fake,' a chert projectile point, and two chert scrapers" (Brown and Cooper 1990:16–17). This assemblage dates between 1848, when the plantation was founded, and 1891, when the plantation was abandoned, probably favoring the later date range (Brown and Cooper 1990). As will be discussed later, the assemblage is intriguing because it contains artifact materials that could be related to the creation of Kongo-influenced *mniski* charms, or magical medicine.

Handler and Lange (1978) identified a possible Obeah man in the burials of Newton plantation, Barbados. Burial 72 contained an old male, who was buried with his head facing the east. This individual wore two copper bracelets on his left arm, and was buried wearing two white metal rings, a copper ring, and a necklace of seven cowrie shells, 21 drilled dog canines, 14 glass beads, five drilled vertebrae from a bony fish, and one large agate bead. Accompanying the burial were a pipe, possibly of African origin, and an iron knife blade (Handler and Lange 1978:125–132). The wealth of the burial goods associated with this individual led to the interpretation that he had been an Obeah man (conjurer). The prone position of another burial, and its isolation from other burial features, has more recently led Handler (1996) to argue that an "African-witch or other negatively viewed person" may be present in the cemetery. It is important to recognize, however, that witches were commonly seen in African society as individuals who, by their own nature rather than spells, could cause harm to others, and is not necessarily an example of a magical practitioner.

Magical Uses in African-American Society

Ethnographic, documentary, and oral historical sources suggest that African Americans exercised magical control over many aspects of their lives, including healthcare, protection from spirits, to maintain family relationships, to attract or dispel love, to gain a job, to attract money, or even

harm one's enemies or rivals (Puckett 1968[1926]; Tallant 1983[1946]; Saxon et al. 1989[1945]; Botkin 1989[1945]; Clayton 1990; Hurston 1990a[1938], 1990b[1935]; Powdermaker 1993[1937]). Magic could be performed through ritual action or through the use of potions or charms. While some charms, potions, and magical ritual could be performed within the home, for many magical tasks and needs, a magical specialist had to be employed.

Medicinal Magic

Magical as well as pharmaceutical means were used to treat diseases that were perceived to be of either natural or unnatural agents. Illnesses in many African-American communities were, and often still are, perceived to be caused by human interference (witchcraft), natural illnesses, or through the interference of spirits or ghosts (Wilkie 1995, 1996a). Magical cures could be used individually, or in conjunction with herbal pharmaceutical remedies. Both sympathetic (i.e., the idea that an object can influence others that have an identity with it) and contagious magic (i.e., the belief that associated objects can have influence on each other) could be found within medicinal magic (Lehmann and Myers 1985). Many magical cures for naturally-caused illnesses or conditions did not require a professional practitioner to be implemented but rather were part of a family's own magico-medical repertoire.

Naturally-occurring medical conditions of a serious nature such as childbirth and changes in child development often received magical aid. For instance, during childbirth, a knife would be placed under the expectant mother's bed in hopes that it would "cut" the pain (Logan as told to Clark 1989:54). Likewise, burning chicken feathers under the mother's bed or having her wear a hat belonging to the father during birth were also believed to ease the pain of contractions (Campbell 1946:114). Once born, a child was not to have its umbilical cord removed until the seventh day (Campbell 1946:35). A pierced penny worn around the neck of an infant was believed to ease the difficulty, pain, and potential danger of teething; a necklace of six plain buttons, or a necklace of rattlesnake rattles, hog teeth, or alligator teeth, would serve the same purpose (Puckett 1968[1926]:346). Each of these magico-medical charms would leave an archaeological trace, although in the context of a midden assemblage, their exact use may not be readily apparent. For instance, researchers (e.g., Wilkie 1994b; Yakubik and Méndez [1995]) have noticed the relatively high proportion of buttons recovered from African-American archaeological sites. In addition to their importance as pieces of adornment, buttons have many recorded magical uses.

The ethnohistorical literature contains numerous examples of charms relating to easing the pain and danger of teething. The fear of an infant's teething period should not be underestimated for throughout the American South both African and Euroamerican populations believed that the condition of teething and the process of weaning made a child more prone to life-threatening diseases (McMillen 1990:151). Physical anthropological investigations of enslaved African-American cemeteries in the American South and Caribbean (e.g., Corruccini et al. 1985; Kelley and Angel 1987; Harris and Rathbun 1989) have demonstrated that African-American skeletal materials exhibit evidence of nutritional stress during childhood. Corruccini et al. (1985:701–702) were able to link the development of hypoplastic conditions in Afro-Barbadian teeth to the period of weaning (approximately three years of age) in a 1660–1820 skeletal population. Excavations of African-American skeletal material from the Cedar Grove Baptist Church, in Lincoln County, Arkansas, included the remains of 32 children (total excavated skeletal population numbered 79), aged between zero to two years. Of this number, 16 of the children were believed to be newborns (Rose and Santeford 1985). This high incidence of mortality for infants (40.5% of the Cedar Grove skeletal population) during the late 19th and early 20th centuries clearly illustrates why magical means of ensuring children's health were so important.

The loss of teeth also had magical significance. Human teeth are commonly recovered archaeologically, often representing deciduous teeth, teeth pulled or dropped due to decay, or pulled for aesthetic or cultural reasons (Handler and Lange 1978). Recovered near a house roofline, however, human teeth can have magical meanings. Herskovits described the following ritual:

> In Trinidad, Haiti, and Dahomey appropriate rituals mark the appearance of the permanent teeth; the essence of one such rite is to throw the first deciduous tooth to fall out on the roof of the mother's house or into some near-by place, asking that the new teeth be strong and beautiful. Parsons reports from the Seas Islands that: "When a chil sheddin teet', take an' put 'em in a corn-cob, an' fling it right over de house." This practice was referred to as "callin' de new teeth back" (Herskovits 1962[1941]:195).

In my research in Louisiana and the Bahamas, I have twice encountered teeth that were recovered just along the roof-drip line, and may represent evidence of magical practice. Turner (1993:116) reports that "in Bahamian folk tradition teeth are not merely discarded but are thrown onto the rooftop, over the shoulder, to bring good luck." The loss of teeth was not an unusual event. Harris and Rathbun (1989:411–412), in their analysis of 36 skeletal individuals from a 19th-century slave cemetery from a South Carolina plantation, found that women in the population lost a mean of 11.6 teeth prior to death, whereas men, who lived a shorter time, lost a mean of 6.5 teeth.

While this discussion has focused upon childbirth and child development, many magical cures are associated with commonly occurring natural illnesses. For instance, in Louisiana, swallowing a gold bead was believed to relieve a sore throat (Saxon et al. 1989[1945]:534). More commonly, however, a wide range of magical treatments is used to cure magically caused illnesses. The treatment of illness in the African diaspora needed to consider not only natural agents of disease but magical causes of disease. Magical cures were often employed, sometimes in conjunction with pharmaceutical cures. Magic intended to harm, which caused illnesses, possession, bodily infestation by reptiles or small animals, and even death, required magical treatments and will be discussed below.

Magic to Harm

Magic to harm, if oral histories and ethnographies are a fair basis for evaluation, is by far the form of magic most feared, although probably the least employed as well. Although archaeologists have recovered little evidence of artifacts intended to cause harm, abundant evidence exists of artifacts apparently used as apotropaics, or devices to turn away evil.

Magic to harm can be performed through the creation of charms—also known as goofers, tobis, hands, gris-gris—or through the performance of elaborate ritual. Hurston (1990b[1935]), once initiated into a New Orleans Voodoo sect, participated in a long and complicated death ritual. The ritual lasted 90 days and involved the sacrifice of chickens, the building and maintaining of an altar, and the burning of black candles (Hurston 1990b[1935]:210–211). Death, however, was not often the result of magic to harm. Often, a person would exhibit an illness commonly associated with magical interference, such as being infested with snakes (the snakes could be seen crawling under the skin). The physical withdrawal of the snakes by a conjurer, the breaking of the original "trick," or a counter "trick" aimed against one's enemy were common cures for magically caused illnesses.

The great majority of magic to harm involves the use of exuvia (body fluids and substances). Dirt removed from footsteps, clothing items, body fluids, skin, hair or finger/toenail clippings, are all commonly involved in magic to cause harm. Puckett (1968[1926]) describes "conjure balls, bottles and bags" in his ethnographic research.

Bottles, used in a variety of ways to conjure or to protect from conjure, are often mentioned in the literature of magic to harm. Bottles or preserve jars are filled with magically meaningful ingredients and buried near doorsteps or houses, or in paths and crossroads. The intended victim, upon passing over the conjure bottle, will be tricked. Puckett (1968[1926]:231) describes "in one case where there was reason to suspect conjuring, a bottle filled with roots, stones, and reddish powder was found under the doorstop, and in the yard more bottles with beans, iron nails and the same powder. The man burned them up and got well again."

Iron nails, needles, bags of red flannel, roots, snakes, snakeskins, insects, keys, and hairballs are just a few of the ingredients described as components of conjure bottles (Puckett 1968[1926]; Hyatt 1978). Preserve jars containing a snake and several insects in addition to something else wrapped up in cloth; vials containing nails, red flannel, and whiskey; and snuff bottles containing vinegar and other liquid ingredients are all discussed as conjure bottles that were employed in the 1920s (Puckett 1968[1926]:231). In addition to bottles and jars, teacups and tin cups were also described as vessels containing conjures (Puckett 1968[1926]; Hyatt 1978).

Conjure bottles, due to their location and contents, should be recognizable archaeologically. Whole bottles, jars, teacups, or tin cups buried near doorways, steps, pathways, or house walls would leave an unmistakable archaeological signature. A review of ethnographic evidence indicates that such vessels were commonly used in the American South and Caribbean. In the Bahamas, bottles containing needles, herbs, and urine would be buried near houses to cause harm (Grace Turner 1996, pers. comm.).

Conjure bottles have been recovered from at least one archaeological setting in the Caribbean, and two in the United States. Excavating at Juan de Bolas plantation in Jamaica, Reeves (1996) recovered two nearly intact bottles that were located upright and adjacent to a former slave house mound. The tops of the bottles had been sheared off during post-depositional horticultural activities, but the bottles were otherwise intact and appeared to contain charcoal and a thin white residue. Samford (1996:107–109) reported the recovery of conjure bottles from the walls of slave cabin sites in North Carolina and Virginia, and has suggested that intact bottles recovered from beneath the floors of slave cabins at the Hermitage plantation, Tennessee, may have also been *minkisi* containers. It is likely that other conjure bottles have been excavated archaeologically but not recognized.

Despite the common practice throughout the diaspora of burying conjure bottles, it is not necessarily likely that these artifacts will be abundant archaeologically. To break the "trick" (misfortune caused by the buried bottle) required that the bottle be found and broken or discarded so that the spell could be ended. Because the bottles were hidden in well-known, archetypal places, part of the intention of the conjure was surely that it be known to the victim. By casting a spell to harm another person through this means, an individual was publicly stating a grievance against another. By actively looking for and finding a conjure bottle, a potential victim was recognizing and acknowledging that they were involved in a serious dispute with another person that could jeopardize their safety. The catalyst that served to ignite the search for conjure would be a spell of bad luck or unexplained ill health, or concern that a particular individual had reason to fear becoming the object of conjure.

Charms to divert evil are commonly mentioned in the oral historical and ethnographic literature. Apotropaics are often worn on the individual. One very common charm for turning away evil is a pierced coin worn on a string around the ankle or neck:

> A silver dime worn about the ankle or neck or placed in the shoe will prevent any trick from exerting its influence against you—this being one of the common charms given by Marie Laveau. Some Negroes openly say that such a coin keeps off evil spirits . . . . Frank

Dickerson says only silver ball will do the work, while others suggest a copper coin in toe of shoe, a silver ring about the finger, or a goose quill filled with quicksilver worn below the knee (Puckett 1968[1926]:288).

Archaeologically, silver coins with holes pierced through them have been recovered from archaeological sites in Virginia, Georgia, Louisiana, and Arkansas (Rose 1985; Adams 1987; Patten 1992; Wilkie 1995; Yakubik and Méndez [1995]). A pierced silver dime and a silver half dollar were found in a late 19th- to early 20th-century African-American cemetery positioned at the necks of two burials (Rose and Santeford 1985:73–75, 115–116).

Red flannel charm bags, commonly made by Kongo peoples (Thompson 1983:129–131), are still popularly used in Louisiana (Fontenot 1994). The flannel bags can contain any number of potentially magical ingredients. The bags can be used either as "fixes" to cause harm or as apotropaics but seem to be most commonly used in the latter capacity. An African-American midwife described one such bag that she obtained to rid herself of a ghost: "After a time I went to a conjure woman to get help to drive off the friendly pirate (the ghost). She made up a strong conjure bag with hog bristles and black cats' hair and a rabbit's foot and dirt from the graves of seven murderers and seven little stones from south-running water all tied up in a red flannel rag greased with snake oil and tied with dead woman's hair" (Campbell 1946:181). It is important to remember that ghosts are not merely a frightening problem, but can be bearers of disease and death. Once in possession of the conjure bag, the midwife was rid of her ghostly visitor.

Animals could also provide magical protection: "If a frizzled hen is kept in the yard she will scratch and destroy all conjuration which will cause discomfort to the family" (Herskovits 1962[1941]:237). This belief is prevalent in West Africa, the Caribbean, and the American South. It is intriguing to wonder if the small guinea fowl charm recovered from the orangery of the Calvert family plantation in Maryland

(Yentsch 1994:214) had any meaning to its holder as a protective device. The importance of plant and animal materials and imagery within African-American magic indicates that archaeologists need to carefully consider the religious and magical implications of floral and faunal materials from African-American sites.

Magic and the Dead

Magical practice relates as well, and not surprisingly, to the treatment and care of the dead. As previously discussed, the dead, as ghosts, have the ability to harm the living, and they must be treated properly to ensure that a loved one completes the journey to the next realm, and to ensure that no malignant spirits remain to harm the living. While it is possible to drive off ghosts with other magical means, as in the case of the midwife and the pirate, it is often easier to anticipate the problem with preventative measures.

The material culture of African-American magic for the dead is found in and above graves, as well as can be seen in the way that the living areas of the deceased are treated. A number of practices are related to the disposal of the deceased's belongings. The understanding that the improper treatment of the dead and their belongings may lead to hauntings is common throughout the American South and Caribbean. In Alabama, Puckett recorded the belief that "unless you bury a person's things with him he will come back after them"(Puckett 1968[1926]:103). In Mississippi, "to keep the deceased from coming back again, the cup and saucer used in the last illness should be placed on the grave. The medicine bottles placed there are also turned upside down with the corks loosened so that the medicine may soak into the grave" (Puckett 1968[1926]:105). Examples of the latter practice have been discovered archaeologically during the excavation of an Arkansas African-American cemetery (Rose and Santeford 1985). Personal belongings from life may decorate the grave: "In South Carolina, bleached sea-shells, broken crockery and glassware, broken pitchers, soap-dishes,

lamp chimneys, tureens, coffee-cups, syrup jugs, all sorts of ornamental vases, cigar boxes, gun locks, tomato cans, teapots, flower pots, bits of stucco, plaster images, pieces of carved stonework from one of the public buildings during the war, glass lamps and tumblers in great number, and forty other kitchen articles are used. On the children's graves were dolls' heads, little china tea-bowls and pitchers, toy images of animals, china vases, pewter dishes and other things which would interest a child" (Puckett 1968[1926]:105).

In many parts of the Caribbean, disturbing a grave can provoke retaliation by *duppies* (ghosts). On Crooked Island, Bahamas, an entire village of houses stands empty, with household belongings intact. The village had been inhabited by old people whose children had moved to other islands. According to older residents of the island, as people died and were buried, the houses were left as they had been so no spirits would be disturbed (June MacMillan 1995, pers. comm.).

Magic and Gender Tensions

If archaeologists are to understand the importance and role of magical and magic-related artifacts recovered from African-American settings, we must remember to situate these artifacts in the places where they are found: households. The overwhelming majority of artifacts recovered that are related to African-American spiritual beliefs have been recovered from households. The spiritual and magical beliefs studied archaeologically are within the context of family life. Be they hidden in root cellars, stored behind hearths, dropped through floorboards, or accidentally dropped or buried in a yard, these artifacts must be understood in the context of the family.

Inherent in the magical practices of Africa and African America is a tension and duality in power between men and women. Men and women, due to their intimate access to one another and their opposing magical makeup, are potentially healing or potentially harmful to one another. As already mentioned, the hat of the father worn during childbirth can ease a woman's labor pains. Likewise, many of the magical charms and spells to harm require access to the victim's exuvia, with sperm, urine, menstrual blood, or excrement being the most powerful magical substances. These substances are protected and disposed of carefully, to avoid their falling into potentially dangerous hands. Powdermaker (1993[1937]:288–289) reported one African-American woman who kept all the hair that she lost in her comb and carefully destroyed it. However, the individuals with greatest access to these substances are other family members.

A man and woman engaged in a sexual relationship and cohabiting in a house without plumbing have a great deal of access to those bodily substances which are most potentially harmful to their mate, and are themselves vulnerable to magical attack from loved ones. Likewise, children, parents, and any extended family living within a house are potentially vulnerable to attack. This circumstance creates a tension within the family. The family must trust its members not to harm each other either directly or indirectly.

In times of marital strife, there is always the potential threat of magical attack and retaliation. Magical attacks that involve substances as strong as urine, semen, menstrual blood, or night soil, can be fatal. Philandering spouses not only endanger themselves by allowing persons outside of the family to gain access to potentially dangerous substances but also threaten the safety and coherence of the family.

Magical spells abound that are intended to destroy marriages, lead another woman's husband away, or bind a man's or woman's affections to another, and so forth (e.g., Puckett 1968[1926]; Hyatt 1978). For instance, in the Bahamas, it is a common Obeah belief that if a woman puts her urine in the bathwater of her husband or sons, they will never abandon her (Grace Turner 1996, pers. comm.). Likewise, African-American women throughout North America have believed that if they put some of their menstrual blood in a man's meal, he will be bound to them forever. Powdermaker (1993[1937]:289) reported hearing that "a woman can hold a man by putting some-

thing in his food," but had not learned what that something was. The intent of the users of love potions was not always sincere: "a young woman has been mentioned who uses love charms to hold men whom she wants only for their money, but who depends solely upon affection to keep the men she really cares for" (Powdermaker 1993[1937]:287). Men were aware of these attempts at magical control and would try to defeat them.

A Bahamian woman told me of a battle over bathwater between her brothers and mother. Her mother had long urinated in their bathwater, unbeknownst to her sons. As the sons neared adulthood, one caught her "fixing" the bathwater, and the sons began to demand that they draw their own baths. While the mother complied, she would create diversions while the baths were being drawn and continued the magical practice whenever possible. Through her actions, she tried to ensure that even when grown and with families of their own, her sons would not fully abandon her. Her sons, by attempting to avoid this binding, were not so much stating a lack of love for their mother, but a desire to become independent of her. Marriage and family life is not just a contract of love and commitment, but also a magical battleground for control.

Given this state of magical combat, and potential issues of control, the division of tasks and activities within the household by gender and age rank can be very important, depending upon the level of stress or strife within a relationship. If a woman suspects her husband of cavorting with another woman, or the husband is thinking of leaving, the act of allowing your mate to prepare a meal versus preparing the meal oneself has new meaning and implications.

Conjurers understood the importance of magic as a means of protecting and healing relationships, and were quick to dispense advice with their medicine. Puckett describes a particularly insightful charm,

A "conjure-woman" in Algiers, La., was given $5 for a bottle of medicine (lemonade) to break a husband of quarreling. Her directions were for the unhappy wife to fill her mouth with the medicine whenever her good man began to quarrel and not to swallow it until he had ceased. Then she was to swallow the medicine and kiss him. So successful was this treatment that several wives came to the doctor upon recommendation for the same prescription (Puckett 1968[1926]:209).

While it may appear that this "magical remedy" is nothing more than dressed-up advice, in the emotional heat of a marital spat, the dictates of a magical recipe are more likely to be heeded than the advice to "just keep quiet until he calms down." While this particular story is sweetly amusing, it also clearly demonstrates that magical solutions to dispute resolution were important.

Outside the realm of marriage, men and women remain potentially dangerous to one another, particularly when lovers. Hyatt (1973, 1974, 1978), when gathering his inventory of magical charms and potions, recorded a wide range of spells related to the prevention of venereal disease. For instance, a woman who rubs earwax on a man's genitals and holds a coin to the roof of her mouth during intercourse could give a man venereal disease (Hyatt 1978:2376). A man could defend himself by holding a penny in his mouth during intercourse (Hyatt 1978:2369). Likewise, a man could test a woman for venereal disease, unbeknownst to the woman, by rubbing the woman's genitals with a bit of his earwax. If the woman complained of a burning sensation, she was "positive" for the disease. In rural Louisiana, African-American men still joke about their lovers passing the "ear-wax test."

That oral traditions suggested that venereal disease could be acquired through the malicious action of a sexual partner illustrates not only the intrinsic danger of members of the opposite sex to one another, but also demonstrates another way in which a strong marriage bond could eliminate the threat of magical harm. Long-term partners would not be well served to inflict venereal disease on a life partner. Sex, outside of the realm of marriage, was a magically dangerous pursuit.

If we are to successfully study gender within African-American households, we must consider the magical dimension of gender relationships, and, likewise, if we are to consider magical practices, then we must consider gender.

Magical and Religious Systems: A Diachronic Approach

While this review of African-American magical uses is by no means exhaustive, it should be evident that magical practices were a pervasive influence on most arenas of daily life. Acts as simple as leaving a footprint or using another person's comb could have profound magical impacts upon one's life. Family relations, child care, personal hygiene habits, the preparation of food, relations with neighbors, were all aspects of everyday life that had magical implications. Threat of magical harm or retaliation for one's actions profoundly shaped important personal and social relations within the African community.

The ways in which magical practice and religion are articulated in African-American society have changed through time. Within traditional West African religions, magical and religious practices were often completely entwined within the belief system. For instance, within Kongo belief systems, the creation of medicine is a magical process that involves the use of a *nkisi*, or charm, which is believed to contain a captured soul of a spirit from the religious pantheon. On some plantations, enslaved Africans and African Americans were discouraged from engaging in religious worship. Organized, African-based religions did continue to be practiced in the New World in the form of Obeahism, Myalism, and Vodun in the Caribbean, Santeria in Cuba, Shango in Trinidad and Brazil, and Voodoo in Louisiana (Herskovits 1962[1941]; Raboteau 1978; Tallant 1983[1946]; Murphy 1988; Brandon 1993).

The extent to which West African religious structures survived the Middle Passage has been a focus of scholarly debate (e.g., Raboteau 1978).

Demographic, political, social, cultural, and geographical factors have all impacted the extent to which enslaved Africans could recreate their religious values throughout the diaspora. As Raboteau summarized:

> The historical circumstances, then, in which religious traditions from Africa have been transmitted to New World societies have varied from society to society. Some traditions extend relatively far into the past of colonial slavery; others have died out with the passage of time; and still others have developed out of more recent contact with Africa. Moreover, Afro-American cults have modified traditions and added new ones. Yet, despite discontinuity and innovation, the fundamental religious perspectives of Africa have continued to orient the lives of the descendants of slaves in the New World (Raboteau 1978:42).

Understanding the myriad of cultural and contextual factors that have contributed to the historical transformations of African religions in the New World is confusing and daunting. Add to the complexity of the situation the secret nature of African-American religious systems during enslavement and beyond, and the task is impossible from documentary sources. Given the temporal nature of the archaeological database, archaeologists are in the best position to contribute to the broader understanding of religions and religious change within the diaspora.

Mechanisms of Religious/Magical Change: Creolization and Syncretism

The processes of culture change that shape the religious and magical developments in the diaspora are creolization and syncretism. Creolization (cf. Joyner 1984; Ferguson 1992) is the process through which a group's "cultural grammar" absorbs a new lexicon. In other words, the ideas that shape cultural action remain the same, but the material way in which they are expressed changes. For example, Ferguson (1992) argues that, while enslaved Africans may have adopted some European foods and products into their diet, the continuity in vessel shapes for their Colono Ware, and continuities in the ways these vessels were used, suggest that enslaved people continued to use these pots and prepare their meals in an African way.

In later African-American archaeological assemblages, the process of creolization can be seen as African-American ethnic values are increasingly expressed through the selection of mass-produced consumer goods. For instance, Wilkie (1996a) has argued that African-American consumer choices in over-the-counter medicines are influenced by the "grammar" of traditional ethnomedical systems. Likewise, Stine et al. (1996) have argued that the relatively high proportions of the color blue among glass beads recovered archaeologically from African-American sites are reflective of active consumer choice. Creolization, as a process, represents retentions in cultural values that become expressed in new ways due to cultural contact and relocation.

Syncretism, most commonly discussed in terms of religious transformations, is the process through which two formally distinct cultural values or icons become fused into a third, new reality (e.g., Thompson 1983). The fusion of the African spirits and Catholic saints within Haitian vodun or Cuban Santeria represents the process of syncretism. The aspects of the respective saint and African deity become merged and inseparable, yet unique and distinct from each original.

In addition to the growth of the North-American born enslaved population, by the beginning of the 19th century, greater numbers of planters were allowing their enslaved peoples to be baptized and practice Christianity. It is clear from ex-slave narratives and accounts from abolitionists that some enslaved people embraced the philosophy and faith of Christianity with great sincerity. With greater access to the theology and rituals of Christianity, enslaved Africans found fertile ground for the expression and elaboration of African religious and magical systems. The syncretic religious and magical practices that arose as a result of the merging of Christian and African theologies remain a largely unrecognized component in archaeological interpretations.

Through time, as more enslaved people adopted Christianity, African traditions became increasingly merged with Christian sacred histories and pantheons. The form in which syncretisms developed was dependent upon a number of factors, including what branch of Christianity was practiced by the enslaved people (Raboteau 1978). For instance, Catholicism includes a broad and diverse pantheon of saints, angels, martyrs, and so on, and incorporates a certain level of mysticism within its theology. As such, Catholicism provided a medium for African Americans to identify, recognize, and continue to worship African deities within the Catholic context, such as in the syncretistic religions of Shango and Santeria. In contrast, the majority of Protestant religions condemn the recognition of other supernatural forces or powers as deviltry, leaving less opportunity to recognize specific African deities. However, the Baptist faith, with its emphasis on water immersion baptism and camp revival meetings—a context in which "shouting" as a religious expression developed— provided a means for continuities in beliefs about water spirits and the religious expression of possession, so important in Yoruban religion (Thompson 1983; Pitts 1993).

As descendants of African populations increasingly embraced different forms of Christianity, traditional magical and magico-medical beliefs diverged in the ways that they were expressed. While attending church services became one means of expressing and experiencing religious worship, magical expressions of belief were increasingly likely to occur outside of the church context. These two facets of religious activity, however, remained linked by a single cosmology. Hortense Powdermaker, working among a rural southern African-American community in the 1930s observed:

> Among the Negroes of Cottonville, many who are deeply religious are not especially superstitious, and

some heartily disapprove of voodoo doctors. Often, however, those who are devoutly religious are also devout believers in current folk superstitions and do not look upon Christianity and Voodoo as conflicting in any way. Some of the "doctors" themselves insist that they work their miracles by the grace of God, and feel that their effectiveness bear witness to their piety (Powdermaker 1993[1937]:286).

Within Catholicism, Africans and African Americans found a spiritual medium that could provide coverage for their own, resulting in the development of syncretic religions such as Santeria, Voodoo, and Vodun. Within these contexts, magical traditions from Catholicism and African-based belief systems were incorporated and merged together. Magic remained an aspect of group, structured religion. In Protestant Christian traditions, while some aspects of worship were compatible, most magical beliefs, while not eliminated, were separated from the realm of organized religion.

Within African-Catholic syncretised religions, apparently traditional Catholic iconography and relics are imbued with new meanings and roles. For instance, Puckett (1968[1926]) reports the importance of "Lucky St. Joseph" in New Orleans. A small gilt figurine of Joseph and the Christ child, kept in a small case, was carried as a good luck charm or for getting a husband by the European-Catholic community. Puckett wrote, "Negroes also carry this Lucky Saint Joseph, but in their case, lacking the spiritual background, they look upon it in much the same fashion as a rabbit's foot, horseshoe, or any other less sacred charm" (Puckett 1968[1926]:564).

However, an interaction between an African-American man, Robert, and his Saint Joseph figurine, as reported by Lyle Saxon, adds another dimension to this interpretation:

> "Yah! Yah! See dat, Saint Joseph!" he (Robert) cried in glee, "I sho' fixed o' dat time!" He addressed a small statue of a saint which stood upside down on the wash-stand, propped in this uncomfortable position between tooth mug and soap dish. And to my further amazement, he reached out his hand, righted the out-

raged saint, and placing him upon the altar beside the Statue of the Virgin, he fell upon his knees and began to pray, rapidly . . . . In response to my questions he told a remarkable story. He had prayed to Saint Joseph that he might have the day off from his work, for he loved the Mardi Gras festivities more than anything else. But it appeared that Saint Joseph did not heed his prayer and he was not chosen as the lucky one that would accompany the children on their all-day wandering . . . he had learned his fate last night and had decided to take desperate measures. This very morning he had quarreled with the saint, "stomped" his foot at him, and turned him upside down against the soap dish for punishment. And now, did I not see that Saint Joseph had come to his senses? Robert had known, the very moment that I came walking into the courtyard . . . St. Joseph sent me in answer to his prayer (Saxon 1988:18).

Saint Joseph is not merely a charm to be carried, like a rabbit's foot; instead, he represents a spiritual power with whom to negotiate and even to bully when not performing satisfactorily. Saxon provides an additional description of Robert's room:

> The walls were covered with pictures of saints in various agonies of torture; Saint Lucy carrying her eyes on a plate, Saint Roch with his sores, followed by a collie that held a cake in its mouth; Saint Somebody else being burned at the stake. I thought them all magnificent. A crucifix hung on the wall, and beneath it was a sort of altar draped in a white lace scarf and bearing three black candles in small candlesticks. A bunch of artificial flowers stood at the foot of a statue of the Virgin Mary (Saxon 1988:17).

It is evident from Saxon's description that Robert was involved to some degree in voodooism. Saxon later describes Robert stopping in the French Quarter to gaze in the window of a voodoo shop. Saxon's work must be viewed with a cautious critical eye, for he was writing memoirs of his childhood, and is known to have confused some dates and events, either accidentally or intentionally. However, Saxon also had a lifelong interest in the supernatural beliefs of African-American Louisiana, and later directed the Federal Writer's Ex-Slave Narratives project in that state, ensuring that interviewers spent a concerted effort in interviews asking about Marie Laveau and Voodoo (Clayton 1990). In any case, Saxon's description does provide some insight into the possible interaction between saint relics and their users.

Throughout Louisiana "Candle Shops," which cater to practitioners of hoodoo and Santeria, stock a wide range of candles decorated with different saints as well as a range of saint medals. "Seven Powers of Africa" candles depict seven saints with the name of their recognized equivalent Yoruban *Orisha*. While the "Seven African Powers" candles are manufactured specifically for practitioners of Santeria, they are bought and used by Louisiana African-American families who do not consider themselves Santerians. Yet, the imagery and the powers of the Santeria deities are familiar and meaningful to these users. In addition to artifacts related to saint iconography that can archaeologically signal continuities in African magical and religious practice, each of the *Orisha* have additional material cultural symbols associated with them (González-Wippler 1992[1973]:15).

Due to the complexity of the relationship between Catholic icons and practice, such as the burning of candles in association with prayer, and syncretised African religions, artifacts that bear Catholic iconography cannot be assumed to represent evidence of strictly Roman Catholic beliefs. Discussing a rosary recovered from an 18th-century African/African-American burial in New Orleans, Orser (1994:38) wrote of the buried individual: "Tooth mutilation is well known in Africa, and it is tempting to suppose that this individual had spent a portion of his life there. The presence of the rosary, however, implies that he had accepted Christianity at some point in his life. We will never know if his conversion occurred in Africa or in his New World home." Orser's attribution of the rosary to a strictly Christian conversion is an oversimplification of a potentially complex situation. The rosary recovered from the burial context in New Orleans is as likely to represent a participation in African syncretic religious belief (of geographic origin in Africa or the New World) as to represent Catholicism.

Likewise, a handmade St. Christopher's medal and rosary recovered from the free-black settlement of Fort Mose in Florida may also represent syncretic religious beliefs rather than pure Spanish Catholicism (Deagan and MacMahon 1995:23, 35). From the Hermitage plantation, Tennessee, three copper-alloy clenched-fist charms, showing the wrist and back of hand, have been recovered from early 19th-century African-American contexts (McKee 1992, 1995). McKee reports that these charms are similar to *figas* and *milagras* used in Brazil and Latin America as votive items, for fertility, good luck, and defense from witchcraft. McKee also recognizes that these artifacts could have Islamic meanings, and could represent the "Hand of Fatima," which was also used to ward off the "evil eye" (McKee 1995:40). A similar charm has been recovered from another planter/slave context in Maryland, from the Calvert site (Yentsch 1994:33, Figure 2.2).

The absorption of Christian iconography by African Americans is visible archaeologically from at least the 18th century to the present, and represents an important direction for further archaeological study. In addition, once a diachronic approach is employed, it is clear that syncretism of African and Christian belief systems was taking place simultaneously as the creolization of African beliefs in other regions. While the processes of creolization and syncretism have been discussed to some extent within the archaeological literature (e.g., Ferguson 1992; Wilkie 1995), as yet, there has been little attempt to situate these processes, and the archaeological evidence of these cultural processes, within a temporal landscape.

A Model for Understanding Religious/Magical Change

Archaeologists have tended to treat African-American magical and religious practices as if they occur synchronically, and have paid little attention to these practices across time and space. In order for researchers to approach African-American magical and religious systems from a diachronic perspective, however, it is necessary for archaeologists to adopt a framework in which to organize and interpret material evidence of African-American religious continuities and transformations. George Brandon (1993), in studying ethnographically the development of Santeria as it spread from its Yoruban origins to Cuba, and eventually to New York City, employed a three-stage framework for understanding the religious transformations he encountered and documented. This three-step framework may likewise prove useful for historical archaeologists studying magical-religious transformations. The three stages, the Formative, Persisting, and Transfomative, were defined by Brandon as follows:

> In terms of religion, a Formative period is when a religion is beginning to assume a different physiognomy than previously, through exposure to other religions, internal developments, economic or political catastrophe, and so forth. What marks this period is exposure, innovation, recoil, or seeking, and these are seen in a number of processes which do not necessarily eventuate in a coherent direction of change. Eventually, though, these developments eventuate in a period of conflict over a small number of alternatives, followed by a taking of positions and the working out of these alternatives until one of more of them becomes a major direction of change. Those alternatives that survive assume a form which is recognizable and whose recognizability can be successfully and consistently reproduced. When this happens it constitutes a period of persistence, and the new form is repeatedly reproduced within a range of variation that assures its uniqueness and coherence. The Transformative stage is simply another version of the Formative stage, with the form that exists during the Persisting stage as its point of departure (Brandon 1993:3).

Brandon is quick to point out that his framework should be seen as one of multilinear, not unilinear, progression. Within the African diaspora, each geographic region will have its own distinctive Formative period, depending upon its political, historical, and social-cultural context.

As the geographic and temporal breadth of African-American archaeology continues to expand, we should be able to evaluate the development of African-American magical and religious systems within their distinct social, cultural, and temporal contexts.

The cultural influences that shape the Formative period are not just the mixing of different West African cultures in the New World setting of enslavement, but also contact with Native American and European cultures. As archaeologists continue to collect archaeological data and interpret them within a contextual framework (Hodder 1986), we will be able to clarify which recurring magical assemblages represent Persisting belief structures and practices, and finally, as we begin to consider our data in a diachronic manner, we can begin to recognize and understand succeeding Transformative and Persisting stages.

Archaeological Expectations of the Model

To effectively employ this model, archaeological assemblages related to African-American magical and religious practices have to be studied across time and space. The development and expression of African-American magical-religious systems will be different in every area of the diaspora. For instance, as will be discussed below, while cosmogram-marked Colono Ware bowls were important to the creation of sacred medicines in 17th- and 18th-century South Carolina (Ferguson 1992), no similar uses of Jamaican African-produced pottery (*yabba* wares) have been reported (Armstrong 1990).

Population dynamics and social and political factors influenced and shaped the processes of creolization and syncretism in different areas. Enslaved populations in different colonies may have been relatively isolated from one another during the 17th and 18th centuries, perhaps leading to the development of distinctive regional religious and magical traditions. Movements of slaves between states became more common during the early 19th century, as growing demand for slaves in the deep south increased, and as

abolitionist movements attempted to eliminate and restrict enslavement on a state-by-state basis (Davis and Donaldson 1975; Genovese 1975, 1989; Gutman 1976). By the period of Reconstruction, African-American populations that had been previously isolated from one another mingled throughout the American South as well as in new, large urban centers such as Chicago, New York, and Philadelphia (Davis and Donaldson 1975). For this later period, regional differences in magical-religious traditions would be expected to lessen, if not disappear.

As defined by Brandon, the Formative period for African-American religions in any part of the diaspora should be archaeologically indicated by a variety of syncretic and creolization events. These events would not necessarily be widespread within a geographic region nor be of particular time depth, since a Formative period would be marked by a variety of competing options. Archaeologically, both Formative and Transformative stages will be difficult to recognize, since these are stages that are characterized by flux and change. The periods of Formative and Transformative stages within a region will have short-lived material correlates. Artifact types or assemblages of limited duration, or single examples of artifacts may be the only material indicators of these stages. The low archaeological profile of these periods, however, does not diminish their importance. The Formative and Transformative periods are the periods of culture change, when the mechanisms of syncretism and creolization are at work. Through documentary evidence it should be possible to understand what contextual influences and events trigger periods of change.

Once a pattern is established within a region, the tradition represents one of Persistence. Periods of Persistence represent phases of stability and are likely to be of greatest visibility in the archaeological record. The repeated recovery of an artifact type, or assemblage of artifact types within a given temporal and spatial context would represent evidence of a persisting magical-religious tradition.

The application of a model such as Brandon's (1993) that explicitly recognizes syncretism and creolization as mechanisms of change to the archaeological study of African-American magical and religious systems is severalfold. First, the stages defined by Brandon have explicit material/artifactual signatures, even if these artifactual signatures may be of short duration or limited distribution. Second, by adopting such a model, magical and religious practices would be placed within a diachronic interpretive framework which acknowledges these practices are not stagnant. Third, the model is intrinsically tied to the sociohistorical cultural context. The model cannot be employed without the researcher considering the cultural landscape in which the artifacts derived meaning. Therefore, the researcher is encouraged to articulate the material with the documentary record, and to maintain a dialectic between these two databases.

Archaeological Examples of the Model Applied

Below, I will provide a brief overview of the published archaeological evidence of African-American spiritual traditions from three geographical regions: South Carolina, the Chesapeake, and Louisiana, and how the application of a diachronic model in these areas could enlighten our understanding of African-American belief systems in these areas. As will be clearly seen, despite the sense within historical archaeology that we have a better understanding of New World African-American religions than ever before, there is no area for which a complete archaeological timeline is available.

South Carolina

South Carolina was home to a large enslaved African population early in its history. The relatively high proportion of Africans to Europeans in South Carolina allowed enslaved populations greater ability to retain African traditions and limit contact with European belief systems and practices (Joyner 1984; Ferguson 1992; Deetz

1993). South Carolina, due to this historical circumstance, is an intriguing area in which to study African and African-American religious traditions.

In South Carolina, Leland Ferguson (1992:110–116) has found evidence of Bakongo-influenced water cults. African-American-produced Colono Ware pottery bowls bear crosses and crosses contained in circles on the interior and exterior bases. Ferguson (1992) has argued, most convincingly, that these symbols bear close resemblance to the Bakongo sign of the cosmos. The cosmogram represents the cycle of life and death, continuity and change, the division between this world and the afterworld, land and sea, sky and earth (Thompson 1981:27–28). Complete bowls bearing these symbols and sherds with these marks have been recovered from rivers and riversides. These bowls may be related to the creation of traditional Kongo sacred medicines, or *minkisi* (*nkisi* = singular), that served to control power emanating from supernatural powers (Ferguson 1992:114). As containers for sacred medicines, the bowls could have once contained any number of magical materials, including stones, white clay, animal remains, shells, broken glass, beads, and so forth.

Ferguson does not propose a date range for the incidence of this cultural manifestation; however, Colono Wares associated with African-American sites date from the 1670s to the early 1800s, after which time they become rare, then disappear all together. The disappearance of Colono Wares does not necessarily mean that the practice of using clay bowls for the preparation of sacred medicine disappeared as well. There is no reason to suppose that American- or European-produced ceramics could not have been used as containers for sacred medicines. Likewise, new containers of organic materials such as wood, gourd, or cloth could have been employed. However, the disappearance of these vessels from the archaeological record does suggest the transition from one Persisting stage to a Transformative stage in the development of African-American religious magical practices in South Carolina.

In South Carolina, it would appear that excavators of 19th- and early 20th-century African-American sites should consider, when evaluating artifacts from these sites, how the magical-religious practices documented archaeologically by Ferguson may have transformed into new cultural and material expressions during this later period.

The Chesapeake

The Chesapeake remains one of the best-studied areas of Colonial America. Unlike South Carolina, where enslaved African people outnumbered Europeans early in the colony's history, in the Chesapeake, the growth of the enslaved population was slower. Africans and African Americans lived in closer contact with Europeans, and the impact of this continued contact is evident in the material culture of enslaved people of the Chesapeake. For instance, unlike the South Carolinian Colono Wares which retain African vessel form shapes, Chesapeake Colono Wares are more likely to take European-influenced forms (Deetz 1993). This difference in historical context should be apparent in the development of African-Chesapeake religious expression.

In the Chesapeake, terra-cotta tobacco pipes have been found with regularity on sites dating between 1640 and 1720 (Deetz 1993:91). Several of these pipes have been found to bear the Nigerian *Kwardata* motif. According to Emerson (1994:43), when placed on a ritual beer vessel the *Kwardata* symbol represents "the transition from youth to adulthood in contemporary Ga'anda society." Emerson states that pipes bearing the *Kwardata* motif have been recovered from sites in Maryland and Virginia, including St. Mary's City, Jamestown, Governor's Land, and Martin's Hundred (Emerson 1994:43). The recovery of these pipes from a number of sites may represent a material expression of a persisting religious tradition within the enslaved population of the Chesapeake.

The placement of a symbol of obvious ritual and religious importance on a new form, a tobacco pipe, reflects some Native American cultural influence as well as a transformation in the original presentation of this symbol. Whether the pipe, and the presumed associated use of tobacco, serves as a substitute for the ritual(s) associated with the traditional beer vessels, or reflects a new, syncretised version of the ritual(s) cannot be determined from the available evidence. These potentially African-American-made pipes disappear early in the 18th century, around the same time that Colono Ware pottery is first found in this region (Deetz 1993). Whether the construction of Colono Ware vessels allowed for a new religious expression is not known. Again, the disappearance of one form of artifactual material expression of religious belief suggests a Transformative process.

Further to the north, in 18th-century Maryland, another set of archaeological finds may represent another manifestation of either Kongo sacred medicines or continuities in the creation of family sacred altars honoring ancestors. Leone (1995; Wilford 1996) has reported the discovery of caches of potentially sacred artifacts associated with hearths and the northeast corners of rooms in two 18th-century houses in Annapolis, Maryland. Curated and hidden artifacts include buttons, doll parts, rings, rock crystals, and pierced disks. Unlike the instances of the cosmogram-inscribed Colono Ware, or the *Kwardata*-adorned tobacco pipes, these artifact assemblages cannot be tied directly to the material cultural expressions of Africa. Instead, the processes of creolization have led to the development of a religious expression which has endowed non-African forms and artifacts with new spiritual meanings. By the date of these caches, the majority of the enslaved population of North America were not Africans themselves, but the descendants of Africans.

Again, the widespread use of these artifacts is suggestive of a Persisting stage of religious expression. The components of Leone's artifact caches include objects that have been recovered from potentially magical contexts at other late 18th- and 19th-century African-American sites in

Virginia and Maryland, such as pierced disks/coins, crystals and doll parts (Klingelhofer 1987; Patten 1992). The recovery of similar artifact caches and similar artifact types suggests the Persistence of a magical-religious tradition dating from the 18th to mid-19th centuries.

Louisiana

Louisiana stands as a distinct region of the deep south for several reasons particular to its history. Settled as a colony by the French and Spanish before becoming acquired by the United States, Louisiana had a strong Catholic religious heritage. After the Haitian Revolution, formerly enslaved Africans from that island migrated to Louisiana, settling in New Orleans during the late 18th century. This immigrant population has often been credited with bringing Voodoo to the city (Tallant 1983[1946]).

Syncretic African-Catholic rituals represent a Persisting component of African-American religious practice in Louisiana from the earliest periods of occupation to the present. The earliest dated African-American religious-magical artifacts recovered from Louisiana are the previously discussed rosary recovered by Charles Orser and Douglas Owsley from a burial dated before 1788 (Orser 1994:38). No other Catholic artifacts are reported from African-American sites until the late 1800s.

By the 1840s, the growth of the sugar industry in Louisiana brought increasing numbers of enslaved people to the state. Contact between previously isolated African-American populations led to a Transformative stage with African Americans in Louisiana adopting artifacts similar to those used by enslaved people in Virginia and Maryland for magical uses. The ensuing Persisting stage appears to bear other similarities to the Chesapeake traditions; at one site, religiously significant artifacts have been found in caches associated with hearths. A pierced 1793 Spanish real, associated with two black barrel glass beads, was recovered from a mid-19th-century slave cabin at Ashland Belle-Helene plantation (Yakubik et al. 1994:10–94). In addition, re-searchers reported that hearth areas of the slave cabins at this plantation may have served as ceremonial centers: "The coin, beads, shells, buttons and smoothed stones were found more frequently near hearths than in other parts of the cabins or in the yards. This may reflect ritual activity occurred within the house, where it could be hidden" (Yakubik and Méndez [1995]:27).

Excavations of hearth areas of slave cabins at Riverlake plantation, which was occupied from the mid-19th century through the mid-20th century, failed to recover evidence of any similar caches of artifacts. The longer duration of occupation at this site may have eliminated any archaeological trace of earlier religious activities around the hearths, suggesting the development of a different Transformative and Persisting tradition. Other religiously and magically important artifacts, such as crystals and projectile points, were recovered from this site, but were recovered from underneath houses and from yard areas. A Catholic St. Anne medal was recovered from a late 19th-century African-American household at Riverlake. While Riverlake plantation was located in the French Catholic parish of Pointe Coupee, the African Americans of the plantation were self-identified Baptists.

Located across the Mississippi River from Pointe Coupee is the predominately Protestant parish of West Feliciana. A rosary medal and a Christ's head relic were recovered from a late 19th- to early 20th-century African-American household in this parish. The occupants were known, through both oral and documentary history, to have been practicing Baptists (Wilkie 1995). Again, the presence of these artifacts in a seemingly contradictory setting—Baptists do not condone the Catholic use of idols—suggests the presence of African nuanced practices. The adoption of Catholic iconography for magical use by Baptists in Pointe Coupee and West Feliciana parish may represent Transformative processes within a very localized area. Pointe Coupe and West Feliciana parish were economically tied during the 19th and 20th centuries. Enslaved, and later freed, African Americans moved across the river between these two parishes seasonally, to work cotton or sugar fields in turn. It seems likely that contact between these Catholic and Baptist populations led to the adoption of each other's magical-religious toolbox during the Persisting stage.

Also recovered from this housesite was an 1855 Britannia pierced penny. The coin has been interpreted as the birth coin of Silvia Freeman, who was born in 1855 and lived in the house (Wilkie 1995). Interestingly enough, Freeman's birthplace is identified from census records as "Virginia." In her case, the magical practice of using coins as protective devices was quite literally brought by her from Virginia. In the example of Silvia Freeman, one can see how religious innovation is ultimately instituted by individuals and their families through time, as they maintain and adapt the magical-religious practices of the proceeding generations.

Summary

The purpose of applying Brandon's (1993) model is not merely to provide a descriptive analysis of where and when different manifestations of African-American spiritual practices can be found. Instead, the model provides an interpretive framework for understanding how African Americans altered their expressions of religious and magical beliefs as their magical-religious needs changed to meet new demands within their communities, and against a changing cultural, social, economic, and political backdrop. As argued above, magical and religious practice is of overarching importance within African-American culture, and influences community relationships, family life, as well as the way individual families view and respond to the world around them. As stated eloquently by Edwards (1995:5), "analyses that treat slave culture as responses only to plantation society in the New World subvert aesthetics, beliefs, craftsmanship, and other issues relevant to African-American research."

The model discussed above offers several benefits for the archaeological study of African-American magical-religious practice. The model provides a vocabulary for describing stages of magical-religious change, and offers a diachronic framework in which to understand data. The intent of the model is not to ignore or simplify the very complex cultural negotiations in which Africans and African Americans participated during the construction of religious expressions. The model provides a means of organizing the limited evidence now available regarding African-American magical-religious tradition and highlights time periods and regions that require further research. It is evident, through the application of a diachronic model, that the archaeological evidence of African-American magical-religious practices from any given area is very incomplete and patchy. While scholars have been able to identify some very important manifestations of African-American spiritual beliefs during and beyond the period of enslavement, we have not directed our investigations in a way that allows us to understand the dynamics of the cultural and social transformations in African-American spiritual traditions, and ultimately, family life. The adoption of an interpretive framework that attempts to contextualize religious change and link the archaeological and documentary records is necessary at this time in the development of the field of study.

Conclusions

A review of ethnographic, oral historical, and documentary evidence indicates that African-American religious and magical beliefs, although geographically and diachronically varied, were pervasive and of great importance to the African-American community. Magical-religious practice influenced every aspect of life, including health care, relationships within the household, gender ideologies, matters of love and marriage, community dispute resolution, and the afterlife. In interpretations of African-American material culture, archaeologists must be careful to recognize the potential magical meaning artifacts may have carried.

Some of the magical-religious artifacts recovered from household middens are distinctive and can be argued to be of religious significance wherever they are found, such as amulets, pierced coins, curated crystals, curated projectile points, and so on, since ethnographic and oral historical evidence identifies them as such. Other artifacts, which are well known to hold multiple functions within African-American households, such as bottles, straight pins, cups and saucers, glass beads, unpierced coins, and buttons, also have, among their other uses, possible magical functions. For many of these artifacts, we can never know if they had magical functions or not but should acknowledge the possibility, although not as an exclusive interpretation.

It is important that archaeologists do not become overly enthusiastic in their attributions of common household materials to magical uses. Doll parts found as part of a cache of religious materials, such as those recovered from Annapolis, may have possessed magical-religious meanings similar to the *figeras* recovered from the Hermitage plantation, or may be distantly culturally related to the meaning behind the "Hand of Power" candles still popular in Voodoo and Santeria shops. However, a doll's hand or foot recovered from mixed household garbage may be merely a broken children's toy. The challenge that archaeologists must face is recognizing contexts in which seemingly mundane artifacts may have had magical and religious meanings. As examples from Levi-Jordan plantation and Annapolis clearly demonstrate, considerations of archaeological and cultural context are necessary if we are to identify distinct African-American traditions.

It is also necessary that archaeologists add a diachronic dimension to their study of African and African-American spiritual traditions. To understand African-American magical-religious practice, archaeologists must also remember that these practices were not static but changed and evolved as African Americans found new ways to express their spiritual values. To understand these transformations, archaeologists must consider the cultural processes of creolization and syncretism: The use of a magical charm does not necessarily represent a continuity in other aspects of African religions, and the embracing of Chris-

tian values does not necessarily dictate an abandonment of African religious practices.

An interpretive model, or framework, has been proposed to structure and organize the available and growing body of archaeological evidence related to magical and religious systems in the African diaspora. The model recognizes three stages of religious process: Formative, Persisting, and Transformative. Archaeologically most visible is the Persisting stage, which represents periods of limited flux in religious processes. As discussed above, archaeologists have identified a number of Persisting magical-religious systems within the diaspora. When particular artifacts or artifact assemblages disappear from the archaeological record, it represents evidence of a Transformative development in religious practice. The documentary record can provide contextual insight into what social, political, demographic, cultural, communal, and so on, influences may have led African Americans to negotiate different magical and religious expressions through time and space.

The model presented was derived from one successfully used to study the development of Santeria in the Americas (Brandon 1993). Like Brandon, I would argue that this model should not be seen as supporting a unlinear evolutionary scheme. Further, I would argue that the purpose of applying a model such as this is not to adopt an evolutionary framework of any sort, but to provide a means of conceptualizing religious changes through time. The use of this model requires archaeologists to articulate the documentary and archaeological records to lead to a better understanding of religious and spiritual change in the diaspora.

The application of this model, provided above, demonstrates that archaeologists still know and understand very little about African-American magical and religious expressions through material culture. To better understand the magical-religious artifacts that we are finding archaeologically, we must better understand the ways in which magic was used in the African-American community. Only then can archaeologists recognize magically meaningful artifacts, representing a general worldview, versus continuities in African religions and the development of syncretic New World religions. Our interpretations of African-American magical-religious artifacts will remain limited and constrained until we attempt to understand the broader worldview that these artifacts represent.

ACKNOWLEDGMENTS

I would like to thank the Louisiana State Division of Archaeology and the National Park Service for funding the archaeological research at Oakley plantation. The recovery of magical-religious items from that site prompted my initial explorations of this topic. I would like especially to thank reviewers Leland Ferguson, Patricia Samford, Daniel G. Roberts, and an anonymous reviewer for their comments on this manuscript. So much material has recently become available on this topic that it is difficult for any individual to stay abreast of the developments. Not only did these reviewers provide thoughtful comments but they were generous in providing offprints and references to additional works. I greatly appreciate their contribution to this manuscript, but take all responsibility for any remaining weaknesses. Finally, I would like to thank Paul Farnsworth, who remains my most challenging reviewer and tireless editor, and Stealth, who has ensured that I completed this research in a timely manner.

REFERENCES

ADAMS, WILLIAM HAMPTON (EDITOR)
1987 Historical Archaeology of Plantations at Kings Bay, Camden County, Georgia. *Reports of Investigation* 5. Department of Anthropology, University of Florida, Gainesville.

ARMSTRONG, DOUGLAS V.
1990 *The Old Village and the Great House.* University of Illinois Press, Urbana.

BOTKIN, B. A. (EDITOR)
1989 *Lay My Burden Down.* Reprint of 1945 edition. University of Georgia Press, Athens.

BRANDON, GEORGE
1993 *Santeria from Africa to the New World: The Dead Sell Memories.* Indiana University Press, Bloomington.

BROWN, KENNETH L., AND DOREEN C. COOPER
1990 Structural Continuity in an African-American Slave and Tenant Community. *Historical Archaeology* 24(4):7–19.

CAMPBELL, MARIE
1946 *Folks Do Get Born.* Rinehart, New York.

CLAYTON, RONNIE W.
1990 Mother Wit: The Ex-Slave Narratives of the Louisiana's Federal Writers' Project. *University of Kansas Humanistic Studies* 57. Peter Land, New York.

CORRUCCINI, ROBERT S., JEROME S. HANDLER, AND KEITH JACOBI
1985 Chronological Distribution of Enamel Hypoplasias and Weaning in a Caribbean Slave Population. *Human Biology* 57(4):699–711.

DAVIS, GEORGE A., AND O. FRED DONALDSON
1975 *Blacks in the United States: A Geographic Perspective.* Houghton Mifflin, Boston, MA.

DEAGAN, KATHLEEN, AND DARCIE MACMAHON
1995 *Fort Mose: Colonial America's Black Fortress of Freedom.* University of Florida Press, Gainesville.

DEETZ, JAMES
1993 *Flowerdew Hundred: The Archaeology of a Virginia Plantation, 1619–1864.* University of Virginia Press, Charlottesville.

DOLLARD, JOHN
1957 *Caste and Class in a Southern Town.* Reprint of 1937 edition. Doubleday/Anchor, New York.

EDWARDS, YWONE DECARLO
1995 "Primitive" and "Folk" in African American Archaeology. Paper presented at the Annual Meeting of The Society for Historical Archaeology Conference on Historical and Underwater Archaeology, Washington, DC.

EMERSON, MATTHEW C.
1994 Decorated Clay Tobacco Pipes from the Chesapeake: An African Connection. In *Historical Archaeology of the Chesapeake*, edited by Paul A. Shackel and Barbara J. Little, pp. 35–49. Smithsonian Institution Press, Washington, DC.

FARNSWORTH, PAUL
1996 Brutality or Benevolence in Plantation Archaeology. Paper presented at the Annual Meeting of the American Anthropological Association, San Francisco, CA.

FERGUSON, LELAND
1992 *Uncommon Ground: Archaeology and Early African America, 1650–1800.* Smithsonian Institution Press, Washington, DC.

FONTENOT, WONDA L.
1994   *Secret Doctors: Ethnomedicine of African Americans.*
        Bergin and Garvey, Westport, CT.

GENOVESE, EUGENE D.
1975   *Roll, Jordan, Roll.* Reprint of 1972 edition. Vintage,
        New York.
1989   *The Political Economy of Slavery.* Wesleyan University
        Press, Wesleyan, CT.

GONZÁLEZ-WHIPPLER, MIGENE
1992   *Santeria: African Magic in Latin America.* Reprint of
        1973 edition. Original Publications, New York.

GUTMAN, HERBERT
1976   *The Black Family in Slavery and Freedom: 1750–
        1925.* Vintage, New York.

HAND, WAYLAND D.
1980   *Magical Medicine: The Folkloric Component of
        Medicine in the Folk Belief Custom, and Ritual of the
        Peoples of Europe and America.* University of
        California Press, Berkeley.

HANDLER, JEROME S.
1996   A Prone Burial from a Plantation Slave Cemetery in
        Barbados, West Indies: Possible Evidence for an
        African-Type Witch or Other Negatively Viewed
        Person. *Historical Archaeology* 30(3):76–86.

HANDLER, JEROME S., AND FREDERICK W. LANGE
1978   *Plantation Slavery in Barbados: An Archaeological
        and Historical Investigation.* Harvard University Press,
        Cambridge, MA.

HARRIS, EDWARD F., AND TED A. RATHBUN
1989   Small Tooth Sizes in a Nineteenth Century South
        Carolina Slave Series. *American Hournal of Physical
        Anthropology* 78:411–420.

HERSKOVITS, MELVILLE
1962   *Myth of the Negro Past.* Reprint of 1941 edition.
        Beacon Press, Boston, MA.

HODDER, IAN
1986   *Reading the Past: Current Approaches to Interpretation
        in Archaeology.* Cambridge University, Cambridge,
        UK.

HURSTON, ZORA NEALE
1990a   *Tell My Horse: Voodoo and Life in Haiti and Jamaica.*
        Reprint of 1938 edition. Harper and Row, New York.
1990b   *Mules and Men.* Reprint of 1935 edition. Harper and
        Row, New York.

HYATT, HARRY MIDDLETON
1973   *Hoodoo-Conjuration-Witchcraft-Rootwork,* Vol. 3.

        Western Publishing, St. Louis, MO.
1974   *Hoodoo-Conjuration-Witchcraft-Rootwork,* Vol. 4.
        Western Publishing, St. Louis, MO.
1978   *Hoodoo-Conjuration-Witchcraft-Rootwork,* Vol. 5.
        Western Publishing, St. Louis, MO.

JOYNER, CHARLES
1984   *Down by the Riverside: A South Carolina Slave
        Community.* University of Illinois Press, Urbana.

KELLEY, JENNIFER OLSEN, AND J. LAWRENCE ANGEL
1987   Life Stresses of Slavery. *American Journal of Physical
        Anthropology* 74:199–211.

KLINGELHOFER, ERIC
1987   Aspects of Early Afro-American Material Culture:
        Artifacts from the Slave Quarters at Garrison Plantation,
        Maryland. *Historical Archaeology* 21(2):112–119.

LAGUERRE, MICHEL S.
1978   *Afro-Caribbean Folk Medicine.* Bergin and Garvey,
        Amherst, MA.

LANGENWALTER, PAUL E. II
1987   Mammals and Reptiles as Food and Medicines in
        Riverside Chinatown. In *Wong Ho Leun: An American
        Chinatown,* Vol. 2, pp. 53–106. The Great Basin
        Foundation, San Diego.

LEHMANN, ARTHUR C., AND JAMES E. MYERS (EDITORS)
1985   *Magic, Witchcraft, and Religion: An Anthropological
        Study of the Supernatural.* Mayfield, Palo Alto, CA.

LEONE, MARK
1995   A Historical Archaeology of Capitalism. *American
        Anthropologist* 97(2):251–268.

LOGAN, ANNIE LEE, AS TOLD TO KATHERINE CLARK
1989   *Motherwit: An Alabama Midwife's Story.* E. P. Dutton,
        New York.

MARWICK, MAX (EDITOR)
1970   *Witchcraft and Sorcery.* Penguin, New York.

MATHEWS HOLLY F.
1992   Doctors and Root Doctors: Patients Who Use Both. In
        *Herbal and Magical Medicine: Traditional Healing
        Today,* edited by James Kirkland, Holly F. Mathews,
        C. W. Sullivan III, and Karen Baldwin, pp. 68–97.
        Duke University Press, Durham, NC.

MBITI, JOHN S.
1970   *African Religions and Philosophies.* Doubleday,
        Garden City, NY.

MCKEE, LARRY
1992   Summary Report on the 1991 Field Quarter Excavation.

Report submitted to The Hermitage, TN.

1995   The Earth Is Their Witness: Archaeology Is Shedding New Light on the Secret Lives of American Slaves. *The Sciences*, March/April:36–41.

MCMILLEN, SALLY G.
1990   *Motherhood in the Old South: Pregnancy, Childbirth and Infant Rearing.* Louisiana State University Press, Baton Rouge.

MUELLER, FRED W., JR.
1987   Feng-Shui: Archaeological Evidence for Geomancy in Overseas Chinese Settlements. In *Wong Ho Leun: An American Chinatown*, Vol. 2, pp. 1–24. The Great Basin Foundation, San Diego, CA.

MURPHY, JOSEPH M.
1988   *Santeria: African Spirits in America.* Beacon Press, New York.

ORSER, CHARLES E., JR.
1994   The Archaeology of African-American Slave Religion in the Antebellum South. *Cambridge Archaeological Review Journal* 4(1):33–45.

PATTEN, M. DRAKE
1992   Mankala and Minkisi: Possible Evidence of African-American Folk Beliefs and Practices. *African-American Archaeology* 6:5–7.

PEARCE, LAURIE
1993   To Whom Do They Belong?: Cowrie Shells in Historical Archaeology. *African-American Archaeology* 9:1–3.

PITTS, WALTER F., JR.
1993   *Old Ship of Zion: The Afro-Baptist Ritual in the African Diaspora.* Oxford University Press, Oxford, UK.

POWDERMAKER, HORTENSE
1993   *After Freedom: A Cultural Study in the Deep South.* Reprint of 1937 edition. The University of Wisconsin Press, Madison.

PUCKETT, NEWBELL NILES
1968   *Folk Beliefs of the Southern Negro.* Reprint of 1926 edition. Negro Universities Press, New York.

RABOTEAU, ALBERT J.
1978   *Slave Religion: The Invisible Institution in the Antebellum South.* Oxford University Press, Oxford, UK.

REEVES, MATTHEW
1996   "To Vex a Teif": An African-Jamaican Ritual Feature. Poster and text presented at The Society for American Archaeology Conference on Historical and Underwater Archaeology, New Orleans, LA.

ROSE, JEROME C. (EDITOR)
1985   Gone to a Better Land. *Arkansas Archeological Research Series* 25. Arkansas Archeological Survey, Fayetteville.

ROSE, JEROME C., AND LAWRENCE GENE SANTEFORD
1985   Burial Descriptions. In Gone to a Better Land, edited by Jerome C. Rose. *Arkansas Archeological Research Series* 25:39–129. Arkansas Archeological Survey, Fayetteville.

SAMFORD, PATRICIA
1996   The Archaeology of African-American Slavery and Material Culture. *The William and Mary Quarterly*, third series, 53(1):87–114.

SANTORIO, ALESSIA ANNE
1994   The Path Least Traveled: Religion and Ritual as Interpretive Frameworks in African-American Archaeology. Unpublished M.A. thesis, Department of Anthropology, University of South Carolina, Columbia.

SAXON, LYLE
1988   *Fabulous New Orleans.* Reprint of 1928 edition. Pelican, New York.

SAXON, LYLE, EDWARD DREYER, AND ROBERT TALLANT
1989   *Gumbo Ya Ya.* Reprint of 1945 edition. Pelican, New York.

STINE, LINDA FRANCE, MELANIE A. CABAK, AND MARK D. GROOVER
1996   Blue Beads as African-American Cultural Symbols. *Historical Archaeology* 30(3):49–75.

TALLANT, ROBERT
1983   *Voodoo in New Orleans.* Reprint of 1946 edition. Pelican, New York.

TERRILL, TOM E., AND JERROLD HIRSCH
1978   *Such as Us: Southern Voices of the Thirties.* University of North Carolina Press, Chapel Hill.

THOMPSON, ROBERT FARRIS
1981   *Four Moments of the Sun.* National Art Gallery, Washington, DC.
1983   *Flash of the Spirit.* Vintage, New York.

TURNER, GRACE
1993   An Archaeological Record of Plantation Life in the Bahamas. In *Amerindians, Africans, Americans: Three Papers in Caribbean History*, by Gerard Lafleur, Susan Branson, and Grace Turner, pp. 107–125. Department of History, University of West Indies, Mona, Jamaica.

WEGARS, PRISCILLA (EDITOR)

1993 *Hidden Heritage: Historical Archaeology of the Overseas Chinese.* Baywood Monographs in Archaeology Series. Baywood, Amityville, NY.

WILFORD, JOHN NOBLE

1996 Slave Artifacts Under the Hearth. *New York Times,* 27 August:C1-1.

WILKIE, LAURIE A.

1994a *"Never Leave Me Alone": An Archaeological Study of African-American Ethnicity, Race Relations and Community at Oakley Plantation.* Ph.D. Dissertation, Archaeology Program, University of California, Los Angeles. University Microfilms International, Ann Arbor, MI.

1994b Archaeological Evidence of an African-American Aesthetic. *African-American Archaeology* 10:1, 4.

1995 Magic and Empowerment on the Plantation: An Archaeological Consideration of African-American Worldview. *Southeastern Archaeology* 14(2):136–148.

1996a Medicinal Teas and Patent Medicines: African-American Women's Consumer Choices and Ethnomedical Traditions at a Louisiana Plantation. *Southeastern Archaeology* 15(2):119–131.

1996b Transforming African-American Ethnomedical Practices: A Case Study from West Feliciana. *Louisiana History* 37(4):457–471.

WILKIE, LAURIE A., AND GEORGE SHORTER

[1997] An Archaeological Glimpse of an African-American Midwife's Life: Excavations at 1MB99. Monograph, in preparation for publication.

YAKUBIK, JILL-KARIN, CARRIE A. LEVEN, KENNETH R. JONES, BENJAMIN MAYGARDEN, SHANNON DAWDY, DONNA K. STONE, JAMES CUSICK, CATHEREN JONES, ROSALINDA MENDÉZ, HERSCHEL A. FRANKS, AND TARA BOND

1994 Archaeological Data Recovery at Ashland-Belle Helene Plantation (16AN26), Ascension Parish, Louisiana. Vol. 1, Investigations in the Quarters and Archaeological Monitoring. Submitted to Division of Archaeology, Louisiana Department of Culture, Recreation and Tourism, Baton Rouge, LA.

YAKUBIK, JILL-KARIN, AND ROSALINDA MÉNDEZ

[1995] *Beyond the Great House: Archaeology at Ashland-Belle Helene Plantation.* Discovering Louisiana Archaeology One. Louisiana Department of Culture, Recreation and Tourism, Baton Rouge, LA.

YENTSCH, ANNE

1994 *A Chesapeake Family and Their Slaves.* Cambridge University Press, Cambridge, UK.

YOUNG, AMY

1996 Archaeological Evidence of African-Style Ritual and Healing Practices in the Upland South. *Tennessee Anthropologist* 21(2):139–155.

1997 Risk Management Strategies Among African-American Slaves at Locust Grove Plantation. *International Journal of Historical Archaeology* 1(1).

LAURIE A. WILKIE
DEPARTMENT OF ANTHROPOLOGY
UNIVERSITY OF CALIFORNIA
BERKELEY, CA 94720-3710

www.ingramcontent.com/pod-product-compliance
Lightning Source LLC
Chambersburg PA
CBHW080944120626
46546CB00010B/2833